THE PROFESSIONAL DIVER'S
HANDBOOK

Editor   David Sisman

Gulf Publishing Company
Book Division
Houston, London, Paris, Tokyo

THE PROFESSIONAL DIVER'S HANDBOOK
published in the United Kingdom by
Submex Limited
19/21 Roland Way,
London, SW7 3RF.

This edition published 1985 by
Gulf Publishing Company
Book Division
P.O. Box 2608
Houston, Texas, U.S.A. 77001.

FIRST EDITION

Library of Congress Catalog Card Number
 85-81110

Produced for Submex by Thomas Telford Ltd, 26–34 Old Street, London EC1P 1JH.

Printed and bound in Great Britain by William Clowes Ltd, Beccles and London.

WHEN ONE is an old professional diver, one reads avidly all that is published concerning this occupation to which one has given so much. Moreover, a book on professional diving is something rare if non-existent; most works are either too general, or sport-biased. I have read this book with great interest and I find that the needs of our profession, as employer and employee have been well anticipated. We have here not a 'diving manual' as taught in schools but a work of reference that concerns all aspects of our profession.

Henri G. Delauze
President, Comex

IT IS HIGH time that a comprehensive and easily read handbook was produced which provides basic information on the wide range of skills expected from a modern oil field diver. Here it is, in one volume that covers diving on everything from BOPs to SBMs. This book should be carried by every trainer diver, and be on the bookshelf of any engineer embarking on a career in subsea technology.

Arne J. Fris
Vice-President Operations, Stolt–Nielsen Seaway Contracting A/S

DIVING has progressed vis-à-vis safety, a subject of utmost importance to me. The very existence of this book cannot help but advance diver safety. For it is a great fund of diving knowledge, a book I can heartily and thankfully recommend. The industry has come a long way. And it's got a long way to go. The Professional Diver's Handbook documents, validates, reaffirms. But more importantly, it teaches and explains—superbly and lucidly—those countless things that can go wrong. And it's also about time!

Andre Galerne
President, International Underwater Contractors, Inc.

THE PROFESSIONAL diver today must have a tremendous range of knowledge. He must be part engineer, scientist, craftsman, rigger, manager, physician and sometimes politician. The diver of twenty years ago did a tough job with rudimentary equipment. There were few tricks to master. Today's professional is expected to work with a wide range of gear: advances in equipment bring almost daily changes. He is now required to do every type of job: drilling support, lay barges, platforms and riser installations, underwater inspections and hyperbaric welding work. This book is an important source of the knowledge which separates the men from the boys on a dive site.

Mike Hughes
Executive Vice-President, Oceaneering International

NOT JUST another pretty book for the shelf but a gap-filling manual for both diving and non-diving readers. For the people actively involved in working in or on the seas and also for the non-diving engineers requiring the wide range of information that is operationally useful to the diver, this book is a basic tool. Not an extra weight for the shelf, therefore, but an easily accessible source of technical information, providing a working knowledge of diving technology for the operators to go with.

Julio E. Melegari
Saipem SpA

A BOOK like this can be a very useful tool to both the new diver learning new skills and to the experienced diver moving into different areas of work. I wish Submex the greatest success in their new endeavour and I am sure that once the 'Professional Diver' reads this reference book he will make it a part of his reference material.

Ken Wallace
President, Taylor Diving and Salvage Co. Inc.

THIS HANDBOOK, the first of its kind, is a unique document that marks a milestone in the development of the diving industry. With such an enormous range of work now carried out by divers, no diver can be expected to be a specialist in all the subjects covered. Even the most experienced of divers will have something to learn from this Handbook. It is an encouraging sign of the industry's professionalism that such a Handbook has been produced, and it will be even more encouraging if it is widely read and used by divers themselves.

Ric Wharton
Joint Managing-Director, Wharton-Williams Taylor Ltd

Contents

Acknowledgments

Acknowledgment is made to the numerous authors and compilers of technical books and journals to which reference was made in the preparation of this Handbook.

List of authors and books consulted

p 2: Whitehead, H. (1976), *An A–Z of Offshore Oil and Gas*, Kogan Page Ltd, London.

p 2: Drawing courtesy of Marathon LeTourneau Offshore Company, Houston.

p 3: Drawing courtesy of British Petroleum Co. Ltd.

p 3: Drawing courtesy of Gusto Engineering BV, Schiedam, The Netherlands.

p 4, 14: Drawings courtesy of Cameron Iron Works Inc., Houston.

p 6, 7, 8, 9, 10, 16: Drawings courtesy of Brown and Root (UK) Ltd, London.

p 7, 9, 18: Drawings courtesy of Shell (UK) Exploration and Production.

p 13: Drawings courtesy of Big Inch Marine Systems Inc., Houston.

p 13: Drawings courtesy of Taylor Diving and Salvage Inc., Belle Chase, Texas.

p 14: Drawing courtesy of Gripper Inc., Houston.

p 14, 15: Drawings courtesy of Hughes Offshore Inc., Houston.

p 17: Drawing by Ron Sandford and reproduced with permission of Mobil North Sea Ltd, London.

p 18, 92: Drawing courtesy of Conoco (UK) Ltd, London.

p 18: Drawing courtesy of The British National Oil Corporation Glasgow.

p 19: Drawings courtesy of Single Buoy Mooring Inc.

p 20, 22, 27: Drawings courtesy of Imodco Inc.

p 46: Turner, J. (1981), The Progress of Photogrammetry in Precise Subsea Measurement. *IUSD*, April/May, 1981.

p 52, 53: AODC (1981), *Code of Safe Practice for the use of High Pressure Water Jetting Techniques by Divers*.

p 54–58, 62–63, 65: Haywood, Dr M. G., *Underwater NDT Course Notes*. Prodive, Falmouth.

p 62, 63, 65: Drawings courtesy of Impalloy Ltd, Bloxwich, UK.

p 67, 222, 225, 226, 227, 231: Reproduced from BR 2808 with the permission of the Controller of Her Majesty's Stationery Office.

p 67–70, 71: *Diving Technical Manual: Underwater Cutting and Welding*, Department of the Navy, Washington.

p 67–70, 100, 103: Zinkowski, N. B. (1971), *Commercial Oilfield Diving*, Cornell Maritime Press, Maryland.

p 71: Drawing courtesy of Solus Ocean Systems Inc., Houston.

p 74, 75, 76: Brand, D., Hotforge Ltd, Aberdeen.

p 77: Brooke-Foster, B., Oceaneering International Services Ltd, Great Yarmouth.

p 77: Diagrams courtesy of ICI, Nobel Explosives Co. Ltd, Ayrshire.

pp 82, 83: Tucker, Wayne C. (1980), *Diver's Handbook of Underwater Calculations*, Cornell Maritime Press, Maryland.

p 88–89: Drawing courtesy of *The Motor Ship*, March 1973, IPC Industrial Press, London.

p 101–104: Dickie, D. E. (1975), *Lifting Tackle Manual*, Butterworth and Co. (Publishers) Ltd, London.

p 106–108: van den Haak, R., *Vryhof Anchor Manual*, Vrijhof Ankers BV, The Netherlands.

p 106–108: Klaren, P. J., Anker Advies Bureau BV, The Netherlands.

p 114–124: Busby, R. Frank, *Unmanned Submersibles*, Elsevier Scientific Publishing Company, New York.

p 114–124: Busby Associates Inc. (1981), *The Undersea Vehicle Directory*, Busby Associates Inc., Virginia.

p 125–126: Milne, Dr P. H. (1980), *Underwater Engineering Surveys*, E. & F. N. Spon, London.

p 112, 127–129, 255, 256: Haux, G. (1982), *Subsea Manned Engineering*, Baillière Tindall, London.

p 173: Drawings and information from Diving Unlimited International Inc., California.

p 174: Drawing courtesy of Kinergetics Inc., California.

pp 174, 215: Virr, L. E., Thornton, A. & Hayes, P. (1981), Review of Thermal Protection, *SUT Divetech '81*. SUT, London.

p 183: Baume, D., Godden, D. & Hipwell, J. (1981), *Language and Procedures for Underwater Communication*, Underwater Technology Unit, North East London Polytechnic.

p 192: Photographs by R. K. Pilsbury and published by permission of the BP Educational Service and from the *Macmillan and Silk Cut Nautical Almanac 1982*, The Macmillan Press Ltd, London.

p 194: Produced from portions of BA chart No. 5011 with the sanction of the Controller, HM Stationery Office and the Hydrographer of the Navy.

p 197: *Macmillan and Silk Cut Nautical Almanac 1982*, The Macmillan Press Ltd, London.

p 199, 200: Drawings reproduced with permission of the Meteorological Office.

p 208, 209, 210: Safar, P. (1981), *Cardiopulmonary Cerebral Resuscitation*, Asmund S. Laerdal, Stavanger, Norway.

p 213, 238, 239: Childs, Dr C. M. and Alcock, Dr S., *Ear Infections in Divers*, Offshore Health Centre, Foresterhill, Aberdeen.

p 213, 238, 239: Allen, M. W., Saturation Hygiene, *J. Soc. Underwater Techn*.

pp 213, 231, 232: Miller, J. N. (1979), *NOAA Diving Manual*, Second Edition, US Department of Commerce, NOAA and OOE, Washington.

p 214, Golden, Surgeon Cdr. F., RN.

pp 218, 222, 223, 224, 228, 229, 230: *US Navy Diving Manual*, Vols I and II, US Department of Navy, Washington.

p 220: Youngblood and Clarke (1978), *Initial Neurological Examination by Non-medical Personnel*.

p 221: Underwater Association for Scientific Research.

p 242: Kemsley, W. F. F. *et al.* (1962), *Brit. J. Prev. Soc. Med.* 16, 189.

pp 242, 243, 251, 252, 292, 293: European Diving Technology Committee (1981), *Guidelines for the Evaluation of Medical Fitness to Dive*. EDTC, Luxemburg.

p 249: Calder, I. M. (1982), Investigation of fatal and non-fatal accidents. In: Cox, R. A. F. (ed.), *Offshore Medicine*, Springer-Verlag, Berlin.

p 257: AODC (1980), *Emergency Diving Bell Recovery*, Addendum to Guidance Notes/Code of Practice.

p 279, 280, 281: Department of Energy, Underwater Engineering Group, AODC (1982), *Guidelines for Safe Diving Practices*.

Many other people, organisations and publications were consulted during the preparation of this handbook, and we apologise if we have forgotten to include any of their names.

Contributors

The production of this book has been an incredible challenge. No one person could have provided all this information. Individual divers, however skilled, tend to have specialised in some particular types of tasks.

Apart from this being one of the main reasons for producing the book, it has meant that the book owes its considerable coverage of subjects to a large number of people and organisations.

We therefore wish to gratefully acknowledge the help given by each person listed below, without whose valuable advice and material this book could never have been written.

In addition, we would like to thank each manufacturer who has checked our copy based on their specific equipment.

Tony Addison, Gas and Equipment Ltd
Kevyn Allen, Submex Ltd
Nic Ashmore, Plymouth Ocean Projects Ltd
Alan Auchterlounie

John Badger, Submex Ltd
Rob Barrett, Underwater Engineering Group, CIRIA
Peter Bates, Luxfer Holdings Ltd
David Baume, North East London Polytechnic
Alan Bax, Plymouth Ocean Projects Ltd
David Beatty, Divemex
Keith Bentley, Phillips Petroleum, Europe-Africa
Doug Brand, Hotforge Ltd
Mike Braun, Submex Ltd
John Breedon
Bernard Brooke-Foster, Oceaneering International Ltd
Andrew Brown, Deepshore Engineering Ltd

Dr Ian Calder, London Hospital
Mike Carrie, Submersible Television Surveys Ltd
Roger Chapman, Sub Sea Surveys Ltd
Mike Chew, Total Oil Marine
Reg Clucas, Clucas Diving and Marine Engineering Ltd
Ray Collyer
Peter Cornish
Prof. Harry Cotton, Welding Institute
Dr Robin Cox, Phillips Petroleum, Europe-Africa
Nic Cresswell, Marathon Oil UK Ltd

Peter Dick, Tokola Underwater Engineering Ltd
John Douds, Comex Services SA

Dr David Elliott, Shell Expro UK Ltd

Chris Fern, Impalloy Ltd
Nic Flemming, Institute of Oceanographic Sciences

Brian Gibbs, Taylor Woodrow Construction Co. Ltd
Hal Goldie, Cameron Iron Works Inc
Terry Gosling, Solus Ocean Systems Ltd
Jeremy Griffiths, Comex Houlder Diving Ltd

Dr Mark Harries, Guy's Hospital
Francis Hayes, London Meteorological Office
Dr Philip Hayes, AMTE, Physiological Laboratory
Mike Haywood, Prodive Ltd
Chris Head, Solus Ocean Systems Ltd
Eila Henderson, Lloyd's Register of Shipping
M. R. Henry, Brown and Root (UK) Ltd
Jack Highley, Sub Sea Offshore Ltd
'Dutchy' Holland, Oceaneering International Ltd
Tom Hollobone, Association of Offshore Diving Contractors

David Jones, David Jones and Partners Ltd

Mike King, Star Offshore Services Ltd

Cyril Lafferty, British Petroleum Development Ltd
Dick Larn, Prodive Ltd
Clive Lloyd, Gas and Equipment Ltd

Ran Macdonald, Trident Underwater Engineering Ltd
Howard McArthur, Solus Ocean Systems Ltd
Bill McIntosh, Conoco North Sea Inc
David Mayo, Dosbouw
Julio Melegari, Saipem SpA
Mike Moncaster, Shell Expro UK Ltd
Robin Morris, Submex Ltd

Len Norris, Cameron Iron Works Inc

Frank Papworth, Taylor Woodrow Construction Co. Ltd
Graham Parker, London Meteorological Office
Surgeon Captain Ramsay Pearson, RN
Sandra Percey, Department of Energy
Geoff Phillips, Shell Expro UK Ltd
Dr Gordon Picken, University of Aberdeen
Ken Pilsbury, BP Educational Service
David Puttock, Ocean Technical Services Ltd

Dr Bob Ralph, University of Aberdeen
Carl Robinson
Don Rodocker, Gas Services Ltd
Per Rosengren, Norwegian Petroleum Directorate

A. Sandford, British Oceanics Ltd
Jack Schmitt, Experimental Diving Unit, USN
Cdr Rob Schroeder, USN
Peter Scoones, Underwater Visual Systems
Mark Scorer, Corrintech Ltd
Peter Sharphouse, British Oceanics Ltd
John Shaw, Shiers Diving Contracts Ltd
Don Shiers, Shiers Diving Contracts Ltd
Bert Simpson, Luxfer Holdings Ltd
Wally Soulsby, Sub Sea Offshore Ltd
Denis Stanley, Submex Ltd
Mike Stock, Submex Ltd

John Towse, AMTE, Physiological Laboratory
John Turner, Camera Alive Ltd

Ken Vaughan, Submex Ltd
D. W. Vories, Conoco (UK) Ltd

Prof. Denis Walder, University of Newcastle-upon-Tyne
David Webster, Offshore Medical Support Ltd
John Westwood, Sub Sea Surveys Ltd
Peter White, Ocean Technical Services Ltd
Don Whittle, Brown and Root (UK) Ltd
Stanley Williams, Royal Institute of Naval Architects
M. Wilton, Maritime Radio Services, British Telecom
Ken Woolley, Ocean Technical Services Ltd

The Staff of the Army Physical Training Corp. at the Royal Military Academy, Sandhurst

Just about every diver builds his own book of essential information. Why? Because until now there has not been available a book containing the practical and useful information that he needs on site.

It is this that has inspired The Professional Diver's Handbook. We have gathered a wide range of information that is operationally useful to the diver. The information that divers themselves are always looking for. There is no padding. We have also tried to fill the gaps that exist in the diving literature. We have assumed that the reader is already a trained diver (this is not another diving manual). We have pitched the level of information assuming the diver's background has not covered that particular subject, so that it provides a working introduction to many subjects. Perhaps the equivalent of about 30 minutes of helpful advice from an experienced Supervisor on each particular subject.

We have tried to make the information easy to understand and readily accessible. We have emphasised illustration since it enables us to convey more information without making it difficult to understand.

Nobody has ever produced a book like this before so we intend to update the book from time to time to improve its usefulness. By this we mean that it is intended as a working book and not just a book to be left on the shelf.

Whilst this book is intended primarily to be useful to the working diver, it will prove invaluable to the trainee diver.

John Bevan

Submex Limited

A very small team produced this book, working cheerfully under considerable difficulties. That it was produced at all is in large measure due to Sue Quatermass, assistant editor. Her lively interest and enthusiasm did more than anything else to keep the project underway. My grateful thanks also to Trevor Vertigan for his meticulous layouts and drawings, and to Diana Mabbs. Don McKinley and Alan Suttie drew the impeccable artwork; David Ledger took care of all the accounts and the marketing of the book. Finally I would like to thank the editors of Thomas Telford, Ann Thompson and Jeremy Swinfen Green and their production controller Elva Tehan for their advice and support.

London
1982

David Sisman

Offshore diving

Offshore drilling rigs are marine versions of conventional land drilling rigs. The main differences are due to the increased distance between the drilling floor and the solid ground beneath—and the behaviour of the water in between. The results have been the development of the marine riser and a seabed blowout preventer stack with its guide base. Both provide considerable work for divers. Details of typical diver tasks concerned with the drilling equipment are given in Section 1.2, Drilling rig support.

Offshore exploration drilling rigs may be supported on barges, jack-up barges, displacement ships or semi-submersible vessels. Some additional diving work is involved with the specialised marine aspects of the vessels. The diving tasks related specifically to the operation of these vessels are described in the following paragraphs.

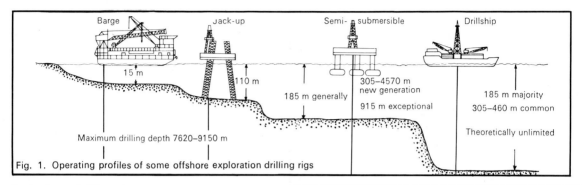

Fig. 1. Operating profiles of some offshore exploration drilling rigs

1. Jack-up drilling rigs

Jack-up rigs are essentially barges fitted with extendable legs. They can only operate in water as deep as their legs will allow. For this reason, jack-up rigs are most suitable for the shallower water sites, usually down to 60 m (200′) although some have been used in depths of over 90 m (300′).

The barge is towed or self-propelled from site to site with its legs jacked up. As this is a rather unstable configuration, the jack-up requires relatively calm weather conditions for transportation. At the drill site the legs are lowered to the seabed. The barge then jacks itself up its legs until it is sufficiently clear of the water to be able to withstand the anticipated sea states. Drilling may then start. After the drilling operations are complete, the barge jacks up its legs and moves on to the next site.

DIVER TASKS
—Usually only air diving is required due to shallow depths of the sites.
—Before a jack-up reaches location, buoys are normally dropped to mark off the centre and leg positions. Divers may be required to do a circular search of these positions to ensure that the legs will be clear of debris.
—Divers may be required to measure the depth of penetration of the legs using an air probe.
—In areas of strong currents, divers will have to check for scour around the legs and if necessary, fill scour holes with sandbags and build a protective wall of sandbags around the base of the legs.

2. Semi-submersibles

Semi-submersibles are mobile working installations designed for use in water depths beyond the reach of jack-up rigs (down to 300 m (1000′)). They are more stable than jack-up rigs and are often self-propelled. They consist of a drilling installation supported on submerged buoyant pontoons that can be ballasted to

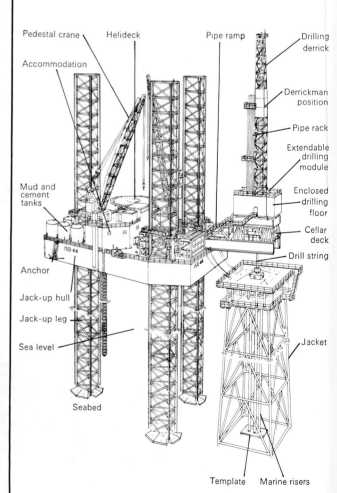

Fig. 2. Jack-up drilling production rig 150-44

adjust their draft. Generally, the lower the platform the more stable it is. Many can operate all year round in the varying sea states.

Once the semi-submersible is on the drill site it maintains location by means of up to eight large anchors or by using computer controlled dynamic positioning. After the required number of wells has been drilled the well heads are sealed off and the semi-submersible moves off to operate in the next location.

DIVER TASKS

—Usually air and mixed gas, bounce or saturation diving.

—When in shallow water the semi-submersible may rest on the seabed and divers may be required to check for debris and penetration of the pontoons.

—If scour is prevalent, divers may be required to infill scour holes or build protective walls with sandbags.

—Inspect thrusters, pontoons and all underwater parts of the structure.

—Assist with rigging of anchor pendant wires.

—Assist with the recovery of any lost or damaged equipment.

3. Drillships

Drillships may be either conventional vessels converted for drilling or may be custom-built. Most have a derrick constructed over a central moonpool through which the drill is run. Drillships can drill in depths of over 1525 m (5000′) and use dynamic positioning to maintain location. Anchors may be used when working in shallow water. Because these vessels tend to pitch and roll more than semi-submersibles, there is greater wear and tear on the drilling equipment and this means more work for the divers.

DIVER TASKS

—Inspect, maintain and repair ship's accessory structures such as moonpool doors.

—Inspect all ship's thrusters and keep them clear of fouling.

—Assist with the recovery of any lost or damaged equipment.

The above tasks all relate to the marine operation of the vessels. The following section describes the diving associated with drilling operations.

Fig. 3. Semi-submersible drilling platform Sedco 703

Rotary table
Draw works
Offices
Galley
Radio room
Mess
Marine control room
Helideck
Lifeboats
Engine exhausts
Generators
Transformers
Elevator
Towing pad
Anchor chain (2 anchors from each footing)
Chain fairlead
Anchor rack
Ballast tanks
Fuel oil tank
Drillwater tank
BOP gantry crane rail
Lower hull
Anchor buoys
Anchor windlasses
Pipe racks
Mud pumps
Revolving crane
Drilling tool storage
Pipe dragway
Bulk cement and mud tanks
Pipe ramp
Revolving crane
Drilling derrick

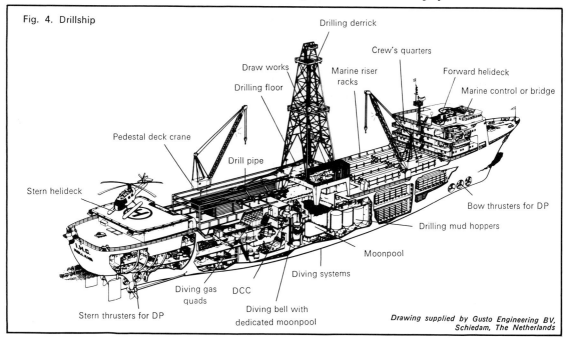

Fig. 4. Drillship

Drilling derrick
Crew's quarters
Forward helideck
Marine control or bridge
Marine riser racks
Draw works
Drilling floor
Pedestal deck crane
Drill pipe
Stern helideck
Bow thrusters for DP
Drilling mud hoppers
Moonpool
Diving systems
Diving gas quads
DCC
Diving bell with dedicated moonpool
Stern thrusters for DP

Drawing supplied by Gusto Engineering BV, Schiedam, The Netherlands

1.2 DRILLING RIG SUPPORT TYPICAL TASKS ON A BLOW-OUT PREVENTER

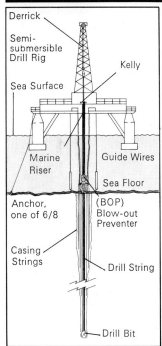

Derrick

Semi-submersible Drill Rig

Kelly

Sea Surface

Marine Riser

Guide Wires

Sea Floor

Anchor, one of 6/8

(BOP) Blow-out Preventer

Casing Strings

Drill String

Drill Bit

Location of the BOP

FUNCTIONS OF THE BOP

A blow-out is what happens when the drill reaches an area of pressure which is higher than the hydraulic head of pressure exerted by the drilling mud inside the drill hole. The result is the uncontrolled blow-out of this mud followed by the oil or gas.

The BOP is responsible for preventing this disastrous outcome and for bringing the well back under control by allowing heavier mud to be pumped down. The blow-out is first prevented by the closing of one or more pairs of rams in the BOP. Rams are hydraulically operated pistons made of steel or tough rubber and are usually placed one on top of each other. There are two kinds, shear (kill) and pipe (choke) rams. When kill rams close they cut through the drill pipe and seal off the BOP stack bore.

Choke rams close and seal round the drill pipe. Both types have locks which keep them hydraulically closed once they have been activated.

Secondly, heavier mud is pumped down two pipes called the kill and choke lines. These are connected to the drill below the rams and can circulate the heavier mud whilst drilling operations and the BOP are shut down.

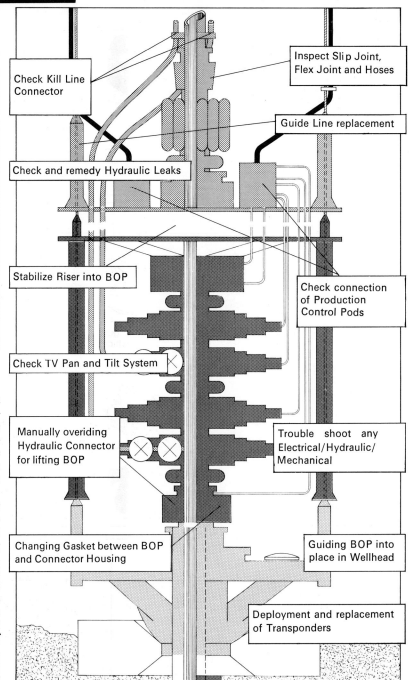

Check Kill Line Connector

Inspect Slip Joint, Flex Joint and Hoses

Guide Line replacement

Check and remedy Hydraulic Leaks

Stabilize Riser into BOP

Check connection of Production Control Pods

Check TV Pan and Tilt System

Manually overiding Hydraulic Connector for lifting BOP

Trouble shoot any Electrical/Hydraulic/Mechanical

Changing Gasket between BOP and Connector Housing

Guiding BOP into place in Wellhead

Deployment and replacement of Transponders

Diagram of a BOP and guidebase showing typical diver tasks

Other diving duties on a drilling rig will include: hull inspection, anchor rack fairlead checks and assistance with attachment of new anchor pennant wires.

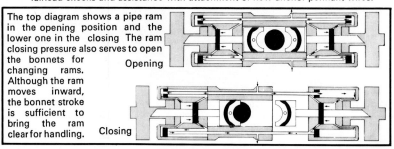

The top diagram shows a pipe ram in the opening position and the lower one in the closing The ram closing pressure also serves to open the bonnets for changing rams. Although the ram moves inward, the bonnet stroke is sufficient to bring the ram clear for handling.

Opening

Closing

TYPICAL DIVER TASKS ON THE BOP

Diver tasks relating to the blow-out preventer are mainly inspection, checking of connections and trouble-shooting any electrical, hydraulic or mechanical malfunction. Some of the more usual tasks are shown on this page. Installations vary, so the diver should study the manufacturer's drawings.

Guiding BOP into place on wellhead

(1) Diver clearing wellhead casing of debris and (2) monitoring by video and intercom as the collet connector locks in between the casing and the BOP.

Guideline replacement
$\frac{3}{4}''$ cables attached to the top of the guideposts run up to the drilling platform where they are spooled onto tuggers and maintained at constant tension. They frequently break and need to be replaced. There are many types, but the usual method is a spelter on the end of the cable which fits into a slot in the guideposts.

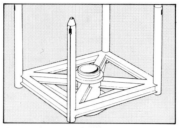

(1) A permanent guide base with four guideposts to which the guidelines must be attached. (2) Diver manually removing top of guidepost assembly.

Checking BOP orientation
Diver observes the bubble in a bull's-eye, mounted on the permanent guidebase, and reports to supervisor on intercom.

Right
Checking and remedying of hydraulic leaks Diver locates hydraulic leaks by visual check and tightens up loose hydraulic fittings.

Right
Changing gasket between BOP and connector housing This may need to be replaced if a leak is discovered when pressure-testing the conductor housing, by pumping fluid through the drill pipe. The gasket shown here is being fitted onto the wellhead casing.

Manually overriding hydraulic connector for lifting BOP The hydraulic connector may not release when the BOP has to be lifted off the guidebase. The diver attaches a tugger line to a key on the collet to release it.

Right
Deployment or replacement of transponders
Transponders are often attached to the guideposts on the permanent guidebase, or on the corners of the lower riser package or even on the seabed around the well.

Inspection of connections
Amongst the many connections that need continual inspection are the riser kill and choke connectors, the production control pods on the riser, and the slip joint, flex joint and hoses.

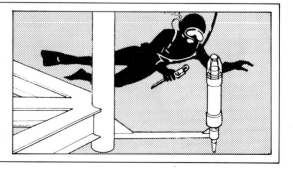

1.3 PIPELAY BARGES

A pipelay barge, sometimes called a lay barge, handles pipeline of single or double sections which are welded together on board. The finished weld is radiographed and the joints coated with bitumen. Finally, the pipe is lowered down the stinger to the seabed as the barge pulls itself forward on its anchors. Pipelay barges are also used for construction tasks such as tie-ins and subsea pile installations.

There are three generations of pipelay barge:
● The first generation are modified flat bottom barges which have the pipeline passed down a sloping deck into the sea.
● The second generation are improved ship shape hulls.
● The third and most recent are semi-submersibles.

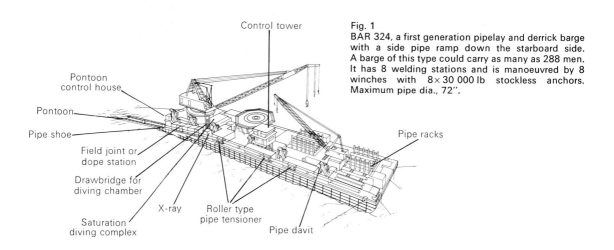

Fig. 1
BAR 324, a first generation pipelay and derrick barge with a side pipe ramp down the starboard side. A barge of this type could carry as many as 288 men. It has 8 welding stations and is manoeuvred by 8 winches with 8 × 30 000 lb stockless anchors. Maximum pipe dia., 72″.

Control tower
Pontoon control house
Pontoon
Pipe shoe
Field joint or dope station
Drawbridge for diving chamber
Saturation diving complex
X-ray
Roller type pipe tensioner
Pipe davit
Pipe racks

Fig. 2
Semac I, a semi-submersible third generation mobile offshore construction platform capable of operating in all weathers. The pipe assembly and stinger are run down the centre of the barge, providing better access to the line up station from both sides, better stability and a balanced mooring system. This barge can accommodate 342 men, and is manoeuvred by 12 winches with 12 × 40 000 lb stockless anchors. Stern truss length 40 m (130′) and stinger length 50 m (170′). Maximum pipe dia., 84″.

Marine control tower
Helideck
Diving operations station
Dope station
Stern truss
Pipe rollers
Stinger buoyancy tanks
CCTV cameras
Floating stinger
Stinger hitch
Stern
Bow
Pontoon
Anchor cable

Most barges are fitted with an articulated arm called a stinger or pontoon which is hinged onto the stern. The completed pipeline is fed through the stinger over a series of rollers and lowered to the seabed.

The third generation semi-submersible barges have the advantage of being able to trim to suit the sea state and are more stable in rough weather.

TASKS IN LAYBARGE OPERATIONS

Diving from a laybarge requires the diver to be familiar with many different diving skills, from diving on the stinger, taking measurements from the pipeline to a jacket, to installing a riser that is to be welded or flanged to the pipeline. It helps to have a good construction background and familiarity with all the necessary installation tools required to make tie-ins, such as bolt tensioning equipment etc.

The work is of two different types:

1. Shallow, surface-oriented, air diving tasks on the stinger to check or maintain its efficient operation. When diving on stingers, divers should have a means of indicating their position day and night and, where possible, have two methods of communication with the surface.

Good weather is particularly important when diving on stingers, since stinger movements in rough weather can make the job considerably more hazardous. In any case, independent surface cover for the diver is essential. Generally, this is provided from an inflatable or the anchor handling vessel carrying suitable communications, standby diver and attendant. Diving operations are supervised from an air station set up just above the stinger hitch.

2. Deeper, possibly mixed gas work on the seabed associated with the pipe, and work on the laydown head and pipeline connections.

TASKS ON THE PIPELAY BARGE

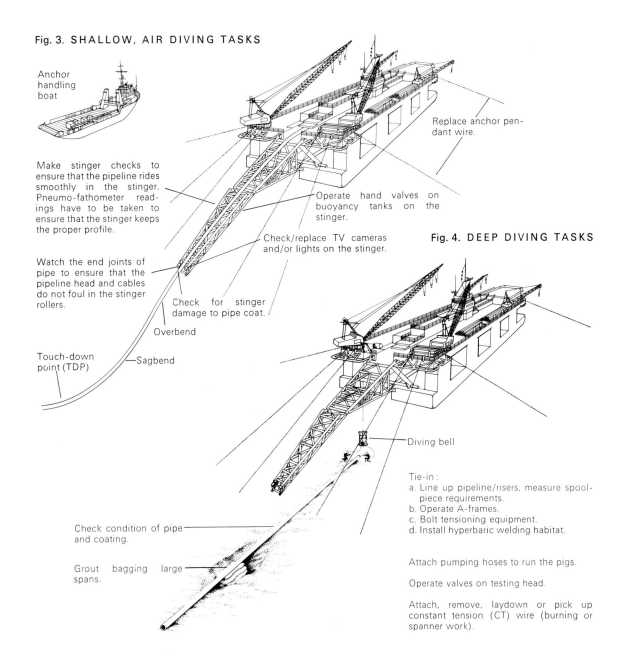

Fig. 3. SHALLOW, AIR DIVING TASKS

Anchor handling boat

Make stinger checks to ensure that the pipeline rides smoothly in the stinger. Pneumo-fathometer readings have to be taken to ensure that the stinger keeps the proper profile.

Watch the end joints of pipe to ensure that the pipeline head and cables do not foul in the stinger rollers.

Touch-down point (TDP)

Sagbend

Overbend

Check for stinger damage to pipe coat.

Check/replace TV cameras and/or lights on the stinger.

Operate hand valves on buoyancy tanks on the stinger.

Replace anchor pendant wire.

Fig. 4. DEEP DIVING TASKS

Diving bell

Check condition of pipe and coating.

Grout bagging large spans.

Tie-in:
a. Line up pipeline/risers, measure spool-piece requirements.
b. Operate A-frames.
c. Bolt tensioning equipment.
d. Install hyperbaric welding habitat.

Attach pumping hoses to run the pigs.

Operate valves on testing head.

Attach, remove, laydown or pick up constant tension (CT) wire (burning or spanner work).

Fig. 5. Stinger valve operation

Opening and shutting specific valves to adjust buoyancy and catenary. Just because the diver has been told a certain valve is open or shut, he should not assume that it is so and should check for himself. Always carry a wrench.

Fig. 6. TV camera replacement

Removal and replacement of CCTV camera(s) on stinger.

Fig. 7. Valve operation

Valves at the testing (pull or laydown) head are opened or closed to flood or dewater the pipe.

Fig. 8. Removal or attachment of the constant tension wire

The cable which lifts or lowers the pipe to the seabed may be removed or replaced at the pulling head. Extreme caution must be exercised by divers when cutting the laydown wire, as there can be over 100 kips (100 000 lb force) tension on it.

Fig. 9. An arrangement of diving equipment on the stern

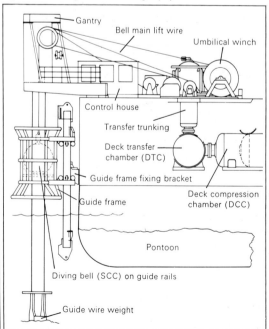

- Gantry
- Bell main lift wire
- Umbilical winch
- Control house
- Transfer trunking
- Deck transfer chamber (DTC)
- Guide frame fixing bracket
- Deck compression chamber (DCC)
- Guide frame
- Pontoon
- Diving bell (SCC) on guide rails
- Guide wire weight

SAFETY

1. In rough weather, diving on the stinger can be very dangerous. If a swell is running, the diver may be drawn in and get caught between the rollers and the pipe if he gets too close. The diver's umbilical may be similarly trapped. Consequently, the diver should stay outside the stinger, especially in poor weather. If a tide is running, the diver should swim along the lee side to keep his umbilical away from the stinger. The saying 'the stinger sucks you in before it spits you out' should be remembered.

2. The decision to wear scuba in place of umbilical supplied UBA should be carefully considered. The diver should always wear an inflatable lifejacket if he uses scuba. In the UK, the use of scuba requires exemption from certain regulations to be given prior to its use.

3. Fins should always be worn when diving around a stinger.

4. All valves on a stinger or on a pipe must be treated with the greatest caution.

5. The barge should not be moved whilst divers are working on the stinger. If this is not feasible, the diver must stay well clear of the stinger during movements.

6. If decompression stops are required, either in the water or as surface decompression, a swift means of recovery from the water is necessary such as a diving basket or wet bell.

1.4 TRENCHING BARGES

Trenching barges are also called 'jet' or 'bury barges'. Their function is to excavate a trench for a pipe or cable in order to protect the pipe or cable from damage and stabilise it on the seabed. The depth of the trench required can be anything from 0.5 m to 5 m (1–15') depending on the area, such as shipping lanes and anchorage grounds. The infilling of the trench is normally left to the natural movements of the seabed. The amount of infilling that eventually occurs varies with the area and the nature of the bottom. The sleds used to produce the trench differ considerably in design depending on the nature of the seabed conditions and the policy of the operator. They may use high pressure water jets with air-lifts, water extruder or a proprietary ploughing system. The diving tasks are associated with checking the physical characteristics of the trench, the status of the pipe and sled, setting the sled and assisting with any problems that may arise.

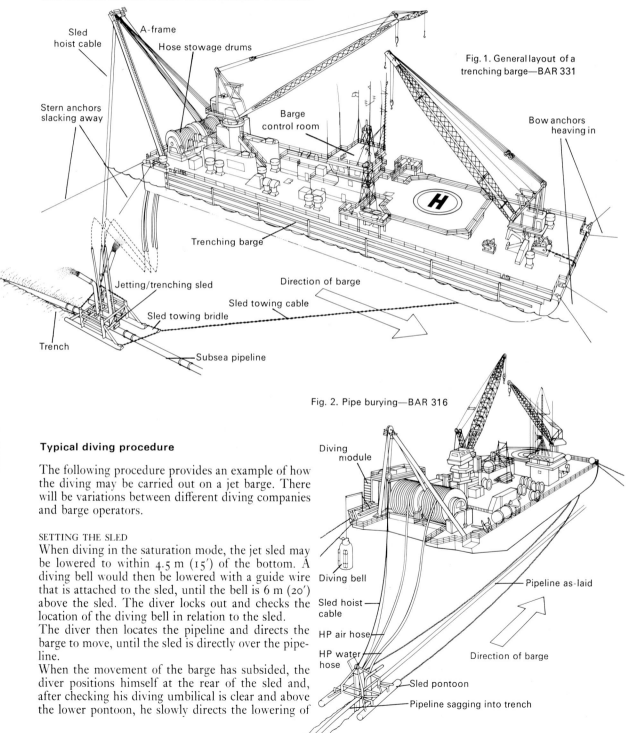

Fig. 1. General layout of a trenching barge—BAR 331

Fig. 2. Pipe burying—BAR 316

Typical diving procedure

The following procedure provides an example of how the diving may be carried out on a jet barge. There will be variations between different diving companies and barge operators.

SETTING THE SLED
When diving in the saturation mode, the jet sled may be lowered to within 4.5 m (15') of the bottom. A diving bell would then be lowered with a guide wire that is attached to the sled, until the bell is 6 m (20') above the sled. The diver locks out and checks the location of the diving bell in relation to the sled.
The diver then locates the pipeline and directs the barge to move, until the sled is directly over the pipeline.
When the movement of the barge has subsided, the diver positions himself at the rear of the sled and, after checking his diving umbilical is clear and above the lower pontoon, he slowly directs the lowering of

the sled over the pipeline.

The diver can lower the sled in zero visibility by standing at the rear of the sled with his feet straddling the pipeline and holding on to the rear air lifts as the sled is slowly lowered over the pipeline.

Once the sled is set, the position of the pipeline in the sled must be checked. Checks should be made of: the front rollers; the towing bridle for possible fouling; the position of the pontoons in relation to the natural bottom; and the rear rollers.

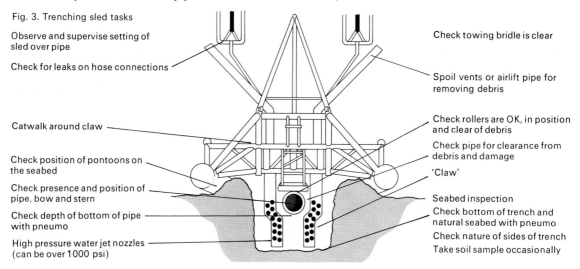

Fig. 3. Trenching sled tasks

Observe and supervise setting of sled over pipe

Check for leaks on hose connections

Catwalk around claw

Check position of pontoons on the seabed

Check presence and position of pipe, bow and stern

Check depth of bottom of pipe with pneumo

High pressure water jet nozzles (can be over 1000 psi)

Check towing bridle is clear

Spoil vents or airlift pipe for removing debris

Check rollers are OK, in position and clear of debris

Check pipe for clearance from debris and damage

'Claw'

Seabed inspection

Check bottom of trench and natural seabed with pneumo

Check nature of sides of trench

Take soil sample occasionally

CHECKING THE SLED

Before any dive is made, the Barge Foreman should always shut down the jetting pressure and air lifts.

There have been a number of fatalities due to divers checking the sled and trench when the water pressure and air lifts have not been shut down. Voice communication with the diver is almost impossible because of the roar of the water pressure, and at least one diver has been sucked out through the air lift.

Once the water and air supplies have been secured, the bell is lowered to within 10 m (30′) of the bottom, and the diver will be required to check the following:

1. Natural bottom depth by pneumo
2. Elevation of the pipe
3. Elevation of trench bottom under pipe at stern roller
4. Position of pipe relative to the rear of the sled
5. Position of pontoons on seabed and orientation relative to pipeline
6. Position of pipe relative to the bow of the sled
7. Towing bridle is clear
8. Condition of pipeline (concrete cracks, etc.) if visibility allows
9. Take a soil sample
10. Pipeline elevation in trench well to stern of trench.

Some important points

The diver should make himself completely familiar with the type of jet sled being used. He should be able to draw a picture of the sled from memory and be able to identify every part of it. As much time as possible should be spent learning the way around the sled whenever it is on the surface because visibility will normally be zero on the bottom.

The diver should:

Identify and memorise any danger areas such as moving parts, cables, rollers etc. Learn how to locate himself by touch alone so as to avoid these danger areas. Take special care of fingers.

Ensure that the sled is at a standstill and that power is shut down before any diving. This includes both the jetting pressure and the air lifts.

Always work in the lee of the sled if there is a current running.

Pay special attention to his umbilical to avoid its becoming entangled or damaged.

Use a helmet for head protection.

Use down-lines and swim-lines whenever possible to provide direction and range in poor visibility.

Use the catwalk on the sled, if provided.

Never get under a sled which is being lowered.

Give accurate measurements in zero visibility by using his body as a measure. Example: standing in a ditch, up to diver hip is 1 m (3′) of cover.

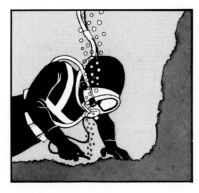

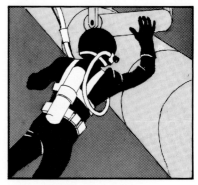

Fig. 4. Checking depth of trench

Diver places pneumo at base of trench for surface readout

Fig. 5. Checking rollers

Diver feels position of rollers on pipe to ensure their proper functioning and positioning.

1.5 PIPELINE CONNECTIONS

Subsea pipeline connections are mainly carried out during the construction phase of an offshore development. Occasionally, at a later date, extra connections may be made or maintenance and repairs carried out.

The applications of subsea pipeline connections or 'tie-ins' commonly carried out include:

—Tie-in of a pipeline to a platform riser.

—Mid-line tie-ins between two or three pipelines (end-to-end or T-pieces) (see also Section 3.3, Underwater welding).

—'Hot taps'—attaching pipes to already operating pipes.

—Placing a valve box in an existing pipeline.

—Repair of a damaged pipeline (see Section 1.8, Pipeline inspection).

—Replacing flexible hoses on SPMs (see Section 1.7, Single point moorings).

Many methods of underwater pipeline connection exist. Those commonly used include:

—Flanged.

—Hyperbaric welded.

—'Flexiforge' (cold forged) by Big Inch Inc.

—'Gripper' connectors by Gripper Inc.

—'Cameron' connectors by Cameron Iron Works Inc.

—'HydroBall/HydroCouple' connectors by Hughes Offshore Inc.

—'Weldball' connectors by Hughes Offshore Inc.

Flanged connections

Flanged pipeline connections are the most common method of pipeline connections used world wide. Flanges come in an assortment of types depending on the operational design requirements.

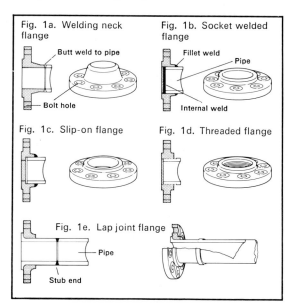

Fig. 1a. Welding neck flange

Butt weld to pipe
Bolt hole

Fig. 1b. Socket welded flange

Fillet weld
Pipe
Internal weld

Fig. 1c. Slip-on flange

Fig. 1d. Threaded flange

Fig. 1e. Lap joint flange

Pipe
Stub end

The swivel ring flange is often used to make it easy to align the bolt holes.

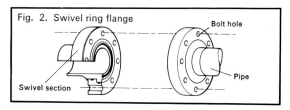

Fig. 2. Swivel ring flange

Bolt hole
Pipe
Swivel section

TYPES OF FLANGE FACINGS

The most commonly found flange facing offshore is the raised face ring joint facing. This is because it is the best for high pressures and temperatures. Another type of flange facing is the flat-face type.

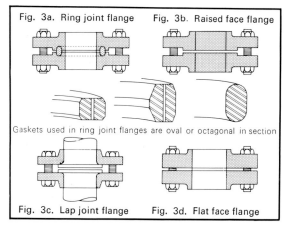

Fig. 3a. Ring joint flange   Fig. 3b. Raised face flange

Gaskets used in ring joint flanges are oval or octagonal in section

Fig. 3c. Lap joint flange   Fig. 3d. Flat face flange

TYPES OF FLANGE BOLT

Stud bolts are much more commonly used on flanges than machine bolts. Stud bolts have the advantage that they are more easily removed if corroded.

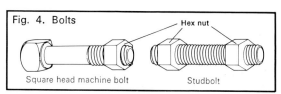

Fig. 4. Bolts

Hex nut
Square head machine bolt   Studbolt

TYPES OF FLANGE GASKETS

Raised face flanges take ring gaskets, and flat faced flanges take full face gaskets. Gasket materials include compressed asbestos and spiral wound, asbestos-filled metal. The latter is particularly useful if the flange has to be repeatedly made and unmade such as in SPM hose changes. The gasket separates cleanly and may be re-useable.

Examples of gasket materials and their applications are given in the following table.

GASKET MATERIAL	APPLICATIONS
Synthetic rubbers	Water, air
Vegetable fibre	Oil
Synthetic rubbers with cloth insert	Water, air
Solid Teflon	Chemicals

Compressed asbestos	Most
Carbon steel (CS)	High pressure fluids
Stainless steel (SS)	High pressure and/or corrosive fluids
Spiral wound:	
SS/Teflon	Chemicals
CS/asbestos	Most
SS/asbestos	Corrosive
SS/ceramic	Hot gases

Hyperbaric welded connection

Hyperbaric welding carried out inside a dry habitat is becoming increasingly used offshore. The welds can be of the highest quality and the results therefore can have the greatest reliability.

There is a considerable amount of diving involved in the preparation for a hyperbaric weld on a pipe. The following procedure is a rough generalisation of a pipeline riser tie-in aimed at giving some idea of the diving tasks involved.

After the pipeline has been set down with its lay-down head in the target area, divers may be needed to remove the constant tension (CT) cable. (See section 1.3, Pipelay barge dive tasks.) Accurate measurements are then made between the riser flange and the pipe to determine the final dimensions of the tie-in spool piece (or pieces). Depending on the distances involved, these measurements can be produced using either a template, a taut wire system or an acoustic transponder system.

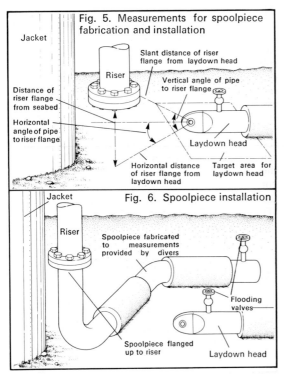

Fig. 5. Measurements for spoolpiece fabrication and installation

Jacket

Riser

Slant distance of riser flange from laydown head

Distance of riser flange from seabed

Vertical angle of pipe to riser flange

Horizontal angle of pipe to riser flange

Laydown head

Horizontal distance of riser flange from laydown head

Target area for laydown head

Jacket

Fig. 6. Spoolpiece installation

Riser

Spoolpiece fabricated to measurements provided by divers

Flooding valves

Spoolpiece flanged up to riser

Laydown head

The spool is fabricated to the required size and configuration. It is lowered to the seabed and manoeuvred into position using surface cranes or davits and diver-operated Tirfors (or equivalent).

The spool may then require to be flooded if it was sent down sealed and dry. Diver-operated valves are provided for this purpose. The riser-to-spool flange is then made up, sometimes only loosely to allow a small swivelling capability on a swivel ring flange.

The ends of the pipe are then carefully cut to allow them to be brought into line ready for the arrival of the alignment frame. Oxy-arc cutting and perhaps some prior seabed excavation by water-jetting may be required to provide access. Various handling systems can be used to manoeuvre the pipe into position including:

—Static 'H' frames.
—Walking-type 'H' frames.
—'Seahorse' subsea cranes.
—Tirfors and dead-man anchors.
—Surface cranes and/or davits.
—Air bags.

Once in line, guide wires are attached to the pipes to guide the descending pipeline alignment frame and welding habitat down over the pipe ends.

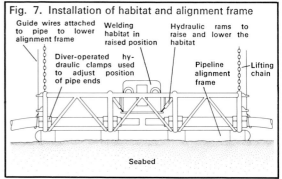

Fig. 7. Installation of habitat and alignment frame

Guide wires attached to pipe to lower alignment frame

Welding habitat in raised position

Hydraulic rams to raise and lower the habitat

Diver-operated hydraulic clamps used to adjust position of pipe ends

Pipeline alignment frame

Lifting chain

Seabed

A combination of the CCTV from ROVs and direct diver supervision can be used for the lowering operation. Divers then operate the hydraulic pipeline clamps to bring the pipe ends into a suitable position to allow the lowering of the habitat. In smaller systems, the habitat may be separate from the main alignment frames.

The access to the habitat can also vary between companies. The bell may mate directly with the habitat to allow a dry transfer. Alternatively, the bell may simply be lowered alongside the habitat and the welder/divers have to lock-out of the bell, swim across to, and lock into the habitat.

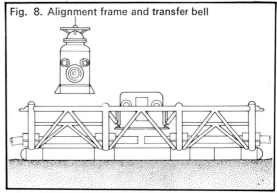

Fig. 8. Alignment frame and transfer bell

Once the habitat is over the pipe ends, the diver installs the door seals.

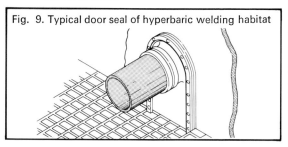

Fig. 9. Typical door seal of hyperbaric welding habitat

Stopper pigs are placed inside the pipe ends and inflated to seal off the inside from the habitat. With door and pipe seals made good, the habitat can be dewatered by blowing down with the appropriate gas mix. The actual gases used for this can vary between diving companies from breathable to un-breathable. In the latter case, the welders would have to wear special masks whilst inside the habitat.

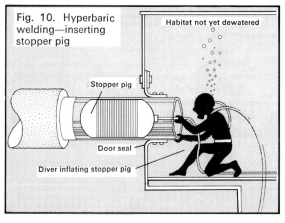

Fig. 10. Hyperbaric welding—inserting stopper pig

Habitat not yet dewatered

Stopper pig

Door seal

Diver inflating stopper pig

The next phase consists of welding preparation and the specialised welding procedure itself, including the installation of a pup piece to close the gap. The pipe ends are bevelled, demagnetised, preheated and MMA, MIG or TIG welded. Following the welding, there is a radiographic examination to check the integrity of the connection. Once the weld is confirmed as meeting the design specification, the exposed pipe metal is wrapped with bitumen tape. The habitat is then flooded and recovered by reversal of the installation procedure.

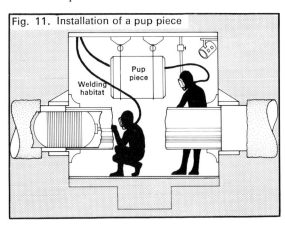

Fig. 11. Installation of a pup piece

Pup piece

Welding habitat

Fig. 12. Alignment of pup piece

Pipe clamp

Fig. 13. Welding pup piece in position

'Flexiforge' pipeline connector

The Flexiforge connector is a means of attaching a flange to the end of a pipe. It incorporates the principle of cold forging the pipe into the flange body. The diver places the Flexiforge end connector on the end of a pipe and inserts into it a hydraulically actuated forging tool. This rotates and expands until its rollers mould the pipewall into a plastic state. As the rollers continue to expand, the pipeline is forged into complete contact with the specially designed grooves of the end connector. When there is complete assurance (using ultrasonic testing) that the forged connection is a mechanical solid the process is terminated and the diver removes the forging tool. The result is that the pipe has been stressed into the plastic range, but the connector has been stressed only into the elastic range. The residual stresses make the end connector function like a steel rubber band.

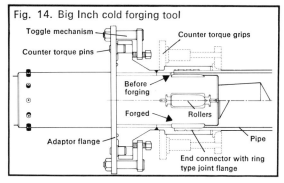

Fig. 14. Big Inch cold forging tool

Toggle mechanism

Counter torque grips

Counter torque pins

Before forging

Forged

Rollers

Adaptor flange

Pipe

End connector with ring type joint flange

Grip and seal mechanical coupling

The 'Gripper' mechanical coupling provides a metal-to-metal sealed flowline connection. The grip and seal is actuated by stud tensioning by the diver.

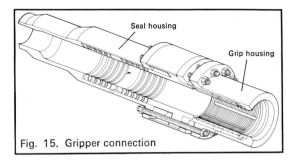

Fig. 15. Gripper connection

Cameron pipeline connector

The Cameron connector is a mechanical connector. The system uses hydraulic actuators to minimise the physical effort of the diver on the seabed. They are easy to operate and provide several reference points for the diver to assure the alignment and position of the hub before connection and pressure testing begins. In addition, the actuator performs the following functions:

—Leads the connection assembly down the guide-wires to the tie-in base on the seabed.

—Moves the hubs together.

—Locks the collet fingers around the two hubs and energises the AX metal seal ring.

—Disconnects and supports tie-in assembly if retrieval of equipment is required.

The hydraulically operated actuators are positioned over the collet connectors at each end of the tie-in assembly and attached to it by means of releasable shoes and swing clamps. Guidewires are passed through the guide funnels on the actuators—from the

guide pins on the seabed to the surface support vessel. Motion compensators on the surface are used to keep these lines tight throughout the operation. The actuators and tie-in assembly are lowered down the guidewires to a close alignment with the hubs of the pipeline on the seabed. When they have landed on the support base and alignment is verified, a control valve in the actuator is operated by a diver (or remote control), and a hydraulic mechanism moves the mating hubs together. Operation by the diver of a second lever activates another hydraulic piston set to move a metal sleeve forward in order to lock the collet fingers around the mating hubs and load the metal seal. The pipeline hubs are now face-to-face. Once a pressure test on the AX seal has been carried out, the actuator is released from the collet connector and retrieved to the surface.

HydroBall/HydroCouple connectors

The external set HydroBall/HydroCouple connector is sealed at the pipe ends, and at the ball-and-socket connection.

The HydroCouple connector is set and sealed onto the pipe end with hydraulic fluid supplied through lines from the surface. The pressure of the fluid forces bi-directional slips against the inner and outer diameters of the connector and the pipe, ensuring a positive and permanent connection. That same pressure seats packers to seal the space between connector and pipe.

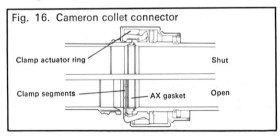

Fig. 16. Cameron collet connector

Clamp actuator ring   Shut

Clamp segments   AX gasket   Open

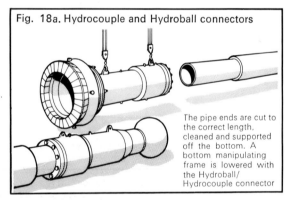

Fig. 18a. Hydrocouple and Hydroball connectors

The pipe ends are cut to the correct length, cleaned and supported off the bottom. A bottom manipulating frame is lowered with the Hydroball/ Hydrocouple connector

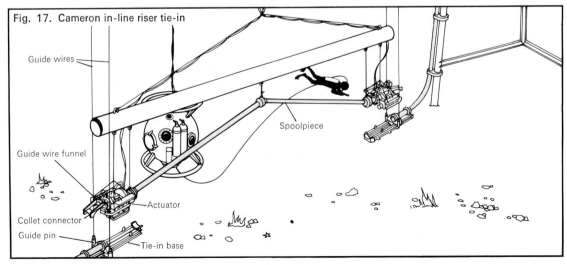

Fig. 17. Cameron in-line riser tie-in

Guide wires

Spoolpiece

Guide wire funnel

Actuator

Collet connector

Guide pin

Tie-in base

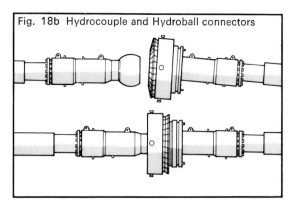

Fig. 18b Hydrocouple and Hydroball connectors

use, it is sealed around the weld area and the water is evacuated from it with an inert gas. The diver is then able to perform standard metal inert gas welding in the dry by holding the gun inside the box.

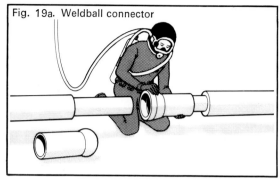

Fig. 19a. Weldball connector

The ball-and-socket portion of the connector uses a mechanical setting procedure. The ball half is moved into the socket and locked in place with lugs. Seals are then set around the machined surface of the ball to complete the connection.

Every seal is then tested through the use of ports, and the pipeline can then be put on stream. The completed connection maintains full pipeline diameter so that pigs and spheres can pass through easily.

Weldball connector

The Weldball connector utilises sleeved ball and socket halves to allow welded pipeline connections at up to 10° misalignment, and 30 cm (12″) or one pipe diameter of end gap. Under special circumstances these design parameters can be exceeded.

The connection is made using an underwater welding procedure that differs from other underwater welding in that the welder works in the wet but welds in the dry through the bottom of a transparent chamber called the Hydrobox. The 'box' may be made in virtually any shape required for a particular job. In

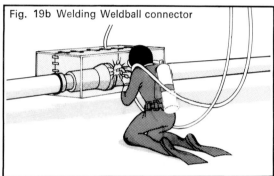

Fig. 19b Welding Weldball connector

A riser-to-pipeline connection for example would be carried out as follows. The ball half of the connector is welded onto the riser before it is put in place. Underwater welders then place the socket half on the pipeline end, fit it to the ball half, and fillet weld it into place in the dry area inside the Hydrobox.

PIGS

A 'pig' is an implement used inside a pipeline in a variety of applications. Pigs are made for cleaning, gauging and proving, separating products, and the inspection and recording of pipeline interiors. The diver may be involved in pigging operations either opening or shutting pipe valves during flooding or dewatering a section of the pipe, or in tracking and locating a pig.

Pigs are so-called because of the squealing sound they emit in operation.

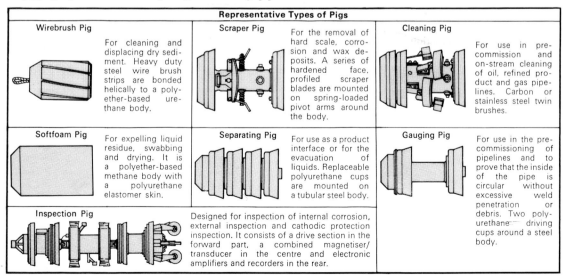

Representative Types of Pigs					
Wirebrush Pig	For cleaning and displacing dry sediment. Heavy duty steel wire brush strips are bonded helically to a polyether-based urethane body.	**Scraper Pig**	For the removal of hard scale, corrosion and wax deposits. A series of hardened face, profiled scraper blades are mounted on spring-loaded pivot arms around the body.	**Cleaning Pig**	For use in pre-commission and on-stream cleaning of oil, refined product and gas pipelines. Carbon or stainless steel twin brushes.
Softfoam Pig	For expelling liquid residue, swabbing and drying. It is a polyether-based methane body with a polyurethane elastomer skin.	**Separating Pig**	For use as a product interface or for the evacuation of liquids. Replaceable polyurethane cups are mounted on a tubular steel body.	**Gauging Pig**	For use in the pre-commissioning of pipelines and to prove that the inside of the pipe is circular without excessive weld penetration or debris. Two polyurethane driving cups around a steel body.
Inspection Pig	Designed for inspection of internal corrosion, external inspection and cathodic protection inspection. It consists of a drive section in the forward part, a combined magnetiser/transducer in the centre and electronic amplifiers and recorders in the rear.				

1.6 FIXED PLATFORMS

Fixed platforms are used extensively offshore in oil production. They can provide a drilling base, production/processing facilities, personnel accommodation, communications and logistic storage and transport facilities.

The design of a platform installation will depend on an evaluation of a number of factors: depth of water, size of field, high or low production, prevailing sea state, nature and contour of sea bottom, production costs and capital requirements. Production drilling can be conducted from a variety of structures.

The minimum platform is a caisson well guard suitable only for a single well, shallow water and sheltered location.

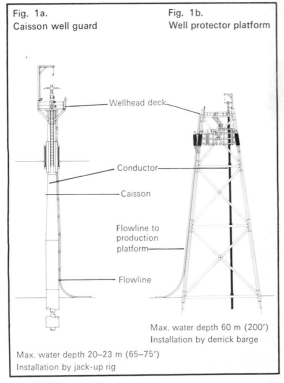

Fig. 1a.
Caisson well guard

Fig. 1b.
Well protector platform

Wellhead deck

Conductor

Caisson

Flowline to production platform

Flowline

Max. water depth 60 m (200')
Installation by derrick barge

Max. water depth 20–23 m (65–75')
Installation by jack-up rig

Next in order of capacity is a well protector platform, a three- or four-legged structure over one or more wells connecting flowlines to a nearby production platform. Some of these are found in the southern North Sea but this design is no longer much used.

Next is a simple production platform which collects the flowlines from surrounding wells in a widely scattered field.

All these platforms provide controls for existing flowlines. More complex and self-contained drilling/production platforms come next. These have the capability of handling as many as 25–30 conductors, of drilling deviated wells in the surrounding field and of processing and separating the oil from gas, water and debris. These larger platforms are usually restricted to depths down to 300 m (1000') and can weigh in excess of 20 000–30 000 tonnes.

Examples of drilling/production platforms are the Minimum, API and the North Sea Tower self-contained drilling/production platforms.

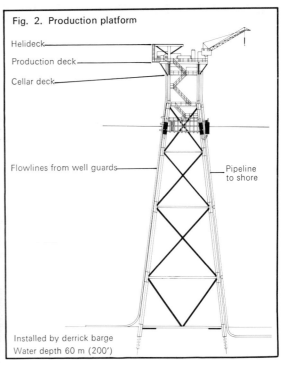

Fig. 2. Production platform

Helideck

Production deck

Cellar deck

Flowlines from well guards

Pipeline to shore

Installed by derrick barge
Water depth 60 m (200')

MULTI-PLATFORMS

The multi-platform system uses separate but interconnected platforms to provide the individual supports for drilling, production and accommodation. This has safety advantages and also allows the drilling to start sooner.

SUBSEA WELL TEMPLATES

These are structures sometimes placed on the seabed through which production wells are drilled by a jack-up or semi-submersible drilling rig. A platform is then placed over the template and the risers connected up. Fixed platforms are usually constructed of steel in the form of a four- to eight-legged framework called a jacket. The topside modules are fixed to the top of this at a height dictated by the anticipated sea states and tidal levels. These steel structures are fabricated ashore and towed out to the well site either on a barge or supported by their own buoyancy. When accurately positioned (siting can be accurate to 2 m) the structure is deballasted and set down. The jacket is secured to the seabed by a series of steel piles.

Concrete is also used to fabricate production platforms but differ from steel in that they are gravity structures depending on their mass for stability and immobility. Ballast tanks built in to the base can be either flooded with seawater or used as storage tanks for oil. The major concrete structures are found in the northern North Sea.

Other types of fixed platform include what are known as compliance platforms.

Where the depth of water or the prevailing sea state precludes the use of fixed platforms, compliance platforms are employed. These may be: a floating platform such as a semi-submersible; a guyed tower which is a steel jacket fixed to a single connection on the seabed and supported by guy ropes; a tension leg platform which is a floating semi-submersible unit held in place over the well by tensioned cables

Fig. 3. North Sea tower—Beryl B

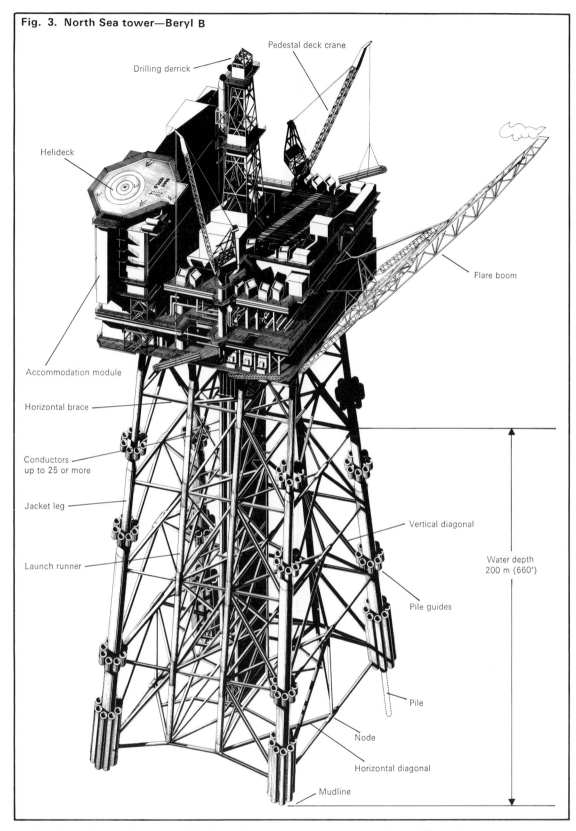

Pedestal deck crane

Drilling derrick

Helideck

Flare boom

Accommodation module

Horizontal brace

Conductors
up to 25 or more

Jacket leg

Vertical diagonal

Launch runner

Water depth
200 m (660')

Pile guides

Pile

Node

Horizontal diagonal

Mudline

anchored to the sea floor immediately under each corner of the platform. In all these compliant units, the aim is to minimise vertical movement of the platform to avoid undue strains on the seabed well connections. Surface and lateral movement may be in the region of up to 10 m (30'), depending on the relationship between the natural period of the waves and the platform period.

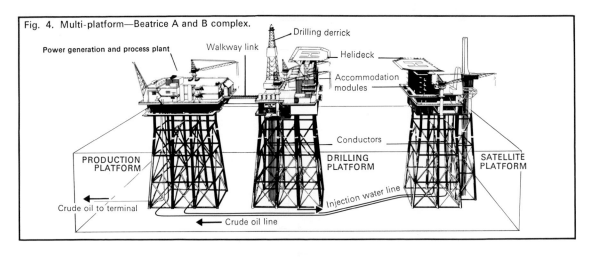

Fig. 4. Multi-platform—Beatrice A and B complex.

Power generation and process plant — Walkway link — Drilling derrick — Helideck — Accommodation modules

PRODUCTION PLATFORM — Conductors — DRILLING PLATFORM — SATELLITE PLATFORM

Crude oil to terminal — Injection water line — Crude oil line

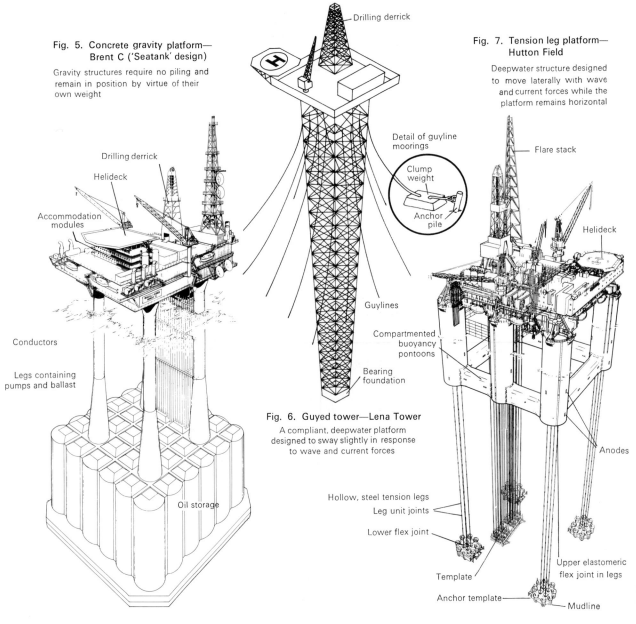

Fig. 5. Concrete gravity platform—
Brent C ('Seatank' design)

Gravity structures require no piling and
remain in position by virtue of their
own weight

Drilling derrick
Helideck
Accommodation modules
Conductors
Legs containing pumps and ballast
Oil storage

Drilling derrick

Detail of guyline moorings

Clump weight
Anchor pile

Guylines
Bearing foundation

Fig. 6. Guyed tower—Lena Tower

A compliant, deepwater platform
designed to sway slightly in response
to wave and current forces

Fig. 7. Tension leg platform—
Hutton Field

Deepwater structure designed
to move laterally with wave
and current forces while the
platform remains horizontal

Flare stack
Helideck
Compartmented buoyancy pontoons
Anodes
Hollow, steel tension legs
Leg unit joints
Lower flex joint
Template
Anchor template
Upper elastomeric flex joint in legs
Mudline

1.7 SINGLE POINT MOORING SYSTEM (SPM)

(1) Applications of SPMs

These fall into two main groups.

FIRST: To export or import crude oil or oil products from onshore/offshore fields or a refinery via some form of storage system. These installations are often multiple, and the loss of one buoy may not be too serious in the terms of lost production. These buoys usually accept ordinary world trade oil tankers.

SECOND: To take the oil straight from the oil field(s) via the production platform. It can be in any depth of water and is often used in the smaller oil fields, in remote locations, or where production does not justify the expense of a pipeline to the shore. The loss of this buoy is much more serious as the oil production may have to stop as soon as the buoy is shut down. These installations usually have dedicated tankers which need little or no assistance in mooring to the buoy.

Divers are heavily involved in installation, operation and maintenance of SPMs. Most are moored within air-diving range though some, for example in the North Sea, require mixed gas diving to reach the lower hoses and seabed manifolds.

(2) Types of SPMs

The most common type of single point mooring is the catenary anchor leg mooring or CALM, of which there are now well over 200 operating around the world, in water depths from under 15 m (50′) to over 65 m (400′) and capable of handling tankers ranging in size from less than 50 000 dead weight tons to the giant VLCCs exceeding half a million dwt.
Other less common types, used mainly where the CALM might show certain disadvantages, are:

—Single anchor leg mooring or SALM, shallow and deep water types.

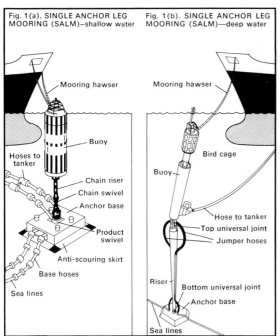

Fig. 1(a). SINGLE ANCHOR LEG MOORING (SALM)–shallow water

Fig. 1(b). SINGLE ANCHOR LEG MOORING (SALM)—deep water

—Vertical anchor leg mooring or VALM of which only a few have been installed and only one is still in operation.

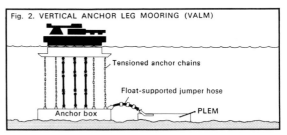

Fig. 2. VERTICAL ANCHOR LEG MOORING (VALM)
Tensioned anchor chains
Float-supported jumper hose
Anchor box
PLEM

—Single point mooring tower or SPMT of which there are two types; the jacket type, in which a jacket is piled to the seabed on top of which is a turntable carrying the mooring gear and pipework and the second type, the spring pile. There is no underbuoy hose system; risers are steel pipes housed within the structure.

—Exposed location single buoy mooring or ELSBM, installed in the North Sea Auk Field in which the mooring hawser and the cargo loading hose are stored on large diameter drums when the berth is unoccupied.

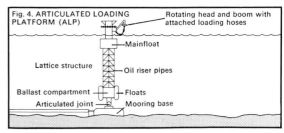

Fig. 3. EXPOSED LOCATION SINGLE BUOY MOORING (SBM)

—Articulated loading platform or ALP.

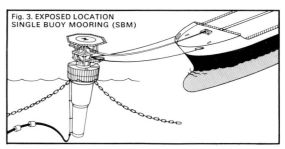

Fig. 4. ARTICULATED LOADING PLATFORM (ALP)
Rotating head and boom with attached loading hoses
Mainfloat
Lattice structure
Oil riser pipes
Ballast compartment
Floats
Articulated joint
Mooring base

The ELSBM, SPAR and ALP are designed for the extreme conditions of the North Sea often in water depths exceeding 90 m (300′).

(3) The CALM

THE MOORING SYSTEM

The mooring system consists of a number of anchor chains laid radially from the buoy. The earlier buoys had eight anchor legs arranged in four pairs; the usual standard is now six.
The size or weight of the chain depends on the size of ship the terminal has been designed to handle, and may vary from 6.5 to 10 cm ($2\frac{1}{2}″$–4″). To prevent the chain from reaching a fully tensioned state causing

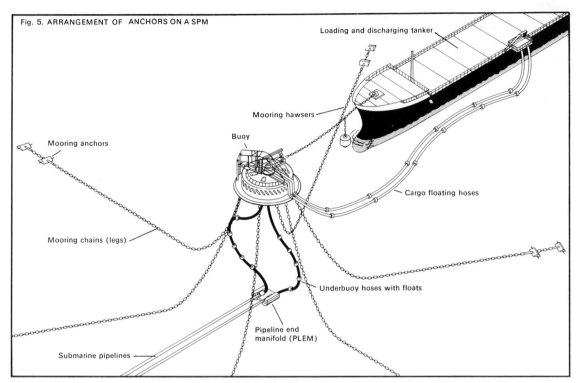

Fig. 5. ARRANGEMENT OF ANCHORS ON A SPM

Loading and discharging tanker

Mooring hawsers

Mooring anchors

Buoy

Cargo floating hoses

Mooring chains (legs)

Underbuoy hoses with floats

Pipeline end manifold (PLEM)

Submarine pipelines

shock loads and, in the extreme, breakage, the size and length are chosen such that the end 27 m (90′) remains on the bottom under the maximum horizontal movement load.

Each leg is some 340–370 m (1100–1200′) long and is attached to either an anchor, a driving pile or a drilled and grouted pile, depending on the nature of the seabed and the required holding power.

When the buoy is installed the anchor chains are pretensioned as accurately as possible to ensure that the buoy is in the correct position.

The mooring load applied by the tanker causes the buoy to move horizontally, lifting chain from the seabed on the side opposite to the applied mooring force, until the system again comes into equilibrium.

SUBMARINE HOSE SYSTEMS

There are three systems

—Chinese lantern, in which the configuration is achieved by the separate attachment of submarine floats. Hose strings are separate. Two or three are usual; four are uncommon but possible.

—Lazy-S, in which the correct configuration is obtained by adjusting the buoyancy of the tanks or by submarine floats. Hose strings are parallel and usually connected together all along their lengths. 2–3 are common; occasionally 4.

—Steep-'S', in which the configuration is achieved with one buoyancy tank of the correct size which is blown dry after installation. The modified Steep-S permits the use of this system in shallower water.

FLOATING HOSE SYSTEMS

Floating hoses are now almost always the integral floating type in which a jacket of buoyant material is built on to the main carcass.

All flotation material is compressible to a degree and if any part of a floating hose system is pulled below the surface the hydrostatic pressure will cause the material to compress, and there will be a reduction in volume and thus buoyancy. That section will become negatively buoyant and progressively pull the rest of the hose string below the surface until it is lying on

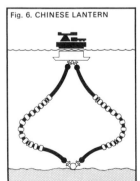

Fig. 6. CHINESE LANTERN

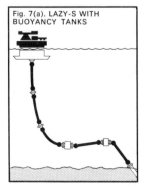

Fig. 7(a). LAZY-S WITH BUOYANCY TANKS

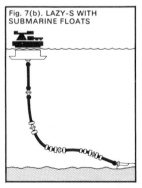

Fig. 7(b). LAZY-S WITH SUBMARINE FLOATS

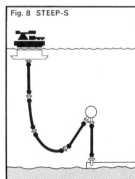

Fig. 8 STEEP-S

the seabed attached only to the buoy by the flange connection at the outboard end of the pipearm. This is known as autosubmersion and usually commences with a hose not fully floated which loses its additional support buoy, i.e. a $\frac{1}{2}$-float rail hose, or if the first hose off the buoy breaks at the flange, which sometimes happens in a spell of heavy weather. The first situation has been overcome by the introduction of the barbell or dumb-bell hose.

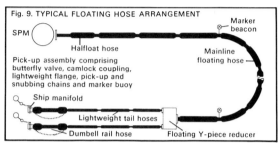

Fig. 9. TYPICAL FLOATING HOSE ARRANGEMENT

Some brands of hose are more prone to these problems than others, depending on the type of material used for the buoyant jacket; the other likely causes of trouble are the Y-piece reducer and concentric reducers sometimes found in floating hose systems. The tank around the Y-piece reducer should always be filled with a closed cell polyurethane foam and concentric reducers should always be fitted with some additional buoyancy. This in itself is vulnerable and needs frequent and regular inspection and repair.

The complete tail and rail hose assembly can often be changed with ease and these together with the first hose off the buoy require a lot of attention.

At a busy terminal, not too far offshore, it is often simpler to have a replacement string made up ashore ready to tow off which requires only one connection to be unbolted and remade.

(4) Tasks on a CALM

INSTALLATION TASKS

(1) Placing the PLEM (pipeline end manifold) and flanging-up with submarine pipelines.

(2) Installing the anchor chains into the buoy hawser pipes and chain stoppers. Checking chain angles and adjusting as and when necessary.

(3) Installing the submarine hoses on the PLEM and buoy. On modern buoys the latter is done in the dry or in waist-deep water in the buoy's centre well. On older buoys, the flanges are underneath and the work is very weather sensitive.

(4) Installing the ship's mooring system. This is usually the last item to install. The systems vary greatly and can be very heavy duty.

(5) Subsea valves operation. The testing and commissioning will include checks for leaks on the PLEM valves, hose strings under the buoy and deck hoses.

These tasks will include:

—use of surface cranes and winches

—rigging: including Tirfors, pull-lifts, chain-hoists, strops and spreaders

—flanging: including impact wrenches (air or hydraulic), spanners, hammers, and placing gaskets

—burning: using oxy-arc above and below water

—welding: possibly on various locking tabs on monkey face plates.

WARNING

When using arc welding on an SPM, beware of the risk of fire, explosion and damage to the bearing carriage through arcing. Always ground to the job.

Maintenance tasks

(1) Marine tasks

Divers may be required to assist with the surface activities on an SPM. These can include the following.

—Dressing the berth. Arrange for the mooring equipment and floating hose-strings to be properly laid out in readiness for the incoming tanker.

—Mooring/unmooring assistance. The handling of hawsers on and off the tanker.

—Hose handling assistance. Bring the ends of the floating hose strings into a position alongside the tanker, near the manifold connection to be hooked on the tanker derrick. When disconnecting, the hose ends need to be unhooked and streamed out clear of the tanker propellor.

(2) Non-diving maintenance tasks

Divers may be required to carry out planned maintenance of the SPM and the diving company may have to provide the power tools, hydraulics, water etc. Typical tasks are shown in Fig. 10.

—Special care is needed to avoid suffocation risk inside buoy compartments. This can be caused by degassing oil or inert gas pockets. Do not enter any compartment which has not been ventilated for a long time even if it had not contained any oil or gas. Never work on your own.

—Special care is also needed due to the explosion risk from degassing oil, especially if using oxy-arc or other hot cutting equipment. Make sure that permission is sought and given before using hot tools. Remember to earth to the job and not to the hull of the buoy. No smoking.

—Avoid the use of spark-producing tools if there is a risk of explosive gases.

—Always turn off the fog-horn (if fitted) whilst working onboard.

(3) Diving tasks

These tasks are divided into:

(a) Work around the structure of the buoy.
(b) Midwater, on the submarine or under-buoy hoses.
(c) Seabed, on the PLEM, pipe and anchor moorings.

Diving tasks around the buoy structure are illustrated in Fig. 11. Care must be taken to avoid injury and overexertion during rough sea conditions.

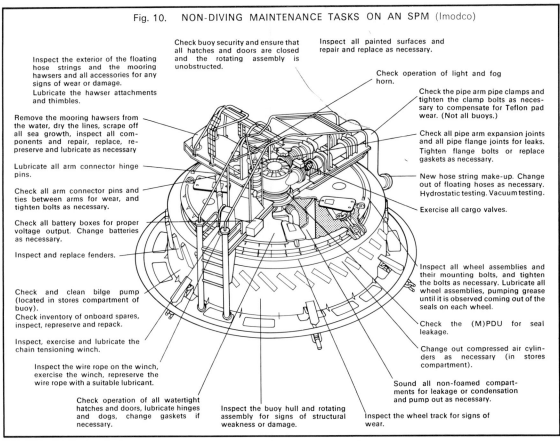

Fig. 10.   NON-DIVING MAINTENANCE TASKS ON AN SPM (Imodco)

Check buoy security and ensure that all hatches and doors are closed and the rotating assembly is unobstructed.

Inspect all painted surfaces and repair and replace as necessary.

Inspect the exterior of the floating hose strings and the mooring hawsers and all accessories for any signs of wear or damage. Lubricate the hawser attachments and thimbles.

Check operation of light and fog horn.

Check the pipe arm pipe clamps and tighten the clamp bolts as necessary to compensate for Teflon pad wear. (Not all buoys.)

Remove the mooring hawsers from the water, dry the lines, scrape off all sea growth, inspect all components and repair, replace, re-preserve and lubricate as necessary

Check all pipe arm expansion joints and all pipe flange joints for leaks. Tighten flange bolts or replace gaskets as necessary.

Lubricate all arm connector hinge pins.

New hose string make-up. Change out of floating hoses as necessary. Hydrostatic testing. Vacuum testing.

Check all arm connector pins and ties between arms for wear, and tighten bolts as necessary.

Exercise all cargo valves.

Check all battery boxes for proper voltage output. Change batteries as necessary.

Inspect and replace fenders.

Inspect all wheel assemblies and their mounting bolts, and tighten the bolts as necessary. Lubricate all wheel assemblies, pumping grease until it is observed coming out of the seals on each wheel.

Check and clean bilge pump (located in stores compartment of buoy). Check inventory of onboard spares, inspect, represerve and repack.

Check the (M)PDU for seal leakage.

Inspect, exercise and lubricate the chain tensioning winch.

Change out compressed air cylinders as necessary (in stores compartment).

Inspect the wire rope on the winch, exercise the winch, represerve the wire rope with a suitable lubricant.

Sound all non-foamed compartments for leakage or condensation and pump out as necessary.

Check operation of all watertight hatches and doors, lubricate hinges and dogs, change gaskets if necessary.

Inspect the buoy hull and rotating assembly for signs of structural weakness or damage.

Inspect the wheel track for signs of wear.

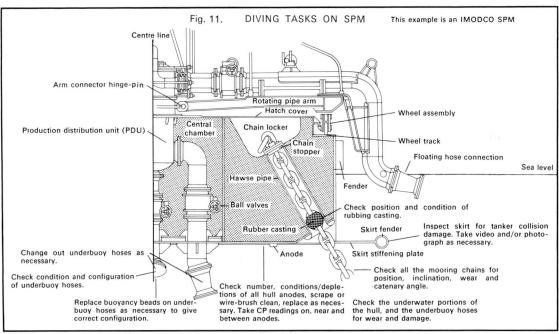

Fig. 11.   DIVING TASKS ON SPM   This example is an IMODCO SPM

Centre line

Arm connector hinge-pin

Rotating pipe arm

Hatch cover

Wheel assembly

Production distribution unit (PDU)

Central chamber

Chain locker

Wheel track

Chain stopper

Floating hose connection

Sea level

Hawse pipe

Fender

Ball valves

Check position and condition of rubbing casting.

Rubber casting

Skirt fender

Inspect skirt for tanker collision damage. Take video and/or photograph as necessary.

Anode

Skirt stiffening plate

Change out underbuoy hoses as necessary.

Check all the mooring chains for position, inclination, wear and catenary angle.

Check condition and configuration of underbuoy hoses.

Replace buoyancy beads on underbuoy hoses as necessary to give correct configuration.

Check number, conditions/depletions of all hull anodes, scrape or wire-brush clean, replace as necessary. Take CP readings on, near and between anodes.

Check the underwater portions of the hull, and the underbuoy hoses for wear and damage.

Notes on surface diving tasks

Chain angle measurement. The chain catenary angle is measured immediately beneath the buoy using a protractor or inclinometer supplied by the manufacturer.

The handbook of basic data and drawings, also supplied by the manufacturer, should specify the angle and make clear whether it is measured from the vertical or the horizontal axis, as this can vary from one manufacturer to another.

Serious errors can occur if the original protractor has been lost or damaged and if a locally made replacement has the scale reversed or wrongly marked so that it reads the opposite.

If the angles are too steep the whole system will be

'sloppy' and movements greater than designed; if the angles are too shallow then the system will be too 'stiff' and loads will exceed planned limits.

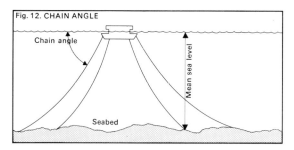

Fig. 12. CHAIN ANGLE

The protractor should look like the one in Fig. 13, which is designed to show the angle between the chain and the horizontal and should be hooked to the chain as close to the stopper as possible.

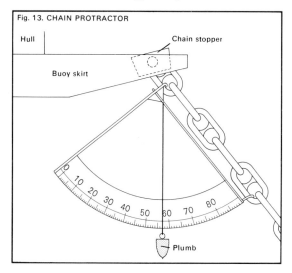

Fig. 13. CHAIN PROTRACTOR

CHAIN WEAR MEASUREMENT

Anchor chains wear most at two places.

(1) At the link in the chain stopper. The maximum tension in a catenary occurs at the point of suspension. The shape of the curve taken by the anchor chain between the stopper and the seabed is called a catenary.

(2) Along the length of each chain where it makes contact with the seabed. Because of the buoy motion, chain in this area is constantly being picked up and laid down and this, coupled with the abrasive nature of the seabed material, causes wear.

Frequent inspection of the links in the stoppers will indicate when these need to be changed.

It is sometimes possible to reverse this particular 'shot' or shackle of the chain if the wear has taken place towards one end. (A shot or shackle is 27 m (90′) in length.) Two types of joining shackle are to be found in making up the required lengths of anchor chains: lugged and lugless or 'Kenter' shackle where this has to pass through the chain stopper. These are illustrated in Fig. 14.

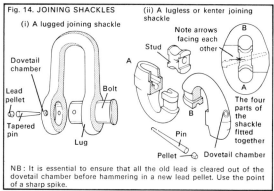

Fig. 14. JOINING SHACKLES

(i) A lugged joining shackle

Dovetail chamber
Lead pellet
Tapered pin
Lug
Bolt

(ii) A lugless or kenter joining shackle

Note arrows facing each other
Stud
The four parts of the shackle fitted together
Pin
Pellet
Dovetail chamber

NB: It is essential to ensure that all the old lead is cleared out of the dovetail chamber before hammering in a new lead pellet. Use the point of a sharp spike.

There are minor differences between the Imodco and SBM designs one of which is the chain stopper arrangements.

In the Imodco buoy each chain passes through a hawse pipe in the hull as shown in Fig. 15. The chain is held in a latch at the top end of the hawse pipe and chafing at the lower end is prevented by a rubbing casting. All these points need frequent inspection.

In the SBM design (also produced by McDermott, where it is called the 'Swivel-Top') the chain stoppers are located in the skirt and consist of a bucket-shape steel casting (which is in two parts, bolted together around the chain) housed in a trunnion mounting frame allowing movement in the vertical plane.

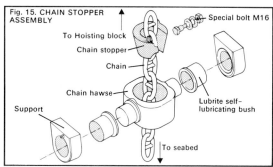

Fig. 15. CHAIN STOPPER ASSEMBLY

To Hoisting block
Chain stopper
Chain
Chain hawse
Support
Special bolt M16
Lubrite self-lubricating bush
To seabed

The Blue Water Terminals buoy, a recent introduction, has a similar arrangement: each stopper is carried in trunnions at the ends of a six-legged spider which is carried in the lower end of the central column. The buoyant hull, which is free to rotate around this column, carries the tanker mooring attachment and the floating hose connection.

BUOY POSITION MEASUREMENT

Another aid to check the buoy position depends on the configuration of the underbuoy hoses.

If these are of the Chinese lantern type the buoy is vertically over the PLEM or seabed manifold, and a plumb-bob dropped from the centre of the underside of the buoy is a useful aid.

With the Lazy-S underbuoy hose system the installation crew may have used a datum—usually a concrete block with a staff on the seabed. The drawing and/or handbook should specify the distance between a mark on the manifold and the position on the seabed vertically below the centre of the buoy.

All measurements should be taken in calm conditions

and ideally at mean sea level. If adjustments to the chain are necessary the handbook and drawings will detail how to rig the buoy derrick and operate the winch.

Pulling up a chain shallows the angle, increases the tension and tends to move the buoy in the direction of that chain. It has the same effect on the chain diametrically opposite, so work on opposite pairs of anchors and not 'around the clock'.

TASKS ON SUBMARINE HOSES

CHECK AND ADJUSTMENT OF CONFIGURATION

Whichever system is adopted, before any adjustments are made, the initial configuration must be measured and drawn as accurately as possible. The following procedures are examples.

(1) CHINESE LANTERN

A plumb line is dropped from the centre of the underside of the buoy; the line can be marked every 3 m (10′) or so with a metal or plastic ·tag. Two divers are necessary, one on the plumb line and one on the hose string to take a series of measurements of the horizontal distance from the plumb line to the midpoint of each hose and each flange connection, recording the depth on the plumb line at each point. Ideally these measurements should be taken in calm conditions at slack water. From them a rough sketch is produced as in Fig. 16 which should later be drawn accurately to scale on squared paper.

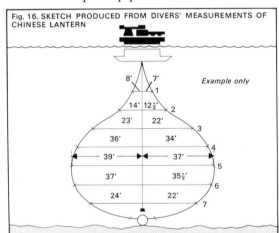

Fig. 16. SKETCH PRODUCED FROM DIVERS' MEASUREMENTS OF CHINESE LANTERN

Removal of floats is largely common sense and practice; if there is a hose company representative present, take his advice.

Do not move more than two floats at a time and allow the system adequate time to settle, particularly with new hoses which will be quite stiff for the first few days in service.

Repeat the above procedure until the recommended configuration is achieved and then produce and file an accurate diagram for future reference.

(2) LAZY-S (WITH FLOATS OR TANKS)

Here only one diver is necessary and if the procedure is not hurried, depths can be recorded from the 'pneumo' gauge. Since the water depth and PLEM offset should be known from measurement,

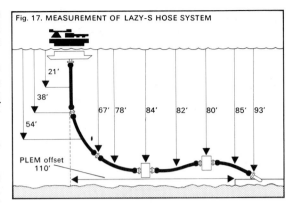

Fig. 17. MEASUREMENT OF LAZY-S HOSE SYSTEM

the diagram in Fig. 17 can be produced.

When installing a new system of this type, the buoyancy tanks will contain just sufficient ballast water to give them a negative buoyancy and will be supported by the crane via a spreader bar. The strings cannot be removed until the hose system is connected to PLEM and buoy and the buoyancy of the tanks adjusted to their approximate position. Final adjustment consists of altering the ballast in each tank until the correct configuration is achieved. For Lazy-S system with floats, adjustments are made by removing or repositioning individual floats. After allowing time for the system to settle after the final adjustment has been made, a record of the configuration should be made, drawn to scale and filed for future reference.

(3) STEEP-S AND MODIFIED STEEP-S

In these systems no adjustments are possible and if correctly designed, neither should they be necessary. For installation, the tank is flooded and, after hook-up, blown dry. However, it is equally important to measure and record the configuration as shown in Fig. 18.

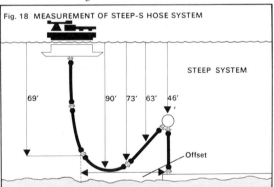

Fig. 18. MEASUREMENT OF STEEP-S HOSE SYSTEM

Since all submarine hose systems are water-filled after installation or a hose change and since the initial configuration is made in this condition, some change is to be expected when oil is introduced into system. The earliest opportunity of checking the oil-filled configuration should be taken and an accurate diagram made for comparison with the water-filled configuration.

REPLACEMENT OF GASKET AT PLEM

—If a recent installation, the gasket will probably be easily extracted intact and only half the bolts will need to be removed. Slacken the other half. Remove the gasket and replace with new one. Replace bolts and tighten them up. (Make sure that the nut is flush with the end of the bolt to prevent fouling/jamming.)

—If the installation is an old one, it will probably be necessary to break the flange completely. The following procedure is an example.

First remove the 3 o'clock and 9 o'clock stud bolts.

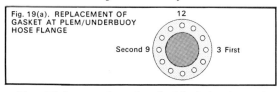

Fig. 19(a). REPLACEMENT OF GASKET AT PLEM/UNDERBUOY HOSE FLANGE

Two Tirfors are then rigged with their wires going through the bolt holes and terminating in a small loop with bulldog clips to prevent them being pulled back through.

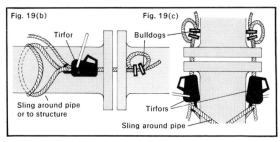

Fig. 19(b)   Fig. 19(c)

These Tirfors must then be tensioned up.

Slacken off the bolts and arrange the 12 o'clock bolt to be held by two turns of the thread.

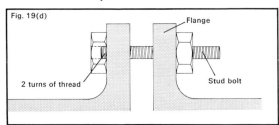

Fig. 19(d)

This will be the last bolt to remove. Remove the remaining bolts and knock off the 12 o'clock nut taking care to avoid any subsequent movement of the hose flange.

Always have the 12 o'clock bolt as the last to undo to reduce the risk of injury due to flange movement. Slacken off the Tirfors to get at the gasket. Remove the gasket and check the flange faces carefully for any damage. Clean as necessary.

Fit the new gasket.

Tension up Tirfors to re-align the flanges—use close tolerance pins/podgers and hammer to help with the final line-up.

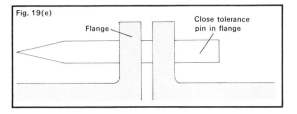

Fig. 19(e)

Replace the bolts and move the pins as necessary. Avoid the use of a hammer on the bolts.

Remove the Tirfor and wire and install the last two bolts.

At all times take care to avoid hands, arms, umbilical etc. becoming trapped between flanges, especially if in bad visibility.

INSTALLATION AND CHANGE-OUT

The Chinese lantern is the simplest system to install since each hose string is handled separately. If it becomes necessary to change one hose in a string, it will usually be easier to remove the whole string, change the hose on the surface and re-install rather than attempt to change a hose underwater.

The same procedures apply to the Lazy-S or to the Steep-S configurations.

With a single hose system of these types, complete removal, change-out on the surface and re-installation is the obvious answer. With twin and multiple hose systems other procedures apply and each can only be assessed on its own merits. When faced with this problem the following points should be considered.

(1) Weather and sea conditions, depth of water, underwater visibility, currents.

(2) How far offshore or from the operating base? (All types of hose strings and systems have been towed from shore assembly to the installation up to distances of 240 km (150 miles). It is often easier to remove a complete system, rebuild it onshore, tow-out and reinstall.) Submarine hoses float when full of air without any additional buoyancy. Use lightweight flanges to blank-off ends.

(3) The type and capacity of crane or derrick available.

(4) Are there enough hands to carry out all duties in the team or can they be provided from local resources?

(5) Are there sufficient pad eyes on both the buoy and the PLEM to rig the necessary tackles, or can extra securing points be provided by bolt-on clamps.

AN EXAMPLE OF AN UNDERBUOY HOSE CHANGE

(a) FLANGE-UP OF HOSE AND PLEM

When replacing an underbuoy hose, the bottom flange is normally made-up first, at least partially, before the underbuoy flange is made-up.

The procedure for manoeuvering and aligning the flanges is basically the same as for the gasket change-out.

The initial closing in of the hose flange is achieved using a guide wire rigged from the surface.

The 3 o'clock wires and 9 o'clock wires are prepared and stowed on the hose flange prior to submergence. They are uncoiled and rigged via the PLEM flange when the final alignment is required. The diver must be careful to avoid injury during the lowering of the hose, especially if the visibility is poor. A knotted tag-line on the hose flange can give the diver an indication of its approach. If the sea surface is rough, the flange can be moving violently and great care is then required to avoid collision, entrapment and entanglement.

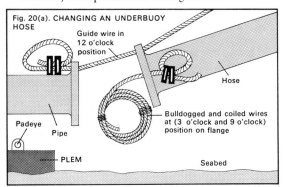

Fig. 20(a). CHANGING AN UNDERBUOY HOSE

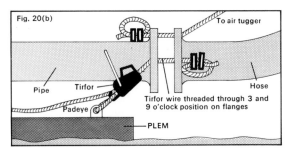

Fig. 20(b)

(b) FLANGE-UP UNDER THE BUOY

This is also similar to the previous arrangement. The hose is played out from the diving support vessel and then winched in below the buoy.

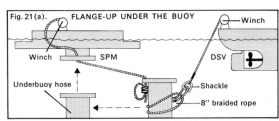

Fig. 21(a). FLANGE-UP UNDER THE BUOY

The winches or Tirfors on the buoy make the final alignment.

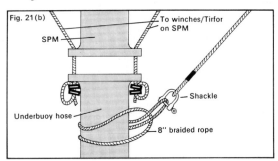

Fig. 21(b)

In poor visibility, the tender must make sure that the diver's umbilical has the absolute minimum of slack to avoid entanglement. For the same reason, if there is a current, the diver should ensure that he remains downstream of the main activity. It is often convenient for the diver to locate himself on a downstream anchor chain to

observe and supervise the flange alignment and closing operation.

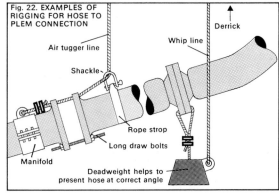

Fig. 22. EXAMPLES OF RIGGING FOR HOSE TO PLEM CONNECTION

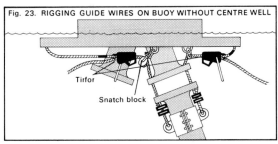

Fig. 23. RIGGING GUIDE WIRES ON BUOY WITHOUT CENTRE WELL

N.B. Later buoys of this type have trunks above the hose connection flanges through which tackles can be rigged.

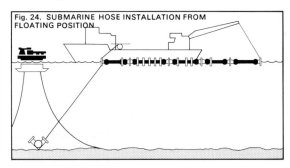

Fig. 24. SUBMARINE HOSE INSTALLATION FROM FLOATING POSITION

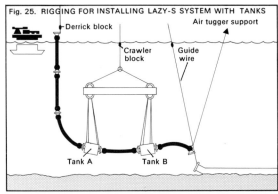

Fig. 25. RIGGING FOR INSTALLING LAZY-S SYSTEM WITH TANKS

N.B. Four-leg slings on tanks prevent kinks in hose adjacent to tanks.

For the Lazy-S system with submarine floats, the 'controlled sink' method can be used in which both ends of each string are closed off with blind flanges equipped with a 5.25 cm (2″) valve through which the sea water can be admitted. When the lower end reaches the area of the PLEM the flange is removed and further control exercised by operating the valve on the top end.

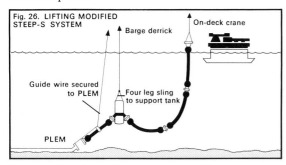

Fig. 26. LIFTING MODIFIED STEEP-S SYSTEM

On-deck crane
Barge derrick
Guide wire secured to PLEM
Four leg sling to support tank
PLEM

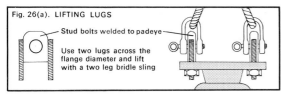

Fig. 26(a). LIFTING LUGS

Stud bolts welded to padeye
Use two lugs across the flange diameter and lift with a two leg bridle sling

Both Lazy-S and Steep-S systems can be installed even in the absence of large crane facilities; after assembly and pressure-testing the tank(s) is(are) flooded till just negatively buoyant such that the depth can be controlled by quite a lightweight tackle during connection to the PLEM. When the top end has been connected to the buoy the tank(s) is(are) ballasted accordingly.

TASKS ON THE PIPELINE END MANIFOLD (PLEM)

VALVE OPERATIONS
These are undertaken according to client requirements.

HYDRAULIC VALVES
—Only a little work is normally required.

—Stab hydraulic line into the open and close sockets to test actuator; observe/feel indicator to check action.

—If difficult, check the ball valve in the socket and hose connector; purge if necessary.

—Check the blank caps are secure over the connector on valve before and after operation.

HAND-OPERATED VALVES
—If the valve wheel has been removed, take a wheel down to turn the valve. If a wheel is not available on site, use a hydraulic tool.

—Clean shaft—use knife to remove marine growth.

—Place the wheel/tool; turn to fully shut or open as required. Make sure the valve is fully home.

—Test by unwinding slightly and retightening.

—Check (see/feel) indicator has moved as expected. Take care because sometimes the indicators can jam and sheer off and not function normally.

—Check with surface control that the pipe pressure confirms the correct valve operation if appropriate.

CONTROL SYSTEM
—Replacement of HP hydraulic hoses.

—Installation of bypass hydraulic hoses.

PILES
—Check the anodes.

—Check for scour.

—Check for damage.

CATHODIC PROTECTION
—Take readings on and near the anode possibly on the continuity strap, e.g. on elbows near pipeline end manifold.

—Make visual checks and calliper checks on the anodes to assess rate of depletion.

PIPELINE TO PLEM CONNECTION
—Check for leaks.

—Can be a flange, or hydroball type or a Cameron etc.

DEBRIS
—Check and remove as necessary from the PLEM and pipeline.

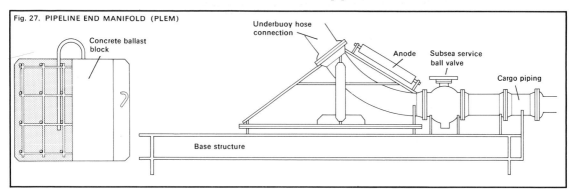

Fig. 27. PIPELINE END MANIFOLD (PLEM)

Concrete ballast block
Underbuoy hose connection
Anode
Subsea service ball valve
Cargo piping
Base structure

1.8 PIPELINE INSPECTION

Pipeline inspection is carried out by divers and manned or unmanned submersibles. This forms part of the routine inspection and maintenance procedure of the owner. The requirements include those of the owners, certifying authorities, insurance companies and governmental bodies.

Pipeline inspection data are a very important part of the operation of oil and gas fields. The highest possible standards of inspection are therefore essential. The following diagrams indicate the type of data that may be required by an oil company client.

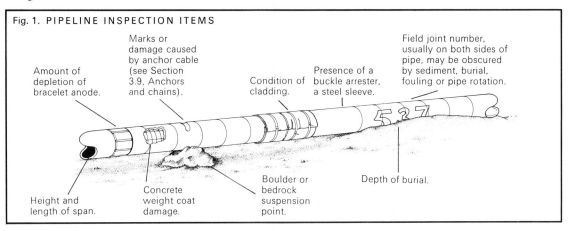

Fig. 1. PIPELINE INSPECTION ITEMS

Amount of depletion of bracelet anode.

Marks or damage caused by anchor cable (see Section 3.9, Anchors and chains).

Condition of cladding.

Presence of a buckle arrester, a steel sleeve.

Field joint number, usually on both sides of pipe, may be obscured by sediment, burial, fouling or pipe rotation.

Height and length of span.

Concrete weight coat damage.

Boulder or bedrock suspension point.

Depth of burial.

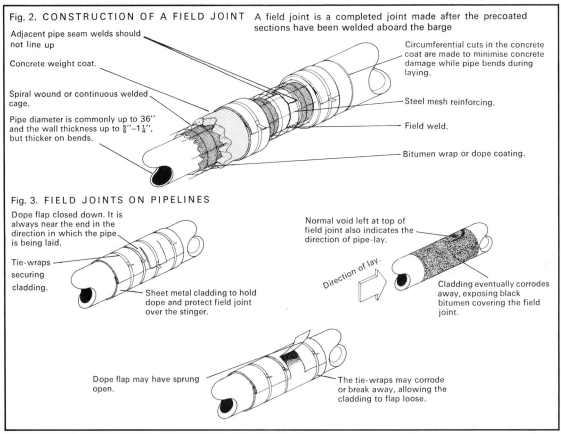

Fig. 2. CONSTRUCTION OF A FIELD JOINT
A field joint is a completed joint made after the precoated sections have been welded aboard the barge

Adjacent pipe seam welds should not line up

Concrete weight coat.

Spiral wound or continuous welded cage.

Pipe diameter is commonly up to 36'' and the wall thickness up to $\frac{5}{8}''-1\frac{1}{4}''$, but thicker on bends.

Circumferential cuts in the concrete coat are made to minimise concrete damage while pipe bends during laying.

Steel mesh reinforcing.

Field weld.

Bitumen wrap or dope coating.

Fig. 3. FIELD JOINTS ON PIPELINES

Dope flap closed down. It is always near the end in the direction in which the pipe is being laid.

Tie-wraps securing cladding.

Sheet metal cladding to hold dope and protect field joint over the stinger.

Normal void left at top of field joint also indicates the direction of pipe-lay.

Direction of lay

Cladding eventually corrodes away, exposing black bitumen covering the field joint.

Dope flap may have sprung open.

The tie-wraps may corrode or break away, allowing the cladding to flap loose.

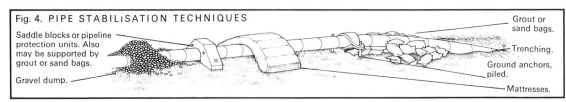

Fig. 4. PIPE STABILISATION TECHNIQUES

Saddle blocks or pipeline protection units. Also may be supported by grout or sand bags.

Gravel dump.

Grout or sand bags.

Trenching.

Ground anchors, piled.

Mattresses.

Fig. 5. PIPELINE TERMINATION

Blind flange.

Pulling head or laydown head.

Laydown head with internal valve(s).

Laydown head with external valve(s). The valves may be protected by a shroud or frame. There may be an extension tube on the inlet/outlet to deflect water or air away from the diver.

Net fitted to open flanged end to catch pigs or spheres.

Caged or recessed bleed valve with flange.

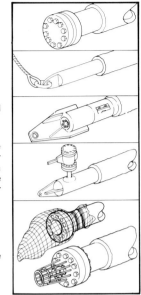

Safety note: Always be aware of the dangers of differential pressures when working on pipelines and valves. There is a possibility of being sucked onto and into valves and pipes when pressure differentials are rapidly altered.

Take care to avoid contact with high concentrations of corrosion inhibitor, oxygen scavenger and dyes that may escape from the pipe. Special care should be taken to avoid contact between these substances and hot water suits, and the possibility of contaminating the bell interior.

Fig. 6. TYPES OF PIPELINE ANODES

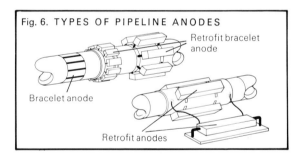

Retrofit bracelet anode

Bracelet anode

Retrofit anodes

Fig. 7. DEBRIS INDENTIFICATION

○ Fishing nets, otter-board and cables.

○ Stud link anchor chain and wire cable.

○ Anchor; see Section 3.9, Chains and anchors for description of types.

○ Boulders that may have been dragged to the pipe by fishing gear.

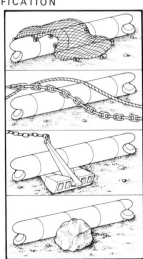

○ Typical anchor scour and mound.

○ Mound of seabed material steeped against one side of the pipe only.

○ Direction of anchor drag.

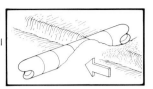

Fig. 8. NATURE OF A TRENCH

The following aspects may be included when describing a trench:

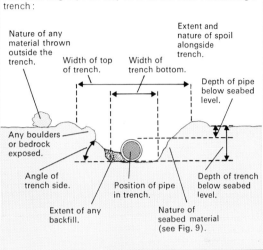

Nature of any material thrown outside the trench.

Width of top of trench.

Width of trench bottom.

Extent and nature of spoil alongside trench.

Depth of pipe below seabed level.

Any boulders or bedrock exposed.

Angle of trench side.

Position of pipe in trench.

Depth of trench below seabed level.

Extent of any backfill.

Nature of seabed material (see Fig. 9).

Fig. 9. NATURE OF THE SEABED

It is helpful to use standardised terms when describing the seabed. The following system is internationally adopted:

Boulder A boulder is a detached rock mass, rounded or otherwise modified by abrasion. The minimum size is 256 mm (about 10") diameter.

Block The same size as boulder, but an angular fragment showing little or no abrasion.

Cobbles Cobbles are similar to boulders but are smaller and range in size from 64 to 256 mm ($2\frac{1}{2}$–10").

Pebbles Rock fragments, rounded or otherwise abraded by the action of water, ice or wind. They range in size from 4 to 64 mm ($\frac{5}{32}$–$2\frac{1}{2}$").

Granules Granules are small rock fragments between 2 and 4 mm in diameter ($\frac{3}{16}$").

Sand Sand is an aggregate of mineral or rock grains between 0.6 and 2 mm in diameter.

Silt Silt is a sediment consisting of particles of sizes from 0.6 mm to 0.004 mm.

Clay Clay is a sediment with particle sizes less than 0.004 mm diameter.

Gravel Gravel is an unconsolidated accumulation of pebbles, cobbles or boulders. This would be referred to as pebble-gravel, cobble-gravel etc.

Conglomerate The consolidated equivalent of gravel is conglomerate and is likewise called pebble- or boulder-conglomerate.

Rubble Rubble is an unconsolidated accumulation of angular rock fragments coarser than sand.

Visual inspection guide

This guide is to assist divers in the inspection of offshore concrete structures. A complete classification of concrete defects is given in the American Concrete Institute code 201. The accuracy of recording features will depend on the class of inspection. Divers should attempt to describe defects fully so that their significance, related to structural integrity, can be assessed by engineers. Careful visual observation is needed because it can be difficult, especially on ROV surveys, to distinguish between defects and normal features. For example, thin wire could be identified as a crack, or white paint as sulphate attack.

1. CRACKS: An incomplete separation into one or more parts with or without space between. Caused by a force sufficient to rip concrete apart

Type of crack	Description	Cause	What to record
Corrosion cracks	Most likely to occur in splash zone or where cover is low. Usually follows line of reinforcement.	Corrosion of reinforcement; corrosion products larger than initial volume of steel giving rise to bursting forces.	Length, width, orientation, surface deposits, location. Covermeters available to measure the cover and position of reinforcement.
Thermal cracking	Most likely to occur in storage cells.	Restricted expansion or contraction of concrete.	Length, width, orientation, location.
Structural overload	For impact most likely to occur in splash zone and cell roofs. Distribution of cracks important for structural analysis.	Excessive applied force e.g. environmental, impact.	Length, width, orientation, location.
Pattern cracking	Pattern formed by interconnection of cracks.	Differential volume change between surface and internal concrete.	Area covered, location, width.
Shrinkage cracking	Possibly in unprestressed concrete. Can form even distribution over surface.	Concrete curing.	Length, width, orientation, location.

2. CONCRETE LOSSES: Loss of concrete section formed after construction

Type of concrete loss	Description	Cause	What to record
Pop out	Shallow, typically conical depressions in the concrete surface.	Development of localised internal pressure e.g. expansion of aggregate particle.	Diameter, depth, location.
Spall	Fragment detached from mass. Depression formed exposing aggregate not covered by laitence.	Corrosion of reinforcement or application of applied force.	Exposed reinforcement, complete dimensional survey, location.
Delamination	A form of 'spall' only the fragment breaks away in a sheet. Thickness of sheet variable 5–100 mm but often to depth of reinforcement.	Corrosion of reinforcement or applied force.	Exposed reinforcement, complete dimensional survey, location.
Chemical attack	Softening of concrete surface possibly white surface appearance.	Sulphate attack.	Area covered, depth, location.
Erosion	Possibly due to particles in fast moving seawater.	Abrasion of concrete surface.	Area covered, depth, location.

3. SURFACE DEPOSITS

Type of surface deposits	Description	Cause	What to record
Exudation	A liquid or viscous gel-like material discharged through a pore, crack or opening in the surface.	Reaction between the alkali in the cement and the aggregate.	Area covered, thickness, hard or soft, location.
Incrustation	A crust or coating generally white in appearance.	Leaching of lime from the cement.	Area covered, thickness, hard or soft, location.
Rust stains	Brown stains on the concrete surface.	Corrosion of embedded steelwork.	Area covered, location.

4. CONSTRUCTION DEFECTS: Defects formed on the concrete surface during construction

Type of construction defects	Description	Cause	What to record
Tearing	Similar in appearance to horizontal cracks on slip formed walls. Normally discontinuous from about 100 mm to several metres long.	Adhesion of the concrete to slip form shutters as they are jacked up.	Width, length, measurable depth, location.
Honeycombing	Voidage between coarse aggregate.	Vibration of concrete insufficient to give complete compaction.	Area covered, estimate of voids percentage, location.
Voidage	Non-designed recess in concrete.	Debris left in shutters.	Length, width, depth, location.
Cold joint	Similar appearance to crack. Distinguished by close examination as line is smooth, not jagged, as if ripped apart. Line is not continuous and rarely straight.	Lack of vibration between concrete layers.	Location, orientation, length.

5. CONSTRUCTION FEATURES: Visible surface features not generally considered as defects

Type of construction features	Description	Cause	What to record
Construction joint	Usually marked on construction drawings. Distinguishable from cracks being more continuous and a smoother line.	Placing of fresh concrete on hardened concrete.	Location if not marked on drawing.
Panel joint	Slight honeycombing and grout wedges a couple of mm wide are sometimes associated.	Marks formed by the joints in formwork.	

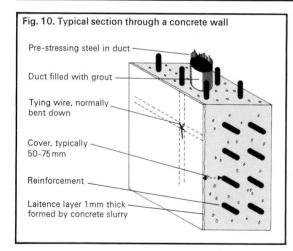

Fig. 10. Typical section through a concrete wall

Pre-stressing steel in duct

Duct filled with grout

Tying wire, normally bent down

Cover, typically 50-75 mm

Reinforcement

Laitence layer 1mm thick formed by concrete slurry

Reporting

Great importance is attached to technical accuracy, detail and standardisation of format and terminology.

VIDEO RECORDING

The following would form an introduction to an inspection record such as a video recording in order to assist future data retrieval and cross-referencing. Every separate tape should carry such an introduction, at least as an audio heading.
Such information can be presented on a video recording as follows:

—Electronic character generator.
—On chalk board.
—On dry wipe board.
—On notice board with removable letters/figures.
—As voice recording.

Title items:
Name of project
Name of client
Name of inspection company
Name of surface support vessel
Name/designation of inspection equipment (submersible, ROV, diver)
Name of pilot/observer/diver
Date : day, month, year
Time : 24 hour clock
Video tape number
Dive number
Geographical location, e.g.:
• North Sea
• UTM co-ordinates or latitude and longitude
• mile post or chainage
• any relevant chart reference numbers
Any relevant drawing reference numbers
Pipe start and finish location
Pipe diameter

Video records are greatly improved if an electronic character generator provides data in real time during the recording on:
—Date and time.
—Gyro compass heading of vehicle (if applicable).
—Depth.
—CP readings, etc.
Additional information can also be added at a later stage when editing tapes, such as arrows indicating areas of interest.

THE COMMENTARY

—Speak clearly and slightly slower than normal.
—Be brief.
—Be positive.
—Avoid 'er . . .' and 'um . . .'.
—Don't be afraid of repetition.
—Never swear.
—Never be flippant.
—Be as informative as possible.
—If the TV is black and white, describe colours.
—Familiarise yourself with the client's terminology.
—Refer to client's drawings.
—Always comment on anything unusual.

Remember: All the engineer on shore has to refer to is the video tape commentary. Make sure it is accurate, make sure it is not ambiguous.

Go through tapes made by you from time to time. Ask yourself—is what I am saying relevant, informative, is the picture I am showing clearly demonstrating what I am saying, is the microphone too close or too far away?

PROCEDURE SUGGESTIONS

Leave one minute of tape free at the start of each tape for later addition of titles.

Tape changes should be at field joints or other readily identifiable points. Stop so that the field joint is in the frame at the end of one tape and the start of the next. If this is impractical, arrange for the next tape to start at an identifiable point covered at the end of the previous tape.

Depths of pipe burial. These are the terms generally used:
a. Pipe lying firmly on seabed.
b. Pipe $\frac{1}{4}$, $\frac{1}{2}$ or $\frac{3}{4}$ buried.
c. Pipe fully buried.
d. Pipe suspended by 5 cm, 10 cm etc.

Scours. The dimensions and position of scours need to be estimated accurately. This is needed to assess the movement of the scours and whether the size of the scour is increasing. This is done by comparison with previous surveys. Scours should only be so called when the seabed drops to the bottom point of the pipe, as opposed to the 'scallop' effects often noticed against the side of pipe. Differentiation between the two is required on the video commentary, with the scallop effects being of much less importance.

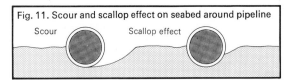

Fig. 11. Scour and scallop effect on seabed around pipeline

Scour   Scallop effect

Spans. Detailed video coverage may be needed of spans. This may require breaking off the survey and turning around to return to the start of the span.

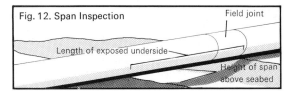

Fig. 12. Span Inspection   Field joint

Length of exposed underside

Height of span above seabed

Estimate dimensions as accurately as possible, if necessary in field joints and pipe lengths. Detailed coverage is required to enable comparison with previous work, to assess whether the span has got larger or smaller.

Damage down to the bare pipe metal. Accurate dimensions are required of such points. The term, 'pipe damage' must not be used lightly. It applies only to the pipe metal itself, not to the concrete coat.

DEBRIS

a. Items of interest are those found essentially within 3 m of the pipe.

b. Large items such as 45 gallon oil drums should be noted, but not small tins etc.

c. Cables and ropes are important; their positions and dimensions must be given.

d. Fishing nets: give dimensions of large pieces and rolls, but ignore small pieces of under 1 m dia.

e. Large items of debris: information about these must be passed to the surface so that the client may decide on the action he might wish to take.

f. Rocks and boulders should be mentioned, but only attach importance to those in excess of 1 m dia.

g. Cladding can be a rusty covering on field joints or be lying beside the pipe at the field joint.

Still photographs. Try to take stills with the video running, even if the tape is not to be presented to the client. This will establish exactly where and when the photo was taken. On the video commentary, mention when you are taking a still. Give full details of the still—what it is; its position; which side of pipe; photo number; film size (35 or 70 mm); gyro axis of camera and depth. The observer can also log these details.

Check-list of items which require to be recorded/described.

The following items may be included in any general pipeline inspection video recording or written report:	
—Orientation of pipe.	—Damage:
—Depth.	—weight coat (see
—Current, direction and	section 3.1, Corrosion
speed.	prevention).
—Nature of seabed, any	—reinforcing wire.
changes.	—bitumen wrap.
—Which side of pipe is being	—pipe metal.
inspected.	—NDT data:
—Weight coat condition	—corrosion potential
(see Section 3.1,	readings.
Corrosion prevention).	—MPI.
—Field joint condition.	—ultrasonics.
—Field joint numbers.	—on bare metal: thickness
—Presence of buckle	(ultrasonic), CP. If
arresters.	specially required, ex-
—Anodes, condition and	pose metal at field joint.
type.	CP may be required on
—Spans, length and height.	nearest anode.
—Nature of trench.	—radiography.
—Burial status.	—Leak detection:
—Anchor mounds in seabed.	—dye.
—Cable marks/damage on	—bubbles.
pipe.	—scouring of seabed.
—Cable marks on seabed.	—water/plankton
—Debris identification,	movement.
description and location.	—rust marks.
—Pig tracking.	

INSPECTION PROCEDURE FOR DAMAGED SUBMARINE PIPELINES

This inspection procedure outlines the type of inspection that may be required on areas of pipeline damage caused by anchor cables.

Many of these activities would be used in other types of inspection. It is essential that the divers, supervisors and NDT personnel know exactly what the procedure will be before commencing the survey. To facilitate the data collection and to make reporting as fast and as accurate as possible the senior NDT supervisor should have a clear idea of the final reporting format very soon after sighting the damage area. The report should include details of the type and frequency of instrument calibration.

1.0 Location, identification and marking

1.1 Position bell over damaged area. Take accurate surface position fix. Record field joint numbers either side of damaged pipe.

1.2 Install a labelled marker pole.

1.3 Establish upstream/downstream directions.

2.0 General area survey

2.1 Carry out a video survey in the immediate vicinity of the damaged area to a radius of about 20 m (66′) and include footage of the damage.

2.2 Record the position of any anchor chains or wires, debris etc., and the direction of chains, trenches, scour, scars etc.

2.3 Record the position of any field joints and any anodes or buckle arresters on the pipeline within the survey area.

3.0 General inspection and surface preparation

3.1 Take still photographs of the damaged area of pipe and any significant findings resulting from section 2.0. above.

3.2 If the sediment and/or marine growth is heavy, remove it using a fan jet. Note if there is any surface corrosion on exposed steel.

3.3 Mark the four clock positions around the damaged area with the 12 o'clock position on the upstream side of the damage.

3.4 Take still photographs from each position at about 45° to the damaged plane. The stand-off distance will be determined by the damage dimensions but each photograph should cover the whole area of interest; take low-level stills along the plane of damage to give indication of groove depth, and profile.

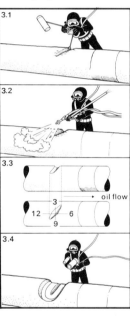

3.5 Remove all weight and corrosion coating up to 100 mm into sound coating. Remove wire reinforcing. Clean to parent metal.

3.6 Make a moulding of any metal surface indentation with Ephophen or similar. Ensure orientation is marked on the moulding.

3.7 Photogrammetry
Adjust the camera separation in accordance with the subject size and lower to the worksite with the appropriate calibration frame. Calibrate the camera by taking six photographs of the frame from at least two different angles, determined by the phototechnician. These will depend upon visibility, size etc. Align camera probes at 90° to the plane of damage and shoot three at 45° either side of the perpendicular.
Shoot a further six of calibration frame on completion.

4.0 Non-destructive testing

4.1 Use hand tools to flush any burr type defects to assist the probe-to-metal contact.

4.2 Carry out MPI.

4.3 Locate the deepest point of damage with a pit gauge and scribe a straight line passing over the point and in the direction of the gauge or dent. Scribe a second line through that point in the direction of the pipe axis. Mark off 10 mm increments on each line the full length of the damaged area.

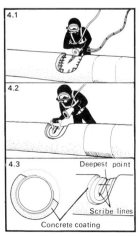

4.4 Take still photographs of the grid.

4.5 Take ultrasonic wall thickness measurements of each grid point using for example a Wells Krautkramer DMU compression probe. Readings to be continued into damaged parent plate on each axis to give a check reading on a parent plate thickness.

4.6 Take cathodic protection potential readings using for example a Roxby Bathycorrometer. One reading for each half square metre of exposed steel will suffice. Take a reading from a standard zinc anode before and after bare metal readings.

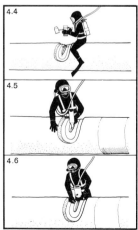

Inspection diving

Inspection is a diver task traditionally applied to exploration well-head diving, and has been based almost exclusively on visual methods such as photography, video, and the diver's eyes.

However, the emergence of certification requirements for fixed production structures in some areas has meant that the requirements for inspection of a high quality has been established. To cater for this, the traditional tasks and methods are now supplemented by additional specialised activities, which include:

—Non-destructive testing (NDT) of nominated areas.
—Corrosion damage inspection.
—Cathodic protection potential surveys: anode inspection measurement.
—Marinegrowth inspection (and removal).
—Debris inspection (and removal).
—Scour and stability inspections.

The basic reason for inspection is to help assess the engineering integrity of a structure. It must be remembered that inspection is a data-gathering task only, and does not normally include interpretation of data significance. Diver inspectors have no qualification to interpret structural integrity from the inspection data that they gather.

The various inspection activities have a basic logical order. Some tasks have to be done prior to cleaning, while others must be done afterwards. For example, most NDT cannot be performed before cleaning, while obviously a marinegrowth survey cannot be performed afterwards.

Once this is understood, the various inspection requirements of a client can be arranged so as to create the most efficient inspection programme. In general terms, programmes are arranged so as to perform:

1. A general initial survey, before any cleaning, to see broadly if there is any obvious damage or problem.
2. General tasks, such as seabed surveys, marinegrowth surveys and corrosion inspection.
3. Appropriate underwater cleaning.
4. Critical inspection tasks in likely areas, in relation to less obvious (or even invisible) defects. The most important of these is cracking. This critical inspection is to detect defects and then, if found, to accurately size them.

The inspection activities discussed in this section relate exclusively to 'certification (and other integrity assurance) inspections'. Exploration 'well-head' inspection tasks are discussed in Section 1.

Inspection is a complex subject, some aspects of which involve theories and formulae beyond the scope of this book. More detailed information may be obtained from other sources, such as u/w inspection training course notes.

GENERALISED SUMMARY OF INSPECTION ACTIVITIES

Inspection category	Inspection activity/summary	Principal reasons for this activity	Items to be inspected	Methods used
1 Initial visual inspection	*Swim the entire structure to detect and note: —Obvious damage; e.g. dents, buckles, tears, missing items etc.	*Structural weakening	*Boat bumpers and fenders etc. *All legs, braces and other structural members	*Divers eyes *And/or photography
2 General visual inspection	*Visual and physical checks	*Loss of design redundancy allowances	*Splashzone coatings *Pitting corrosion *Riser clamps and conditions *Surface condition of anodes *Etc.	*And/or CCTV *Sketches *Measurements *Documentation
3 Seabed survey May be performed concurrently with 2	*Debris survey: to detect and record all metallic and other debris	Debris can cause: *Diversion of corrosion protection from the structure to the debris (thereby damaging the structure) *Hazards to divers, submersibles and remotely operated vehicles	*All underwater items
			*Seabed to a nominated distance from the structure	
	*Scour and abrasion survey, comprising: —Soil levels —Evidence of rocking etc. —Integrity of scour prevention devices	*Possible movement and instability of the structure, and *The associated structural stresses unaccommodated in the design calculations	*Piles, legs, and horizontal members etc. at the mudline	
4 Marinegrowth survey May be performed concurrently with 2	*Measure the thickness of the marinegrowth *Plot distribution patterns *Distinguish between 'soft' and 'hard' growths	Excess marinegrowth attached to a structure may: *Induce unacceptable physical loads to a structure, by either/both: —Deadweight loading —Wave loading *Provide discomfort to divers	*Mainly the splashzone *Normally to El+30' to −60' (the hard growth zone) *(possibly some other locations in special circumstances)	*Measurements of thicknesses *Mapping of patterns etc *Photography *CCTV *Sampling/specimens on some occasions
5 Corrosion inspection	*Assess the integrity of the protection systems, by: —Checking coatings	*Assurance as to continued protection against corrosion, by: —Assurance of the effectiveness of the systems *Provide assistance in the scheduling of anode replacements	*Nominated/random areas	*Physical checks
	—Measure dimensions of sample anodes		*Nominated/random anodes	*Measurements
	—Check electrical continuity of anodes		*All (or most) anode connections—continuity straps	
	—Take CP potential readings		*Nominated areas—normally 4 cardinal points around: —Legs (at node levels) —Risers/conductors —Etc.	*CP potential readings
	—Measure flux-densities			*Flux-density readings
	*Determine if any corrosion damage is evident, by: —Measuring the steel thicknesses	*Ensure that material corrosion losses have not: —Exceeded the design allowances —Reduced material thicknesses below an acceptable level		*Ultrasonic thickness readings
	—Measuring the depths of corrosion pits		*Worst detected examples of pitting corrosion	*Pit gauges, or pit moulds
6 Cleaning	*General removal of marinegrowth fouling	*To remove excess loadings	*Splashzone areas	*Any satisfactory method: —Hand tools e.g. wire strops, brushes etc. —Mechanical power tools (pneumatic and/or hydraulic etc.) —High pressure waterjet with or without: Dry sand, or slurry —Grit entrainment
	*Special cleaning, to 'bright metal', for —the close and critical inspections	*To remove all matter (including: marinegrowth, paint or bituministic coatings, corrosion product, scale, etc.). thereby enabling the close and NDT inspection to be able to be performed validly	*All welded joints nominated for: —Close visual inspection —Critical (NDT) inspection —Critical defect sizing	
7 Critical inspection — Close visual inspection / NDT inspection	Rapid scan' crack detection — For: *Visible cracking defects / For: *Invisible (to the human eye) cracking defects	Cracking defects would negate the designed redundancy allowances—possibly to a dangerous degree Cracks would normally result from: *Continual and/or cyclic stresses (causing fatigue cracking) *Physical impact (e.g. from a vessel, a dropped pile, or similar)	*Nominated high-stress low-fatigue node joints *Known or suspected defects *Previous repairs	*Divers eyes *Close-up photography *Close-up CC videography *Appropriate NDT, e.g. —Magnetic particle inspection —Electro-magnetic interrogation —Or other suitable method
7 Critical inspection — Further defect investigation	Detail defect sizing — *To establish the dimensions of any detected crack defects	*To enable engineers to better understand the defect, and to: —Facilitate the decision as to whether repair is necessary —Enable an appropriate repair method to be developed	*Nominated relevant defects detected in 7 and/or 8	*Appropriate NDT *Photogrammetry

2.1 INSPECTION PLANNING

1. Planning considerations

Planning of inspection programmes is very important, as ineffectual and inapplicable schemes are costly. Careful initial planning will ensure that no unnecessary activities are allowed to intrude.

The most efficient intervention method should be selected, whether by vehicle or diver; and if by diver, whether vertical or horizontal working would be the most advantageous.

The selection of equipment most appropriate to the specific tasks can greatly increase efficiency and this is especially important with photography, video and NDT. However, where alternative techniques are possible, particularly in the case of NDT, cost effectiveness must not be allowed to interfere with the validity of the tests. There is no value in a client's expenditure for testing that merely goes through the motions.

Inspection programme planning must be based on experience and an awareness of both the underlying engineering objectives and the available resources and capabilities.

2. Typical inspection programme

A typical planned inspection programme is shown in Table 1, together with the summarised principal reasons for each activity, the items to be inspected and the commonly used methods. Although this programme is typical, individual programmes may emphasise different aspects according to the client's particular requirements.

2.2 VISUAL INSPECTION

1. The role of visual inspection

The bulk of inspection data is derived from visual inspection techniques. Visual inspection is used to inspect structures for obvious damage such as missing parts, dents, buckles and tears; and to observe and record underwater conditions and features. Underwater visual inspection is carried out by the human eye, still photography and closed circuit television (often referred to as CCTV or video). These methods are used in conjunction with verbal and written reports from the underwater inspector, who may be a diver or submersible pilot. Both manned and remotely operated vehicles are normally fitted with still and video cameras.

Still photography and CCTV are frequently used together as each has its own advantages. Still photography provides the necessary high definition required for detailed analysis, while video on the other hand, though having poorer resolution, provides a continuous real-time image of events that can be monitored by surface engineers and recorded for later viewing. A typical example of this might be during a pipe survey. The diver or submersible pilot would follow the pipeline with a TV camera, and whenever high definition details are required he would use a still camera.

It must be remembered that visual inspection can only detect visible defects. While this seems obvious, cracking defects can be very difficult to find by visual methods (although once found they may then be able to be 'seen'), and may indeed be invisible to the naked eye or camera. Detection of cracks is discussed in Section 2.8.

2. Close visual inspection

Close visual inspection is an important component of the 'critical' stage of most inspection programmes. There are two principal forms: the use of the human eye from close quarters whether as part of an NDT inspection or not, and the production of close-up photographs so as to study small details in high definition enlargements (see Section 2.3). Close-up videography may also be used in some circumstances providing that the video camera has an adequate close-focus capability.

3. The human eye

The human eye is invaluable in locating and identifying areas of interest, to place and use specialist equipment, and to observe and make assessments on a continual basis. It would be very difficult to perform inspection at all without the human eye. However there are limitations as well as advantages.

a. ADVANTAGES OF THE EYE
—Has a stereo capability.
—Has a colour capability.
—Is connected to the reasoning logic of the human brain.
—Is adaptable to a wide range of ambient light conditions.
—Requires no instrumentation to buy, carry or maintain.
—Requires no external power requirements.
—Is intrinsically hazard-free.
—Is versatile.

b. DISADVANTAGES
—Requires human presence.
—No permanent record is produced.
—May have defects.
—Has no capability to enlarge images.
—Adjusts slowly to low light conditions (cannot compete with low-light CCTV).
—Are not always objective in assessing what they see.
—No remote or third party viewing.
—Has difficulty in assessing size and distance.
—Is sensitive to damaging irradiations (e.g. from welding).

The value of human eye observation is largely dependent on a log of what the eyes have seen. For this reason it is essential that inspectors should provide continual verbal commentary for recording, for subsequent analysis and correlation with photographic and videographic records.

As a result of these factors, the diver's eyes are used for initial surveys first to identify and locate areas of interest and then to place specialist equipment.

4. The underwater problems

There are four factors which between them are responsible for all the optical problems of underwater visual inspection.

  (i) Visibility.
 (ii) Lighting.
(iii) Refraction.
(iv) Filtration.

(i) VISIBILITY
Visibility is dependent upon the amount of suspended particles and algae in the water between the viewing point and the subject, and upon the strength, type and position of the source of light.

Visibility does not necessarily correlate to the amount of light and a lack of visibility may not mean that it is dark. Low visibility conditions are like being in a fog. Regardless of whether it is night or day in a fog (i.e. dark or light), the addition of light can sometimes hinder seeing.

As regards the sediment and algae matter in the seawater, the best visibility is often just before or just after slack water after a period of calm. It should be remembered that slack water is not always at high or low water, and it is important to avoid disturbing the seabed and surrounding area. To get the best photographic and video results the lens-to-subject distance should be kept to a practical minimum—never more than $\frac{1}{3}$ of the ambient visibility distance.

There are many ways of overcoming bad visibility when one cannot wait until the conditions are right. Known as 'clear water systems' they are simple to operate and depend upon the ingenuity of the photographer. One example might be when a close-up of a weld is required in 6″ visibility. Squashing a transparent plastic bag filled with clean tap water between the camera and the weld would produce a reasonable result. Another solution might be to construct an enclosure around the camera and subject, and pump clear water into it to replace the turbid water. Most of these techniques are really only suitable for close-up work.

(ii) LIGHTING—AMBIENT LIGHT
The lower the sun in the sky the more light reflects off the surface and the less light passes through into the water. Providing that the sun is high enough in the sky to penetrate the surface, available light from the sun is normally adequate for human eye and video inspection at shallow depths, say up to 10 m. Wave motion will also deflect the sun's rays off the surface, while some reflection may occur from the bottom.

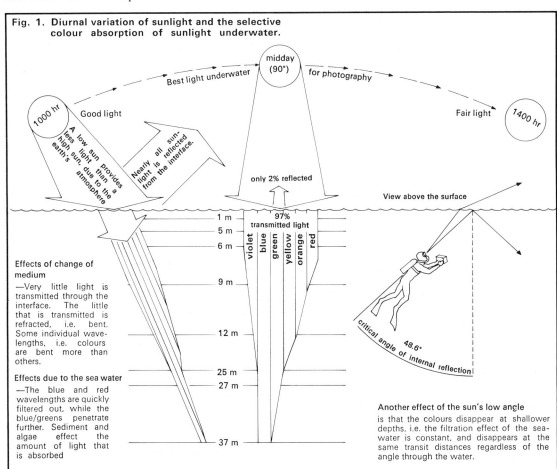

Fig. 1. Diurnal variation of sunlight and the selective colour absorption of sunlight underwater.

With an increase in depth, the daylight diminishes rapidly because of absorption and filtration, and some form of artificial illumination becomes necessary. This can be provided by fixed lights for human eye and video inspection, or in the case of still photography by electronic flash. Ambient light is not appropriate for most underwater photography. For the inspection of large areas, i.e. structural inspection, available light is preferred because it gives a more even illumination. However, available light is not normally adequate for most offshore video and photographic requirements.

Fixed lights and electronic flash give good illumination but are restricted to relatively small areas.

(iii) REFRACTION

When light passes from any transparent medium to another (for example, sunlight passing from air to seawater) the differences in densities affect the light velocities and, according to Snell's Law, three things happen.

(1) The light both reflects from and penetrates the seawater.

(2) The light is refracted (i.e. bent) (See Section 2.3, p 41-42, Optics).

(3) Some individual wavelengths (i.e. colours) bend more than others.

The degree of these effects is entirely dependent on the light's angle of incidence to the water surface.

(iv) FILTRATION

Seawater acts as a progressive colour filter with its own colour cast and degree of absorption. The more water that is traversed by the light, the more density the colour filter has and the greater the filtration effect. Even in clear water, at depths in excess of 10 m most of the colour has been filtered out.

The exact colour of this filter depends on the location, time of day, and the suspended matter in the water. But in general terms the filtration colour is cyan (blue) in appearance, due to the progressive absorption of the red end of the spectrum. All seawater contains sediment and algae etc. to varying degrees, which result in water that may be quite clear or very turbid.

In shallow coastal waters, dyes from suspended particles usually tint the sea with yellow which, added to the existing cyan, makes the sea appear green. At a certain depth the dyes cancel out the water colour filter, absorbing all the blue light as well as the red and other colours. So, although the water may be clear, very little light will get through it. In other words, the filtration effect of the water reduces the amount of light available in the water (which has already been reduced at the air/water interface) and eventually it will absorb all the colours until no light remains at all.

To put back the colour and light that have been lost, it is necessary to use some form of supplementary lighting; fixed lights for human eyes and video inspection, and electronic flash for still photography. When colour values are important to colour photography and video recording, the diver should place a colour card (guide) within the picture area for subsequent analysis and comparison.

○ Make sure there is a photo identification plate in every exposure detailing the location and date.

2.3 STILL PHOTOGRAPHY

Still photography is invaluable to underwater inspection for topside analysis by engineers. It is a relatively simple and economical means of securing high definition permanent records from which engineers can obtain a great deal of information. However, in order to achieve its potential, it is necessary to recognise the inherent capabilities and limitations, and to understand the problems of the seawater environment.

1. Capabilities and limitations

a. CAPABILITIES
—High detail (i.e. good resolution) possible.
—Relatively inexpensive.
—Magnification of images/small detail possible.
—Stereo.
—Colour capability.
—Large film loadings.
—System controls can be simplified/pre-set.
—Easy low-cost duplication of records.
—Digital data recording on photographs.
—Critical measurements in three planes.

b. LIMITATIONS
—For best results (for offshore-related work), artificial lighting is preferable in most conditions.
—No real-time remote viewing, and no real-time record of movement.
—Moderate skill required.
—Requires idents in each photograph.
—Requires a chemical process before results are available.
—Success of results cannot be determined until after film processing.
—Difficulties in black and white interpretation.

2. The photographic problems

The environmental problems of visibility, sufficient light and colour casts discussed in Section 2.2 (4), produce specific problems for underwater photography, all of which are related to lighting. Low levels of available light and associated colour saturation problems will be eliminated by correct application of artificial light sources.

This lack of the correct colour light causes two main problems: a level of darkness which results in contrast problems, and false colours (or colour casts).

a. CONTRAST/BRIGHTNESS

Contrast (i.e. the brightness range) is the relationship between the brightest and darkest points within the overall picture. When there is a great difference between them the contrast is said to be high (or 'crisp') and when there is little difference the contrast is low (or 'muddy'). Image quality is directly related to good (high) contrast. Brightness may be described as an illumination level and there can be a range of light levels from one area in a photograph to another. Whilst this would appear to provide good contrast, it may look disappointing in the finished photograph. However, this is not a problem of contrast, but one of poor lighting.

There are a number of reasons for low image contrast.

(i)   The subject itself may lack contrast (i.e. all of it may be shades of one colour, or all white or all black etc.). This is known as 'subject contrast' and although different, can effect 'image contrast'.

(ii) There is insufficient light illuminating the subject.

(iii) The photographic image has been underexposed, or overexposed. (It must be remembered that underexposure does not necessarily mean that the subject was not adequately lit; it could be that much of the light could not penetrate the sediment within the water between the subject and the camera.)

(iv) The film has been over or underdeveloped.

(v)   A combination of the above, in particular Nos (iii) and (iv).

In underwater terms, subject contrast problems may lie in photographing an area of corrosion, for example, high contrast would exist where there is a bright flared reflection from a bare metal surface which is against a totally unlit seawater background. Should a photograph have a low contrast which is not caused by subject contrast, it is likely that there has not been enough light reaching the film (assuming that the process has been correct).

In underwater photography contrast is best controlled by correctly lighting the subject (see 3a, b).

However, some compensation is possible during processing (see 4d).

b. FALSE COLOUR

The manufacturers of colour film assume that the light to be used will be either of two types: sunlight or flash (colour temperature of approximately 5500°K); or tungsten/quartz floods (3200°K).

These are the common reasons for false colour in photographs:

Reasons in principle	Relevance underwater
The light used was inappropriate to the film type	Tungsten type film used with electronic flash
No filter, or an incorrect filter was used to correct the light source	Daylight type film was used with fixed continuous lights
Assuming correct type of light: —That light became filtered	Either type of film was used with light that had become: —Filtered by the seawater —Filtered by reflection off a large non-white surface
Faulty colour process	

All of these can be controlled. Assuming that the processing is correct, the principal remedy for false colour is to ensure that the light suits the film being used and the underwater conditions; that is, that there is enough light and that only minimal filtration is allowed to occur by having the camera and the light source close to the subject (see 3b).

c. BACK SCATTER

Back scatter is also a problem of lighting. It results from the light reflecting off suspended particles in the seawater and back into the camera. (In principle this is similar to the previously mentioned on-land problem, the effect of car lights on fog.)

To avoid back scatter, the flash should be mounted to the side of and well in front of the camera so as not to light the seawater in front of the camera (see 3b).

d. OTHERS

The photographic problems of refraction and optics are fully dealt with in 4).

3. The essentials of lighting

Available light underwater is not an ideal source for the reasons previously mentioned, i.e. variable, low in contrast, incorrect colour rendition etc.

Correct lighting should ideally be:

a. Strong enough to provide high contrast image without extra enhancement of the medium, i.e. push processing film image enhancement of video.

b. Light evenly spread over the required area.

c. The correct colour temperature for the film or video camera being used.

The technical quality of a photograph is directly related to the quality of light forming the image; in broad terms the more light, the better the quality. While there can, in theory, be too much light, this is rarely a practical problem underwater. The main underwater lighting problem relates to the placement of the light.

Before defining the essentials of correct lighting, it should be remembered that detail should be visible in both the brightest highlight and the darkest low light areas. Even if an underwater photograph is sharply focused and has bright saturated colours, it is not a good photograph for engineering purposes unless detail can be seen in it.

Every light casts shadows and the brightness range (i.e. the contrast gradient) between the brightest areas and darkest shadows may be in the order of 20:1. However, the latitude of most photographic emulsions is not as wide, typically about 15:1–17:1. If detail is to be seen in the highlights *and* the shadows of the film, additional light must illuminate the shadow areas. This is the reason that some photographers use more than one light. They use a main (prime) light with one or more modelling (fill-in) lights at a 3:1 relationship, that is to say, the main light is three times brighter than the secondary one. While 3:1 would be difficult to attain underwater, the principle is worth pursuing.

Using more than one light source will give fine detail and even lighting, but may produce flat working results. In some circumstances a single light source may be preferred if surface texture is required.

a. TYPE OF LIGHTING

There are two types of artificial light sources used underwater—fixed lamps and electronic flash. Fixed lamps are usually available to the diver or vehicle, but may be of mixed colour temperatures: some have a yellow bias, others a green. Some of these may be adequate for video but not for still photography. As fixed lamps require external power, are bulkier and heavier, involve the use of exposure meters, and are significantly lower powered, so there is little benefit in their use for underwater still photography, except in certain specialised applications.

Electronic flashguns, sometimes called 'strobes'—(see note) should always be used for the following reasons:

—They provide the appropriate power necessary.

—They have the correct colour temperature for daylight film.

—They are compact and easily carried.

—They are inexpensive.

NOTE:

A 'strobe' is defined as a rapidly flashing light (such as is found in discotheques). While a strobe can be used for multiple image photography, or indeed for normal flash photography by slowing its flashing rate down to one at a time, the equipment normally used underwater cannot have its flashing uprated, and is not a strobe. 'Strobe' is often used in the USA to describe an electronic flash.

b. PLACEMENT OF THE LIGHT SOURCE

The placement of additional lighting is important and is frequently the difference between a good and a bad photograph—particularly underwater photographs. However, a compromise is often necessary between what is ideal and what is possible.

There are two main points to bear in mind:

First; in order to reduce the volume of seawater between the subject and lens, the diver needs to take his photographs from as close to the subject as practicably possible.

Second; in order not to light the seawater (sediment/algae) in front of the lens, he needs to offset the light from the camera axis. Unfortunately this tends to light only one side of the subject. The closer the light, the more severe is the problem. The previous recommendation for the use of more than one flash substantially reduces the problems of uneven lighting.

The following principles for the placement of lights should always be considered:

For all work	Keep the flash unit(s) offset from the lens axis wherever possible so as not to light the water in front of the lens and induce back scatter. If necessary utilise a 'barn door' principle. Ensure that the unit's angle of illumination is adequate for the subject size/flash position and the camera lens acceptance angle.
For close-up work (for subjects of say 5–50 cm (2–20″) in size)	Where the camera is close to the subject it is important to keep the illumination as even as possible across the subject. Therefore when using: —One flash unit. Keep the unit a reasonable distance back from the subject. —Two flash units. Place the units closer, ensuring that the distances from the subject are equal. Ensure that a shadow of the camera or diver is not cast onto the subject.
For medium and distance work (for subjects of say 50–150 cm (20–60″) in size)	Keep the flash unit(s) in front of the camera plane (about 23–30 cm) (9–12″) wherever possible. Ensure that the flash unit(s) do not intrude into the field of view.

4. Camera optics and features

There is as yet no one camera that is ideal for all underwater situations. There are specialist cameras that can do one job really well, and there are others that can be adapted to do many tasks moderately well. Selection of a camera system will depend upon its particular features and their suitability to the work objectives. However, there is one subject common to all cameras—the optics.

a. UNDERWATER OPTICS

As previously stated, whenever light passes from one medium to another it is refracted (bent). Underwater photography involves using light that passes through three different mediums. From the water it passes through multiple glass and air interfaces. Lens manufacturers make all necessary air/glass corrections, but some manufacturers of underwater cameras may not have been fully corrected for the initial water/glass/air interface.

For any given camera format, different focal length lenses will produce differently scaled images of the same subject from the same distance. A wide angle

	35 mm Format					70 mm Format				
	Nominated specs (in air at infinity)		As used underwater (in water at closest focus)*			Nominated specs (in air at infinity)		As used underwater (in water at closest focus)*		
	Focal length	Angle of view		Focal length	Angle of view	Focal length	Angle of view		Focal length	Angle of view
Wide Angle	21 mm	92°	C	23 mm	86°	38 mm	90°	C	47 mm	79°
			U	30 mm	71°			U	63 mm	63°
	28 mm	75°	C	30 mm	71°	50 mm	75°	C	60 mm	66°
			U	40 mm	47°			U	80 mm	62°
	35 mm	63°	C	37 mm	60°					
			U	50 mm	47°					
Standard	50 mm	47°	C	53 mm	44°	80 mm	52°	C	89 mm	47°
			U	71 mm	34°			U	118 mm	26°
Telephoto	85 mm	29°	C	91 mm	27°	120 mm	36°	C		
			U	121 mm	20°			U		
	100 mm	24°	C	107 mm	23°					
			U	142 mm	17°					

C indicates that refraction corrections have been made.
U indicates that refraction is uncorrected.
*Typical; as there are variations between lens designs and manufacturers.

lens will cover a large area and objects in it will appear small. A telephoto lens will cover a small area and objects will appear large. Most formats have a standard lens which gives an angle of view similar to that of the human eye. The angle of view of a lens is termed the acceptance angle.

Specific focal lengths for any given angle vary with the size of the camera format. However, should a lens be encapsulated for underwater use the design of the port can significantly change the acceptance angle. Considering that seawater has a different refractive index to air and glass (i.e. 1.33, against nearly 1.0 and anything between 1.5 and 1.8), anticipated angles of acceptance can be changed significantly.

Such uncorrected underwater optics will, for example, change a 35 mm lens (63°) at infinity to a 50 mm lens on a 35 mm format (47°) at close focus. This means that the image will be about one third larger and in order to picture the whole subject, a greater distance must be put between the camera and the subject. This introduces unnecessary attendant problems of lower contrast, less light and colour, visibility losses and significantly less depth of field, making focusing more difficult.

b. OPTICAL CORRECTIONS
The solution to the problem is quite simple. The refraction can be reduced by the use of a domed port instead of a flat port. For full underwater correction an Ivanoff corrector is required.

c. ANGLES OF VIEW
The angle of view of a lens will determine the stand-off distance necessary to cover a given subject. As the seawater is the main degrading factor, it is important to reduce the amount of the water between the subject and lens by reducing the stand-off.

STANDARD LENS. Most subjects for underwater inspection would be in the order of 1–2 m in size, up to a maximum of about 3 m. Should a 'standard' lens be used, the subject is often too large to fit into the frame; to enable it to fit it would be necessary to go

Effects of refraction on the angle of view

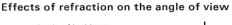
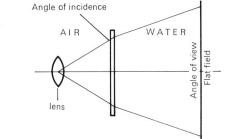

Fig. 1. Flat port lens giving reduced angle and colour.

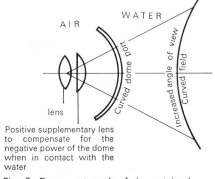

Fig. 2. Dome port, angle of view retained.

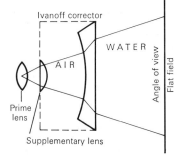

Fig. 3. The Ivanoff corrector.

further away from the subject—thereby increasing the stand-off distance. However, this would increase degradation.

TELEPHOTO (LONG FOCUS) LENSES have limited applications in conventional underwater inspection photography.

WIDE-ANGLE LENSES are most suitable underwater as they provide the maximum image from the shortest stand-off distance. In addition they are usually close-focusing and have a large depth of focus. The most useful lenses for underwater have an angle of acceptance of about 92°–63° (i.e. 21–35 mm focal lengths in 35 mm format; and 38 mm–50 mm in 6×6 cm format).

There is a disadvantage in that wide angle lenses distort perspective; objects closer to the lens will appear to be much larger in relation to things further away.

Many of the qualities of a wide angle lens are thrown away when the lens is placed behind a flat port in a housing, as its angle of acceptance is reduced. A corrected port, or a specially designed underwater lens is the best answer.

CLOSE-UP OR SUPPLEMENTARY LENSES are convenient in that they can be fitted and removed underwater from Nikonos and certain similar cameras. They may also be used with any camera encapsulated in a housing to give a system which must be dedicated to close-up work for that particular dive. These lenses are sometimes difficult to fit to certain specialist underwater cameras.

Extension tubes are useful for closer focusing distances than can be managed by the use of close-up lenses, say for magnifications of 1:0.4 and greater, but they do need an exposure allowance.

MACRO LENSES are designed for close-ups of small objects and are satisfactory behind a flat port. These lenses focus down to close distances and are often used with extension tubes. They are usually of a 50 mm focal length or longer but can be used only with SLR cameras in housings.

d. CHOICE OF FILM

Colour or black and white

Colour film is used in nearly all underwater photographic inspection work because there is so much more information to be obtained from it than from black and white film. Modern colour films now have greatly increased speeds. For general inspection colour film may be up-rated. Black and white film is only used for special purposes where colour would be irrelevant or if higher resolution is required.

Compared to black and white film, colour has some disadvantages, two of which are:
1. Narrow latitude.
2. The degree of precision required in processing.

Latitude is the film's tolerance to under- and over-exposure. Black and white film can allow a variance of as much as four f-stops, whereas colour film can tolerate only half an f-stop. A wide latitude film is best underwater, where exposure is uncertain. Negative colour film has more latitude than reversal colour film and allows some colour correction at the printing stage.

Colour processing must be carried out to close temperature tolerances, and the time interval of each stage carefully controlled.

In low light conditions the effective ISO (ASA) value of the colour film may be increased up to four times, but this would require special processing. Black and white films are available that can be up-rated to as much as 3200 ISO with little quality loss. Care would have to be taken in the processing not to lose shadow detail. The newly introduced dye-coupled black and white films combine extreme speed with high resolution and low granularity. Examples of these films are Agfa Vario XL or Ilford XPI.

The film speed may be uprated by extending the first developer times. As a general guide, the first developer time should be multiplied by one third for every one stop increase in film speed.

Example: Normal first developer time = 6 min.
1 stop increase = $6 \times \frac{1}{3}$ = 8 min.
2 stop increase = $8 \times \frac{1}{3}$ = $10\frac{1}{2}$ min.

FILM SPEED

Films are made for specific purposes. Their sensitivity is rated at speeds between 25 and 2750 ASA, now called ISO (International Standard Organisation). Slow films, 25 to 125 ISO, are fine-grained and the resolution is high. This is especially important if there is to be considerable enlargement of the photographs. Slow-speed film should be used unless the available light is insufficient, when a high-speed film is preferable.

e. THE END PRODUCT

The prime consideration is what ultimately is going to be done with the information obtained. Many of the pictures taken underwater are processed on site, so that the original transparencies can be looked at by

Table showing processing adjustments for different speeds of reversal films				
200 ISO Film (Daylight)	**160 ISO Film** (Tungsten)	**64 ISO Film** (Daylight)	**50 ISO Professional Film** (Tungsten)	Change the time in the first developer by
800	640	250	200	$+5\frac{1}{2}$ mins
400	320	125	100	$+2$ mins
Normal 200	Normal 160	Normal 64	Normal 50	Normal
100	80	32	25	-2 mins
Reversal films are developed in E6 process. Negative films in C41 chemistry.				

COMPARATIVE SPECIFICATIONS OF UNDERWATER STILL CAMERAS

Manufacturer	Model	Format	Shots Per Load (max.)	Standard Lens	Focus Parameters	Underwater Corrector	Diagonal Angle of View	Speed and Aperture Setting Method	Focus Method
Alpa-Rebikoff	U-PHOT DR-8	24 × 36 mm	36	35 mm f2.8	50 cm to 10 m	Ivanoff	55°	preset	manual
Alpa-Rebikoff	DR-80	24 × 36 mm	800	21 mm f3.4 Schneider	fixed 1.5 m	Ivanoff	92°	preset	fixed 1.5 m
Benthos	374	24 × 36 mm	400	2.8 mm f2.8 Nikkor	600 mm to ∞	no*	60°	preset 1/100 sec or remote	manual
Benthos	378	24 × 36 mm	400	2.8 mm f2.8 Nikkor	600 mm to ∞	no*	60°	preset 1/100 sec or remote	manual
Hasselblad	500 ELM	6 × 6 cm	72 or 200 magazine by special order	50 mm/f4 Distagon 80 mm/ f2.8 Planar	150 mm to ∞ with 50 mm	dome with supplementary positive lens	72° 25°	manual through housing	
Nikon	Nikonos III	24 × 36 mm	36	80 mm 35 mm 28 mm 15 mm	0.8 m to ∞	no no u/w lens u/w lens	lens dependent (94°–22°)	manual	manual
Nikon	Nikonos IV-A	24 × 36 mm	36	80 mm 35 mm 28 mm 15 mm	0.8 m to ∞	no no u/w lens u/w lens	lens dependent (94°–22°)	manual aperture, automatic shutter speed	manual
Osel	Hydroscan automatic camera	24 × 36 mm	250	30 mm f16 or 50 mm f16	fixed 90 mm	yes no	55° 34°	fixed	fixed
Photosea	1000	24 × 36 mm	250	28 mm f3.5 u/w Nikkor	300 mm to ∞	no*	60°	fixed 1/100 sec	manual
Photosea	2000 (stereo)	24 × 36 mm stereo pairs	100 (250 single frames)	2.8 mm f3.5 Nikkor	300 mm to ∞	no*	60°	fixed, preset	
UMEL	SWC	24 × 36 mm	400	35 mm f2.8 Nikkor	15 mm to ∞	dome	55°	manual preset	manual preset
UMEL	DHC/70	6 × 6 cm	70 or 200	38 mm f4.5 Biogon	15 mm to ∞	dome	90°	manual through housing	
U.V.S.	MD 600 OM	24 × 36 mm	36	21 mm to 50 mm	from front element to ∞	Ivanoff	lens dependent (90°–47°)	preset or automatic	manual preset
U.V.S.	MD 600 ON 250	24 × 36 mm	250	21 mm to 50 mm	from front element to ∞	Ivanoff	lens dependent (90°–47°)	preset or automatic	manual preset

Addresses of manufacturers and main distributors: still photography

Victor Hasselblad Aktiebolag,
Ostra Hamngatan 3, Box 220,
40123 Gotenborg 1, Sweden.
Tel: (031) 171960   Tlx: 2279

Hasselblad (GB) Ltd,
York House, Empire Way, Wembley,
Middlesex, HA9 0QQ, UK.
Tel: 903 3435   Tlx: 922866

Photosea System,
11120 Roselle Street, Suite J,
San Diego, Ca. 92121, USA.
Tel: (714) 452 8903   Tlx: 181797

Bennico Ltd,
62 Marischal Street,
Aberdeen, AB1 2AL, UK.
Tel: (0224) 27226/7   Tlx: 739206

Tamtech Ltd,
Unit 11, Kirkhill Place,
Kirkhill Industrial Estate,
Dyce, Aberdeen, AB2 0ES, UK.
Tel: (0224) 723697

UMEL,
Oakhanger Industrial Estate,
Bordon,
Hampshire, GU35 9HH, UK.
Tel: (04203) 3883   Tlx: 858893

Alpa Pignons SA,
CH-1338 Ballaigues, Switzerland.
Tel: (021) 83 2285   Tlx: 24737

Benthos Inc,
Edgerton Drive, North Falmouth,
Mass. 02556, USA.
Tel: (617) 563 5917   Tlx: 940884

ExplorOcean Technology,
63 Windmill Road,
Sunbury-on-Thames,
Middlesex, TW16 7DT, UK.

OSEL,
Boundary Road,
Harfreys Industrial Estate,
Great Yarmouth, Norfolk, UK.
Tel: (0493) 59916   Tlx: 975084

Nikon (Nippon),
Kogaku KK Fuji Building,
No 2–3 Marumouchi,
No 3 Chome Chiyoda, KU,
Tokyo 1000, Japan.

Nikon UK Ltd,
20 Fulham Broadway,
London, SW6 1BA, UK.
Tel: (01) 381 1551

U.V.S.,
195 Carshalton Road,
Carshalton, Surrey, UK
Tel: (01) 642 3656

Note: *These cameras use the 28 mm underwater Nikkor lens behind a flat port; consequently their performance is slightly impaired when compared with results obtained with the same lens used in direct water contact, as intended.

Max. Depth	Data Back	Dimensions	Weight		Options	Comments
			Air	Water		
200 m	no	180 × 300 mm	3.5 kg	0.9 kg	matched flash unit	automatic motordrive operation; 2 frames/sec
450 m	yes	410 × 150 mm	7.5 kg	0.3 kg	matched flash unit	automatic or remote operation up to 2 frames/sec
1000 m	data chamber standard	385 × 120 mm	7.2 kg	3.17 kg	matched flash unit; wide angle lens; altimeter	lightweight, titanium housing; cassette is daylight loading and unloading
675 m	data chamber standard	320 × 114 mm	3.9 kg	0.4 kg	matched flash unit; diver option available	ultra lightweight filament wound epoxy and delrin housing; 'quick twist' frontal loading; daylight loading and unloading
200 m	no	430 × 350 mm	12.5 kg	neutral	interchangeable lenses; interchangeable film magazines	standard 6 × 6 system camera fitted to makers' own underwater housing; reflex viewfinder; flash synchronized at all speeds, via EO outlet
50 m	no	144 mm wide 99 mm high 72 mm deep	0.78 kg	0.3 kg (appx.)	many system attachments and lens options from Nikon and independent suppliers	standard 35 mm diver camera, shallow water. Discontinued: replaced by Nikonos IV-A
50 m	no	149 mm wide 99 mm high 83 mm deep	0.9 kg	0.35 kg (appx.)	many system attachments and lens options from Nikon and independent suppliers; dedicated automatic flash; lenses from 15 mm to 80 mm; close-up outfit available	automatic exposure version with limitations and advantages compared with previous model; non-automatic when 15 mm Nikkor fitted
300 m	no	490 × 150 mm	8.2 kg	1.3 kg negative	probe system; long stand-off options	completed ring flash, automatic operation, weld inspection camera
600 m	no	320 × 108 mm	3.8 kg	1.1 kg	matched flash unit; deep water variants available	A purpose built underwater camera
600 m	yes	320 × 108 mm	4.3 kg	1.5 kg	matched flash unit	lightweight, compact stereo system; can be used for single frames also
1500 m	optional	600 × 115 mm	7.64 kg	2.7 kg	matched flash unit; pairable for stereo photography	A purpose built underwater camera
600 m	no	410 × 150 mm	11.5 kg	1.3 kg	matched flash unit; pairable for stereo photography; special version available for u/w photogrammetry	uses modified Hasselblad 70 mm SWC (motor driven); provides photogrammetric quality when a fiducial plate and a Reseau plate are fitted
600 m	optional	180 × 165 mm	5 kg (appx.)	0.4 kg (appx.)	unit pairable for stereo and photogrammetric work; probe attachments	auto, remote, hand-held options; 3 frames/sec max.; lens option 21 mm to 50 mm fully corrected; Reseau plates fitted for photogrammetric work
600 m	optional	180 × 165 mm	5 kg (appx.)	0.4 kg (appx.)	unit pairable for stereo and photogrammetric work; probe attachments	auto, remote, hand-held options; 3 frames/sec max.; lens option 21 mm to 50 mm fully corrected; Reseau plate fitted for photogrammetric work

Photogrammetry

UMEL,
Oakhanger Industrial Estate,
Bordon, Hampshire,
GU35 9HH, UK.
Tel: (04203) 3883   Tlx: 858893

Camera Alive Ltd,
St David's House,
272 Broomhill Road,
Aberdeen, AB1 7LP, UK.
Tel: (0224) 325 777   Tlx: 739 168

Hunting Surveys Ltd,
Elstree Way, Borehamwood,
Hertfordshire, WD6 1SB, UK
Tel: (01) 953 6161   Tlx: 23517

Neptune Surveys Ltd,
1 Atholl Place,
Edinburgh, EH3 8HP, UK.
Tel: 031 228 1446   Tlx: 72465

Closed circuit TV

Osprey Electronics,
E27 Wellheads Industrial Centre,
Dyce, Aberdeen, AB2 0GD, UK.
Tel: (0224) 770101   Tlx: 739575

Subsea Systems,
753 W. Washington Ave,
Escondido, Ca. 92025, USA.
Tel: (714) 747 4223   Tlx: 695409

UDI Group Ltd,
Woodside Road,
Bridge of Don Industrial Estate,
Aberdeen, AB2 8EF, UK.
Tel: (0224) 703551   Tlx: 73361
After 5 30: Air call (0224) 871183

Kinergetics Inc,
6029 Reseda Blvd,
Tarzana, Ca. 91356, USA.
Tel: (213) 345 2851   Tlx: 696399

Kinergetics,
11 Greenfern Place, Mastrick,
Aberdeen, AB2 5JR, UK.
Tel: (0224) 681 020   Tlx: 739675

Hydro Products Inc,
11777 Sorrento Valley Road,
San Diego,
Ca. 92121, USA.
Tel: (714) 453 2345
Tlx: 910 322 1133

Hydro Products Ltd,
Unit 6 Wellhead Crescent,
Wellhead Industrial Estate,
Dyce, Aberdeen, AB2 0GA, UK.
Tel: (0224) 770145   Tlx: 739682

IBAK Helmut Hunger GmbH & Co. KG,
Postfach 6260, D-2300 Kiel 14,
West Germany.
Tel: (0431) 72701   Tlx: 292824

Techmation Limited,
58 Edgware Way,
Middlesex, HA8 8JP, UK
Tel: (01) 958 3111   Tlx: 262245

the client or engineers to guarantee results without delay. Reversal films which produce transparencies tend to be used for this reason.

There are two ways of presenting the finished product.

—Reversal: The original film is developed to become a positive transparency, which can be viewed by projection. Colour prints may be produced from the transparency by means of a reversal paper. The results tend to be rather contrasty, losing detail in the highlights and/or the shadow areas in the print. On the other hand, this sort of print can achieve a high degree of resolution.

—Negative: The advantages of 'negative' over 'reversal' film are its wider latitude, its cheapness, and its quickness to process initially. Its comparative disadvantages are that the original negative film has to be converted to a positive print or to a transparency before it can be viewed. The print, however, can be of a superior quality to a conventional reversal print and cheaper to produce. Duplicate transparencies can be readily and inexpensively produced on print film. Negative film is probably the most suitable for recording data.

PHOTOGRAMMETRY

Photogrammetry is a form of stereo photography from which measurements of all three dimensions can be obtained (length, breadth and thickness). The technique is being increasingly used in offshore inspection, particularly for evaluating and monitoring corrosion and damaged areas. Photogrammetry differs from stereo photography mainly in the precision of the camera construction and the lens optics, and in the provision of a Reseau plate in the film plane. This holds the film flat and superimposes accurate register marks on the film to aid analysis of the results.
The photographic stage is only the first part of the photogrammetric process. The photographs must be observed in a special machine to identify the points that have to be measured. The output from this

f. MONO OR STEREO PHOTOGRAPHY

Mono
Mono photography is the simplest way of producing good quality still reproductions. Most black and white or colour still photography will be mono, but stereo reproduction seems to be becoming more popular in inspection specifications.

Stereo
Stereo photography is a technique for producing three-dimensional photographic images by simultaneously taking two photographs of the same subject from slightly different camera positions. The resulting prints have to be viewed in a special viewer. Stereo images give the viewer the ability to assess distances between objects and to evaluate contours of objects that would not be possible using mono images. Stereo images would be produced when the maximum amount of visual assessment is required: for instance, a dent in a tubular bracing would be more apparent and possibly only obvious in a stereo image. The combination of stereo and colour can provide topside personnel with information which cannot be achieved by mono alone. Stereo photography is not to be confused with photogrammetry, which is described below and is a technique employed when accurate measurement is required.

machine must then be further processed by a computer to obtain the results of the type required, and to introduce corrections for the inherent optical distortions present in every camera as well as for the refractive index of water. The drawings made from these results can show measurements of discrete points, dimensions, profiles etc. Where part of a structure is damaged and needs to be repaired, the use of photogrammetry can lead to the manufacture of a piece that will exactly fit the damaged area.
The use of photogrammetric cameras is dependent on the correct photographic procedures and computations being available. With a correctly designed system, even an untrained diver can obtain results that can be used as photogrammetric measurements.

Photogrammetry has the following advantages over conventional measuring techniques.

1. It is a non-contact measuring technique so there is little or no interference with the subject.

2. It allows underwater measurement of objects that are difficult to measure by other techniques because of their shape or size or physical position. Complex subjects may require photographic coverage from several positions.

3. The total effort does not increase proportionally with the number of points to be measured.

4. The amount of information is very high when compared with other measuring techniques.

5. The data acquisition and data processing stages are separate.

6. The data acquisition is fast, limited only to the time taken to photograph the subject. The saving in offshore time is considerable.

7. The data are stored in a permanent form. Measurements can be taken at any time in the future of any part of the subject, thus avoiding the costly remobilisation of a submersible or diving spread should additional measurements be needed.

8. The results may be presented in a number of ways, as separate points, dimensions, contour maps, cross-sections, or even as volumes. Reporting may be tailored to the exact needs of the job.

9. It is a very precise technique, with an accuracy of 1:1000 (subject stand-off distance to accuracy), which is equivalent to 0.1 mm in a 1 m² field of view. This precision is only obtainable with correct use of suitable equipment.

Photogrammetric systems are available from several sources including Neptune Surveys and the Association of Camera Alive Limited, Hunting Surveys Limited and Underwater and Marine Equipment Limited, known as UMEL.
Neptune Surveys use a system with two Hasselblad MK 70 photogrammetric cameras, with 60 mm Biogon lenses behind Ivanoff correction systems (70 mm film, 70 exposures). The UMEL system is basically two modified Hasselblad SWC cameras on 70 mm film allowing 200 exposures with one magazine. The optical system is dome-corrected for underwater use; a fiducial plate and a Reseau plate are fitted. The housing is only 15.2 cm dia.× 43.2 cm long (6× 7″) and weighs 1.4 kg (3 lb) in water. It can be used down to 600 m (2000′) without pressure compensation.

2.4 CLOSED CIRCUIT TELEVISION

1. Monochrome CCTV systems

Underwater CCTV, particularly when used with wide-angle lenses can give better overall images than can be perceived by the diver. Typically, twice the diver's angle of view can be achieved. The tonal compression and the ability to alter the contrast and intensity at the surface monitor combine to give this effect.

CCTV systems run on a low voltage supply of between 9–18 volts, and the output is a video signal out. Systems standards for the UK are 625 lines, 50 cycles; and for USA, 525 lines, 60 cycles.

Some systems incorporate an audio channel into the umbilical, which may be used for a diver communication link with the surface.

A variety of lighting systems are available. The quality of the lighting for CCTV is important; the type of lamp used is of secondary importance; soft even wide-angle illumination is required for TV cameras.

Picture interference on CCTV can be introduced from many different sources, for example: platform supplies and radio interference. These and others can be minimised by the use of an independent supply such as batteries or voltage or frequency stabilisers. ROVs present a different problem which might be solved by either transmitting the umbilical signal as a radio frequency (rf) or digitally.

Table 2 shows a selection of the types of monochrome CCTV cameras available.

The majority of underwater CCTV systems use standard Vidicon tubes. The larger sizes, around 1″, are mostly mounted on submersibles. The smaller sizes, $\frac{2}{3}$″ and below are mounted on the diver's helmet or are hand-held.

A Vidicon requires a lot of light compared with silicon diode (SiD) systems (Newvicon, Chalicon and Saticon). The SiD systems can be used without supplementary lighting at greater depths and are suitable in turbid water where there is a lot of back-scatter which might be a problem with additional lighting.

A silicon intensified target (SIT) system is designed for depths where there is little ambient light. Back-scatter problems are minimised because a low power light source is required. A SIT can produce excellent results with a weak diver's torch covered with a diffusing material such as a handkerchief. SIT cameras can record images at light levels as low as 0.0005 foot candles whilst maintaining a horizontal resolution of 300+ lines.

2. Colour CCTV systems

To date, CCTV colour cameras have been land cameras fitted into underwater housings.

As stated previously, the amount of extra information provided by colour is considerable, even though the picture may be less sharp or lack some detail.

There are three basic types of colour video cameras:
1. Single tube cameras.
2. Three tube cameras.
3. CCD cameras (charge coupled device).

Single tube cameras use a tube which has red/green and blue vertical stripes on the face plate which give three separate signal colours. They are limited in resolution because of the shaved face plate. (Typical resolution is between 200–350 TV lines.) Three-tube cameras use a beam-splitting system and three separate tubes to record the red/green and blue separate images. The resolution is then similar to a black and white image given by equivalent tubes i.e. between 300–500 lines. The average 600 lines per frame on TV compares unfavourably with the 3600 lines per frame resolved by a still camera. However, since the colour can present so much more information than monochrome, it is not significant.

The characteristics of a single tube camera are:

a. It is electronically simple.

b. It is compact, which makes it capable of being fitted into a small underwater housing, a significant factor in underwater equipment.

c. It does not have the image restriction problems of a three-tube camera and does not go out of register.

The characteristics of a three-tube camera are:

a. It incorporates three tubes, each dedicated to an individual colour, red, green and blue.

b. It has a good image quality, superior to the single tube. It should be said, however, that a top quality single tube is equal to the lower end of the three-tube range.

c. It is complex. One particular result of this complexity is that registration of the tube images are prone to drift, either electronically or because of physical damage, the result of which is an overall degradation of quality. Image drifting is a problem with three-tube cameras and a qualified technician is needed to re-register these cameras regularly.

d. It is more expensive than a single tube, ranging from £6000 to £30 000.

The sensitivity of CCTV colour systems is about the same as the Vidicon monochrome cameras; the amount of light required and most of the other problems encountered with a Vidicon are similar. Colour systems, in common with Vidicons, require a reasonable level of illumination and a low lighting contrast range (about 3:1). Although they will not automatically compensate for red or blue light, it is possible to adjust for minor colour differences.

NOTE:
Colour correction of a high order can be achieved, but it is important that any modification of the colour imaging characteristics of CCTV cameras used underwater is carried out by experienced personnel.

If inexperienced manipulation of the electronic functions is carried out, the resulting images can result in all the benefits of colour being thrown away. Colour CCTV cameras can produce a satisfactory image on a black and white monitoring screen, but not the other way around.

COMPARATIVE SPECIFICATIONS OF MONOCHROME CCTV SYSTEMS

Manufacturer	Model	Tube type	Tube size	Resolution	Focal length standard focus method	Diagonal angle of view	Under-water corrected	Focal para-meters	Weight Air	Water
Hydroproducts	TC-125	Vidicon	1''	650 lines	12.5 mm f1.4/ remote	65°	yes in standard form	75 mm to ∞	5.4 kg	3.6 kg
Hydroproducts	TC 125 SDA	silicon diode array	1''	500 lines	12.5 mm f1.4/ remote	64°	no	75 mm to ∞	5.4 kg	3.6 kg
Hydroproducts	TC 125 SIT	silicon intensified target	1''	550 lines	12.5 mm f1.4/ remote	65°	yes	300 mm to ∞	11.9 kg	7.8 kg
IBAK	L70	electron bombarded silicon	1''	550 lines	12.5 mm to 75 mm f1.8	46°	yes	10 mm to ∞	5 kg 3 kg	2 kg stainless 0 kg titanium
IBAK	UF9	Vidicon or Pasecon	⅔''	true 600 lines	6.5 mm f1.8 (4.0 mm f1.4)	110°	yes	fixfocus 250 mm to ∞ sharp	1.7 kg	1.15 kg
Kinergetics (originally Gen. Aquadyne)	Observer II System	Vidicon	⅔''	550 lines	8.5 mm f1.5/ fixed	65°	yes	7.5 mm to ∞	2.8 kg	0.7 kg
Kinergetics	Observer V	Vidicon	⅔''	550 lines	8.5 mm f1.5/ fixed	65°	no	10 mm to ∞	2.8 kg	0.8 kg
Osprey Electronics	Ondine OE 1300A	silicon diode array	1''	650 lines	12.5 mm f1.4/ remote	49°	optional	10 mm to ∞	3:65 kg	1 57 kg
Osprey Electronics	OE 1311A	Vidicon Chalnicon Ultricon	⅔''	(V)550 lines (C)650 lines (U)400 lines	12.5 mm f1.3/ remote	49°	yes	10 mm to ∞	3.25 kg	1.0 kg
Osprey Electronics	OE 1321A	silicon intensified target	1''	500 lines	6.5 mm f1.8/ fixed	110°	yes	150 mm to ∞	4 kg	0.8 kg
Osprey Electronics	OE 2300A	silicon intensified target	1''	450 lines	24 mm f2.5/ remote	80°	yes	150 mm to ∞	11 kg	0.5 kg
Sub Sea Systems	CM-8	1) Vidicon 2) Ultricon 3) Newvicon 4) SDA	⅔''	550 lines	4.3 or 8 mm f1.7/ remote	65°	yes	50 mm to ∞	1.63 kg	0.68 kg

COMPARATIVE SPECIFICATIONS OF COLOUR CCTV CAMERAS

Manufacturer	Model	Tube type	Tube size	Resolution	Focal length standard focus method	Diagonal angle of view	Under-water corrected	Focal para-meters	Weight Air	Water
Hydroproducts	Hydro-colour TC-181	single Vidicon	1''	260 lines	11.5 mm to 70 mm f1.8	68° dia. to 15° dia. zoom	yes	25 mm to ∞	6.6 kg	1.1 kg
IBAK	UFK-22	single Vidicon	1''	250 lines	6.5 mm f1.8/ fixed	97°	yes	600 mm to ∞ or 300 mm to ∞	7.5 kg	0 3 kg
Kinergetics	Observer I	single Vidicon	1''	260 lines	12.5 mm f1.5/ remote	50°	no	100 mm to ∞	8 kg	0 3 kg
Osprey Electronics	OE 1330A	single Vidicon	1''	260 lines	12.5 mm f1.4/ remote	65°	yes	50 mm to ∞	5.5 kg	neutral
Osprey Electronics	OE 1340A	three tube Saticon	3 × ⅔''	400 lines	12.5 mm f1.4/ remote	47°	no	50 mm to ∞	26 kg	0.5 kg
Sub Sea Systems	CM-40	single Vidicon	1''	260 lines	12.5 mm f1.5/ remote	65°	yes	50 mm to ∞	5 kg	0.9 kg

Max. depth	Housing size	Special features	Manufacturers' recommendations	Mounting type
610 m	530 mm ×76 mm	wide angle and zoom lenses; UK or USA standard; 3 and 12 m depth housings	for high resolution TV viewing e.g. crack evaluation in NDT	hand held pistol grip, light assembly or bulkhead mounted
610 m	530 mm ×76 mm	autofocus, wide angle and zoom lenses; 3 and 12 m depth housing; UK or USA TV standards	low light conditions	hand held or bulkhead mounted
610 m	590 mm ×100 mm	wide angle or zoom lenses; incorporating neutral density filter at f.22; UK or USA TV standard	ultra low light conditions	hand held or bulkhead mounted
500 m 1000 m	500 mm ×100 mm	zoom lens and monitor—viewfinder	standard stainless steel housing for 500 m; titanium for 1000 m and low weight	hand held mounting device on request
500 m	255 m	two separately switchable u/w lights standard; stainless steel housing standard; diver communication and superimposed time available	easy to handle diver camera	hand held
120 m	240 mm× 150 mm ×70 mm	camera and lights integral with helmet	fully integrated system, including recorder and surface console	integral with helmet
900 m	240 mm× 150 mm ×70 mm	incorporates lighting set	none	hand held or helmet mounted
750 m	485 mm ×86 mm	UK or USA TV standard; long line amp; deep water housing	low light conditions burnproof tube	hand held or bulkhead mounted
750 m	350 mm ×100 mm	lens and tube options; radio frequency modulator; UK or USA TV standard; long line amp; deep water housing; 6.5 mm wide angle lens; balanced output, external synchronisation	rugged conditions low light level burnproof tube optional	hand held, helmet or bulkhead mounted
750 m	415 mm ×100 mm	12.5 mm f1.4 lens; radio frequency external synchronisation; UK or USA TV standard; long line amp; deep water housing; balanced output	ultra low light conditions	hand held or bulkhead mounted
750 m	460 mm ×178 mm	incorporates 250 shot 35 mm camera which utilises same lens and includes data chamber with entry from surface	surface control unit allows remote adjustment of focus, still camera iris (f stop) & entry data	hand held or bulkhead mounted
760 m +50%	246 mm ×71 mm	auto iris required for all tubes except vidicon options; external synchronisation; zoom lens; wide angle lens (4.5 mm); balance line video; alum/stainless housing	(1) rugged conditions with good visibility; (2) used to view welding operations; (3) low light operations; (4) similar to Ultricon tube	hand held, helmet mounted or for ROV operations

Max. depth	Housing size	Special features	Manufacturers' recommendations	Mounting type	Colour system
610 m	350 mm ×150 mm	macro focus with zoom lens (6:1); auto colour balance; auxiliary inputs for depth, CP and other sensors; optional auto-focus is available upon request	integrated system includes surface console; exposure and colour controls automatic	hand held with pistol grip integral with 500 W quartz iodide light	NTSC or PAL version available
500 m	365 mm ×180 mm	PAL system optional; includes lighting set 2×35 W	streamlined housing of galvanized aluminium	hand held	PAL
450 m	355 mm ×170 mm	3400°C lighting set	none	hand held	PAL
750 m	380 mm ×140 mm	RF modulation; balanced output; NTSC and Secam optional; long line amplifier	fully self-contained including auto iris and remote focus; no operator adjustment necessary for accurate colour	hand held or bulkhead mounted	PAL
750 m	580 mm ×254 mm	RF modulation; balanced output; NTSC and Secam optional; external synchronisation; long line amplifier; deep water housing	telemetry control unit used to adjust red, blue, pedestal focus and call up colour bar generator via a single wire	hand held or bulkhead mounted	PAL
305 m	355 mm ×160 mm	PAL or NTSC system; options: long line amplifier; deep water housing; divers viewfinder; dual lights colour balance; balance video output	remote operation of focus and red/blue balance at surface console; auto iris lens	hand held or bulkhead mounted	NTSC or PAL available

Thalium iodide, sodium and mercury discharge lighting are not suitable for colour TV. Tungsten halogen or straight tungsten lighting is required.

There are many applications especially suitable for colour TV apart from inspection: offshore construction, salvage, marine fouling identification and marine environmental studies to name but a few.

3. Stereo CCTV systems

All the advantages of stereo in still photography apply equally to a CCTV stereo system. Miniaturisation has made it possible to mount two CCTV cameras alongside each other on a single fixed mount. The spatial impression given to the observer greatly enhances the information presented. Stereo is particularly useful in inspection work, differentiating between corrosion and dirt and other damage to structures.

Where the camera is mounted on a ROV or submersible which operates a manipulator, the stereo system is a considerable advantage in gauging distance by giving a sense of depth. Unfortunately, stereo video is difficult to record because stereo CCTV recorders do not yet exist. However the main benefit of stereo is to facilitate real-time dexterity and information.

Applications for stereo TV are listed below.

1. Positioning tasks using manipulators or other systems.

2. Precise control of ROVs.

3. Inspection and video tape documentation (diver or submersible vehicle).

4. Enhanced optical search and detection.

5. Subsea equipment positioning in drilling and production operations.

6. Mating of structures in offshore construction.

7. Internal pipeline inspection.

2.5 GENERAL SURVEY INSPECTIONS

Seabed surveys

Tide and current movement around the base of a structure or pipeline may produce shifting of the seabed levels. Scour may leave portions of a structure (particularly leg bases) or a pipeline unsupported, resulting in movement, rocking, displacement, or even rupture of the structure or pipeline. Scour prevention devices, such as artificial seaweed mats, can effectively prevent or control scouring problems, but regular seabed inspections are still required to check their continued effectiveness.

Debris surveys

Debris means any material that should not be there, such as lost fishing nets, anchor cables, wire ropes, girders and scrap material dropped over the side from offshore platforms and vessels.

Debris is a serious problem, not only because it may create a hazard to divers, submersibles and ROVs, but also because it can interfere with corrosion protection systems and may even cause fretting, wear and resultant accelerated corrosion.

For these reasons, debris surveys, to locate and record the positions of all debris so that it may later be removed efficiently and safely, are essential.

Every offshore structure has a limit to the amount of weight and wave loading that it can safely endure.

Marinegrowth surveys

Marinegrowth can jeopardise the safety of a structure by increasing not only the weight of the structure itself, but also its surface area, which means that the impact of waves and currents is increased. If marinegrowth becomes excessive, important equipment may have to be removed from the deck, or the structure may become unsafe. Regular surveys are needed to help determine when the removal of marinegrowth will be necessary.

Such surveys need to measure the thickness of the growth, the amount of the structure that is affected, and whether the growth is 'soft' or 'hard', as each type has different significance due to different weights per volume.

2.6 CORROSION INSPECTION

Corrosion surveys are essential to any inspection programme. As steel and salt water are a very corrosive combination, much attention is directed to the problem. (See Section 3.1, Corrosion prevention, for a full explanation.)

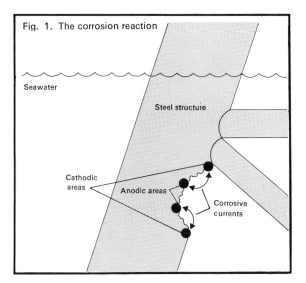

Fig. 1. The corrosion reaction

There are many different types of corrosion, each produced by different causes. They may occur alone or simultaneously. Some of these types are listed below:

1. Dissimilar metals in close proximity (galvanic).
2. Fretting corrosion.
3. Biological corrosion.
4. Stress corrosion and fatigue.
5. Erosion corrosion.
6. Crevice corrosion and concentration cell corrosion.
7. Hydrogen attack and embrittlement, etc, etc.

The two that are of the most interest to the diver are 'general corrosion' (an even loss of metal) and 'pitting corrosion' (localised areas of concentrated metal loss). The present engineering approach to these problems has two prime aspects:

1. To build-in at the design stage, an extra thickness of steel as a corrosion 'allowance', normally about 20–30 mm in the splash zone.
2. To attempt to prevent corrosion. The main protection methods are cathodic protection and protective coatings, which are described fully in Section 3.1, Corrosion prevention.

Corrosion inspection has three important objectives:

1. To find out if the corrosion protection systems are actually working, by checking:
a. That the coating is intact.
b. That the coating remains bonded to the steel.
c. That the anodes are still in place.
d. That the electrical circuit still exists between the anode and the structure (check continuity strap).
e. That the electrical potential between the structure and the seawater is adequate by comparison against a reference half-cell indication, using a CP meter.

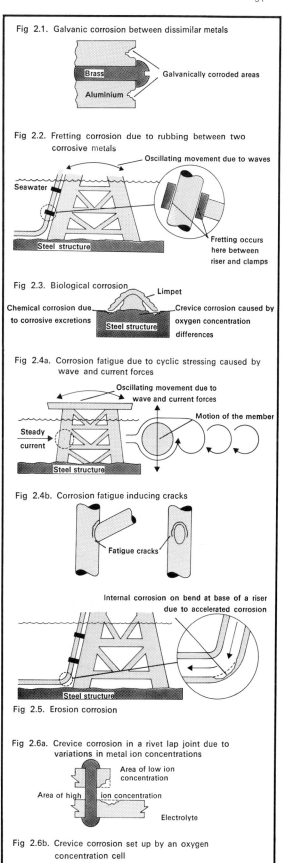

Fig 2.1. Galvanic corrosion between dissimilar metals

Fig 2.2. Fretting corrosion due to rubbing between two corrosive metals

Fig 2.3. Biological corrosion

Fig 2.4a. Corrosion fatigue due to cyclic stressing caused by wave and current forces

Fig 2.4b. Corrosion fatigue inducing cracks

Fig 2.5. Erosion corrosion

Fig 2.6a. Crevice corrosion in a rivet lap joint due to variations in metal ion concentrations

Fig 2.6b. Crevice corrosion set up by an oxygen concentration cell

2. To find and measure corrosion damage by:
a. Measuring the thickness of steel for general corrosion, using ultrasonic thickness meters, commonly called 'D' meters.
b. Measuring the extent and depth of pitting corrosion, using pit gauges.

3. To help plan the maintenance of corrosion protection systems by:
a. Measuring the dimensions of anodes to find the rate of erosion and thereby estimate the remaining life of an anode.

b. Assessing the condition of the protective coating to find out if and when maintenance is required.

Fig 3.1. General corrosion

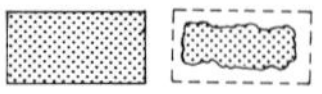

A general thinning of the entire steel surface due to the movement of the anodic areas

Fig 3.2. Pitting corrosion

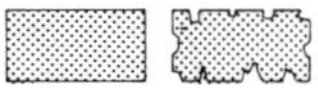

Pitting where the anodic areas are stationary

2.7 UNDERWATER CLEANING

Cleaning is performed for one of three reasons:
1. To remove excessive marinegrowth.
2. To prepare a surface for close visual and critical (NDT) inspection.
3. To unblock seawater intake.

Removal of the marinegrowth alone is normally adequate for close visual inspection. Critical NDT inspection, however, requires the removal from the metal surface of everything including paint, coatings, scale, etc. so as to leave a bright shiny metal surface.

Cleaning methods range from the slow, simple and inexpensive to the fast, complex and expensive. (See Table 2 which provides a summary of cleaning methods and their applications.)

High pressure water jets provide the most effective underwater cleaning technique. It is, however, comparatively expensive since the cost is directly related to the pressure used. The cost of the operation can be significantly reduced by a reduction of the pressure requirement or by the addition of an abrasive (sand or grit) to the water, either dry or as a wet slurry.

When using an abrasive, the water pressure can be reduced. For example, pressures up to 1020 bar

(15 000 psi) are employed when using HP water alone, whereas pressures of only 140–420 bar (2000–6000 psi) at the gun can give excellent results when abrasives are used. The addition of abrasives improves efficiency and provides a faster operation.

Other applications of the high pressure water jet are in cutting timber or concrete.

SAFETY

The high pressure water jetting gun is a potentially dangerous tool and needs handling with great care. All divers using such equipment must be trained in its use.

The following precautions should be observed by divers.
1. At no time should there be more than one diver working in an area where jetting is taking place.
2. The signal to start the high pressure water supply should only be given by the diver when he is ready to start jetting.
3. Under no circumstances should the diver adjust the operating trigger in order to maintain an open position.

CLEANING METHOD				GENERAL MARINEGROWTH REMOVAL	SPECIAL CLEANING FOR CLOSE AND CRITICAL (NDT) INSPECTION	
					AIR RANGE WORK	GAS RANGE WORK
Hand Tools	Wire strops			Excellent. Fast and inexpensive	Not suitable	
	Wire brushes				Not suitable (very slow)	
Power Mechanical Tools	Brushes and grinders			Not suitable (very slow)	Not suitable (worsens defect: e.g., peening of its edges)	
	Chipping hammers					
	Needle guns					
HP Waterjets	HP Water (alone)		Flow requirements	Excellent. Fast and effective (but very expensive comparatively).	Not recommended (slower than with grit entrainment and requires much higher pressures, therefore more costly)	
			HP water: to 15000 psi/1030 bar at 12 gpm			
	HP WATER + GRIT ENTRAIN-MENT	Dry Grit	HP water to 3500 psi/240 bar at 10 gpm	Not recommended	Optimum method. Fastest and most efficient. Lowest (non-manual) cost	Possible (but slurry better due to dry sand problems)
			Air supply: Approx. 150 psi/10 bar at 120 cfpm			
		Wet Slurry	Slurry: to 4500 psi/300 bar at 8 gpm		Adequate (but dry method is simpler and cheaper)	Optimum method. Fastest and most efficient. Lowest (non-manual) cost

4. A strong guard should be fitted around the trigger to prevent inadvertent operation.
5. Jetting is noisy. The wearing of helmets instead of masks is recommended.
6. The retrojet cover should be long enough to prevent damage to the diver's equipment. The length of the lance should be sufficient to give safe working and good visibility for the diver. It should also include a handle/shield to prevent self-inflicted injury.

7. Abrasives can interfere with other equipment such as suit inflation valves etc. Care should be taken to clean all equipment after every dive.
8. The diving supervisor should always be in direct contact with the technician running the pumps who should be standing by his pump whilst it is running. It is imperative that clear communications exist at all times between the supervisor, the pump technician and the diver.

See Section 12.1, First aid, for the treatment of water-jetting injuries.

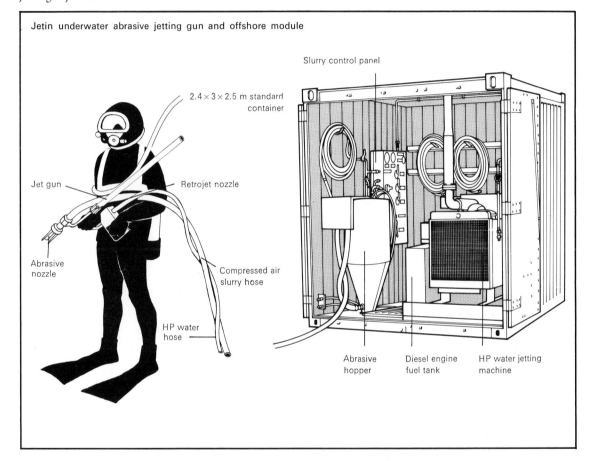

Jetin underwater abrasive jetting gun and offshore module

Slurry control panel

2.4 × 3 × 2.5 m standard container

Jet gun

Retrojet nozzle

Abrasive nozzle

Compressed air slurry hose

HP water hose

Abrasive hopper

Diesel engine fuel tank

HP water jetting machine

2.8 NDT INSPECTION

The harsh marine environment and the high loads imposed on offshore installations can result in the formation of defects underwater. These defects start as minor flaws and, if not discovered at an early stage, may develop into dangerous faults. The role of the NDT diver/technician is to provide information on those defects, or the lack of them, so that the underwater condition of the structure can be assessed by the topside engineers.

NDT was initially developed on land installations. However, underwater NDT is now emerging as a valid engineering discipline. This has largely been due to the certification requirements for offshore production installations.* However, NDT requires considerable skill in operation and experience in interpretation on the part of the diver; hence the need for an NDT qualification.

The prime purpose of NDT is to confirm that there are *no* defects in an inspected area. Assurance of structural integrity does not come from knowing that there is a crack, but from knowing that there are no cracks. For example, a new weld is radiographed to attest that it has no defects. If, however, defects do exist, the radiographer must be able to recognise them so as to prevent the defective weld from being passed as clean.

Each NDT technique may be applied wrongly, resulting in invalid data, so it is important that an NDT technologist specifies the correct technique for a particular inspection. A certain technique may be chosen to examine an area because that technique may have proved successful elsewhere. Use of invalid NDT may well find defects, but it may miss more important ones.

Within the NDT process of seeking to report no defects, indications of possible defects may be found which must be confirmed or cleared. If significant defects are confirmed, they must be repaired and re-tested so that a report can be issued attesting that the inspected item now has no significant defects.

The purpose of NDT

At the present time, underwater practices are still in a developing stage and changing almost daily. Consequently, the following information is intended to help divers gain a general understanding of the subject rather than to give detailed instructions.

Any inspection method which does not destroy the item under test is an NDT method. Visual inspection and photography are recognised NDT methods. Serious defects are, however, not always visible and some other means of detection is required.

A diver having an X-ray of his chest or long bones is being tested by NDT. One of the oldest methods, radiography, shows the aptness of the name 'non-destructive'. A radiograph can be made of steel (or anything else) and, under appropriate circumstances, show graphically the internal defects without destroying the article.

NDT in practice

There are more than 50 NDT methods, none of which can be universally applied to all problems. Each has its own advantages, disadvantages and applications. Apart from being used to discover defects, visible and invisible, they may also size them.

Defect sizing, i.e. measuring length, breadth and height, is more demanding than defect detection in terms of both time and cost. Care is needed to select which NDT method should be applied. For this reason, it is advisable to consider NDT practice under two main categories:

1. 'Rapid' scanning methods which include magnetic particle inspection, compression wave ultrasonics, electromagnetic interrogation, the Harwell ultrasonic torch, radiography and AC potential drop methods. Although these methods are referred to as rapid, they are only so in relation to critical sizing methods.
2. Critical sizing methods including shearwave ultrasonics and AC potential drop methods.

Most rapid scan methods can take a considerable time to perform, but are rapid compared to the inspection times necessary should sizing methods be employed for defect detection.

Rapid scanning methods

a. MAGNETIC PARTICLE INSPECTION

MPI is sometimes known as MPCD (magnetic particle crack detection) and can only be applied to ferrous metals. It is based on the fact that where a magnetic field exists within a ferrous metal, the magnetic flux (lines of force) will jump over and concentrate at any discontinuity in the metal. This is known as 'flux leakage' and occurs because one

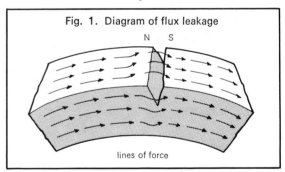

Fig. 1. Diagram of flux leakage

lines of force

side of the crack acts as a north and the other side as a south pole. Thus magnetisable particles are attracted even to the edges of a hairline crack and bridge the gap, forming a concentration along the length of the defect. When this concentration can be seen, it reliably indicates an otherwise invisible crack.

For underwater MPI to be successful the following three conditions must exist:
—There must be adequate magnetic flux in the metal being tested.
—Suitable ferrous particles must be applied and allowed to be attracted by the flux leakage.
—The particles must be appropriately illuminated.

* UK Offshore Installations (Construction and Survey) Regulations 1974.

(i) Provision of magnetic flux.
A magnetic field may be created within the metal by applying either a magnet or an electric current. Currents may be passed either close to the metal through an insulated coil or conductor, or actually through the metal by the use of prods. These are called 'current flow techniques'. 'Flux path' techniques involve the passing of magnetism into the steel under test from either a permanent or an electro-magnet. Each technique has limitations and inappropriate usage may invalidate the test results.

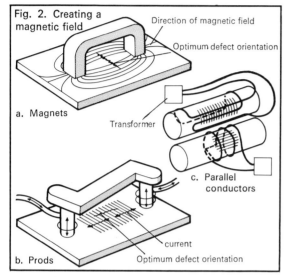

Fig. 2. Creating a magnetic field

Direction of magnetic field

Optimum defect orientation

a. Magnets

Transformer

c. Parallel conductors

current

b. Prods   Optimum defect orientation

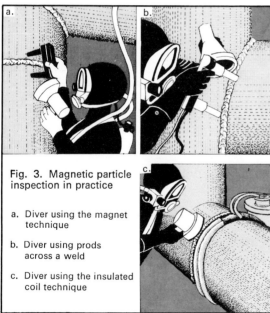

Fig. 3. Magnetic particle inspection in practice

a. Diver using the magnet technique

b. Diver using prods across a weld

c. Diver using the insulated coil technique

Important aspects of flux provision are that the flux:

a. is applied *into* the steel (not merely in its vicinity)

b. is neither too little nor too much (between 7200–12 000 gauss, 0.72–1.2 Tesla)

c. direction is appropriate for the direction of the defect being sought (the two directions should ideally be perpendicular)

The strength of the magnets or currents to be used depends on the permeability of steel, i.e. its ability to be magnetised, and specific values for each test must be determined from a relevant Standard or Specification.

(ii) Particle indicators.
Having established the magnetic field, each ferrous particle is highlighted with fluorescent dye; under the influence of the magnetic field, the particles concentrate along the edges of any defect that may exist. In order to see this concentration, the fluorescent-coated particles must be irradiated using ultraviolet light in dark ambient light conditions (less than 10 lux). The fluorescent particles must also be maintained in suspension by constant agitation of the ink. (The irradiation requires wavelengths in excess of 3500 Å (350 nm)* and the light intensity on the testpiece should be not less than 1000 W/cm² and no more than 3000 W/cm².) Viewing and interpretation of the results can then take place.

The diver inspector can prejudice the certainty with which the leakage fields are detected by:
a. Not having sufficient concentration of magnetic particles in the ink.
b. Having insufficient output from the ultraviolet light.
c. Using light of the wrong wavelength.

MPI is a very reliable crack-detection method, but only when the correct technique is chosen for a particular job, when the procedure is complied with throughout the test and when the diving inspector performing the test is adequately trained, qualified and experienced.

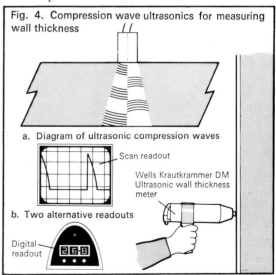

Fig. 4. Compression wave ultrasonics for measuring wall thickness

a. Diagram of ultrasonic compression waves

Scan readout

Wells Krautkrammer DM Ultrasonic wall thickness meter

b. Two alternative readouts

Digital readout

Accurate interpretation is totally in the hands of the diver inspector until such time as techniques are developed to enable the transmission of the details of leakage field distributions to take place.

b. COMPRESSION-WAVE ULTRASONICS
CW ultrasonics is primarily used in underwater corrosion surveys to measure the thickness of metal.

* Å = Angstroms; nm = nanometres

Very high frequency sound waves (2.5–6 MHz) are applied at right angles to the metal testpiece surface via a diver hand-held probe. The sound waves travel through the metal and reflect off the back wall. The time taken to return to the probe is measured and, since the rate at which sound travels through any metal is known, this measurement can be used to determine the thickness of the metal.

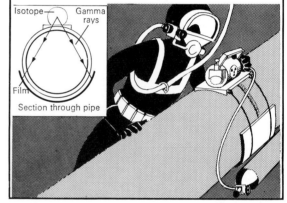

Fig. 5. Diver measuring wall thickness with a Seaprobe P200 digital readout gauge

The data are displayed on either a cathode ray tube screen ('A' scan) or a digital readout on a diver-carried unit. Digital meters are simple to use and are accurate when used appropriately and correctly.

c. ELECTROMAGNETIC DETECTION (EMD)

EMD is based on detecting the change of permeability and polarity, a condition which occurs where there is any defect in metal. It is a recently developed technique which, compared to other NDT methods, requires less preparatory surface cleaning and less operator skill, training and expertise.

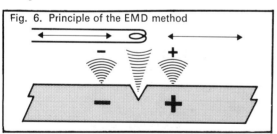

Fig. 6. Principle of the EMD method

d. THE HARWELL ULTRASONIC TORCH

The Harwell ultrasonic torch carries out the same function as MPI at much the same workrate.

The torch uses microprocessor control to apply ultrasonic waves to the surface of the testpiece from

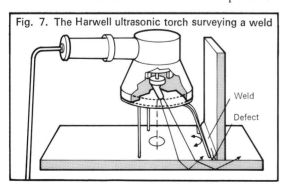

Fig. 7. The Harwell ultrasonic torch surveying a weld

Weld

Defect

a fixed stand-off distance. The return signals are displayed on a screen and provide data on the location and size of the defect.

e. RADIOGRAPHY

A serious weakness of radiography is its poor ability to detect cracks. Its use underwater is therefore of limited value. It is, however, sometimes used to assess blockages in pipelines or to detect internal corrosion of pipelines.

It operates on the same principle as X-rays. A radiographic photosensitive plate is placed on one side of the pipeline while the unit that emits the radiographic rays is placed opposite it on the other side of the pipe. When the diver exposes the isotope in the unit, he moves away while the rays travel through the pipeline to expose the film. After sufficient time for a correct exposure, he returns to reshield the isotope. He returns the equipment to the surface where the film is developed and viewed.

Fig. 8. Gammagraphy used in pipeline survey and inspection

Isotope — Gamma rays

Film

Section through pipe

f. AC DROP METHODS (AC-D)

Although it can be used as a rapid scanning method, AC-D may be more valuable as a means of defect sizing. (See Critical sizing methods.)

Critical sizing methods

Critical sizing methods should ideally provide accurate data regarding defect dimensions, position and orientation. Existing methods are very good for determining the length of surface-breaking defects, but questionable as to defect depth and subsurface orientation. The best available methods are shearwave ultrasonics and AC drop methods; the former is used to determine the position and depth of a subsurface crack, while AC drop methods may be able to measure the depth of some surface-breaking cracks.

a. SHEARWAVE ULTRASONICS

'Shearwave' indicates that ultrasound is introduced in to the metal testpiece at an angle (usually 30°–70°) and is therefore often known as 'angle working'. The frequencies used are normally around the 5 MHz level. Shearwave ultrasonics are mainly used for flaw detection in welds and parent materials.

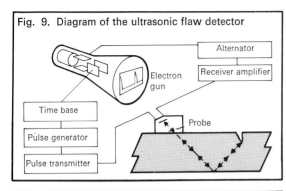
Fig. 9. Diagram of the ultrasonic flaw detector

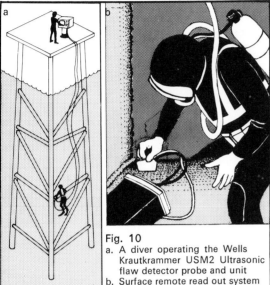
Fig. 10
a. A diver operating the Wells Krautkrammer USM2 Ultrasonic flaw detector probe and unit
b. Surface remote read out system

The operator has a choice of manual or automated application, the latter being more valuable underwater. Manual application requires considerable training and skill and is difficult enough on land. The underwater environment only compounds the problems. Useful results are only obtained if quality controls on the operator's skill and technique are of the highest order.

Fig. 11. The Corroscan automatised underwater shear-wave and ultrasonic flaw detector

top
side
ampl
T-scan display

top
side
Weld
defect in weld

Automated computer-controlled use has, however, considerable potential underwater, especially for use on circumferential butt joints. The SVC 'P' scan system (Danish) appears to be the most effective currently available. Current techniques however, are not yet sufficiently advanced to be able to cope with the more complex structure of crack detection on node joints.

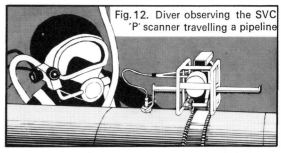
Fig. 12. Diver observing the SVC 'P' scanner travelling a pipeline

b. AC DROP METHODS (AC-D)

AC-D methods are used to measure the depth of surface-breaking cracks. AC-D operates on the 'skin' effect of AC electrical currents, i.e. currents travel mainly along the surface (skin) of the metal. The distance that a current travels between two contact points is measured; should a crack exist along this path, the distance travelled will increase by the distance up and down both faces of the crack. From this data the depth of the crack can be calculated.

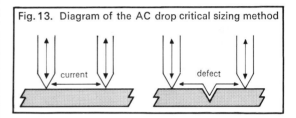
Fig. 13. Diagram of the AC drop critical sizing method

current   defect

Summary of suitability of NDT methods and their applications.

*** Very suitable   ** Possible   * Sometimes possible

TECHNIQUE	APPLICATION	SUITABILITY UNDER-WATER
VISUAL INSPECTION	Surface condition of all materials at low cost. Always primary method of inspection.	***
MPI	Surface and near surface defects on ferromagnetic materials only. To detect and monitor fatigue cracks.	***
MAGNETOGRAPHIC TAPE	As for MPI.	**
ULTRASONICS	Thickness testing.	***
	Laminations and other planar defects such as cracks.	***
	Volumetric defects.	*
RADIOGRAPHY	Volumetric defects (provides permanent record).	***
	Planar defect.	*
CORROSION POTENTIAL MEASUREMENT	Metallic components immersed in an electrolyte.	***
STRUCTURAL MONITORING —VIBRATION ANALYSIS	Gross structural defects.	***
	Gross structural defects.	**
—ACOUSTIC EMISSION	Nature and location of defects on a structure.	

2.9 INSPECTION QUALIFICATIONS

As inspection is a major diver activity offshore, it is to the advantage of everyone in the diving industry for divers to have a sound training in NDT and a recognised qualification.

Qualifications are, however, only of real value when they are supported by a track record of supervised practical training and experience.

The normal NDT qualification process involves a balance of:

1. Formal training (theoretical and practical).
2. Ideally, a period of supervised practical experience.
3. Formal examination (theoretical and practical).

The type of training, experience and examination determines whether a diver is granted 'Approval' or 'Certification' in underwater inspection and NDT. Approval may be granted by a Certification Authority (CA) after an experienced diver has successfully completed a suitable course (different levels for Lloyd's or DnV). Certification goes on from there, requiring an additional higher level examination such as CSWIP (Certification Scheme for Weldment Inspection Personnel) or the equivalent.

In other words, a certified diver has a formal certificate such as CSWIP, while an 'Approved' man may work without a certificate, having satisfied the CA as to his competence.

The most common underwater qualifications are:

○ CSWIP certification: acceptable to Lloyd's and DnV.
○ DnV certification: granted when the technician has an approved formal qualification such as CSWIP.
○ ASNT certification: which may need CA on-the-job endorsement.
○ DnV approval: the DnV Blue Record of dive added to a diver's logbook, besides being acceptable to DnV, may be considered by Lloyd's.
○ Lloyd's approval: acceptable to Lloyd's but less likely to be considered by DnV.

The main courses relating to North Sea underwater NDT work are offered by:

Det Norske Veritas (DnV), PO Box 300, N-1322 Hoevik, Norway. Tel: (02) 129 955

*Fort Bovisand Underwater Centre, Plymouth, Devon, PL9 0AB, UK. Tel: (0752) 42570 & 45641

Lloyd's Register, Garrett House, Manor Royal, Crawley, West Sussex, RH10 2QN, UK. Tel: (0293) 26404

*Prodive, Service Area, Falmouth Oil Exploration Base, Falmouth Docks, Falmouth, Cornwall, TR11 4NR, UK. Tel: (0326) 315691

*School of Applied NDT (SANDT), Abington Hall, Abington, Cambridge, CB1 6AL, UK. Tel: (0223) 891162

*Scottish School of NDT (SSNDT), Paisley College of Technology, High Street, Paisley, Renfrewshire, TA1 2BE, Scotland. Tel: (041) 887 1241

Most of the courses run for 8 days.

Successful course completion (marked by the end-of-course theoretical and practical examination) enables the diver to be granted the appropriate approval. In the case of the four schools marked with an asterisk (*), which run CSWIP approved courses, the diver may sit the CSWIP Phase 7 (3.1D –Diver Inspector) $1\frac{1}{2}$ day examination after a minimum period of 1 month between his course and the examination. Besides this new 3.1D underwater qualification, the appropriate CSWIP land-based qualification is accepted for underwater work at the present time.

The following table shows the qualifications structure for the UK, USA and Europe. In this table, the CSWIP section has been expanded to show details of each phase of the scheme; but other schemes have similar structures which may be acceptable for underwater work.

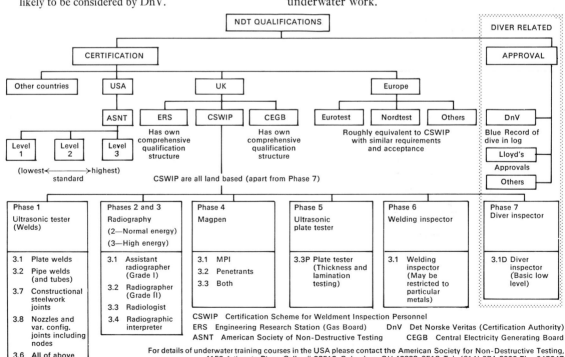

CSWIP   Certification Scheme for Weldment Inspection Personnel
ERS   Engineering Research Station (Gas Board)   DnV   Det Norske Veritas (Certification Authority)
ASNT   American Society of Non-Destructive Testing   CEGB   Central Electricity Generating Board

For details of underwater training courses in the USA please contact the American Society for Non-Destructive Testing, 4153 Arlingate Plaza, Caller # 28518, Columbus, OH 43228-0518. Tel: (614) 274 6003 Tlx: 245347

Applied techniques

3.1 CORROSION PREVENTION

A solution which will conduct electricity is known as an electrolyte. Sea water is such a solution, and is considered in that context in this section.

When two metals are submerged together in seawater, an electrochemical reaction occurs, which produces a potential (or voltage difference) between them. This can also occur between different parts of a single piece of metal, where localised variations may produce a potential difference because of variations in temperature, stress, fabrication (e.g. mill scale, or slag inclusions in steel), or the environment (e.g. marinegrowth or variable silting).

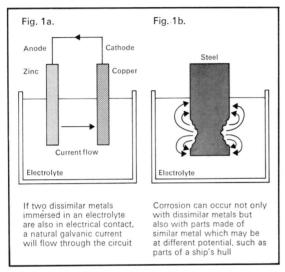

Fig. 1a. Fig. 1b.

If two dissimilar metals immersed in an electrolyte are also in electrical contact, a natural galvanic current will flow through the circuit

Corrosion can occur not only with dissimilar metals but also with parts made of similar metal which may be at different potential, such as parts of a ship's hull

This potential difference causes a current to flow in the metal from an area with a positive potential to another more negative area, and the circuit is then completed by the current leaving the metal and returning to the first area through the seawater. In simple, practical terms, areas where this circulating current *leaves* the metal and enters the seawater are corroded. Potential at these points moves in a positive direction and they are called ANODIC areas. Similarly, areas where the current *enters* the metal from the electrolyte are protected from corrosion. Their potential moves in a negative direction so that they are called CATHODIC areas.

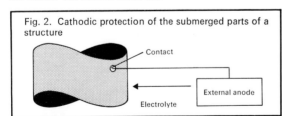

Fig. 2. Cathodic protection of the submerged parts of a structure

Corrosion protection is based on the elimination of the anodic areas. Four main techniques are used.

1. Selection of materials.

2. Protective coatings.

3. Cathodic protection.

4. Corrosion inhibitors.

Selection of Materials

Since it is the dissimilarity between metals that produces the electrochemical process that leads to corrosion, the use of compatible metals is the first step in corrosion prevention since this results in low potential differences and hence low corrosion rates. This is particularly important for structures consisting of many components.

It should be appreciated that this reaction is not limited to steel—any metal will tend to behave in a similar way if immersed in an electrolyte. The following table shows the order in which various metals tend to corrode. It is called the GALVANIC SERIES and is determined from the natural potentials of each metal relative to the others.

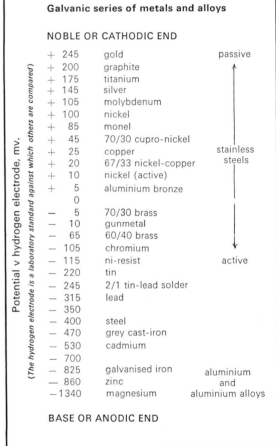

Galvanic series of metals and alloys

NOBLE OR CATHODIC END

Potential v hydrogen electrode, mv.
(The hydrogen electrode is a laboratory standard against which others are compared)

+ 245	gold	passive
+ 200	graphite	
+ 175	titanium	
+ 145	silver	
+ 105	molybdenum	
+ 100	nickel	
+ 85	monel	
+ 45	70/30 cupro-nickel	
+ 25	copper	stainless steels
+ 20	67/33 nickel-copper	
+ 10	nickel (active)	
+ 5	aluminium bronze	
0		
− 5	70/30 brass	
− 10	gunmetal	
− 65	60/40 brass	
− 105	chromium	
− 115	ni-resist	active
− 220	tin	
− 245	2/1 tin-lead solder	
− 315	lead	
− 350		
− 400	steel	
− 470	grey cast-iron	
− 530	cadmium	
− 700		
− 825	galvanised iron	aluminium
− 860	zinc	and
−1340	magnesium	aluminium alloys

BASE OR ANODIC END

Stainless steel itself is 'stainless' because it forms a very thin skin of its oxide (or corrosion product) on the surface of the steel, and this oxide film insulates and protects the surface. However, the oxide film can be broken down by voltage stress, so that stainless steel will corrode rapidly when in contact with the wrong metal, and once it has started corroding, it becomes active and moves much further down the galvanic series.

The galvanic series lists metals in order of their electrical potential in seawater, showing that any metal will tend to be 'protected' by any other below it in the series. In other words, zinc in contact with mild steel will corrode to protect the steel: while mild steel in contact with cast iron will corrode to protect the cast iron and so on up the series.

The significance of this can be shown by the example of a mild steel cover secured by stainless steel bolts. The cover will corrode rapidly around the bolts (where it is in contact with the stainless steel) with disastrous results.

Protective coatings

The main aim of a coating is to provide an electrically insulating cover to the metal which will prevent discharge of current. To be effective it must be a good insulator, be well bonded to the metal and must maintain these properties for many years. Unbonded coatings which allow water to penetrate behind them are a corrosion hazard which can be most difficult to detect.

Coatings for subsea service must be highly chemical-resistant and offer long term protection because of the high cost and difficulty of replacing them.

Insulating coatings consist of various plastics and epoxies, either in the form of tapes or as coatings of various thicknesses. Typical of these are the epoxy-phenolic coats, zinc-rich primers, polyamide epoxies and urethanes. Metal and concrete coatings are encountered regularly in offshore work.

A casing of Monel Metal is sometimes placed around the members of offshore installations, throughout the splash zone. This is to give physical protection to the structure in the most corrosive area, where the metal alternates between being wet in air and being fully submerged. Regular coatings normally suffer extensive mechanical damage in this area, and atmospheric corrosion is very rapid in the wet conditions.

Concrete coatings are also frequently used on offshore pipelines. They act as weight coatings to overcome the buoyancy of the line and to ensure that it stays in place on the seabed. The concrete is applied over an epoxy or bitumen coating which provides corrosion protection.

However if the concrete weight coat and bitumen coating is damaged, a severely corrosive galvanic cell is produced between the encased steel and any exposed steel.

Cathodic protection

Another method of eliminating the anodic areas is to overcome the discharging current by introducing a separate source of current of such polarity as to ensure that the structure receives current over its entire surface area. By doing this, the potential of the structure becomes more negative, or more cathodic; hence the term 'cathodic protection'.

Cathodic protection can be achieved by the use of either of two different types of anode.

I. SACRIFICIAL ANODE

To protect a steel structure, a more active metal than the steel is selected from the galvanic series and is placed in contact with the steel below water level. Current flows as a result of the electro-chemical difference, from the active metal, through the seawater, to the steel. Thus the active

metal becomes anodic and corrodes, whilst the steel becomes cathodic and is protected, so that in fact the active metal corrodes in order to protect the steel.

Magnesium in fresh water, zinc and aluminium in seawater are the most commonly used metals for this anode type and 'sacrificial anodes' are so called because they use no external power supply to activate the protective process. All of these metals corrode at known rates, so that their life expectancy can be estimated and maintenance replacement programmes specified in order that new anodes can be installed before the old ones are entirely used up.

Typically, a large platform anode can produce around 4 amp DC at about 0.25 V (power level 1W). The current is only transmitted over relatively short distances.

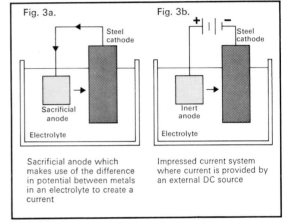

Fig. 3a.   Fig. 3b.

Sacrificial anode which makes use of the difference in potential between metals in an electrolyte to create a current

Impressed current system where current is provided by an external DC source

2. IMPRESSED CURRENT

Impressed current anodes have the same overall effect as sacrificial anodes, but with the former, the protective current is derived from an external power source. Because of this, an anode material which will have the lowest possible corrosion rate when conducting the protective current into the seawater is used. Lead/silver/antimony alloys, or alternatively titanium or platinum with a very thin niobium covering, are the most common materials.

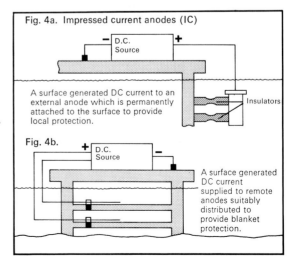

Fig. 4a. Impressed current anodes (IC)

A surface generated DC current to an external anode which is permanently attached to the surface to provide local protection.

Fig. 4b.

A surface generated DC current supplied to remote anodes suitably distributed to provide blanket protection.

Typical operating power for a single impressed current anode may be around 50 amp, 20 V DC (100 W) so that high power levels can be achieved with few anodes, and long distances can be covered.

Comparative aspects of the two types of cathodic protection

Cathodic protection system	Advantages	Limitations
SACRIFICIAL ANODE SYSTEM	Power is not required Little supervision once installed System is operating as soon as the structure is installed Does not cause interference to other structures in the vicinity	May cause excessive drag on structural members The protection is limited and depends upon total surface area of the anodes Excessive weight of metal may be overcome if the mechanical design allows for it Difficult to replace after permanent failure or at the end of their working/design life
IMPRESSED CURRENT SYSTEM	Saving in weight and drag Provided the power is available, protection may be increased to any desired value as long as the anode material can still operate Integral monitoring systems can easily be built	If the power fails, protection is lost The power source must be connected to the structure correctly The system must be continually monitored Possible hazard to divers The electrical cables must be well protected; damage to them will result in failure of the system Too much power can be applied which may damage paint coatings increase fatigue crack growth and cause hydrogen embrittlement

Corrosion inhibitors

These are chemical systems, normally only used as additives to water in closed systems, or in circulating water systems in refineries, etc., so that the diver involvement is rare.

Corrosion inhibitors of many types are used, depending on the metal to be protected and on the actual application. However, they fall into two main categories:

1. Where a protective film is deposited onto the surface of the structure, pipes, etc., out of the liquid.

2. Where the chemicals in the inhibitor react on the surface of the steel and with the steel itself, to

form a protective skin in a similar way to the oxide layer on stainless steel.

Insulation

It will be appreciated that a galvanic cell such as, for example, a zinc anode on a steel ship's hull, will only experience current flow if a very low resistance contact exists for the current return path. This is made deliberately in the case of an anode, by direct welding of the anode's steel core to the hull, but other cases may not be as beneficial as this. The example of a stainless steel bolt/washer in a steel panel has already been quoted, but another typical case is the cast iron body of a valve in a steel pipeline. With no protection, the steel will be anodic to the cast iron, and will corrode because they are in contact through the (normally) bolted flanges. Corrosion due to this cell would be prevented by insulating the flanges each side of the valve. It is more common to apply a cathodic protection system which will tend to equalise the potentials of the two metals, both at a protective level.

Reference electrodes

In order to measure levels of protection, the electrochemical reaction between two metals in an electrolyte is again used.

A selected metal surrounded by a saturated solution of its own salts, for example, a silver electrode in a silver chloride paste, is placed near the metal, say steel, to be monitored. Since the silver chloride paste is saturated, the silver electrode can be considered to be in a stable and unchanging environment, but the steel is subject to any of the normal variations and stresses that it will encounter in its normal working situation. Therefore, if the voltage between the steel and the silver is measured it can be assumed that this voltage level is only changed according to the effect of the environment upon the steel, so that the voltage is a direct indication of the corroding or protected condition of the steel.

The other most common type of reference electrode used in submerged applications is high purity zinc, which, for most practical purposes, has a stable voltage when directly immersed in seawater. This means that it can be assembled into a much more rugged electrode unit and it is often favoured for this reason.

Table showing the expected range of potentials in seawater of the most common metals used in marine installations.

Metal	Measured with reference to the silver/silver chloride half cell in mV
Unprotected iron and steel	−400 to −650
Cathodically protected iron and steel	−800 to −900
Zinc	−1000 to −1050
Monel	−50 to −150

Diver operations

These are generally associated either with the installation of a system, or with the monitoring of its operation.

Fig. 5a. Practical use of the portable corrosion meter

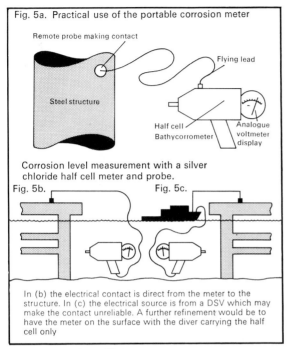

Remote probe making contact

Flying lead

Steel structure

Half cell
Bathycorrometer

Analogue
voltmeter
display

Corrosion level measurement with a silver chloride half cell meter and probe.

Fig. 5b.   Fig. 5c.

In (b) the electrical contact is direct from the meter to the structure. In (c) the electrical source is from a DSV which may make the contact unreliable. A further refinement would be to have the meter on the surface with the diver carrying the half cell only

Installation of sacrificial anodes

A sacrificial anode cathodic protection system design first identifies the total tonnage of anodic material required for a specified life, and this tonnage is then subdivided into individual anodes, each of which produces a proportion of the total current required for protection. The actual current produced by an anode depends on a number of factors, but, for a given material in seawater, the most significant are the dimensions and shape of the anode.

Thus the designer calculates the optimum quantity and size of anodes, and then specifies their location to achieve the most even current distribution.

The anodes are then fitted by either welding, clamping or bolting.

Fig. 6. A diver inspector taking cathodic protection potential measurements using a Roxby Bathycorrometer Mk V with remote probe

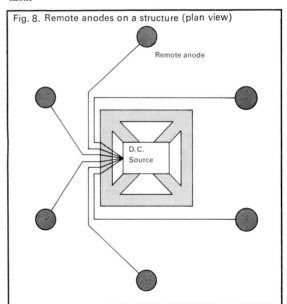

Fig. 7. Rectangular and pipeline anodes

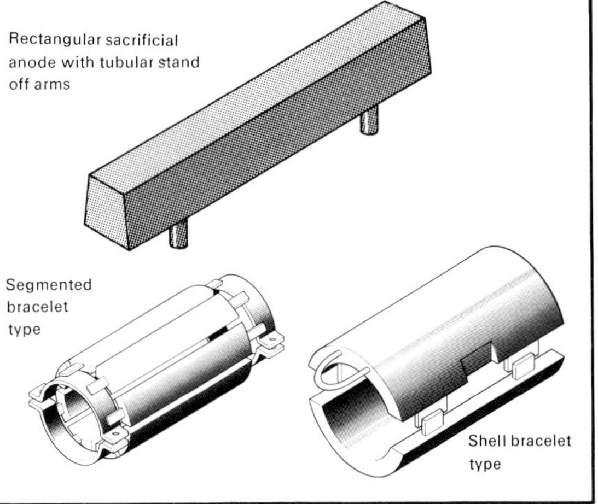

Rectangular sacrificial
anode with tubular stand
off arms

Segmented
bracelet
type

Shell bracelet
type

Installation of impressed current systems

The most significant difference between sacrificial and impressed current systems, as already discussed, is that the impressed current system requires a DC power source, such as a transformer–rectifier, which will be mounted out of the water. At the same time, the anodes must be permanently below water, so that the cable connection between transformer–rectifier and anode must inevitably run through the 'splash zone' and be subject to wave action. Fixing of conduits, etc., must take this into account when mounting impressed anodes on a structure.

An assembly, or array, of impressed current anodes may also be located on the seabed remote from the protected structure. This is mainly pre-assembled above water and lowered directly into position.

The fitting of retrofit anodes is another common diver task.

Fig. 8. Remote anodes on a structure (plan view)

Remote anode

D.C.
Source

Installation of monitoring systems

Permanent reference electrodes are installed to enable periodic measurements to be made at designated positions on a structure and these may be used with either type of cathodic protection system. They

are normally connected by cables to a monitoring/
control panel above water, and again these cables
must be suitably installed and protected.

Corrosion rate

As previously mentioned, anodic or corroding areas
are those where current is passing from the metal
into the electrolyte, and it will be appreciated that
higher current levels will result in more rapid corrosion. We can define corrosion rate in terms of
current flow, and a typical figure is that for steel:

    1 amp flowing for 1 year will remove approximately
    10 kg of steel.

This is a relatively low current, but 10 kg represents
a large piece of steel out of a pipe wall and would be a
major leak in a pipeline.

Current level, according to Ohm's Law, is equal to
voltage divided by resistance. Therefore high voltage
or low resistance will cause high current, and rapid
corrosion. It should be noted, however, that high
voltage in this context will still be extremely low—in
most cases less than 1.0 V.

The specific resistance, or resistivity, of the water is the
electrical resistance of a 1 cm cube of the water,
measured between two opposite faces of the cube, and
is normally stated as ohm−cm. This gives a means
of measuring the corrosivity of the water, and the
following levels are generally accepted.

Typical Resistivities and Current Densities of Bare Steel		
0–2,000 ohm/cm = severely corrosive		
2,000–10,000 ohm/cm = moderately corrosive		
10,000 ohm/cm and higher = unlikely to be corrosive		
Ocean Area	Resistivity (Ohms/cm)	Current Density (milli Amps/m²)
North Sea	30	130–180
Gulf of Mexico	20	65
Australia (South)	20	130
West Africa	20	85–130
Indonesia	19	65
Gulf (Middle East)	15	110
Buried pipelines	70–100	50
Saline mud	70–100	11–30
Estuarine water	750–1,000	—

3.2 UNDERWATER CUTTING

There are four underwater cutting processes generally in use.

(1) Oxy-arc (carbon and steel electrodes)

(2) Thermic cutting (Kerie Cable and Broco Rods)

(3) Gas cutting (Oxy-hydrogen torch)

(4) Shielded metal arc (SMA) (also known as manual metal arc MMA)

Of these, Oxy-arc is probably the most widely used. Shielded metal arc can cut steels which are resistant to oxidization and corrosion, and non-ferrous materials, and is useful where no oxygen is available. Oxy-hydrogen cutting is performed with a torch rather than with a cutting electrode and an experienced operator can achieve a very neat cut in thick metal. Thermic cutting will burn through almost anything, including reinforced concrete.

Operating principles

Oxy-arc is a cutting process which exploits the chemical reaction between oxygen and the base ferrous metal at very high temperatures. This heat is initiated and maintained by an electric arc between the electrode and the base metal and by the chemical reactions in the work and the electrode itself. In other words, a spot on the base metal is made hot by the electric arc, which is formed between the base metal and the tip of the hollow tubular arc cutting electrode. Preheating is instantaneous, a jet of oxygen is directed at the preheated spot at the same time as the arc is established and cutting commences. In practice the oxygen flow is turned on prior to forming an arc so that the oxidized steel will be blown away from the line of cut, also preventing fusion between rod and metal and possible sealing of the tip when using steel electrodes. For the same reason the oxygen flow is maintained for a short period after breaking the cutting arc.

EQUIPMENT

The equipment used for oxy-arc cutting and shielded metal arc cutting is basically the same as shielded metal arc welding.
1. DC welding generator
2. Oxygen supply
3. Oxygen coupler
4. Oxygen regulator
5. Earth or ground plate
6. Work or base metal
7. Knife switch or electrical contactor
8. Solenoid valve
9. Cutting electrode
10. Cutting torch and spares
11. Cable connector
12. 400 amp cable (supply and return)
13. Oxygen supply hose
14. Scraper

The equipment required for oxy-hydrogen cutting is:
1. Oxygen supply
2. Oxygen manifold
3. Oxygen regulator
4. Hydrogen supply
5. Hydrogen manifold
6. Hydrogen regulator
7. Compressed air supply
8. Compressed air regulator
9. Electrical igniter
10. Cutting torch
11. Oxygen hose, 30 m (100 ft)
12. Hydrogen hose, 30 m
13. Oxygen hose for compressed air, 30 m
14. Wrenches
15. Scraper

Fig. 1. Two types of underwater oxygen arc cutting torches

Torch head insulator jacket — Cable — Insulator coupler — Torch handle — Base nipple — Torch head — Flash arrester cartridge — Collet locknut — Collet — Inlet nipple — Handle screw — Trigger valve assembly — External washer — Internal washer — Collet locknut

a) Craftsweld torch   b) Broco torch

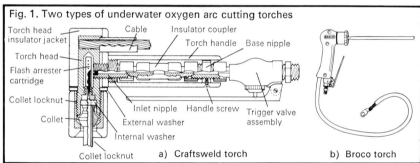

Fig. 2. 'Seafire' gas cutting torch

Operational functions of gases in underwater cutting torch
A ☐ Air
B ■ Oxygen cutting jet
C ▨ Oxygen
D ▨ Mixed oxygen and hydrogen
E ▨ Hydrogen

Fig. 3. 'Seafire' regulator

Outlet valve — Hose connection 3/16" — Pressure adjusting spring — Diaphragm — Main valve — Bottle nut (wing) — Felt filter — Safety valve

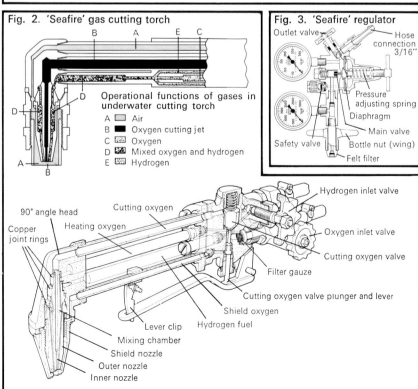

90° angle head — Cutting oxygen — Hydrogen inlet valve — Copper joint rings — Heating oxygen — Oxygen inlet valve — Cutting oxygen valve — Filter gauze — Cutting oxygen valve plunger and lever — Shield oxygen — Hydrogen fuel — Lever clip — Mixing chamber — Shield nozzle — Outer nozzle — Inner nozzle

Factors in planning underwater oxy-arc cutting operations

(1) Sea state; tidal state; rate and direction of tidal stream; weather forecast.

(2) Visibility underwater.

(3) Setting up the equipment, which entails
(a) determining amperage, depending on length of cables, depth at the work position, and the thickness of plate to be cut. An amperage of between 300 and 500 amps would be required. Excess cable should be laid out in straight lines or snaked out in large 'U's, as coiling reduces efficiency of burning.
(b) a low voltage, between 60 and 90 V d.c. at straight polarity (electrode negative)
(c) the electrode cable to be connected to the **negative** terminal at the electric supply generator
(d) a safety switch or contactor to be fitted in the negative lead
(e) adequate cylinders of commercial grade oxygen (99.5% pure). A manifold to connect the cylinders if more than one is used, and to minimize interruptions due to cylinder change
(f) an oxygen regulator which can be set to furnish a pressure of 4–6.8 bar (60–100 psi) above ambient pressure.
(g) selection of the type of electrode. These are
   (i) carbon electrodes
   (ii) tubular steel electrodes
   (iii) ultrathermic electrodes.
All must be suitably waterproofed and insulated. Ultrathermic electrodes may need an adaptor to fit into some torches.

(4) The provision of a steady stage or platform from which to cut. If nothing else is available use magnetic holds.

(5) Proper cleaning of the line of cut. Where neatness of the cut is important a cutting template is useful. On a pipeline, a strap or rope wrapped around the pipe so that the outline can be followed is often useful. On more complex structures, a cutting template may be designed for the job.

(6) Securing of a ground (earth) clamp to workpiece.

(7) Ground or earth plate connected to the **positive** terminal of the electrical supply.

(8) When cutting through thick steel, it will be useful to have some tool, such as a kitchen knife, to push all the way through the cut to check for bridging.

COMMON PROBLEMS ENCOUNTERED WITH UNDERWATER OXY-ARC CUTTING TORCHES

1. Worn or damaged collet, possibly causing poor electrical contact or an oxygen leak.

2. Worn or damaged Blow-Out Preventer or spring.

3. Sealing washers need replacement.

4. Oxygen valve/torch seized up through corrosion.

5. Torch insulation broken down.

6. Poor electrical contact between cable and torch.

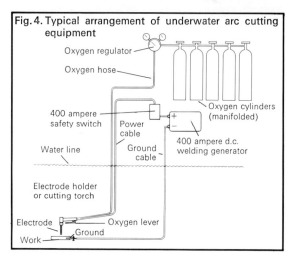

Fig. 4. Typical arrangement of underwater arc cutting equipment

CARBON ELECTRODES

Carbon electrodes are usually 20.3 cm (8 in) long and 9.5 mm ($\frac{3}{8}$ in) diameter. These electrodes have the following characteristics.

(a) Cutting technique is simple.

(b) Economy; they oxidize more slowly than the other types of rod and therefore will cut more linear plate per rod on plate up to 25 mm (1 in) thick (average speed 0.3 m/min (1 ft/min) on 12.7 mm ($\frac{1}{2}$ in) plate).

(c) Cheapness; they are half the price of tubular steel.

(d) Limited cutting at one pass on plate over 25 mm thick unless cut is opened up.

(e) Poorly insulated unless plastic coated.

(f) They break easily.

TUBULAR STEEL ELECTRODES

These widely used burning electrodes are of tubular steel, usually 35 cm (14 in) long and 8 mm ($\frac{5}{16}$ in) OD, with a bore of approximately 3 mm ($\frac{1}{8}$ in).

Their characteristics are

(a) cutting technique is simple

(b) up to 5.1 cm (2 in) thickness of metal can be cut at one pass with practice

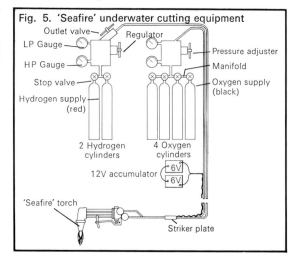

Fig. 5. 'Seafire' underwater cutting equipment

(c) cutting is performed very rapidly, depending on the metal thickness, oxygen pressure, water depth, current and operator skill; (average speed 0.7 m/min (27 in/min) on a 12.7 mm ($\frac{1}{2}$ in) plate

(d) neat trim cuts are produced

(e) power requirement is within 400 amps

(f) have a short burning life.

ULTRATHERMIC ELECTRODES

Ultrathermic electrodes differ from tubular steel electrodes in construction, being composed of seven mild steel small rods inside a steel tube. One of the seven rods is a special alloy which will burn independently once an arc is struck and oxygen is flowing through the tube. It is about 46 cm (18 in) long and comes in two diameters, 9.5 mm ($\frac{3}{8}$ in) and 6.3 mm ($\frac{1}{4}$ in).

Ultrathermic electrodes have the following characteristics.

(a) Cutting technique is simple.

(b) They allow electrical cut-off. The electrodes will go on burning if the oxygen flow is maintained so provision should be made for the rapid isolation of the oxygen supply.

(c) Cutting is performed as rapidly as tubular cutting electrodes.

(d) They may be used for cutting both ferrous and non-ferrous metals.

(e) Power requirement is only approximately 150 amps which allows a much smaller and lighter welding set to be carried. A 150 amp set can be carried by one man, whereas a typical 400 amp set could weigh as much as $\frac{1}{2}$ ton.

(f) The electrodes are costly.

(g) Their burning life underwater is about one min.

INDUSTRIAL THERMIC LANCES

The thermic lance is a steel tube, 3.2 m (10$\frac{1}{2}$ ft) long by 9.5 mm ($\frac{3}{8}$ in) diameter, packed with a number of mild steel rods. Owing to the very high temperatures produced, the lance will burn through almost anything—steel, non-ferrous metals, rock and concrete —but the risk of explosion makes the cutting of non-ferrous metals highly dangerous. One of its special applications underwater is to cut holes in reinforced concrete. It is difficult to handle because of its length and it has a high rate of oxygen consumption. One lance will burn for 6 minutes. Thermic lances are currently more evident offshore as, although the cut is not as good as with oxy-arc, less cutting skill is needed to operate them.

Fig. 6. Thermic lance holder (Saffire BOC)

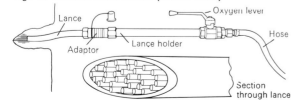

An improvement on the thermic lance is the Clucas Thermal-Arc System which operates on the same principle, but instead of a rigid bar, the consumable agent is a 30 m (100 ft), 12 mm or 6 mm diameter, flexible plastic covered cable of high tensile steel wire called Kerie Cable. Its advantages are its ease of handling and its average burning time of nearly one hour. Kerie Cable will burn at the rate of 27 m (88.6 ft) in one hour, or 0.5 m/min. The electrical circuit is used only for igniting the thermic cable and is not used during the actual burning. The reduced temperature of Kerie Cable (2700°C) prevents the cutting of non-ferrous metals. This reduction has been made for safety reasons. The cut using this equipment is broad compared with that of carbon or tubular steel electrodes.

SOME CHARACTERISTICS OF KERIE CABLE:

(a) 30 m (100 ft) of 12 mm will provide 45 minutes of continuous cutting.
(b) 30 m (100 ft) will consume approximately 3 oxygen cylinders at 0–18 m (0–60 ft) depths.
(c) Typical oxygen consumption would be as follows: three 6794 l (240 ft³) cylinders of oxygen will be consumed for every 30 m (100 ft) of depth, when set to a surface pressure of 27 bar (400 psi) plus ambient pressure; in this case, 27 bar (400 psi) + 4 bar (59 psi) = 31 bar (459 psi).

THE EQUIPMENT REQUIRED FOR THERMIC ARC CUTTING IS:

1. Oxygen supply
2. Three-cylinder oxygen manifold
3. Control unit
4. (a) 30 m (100 ft) length of 12 mm ($\frac{1}{2}$ in) Kerie Cable (b) or, 15 m (50 ft) length of 6 mm ($\frac{1}{4}$ in) Kerie Cable, (c) or, a number of
   $3\frac{1}{2}$ m (10 ft) thermic lances
5. 30 m (100 ft) extension lead
6. One or two 12 volt Batteries
7. Wire wool for surface ignition
8. Heavy duty wire cutters
9. Insulating sleeves

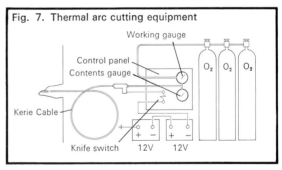

Fig. 7. Thermal arc cutting equipment

Safety
(1) Do not cut into a compartment without first ascertaining that there are no explosives or inflammable substances on the other side.
(2) Be careful to vent inflammable gases generated by the arc which may become trapped in an enclosed compartment during electric cutting. Oxy-Arc cutting will produce hydrogen. Hydrogen is also a hazard when gas cutting by oxy-hydrogen. Care should be taken when cutting in habitats or hyperbaric enclosures on or above the sea or river beds, especially in mud, as trapped methane gas may cause explosions.
(3) Ensure that all cable connections and metallic parts are properly insulated.

(4) Make certain that the electrical supply is earthed before starting operations, i.e. earth the frame of the welding set.

(5) Make certain that all electrical connections are securely made and insulated before starting operations.

(6) Make certain that you position the earth so that you cannot accidentally become part of the circuit by standing between the earth and the electrode.

(7) The electrical current must never be on except when you are actually cutting or have the torch poised to do so. The safety switch should be kept open at all times except when directed by the diver/cutter to close it.

(8) Never pass the torch from the water to the tender unless the power is off. Divers must never surface while the power is on.

(9) Never hold the cutting torch so that it points towards you.

(10) Always wear adequate rubber gloves.

(11) Be careful that pieces of metal cut from the work do not entangle your lines or fall on you. Cut carefully so as to prevent dropping slag or molten metal making bodily contact.

(12) Cutting non-ferrous metals is always dangerous with any heat cutting process. It may be preferable to use explosives or other cold cutting techniques.

(13) It is strongly recommended that divers should wear a full helmet apparatus when cutting underwater.

Some characteristic features of the cutting processes

Legend: ■ = recommended, (blank) = unsuitable

Feature	OXY-ARC Electrode Carbon	OXY-ARC Electrode Tubular	THERMIC Ultra-electrode	THERMIC Thermic lance	THERMIC Kerie Cable	SMA/MMA	OXY/HYDRO
Cuts all standard thicknesses	■	■	■	■	■	■	■
Cuts ferrous metals	■	■	■	■	■	■	■
Cuts non-ferrous metals			■	■	■	■	
Cuts oxidization/corrosion resistant materials			■	■	■	■	
Cuts laminated plating	■	■	■	■	■		■
Cuts non-metals				■	■		
Cuts rapidly			■	■	■		
Cuts neatly and precisely	■	■	■				■
Needs experience/skill						■	■
Ease of handling	■	■	■			■	■
Requires oxygen	■	■	■	■	■		■
Requires fuel gas							■
Requires electrodes	■	■	■			■	
Instant start	■	■	■	■	■	■	■
Burns after current switch off			■	■	■		
Electric shock hazard	■	■	■			■	
Protective clothing should be worn	■	■	■	■	■	■	■
Requires preheating							■
Explosion hazard	■	■	■	■	■	■	■

There are other factors to take into account when selecting which process to use, such as the operating conditions; available equipment and its weight and bulkiness; the training and experience of the operators.

3.3 UNDERWATER WELDING

The two basic arc welding processes are:

1. **Flux shielded arc welding.** Typically manual metal arc welding in which short, flux-coiled electrodes are used. The electrode is burnt and consumed in the process, providing the metal necessary to fill the weld. This method is the most widely used and is known as manual metal arc (MMA) or shielded metal arc (SMA).

2. **Gas shielded arc welding.** Typically tungsten inert gas welding (TIG) in which an arc is struck between a non-consumable tungsten electrode and the workpiece. Filler-material in the form of bare metal rod is added into the molten pool by the diver/welder. An alternative method is metal inert gas welding (MIG), in which an arc is struck between a consumable bare metal wire electrode fed from a reel into the weld pool. These gas shielded methods are being adopted increasingly underwater.

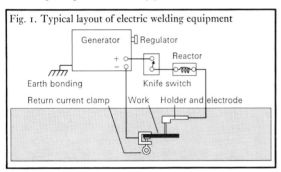

Fig. 1. Typical layout of electric welding equipment

There are three underwater welding methods.

1. **Dry hyperbaric welding** using either the semi-automatic or the manual metal arc welding processes. The weld area can be enclosed in three ways:

(a) FULL-SIZED HABITAT: an open-bottomed chamber enclosing the whole weld area, the welder and his equipment and filled with an appropriate gas mixture at ambient pressure. The diver/welder may be dressed in lightweight diving equipment or he may change headgear into a surface type breathing apparatus and coveralls.

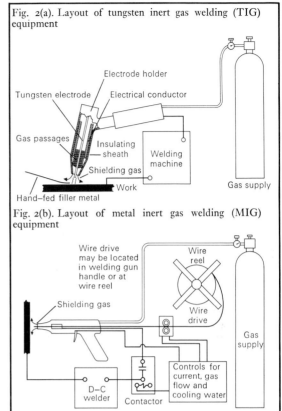

Fig. 2(a). Layout of tungsten inert gas welding (TIG) equipment

Fig. 2(b). Layout of metal inert gas welding (MIG) equipment

(b) MINI-HABITAT: a small chamber enclosing the weld area and the upper half of the diver/welder's body. The water in the chamber is displaced by an inert gas or by air, and the welding is performed by one of two processes referred to above.

(c) PORTABLE DRY BOX: this encloses the weld area only. Metal inert gas (MIG) or gas metal arc (GMA) is normally used. A gas is introduced to displace the water in the box, usually an argon mixture. The box is transparent; the diver works from outside in the water and reaches into the opening on the underside of the box. A vent in the top of the box would help to clear the welding fumes.

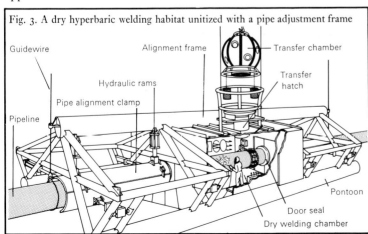

Fig. 3. A dry hyperbaric welding habitat unitized with a pipe adjustment frame

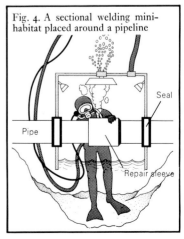

Fig. 4. A sectional welding mini-habitat placed around a pipeline

2. One-atmosphere welding.

The diver/welder is transported in a one-atmosphere transfer submersible to an underwater chamber in which the environment is maintained at one atmosphere. Water sealing is a problem with this method.

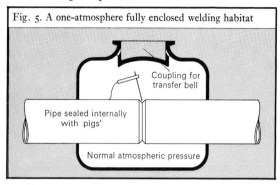

Fig. 5. A one-atmosphere fully enclosed welding habitat

Coupling for transfer bell

Pipe sealed internally with 'pigs'

Normal atmospheric pressure

In terms of process, dry hyperbaric welding and one-atmosphere welding are the same except that dry hyperbaric welding is conducted under pressure.

3. Manual metal arc or Shielded metal arc wet welding.

Basically the same equipment is used as for surface welding, but with insulated cable joints and torch and waterproof electrodes. Until recently, wet welding was estimated to be about 25% inferior to surface welding, but a newly developed technique is proving that it can be more reliable than thought originally. Manual metal arc welding is the most widely used wet process today and is carried out by creating an electric arc between a flux-covered metal electrode and the workpiece. The heat developed by the arc results in the melting of the parent metal parts, the core wire and the flux covering. The flux covering decomposes, under the action of the arc, into gas which shields the molten metals from the surrounding water.

There are two techniques used with this process, one is the 'touch' or 'drag' technique where a constant contact is maintained between the electrode covering and the work. The electrode is dragged across the work and pressure applied by the diver/welder so that the weld metal is deposited in a series of beads or strings. This technique is ideal for fillet welding and suitable for most underwater work.

The second is the 'manipulative' or 'weave' technique in which the welder holds a constant arc which he controls by manoeuvring the electrode, but does not apply pressure to it. Beads can be applied with a significant weave, but this technique calls for a very expert and experienced operator. The main metallurgical problem with all wet welding methods is the high rate of cooling of the molten weld pool.

Wet welding is used for temporary welds on anodes and not for structural quality welds. Welds on anodes are necessary for electrical continuity. Anodes are mainly welded by standard cad welding (thermic welding). Cad welding is currently receiving a great deal of attention and has been approved by Lloyd's. Explosive welding is considered under 'Anodes' or 'Cathodic protection' as it has no other area of application.

Factors in planning underwater welding operations

1. Sea state; state of tide; rate and direction of tidal stream; weather forecast.
2. Visibility underwater, especially where there might not be a groove to follow in the workpiece.
3. Setting up the equipment, which entails
   (a) ensuring that the welding generator is of the variable voltage type
   (b) determining amperage, which is dependent on the size of the rod. The larger the rod, the higher the amperage—usually 200–300 A
   (c) setting the correct voltage values on the welding set for the type of work and depth
   (i) overhead welding (in this case only, the polarity is reversed and the amperage dropped)
   (ii) vertical-up welding
   (iii) down-hand welding
   (d) adjust voltage for operating depth (10 V per 30 m)
   (e) connect diver's torch cable to **positive** terminal on generator supply on MIG and MMA; negative for TIG
   (f) check that all joints and the torch are properly insulated
   (g) check that the correct electrodes are being used, waterproofed and stored in some sort of container to keep them dry until required.

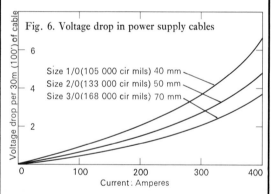

Fig. 6. Voltage drop in power supply cables

Size 1/0(105 000 cir mils) 40 mm
Size 2/0(133 000 cir mils) 50 mm
Size 3/0(168 000 cir mils) 70 mm

Voltage drop per 30m (100') of cable

Current: Amperes

4. Provision of a steady stage or platform from which to weld.
5. Proper cleaning of work surfaces to bright shiny metal free from any surface coating, corrosion or marine growth.
6. Securing of ground (earth) clamp to work. This is especially important when welding pipelines together, each of which may have different magnetic polarities, making it necessary to earth them in more than one place.

SAFETY
(1) The electrical power source must be insulated, high and low voltage d.c.
(2) Welding machine frame must be earthed before starting operations.
(3) All electrical connections must be clean and securely made before starting operations.
(4) Use only torches specifically made for underwater use.*
(5) Torches and joints in the cable should be properly insulated.*

(6) Only change or tighten the electrode when no current is in circuit.

(7) Never point the electrode holder towards yourself.

(8) Do not let any metallic part of your diving equipment touch the electrode.

(9) The current should be off at all times except when actually welding. The tender should not close the circuit unless specifically directed by the diver/welder. The earth should be positioned so as to prevent the diver/welder getting between the electrode and the workpiece, thus making him part of the secondary circuit.

(10) Always wear rubber gloves to insulate your hands, especially when wet welding. For dry hyperbaric welding, leather or asbestos gloves are preferred to protect the operator's hands from the heat of the welding arc.

(11) Always use the appropriate grade of welding filter to protect your eyes.

(12) Inspect metallic parts of your diving equipment for electrolysis.

(13) When working in an enclosed area make certain that no escaped gases are being trapped nearby underwater.*

(14) Do not weld unless you know that in the vicinity of the welding there is no hazardous material that might be affected by the heat generated.

* Especially when wet welding.

Welding habitats

(1) Structure repairs

(a) Precautions with regard to supply boat loadings, debris and dumping cement, etc., to be observed as for other diving operations.

(b) No submersible craft are to approach the work site without prior consultation with the Diving Supervisor.

(2) Pipeline tie-ins or repairs

1 (a) and (b) above plus the following.

(a) Valves and by-passes at both ends of pipeline and any interconnecting pipeline systems to be shut and locked.

(b) Where possible, risers to be drained to sea level and pig traps, etc., opened.

(c) Platform shore terminal personnel must be instructed forcibly not to undertake any actions which could result in a variation of pressure in the pipeline being worked upon.

(d) No pressure tests are to be performed on any interconnected pipelines during hyperbaric operations.

(e) No operations which can result in abnormal noise or vibration being transmitted down the pipeline can be permitted without full consultation with the Diving Supervisor (e.g. drilling operations, piling, etc.).

(f) The electrical neutrality of the pipeline is to be maintained at all times.

(g) No marine operations to be undertaken near a pipeline which could conceivably result in distortion of the alignment of the pipe(s) (e.g. anchor movements, positioning pipeline covers).

3.4 EXPLOSIVES

Theory

An explosion is a chemical reaction in which the original material is rapidly converted into a gas so that pressures of about 50 000 bars and temperatures of about 3000°C are created. This reaction is called detonation; it can travel at speeds from 1500 m/sec to 9000 m/sec. Slower reactions are propagated by thermal conduction and radiation and are known as deflagration.

Underwater, the reaction forms a sphere of gas which displaces the surrounding water at speeds greater than sound (about 1500 m/sec in water) and produces an intense pressure wave. As the gas expands, so the pressure drops.

The most important phenomenon associated with underwater explosions is the action of the sphere of gas between detonation and venting to the surface.

The bubble oscillates for up to 10 cycles, creating diminishing secondary pressure pulses, and is attracted towards rigid boundaries rather than to a free surface. The effect of this bubble pulse must be taken into account when planning underwater explosions.

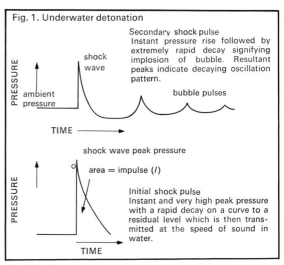

Fig. 1. Underwater detonation

Secondary shock pulse
Instant pressure rise followed by extremely rapid decay signifying implosion of bubble. Resultant peaks indicate decaying oscillation pattern.

Initial shock pulse
Instant and very high peak pressure with a rapid decay on a curve to a residual level which is then transmitted at the speed of sound in water.

Applications

Many underwater tasks can be most efficiently carried out by the use of explosives. Typical applications include:

Product	Description	Depth limitation	Duration of immersion	Velocity of detonation
Special gelatine (90%) Special gelatine (80%)	Nitroglycerine medium strength gelatinous explosive obtainable in various cartridge sizes or bulk packing	Down to 6 m	A few days	2500 m/s to 5000 m/s
Subgel Fortex	High density strength nitroglycerine-based explosives	Down to 46 m	Several weeks	5–6000 m/s
Plaster gelatine	Nitroglycerine high strength gelatinous putty	Down to 45 m	Several weeks	6300 m/s
Submarine blasting	Nitroglycerine high strength, high density, rubber-like explosive. Cannot be moulded	In excess of 300 m	Several weeks	7500 m/s
PETN Plastic explosive 1509	PETN and plasticiser high density medium sensitivity explosive. High brisance	No limit	Several months	8400 m/s
RDX Plastic explosive PE4, C4, T4	High brisance, stable explosive	No limit	Several months	8700 m/s
Nitromethan (sensitised)	Liquid propellant based explosive, requires sensitising with an amine. Suitable for shaped charge operations	No limit if sealed in container	Requires sealed container	6300 m/s
Hydrazine Astrolite	Liquid propellant based explosive sensitised with appropriate nitrate compound; difficult to handle unless purchased in twin bottle mixer packs (astro-Pak)	No limit if sealed in container	Requires sealed container	8700 m/s
Cast explosives Pentolite RDX/TNT	Pourable mixture of TNT and PETN 50/50. More stable than Pentolite	Unlimited Unlimited	Unlimited Unlimited	7400 m/s 7400 m/s
Slurry explosives Methylamine Nitrate (man)	Special slurries can be used in trenching charges	25 m	Unlimited	Up to 6200 m/s
Detonating cord	Waterproof coated cord with a PETN filling	Dependent on cord size	Ends have to be sealed	6500 m/s to 8200 m/s depending on cord size

Table title: Explosives recommended for underwater use

—Fragmentation of rock pinnacles, bed rock, hard coral and conglomerates prior to dredging.

—Cutting or clearing of trenches for cables and pipelines in rock, conglomerates and soft sediments.

—Breaking and scattering wrecks and obstructions.

—Dismantling of seabed structures prior to their recovery, e.g. wellheads, anchor chains, platforms etc.

—Repair and maintenance tasks such as pipeline weight coat removal, pipeline venting, removal of marine growth, cleaning of areas prior to inspection and explosive welding and swaging.

Types

Most commercial explosive is nitro-based and is available with high or low detonating velocities.

Low explosives, such as cordite and gunpowder, burn at rates up to 300 m/sec. High explosives detonate at 3000–9000 m/sec and develop large amounts of energy which produce a shattering effect known as 'brisance'.

High explosives, which are used almost exclusively underwater, are of two types:

—PRIMARIES, such as fulminates and lead azide, which can be easily detonated by heat, friction or shock. They are mostly used in detonators and require careful handling.

—SECONDARY explosives are more stable, have much greater strength and, being safe to handle and transport, are used as main charges. All need a detonator to initiate them.

The most stable types may also require boosting by a commercial PETN booster (about 14.5 gm ($\frac{1}{2}$ oz) is usually sufficient) or by taping a dozen short strands of sealed detonating cord around the detonator; a single strand of cord is not enough.

Techniques

DRILLING AND BLASTING

The most economic method of using explosives is to insert and tamp the charge into a predrilled hole. This is most suitable when the bench height (the thickness of rock to be removed) is more than 2 m (6′).

For small operations a hand-held rock drill is sufficient. A template should be used by the diver to ensure that the holes, which should be plugged as they are drilled, are correctly spaced. Drilling should never be undertaken closer than 2 m (6′) to a charged hole.

Drilling of multiple holes can also be carried out from the surface, using one or more drill heads. Here the diver's role is confined to assisting with the lining up of the drill(s) and to the laying and wiring of the charges.

Where an overburden is likely to cause problems, the drill is passed through an outer casing which penetrates the sediment and the surface of the base rock; the charge is then loaded directly from the surface and the risk of the hole filling is eliminated.

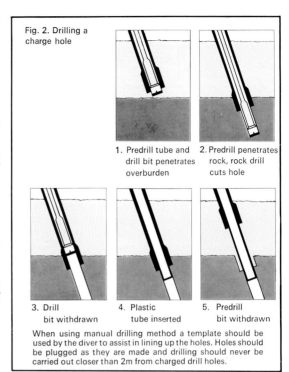

Fig. 2. Drilling a charge hole

1. Predrill tube and drill bit penetrates overburden

2. Predrill penetrates rock, rock drill cuts hole

3. Drill bit withdrawn

4. Plastic tube inserted

5. Predrill bit withdrawn

When using manual drilling method a template should be used by the diver to assist in lining up the holes. Holes should be plugged as they are made and drilling should never be carried out closer than 2m from charged drill holes.

CALCULATION OF CHARGES

Calculation of charges is usually the responsibility of an explosives expert rather than a diver. However, as a rough guide, about 1 kg per cubic metre of low velocity underwater explosive should ensure good fragmentation and allow for misfires; this can be reduced by 10% if the holes are drilled at an angle of 3:1.

In general, about two thirds of a hole is filled with explosive. Spacing between holes will depend on the charge concentration while the depth of drilling should equal the bench height plus the hole spacing.

BULK BLASTING/PLASTER SHOOTING

This involves the use of bulk explosives to break up submarine rock or to create trenches in silt and sand. It is best used in depths of 8 m (25′) or more because it relies on the head of water to tamp down the charge and because it can produce high levels of waterborne shock and vibration. A typical pattern would involve 22.5 kg (50 lb) charges spaced at 2 m (6′) intervals.

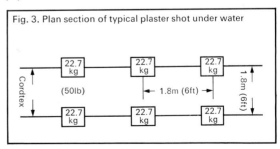

Fig. 3. Plan section of typical plaster shot under water

A trench through soft material can be blasted by using a single line of boreholes. Approximately $\frac{1}{2}$ kg (1 lb) of explosive per 75 cm (30″) centres should give a trench 1 m (3′) deep by 2 m (6′) wide at the mudline.

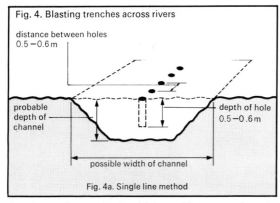

Fig. 4. Blasting trenches across rivers

distance between holes
0.5−0.6 m

probable depth of channel

depth of hole
0.5−0.6 m

possible width of channel

Fig. 4a. Single line method

An alternative method, which enables a trench to be blasted in one operation, is to attach charges to a weighted rope; initiation is effected by high strength detonating cord threaded through the top of the charges (Fig. 4b).

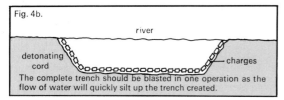

Fig. 4b.

river

detonating cord

charges

The complete trench should be blasted in one operation as the flow of water will quickly silt up the trench created.

SHAPED CHARGES

An alternative to drilling and blasting or plaster shooting to break up bed rock or to create an underwater trench is to use shaped trenching charges.

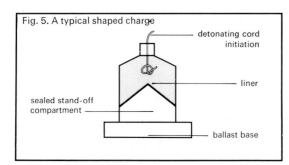

Fig. 5. A typical shaped charge

detonating cord initiation

liner

sealed stand-off compartment

ballast base

They are particularly effective if a cut of 2 m (6′) or less is required or if the water depth restricts drilling/blasting or plaster shooting. The charge is held in a container with a sealed conical inner liner which directs the explosive force downwards. It is, however, important that any overburden should be cleared away to ensure optimum effect.

Depending on the rock material, charges are usually spaced 1–2 m (3–6′) apart. For small operations, charges can be loaded by hand; large operations require a recoverable laying frame holding 30–90 charges. Diver assistance may be required.

Shaped charges are normally deployed under the supervision of an explosives engineer.

CUTTING CHARGES

Most of the specialised cutting charges now available are normally used under expert supervision.

A simple cutting charge can be made by sealing a

length of copper pipe at both ends and forming a saddle of high velocity explosive, such as PE4, along its length. About 170–225 gm (6–8 oz) per foot of 13 mm ($\frac{1}{2}$″) bore pipe will cut up to 1.6 cm ($\frac{5}{8}$″) mild steel.

LIQUID EXPLOSIVES

If the charge case has not been supplied by the manufacturer, it is important that his directions be followed exactly—some explosives are not compatible with steel—and that the charge is made up in strict compliance with the stated specifications.

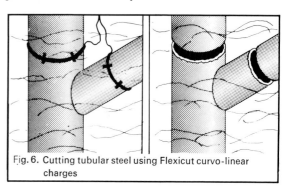

Fig. 6. Cutting tubular steel using Flexicut curvo-linear charges

WELLHEAD REMOVAL

For most applications approximately 34 kg (75 lb) of high density explosive is sufficient. For a $9\frac{5}{8}$″ casing a container about 18 cm ($7\frac{3}{4}$″) in diameter by 117 cm (46″) long will be required: for $13\frac{5}{8}$″, the dimensions should be about 29×56 cm ($11\frac{1}{2} \times 22$″). The container, which need not be waterproof, should be designed so that the explosive can be initiated simultaneously from both ends with EBW detonators and boosters.

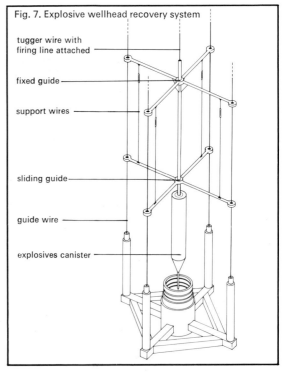

Fig. 7. Explosive wellhead recovery system

tugger wire with firing line attached

fixed guide

support wires

sliding guide

guide wire

explosives canister

The charge is lowered in its container into the well casing from the surface, supported by a T-piece and slung between guide wires.

The depth at which the charge is placed will depend on the lifting gear available on the recovery vessel—casing cut 6 m (20') below the surface will typically demand a pull of 90 tons to remove it.

Initiation

There are two types of detonator:

—PLAIN. Designed to be fired by spark from a safety fuse. When supplied with the fuse already fitted these are known as capped fuses and usually have a bean pole connector for use with plastic igniter cord. Alternatively they may be supplied with a separate fuse for use for single shot firing or for charges linked with detonating cord.

—ELECTRIC. Particularly suitable for use underwater, these are more safe in that they allow greater control over initiation. Instantaneous and time delay types are available.

Conventional detonators contain a primary explosive which is sensitive to both shock and friction and they can therefore create hazards when handled underwater or in atmospheric diving systems. For most subsurface use, exploding bridgewire detonators are recommended; in these the primary explosive has been replaced by a short length of gold wire which requires a special exploder with an output of 3000 volts at 1000 amps.

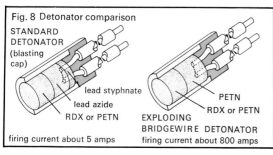

Fig. 8 Detonator comparison
STANDARD DETONATOR (blasting cap)
lead styphnate
lead azide
RDX or PETN
firing current about 5 amps

PETN
RDX or PETN
EXPLODING BRIDGEWIRE DETONATOR
firing current about 800 amps

The point from which the charge is initiated has an important effect on efficiency. The explosive should always be placed between the detonator and the area where the effect is required. A cone- or prism-shaped charge initiated from the apex is more efficient than a cylindrical charge.

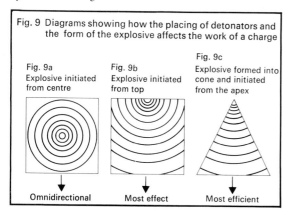

Fig. 9 Diagrams showing how the placing of detonators and the form of the explosive affects the work of a charge

Fig. 9a
Explosive initiated from centre
Omnidirectional

Fig. 9b
Explosive initiated from top
Most effect

Fig. 9c
Explosive formed into cone and initiated from the apex
Most efficient

Simple precautions must be taken for successful initiation with detonating cord. The cord should be securely taped to a small rope for its full length to prevent kinks and sharp angles which will cause misfires. Where the cord is to be taken round an angle, it is advisable to pass it through a length of spare hose or tape several strands of sealed detonating cord around the angle to the main firing line. The firing cable should be secured to the detonating cord before the detonator is attached and both should be tied off to ensure that no strain can be placed on the cable or the charge pulled out of position—a detonator can be accidentally fired if the leads are jerked from it. Similarly, spare lead wires should be firmly taped over.

FIRING CIRCUITS

Many operations involve the simultaneous firing of several charges; for most applications a simple series circuit (Fig. 10 a) is sufficient. The parallel circuit (Fig. 10 b) reduces the possibility of misfires but it is not normally employed with an exploder where more than three detonators are used because of the large currents required—in this event mains firing is advisable.

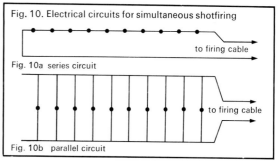

Fig. 10. Electrical circuits for simultaneous shotfiring
to firing cable
Fig. 10a series circuit
to firing cable
Fig. 10b parallel circuit

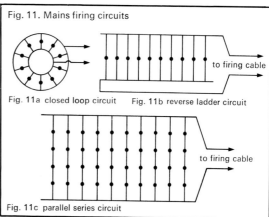

Fig. 11. Mains firing circuits
to firing cable
Fig. 11a closed loop circuit   Fig. 11b reverse ladder circuit
to firing cable
Fig. 11c parallel series circuit

For very large rounds the parallel/series (Fig. 14c) circuit is normally used with mains firing. For proper distribution, this should be in the form of a closed loop (Fig. 11 a) or a reverse ladder (Fig. 11 b).

Safety precautions

EXTRANEOUS ELECTRICITY

Many detonators can be accidentally initiated by stray electrical charges caused by:

—LIGHTNING. At the first sign of lightning, all detonators should be removed and placed in secure storage and the area cleared of personnel.

—STATIC ELECTRICITY. This can be generated by snow, dust storms and other atmospheric conditions as well as by the moving parts of machinery. For safety, shot-firing cable should be laid carefully and all detonator leads shorted and earthed. Leads should not be unearthed and connected up until everything is ready for firing. Earth yourself before handling detonators.

—STRAY ELECTRIC CURRENTS. All machinery and metal structures should be properly earthed.

—GALVANIC ACTION. Electric currents can be created by the joining of two dissimilar metals. To avoid this hazard, always use a non-metallic tool for loading shot holes, and do not mix metals in charge cases.

—ELECTRO-MAGNETIC RADIATION. Any transmitting device can set off a detonator. For safety the following minimum distances should be observed.

Walkie-talkie and car transmitters	10 m
Transmitters up to 1 kW	300 m
Transmitters 1–10 kW	1 km
Transmitters 10–100 kW	7.4 km
Transmitters 100–1000 kW	10 km

Detonator wires should not be unwound until they are ready for use. Twin firing cables should always be used and the ends of the leads kept together and not splayed so that they form a dipole. The firing cable should be laid directly away from any source of radiation, such as a transmitter. The cable should never be suspended.

DETONATING CORD
Remember that detonating cord is an explosive—it can be fired by a sharp blow.

MISFIRES—ELECTRICAL
Retest the circuit with an ohmmeter—if it appears complete, attempt to fire again using a different initiation source. If this is unsuccessful, wait for 30 min, recover the charge and inspect all joints— internal breaks will sometimes show only when the firing cable is under tension. Replace all charges with new ones—do not attempt to remove a detonator from a charge.

MISFIRES— DETONATING CORD
Wait for 30 min and then check that all joints were sealed and dry and that all junctions were facing the initiation point. Wet detonating cord will not fire.

Explosives—general safety
Remember:

EXPLOSIVES ARE SAFE UNTIL YOU FOR-GET THAT THEY ARE DANGEROUS.

Don't trust your memory—always refer to the safety guides or to the manufacturer's instructions, where appropriate.

The following rules should always be observed.

(1) Basic explosive, without firing caps, is a fire hazard—so no smoking or naked lights and ensure that sparks cannot be created in the work area.

(2) Never use steel for tamping explosive—use wood or non-ferrous metal.

(3) Never stow explosive in rusty steel cans—nitroglycerine can be absorbed by the rust which then becomes hypersensitive to shock or friction.

(4) Protect all explosives from sub-zero temperatures —most become extra sensitive, and therefore dangerous, when frozen.

(5) Don't leave detonating cord lying around.

(6) Never leave explosives unattended.

(7) Keep the work area free of unnecessary personnel.

(8) Do not allow untrained personnel to handle explosives.

DETONATORS AND FIRING CAPS
These provide the greatest hazard—always handle them with extra care.

(1) Never stow detonators with bulk explosive.

(2) Always keep detonators in their cases until they are required for use.

(3) Never work near power cables or electric meters—they can cause electrostatic hazards.

(4) Ensure all radio and radar transmitters are switched off before you handle detonators or primed charges.

(5) Never work in an electric, thunder or sand storm.

(6) Only one man should handle detonators.

(7) Ensure that the ends of detonators and firing leads are shorted together.

(8) Always use proper dynamo exploders for initiating charges.

(9) Check all firing cables and detonators with a safety ohmmeter before you connect up.

(10) Place all detonators in a safe place before testing.

(11) Consult the safety guide to radiation frequency hazards before you handle detonators.

(12) Secure all firing cables before placing detonators —if the leads are jerked from a detonator, it could fire.

(13) When operating from small boats, a buoy should mark the position of the charge. Another buoy should be laid up or down tide of the charge area to enable the boat to be moored and the engine stopped to avoid electrical interference.

3.5 EXPLOSIVE TOOLS   SUBMARINE BOLT DRIVING GUN

One form of the velocity power tool is an explosively actuated gun which instantaneously drives a solid or hollow bolt into steel plate above or below water. The projectile is driven by the explosive energy of a cartridge, which can be varied according to the amount of penetration desired and the thickness of the plate. Main uses are the rapid attachment of steel plate patches, splinter boxes, etc., the construction of cofferdams and the attachment of eye plates and other fixtures for lifting and salvage purposes.

COX NO. 2 SUBMARINE BOLT DRIVING AND PUNCHING GUN

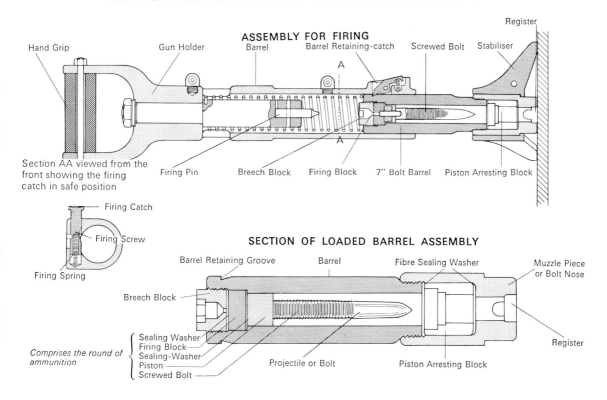

ASSEMBLY FOR FIRING

Hand Grip · Gun Holder · Barrel · Barrel Retaining-catch · Screwed Bolt · Stabiliser · Register

Section AA viewed from the front showing the firing catch in safe position

Firing Pin · Breech Block · Firing Block · 7" Bolt Barrel · Piston Arresting Block

Firing Catch · Firing Screw · Firing Spring

SECTION OF LOADED BARREL ASSEMBLY

Barrel Retaining Groove · Barrel · Fibre Sealing Washer · Muzzle Piece or Bolt Nose

Breech Block

Comprises the round of ammunition { Sealing Washer · Firing Block · Sealing-Washer · Piston · Screwed Bolt }

Projectile or Bolt · Piston Arresting Block · Register

GUN

This is an explosively actuated gun, which instantaneously and without previous preparation of the plate, drives at high velocity, special steel alloy threaded bolts into steel plate up to 1 inch thick. It is equally effective above and below water, and performs its work without recoil shock to the operator. The gun is easily handled and will operate at any depth.

BOLTS

The bolt is of special 100-ton tensile steel with a shearing strength of 10 tons per bolt. Also available are hollow bolts incorporating a seal removable from the operating side of the structure which can be driven into steel plate 1" thick.

TASKS

Rapid attachment of steel plate patches, wooden patches, securing bolts, lifting bolts, and cofferdam work. Hollow bolts can be used to supply air for breathing; compressed air for lifting; introducing wires for electrical circuits; supplying external foam or CO_2 gas line for extinguishing fires, etc.

COX GUN SET COMPRISES:

Cox Submarine Gun
  Bolting Barrel
  Punching Barrel
  Reloading Box
  Elastic Slinging Cord

Steel Plate Bolting Equipment

Bolt Ammunition

Steel Plate Punching Equipment

Punch Ammunition
  Wooden patch and timber construction equipment
  12" extension bolts, wing nuts, washer plates
  18" extension bolts, wing nuts, washer plates
  24" extension bolts, wing nuts, washer plates
  15" timbering barrels
  Wooden ferrules

Air Bolt Equipment
  Air Bolt Barrels (12")
  Air Bolt Adaptors
  Air Bolt Ammunition

3.5b TORNADO T6U AMPHIBIOUS CARTRIDGE HAMMER

The Tornado T6U is an explosively actuated hammer designed to fire threaded studs or rivets into naval quality steel plate up to 25 mm (1″) thick. It consists of two parts, a hand set and a barrel assembly which can be changed to allow it to be used above water. A blank safety cartridge is loaded into the breech together with the appropriate fastener. After taking up the safety pressures the tool is fired.

The hammer may be used to fix steel plates onto steel or concrete surfaces underwater, to fix eyebolts to lift large submerged objects, to fix demolition charges to piers, etc.

TORNADO TYPE T6U UNDERWATER HAMMER

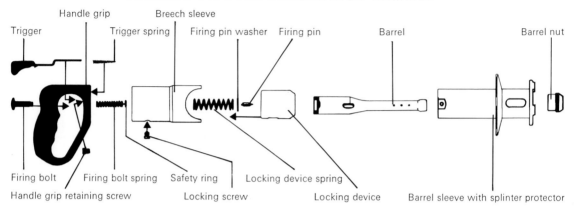

OPERATION

1. Select a cartridge and stud, together with the appropriate barrel, suitable for the thickness of steel. There are two sizes of bore for underwater use, $\frac{5}{16}$″ and $\frac{3}{8}$″. The $\frac{1}{4}$″ bore is for above-water use only. The table below may be used as a guide for selecting the correct stud and cartridge.

2. If possible, test penetration by firing a test shot into the same thickness of steel out of the water using the T6 front section for above water use with its yellow splinter shield. With correct penetration the full shaft is embedded, leaving the threaded portion proud. Adjustments can be made by positioning fasteners in the breech to allow more or less space between the stud and the cartridge (less or more penetration respectively).

3. Insert stud into barrel.

4. Insert cartridge into breech.

5. Close and lock breech by turning handgrip to the right.

6. Lower gun to the diver in the water.

7. Before firing, check what is on the other side of the steel plate and confirm that it does not present any problem.

8. Place muzzle at right angles to surface.

9. Push hammer firmly against surface to take up full safety pressure. Where a firm standing is not available, the diver may need extra weights in order to exert this pressure. Always keep the hands behind the protective shield.

10. Squeeze trigger whilst maintaining firm contact with the surface.

11. A final adjustment to the penetration may be necessary because of the effect of depth.

It is preferable to reload on the surface, especially where the water is murky. This is because debris may enter the breech and cause the hammer to misfire. Two or three guns may be used in rotation to ensure fast continuous fixing.

After use, wash parts separately in Bo5 oil using washing tanks provided. Allow to dry for 15 min. Do not wipe. Bo5 oil is reusable after settlement.

If the gun fails to fire, check that it is at right angles to the surface and that the full safety pressure has been taken up. If it still misfires return the hammer to the surface to be reloaded. If the hammer is to be reloaded underwater:

—Wait 1 min before opening breech.
—Check that cartridge has been struck correctly.
—If struck, let cartridge slip out of breech. If it does not, eject it by pushing ram-rod down muzzle, pointing muzzle away from the body.
—If not struck, check firing pin and change it if broken.
—Never attempt to remove a damaged cartridge any other way.

If the hammer repeatedly misfires, strip the tool completely. Check all components for damage and replace as necessary. Thoroughly clean and wash in Bo5 oil.

Note:
—Only $\frac{5}{16}$″ and $\frac{3}{8}$″ studs must be used underwater.
—Do not fix through thin, non-resistant material.
—Do not fix nearer to the edge than 5 cm (2″) in concrete and 2 cm ($\frac{3}{4}$″) in steel.
—Do not exert pressure on the muzzle of a loaded hammer except when fixing.
—Do not drop a loaded hammer.
—Always fix at right angles to the work surface.
—Always assume the hammer is loaded until proved otherwise. Never point it at anyone or any part of the body.

3.6 BUOYANCY

There are several methods of providing buoyancy to raise sunken objects, ranging from the historical method of displacing water with air, either by filling the object itself or by providing air held in some sort of container, to the filling of a vessel with modern plastic foam.

The successful application of buoyancy methods to raising sunken objects depends on a full understanding of all the factors involved, some of which are given below.

(1) The location of the sunken object and its attitude on the sea bed.

(2) Identification of the object. In the case of a shipwreck, the availability of ship's plans can be of enormous help in calculating the centre of gravity, details of fixings, capacity of compartments and displacement weight.

(3) The depth of the water. This will govern the bottom time of divers securing the lifting gear, as well as the amount of gas needed to provide the buoyancy.

(4) The nature of the sea bed, in particular its load bearing capacity which might cause sinkage resulting in the need to provide a break-out force, and which will depend on the contact area of the object, before the lifting can be attempted.

(5) The amount of burying or overburden of the object, including sand or mud that may be inside; it may be necessary to remove this material by air lifts or water jets before attempting lifting.

(6) The structural strength and integrity of the object and whether its condition is compatible with the chosen method of lift; also the object's stability submerged or afloat, its seaworthiness and watertightness.

(7) The structural integrity of the attachment points to which lifting strops may have to be attached.

(8) The material of which the object is constructed, which may be more than just one material.

(9) The necessity to effect underwater repairs before raising.

(10) The probability, in the case of vessels, of fuel in tanks, cargo in holds, and the desirability of removing these before lifting.

(11) The best method for the lifting, bearing in mind all the foregoing plus the logistics of the operation.

(12) The necessity for a complete plan of action, involving precise briefings and the establishment of a good underwater communications system.

(13) The vital importance of keeping the centre of buoyancy above the centre of gravity. The centre of gravity is that point at which the object will balance and where the entire weight is concentrated. An object suspended in air will always move so that its centre of gravity is below the point of support. A suspended object under water, however, will also be influenced by its centre of buoyancy which will affect its trim and stability.

(14) The safety of the divers and surface crew. Raising objects can be a very hazardous operation.

(15) The arrangements for disposal once the object is near the surface.

(16) The Law relating to wreck and salvage (in the UK: *Part 9, The Merchant Shipping Act, 1894*).

(17) The preservation of raised objects to avoid deterioration in air.

(18) Tidal information: times and heights of high and low water; range of the tide; rate and direction of tidal streams.

(19) Finally, the present and the forecast weather and sea state.

The following examples show how typical problems of lifting submerged objects might be tackled. Every operation has its own particular difficulties. Large scale lifting is best left to specialists as the calculation of buoyancy and weight distributions are complex.

Submerged weight

Archimedes' principle states that any object wholly or partially immersed in a liquid experiences an upthrust equal to the weight of the liquid displaced.

Salt water weighs 1.026 tonne/m³ (64.04 lb/ft³)

Fresh water weighs 1.0 tonne/m³ (62.37 lb/ft³)

Air weighs so little compared to any equal volume of water that it lifts virtually the same as it displaces, i.e. 1.026 tonne/m³ (64 lb/ft³)

The weight of an object in water is less than its weight in air and the difference depends on its volume, which is directly proportional to the upthrust or buoyancy force. Lead is so dense that its weight is not significantly affected under water, whereas aluminium will lose about 38% of its weight under water. The diver will lose almost 100% of his weight under water because the body's density is nearly the same as that of water. The weight of an object is its density multiplied by its volume. The density of a material is its weight per unit volume expressed in Kg/cm³ or lb/ft³.

(See Table on page 84)

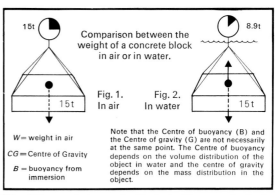

15t   8.9t

Comparison between the weight of a concrete block in air or in water.

Fig. 1.   Fig. 2.
In air   In water
15t   15t

W = weight in air

CG = Centre of Gravity

B = buoyancy from immersion

Note that the Centre of buoyancy (B) and the Centre of gravity (G) are not necessarily at the same point. The Centre of buoyancy depends on the volume distribution of the object in water and the centre of gravity depends on the mass distribution in the object.

The difference between the blocks in Figs. 1 and 2 is the weight of the water *displaced* by the object.

The difference (buoyancy force)= volume of object ×
density of sea water. The volume of an object is its length
× breadth × height (if the object is a solid cuboid, i.e.
shaped like a tank or box as the Figure shows).

If the buoyancy force is subtracted from the air weight of
the object, the result will be the submerged weight of the
object.

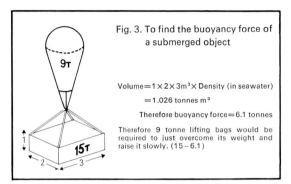

Fig. 3. To find the buoyancy force of
a submerged object

9т

Volume=1 × 2 × 3m³ × Density (in seawater)

=1.026 tonnes m³

Therefore buoyancy force=6.1 tonnes

Therefore 9 tonne lifting bags would be
required to just overcome its weight and
raise it slowly. (15−6.1)

15т

Weight calculations

To calculate the weight of a submerged object:
(a) First find the weight of the object in air by multiplying
the object's density by the volume of the material. If the
object is solid this can be obtained from its external
dimensions. If, however, the object contains an enclosed
volume, then the volume of the material is obtained from
its internal and external dimensions. (It is assumed here
that the enclosed volume is free-flooding.)

$$W_{air} = p_0 V_0$$

where: W_{air} = weight of the object in air expressed in kg
or lbs

p_0 = density of the object (in kg/m³ or lbs/ft³)

V_0 = volume of material in the object (in m³ or
ft³) (calculated dimensions)

(b) To calculate the weight of a submerged object, the
weight of the volume of water displaced by the object must
be subtracted from its air weight:

$$W_{sub} = W_{air} - W_w$$

where: W_{sub} = submerged weight of object

W_{air} = weight of object in air

W_w = weight of water displaced by object

Weight may be expressed as density × volume, so that in
sea water it becomes:

$$W_{sub} = p_0 V_0 - p_w V_0$$

$$W_{sub} = V_0(p_0 - p_w)$$

where: W_{sub} = submerged weight of object (in kg or lbs)

V_0 = volume of material in the object (in m³ or
ft³)

p_0 = density of object (in kg/m³ or lbs/ft³)

p_w = density of water (in kg/m³ or lbs/ft³)

(To find weights and densities consult the Tables on p 84)

Example one

What is the weight of a block of concrete measuring
46 × 30 × 23 cm (18 in × 12 in × 9 in)? How much will it
weigh under water?

(a) IN AIR

In metric units | *In imperial units*

$W = pV$	$W = pV$
$p = 2403$ kg/m³	$p = 150$ lb/ft³
(from density table)	(from density table)
$V = 46 × 30 × 23$ cm³	$V = 18 × 12 × 9$ in³

Convert to m³: | Convert to ft³:

$$= \frac{46 × 30 × 23}{10^6}$$ | $$= \frac{18 × 12 × 9}{1728}$$

$$= 0.03174 \text{ m}^3$$ | $$= 1.125 \text{ ft}^3$$

$W =$ | $W =$

(2403 kg/m³) × (0.03174 m³) | (150 lb/ft³) × (1.125 ft³)

$= 76.27$ kg | $= 168.75$ lbs

(b) UNDERWATER (SALT WATER)

$W_{sub} = V(p_0 - p_w)$	$W_{sub} = V(p_0 - p_w)$
$V = 0.03174$ m³	$V = 1.125$ ft³
$p_0 = 2403$ kg/m³	$p_0 = 150$ lbs/ft³
(from table)	(from table)
$p_w = 1026$ kg/m³	$p_w = 64.04$ lbs/ft³
(from table)	(from table)

W_{sub} | W_{sub}

$= 0.03174 × (2403 - 1026)$ | $= 1.125 × (150 - 64)$

Weight= 43.7 kg | Weight= 96.7 lbs

Lifting methods

A sunken object may be lifted off the sea bed in various
ways, depending largely on its size and weight, its structural integrity and its flotation capability.

Common methods are:

(1) By lifting with a floating crane, such as sheerlegs, or
from salvage pontoons equipped with multiple winches.
This method would require strops to be passed either
underneath the sunken object or attached to suitable points
on it.

(2) By attaching air-lift bags, which would then be inflated
under water, to anchorage points on the object. Variations
of this might be to place airbags within the structure or to
secure submersible salvage pontoons alongside the sunken
object which would then be pumped full of air from the
surface.

(3) By closing the main compartments to make them airtight and then pumping into them a gas or a liquid that is
lighter than water.

(4) As an alternative to (3), when it might be impossible to
secure an airtight integrity of the main compartments,
pumping in a very light flotation material might be effective. Such a material might be expanded polystyrene.
Syntactic foams come in many forms and sizes; one of
these, Eccofloat, consists of hollow epoxy fibreglass spheres.

Lifting calculations

As air weighs virtually nothing compared with an equal
volume of water, its lifting capacity equals the weight of
the water it displaces (1026 kg/m³ or 64 lb/ft³). However,
it is necessary to subtract the air weight of the lifting
container (which contains the air) from the lifting capacity
of the air.

i.e. $LC = (p_w V_c) - W_c$

where: LC = lifting capacity in kg or lbs

p_w = density of water in kg/m³ or lbs/ft³

V_c = volume of container in m³ or ft³

W_c = weight of container in kg or lbs

Thus:

IN METRIC UNITS   IN IMPERIAL UNITS

Sea water LC Sea water LC
$= (1026\,\text{kg/m}^3 \times V_c) - W_c$ $= (64\,\text{lb/ft}^3 \times V_c) - W_c$

Example two
If a 55 US gallon (0.208 m³) drum weighs 9.07 kg (20 lbs), what is its lifting capacity in sea water?

$V_c = 0.208$ m³ (55 gal)

$W_c = 9.07$ kg

$LC = (p_w V_c) - W_c$

$= (1026\,\text{kg/m}^3 \times 0.208\,\text{m}^3) - 9.07$ kg

$= 213.41 - 9.07$ kg

$= 204$ kg approx.

Example three
A pipe-handling frame is to be salvaged. The plan is to lighten it with air and then lift it off the bottom by crane and winches. It is a rocky bottom, so there will be no problem with break-out force. The task is to lighten the frame until it is almost neutral. The frame weighs 20 long tons (UK tons) (20 320 kg) out of the water and is all steel. If it is to be lightened to 2 tons (2032 kg), how many 1000 gallon (3.875 m³) steel fuel drums, each weighing 1 ton (1016 kg), will be required? The fuel drums will only lighten the frame, not lift it.

$$LC = (p_w V_c) - W_c$$

Density of steel (P_o) from Table 1 is 7770kg/m³ (485lb/ft³)

In metric units   *In imperial units*

Volume of steel in frame (V_o) is

$\dfrac{20\,320\,\text{kg}}{7700\,\text{kg/m}^3} = 2.62$ m³ $\bigg|$ $\dfrac{44\,800\,\text{lbs}}{485\,\text{lb/ft}^3} = 92.37$ ft³

Weight of frame in water (from p.82)

$= W_{air} - W_w$ $\bigg|$ $= W_{air} - p_w V_o$

$= 20\,320 - (2.62 \times 1026)$ $\bigg|$ $44\,800 - (92.37 \times 64)$

$= 17\,630$ kg $\bigg|$ $= 38\,888$ lbs

To reduce the frame weight to 2 tons (2032 kg) the fuel drums need to lighten the frame by:

$17\,630 - 2032 = 15\,598$ kg $\bigg|$ $38\,888 - 4480 = 34\,408$ lbs

Applying this to the formula:

$LC = (p_w V_c) - W_c$ if N = number of drums

$15\,598 =$ $\bigg|$ $34\,408 =$ (1 m = 3.28 ft)
$(1026 \times 3.875 \times N) - 1016\,N$ $\bigg|$ $[64 \times 3.875 \times (3.28)^3 \times N] -$
  $\bigg|$ $2240\,N$ (m³)

$15\,598 =$ $\bigg|$ $34\,408 =$

$N[(1026 \times 3.875) - 1016]$ $\bigg|$ $N(64 \times 136.74 - 2240)$

$15\,598 = N(2960)$ $\bigg|$ $34\,408 = N(6511)$

$N = 5.27$ $\bigg|$ $N = 5.28$

Therefore use 6 lifting drums.

Example four
A 51 tonne steel MFV heavily laden with fish capsized after being pooped by a following sea. The MFV was located upright and seemingly undamaged, lying on sand and mud in 65 m of water. The problem was to calculate the amount of lift necessary to raise her to the surface for eventual towing to harbour.

CALCULATIONS:

1. Weight of MFV   51 tonnes
   (in displacement tons) Convert 51 tonnes to kg:
   assuming totally flooded $51 \times 1000 = 51\,000$ kg

2. Density of steel   7770 kg/m³ (from Tables)

3. Displacement $51\,000 \div 7770 = 6.564$ m³
                          of sea water. This is
                          equivalent to 6.564×1026
                          $= 6735$ kg of sea water

4. Lift required $51\,000 - 6731 = 44\,265$ kg
                          $= 44.265$ tonnes(45 tonnes)

5. It was decided to use 5 tonne lifting bags:
   Therefore number of lifting bags required
   $= 45$ tonnes $\div 5$ tonnes $= 9$ lifting bags

6. For several reasons, detailed below, a 150% lift was used (68 tonnes instead of 45)

Thus:

$$68 \div 5 = 13.6$$

Therefore 14 lifting bags were used.

In the example above no allowances were made for residual fuel or cargo, as both were found to have dispersed in the 8 months that the ship had been submerged.

The decision to use 5 tonne lifting bags was influenced by

(1) the ship was comparatively new so that the attachment points might well be secure and the hull structurally sound
(2) an all-up high buoyancy lift was needed
(3) the depth of 65 m restricted the divers' bottom working times.

Although a lift of 45 tonnes was estimated, in the end a lift of 68 tonnes was employed. One reason for this was that open-bottomed lift bags were used and these have a tendency to dump air and lose buoyancy at the surface. The second reason was to provide a break-out force. At least 150% of the estimated buoyant lift should be applied to a sunken object if open-bottomed lift bags are used. It is preferable to jet around the base of the object to assist break-out. Great care must be exercised to avoid over-buoyancy.

The lift bags were secured symmetrically around the hull and filled systematically bow and stern to only about one quarter full so as to allow them to expand on the surface. It may be necessary to carry out the lift in several stages, by towing the partly submerged object into shallow and sheltered water before readjusting the lift bags to achieve a higher lift.

SAFETY

(1) Formulate a definite plan of operation so that personnel can work as a co-ordinated team.

(2) Be sure that all rigging is in good condition, within test dates and free of kinks.

(3) Know the safe working load (SWL) of the tackle being used. Check documentation.

(4) Be prepared for structures to collapse, especially if the object has been submerged for a long time.

(5) Be sure that all divers are clear from beneath the object while it is being raised, and watch out that they do not get entangled in lifting lines.

(6) All personnel must stay clear of rigging under strain.

(7) Be ready to control the object immediately upon surfacing. Buoyancy may easily change at this moment and become unstable.

(8) Keep an eye on the weather forecast.

Table 1. Table of density values

Material	Density kg/m³	lb/ft³	Material	Density kg/m³	lb/ft³
Gold	19304	1205	Aluminium	2707	169
Mercury	13537	845	Concrete	2403	150
Lead	11342	708	Magnesium	1730	108
Silver	10493	655	Sea water	1026	64.04
Copper	8955	559	Fresh water	999	62.36
Brass	8234	514	Oak wood (dry)	705	44
Steel	7770	485	Pine wood (dry)	433	27
Zinc	7129	445	Balsa wood (dry)	128	8
Granite	2723	170	Styrofoam	16	1

Table 2. Weights of various materials

Material	Weight per m³ in kg	ft³ in lb	Material	Weight per m³ in kg	ft³ in lb
Aluminium	2691	168	Lead	11342	708
Asbestos	2003–2804	125–175	Limestone	2675–2739	167–171
Asphalt	1105–1506	69–94	Magnesium	1746	109
Basalt (piled)	1538	96	Manganese ore (loosely piled)	2643–3204	165–200
Brass	8394	524	Mercury (15.6°C/60°F)	13 569	847
Brick, common	1794	112	Monel, metal	8971	560
Bronze, metal	8715	544	Mortar rubble, granite, limestone, marble	2403–2483	150–155
Cadmium	8635	539	Nickel	8731	545
Cement, Portland	1506	94	Nitrates (loosely piled)	1602	100
Cement, Portland (set)	2483	155	Oils, mineral	929	58
Chalk	2195	137	Paper	929	58
Chromium	6857	428	Petroleum, crude	881	55
Clay (wet)	2643–3124	165–195	Riprap, sandstone	1442	90
Coal, anthracite	1554	97	River mud	1442	90
Coal, bituminous	1346	84	Rubber	929	58
Cobalt	8843	552	Sand	1442–1602	90–100
Coke	1202	75	Slate, shale	2595–3284	162–205
Concrete masonry	2323	145	Steel	7769	485
Copper ore	4197	262	Tar, bituminous	1202	75
Cork	256	16	Tin	7337	458
Corn, bulk	593	37	Tungsten	18 904	1180
Glass	2884–3140	180–196	Water (freezing point)	999.92	62.417
Gravel	1602–1922	100–120	Water (standard, 16.7°C/62°F)	998.911	62.354
Iron, cast	7209	450	Water, sea (16.7°C/62°F)	1024.255	63.936
Iron ore, hematite (loose)	2403	150	Zinc	7049	440
Kerosene	817	51			

MASS	Metric tonne	Long ton	Short ton	Pound	Kg
Metric Tonne*	—	0.984	1.102	2205	1000.0
Long ton	1.016	—	1.120	2240	1016.05
Short ton	0.907	0.893	—	2000	— 5
Pound	0.000453	0.000446	0.0005	—	2.20462

* In converting crude oil to kilolitres or cubic metres, 1 metric tonne is approximately equal to 1.16 kilolitres or 1.16 cubic metres.

AIR LIFT BAGS

There is a considerable range of air lift bags now available. It is essential to choose the correct type and size for each individual application if their use is to be successful. The choice of the wrong bag would probably mean a failed job and perhaps even considerable risk to personnel. The main factors affecting the choice of bag may be grouped as under:

1. Buoyancy required   2. Vertical lift or static buoyancy

3. Depth of operation   4. Degree of required control

The following 2 pages show the J W Automarine range.

AIRCRAFT RECOVERY BAG ARB1

Pressure relief valves set to expel air at 0.14 kg/cm² capable of releasing in excess of 2000 litres per minute. Air Cylinder supplied separately to required capacity with pressure reducing valve and hose. Totally enclosed 1 ton lift capacity designed to give buoyancy to ditched aircraft.

Lift capacity (kg)	1000
Overall length (m)	1.5
Overall diameter (m)	1.0

MINOR RANGE M5

Diver controlled dump valve with lanyard and push button operation. Open hemmed to allow excess air to vent off during ascent. Suitable for a variety of tasks including the recovery of small items and as buoyancy aids for tools and equipment employed underwater.

Lift capacity (kg)	250
Overall length (m)	1.5
Overall diameter (m)	0.75

PROFESSIONAL RANGE PR1, PRIV, PR2

Diver controlled dump valve with lanyard and push button operation. Air inlet connection hose with quick release coupling welded within bag for inflation. Open hemmed to allow excess air to spill away during ascent and designed to perform a variety of tasks from vessel and aircraft salvage to providing buoyancy for towing operations.

	PR1	PRIV	PR2
Lift capacity (kg)	1000	1500	2000
Overall length (m)	2.3	2.75	3.0
Overall diameter (m)	1.35	1.35	1.35

SPORT DIVER LIFT BAG SPD2

Diver controlled dump valve with lanyard and push button operation. Open hemmed to allow excess air to vent off during ascent. The SPD2 is capable of a large variety of underwater tasks, such as the recovery of lost outboard motors, anchors etc.

Lift capacity (kg)	100
Overall length (m)	1.0
Overall diameter (m)	0.6

PROFESSIONAL RANGE, PR3, PR5, PR10

Diver controlled dump valve with lanyard and push button operation. Air inlet connection hose with quick release coupling welded within bag for inflation. Open hemmed to allow excess air to spill away during ascent. Same capabilities and uses as the PR1 range but with greater lift.

	PR3	PR5	PR10
Lift capacity (kg)	3000	5000	10000
Overall length (m)	3.9	4.2	5.2
Overall diameter (m)	1.5	2.0	2.95

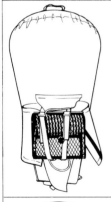

AUTO LIFT BAG ALB IV

The ALB contains its own supply of compressed air or solid propellant gas, obviating the need for surface airline connections, when used with propellant gas, the ALB is capable of operation to depths of 61 ats (2000 feet). The ALB is open bottomed to allow excess gas/air to spill away during ascent. Diver controlled dump valve with lanyard and push button operation.

Lift capacity (kg)	1500
Overall length (m)	2.35
Overall diameter (m)	1.35

TOTALLY ENCLOSED RANGE, T2C, TSC, T10C

¾ inch inlet valve made of brass with quick release coupling. High volume (2265 litres/minute) air pressure relief valve set at 0.14 kg/cm². Totally enclosed for ease of handling these bags combine lifting capabilities with long towing operations. Extensive service with towing underwater pipe and cables.

	T2C	T5C	T10C
Lift capacity (kg)	100	250	500
Overall length (m)	0.85	1.0	1.15
Overall diameter (m)	0.4	0.6	0.8

MINE RECOVERY BAG PRIVM

The PRIVM is the military version of the ALBIV, manufactured to Ministry of Defence requirements, primarily for mine recovery, though used for any lifting operation. Diver controlled dump valve with lanyard and push button operation.

Lift capacity (kg)	1500
Overall length (m)	2.35
Overall diameter (m)	1.35

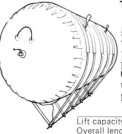

TOTALLY ENCLOSED RANGE T1, T2, T3, T4, T5

¾ inch inlet valve made of brass with quick release coupling. High volume (2265 litres/minute) air pressure relief valve set at 0.14 kg/cm². Same capabilities and uses as the TC range but with greater lift.

	T1	T2	T3	T5
Lift capacity (kg)	1000	2000	3000	5000
Overall length (m)	1.5	2.0	2.2	3.5
Overall diameter (m)	1.0	2.2	1.4	1.4

	lifting capacity		displacement		ABSOLUTE DEPTH											
					ats	1	2	3	4	5	6	7	8	9	10	25	50
					metres	0	10	20	30	40	50	60	70	80	90	240	490
Airbag model number					feet	0	33	66	99	132	165	198	231	264	297	825	1650
	lbs	kgs	lbs	litres		AIR REQUIREMENT AT DEPTH											
SPD1	75	34	1.2	34	ft³	1.2	2.3	3.5	4.7	5.9	7.0	8.2	9.4	10.5	11.7	29.3	58.5
					litres	3.4	68	102	136	170	204	238	272	306	340	850	1700
SPD2 M2 T2C	220	100	3.5	100	ft³	3.5	6.9	10.3	13.7	17.2	20.6	24.0	27.5	30.9	34.3	85.7	171.5
					litres	100	200	300	400	500	600	700	800	900	1000	2500	5000
M5 T5C	550	250	8.6	250	ft³	8.6	17.1	25.7	34.3	42.9	51.5	60.1	68.7	77.3	85.9	214.7	429.5
					litres	250	500	750	1000	1250	1500	1750	2000	2250	2500	6250	12500
M10 T10C	1100	500	15.7	500	ft³	15.7	31.2	46.8	62.4	78.1	93.7	109.3	124.9	140.5	156.2	390.5	781.0
					litres	500	1000	1500	2000	2500	3000	3500	4000	4500	5000	12500	25000
PR1 T1 ARB	2200	1000	34.4	1000	ft³	34.4	68.7	103.1	137.4	171.8	206.2	240.5	274.9	309.3	343.7	859.2	1718.5
					litres	1000	2000	3000	4000	5000	6000	7000	8000	9000	10000	25000	50000
PRIVM ALBIV	3300	1500	51.6	1500	ft³	51.6	103.1	154.6	206.2	257.8	309.3	360.9	412.4	464.0	515.6	1289.0	2578.0
					litres	1500	3000	4500	6000	7500	9000	10500	12000	13500	15000	37500	75000
PR2 T2	4400	2000	68.8	2000	ft³	68.8	137.5	206.2	275.0	343.7	412.5	481.2	550.0	618.7	687.5	1718.5	3437.5
					litres	2000	4000	6000	8000	10000	12000	14000	16000	18000	20000	50000	100000
PR3 T3	6600	3000	103.2	3000	ft³	103.2	206.2	309.3	412.0	515.6	618.7	721.8	824.9	928.0	1031.2	2578.0	5156.0
					litres	3000	6000	9000	12000	15000	18000	21000	24000	27000	30000	75000	150000
PR5 T5	11000	5000	171.89	5000	ft³	171.9	343.7	551.6	687.4	859.3	1031.2	1203.0	1374.9	1546.8	1718.7	4296.7	8593.5
					litres	5000	10000	15000	20000	25000	30000	35000	40000	45000	50000	125000	250000
PR10	22000	10000	343.8	10000	ft³	343.8	687.5	1031.2	1375.0	1718.7	2062.5	2406.2	2750.0	3093.7	3437.5	8593.5	17187.5
					litres	10000	20000	30000	40000	50000	60000	70000	80000	90000	100000	250000	500000

SUBSALVE LIFT BAGS

Another range in air lift bags is manufactured by Subsalve Industries Inc., USA. They produce two main types of open-bottomed, self-venting bags, the Professional and Commercial ranges, and a series of enclosed flotation bags. A particular feature of Subsalve bags is the choice of material: either a 0.050 in thick Neoprene of 1250 lbs/in tensile strength, or a vinyl-coated Kevlar/polyester fabric 0.050 in thick and 750 lbs/in tensile strength.

Commercial

Model	A		B		C		Lift capacity		Weight		Cube	
	cm	in	cm	in	cm	in	kg	lbs	kg	lbs	m³	ft³
100	76.2	30	71.1	28	25.4	10	62.6	138	2.3	5	0.015	0.53
200	88.9	35	76.2	30	30.5	12	108.9	240	3.2	7	0.015	0.53
500	127	50	101.6	40	35.6	14	424.7	535	5.0	11	0.05	1.7

Professional

Model	A		B		C		Lift capacity		Weight		Cube	
	cm	in	cm	in	cm	in	kg	lbs	kg	lbs	m³	ft³
1000	127.0	50	88.9	35	25.4	10	499.0	1100	6.3	14	0.048	1.7
2000	152.4	60	116.8	46	25.4	10	952.6	2100	11.8	26	0.12	4.2
6000	228.6	90	170.2	67	40.6	16	2812.3	6200	22.7	50	0.23	8.0
12 000	269.2	106	208.3	82	40.6	16	5670	12 500	61.2	135	0.31	11.0
20 000	355.6	140	248.9	98	40.6	16	9366.8	20 650	93.4	206	0.43	15.0

Enclosed flotation bags

Model	A		B		C		Lift capacity		Weight		Cube	
	cm	in	cm	in	cm	in	kg	lbs	kg	lbs	m³	ft³
500	124.5	49	71.1	28	45.7	18	244.9	540	5.4	12	0.015	0.53
1000	152.4	50	96.5	38	61.0	24	489.9	1080	9.1	20	0.048	1.7
2000	137.2	54	121.9	48	76.2	30	979.8	21·60	14.5	32	0.048	1.7
3000	147.3	58	142.2	56	101.6	40	1451.5	3200	18.1	40	0.119	4.2

CANFLEX LIFTING BALLOONS WITH CABCO

A third company, Canflex Manufacturing Inc., Canada, produce a range of 9 open-bottomed self-venting bags. Canflex have a unique Cabco hose system which provides a continuous automatic buoyancy-controlled lift. The smaller units need only the diver to inflate the bag initially without adjustment. The larger units should be adjusted and tripped by the diver. When several bags are being used to raise a heavy lift, load balancing can be effected by using a hose connection, and if fitted with Cabco hoses the quick release systems should be operated remotely.

Specifications

MODEL	LIFT		HEIGHT			WIDTH			VOLUME		SHIPPING WEIGHT	
	kg	lbs	m	ft	in	m	ft	in	m³	m³	kg	lbs
SL50	50	110	0.7	2	3	0.7	2	3	0.05	1.82	1.1	2.43
SL100	100	220	0.8	2	7	0.8	2	7	0.1	3.62	1.4	3.09
SL500	500	1100	1.2	3	11	1.2	3	11	0.51	18.12	4.5	9.92
CL1	1000	2200	1.8	5	11	1.2	3	11	1.03	6.23	8.6	18.96
CL2	2000	4400	2.2	7	3	1.5	4	11	2.05	72.47	13.6	29.98
CL3	3000	6600	2.6	8	6	1.7	5	7	3.1	108.69	22.7	50.04
CL5	5000	11 000	3.1	10	2	2.0	6	7	5.1	181.16	28.2	62.17
CL10	10 000	22 000	3.9	12	9	2.6	8	6	10.25	362.33	45.0	99.21
HL25	25 000	55 000	5.2	17	1	3.5	11	6	25.63	905.82	85.0	187·39

3.6 SHIP WORK DIVER TASKS ON A STANDARD CARGO VESSEL

This drawing of a typical cargo ship, an Austin and Pickersgill SD15, shows the approximate position of various underwater fittings that might require the services of a diver. No two vessels are exactly alike, so that the diver would need to consult the ship's plans for their exact location and type. Lloyd's Register, amongst other classification societies, issue a list of rules for their LR classification in-water survey. These precisely detail the diver tasks required.

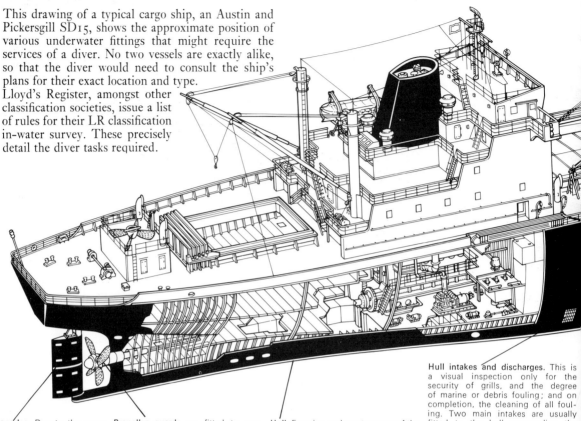

Sacrificial anodes. Due to the many dissimilar metals around the stern, a number of sacrificial anodes may be fitted. Check each anode as in item (e) of 'Rudder, stock and bearings'.

Propeller guards are fitted to prevent wires or ropes fouling the propeller. They are circular plates that cover the gap between the aft end of the propeller shaft and the forward face of the propeller.

Hull. Examine underwater areas of the hull for leaks and damage. Look out for pockets of air trapped under a flat-bottomed hull and measure their depth.

Hull intakes and discharges. This is a visual inspection only for the security of grills, and the degree of marine or debris fouling; and on completion, the cleaning of all fouling. Two main intakes are usually fitted to the hull surrounding the engine room—one high and one low. There may be many more intakes and discharges elsewhere in the hull. The senior engineer on watch must be aware that divers are at work.

Preparation for working on a ship's bottom

—Diver is to be negatively buoyant so as to increase his purchase when using tools underwater.

—If diver is wearing a standard dress or is heavily weighted, the tender must be alert in case the diver should fall off his stage.

—The underwater staging and bottom lines must be securely and properly rigged for the work. If diving is from a boat, it must be moored so that it cannot break adrift whilst the diver is down. If diving is in tidal waters, both boat and underwater stages are to be secured so that they do not drift.

—All tools likely to be required for the task should be ready at the work site.

—The diver should be briefed in exactly what he is expected to do, and shown any relevant ship's plans or fitting diagrams.

—It is often difficult for the diver to be sure that he has reached exactly the right fitting, especially when there are several similar ones close together. There are various ways of guiding him. Someone inside the ship close to the fitting can tap with a hammer on the hull, or air can be pumped through an outlet to produce bubbles as a guide.

—Before diving, the senior engineer on watch must ensure that the main engines are shut down and the shaft brakes on, with warning signs displayed in the engine room and on the bridge. There is a tendency for some propellers to turn, even when the engine may be in neutral. This is particularly true of steam turbine engines whilst cooling down.

—Because of the possible suction effects on divers working on main inlets, the circulating pumps must be stopped and the main inlet and discharge valves shut. Overboard discharges are to be secured. Sonar equipment should not be energised and their power switches should be tagged to that effect. The stabiliser breaker is to be opened and a warning board affixed to it. If an impressed current cathodic protection system is fitted, it must be switched off before divers enter the water. Flag A should be flown and the deck officer kept acquainted with the progress of the diving operation. Others that need to be informed might be the Harbour or Berthing Master.

—The diving supervisor must be aware of the state of the tide especially the depth of water beneath the ship's bottom on the ebb.

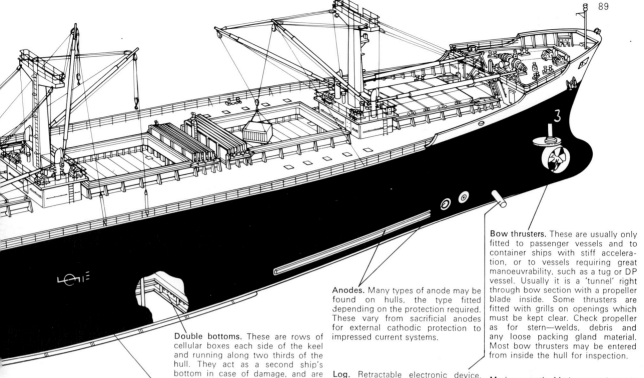

Bow thrusters. These are usually only fitted to passenger vessels and to container ships with stiff acceleration, or to vessels requiring great manoeuvrability, such as a tug or DP vessel. Usually it is a 'tunnel' right through bow section with a propeller blade inside. Some thrusters are fitted with grills on openings which must be kept clear. Check propeller as for stern—welds, debris and any loose packing gland material. Most bow thrusters may be entered from inside the hull for inspection.

Anodes. Many types of anode may be found on hulls, the type fitted depending on the protection required. These vary from sacrificial anodes for external cathodic protection to impressed current systems.

Double bottoms. These are rows of cellular boxes each side of the keel and running along two thirds of the hull. They act as a second ship's bottom in case of damage, and are often filled with fuel or water.

Log. Retractable electronic device. Check free movement—extended and retracted; measure protrusion if necessary; check for damage, corrosion and marine fouling.

Marine growth. Marine growth needs to be removed periodically because the friction it causes increases fuel costs and reduces the ship's speed. It can also cause corrosion by breaking through the protective antifouling. Check and report on percentage coverage, thickness, density and nature, especially around intakes close to discharges where hot fluids will encourage rapid growth. Marine growth cleaning is usually done with divers using brush carts.

Fin stabilisers. Check travel, port and starboard. Hydroplane to full dive then mark ship's side with crayon at trailing edge. Then full rise and mark. Neutral and mark. Measure distance from centre mark to top and bottom marks.

Bilge keel. Check for security, broken welds, condition of sacrificial anodes, physical damage or distortion.

Load line. Load line markings, i.e. Lloyd's Register, Bureau Veritas etc., are normally 'cut-out' steel markings welded on hull. These marks are usually situated slightly above the water line depending on the trim. Marks are welded bead, not plate. Check for any sign of welds allowing marks to fall off or for any sign of damage by rubbing.

Rudder, stock and bearings

Starting at the top, inspect:

(a) Rudder stock: check stock for cracks and connection to rudder for loose or missing bolts or nuts.

(b) Upper support housing: look for obvious wear, loose or missing bolts or nuts, the security and effectiveness of locking devices and any missing components. The space between the upper bearing gland and rudder should be free of debris.

(c) Top portion of rudder: check for missing filling plugs, corrosion and damage.

(d) Inspection plates: check for security of all bolts or nuts, and that no gasket material is hanging loose or parts of gaskets missing.

(e) Sacrificial anodes: check degree and coverage of pitting. Measure pits and report average depth and maximum depth of pitting. Check and report percentage waste. Take three circumferential and one length measurements to compare with the original (as new) size. Check if securely attached. Check securing lugs for corrosion or if in good condition. Check and report if anodes are secured by bolts, welded lugs or any other means.

(f) Lower portion of rudder: check drain plugs, lower inspection plate(s), anodes and lower bearing. NB. If rudder can be moved, with diver on propeller shaft and clear of movement, the rudder should be set amidships and position checked for alignment; then hard to port/starboard and the

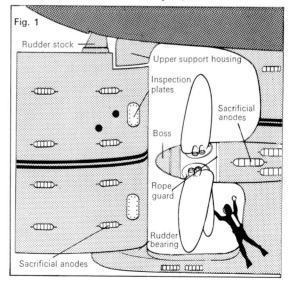

Fig. 1

Rudder stock

Upper support housing

Inspection plates

Sacrificial anodes

Boss

Rope guard

Rudder bearing

Sacrificial anodes

full travel checked and measured in degrees if possible. Measure rudder tracking edge to prop boss when rudder hard to port and hard to starboard.

Propeller and shafting

(a) Check boss for damage, locking devices, and that no significant gap exists in any joints.

(b) Check each blade for chipping, cracks, distortion, 'polishing'. If any damage has occurred, take detailed measurements of all dimensions of any damage. Report with a sketch and carefully note which blade it is on in that particular position.

(c) If variable pitch, check each blade's securing flange, nuts and locking devices. Check that no debris, i.e. wire, rope, nylon etc., has intruded on fittings. With diver well clear of propeller, but within good visibility range, check each blade as it is 'feathered'. Then turn from full-ahead position to full-astern. Measure this angle if practicable.

(d) Report on all blades in sequence.

(e) Check ropeguard for security, fixtures and securing bolts and locking devices. Check that no line

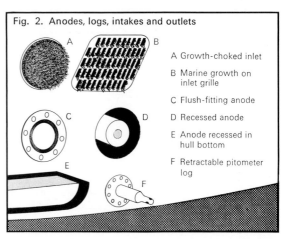

Fig. 2. Anodes, logs, intakes and outlets

A Growth-choked inlet

B Marine growth on inlet grille

C Flush-fitting anode

D Recessed anode

E Anode recessed in hull bottom

F Retractable pitometer log

or wire rope has entered the gap between guard and propellor.

(f) If 'A' brackets are fitted, check for damage and any cracks, particularly the welds or attachment devices to both hull and shaft housing.

(g) Clear ropes and debris and check main stern gland(s) for wear or damage.

(h) Check all bearings and shafts for oil leaks.

3.8 ENGINEERING DRAWINGS

The interpretation of mechanical drawings relating to the installation and inspection of subsea structures is an important aspect of the diver's work. Finding the correct drawing relating to a particular aspect of a subsea structure is often a time consuming job. It is therefore necessary to understand the way in which the drawings of any platform or subsea installation are organised. A system of drawings is often referred to as a family tree and usually has a master drawing number. A typical family tree of drawings for a subsea structure appears in a simplified form in Fig. 1.

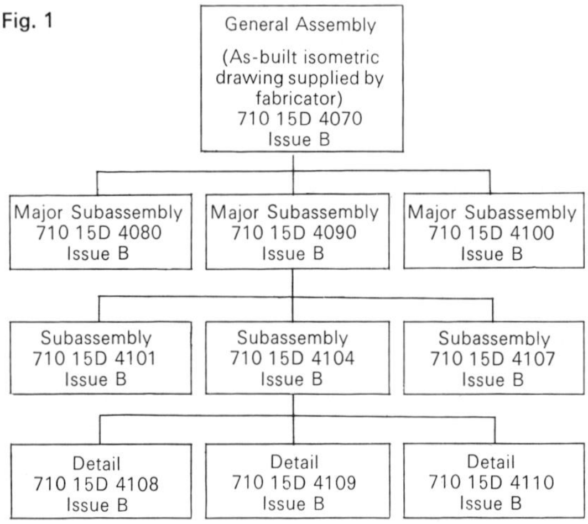

The detailed drawing for any part of a subsea structure usually has its own drawing number and can be found by reference to the drawing list.

Every drawing or print should contain a panel showing the technical details of the drawing. This panel is normally found in the lower right hand side of the sheet and might contain the following information:

—Title of the drawing.

—Name of the owner.

—Location of the project.

—Project or contract number.

—Drawing number.

—Number of drawing sheet; there can be several drawings against one drawing number.

—Revision number.

—Date on which the drawing was issued or revised.

—Scale.

—Key plan, showing geographical orientation.

—Projection.

—Notes: these might specify details such as the units in which dimensions are stated, mechanical tolerances, materials etc.

—Legend: explanation of symbols.

A typical drawing panel is shown in Fig. 2.

Fig. 1

General Assembly (As-built isometric drawing supplied by fabricator) 710 15D 4070 Issue B

Major Subassembly 710 15D 4080 Issue B — Major Subassembly 710 15D 4090 Issue B — Major Subassembly 710 15D 4100 Issue B

Subassembly 710 15D 4101 Issue B — Subassembly 710 15D 4104 Issue B — Subassembly 710 15D 4107 Issue B

Detail 710 15D 4108 Issue B — Detail 710 15D 4109 Issue B — Detail 710 15D 4110 Issue B

Fig. 2

Orientation/ Key plan			
Notes			
Projection			
Legend			
REVISIONS	Drawn by	TITLE OF DRAWING	PROJECT OR CONTRACT NO. AB 0190
ISSUE or REVISION NO. date	date		
	Checked by		DRAWING NO. 710 15D 4110
Revised by date	date	Name of owner	
APPROVALS date date date	Scale	Location of project	REVISION NO. 3
			SHEET 2 OF 10

The issue of a drawing is important since modifications could have been made to the structure since it was first drawn up. Changes in issue are recorded on the family tree and appear on the drawing as a number or letter against the word 'Issue'. The issue number of every drawing should be checked before use against the current build standard of the structure. Always use the latest issue. Care must be taken to distinguish early conceptual drawings from 'Approved for construction' drawings.

The units in which the dimensions are shown on drawings vary. The units are usually defined on the drawing and different units can be used for different parts of the structure, i.e.: dimensions of tubular sections can be expressed in millimetres whilst figures for elevations can be given in metres on the same drawing.

Most mistakes during construction occur when dimensions on drawings are not properly defined, or are misinterpreted.

The three types of platform drawings which will most commonly be encountered by the diver are as follows:

—Perspective drawing or three-dimensional view (Fig. 5). Sometimes this is shown as an isometric drawing.

—Elevation drawing, or side view (Fig. 3).

—Plan drawing, or top view; view looking vertically down on a structure (Fig. 4).

Because of the height and shape of structures, it is usual practice to have a large number of separate plan drawings made at various levels on the structure. These different plan drawings are defined by reference to the elevation at which the drawing was made, e.g. 'Plan view at − 30.000' means that the drawing depicts a horizontal section of the platform 30 m below lowest astronomical tide (LAT).

Superimposed on any of the above three types of drawings can be stated:

—Type of steel.

—Type of welds.

—Extent of reinforcing.

—Finish.

These symbols are generally defined in the overall drawing list legend.

Perhaps the most useful drawing available to the diver involved in inspection or construction work on offshore platforms is the as-built platform isometric drawing. This gives a three-dimensional view of the platform from which a lot of useful information can be extracted:

—Position of pile guides.

—Orientation of nodes and weldments.

—Position of risers.

—Number and identification system used for jacket legs.

—Location of horizontal and diagonal support bracings.

—Relative sizes and positions of the various parts.

Isometric drawings often include information on the depth at various points on the structure. This is generally given as a figure in metres, prefixed by the word 'Elevation' (EL) and either a positive or negative sign depending on whether the location is above or below the surface. Depths shown in this way are normally referred to as Lowest Astronomical Tide (LAT). Care must be taken to avoid any confusion as sometimes the elevation figures refer to height above the seabed rather than the depth below the LAT.

Very often it is useful to make one's own working sketch of a particular part of the structure for reference purposes underwater. Since components such as bracing joints and nodes involve members running in different directions, the sketch must have a reference to a directional axis, e.g.: Leg D Node 6 looking North.

Note: A primary aspect of any underwater inspection is to check that the actual structure conforms to the as-built isometric drawings and to note any discrepancies.

Master drawings, i.e. the originals, are usually kept ashore. Prints can be made in the following ways:

Photocopying.
Dye line printing.
Radio facsimile.

After duplication, prints should be folded in such a way that the title block and drawing number remain visible. Drawing sheets should be handled by the borders and should not be left in strong sunlight, otherwise they will fade.

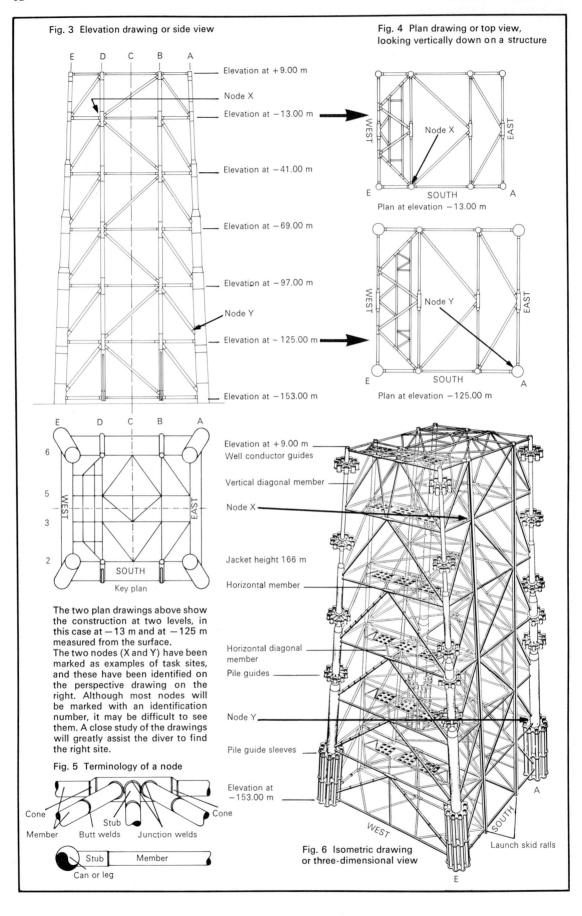

Fig. 3 Elevation drawing or side view

E D C B A

Elevation at + 9.00 m

Node X

Elevation at − 13.00 m

Elevation at − 41.00 m

Elevation at − 69.00 m

Elevation at − 97.00 m

Node Y

Elevation at − 125.00 m

Elevation at − 153.00 m

Fig. 4 Plan drawing or top view,
looking vertically down on a structure

WEST   EAST

Node X

E   SOUTH   A

Plan at elevation − 13.00 m

WEST   EAST

Node Y

E   SOUTH   A

Plan at elevation − 125.00 m

E D C B A

6

5

3

2

WEST   EAST

SOUTH

Key plan

The two plan drawings above show
the construction at two levels, in
this case at − 13 m and at − 125 m
measured from the surface.
The two nodes (X and Y) have been
marked as examples of task sites,
and these have been identified on
the perspective drawing on the
right. Although most nodes will
be marked with an identification
number, it may be difficult to see
them. A close study of the drawings
will greatly assist the diver to find
the right site.

Fig. 5 Terminology of a node

Cone   Cone

Stub

Member   Butt welds   Junction welds

Stub   Member

Can or leg

Elevation at + 9.00 m
Well conductor guides

Vertical diagonal member

Node X

Jacket height 166 m

Horizontal member

Horizontal diagonal
member

Pile guides

Node Y

Pile guide sleeves

Elevation at
− 153.00 m

WEST   SOUTH

E

A

Launch skid rails

Fig. 6 Isometric drawing
or three-dimensional view

3.9a PURCHASES AND TACKLES

Rigging for hoisting, pulling or hauling heavy objects consists of a purchase, which is a mechanical device to increase power or force by means of blocks or pulleys rove with a rope or chain, or by levers, ratchets or gears. There are many such devices available—the traditional block and rope tackle, jacks, come-alongs, lever hoists, and hand winches. Most of these can be operated manually, hydraulically or electrically, but the manual types are mainly used underwater. The choice of the equipment to be used depends on

1. availability of equipment.

2. the weight of the object to be handled.

3. the size and physical nature of the object.

4. the distance the object has to be moved.

5. the rated power of the equipment.

6. access: enough room to operate equipment.

Traditional tackle

A single block used for a straight lift (a single whip) imparts no mechanical advantage because the block does not move. A purchase consists of a rope rove through two or more blocks in such a way that a pull applied to its hauling part is increased by an amount depending upon the number of sheaves in the blocks and the manner in which the rope is rove through them. Put another way, the gain in the power is equivalent to the number of parts (of rope) which enter and leave the moving block of the tackle, depending on whether the tackle is rigged to advantage or disadvantage. As its name implies, a tackle rigged to advantage gains the maximum increase in power.

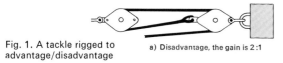

Fig. 1. A tackle rigged to advantage/disadvantage

a) Disadvantage, the gain is 2 :1

b) Advantage, the gain is 3 :1

The amount by which the pull on the hauling part is multiplied by the tackle is called its mechanical advantage (M.A.) and, if friction is disregarded, this is equal to the number of parts of the fall at the moving block. In Fig. 3 for example, there are two parts at the moving block, therefore the M.A. is 2; in other words, a pull on the hauling part of 51kg would, if friction were disregarded, hold a weight of 102kg.

To raise a load 1 ft The lower block must be raised 1 ft, and consequently each working rope will be shortened 1 ft. All the sheaves in a set of blocks will rotate at different rates Consequently, the sheaves nearest the lead line wear out fastest.

To estimate the pull required, in the hauling part of any tackle, to hoist a given weight, divide the weight by the mechanical advantage of the tackle. Conversely, the weight which can be hoisted by a given pull on the hauling

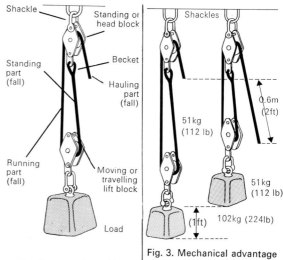

Fig. 2. Parts of a tackle

Fig. 3. Mechanical advantage and velocity ratio

part of a tackle can be found by multiplying the pull by the mechanical advantage of the tackle.

There can be many combinations, such as two tackles rigged together, or using blocks with multiple sheaves. It should be remembered however, that friction in the bearings of the sheaves reduces the mechanical advantage by about one tenth of the weight to be hoisted for each sheave of the tackle. Mechanical advantage is gained only at the expense of speed of working.

The ratio between the distance moved by the hauling part and that moved by the moving block is called the velocity ratio (VR) and is always equal to the number of parts of the fall at the moving block.

The difference between the MA and the VR is the amount of friction.

Be sure to check that the blocks, ropes and shackles used are within the safe working load for the weight.

The Reeving of Tackle Blocks

In reeving a pair of tackle blocks, one of which has more than two sheaves (as in 4), the hoisting rope should lead from one of the centre sheaves of the upper block. When so reeved, the hoisting strain comes on the centre of the blocks and they are prevented from toppling (which would cause injury to the rope by cutting across the edges of the block shell).

To reeve by this method, the two blocks should be placed so that the sheaves in the upper block are at right angles to those in the lower one, as shown in Fig. 4. Start reeving with the becket, or standing end of the rope.

It is good practice to use a shackle block as the upper one of a pair, and a hook block as the lower one. A shackle is much stronger than a hook of the same size, and the strain on the upper block is much greater than on the lower one. The lower block supports only the load whereas the upper block carries the load as well as the hoisting strain. A hook is more convenient on the lower block because it can more readily be attached or detached from the load.

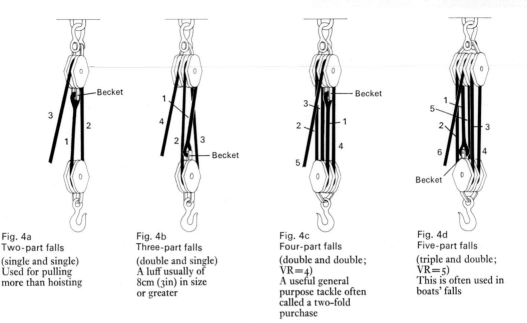

Fig. 4a
Two-part falls
(single and single)
Used for pulling
more than hoisting

Fig. 4b
Three-part falls
(double and single)
A luff usually of
8cm (3in) in size
or greater

Fig. 4c
Four-part falls
(double and double;
VR=4)
A useful general
purpose tackle often
called a two-fold
purchase

Fig. 4d
Five-part falls
(triple and double;
VR=5)
This is often used in
boats' falls

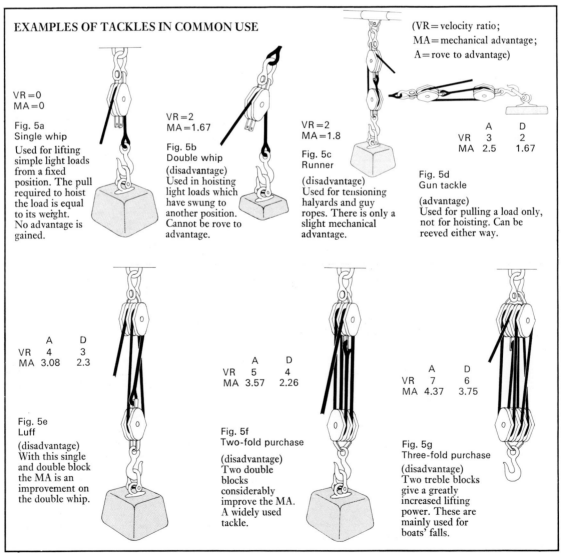

EXAMPLES OF TACKLES IN COMMON USE

(VR = velocity ratio;
MA = mechanical advantage;
A = rove to advantage)

VR = 0
MA = 0

Fig. 5a
Single whip
Used for lifting
simple light loads
from a fixed
position. The pull
required to hoist
the load is equal
to its weight.
No advantage is
gained.

VR = 2
MA = 1.67

Fig. 5b
Double whip
(disadvantage)
Used in hoisting
light loads which
have swung to
another position.
Cannot be rove to
advantage.

VR = 2
MA = 1.8

Fig. 5c
Runner

(disadvantage)
Used for tensioning
halyards and guy
ropes. There is only a
slight mechanical
advantage.

	A	D
VR	3	2
MA	2.5	1.67

Fig. 5d
Gun tackle

(advantage)
Used for pulling a load only,
not for hoisting. Can be
reeved either way.

	A	D
VR	4	3
MA	3.08	2.3

Fig. 5e
Luff
(disadvantage)
With this single
and double block
the MA is an
improvement on
the double whip.

	A	D
VR	5	4
MA	3.57	2.26

Fig. 5f
Two-fold purchase

(disadvantage)
Two double
blocks
considerably
improve the MA.
A widely used
tackle.

	A	D
VR	7	6
MA	4.37	3.75

Fig. 5g
Three-fold purchase

(disadvantage)
Two treble blocks
give a greatly
increased lifting
power. These are
mainly used for
boats' falls.

3.9b PULLING AND LIFTING TOOLS THE TIRFOR MACHINE

The Tirfor is a hand-operated pulling and lifting machine with an unlimited rope travel. It works by pulling directly on the rope, the pull being applied by means of two pairs of self-energizing smooth jaws which exert a grip on the rope in proportion to the load being lifted or pulled.

These devices are designed for land use but are successfully employed underwater with some additional care and maintenance.

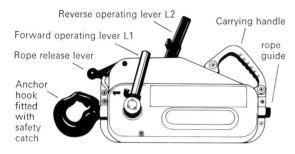

Reverse operating lever L2
Forward operating lever L1
Rope release lever
Anchor hook fitted with safety catch
Carrying handle
rope guide

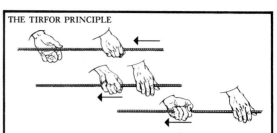

THE TIRFOR PRINCIPLE

The general principle may be described as a 'hand-over-hand' principle, like a sailor pulling on a rope: while one hand pulls, the other one changes position in order to pull in turn.

The two hands represent the two jaw grips of the Tirfor; they grip the wire rope without damaging it and alternately haul it during forward motion and clamp it during reverse motion. The effort is transferred to the jaws by means of two levers—one for forward motion and the other for reverse motion—which acts by a cam system on the keys that command the automatic clamping of the jaws on the rope.

Functioning of the Keys

The jaw grips are made of two jaws which can be brought together (clamping) or separated (unclamping) by means of keys actuated by levers called jaw links. When the jaw-link is moved to the left the jaws are clamped on the wire rope in order to draw

Fig. 1

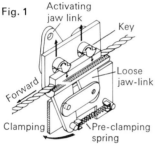

Activating jaw link
Key
Forward
Loose jaw-link
Clamping
Pre-clamping spring

it or maintain it in position. When the jaw-link is moved to the right the jaws are unclamped in order to allow the wire rope to slip through, but only in the direction opposed to the motion of the wire rope.

Reverse motion:
Fig. 4
Reverse motion is obtained by a to-and-fro motion of lever L2. If the lever is actuated to the right, grip M2 clamps and is drawn by the rope to the right, while M1 opens itself slightly to let the cable

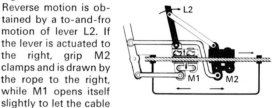

glide while controlling its motion (Fig. 4). Inversely, if lever L2 is actuated to the left, grip M2 is clamped on the rope and grip M1 opens slightly to allow the rope to glide under control.

Fig. 5

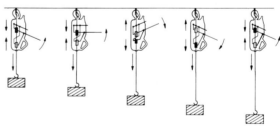

This to-and-fro motion of the lever L2 causes the progression of the rope from the left to right, hence the lowering of the load (Fig. 5).

Forward motion:
Forward motion is obtained by a to-and-fro motion of the lever L1. If the lever is actuated to the right, grip M1, acted upon by connecting rod B1, clamps and draws the rope to the left. Simul-

Fig. 2

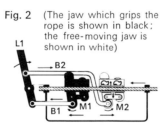

(The jaw which grips the rope is shown in black; the free-moving jaw is shown in white)

L1
B2
B1 M1 M2

taneously, grip M2 opens itself slightly and moves to the right (Fig. 2). If, thereafter, lever L1 is actuated to the left the movements are simply reversed.

Fig. 3

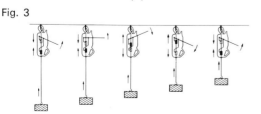

The power stroke lever L1 thus controls the progression of the rope from right to left, namely the pulling or lifting of the load (Fig. 3).

Release
For ease of operation it must be possible to open simultaneously both jaws to introduce the rope, tension it or to disengage the machine.

Fig. 6

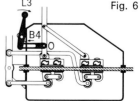

L3
B4
O

To release simultaneously the jaws of the two grips it is necessary to pull on the reverse mechanism at 'O'. A release system L3–B4 performs this function (Fig. 6).

BASIC RANGE OF TIRFORS

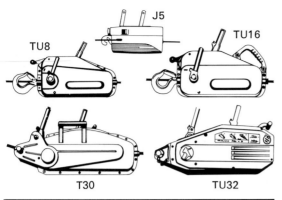

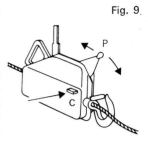

TIRFOR MODEL		J5	TU8	TU16	T30	TU32
Pulling capacity	tonnes	0.8	1.2	2.5	5.0	5.0
Lifting capacity (SWL)	tonnes	0.5	0.8	1.6	3.0	3.2
Weight	kg	3.5	8.2	18.0	28.0	27.0
	lb	7.7	18.5	40.0	59.5	59.5
Diameter of wire rope	mm	6.5	8.2	11.3	16.3	16.3
	inch	0.256	0.323	0.445	0.642	0.642
Minimum breaking strain of wire rope	tonnes	3.0	4.8	8.1	16.8	16.8
Standard length of wire rope	m	10	20	20	20	20
	ft	32.8	65.6	65.6	65.6	65.6

Safety factors are 5:1 lifting and 3:1 pulling.

Operating instructions

Lubricate the unit generously before starting. (See section on Maintenance and lubrication.)

(1) Uncoil the special Tirfor Maxiflex wire rope in a straight line, to prevent loops untwisting the strands or forming kinks when under pressure.

(2) With the left hand, push in and maintain pressure on release catch C (Fig. 7). With the right hand pull the rope release lever P away from the hook until it is vertical. Release catch C. Continue to pull back on the rope release lever P until it locks into position. Both jaws are now open.

Fig. 7

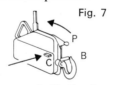

(3) With the machine placed on the ground, insert the fused and tapered end of the rope at A. This is the best position for feeding the rope between the jaws. Push the rope through until it emerges at B (Fig. 8(a)).

Fig. 8(a)

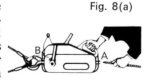

(4) Anchor the machine and the cable hook with the correct slings and ensure that the safety catch C is closed

(5) Pull the wire rope by hand until the rope becomes tight on the load. (Fig. 8(b)).

Fig. 8(b)

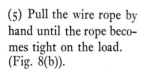

(6) To engage the machine on the rope, ease the rope release lever P away from the hook, press and maintain pressure on the release catch C on the side of the machine. Allow the release lever P to travel slowly back to its original position (Fig. 9). Release catch C.

Fig. 9

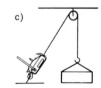

(7) The rope is now firmly fixed between the jaws of the machine. To operate the machine, place the operating handle on the forward operating lever L1 and lock it into position by twisting; now move the handle to and fro. The rope moves through the machine on both forward and backward strokes of the lever.

Use of Tirfors

Tirfor machines can be used for any lifting and pulling job within the rated capacities of the machines. They are particularly useful for longer pulls and higher lifts than can be done with other equipment due to the fact that any length of rope can be used. The diagrams below show the various ways in which Tirfors are used.

HORIZONTAL OR ANGLE PULLING:

The unit can be anchored by its hook, using a sling or a chain, to any fixed point, pad eye or support column, etc. (Fig. 10).

Fig. 10

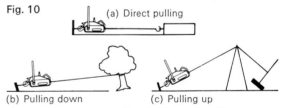

(a) Direct pulling

(b) Pulling down

(c) Pulling up

HEIGHT OF ANCHORAGE. For horizontal pulling, or for angles of up to 45°, secure the anchor hook about six inches above the ground. For angles between 45° and 90° the recommended height above the ground is two feet.

LIFTING:

There are several ways of using a Tirfor as a lifting machine.

Fig. 11

a) b) c)

11a. The machine can be anchored by its hook to a fixed point above the load, and the load lifted toward the machine.
11b. The machine can be anchored directly to the load, and the rope hook anchored directly above it. In this case the rope remains static and the machine and load climb the rope.
11c. The most popular use is to anchor the machine by its hook to a fixed point as near to the sea bed or deck as possible, and to take the rope over a pulley fixed directly above the load. This system is convenient for the diver and keeps him away from the danger of the load.

Sheave blocks

The minimum diameter of the pulley wheels used in sheave blocks are given here for two Tirfor machines, together with the suitable Tirfor Maxiflex steel wire rope.

Tirfor model number	Minimum pulley diameter		Suitable for steel rope of diameter	
	mm	ins	mm	ins
TU16	203	8	11.3	$\frac{7}{16}$
T35	229	9	16.3	$\frac{5}{8}$

When using multi-sheave blocks, always ensure that the blocks are suitable for the total load to be lifted and that the top anchorage for the combination is sufficient to carry the total load of the machine, the tension in the lead rope, the weight of the blocks and the load to be lifted.

SHEAVE BLOCK COMBINATIONS:
For increasing size of load to be lifted

Fig. 12.

P = Load at head block

W = Load at moving block

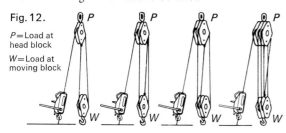

Block combinations	1+1		2+1		2+2		3+2	
No. of falls	2		3		4		5	
	W	P	W	P	W	P	W	P
		max		max		max		max
TU16 load in pulling rope 1600 kg (1.6 tons)	kg 2260	4800	4120	6400	5310	8000	6400	9600
	tons 1.32	4.73	4.05	6.30	5.24	7.88	6.30	9.45
T35 load in pulling rope 3000 kg	kg 5340	9000	7730	12000	9970	15000	12000	18000
	tons 5.25	8.86	7.61	11.80	9.82	14.75	11.80	17.72

Frictional losses are not assumed when calculating P (the load in the block anchor sling and anchor). The weight of the blocks has been ignored, thereby giving a safer figure.

Hence, in the case of the three and two combination for the TU16, P max is 9.5 tons. The anchor sling should have a safe working load of at least 9.5 tons, and a breaking load of 45 tons.

NOTE: When calculating the load which can be lifted over blocks an allowance is made for loss of effort required to overcome friction in sheaves. This figure can vary between 5% and 10%. In the Table above a factor of 8% per sheave has been applied.

Increase of lifting and pulling power

Fig. 13

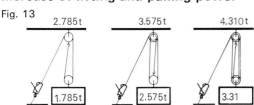

The diagrams in Fig. 13 show how the lifting or pulling power of the Tirfor machines can be increased by using multiple sheave blocks. For the most correct applications we have calculated in each case the weight which can be lifted and the efforts on the pulleys or hooks when applying a one ton load in the Tirfor used. An allowance for friction of approximately 8% per sheave has been made. The weight of the pulley has been neglected.

When using the Tirfor for pulling purposes it should be remembered that the necessary pulling effort is not equal to the weight of the load to be moved. The figures apply to effort and not weight of the load. As work is equal to effort × displacement, the working speed is reduced inversely in proportion to the effort.

Advice on using Tirfors

Use only Tirfor Maxiflex wire rope. Make absolutely sure that the lifting or pulling effort to be exerted is within the rated capacity of the machine. Ensure that there are no obstructions around the machine which could prevent the rope, machine and anchor from operating in a straight line.

Never operate forward/reverse levers at the same time.

Never anchor the machine by the tip of its hook.

Levers L_1 and L_2 must move freely at all times.

Ensure that both the anchor sling and the anchorage are of sufficient strength to hold the load.

The length of the machine anchoring sling should be such that the machine is comfortable to use.

If the Tirfor is being lowered to a worksite from the surface, it may be useful to tie down the rope release lever P to avoid its accidental operation.

Always check the operation of the Tirfor, including the feeding of the wire rope and its smooth running, on the surface before sending it down.

Try to arrange the working location of the Tirfor to be near a good anchorage point to pull against. Pulling is always easier than pushing.

If extended periods of submersion of the Tirfor are anticipated, it should be regarded as a consumable as the sea water will cause corrosion.

Maintenance and lubrication

Lubrication should be carried out at regular intervals to ensure that all the rope gripping mechanisms are working freely. Before putting a machine into service, lubricate generously, and before each application.

A lack of lubricant sometimes brings about a condition known as 'pumping'. As the operating handle is pulled down the machine climbs up the rope about an inch, but when the operating handle is moved up again the machine moves down the same inch. It must be stressed that while this situation is inconvenient, it is not dangerous as there is no risk of the machine releasing its load and slipping. The normal procedure is then to lower the machine back to the ground on the lever L_2 which is unaffected by the 'pumping' action of the lifting lever L_1. The Tirfor should then be thoroughly lubricated with a good quality gear oil (grease for underwater application) and it will recommence working normally.

NOTE:

(1) After use the Tirfor must be washed in fresh water to remove all the sea water, and then re-lubricated.

(2) If the machine is very dirty or clogged, soak it in paraffin, diesel or some proprietary cleansing fluid such as Jizer; then lubricate.

(3) If the Tirfor cannot be washed and greased immediately after being brought to the surface, it may be temporarily stored submerged in diesel fuel oil.

(4) Excess lubrication cannot cause the wire to slip.

(5) Greases and oils containing additives such as molybdenum disulphide must not be used in these machines.

Care of Tirfor Maxiflex steel wire rope

The Tirfor steel wire rope supplied with the machine is designed and manufactured *specially for use with the Tirfor and no other rope should be used*. Ordinary wire ropes deform under the pressure of the jaws, causing the machine to malfunction.

(1) The wire rope should be reeled and unreeled in a straight line to prevent loops or kinks.

(2) Kinked rope will not work in the Tirfor; for this reason, never use the rope as a sling (i.e. passing the rope around an object and then hooking onto the rope again). Always use a separate wire rope sling.

(3) The wire rope outlet of the machine should not be obstructed. The rope must be able to pass freely to prevent it being forced back into the unit.

(4) Ensure that the end of the wire, which is to be fed through the Tirfor, is tapered and free from burnt metal beads or free wire strands which will not allow the wire to pass through.

(5) Avoid subjecting the wire rope to abrasion by rubbing over sharp edges. Be sure that the wire rope is wiped clean before inserting it into the machine.

(6) For longer life and better performance the wire rope should be maintained lubricated.

(7) To avoid unlaying the strands, never allow a loaded rope to rotate.

The data presented here are based substantially on information provided by Tirfor Limited. Further details may be obtained from their head office: Tirfor Limited, Halfway, Sheffield S19 5GZ, England.

RATCHET/LEVER HOISTS

These hand-powered rigger's tools have many applications in underwater work, mainly for exerting lateral pull and accurately positioning awkward loads such as heavy riser clamps. Never use a cheater pipe for extra leverage; change to a larger unit.

Before using these hoists it is important to ensure that
(1) the reverse mode works properly
(2) the hoist is not too great for the tool's rated capacity
(3) the chains are not kinked.

There are many of this type of hoist, of varying lifting capacities. Among the better known are the following:

Table of Specifications							
Make and model	Type	Lifting capacity	Standard lift		Effort required to lift SWL		Comments
		tonnes	m	ft	kg	lb	
ELF (TIRFOR) **75IR** **1501R** **3001R**	Roller chain	0.75 1.5 3.0	1.5 1.5 1.5	4.92 4.92 4.92	36 36 45	80 80 100	These hoists are for use in the vertical plane
ELF (TIRFOR) **752L** **1502L** **3002L**	Link chain	0.75 1.5 3.0	1.6 1.75 1.9	5.5 5.75 6.25	36 36 45	80 80 48	Lever only. Incorporate reduction gear
MORRIS **LEVALIFT** **116**	Roller chain	0.75 1.5 3.0 0.75	1.676 1.676 1.905 1.676	5.50 5.50 6.25 5.50	36 36 45 36	80 80 100 80	
MORRIS **LEVALIFT** **117**	Link chain	1.5 3.0 4.5 0.75 1.5	1.753 1.905 1.905 1.4 1.35	5.75 6.25 6.25 4.6 4.4	36 45 48 38 45	80 48 107 84 99	
YALE PUL-LIFT **MODEL C**	Roller chain	1.5 3.0 4.5 6.0 0.75 1.5	1.35 1.35 1.35 1.35 1.5 1.5	4.4 4.4 4.4 4.4 4.9 4.9	42 38 40 44 42 37	93 84 88 97 93 82.5	Double strand
YALE PUL-LIFT **MODEL D**	Link chain	2.5 (sp) 2.5 5.0 (sp) 5.0 0.75	1.5 1.5 1.5 1.5	4.9 4.9 4.9 4.9	33 33 38 38 30.8	73 73 84 84 68	
FELCO **ROTOLIFT**	Link chain	1.5 3.0 6.0			24.0 26.3 28.5	53 58 63	

CHAIN HOISTS AND TROLLEYS

Not all these trolleys are used under water as they are designed to be suspended from fixed girders. They do, however, have many applications on platforms or on shore.

MAKE	TYPE	LIFT. CAP.	EFFORT REQUIRED TO LIFT SWL	
		tonnes	kg	lb
MORRIS LITALIFT 127	Chain	0.5	14.9	33
		1.0	29.9	66
		1.5	23.5	52
		2.0	32.2	71
		3.0	35.8	79
		4.0	45.4	106
MORRIS LITALIFT 128	Hook suspension type trolley	5.0	53.5	118
		10.0	57.0	126
		15.0	61.2	135
		20.0	65.8	145
MORRIS 164	Trolley	0.5		
		1.0		
		1.5		
		2.0		
		3.0		
		4.0		
		5.0		
		7.5		
		10.0		
		15.0		
		20.0		
VERLINDE	PHR-0-1 chain block (1 fall)	0.5	26.0	57.3
		1.0	27.0	59.5
VERLINDE PHR-1-3	Hook suspension type PHR chain block (2 falls)	1.6	26.0	57.3
		2.0	32.0	70.5
		3.2	37.0	81.6
		4.0	26.0	57.3
		5.0	32.0	70.5
		6.3	40.0	88.2

MAKE	TYPE	LIFT. CAP.	EFFORT REQUIRED TO LIFT SWL	
		tonnes	kg	lb
VERLINDE PHR-3	Hook suspension type PHR chain block (3 falls)	8.0	38.0	83.8
		10.0	39.0	86.0
		12.5	49.0	108.0
VERLINDE PHR-3	Hook suspension type chain block (6–8 falls)	16.0	38	83.8
		20.0	39	86.0
VERLINDE GIRDER TROLLEY	Girder trolley	0.5		
		1.0		
		0.2		
		3.2		
		5.0		
FELCO TROLLEY		0.25		
		0.50		
		1.0		
		1.5		
		2.0		
		3.0		
		4.0		
		6.0		
		8.0		
		10.0		
		16.0		
		20.0		
FELCO CHAIN BLOCK	(1 fall)	0.5	26	57.3
		1.0	25	55.1
		2.0	42	92.6
	(2 falls)	4.0	44	97.0
	(3 falls)	6.0	46	101 4
	(4 falls)	8.0	49	108.0
	(5 falls)	10.0	52	114.6
	(8 falls)	16.0	61	134.5
	(10 falls)	20.0	63	139

FACTORS AFFECTING CHOICE OF PULLING MACHINE

TIRFOR	RATCHET/LEVER OR CHAIN HOISTS Roller chain and Link chain	
Used for long distance movement of objects and where the distance between the pulling points may not be known accurately.	Used when the movement of an object is not required to be great and when the starting distance between two points is fairly well known.	
If overloaded, can fail in the seized mode and require cutting away Some models fitted with a shear pin. Reverse operation still possible It may also fail by gradually allowing the cable to slip through.	If overloaded, can fail by breaking of the chain. Ratchet wheel mechanism may fail but load still safely held.	
Tends to be used for the smaller pulling loads.	Tend to be used for the heavier pulling loads.	
Machine is bulkier than the equivalent strength ratchet hoist	Smaller in size than a Tirfor of equivalent strength.	
Gives better control of smaller movements due to continuous pull over fractions of a stroke.	Minimum distance of a pulling movement is limited to the length of link of the chain or to the ratchet movement. This could be between 5 and 1 mm, depending on capacity. Smaller stroke movements not possible unless blocks are used.	
Operation requires greater dexterity and mental concentration. This can be a problem especially in bad visibility.	Simpler mode of operation than Tirfor. Therefore easier to use in bad visibility and under effect of nitrogen narcosis in deep air diving. Also less likely to be incorrectly used.	
Uses a separate handle which needs to be carried separately by diver, committing another hand. If the handle is dropped accidentally it could hold up the dive although a handle can be attached to the machine by a short chain.	All one piece construction with nothing to fall off or get lost.	
Cable feeds freely through machine, but damaged cable will jam. Needs normal maintenance to avoid corrosion and seizing.	Roller chain feeds better than link but can jam due to seized/corroded links. Sensitive to sideways bending. Maintenance on roller chain to avoid seizing of links.	Link chain can get into tangles and jam the machine. Can be a problem in bad visibility. Needs normal maintenance to avoid corrosion and seizing.

Cordage may be divided into two main types, natural or synthetic fibre ropes. Natural fibre ropes are constructed of short overlapped vegetable fibres twisted together into yarns and again into strands and finally into 3/4 stranded hawser laid rope. They are made from manila, sisal or hemp; manila is the strongest and most durable.

Synthetic, or man-made fibre ropes are replacing natural fibres in the marine environment. In general, synthetic fibres are stronger and lighter, rot resistant, and do not stiffen when wet or freeze in low temperatures. They are more elastic and shock resistant, are longer lasting and easier to handle. They do have, however, a low melting point, so care should be taken where there is much friction. Unlike natural fibres, individual synthetic fibres are manufactured to run the entire length of a rope.

The important features of the different types of synthetic fibres are as follows:

1. NYLON (Perlon, Enkalon)	This is the strongest of the synthetics. Good resistance to abrasion and weathering. Extensively used for towing because of its elasticity.
2. POLYESTER (Dacron, Terylene)	Almost identical with Nylon, except that it has little elasticity. Its low stretch properties make polyester ideal for lifting.
3. POLY-PROPYLENE (Ulstron, Nelson, Prolene)	Lower strength than the former two fibres, and has a relatively low melting point. Light in weight and buoyant; much used for mooring and spring lines.
4. POLYETHYLENE (Courlene, X3)	Similar to polypropylene.
5. BLENDS	There are many combinations of the above to suit special applications.
6. ARAMID POLYAMIDE (Kevlar, Kexlon)	This is a new product claimed to have the same strength as wire ropes at 1/5th of the weight. It is corrosion free, lasts longer and is cheaper than wire rope.

Nos 2, 3 and 4 have good electrical insulating properties, important when working near power lines.

Synthetic fibre ropes may be hawser laid, or 8 to 16 strand plaited, or braided. Braid line consists of a braided core enclosed in a braided sheath and is the strongest form of nylon rope. It has the advantage it will neither twist nor kink.

The elasticity and slipperiness of synthetic ropes may make conventional knots and bends unreliable. It is often better to use a climber's or angler's knot, or to secure free ends with an extra hitch or tuck. Each diver will have his own preferences, but those illustrated are recommended.

Synthetic ropes may be spliced but it may be complicated if there are many strands. There are many connectors and terminations available which offer a more practical solution.

Clove hitch
for temporarily making fast to a spar or stanchion. Non-jamming, may slip.

Constrictor knot
for securing tools or lines to pipes. More secure than clove hitch. Self-jamming.

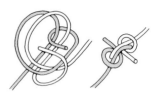

Double sheet bend
for joining different sized ropes.

Hunter's bend
Non-jamming, but unlikely to slip.

Double bowline
the most versatile of all knots, ideal for lifelines. Non-jamming.

Fisherman's bend
for securing to anchors and shackles. Self-jamming—will not slip.

Timber hitch
for vertical lifts or towing long objects.

All self-jamming.

Rolling hitch
a hitch that will not slide for securing to slippery cylindrical surfaces or a rope to a wire.

Tarbuck knot
a lifeline knot providing a loop which will not tighten but can slide up and down a spar.

Rope strength losses

Knots (loops, turns and locking crosses) in ropes reduce its strength by	55%
Hitches (knot tied around an object)	25%
Bends (two ropes tied together)	50%
Kinks	30%
Splices	10%

Rope is described by its diameter in millimetres.

In the UK, rope has been traditionally measured by its circumference in inches, but this is no longer correct.

3.9d WIRE ROPES

The diver will inevitably find himself handling a variety of wire ropes, each of which has been made to withstand the demands of a particular task. The rope's characteristics will be determined by:

1. Grade of wire.
2. Number and pattern of wire in a strand.
3. Type of lay.
4. Preforming.
5. Type of core.

Wire rope is used for both standing and· running rigging, the requirements for which are different. Standing rigging is made of minimum stretch wire, whereas running rigging needs to be flexible.
Wire rope is manufactured in grades signifying degrees of strength, toughness, abrasion and corrosion resistance. A commonly used grade would be Grade 160 (102 ton f/in²) (16.58 tonne f/cm²).

CONSTRUCTION

A single wire is a long slender solid rod. A strand is made up of several wires twisted around a central wire. The number of wires in a strand affect the rope's flexibility and resistance to bending fatigue, and its resistance to abrasion. The greater the number of wires, the more flexible the strand. Most strands consist of seven wires, a straight centre wire with six smaller diameter wires winding helically around it.

Fig. 1. Composition of wire rope

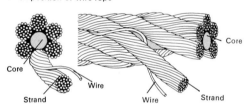

The construction specification of a wire rope is indicated by the number of strands and the number of wires in each strand.

Fig. 2. Some representative wire rope constructions

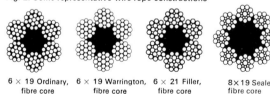

6 × 19 Ordinary, fibre core   6 × 19 Warrington, fibre core   6 × 21 Filler, fibre core   8 × 19 Seale fibre core

The wires in the strands may be all the same size, or be a mixture of sizes. Amongst the many variations of these, the most commonly used are the 19 and the 37 wire strand ropes (see Fig. 3a and b).

Fig. 3(a). Variations of basic 19-wire construction

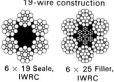

6 × 19 Seale, IWRC   6 × 25 Filler, IWRC

Fig. 3(b). Variations of basic 37-wire construction

6 × 31 Warrington Seale, IWRC

In wire rope, the strands are usually twisted around a hemp centre; in a cable the strands lie parallel to each other inside a flexible metal duct. These are sometimes called tendons.
Strands are classed according to their shape; round, flattened or concentric strand ropes, and locked coil ropes. Most are round strands.

Fig. 4. Strand classification

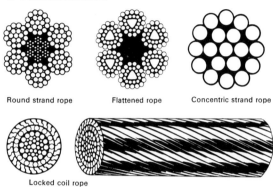

Round strand rope   Flattened rope   Concentric strand rope

Locked coil rope

'Rope lay' is the direction of rotation of the wires and the strands, clockwise or anticlockwise. Lay affects flexibility and wear. In regular lay ropes the wire in the strands are laid one way whilst the strands are laid the opposite way. This lay offers good resistance to kinking and twisting and makes them easy to handle.
In Langs lay ropes, both the wire and the strands are laid in the same direction. Langs lay ropes have greater resistance to abrasion and are very flexible, but liable to kinking.
Unless otherwise stated, the standard rope is a right regular lay.

Fig. 5. Rope lay

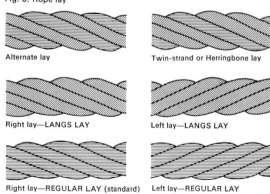

Alternate lay   Twin-strand or Herringbone lay

Right lay—LANGS LAY   Left lay—LANGS LAY

Right lay—REGULAR LAY (standard)   Left lay—REGULAR LAY

Preforming a rope is a manufacturing process which shapes the wires and strands so that they do not tend to straighten out when cut.

Fig. 6. Preforming

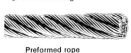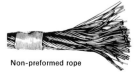

Preformed rope   Non-preformed rope

Cores form the heart of a rope around which the strands are laid, and prevent them from jamming against each other when flexing. Cores may be of fibre or wire. Wire cores stretch less and are stronger, but are less resilient and resistant to shock than fibre cores.

The size of a wire rope is its length measured in metres and its diameter in millimetres. Be careful to measure diameter at its widest as shown in Fig. 7.

Fig. 7. Measuring the diameter of a rope

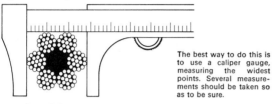

The best way to do this is to use a caliper gauge, measuring the widest points. Several measurements should be taken so as to be sure.

SAFE WORKING LOADS

The load on a wire rope should be only a fraction of its breaking load. This fraction is called the factor of safety (FoS) and varies between 5 and 10, according to whether the rope is used for carrying personnel.

TO FIND THE SAFE WORKING LOAD

$$\text{Factor of safety} = \frac{\text{Min. breaking strength of the rope}}{\text{Max. safe working load (SWL)}}$$

The maximum safe working load (SWL) is calculated as follows:

$$\text{Maximum SWL} = \frac{\text{Min. breaking strength of the rope}}{\text{Factor of safety}}$$

$$= \frac{\text{Min. breaking strength}}{5}$$

EXAMPLE

If the wire rope catalogue gives the breaking strength of the rope as 10 tonnes, the maximum SWL is:

$$\text{Maximum SWL} = \frac{10 \text{ tonnes}}{5} = 2 \text{ tonnes}$$

The minimum breaking loads are found in BS 302, or in the manufacturer's rating tables. If the manufacturer quotes the breaking strength, that figure must be divided by the FoS to get the SWL. A useful rule of thumb method of calculating the approximate SWL is:

SWL = Rope dia. × Rope dia. × 8

EXAMPLES:

(a) $\frac{1}{2}$″ diameter rope   SWL = $\frac{1}{2} \times \frac{1}{2} \times 8$ = 2 tonnes

(b) 1″ diameter rope   SWL = $1 \times 1 \times 8$ = 8 tonnes

[1 tonne = 0.98 ton = 1000 kg]

Although wire rope looks indestructible, a programme of periodic inspection is necessary. Wire rope in constant service must be inspected weekly, with a thorough examination every month. A wire rope inspection report should be logged by a competent person, which will give an indication of when the rope should be taken out of service. When a rope is considered to be unfit for service it must be destroyed, not left discarded. The kind of defects that an inspector would look for are signs of abrasion, wear, fatigue, corrosion, kinking and evidence of incorrect reeving.

END FITTINGS AND CONNECTIONS

Splicing of wire rope is best left to riggers. The average diver will probably use the special fittings available. Care must be exercised to ensure that the fittings are of the correct load rating (SWL) and installed correctly.

END FITTINGS

Swaged socket attachments are used on permanent types of installations such as pendants. The steel sleeve is hydraulically compressed over the rope. They are not suitable where there is much movement as ropes tend to crack at the socket entry. 100% efficient.

Fig. 8. End fittings

(a) Swaged socket   (b) Spelter socket   (c) Wedge socket

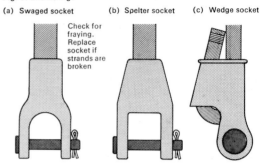

Check for fraying. Replace socket if strands are broken

Zinc (spelter) sockets are the most reliable of terminal fittings, made by setting the rope in molten zinc in a white metal capping. 100% efficient.

Wedge sockets are simple and easy devices for anchoring a wire rope and can be just as easily detached. Care must be taken to prevent the wedges being forced out. 70% efficient.

CONNECTIONS

The most common method of making an eye or attaching a wire rope is with cable or Crosby clips (U-bolt and saddle type) or with 'fist grips' (double integral saddle-and-bolt type). U-bolt clips must always be fitted with the U-bolt section on the dead or short end of the rope, and with the saddle on the long end.

Fig. 9. Connections

(a) Cable clip or Crosby clip

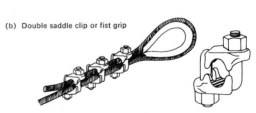

(b) Double saddle clip or fist grip

Connections are probably the largest single known cause of mooring failures and should always be suspect in failures from unknown cause. Connectors are the weakest point in the system.

3.9e SLINGS

Slings for attaching a purchase to a load come in many different types and materials. It is important to use a specific configuration of legs and to position them correctly around the load. The aim is to keep the centre of gravity as low as possible. The misuse of slings is a frequent cause of accidents. Slings must be of more than sufficient strength to lift the load. The safe working load may be found in the manufacturer's SWL table.

All these points are important because it is essential in a lifting operation that the load is rigged so that it is stable. A stable load is one in which the centre of gravity is directly below the main hook and below the lowest point of attachment of the slings.

The centre of gravity of an object is that point at which the object will balance. The entire weight is concentrated at this point. A suspended object will therefore always move so that its centre of gravity is below the point of support. The hook must always be directly above this point. A load which is slung above and through the centre of gravity will be stable and will not slide out of the slings. In practice, the centre of gravity is determined by judgement, or by cautious trial and error methods, lifting a little at a time. For crane signals see Section 7.7.

The angle between the legs of the sling and the load has a great effect on the stress imparted by the load. The lesser the angle, the more tension the legs have to bear. As a general rule, the angle should be kept greater than 45°. Avoid angles below 30° which would considerably increase the load on each leg. In practice, the angle at the hook between the slings is limited to between 0°–120°. Fig. 1 demonstrates the increase of tension with the decrease in angle.

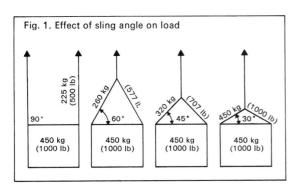

Fig. 1. Effect of sling angle on load

The most common configurations of slings and their specific applications are shown in Figs. 2, 3 and 4.

Fig. 2. Bridle hitches—for hoisting objects that have lifting lugs or attachments.

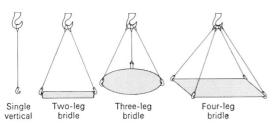

Single vertical | Two-leg bridle | Three-leg bridle | Four-leg bridle

Fig. 3. Basket hitches—for hoisting objects that can be balanced.

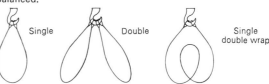

Single | Double | Single double wrap

Fig. 4. Choker hitches—not suitable for loose bundles from which material may fall.

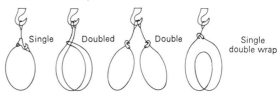

Single | Doubled | Double | Single double wrap

There are many uses for slings besides lifting loads and the choice of the material of which the sling is made depends on the job it is required to do.

WIRE ROPE SLINGS

These are the most widely used underwater because of their great strength and stability. Wire rope has considerable reserves of strength in the case of a failure. However, it is often forgotten that wire rope needs care and maintenance. Kinks must be avoided and attention must be paid to not exceeding its safe working life.

Fibre rope slings are pliant and grip a load well without damaging its surface. They are only used for light loads and they are rarely used underwater.

Fig. 5. Endless or grommet sling

These can be used in many configurations, and the one shown on the right is in the choker hitch configuration. Ensure that the splice is clear of load or hook.

Nylon rope slings between a chain choker and the crane hook are occasionally used to impart a moving force to an object, such as when picking up a pipe to line-up two flanges. The stretch in nylon can usefully act as a shock-absorber between the diving support vessel and the load when there is much swell. Nylon is stronger than fibre rope.

SYNTHETIC WEB SLINGS

These are not used extensively underwater but they do have several advantages.
1. They are not affected by moisture.
2. Being flexible, they mould to the shape of the load.
3. They are non-sparking and can be safely used with explosives.
4. They minimise twisting and spinning.

Fig. 6. Two types of synthetic webbing slings

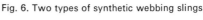
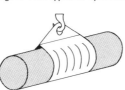
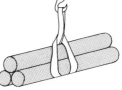

CHAIN SLINGS

These are the strongest of all types of sling and need minimal maintenance. Chain is very hard wearing and is the safest type of sling for lifting. Chain has a better grip on cylindrical surfaces than wire rope and should be used when slipping might occur. A good example of chain use is when lining up two flange bolt holes. A chain sling would be most effective in imparting a rolling force to the pipe. Chain should also be used when rigging has to pass over rough surfaces or sharp edges.

Safety factors when using slings

—Determine the load weight before lifting it.
—Be sure of the safe working load (SWL) of the equipment being used. Do not exceed it.
—Inspect all lifting gear regularly.
—Destroy defective equipment so that others cannot use it inadvertently.
—Watch the weather. Wind and swell can affect control of a hoist.
—Extreme caution should be exercised in temperatures below freezing ($0°C$, $32°F$) to ensure that no equipment is shock-loaded.
—Be careful to avoid electrocution caused by the contact of a hoist with a power line.
—Avoid sharp bends, kinks, pinching or crushing.

HOOKS ON SLINGS

Open hooks are not generally used underwater because of their tendency to become unhooked. Snap hooks or shackles are more reliable. There are some rules about using hooks:

1. With a 2-leg bridle hitch, when picking up a long load, the hooks should point outward. The exception is when lifting a joint of pipe by its ends, when the hooks would point inwards, as in Fig. 7(a).
2. With choker hitches, the bill of the hook should always point down. When picking up a joint of pipe with a double choker hitch the hooks should point down and outwards (Fig. 7(b)). As a general rule hooks must point down on vertical lifts.
3. Try to centre a crane hook as near as possible over a load.

Fig. 7. Lifting a pipe joint
(a) with a bridle hitch   (b) with a double choker hitch

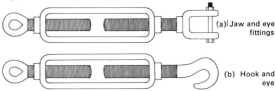

Fig. 8. Sling hooks

Sling   Snap   Safety   Sliding choker   Standard choker

RIGGING FITTINGS

Amongst the many varieties of rigging equipment there are special fittings for each particular application. All rigging fittings should be checked to ensure that they are of adequate strength to cope with the job, and must suit the rope or chain being used.
The following are some fittings most likely to be used by the diver.

SPREADER BARS AND EQUALISING BEAMS

These are used to prevent long loads from tipping during lifting and also avoid the use of low sling angles. Be sure to check that the bar is of the appropriate strength and material for the load.

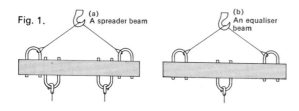

Fig. 1.   (a) A spreader beam   (b) An equaliser beam

TURNBUCKLES

Sometimes called rigging screws, turnbuckles are used to adjust the length or tension of rigging. The end fittings are selected to suit the particular application. If there is any vibration, the end fittings should be locked to the body to prevent it loosening.

Fig. 2 Turnbuckles

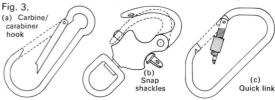

(a) Jaw and eye fittings

(b) Hook and eye

Other rigging fittings used for attaching lifting gear are: carbine or carabiner hooks and quick links. These are usually of small size and most handy used for attaching lifting bags or tools to the diver's person.

Fig. 3.

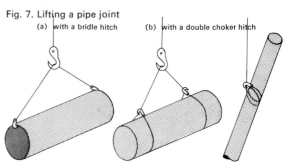

(a) Carbine/carabiner hook
(b) Snap shackles
(c) Quick link

Thimbles are made of galvanised gunmetal or mild steel and are used as linings to eye splices to reduce the wear from an attached shackle. They also greatly increase the strength of the eye. Thimbles are usually heart-shaped, but some are round or solid according to their purpose.

Fig. 4. Thimbles

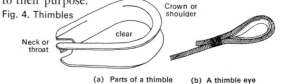

Crown or shoulder
clear
Neck or throat

(a) Parts of a thimble   (b) A thimble eye

SHACKLES

Shackles are made of wrought iron, mild steel or forged alloy steel; they are coupling links for joining chains to wires or ropes, or to a fitting. Shackles are more secure than hooks and should always be used between a tension member and a load.

Although there are specialized shackles for every purpose, there are two main types, straight shackles and bow shackles.

The size of a shackle is determined by the diameter of the metal in the bow section. The safe working load may be found in tables supplied by the manufacturer and is often stamped on the shackle itself.
Proof load = twice the safe working load.
Minimum breaking strength = 4 to 6 times the safe working load.

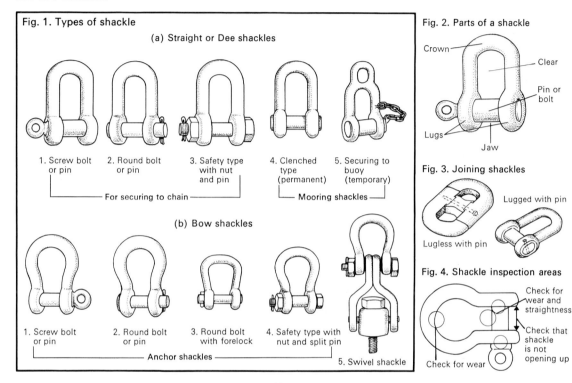

Fig. 1. Types of shackle

(a) Straight or Dee shackles

1. Screw bolt or pin   2. Round bolt or pin   3. Safety type with nut and pin   4. Clenched type (permanent)   5. Securing to buoy (temporary)

—— For securing to chain ——   —— Mooring shackles ——

(b) Bow shackles

1. Screw bolt or pin   2. Round bolt or pin   3. Round bolt with forelock   4. Safety type with nut and split pin

—— Anchor shackles ——   5. Swivel shackle

Fig. 2. Parts of a shackle

Crown   Clear   Pin or bolt   Lugs   Jaw

Fig. 3. Joining shackles

Lugged with pin   Lugless with pin

Fig. 4. Shackle inspection areas

Check for wear and straightness   Check that shackle is not opening up   Check for wear

Apart from the obvious necessity of using a shackle that is rated for the load weight, there are some definite right and wrong ways of using them. A shackle must never be pulled at an angle because this may pull the legs apart, as well as greatly reducing the shackle's lifting capacity. Always centralize the load on the bolt as shown in Fig. 4(b), packing with spacers if necessary.

For the diver there are several advantages in using a safety shackle (Fig. 1(a)(3)). Once the bolt is rammed home the load is secure and the diver will not have to take the weight or tension while he is screwing on the nut. When using a screw pin shackle the weight of the load has to be supported by the diver until the bolt is home and screwed up. A safety shackle bolt is secure from coming undone and is therefore safer; it can be made even more secure by inserting a pin or wire through the hole in the bolt.

The diver should ensure that he takes with him the right tool for screwing or loosening shackle bolts when proceeding to work under water. Whenever working with rigging which will be under tension, the diver should exercise great care to see that he and his umbilical are well clear.

Never substitute an ordinary bolt for a missing shackle pin.

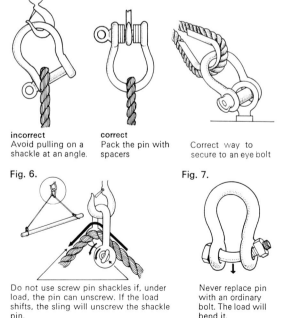

Fig. 5. Right and wrong ways of using a shackle

incorrect
Avoid pulling on a shackle at an angle.

correct
Pack the pin with spacers

Correct way to secure to an eye bolt

Fig. 6.

Do not use screw pin shackles if, under load, the pin can unscrew. If the load shifts, the sling will unscrew the shackle pin.

Fig. 7.

Never replace pin with an ordinary bolt. The load will bend it.

3.9f ANCHORS

There is an appropriate anchor for every type and size of vessel or installation, depending on the particular function the anchor is required to perform; the nature of the seabed where the anchor will be used; and the prevailing weather conditions. The seabed, as far as anchors are concerned, may be categorised into three types:

—Mud or silt, which offers little resistance to forces.

—Sand, which provides good holding for specifically designed anchors.

—Rock, where it is only the deadweight anchors which hold. Occasionally a fluke will catch.

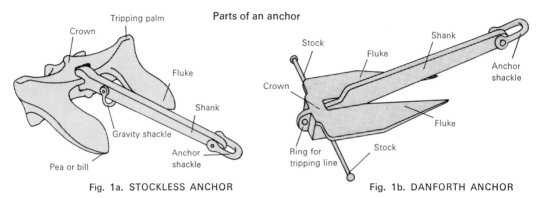

Parts of an anchor

Fig. 1a. STOCKLESS ANCHOR

Fig. 1b. DANFORTH ANCHOR

The holding power of an anchor is its efficiency expressed in terms of holding power per pound of its own weight. This is greatly affected by the fluke/shank angle, depending on the relationship between the flukes to the length of the shank, and to the tripping palm or stock stabiliser which turns the anchor to its correct burial position. The holding power of an anchor in sand can reach 35 times its own weight, but only about twice its weight in mud. The essentials for good holding power are the reliable opening of the flukes at the tripping palm areas and good fluke design to maximise deep penetration and stability.

The flukes will penetrate the seabed according to their design and the nature of the bottom. As an approximate guide, the angle of penetration (fluke/shank angle) should be as follows:

—In mud, approximately 50°.

—In sand, around 30°.

—Where the seabed is hard to variable, approx. 45°.

Fig. 2a. In hard soil, an anchor with a fluke angle of 32° will give the greatest holding power.

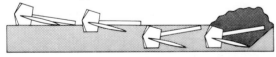

Fig. 2b. In hard soil, a 50° fluke angle will obstruct penetration and the anchor will keel over at its stock stabilisers.

Drag is the distance required for the anchor to be pulled over the bottom before attaining any holding power. An anchor will drag if it is of a type unsuitable for that particular sea bottom, or if insufficient cable is laid out.

Originally, ships' anchors were only required to hold a vessel in shallow water in the event of a propulsion or steering gear failure. It is the weight of the chain, not the anchor, that moors them. The anchor is only a nail in the seabed to stretch out the chain. The general rule is for the weight of the laid-out chain to be six times the weight of the anchor. To function properly, the anchor ought to be as nearly horizontal as possible as this position tends to drive the flukes into the seabed. To ensure this horizontal position, the seamanlike practice is to lay out a length of anchor cable or wire at least three times the depth of water. The ship's bow turns into the wind and rides to a long sloping catenary.

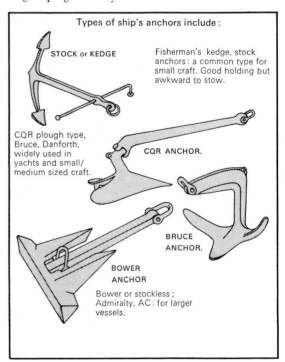

Types of ship's anchors include:

STOCK or KEDGE — Fisherman's kedge, stock anchors: a common type for small craft. Good holding but awkward to stow.

CQR plough type, Bruce, Danforth, widely used in yachts and small/medium sized craft.

CQR ANCHOR.

BRUCE ANCHOR.

BOWER ANCHOR — Bower or stockless; Admiralty, AC: for larger vessels.

CHARACTERISTICS OF ANCHOR TYPES

Anchors can be broadly classified into three groups:

1. Dragging anchors, which rely on their weight and, to some degree, on hooking or suction to the seabed for their holding power.

2. Burial anchors, which do not rely on weight but depend on the withdrawal resistance of their large flukes.

3. Embedment anchors, which are a form of burial anchor penetrating into the seabed by means of an explosive/hydrostatic/pneumatic charge.

DRAGGING ANCHORS

This type of anchor and anchor chain has a resistance to drag equal to its own weight in sandy soils. On a clay bottom its resistance is about 30%, and on mud it is even less. Dragging anchors would be unacceptable for use in a pipelay or derrick barge. Representative types of dragging anchors include clump, mushroom, fisherman or kedge, and stockless.

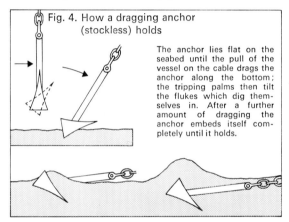

Fig. 4. How a dragging anchor (stockless) holds

The anchor lies flat on the seabed until the pull of the vessel on the cable drags the anchor along the bottom; the tripping palms then tilt the flukes which dig themselves in. After a further amount of dragging the anchor embeds itself completely until it holds.

BURIAL ANCHORS

The early stockless anchors were unstable and tended to turn the anchor so that the flukes pointed upwards and did not bite into the seabed, so stockless anchors were developed with stabilising stocks protruding through the head or crown. Unfortunately these have the disadvantage that the pendant wire is easily fouled around the stock; dropping could sometimes bend or break it. If a burial anchor such as a Danforth falls onto hard bottom, the results will probably be as shown in Fig. 2b. Should it fall onto soft bottom however, it may behave as in Fig. 5. At first, its heavy head will make it sink with the flukes pointing upwards, but as soon as a horizontal pull is exerted, the anchor will slide up on the flukes. The small tripping area on a Danforth could result in the flukes not turning around.

Fig. 5. Behaviour of a Danforth burial anchor in a soft bottom.

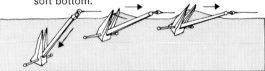

To overcome these problems, a new generation of stockless anchors has been developed, such as the Flipper-Delta anchor.

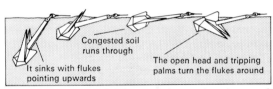

Congested soil runs through

It sinks with flukes pointing upwards

The open head and tripping palms turn the flukes around

Fig. 6. Behaviour of Flipper Delta anchor in a soft bottom.

GROUP	CLASS	CHARACTERISTICS	TYPICAL EXAMPLES	
DRAGGING ANCHORS	A	Clump types are simply weights, consequently effective in all grounds.	CLUMP.	
	B	Stock anchors with small fluke area and stabilisers at the front and the shank.	STOCK or KEDGE. MOORING ANCHOR.	
	C	Anchors with a square shank, no stock stabilisers, the stabilising resistance being built into the fluke design. Efficient in sand/heavy mud but drag on soft mud, shingle or shell.	US NAVY STOCKLESS, BEIJERS, UNION.	
	D	Anchors with extremely short thick stabilisers hinged at the rear and relatively short, more or less square shanks. Not efficient in soft mud.	AC14, STOKES, SNUGSTOW.	
BURIAL ANCHORS	E	Anchors with hinge and stabilisers at the rear and with relatively long shanks and stabilisers. Suitable for all bottoms and for sand and mud if allowed to settle.	DANFORTH, MOORFAST, STATO, BOSS.	
	F	Anchors with large hollow flukes, hinged near the centre of gravity and with relatively short shank and stabilisers. Effective in all bottoms, specially in soft ground.	STEVIN/STEVFIX, STEVMUD, FLIPPER-DELTA.	
	G	Anchors with 'elbowed' shank giving deep penetration. Effective in all bottoms.	BRUCE, BRUCE TS, HOOK, CQR.	

GROUP	CLASS	CHARACTERISTICS	TYPICAL EXAMPLES	
BURIAL ANCHORS	H	Anchors with ultra penetration and high holding power. Particularly effective in soft ground.	DELTA, KITE, WISHBONE (STEVPRIS).	
EM— BEDMENT ANCHORS	I	Anchors with ultra penetration, high HP to fluke weight ratio. Usually a single fluke attached to a long pendant. Does not rely on cable weight. Suitable in hard bottom.	QMC TENSION PILE, PEA (PROPELLANT EMBEDMENT ANCHOR), REA (RAFOSS EXPLOSIVE ANCHOR).	

Anchoring systems in use offshore have quite separate requirements from ships' systems and may be divided into two aspects:

For fixed installations, such as a guyed tower, capable of withstanding the most severe environmental conditions and requiring that the integrity of the structure be safely maintained by direct permanent contact with the seabed. Systems commonly in use are piled or gravity anchors.

For mobile installations, such as semi-submersibles, SPMs, DSVs or pipelay barges, where the environmental criteria would allow operations to continue. Mobile systems incorporate special anchors, chain cables and wires tensioned by dedicated winches such that the installation can be securely moored in all conditions. This is known as a marine system, but it should be appreciated that the mode of working a mooring system for a semi-submersible is entirely different from that for a ship. The increased depth of water (up to 610 m (2000′)), the inability to turn into the wind to face the prevailing weather, and the lack of a compensating catenary effect, all require different design approaches. These would involve the design of the anchors, a much longer scope of wire, increased horsepower on the winches and a planned geometry of layout. It should be noted that, regardless of whether an installation is classed as a ship or not, if it is involved in mineral exploitation in the UK waters, it is by definition an offshore installation and therefore must comply with DEn requirements.

Pendant or pennant wires and buoys

To facilitate breaking out mooring anchors, a pendant wire is secured to the crown of the anchor and located by means of a surface marker buoy. These pendant wires may be of a considerable length dictated by the water depth. Because of the rise and fall, the pendant may slacken and foul its own anchor. Supporting the pendant on a spring buoy reduces fouling and chafing.

Chasers

Pendant buoys have a way of getting lost. Fitting a chaser around the mooring line eliminates the need for them. To lay the anchor, the chaser is positioned around the shank near the crown and is towed out from the installation by the anchor handling boat. At the planned site, it is lowered to the seabed by the pendant wire. To recover the anchor, the same procedure is followed, the handling boat towing the chaser out to the anchor until it is arrested by the anchor crown, when it can be broken out and raised.

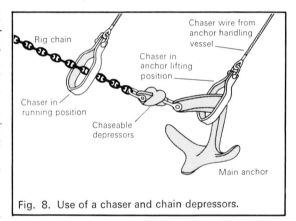

Fig. 8. Use of a chaser and chain depressors.

Anchor cradles or cow-catchers

Mooring anchors on installations are usually stowed on cradles or racks protruding from the side. The transfer of the anchor, chaser and pendant to the anchor handling boat is more easily accomplished from the cradle. Another method is to use davits.

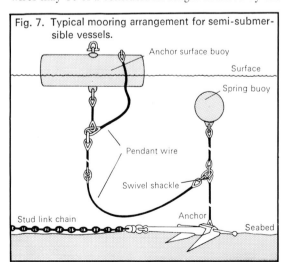

Fig. 7. Typical mooring arrangement for semi-submersible vessels.

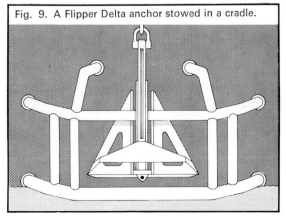

Fig. 9. A Flipper Delta anchor stowed in a cradle.

Operational equipment

4.1 SUBMERSIBLES

The difference between a submarine and a submersible is one of autonomy, of size and independence from surface support. Whereas a submarine carries its own fuel to recharge its batteries, a submersible relies on a support ship for its power requirements. Almost all submarines have been designed for military purposes whilst submersibles have been designed mainly for commercial use.

There are basically two types of submersible used in underwater work:

Manned submersibles.

Unmanned remotely operated vehicles (ROVs).

Each is part of a fully integrated system: vehicle, surface support vessel, handling gear, logistic and maintenance support.

The applications of the two systems can be complementary and often overlapping. There are certain tasks that can be performed only by a manned submersible, but there are many others that can be done by either. Determining factors are: safety of personnel, economics, logistic support requirements, surface support, deck-loading and space limitations, operating depths, duration of dives, visibility, current and other environmental conditions, urgency and complexity of the task, and the user's operating policies. The choice between using one type rather than the other does not always fall into an either/or category. Sometimes both are used together or even with divers.

In offshore diving the most important and frequent diver functions are:
1. Inspection and NDT.
2. Simple repair.
3. Repair of modules *in situ*.
4. Equipment salvage.
5. Debris clearance.
6. Measurements and alignment.
7. Structural repair.

Diving support services and life support systems are most affected by increased operational depths, and seem to grow arithmetically with size and cost. The cost of supporting divers at hyperbaric pressures exceeding 15 atmospheres has also become much more expensive. Offshore exploration depths are approaching both physical and economical barriers to the use of man in the sea. The alternatives to deep hyperbaric diving are manned 1 atmosphere systems and unmanned remotely controlled systems, which involve the redesign of subsea installations to make up for their lack of dexterity.

Not all the systems in the Table are capable of performing the ten functions listed. Table 1 evaluates diver alternative work systems and shows that man-in-the-sea is best, but more costly and in a greater state of risk at depth.

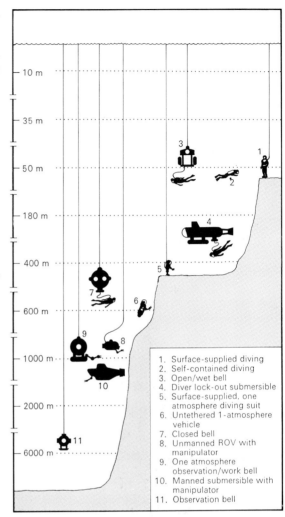

1. Surface-supplied diving
2. Self-contained diving
3. Open/wet bell
4. Diver lock-out submersible
5. Surface-supplied, one atmosphere diving suit
6. Untethered 1-atmosphere vehicle
7. Closed bell
8. Unmanned ROV with manipulator
9. One atmosphere observation/work bell
10. Manned submersible with manipulator
11. Observation bell

The normal operating depths and capabilities of a range of submersibles are shown above.

Table 1. Diver and Submersible capabilities compared

Rating: 1 2 3 4 5 → better

	Method of intervention	Visual inspection	Photography	CCTV	NDT	Seabed survey	Debris clearance	Salvage	Manipulative tasks	Mid-water operations	Vertical excursions	Large area coverage	Personnel safety	Payload
MANNED / ADS	Walking	3	2	2	2	2	3	2	3	1	1	1	4	1
MANNED / ADS	Thrusters	4	2	2	2	2	3	2	3	4	5	2	4	1
MANNED	1 at tethered, 1 man sub	4	3	2	2	3	3	3	2	4	5	3	4	2
MANNED	1 at tethered, observation bell	4	4	3	2	3	3	3	3	4	5	3	4	4
MANNED	1 at untethered, multi-man sub	4	4	5	2	5	3	3	2	4	5	5	4	5
ROV / TETHERED	Free-swimming — Large	4	4	4	2	5	3	3	3	4	5	5	5	4
ROV / TETHERED	Free-swimming — Small	3	3	2	1	3	–	–	–	4	5	4	5	1
ROV / TETHERED	Bottom crawling	2	3	3	2	4	2	2	3	–	–	4	5	5
ROV / TETHERED	Towed	1	1	2	–	4	–	–	–	3	4	5	5	5
ROV	Untethered Free-swimming	1	1	1	–	1	–	–	–	1	1	2	5	4
	Diver	5	5	5	5	2	5	5	5	5	5	2	3	1

Note: ADS manipulative capability is increased if anthropomorphic arms are used.

MANNED SUBMERSIBLES

Manned submersibles can be categorised into six main groups. Representative examples of each group are shown in brackets at the end of each paragraph.

1. Atmospheric diving suits (ADS):

One man crew; 1 atmosphere; human-powered, with a surface tether and hard wire communication line. (Jim, Sam, etc.)

2. One atmosphere, tethered one-man submersibles:

One man crew; 1 atmosphere; electrically powered from surface and with emergency batteries; some midwater movement capability from thrusters; Mantis is also capable of ROV operations. (Wasp, Spider, Mantis, etc.)

3. One atmosphere, tethered observation/work bells:

(i) Two man crew; battery powered; electro-mechanical lift-line for TV and comms; horizontal thrusters; some have advanced manipulators. (Arms I & II, OMB.)

(ii) Two or three man crew; electrically powered from surface; fixed reversible thrusters; emergency battery power; advanced manipulators. (Arms IV, OB (MOB), Checkmate.)

4. One atmosphere, untethered submersibles:

Two or three man crew; self-powered by batteries and independent of movement from the support ship; range limited only by the power supply. (Pisces I–XI, LR2 & 3, PC1601/2, etc.)

5. Diver lock-out vehicles:

Two or three man crew; 1 atmosphere control section with adjoining separate lock-out chamber for two or three divers.

(i) Battery powered. (Taurus A, LR4 & 5, LS-200-12 (SM358), Mermaid, etc.)

(ii) or with surface umbilical for power. (PC 1803)

6. One atmosphere transfer vehicles:

For transferring personnel in and out of underwater chambers, including rescue from a sunken submarine.

(i) Specifically constructed (DSRV, PC 1601/2, etc.)

(ii) or modified diver lock-out submersibles. (PC1801, Taurus A and LR5, etc.)

UNMANNED SUBMERSIBLES

Unmanned, tethered submersibles or ROVs (remotely operated vehicles) fall into four main groups.

1. Free-swimming, tethered vehicles:

Surface umbilical powered for use in mid-water or on the seabed; controlled from the surface or a manned submersible.

(i) Small observation vehicles: several capable of simple NDT work. (RCV 225, Scorpi, UFO300, Trec/Mk II, etc.)

(ii) Larger survey vehicles which can undertake varied tasks from pipeline survey to BOP work. (Angus, Consub 2, Scorpio, Trov/Hysub, etc.)

2. Bottom crawling vehicles:

There are several heavy duty bottom-crawling tethered vehicles built to carry out a variety of tasks such as pipeline surveys, visual TV inspection, debris clearance and cable burial. Because of their weight and stability, these tractors can perform tasks outside the capabilities of a submersible or ROV, such as operating in strong currents or lifting heavy loads. (Seabug, Seadog, Kvaener Myren, Eager Beaver, etc.)

3. Towed vehicles:

Powered and propelled by a surface support ship via an umbilical. (Teleprobe)

4. Untethered vehicles:

Self-powered from batteries; preprogrammed or surface-controlled by acoustics (telemetry). (Spurv, etc.)

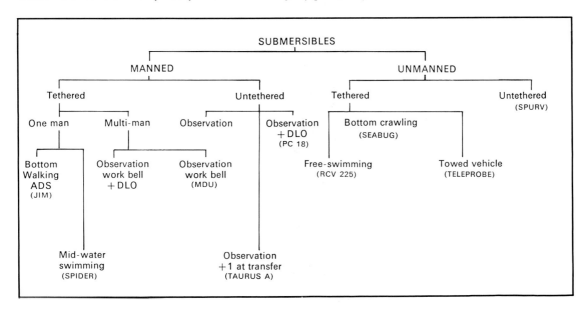

4.2 MANNED SUBMERSIBLES

Manned submersibles have an advantage over ROVs in the combination of human eye, hand and brain to make real-time observations and decisions. This provides the ability to react immediately to alter plans in response to a changing situation. Although only humans have this unique capacity for interaction, they do require life-support systems that are complex, expensive and indispensable. Their time-on-bottom can be further limited by weather, sea state and human endurance. Those not connected by an umbilical link with the surface have more freedom to move independently of the support vessel and avoid becoming entangled in underwater obstructions. The launch and recovery of most submersibles require the specialised equipment of a dedicated support vessel. Submersibles are particularly vulnerable when passing through the air/water interface. A sea state 4–6 is about the limit for them, depending on the spread.

As operating depths continually increase, the physical and economic barriers to the extended use of man-in-the-sea have forced the search for alternatives to deep hyperbaric diving. The major effort has been directed to 1 atmosphere systems and to unmanned ROVs. Because both systems lack the manual dexterity of the diver, a third area of development has been the im-improved capability of mechanical arms as well as the redesign of fittings on subsea equipment to accommodate them, such as simpler valving on well heads, etc.

Atmospheric diving suits and one-man 1 atmosphere submersibles

These craft are being increasingly employed in drilling support, particularly at depths between 100–300 m (330–1000'). Both types of craft are well suited to quick intervention in case of emergency, and also for search and identification in limited areas for such objects as sunken ships, downed aircraft etc. Their interaction with diving may be restricted to providing emergency back-up facilities for diving spreads, particularly in remote parts of the world.

1. Manned, tethered ADS (atmospheric diving suit)

JIM. A bottom-oriented, human-powered ADS. 15 Jims have been made to date. Bodies are constructed from magnesium alloy. Aluminium alloy limb joints are fluid filled.

Specifications for ADS type II
Overall height: 1.98 m (6' 6")
Maximum width: (Front) 1.04 m (3' 5")
Weight in air: 414 kg (910 lb)
Weight in water: 27 kg (60 lb) approx.
Maximum operating depth: 457 m (1500')
Life support: Oxygen make-up. Lung-powered scrubber via oral/nasal mask

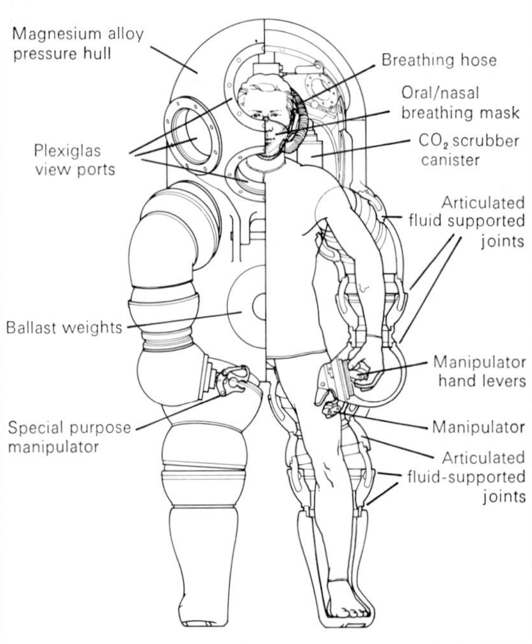

Life support duration: Approx. 72 hr, limited by adsorbent
Communications: Wire line and emergency through-water
Payload: Various
Builder: UMEL, Hampshire, England

2. One atmosphere, tethered one-man submersibles

SPIDER. A self-propelled inspection system with very good manoeuvrability provided by six independent variable thrusters. It can hover mid-water or anchor by extendable suction pads and is operated in the vertical mode. The hull is of GRP and electrically insulated. Articulated arms have powered claws. One set of emergency batteries provides 30 min. of power for thrusters; second set, 72 h power for communications. Spider is an integrated system which can be operated from any vessel of opportunity.

Fig. 1. JIM

- Magnesium alloy pressure hull
- Breathing hose
- Oral/nasal breathing mask
- CO_2 scrubber canister
- Plexiglas view ports
- Articulated fluid supported joints
- Ballast weights
- Special purpose manipulator
- Manipulator hand levers
- Manipulator
- Articulated fluid-supported joints

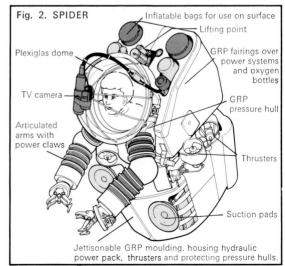

Fig. 2. SPIDER

- Inflatable bags for use on surface
- Lifting point
- Plexiglas dome
- GRP fairings over power systems and oxygen bottles
- TV camera
- GRP pressure hull
- Articulated arms with power claws
- Thrusters
- Suction pads

Jettisonable GRP moulding, housing hydraulic power pack, thrusters and protecting pressure hulls.

Specifications
Length: 1.5 m (5′ 3″)
Width: 1.3 m (4′ 3″)
Height: 2.2 m (7′ 5″)
Weight in air: 1025 kg (2360 lb)
Weight in water: Neutral
Maximum operating depth: 610 m (2000′)
Life-support: Oxygen make-up with electrically
  powered scrubber, with oral-nasal lung
  powered back-up.
Life-support duration: 80 hr
Communications: Hardwire through umbilical.
  Acoustic standby
Speed: 2 kt
Payload: 27 kg (60 lb)
Builder: Slingsby Engineering Limited, Yorkshire,
  England.

WASP. Similar in design to Jim but without legs and
operated in the vertical mode. Wasp is a laminated
GRP-aluminium ADS which can be manoeuvred by
thrusters operated by batteries. It has a mid-water
capability and can operate in currents up to 1.5 kt.
Trim is maintained by foot-operated pumps. Articulated arm manipulation.

Specifications for ADS type Wasp
Overall height: 2.6 m (8′ 6″)
Maximum width: 0.914 m (3′)
Weight in air: 454 kg (1117 lb)
Weight in water: Neutral (± 13.6 kg (30 lb))
Maximum operating depth: 610 m (2000′)
Life support: Oxygen make-up, re-circulation with
  electrically powered scrubber. Oral-
  nasal lung powered back-up
Life support duration: 86 hr
Communications: Wire line and emergency through-
  water
Speed: 1.8 kt
Payload: Operator + 30 kg (66 lb)
Builder: OSEL Group, Great Yarmouth, England

MANTIS. Has the capacity for bottom or mid-water
work and is unusual in that it can also be operated as
an ROV. Its small size enables it to approach restricted areas inaccessible to larger submersibles. Mantis
is operated in the horizontal mode. Although powered
via an umbilical, in an emergency it can operate for
4 hr on its own batteries. Manipulators can be
operated by remote control.

Specifications
Length: 2.5 m (8′)
Width: 1.37 m (4′)
Weight in air: 1600 kg (3500 lb)
Weight in water: Neutral (± 27 kg (60 lb)) trim
Maximum operating depth: 710 m (2300′)
Life-support: Oxygen make-up with electrically
  powered scrubber. Oral-nasal lung
  powered back-up
Life-support duration: 86 hr
Communications: Hardwire through umbilical.
  Acoustic standby
Speed: 2 kt DC main thrusters. 3 kt AC and electro-
  hydraulic thrusters
Payload: 200 kg (448 lb)
Builder: OSEL Group, Great Yarmouth, England

3. Observation/work bells

These craft have been used for drilling support in
deep water, for assistance during pipelaying and
carrying out similar tasks to those performed by free-
swimming submersibles. They differ from conventional diving bells in that observation bells' crew are
maintained at atmospheric pressure and usually have
some degree of independent movement. However,
many observation bells can be connected to submersible compression chambers. They are usually
launched and recovered through a moonpool on a
dedicated vessel. Although these craft may run off
vessels fitted with diving spreads, the only likely
diver-requirement would be in a rescue situation or
for surface swimming if the bell is forced to surface
away from its handling system.

OCEAN ARMS I & II. Both are two to three man deep
diving bells, self-propelled by two 5 hp electric
motors powered by the bell's own batteries. Both are
equipped with 'Arms' manipulators plus a grabber
type manipulator. Arms stands for atmospheric roving

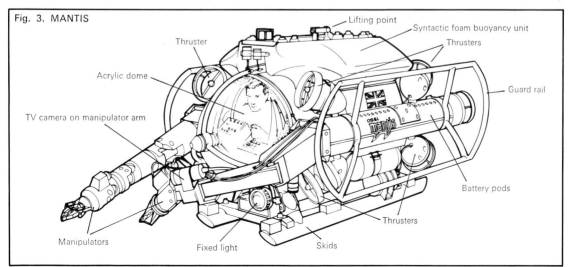

Fig. 3. MANTIS

Lifting point
Syntactic foam buoyancy unit
Thruster
Thrusters
Acrylic dome
Guard rail
TV camera on manipulator arm
Battery pods
Thrusters
Manipulators
Fixed light
Skids

manipulator system, a highly advanced manipulator which can be fitted to most submersibles. The system has two primary components, a master-controller operated from within the bell, and a limited slave-manipulator mounted on the hull. A special feature is the 'force feed-back' which allows the operator to feel the work he is performing. The umbilical cable acts as a lifting wire with a communications/TV link.

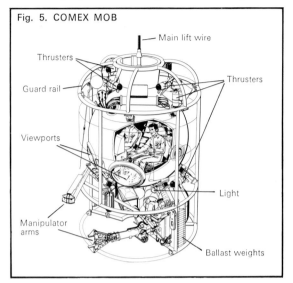

Fig. 4. OCEAN ARMS II

COMEX OB 1000-10 (MOB 1000). This 1000 m (3300') bell is a subsea observation and manipulation unit operated by two pilots at atmospheric pressure. It can manoeuvre within a 500 m (1650') radius from the mother ship. Manoeuvring control by eight fixed reversible propellers. Two sophisticated manipulators

Fig. 5. COMEX MOB

Specifications
Height: 3.5 m (11' 6")
Diameter: 2.6 m (8' 6")
Weight in air: 7711 kg (17 000 lb)
Weight in water: 227 kg (500 lb) positive when winched off clump weight. 318 kg (752 lb) negative with clump weight
Maximum operating depth: 914 m (3000')
Life support: Oxygen make-up with electrically powered CO_2 scrubber
Life support duration: Normal 8 hr, max. 144 hr
Communications: Surface and underwater hardwire telephone
Speed: 2 kt submerged max.
Payload: 227/454 kg (500/1000 lb)
Builder: Perry Oceanographics Inc., Florida, USA

OCEAN ARMS IV. This is also a two-man work bell equipped with Arms and a grabber manipulator; it differs from I and II in that it is supplied with power via an umbilical from its surface support vessel. Manoeuvring is by two 8 hp electric motors powering two fixed reversible variable thrusters. A 726 kg (1697 lb) clump weight controls vertical movement up to 24 m.

Specifications
Height: 2 m (6')
Beam: 2.2 m (7')
Weight in air: 6.3 tonnes
Maximum operating depth: 457 m (1500')
Life support: Oxygen make-up, electrically powered sodalime CO_2 scrubber
Life support duration: 180 man hr
Communications: Two: one hardwire, one through-water acoustic
Speed: Max. 3 kt
Payload: 567 kg (1247 lb)
Builder: Can-Dive Services, 250 East Esplanade, North Vancouver, BC, Canada V7L 1A3

Specifications
Height: 3.85 m (12' 6")
Diameter: 2.65 m (8' 8")
Weight in air: 9642 kg (21 280 lb)
Weight in water: 350 kg (784 lb)
Maximum operating depth: 1000 m (3300')
Life-support: Oxygen make-up, with electrically powered CO_2 scrubber
Life-support duration: 144 hr
Communications: Interphone, through water communications for emergency use
Speed: 2 kt
Payload: 300 kg (672 lb)
Builder: Comex Industries, Marseilles, France

4. One atmosphere, untethered submersibles

These vehicles usually operate from a dedicated support ship. They are ideally suited to survey and inspection work over long distances or in large areas, and may be employed for inspection and NDT tasks around platforms and other structures. They are not likely to work with divers, but diver/swimmers might be required to support launch and recovery from support vessels.

LR2. A very manoeuvrable, high payload, fibreglass submersible; battery-powered; one 10 hp main propulsion motor and two 5 hp lateral thrusters. Two additional transverse 5 hp thrusters are fitted. Emergency batteries. A client engineer can be carried in addition to the two crew.

Specifications
Height: 2.6 m (8' 6")
Beam: 3 m (10')
Length: 7.3 m (24')
Weight in air: 13 200 kg (29 120 lb)

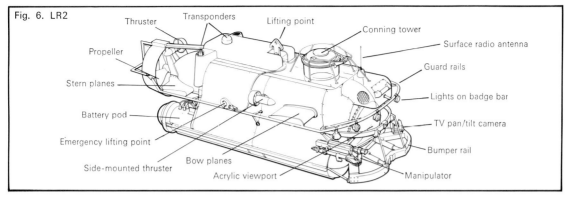

Fig. 6. LR2

Thruster — Transponders — Lifting point — Conning tower — Surface radio antenna — Guard rails — Lights on badge bar — TV pan/tilt camera — Bumper rail — Manipulator — Acrylic viewport — Bow planes — Side-mounted thruster — Emergency lifting point — Battery pod — Stern planes — Propeller

Maximum operating depth: 366 m (1200′)
Life support: Oxygen make-up and electrically powered CO_2 scrubber
Life support duration: 7 days (for 3 occupants)
Communications: VHF, line-of-sight to horizon on surface. Through-water when underwater
Speed: Max. 2 kt
Payload: 544 kg (1200 lb)
Builder: Slingsby Engineering Limited, Yorkshire, England

PC 1602. A four man crew medium-sized deep diving submersible, capable of dry transfers. It is constructed of HY-100 steel in three nested spheres. The centre sphere allows dry transfer at 1 atmosphere at great depth. Power is provided from its own batteries to one 10 hp electric motor driving the main propeller, two lateral and two 1 hp bow thrusters. Two Perry fixed rate electro-hydraulic manipulators are standard equipment. Emergency batteries.

Specifications:
Height: 2.9 m (9′ 6″)
Beam: 2.4 m (8′)
Length: 7.6 m (25′)
Weight in air: 15 700 kg (35 000 lb)
Maximum operating depth: 915 m (3000′)
Life support: Oxygen make-up
Life support duration: Max. 100 man hr
Communications: Surface and sub-surface u/w tele-phones, VHF radio-telephone
Speed: Max. 2 kt
Payload: 340 kg (750 lb)
Builder: Perry Oceanographics, Florida, USA

PISCES VIII. A very deep diving submersible used extensively for positioning tasks on the installation of guide bases and BOP stacks, and for entry and re-entry manoeuvres. Pisces VIII has been found to be a more efficient, faster technique than sonar TV systems acting alone. Spherical pressure hull of HY-100 steel. Batteries power two 5 hp reversible side thrusters. One heavy duty and one general purpose manipulator. Two to three crew.

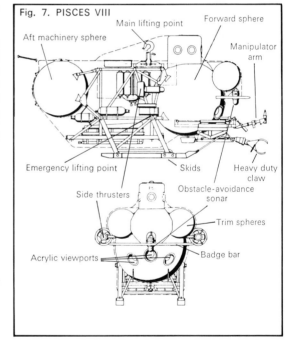

Fig. 7. PISCES VIII

Aft machinery sphere — Main lifting point — Forward sphere — Manipulator arm — Emergency lifting point — Skids — Heavy duty claw — Side thrusters — Obstacle-avoidance sonar — Trim spheres — Acrylic viewports — Badge bar

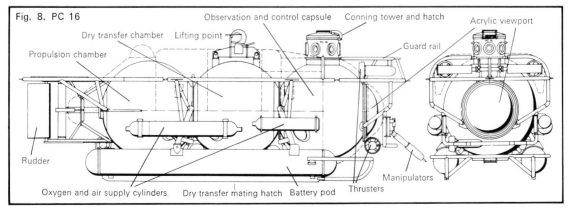

Fig. 8. PC 16

Propulsion chamber — Dry transfer chamber — Lifting point — Observation and control capsule — Conning tower and hatch — Acrylic viewport — Guard rail — Rudder — Oxygen and air supply cylinders — Dry transfer mating hatch — Battery pod — Thrusters — Manipulators

Specifications

Height: 3.2 m (10′ 7″)
Beam: 3.3 m (10′ 8″)
Length: 6.2 m (20′ 5″)
Weight in air: 11 542 kg (25 445 lb)
Maximum operating depth: 1000 m (3280′)
Life support: Oxygen make-up with electrically powered scrubbers
Life support duration: 168 man hr
Communications: Underwater 27 and 9 kHz telephone, surface VHF radio
Speed: 2 kt
Payload: 204 kg (450 lb)
Builder: International Hydrodynamics Ltd, Vancouver, BC, Canada

5. Diver lock-out submersibles

These combine the versatility, endurance and hardware capabilities of the manned submersible with the manual dexterity of the diver. DLO submersibles can be used in various modes, such as seabed lock-out, mid-water lock-out whilst fixed to a structure, 1 atmosphere transfer and submarine rescue. One pressure hull section is at 1 atmosphere, the other can be brought to ambient pressure. One of the chief advantages of the DLO submersible over other systems is its mobility. Divers can be transported to the work site which can be any distance away from the support vessel and they can observe and plan their work before entering the water. The submersible's underwater navigation systems can position it ± 2 m with respect to the surface. The divers can be directly monitored by a supervisor remaining within the submersible. The DLO submersible provides a high level of diver safety and rescue. Variable buoyancy tanks enable the pilot to compensate for its diver's movements. Some DLOs' lock-out chambers are preheated. DLOs can be used as hyperbaric lifeboats in emergencies.

The main limitation of DLO submersibles is presently their limited power to supply the thrusters, diver heating and electronic instrumentation, etc.

The combination of diver and submersible is particularly effective for underwater pipeline or rig maintenance, search and recovery operations and underwater operations with hydraulic tools. DLO submersibles are generally run from dedicated support ships with built-in transfer locks and DCCs. The MDU (mobile diving unit) is a hybrid vehicle combining the capabilities of a lock-out vehicle with an observation bell and receives all services via an umbilical.

TAURUS A. One of the largest DLO submersibles built with a long range and many capabilities. It is capable of effecting a dry transfer of 10–22 personnel at one time. Usually carries two crew and one observer in forward cylindrical steel compartment plus two to three divers in spherical dry transfer chamber. Manoeuvred by two 5 hp stern thrusters, two lateral and one 5 hp transverse thruster, powered by 975 Ah (134 kWh), 120 V batteries. 24V auxiliary and 12V emergency batteries.

Specifications

Length: 10.4 m (34′)
Beam: 4 m (13′)
Height: 3.7 m (12′)
Weight in air: 24 040 kg (53 000 lb)
Maximum operating depth: 335 m (1100′)
Life support: Oxygen carried externally. CO_2 removed by sodalime and/or LiOH.
Life support duration: 168 man hr (minimum)
Communications: Surface VHF FM transceiver; underwater telephone transceiver —supervisor to lock out. Unscrambler fitted in 1 atmosphere compartment; pinger receiver
Speed: 2.7 kt
Payload: 907 kg (2000 lb)
Builder: International Hydrodynamics Limited, Vancouver, BC, Canada

LS-200-12 (SM 358). Capable of observation missions to 300 m and DLO missions to 200 m. Two to three man crew. Two divers and one bellman can operate for 4 hr bounce diving to 100 m, or 2 man hr. Saturation diving to 200 m, with decompression aboard support ship. Manoeuvred by a main swivel thruster and three lateral and vertical thrusters. Battery-powered, 48 kWh. Two hydraulically powered manipulator and gripping arms.

Specifications

Length: 7 m (23′)
Beam: 2.5 m (8′)
Height: 2.8 m (9′)
Weight in air: 12 473 kg (27 500 lb)
Maximum operating depth: 300m (1000′) observation;

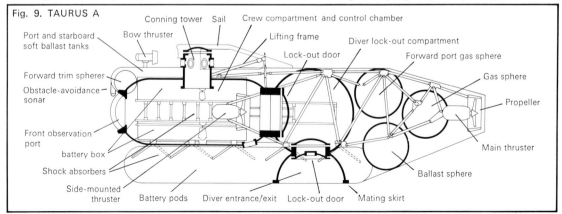

Fig. 9. TAURUS A

Conning tower Sail Crew compartment and control chamber
Port and starboard soft ballast tanks Bow thruster Lifting frame Diver lock-out compartment
Lock-out door Forward port gas sphere
Forward trim spheres Gas sphere
Obstacle-avoidance sonar Propeller
Front observation port Main thruster
battery box Ballast sphere
Shock absorbers
Side-mounted thruster Battery pods Diver entrance/exit Lock-out door Mating skirt

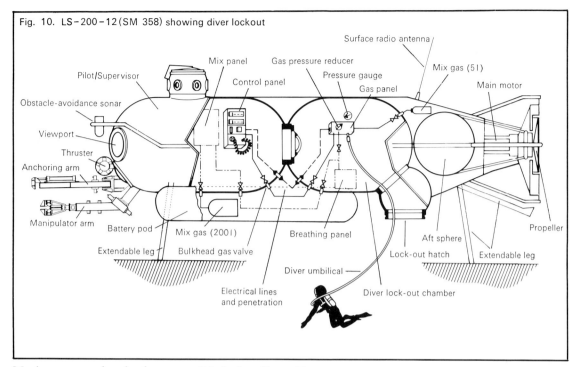

Fig. 10. LS-200-12(SM 358) showing diver lockout

Maximum operating depth: 200 m (660') for diver
lock-out
Life support duration: Normal endurance 3–8 hr;
diver lock-out 4 man hr.
Communications: Three systems: intercompartmen-
tal telephone, submersible to
diver, unscrambler intercom. Submersible to surface 100 W ultrasonic telephone
Speed: 3 kt. Operating range: 15 km at 2 kt
Payload: 300 kg (672 lb)
Builder: Comex Industries, Marseilles, France

Other than the US Navy deep submergence rescue
vehicles (DSRV), only two other 1 atmosphere
transfer submersibles have been built, neither of
which have yet been used for transfer work. If the
development of neutrabaric underwater chambers
progresses, personnel will be required to transfer
between the submersible and the underwater chamber
to do their work.
Unlike divers entering and leaving an SCC at
ambient pressure, non-diving personnel will transfer
at atmospheric pressure into capsules where there is
an external overpressure. Many of the larger atmospheric underwater habitats have a dedicated transfer
bell on guide wires. When conditions prevent this, a
submersible is the only feasible solution.

USN DEEP SUBMERGENCE RESCUE VEHICLE (DSRV).
These can carry a crew of three, one pilot and two
others and can rescue up to 24 persons per trip. They
are constructed of HY-140 steel and composed of
three interconnecting 2.3 m dia. spheres. DSRVs can
hover in a 1 kt current.

Specifications:
Length: 15 m (49' 3")

Beam: 2.4 m
Weight in air: 30 500 kg
Maximum operating depth: 1050 m
Life support duration: 24 hr min. for 27 persons.
Emergency individual life
support for 3 hr min.
Communications: Includes 8.0875 kHz underwater
telephone
Speed: 5 kt
Payload: (4080 lb)
Builder: Lockheed Missiles and Space Co., Sunny-
vale, California, USA

6. One atmosphere transfer submersibles

PC1801. A medium/small submersible with both a dry
transfer and a diver lock-out facility. It is designed for
offshore oil work; one steel 1 atmosphere compartment for pilot and observer; a second compartment
for diver lock-out or dry transfer plus a medical lock.
Batteries drive one 10 hp electric motor driving main
stern propeller, which can pivot. Two auxiliary
thrusters to provide low speed manoeuvrability. Two
manipulators and a comprehensive array of equipment.

Specifications
Length: 6.4 m (21')
Beam: 2.4 m (8')
Height: 2.7 m (8' 9")
Weight in air: 10 000 kg (22 400 lb)
Maximum operating depth: 310 m (984') Diver lock-
out 200 m (650')
Life support: Oxygen make-up, electrically powered
CO_2 scrubber
Life support duration: 8 hr; max. 7 man days
Communications: Underwater telephone
Speed: 2½ kt submerged max.
Payload: 454 kg (1000 lb)
Builder: Perry Oceanographics Inc., Florida, USA

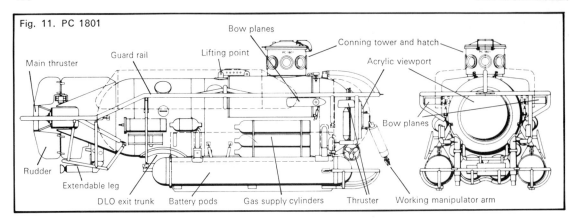

Fig. 11. PC 1801

Main thruster — Guard rail — Lifting point — Bow planes — Conning tower and hatch — Acrylic viewport — Bow planes — Working manipulator arm — Thruster — Gas supply cylinders — Battery pods — DLO exit trunk — Extendable leg — Rudder

4.3 UNMANNED VEHICLES

The high cost of putting a man into the water either as a diver or in a manned submersible, with all their attendant support, has contributed to the development of the ROV (remotely operated vehicle).*
ROVs are built in many different forms and sizes depending on the tasks they are required to perform. The advantages of ROVs are their unlimited operational endurance at the work-site and their ability to perform in hazardous areas. There is also a considerable economy in not having to provide life support systems and safety provisions during launch and recovery operations.

ROVs have many industrial, military and research applications. Their functional performance in industry can be listed as follows:

(i) Inspection and maintenance—locating and/or checking the condition of structures and performing simple maintenance tasks.

(ii) Monitoring—the observation and measurement of tasks.

(iii) Exploration drilling support—observation of wellhead systems, positioning of drill string, changing sela and operating valves.

(iv) Survey—the measurement and sampling of bottom features.

(v) Diver assistance—support of diver activities.

(vi) Search and identification—the location and identification of objects on the sea floor.

(vii) Installation and retrieval—assistance with installation of fixed structures and the retrieval of objects.

(viii) Cleaning.

1. Free-swimming, tethered vehicles

This category comprises the majority of ROVs ranging from the very small (RCV 225) to the large (Consub 2). Free-swimming ROVs (F/S ROVs) are integrated systems, consisting of an underwater vehicle, a deployment unit and a control station on the support vessel. No two systems are the same; each one is designed for a specific task. The vehicle carries the necessary equipment, such as lights, TV cameras and a manipulator. All vehicles have their own means of propulsion by thrusters, but they are tethered to the support ship which supplies the electric power. In strong currents, the drag on the tether can cause manoeuvring difficulties. To reduce this drag, some vehicles are deployed from an underwater launcher or 'garage' lowered to the operating depth by a deployment unit on the support vessel. The control station supplies the power to the vehicle and a control display monitors the vehicle's movements which are directed by an operator using a hand controller. The ROVs endurance is limited only by that of the surface operator.

F/S ROVs can be easily entangled by underwater obstructions and, as yet, their CCTV does not provide the three-dimensional viewing necessary for complex manipulative tasks.

F/S ROVs can normally be launched or retrieved in a sea state 5, but this would depend on the type of deployment unit and the support vessel. F/S ROVs are particularly suited to inspection tasks, blow-out emergencies and automatic pipeline tracking, and they are being used increasingly for manipulative work tasks. Many new developments such as fully automatic pilot capabilities, automatic depth keeping (ADK), pipeline sensors, and real time computer-controlled navigation and data processing have made the F/S ROVs a realistic and cost-effective alternative to manned submersibles, work bells or divers. Specially dedicated support vessels with dynamic positioning and automatic tracking make control of the F/S ROVs more reliable.

Small observation vehicles

RCV 225. Probably the most widely used ROV to date. The small ROV is often referred to as a 'remote eye ball', being little more than a tethered free-swimming TV camera. The vehicle is part of a complete system which is easily transportable. Its spherical syntactic foam hull is positively buoyant and is propelled by four electric thrusters. It carries two 45 W tungsten

* RCV is the exclusive trade name of ROVs manufactured by Hydro Products, California.

halogen lights and a low-light level SIT TV camera. Orientation at short range by TV. It can also be modified to carry Photosea 1000 and perform CP profiles by interfacing with a suitable probe.

Specifications, vehicle only
Height: 51 cm (1' 8")
Width: 66 cm (2' 2")
Depth: 51 cm (1' 8")
Weight in air: 82 kg (180 lb)
Weight in water: 2 kg (4½ lb)
Total shipping weight of complete system: 2520 kg (5600 lb)
Maximum speed at surface: 1.7 kt
Maximum speed at depth: 1 kt at 2012 m (6600')
Maximum operating depth: 2012 m (6600')
Deployment cable capacity: 400 m (1350')
Tether cable capacity: 120 m (400')
Builder: Hydroproducts, San Diego, California, USA

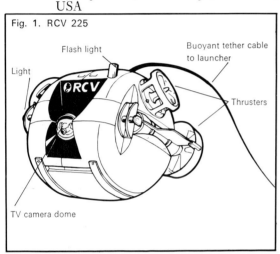

Fig. 1. RCV 225

Light
Flash light
Buoyant tether cable to launcher
Thrusters
TV camera dome

UFO 300. 'UFO' stands for underwater flying observer —a miniaturised inspection vehicle, primarily for use on offshore structures. Its small size makes it easily transportable and particularly suitable for inspection in areas inaccessible to larger vehicles. Four ¼ hp electric motors provide 12 lb thrust through ducted

jets. The system comprises a vehicle, deployment unit, and control console. SIT low light level TV camera, two 20 W halogen lights. Stereo-paired TV cameras or a Photosea 1000 35 mm camera available to retrofit.

Specifications
Length: 1.117 m (3' 8")
Weight: 66 cm (2' 2")
Height: 45.7 cm (1' 6")
Weight in air: 81.6 kg (180 lb)
Weight in water: Positively buoyant hull with 4.5 kg (10 lb) lead ballast
Maximum operating depth: 457.2 m (1500')
Maximum speed: 2 kt
Payload: 6.8 kg (15 lb)
Operators: 3
Builder: Submersible Television Surveys Ltd, Peterhead, Scotland and OSEL, Great Yarmouth, England

Larger observation/work vehicles

SCORPIO. An open-framed lightweight vehicle which is easily modified to suit individual tasks. It is widely used for exploration drilling support and pipeline inspection. Standard equipment includes a CTFM sonar, pan/tilt TV camera, a five-motion manipulator, automatic depth and heading control, a 1066 m tether cable, hydraulic reel and winch, operator controls, sonar and TV displays. It is propelled by four 5 hp hydraulic thrusters.

Specifications
Length: 2.1 m (7')
Width: 1.8 m (6')
Height: 1.5 m (5')
Weight in air: 907 kg (2000 lb)
Maximum operating depth: 914 m (3000')
Maximum speed: 2½ kt submerged
Payload: 40.8 kg (90 lb)
Operators: 3
Builders: Ametek Straza Division, California, USA

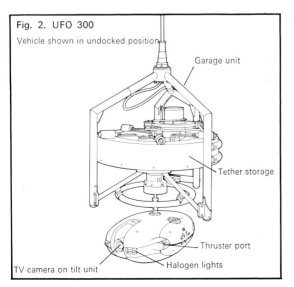

Fig. 2. UFO 300

Vehicle shown in undocked position

Garage unit
Tether storage
Thruster port
TV camera on tilt unit
Halogen lights

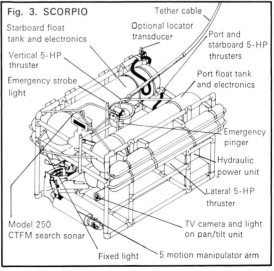

Fig. 3. SCORPIO

Starboard float tank and electronics
Vertical 5-HP thruster
Emergency strobe light
Optional locator transducer
Tether cable
Port and starboard 5-HP thrusters
Port float tank and electronics
Emergency pinger
Hydraulic power unit
Lateral 5-HP thruster
TV camera and light on pan/tilt unit
Model 250 CTFM search sonar
Fixed light
5 motion manipulator arm

CONSUB II. Designed for underwater surveys and inspection in offshore operations. Its open-frame construction/configuration caters for a variety of applications but is particularly suited to pipeline surveying. A special feature of Consub II is the mounting of the TV cameras on a rotating platform which is stabilised in azimuth in relation to the rest of the vehicle, so that Consub II will travel in whatever direction the pilot points the camera. The Consub II system uses a PDPII computer to control underwater navigation, automatic vehicle control, data collection and processing etc. These capabilities are of considerable use in survey work in producing immediate preliminary charts. Consub II is powered by the support ship via an umbilical and is propelled by four fixed reversible 12.5 hp thrusters.

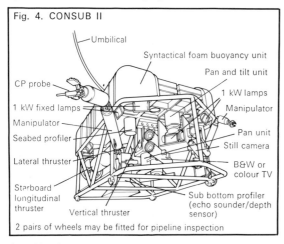

Fig. 4. CONSUB II

Umbilical
Syntactical foam buoyancy unit
Pan and tilt unit
CP probe
1 kW lamps
1 kW fixed lamps
Manipulator
Manipulator
Pan unit
Seabed profiler
Still camera
Lateral thruster
B&W or colour TV
Starboard longitudinal thruster
Sub bottom profiler (echo sounder/depth sensor)
Vertical thruster

2 pairs of wheels may be fitted for pipeline inspection

Specifications
Length: 3.7 m (12')
Width: 2.1 m (7')
Height: 1.7 m (6')
Weight in air: 2948.4 kg (6500 lb)
Maximum operating depth: 610 m (2000')
Tether: 914 m (3000')
Maximum speed: 2 kt submerged for unlimited time
Payload: 454 kg (1000 lb)
Operators: 7
Builder: British Aerospace, Bristol, UK

TROV (SMT). 'Trov' stands for tethered remotely operated vehicles. The Trov vehicle consists of a free-flooding aluminium frame designed to accommodate a large array of components. Power is supplied from the surface via an umbilical and drives two fore and aft 7 hp thrusters, plus a third laterally and a fourth vertically. In addition to the fixed ballast of syntactic foam that maintains the ROV at neutral buoyancy, Trov has a variable air ballast system to adjust trim when lifting loads or using special tools.
Standard equipment includes two manipulators, a location system, an echo-sounder, a pinger, two CCTVs and a video system.

Specifications for Trov 9
Length: 2.7 m (9')
Width: 1.3 m (4' 2")
Height: 1.3 m (4' 2")

Umbilical length: 1067 m (3500')
Weight in air: 1633 kg (3600 lb)
Weight in water: neutral
Maximum operating depth: 914 m (3000')
Maximum speed: 2 kt
Payload: 136 kg (300 lb)
Operators: 2
Builders: International Submarine Engineering Ltd, Canada

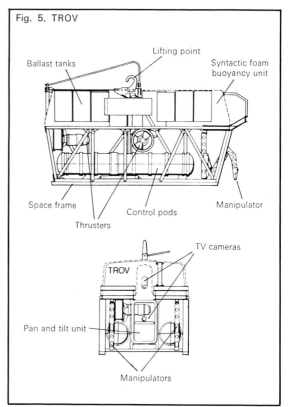

Fig. 5. TROV

Ballast tanks
Lifting point
Syntactic foam buoyancy unit
Space frame
Control pods
Manipulator
Thrusters
TV cameras
TROV
Pan and tilt unit
Manipulators

2. Bottom crawling tethered vehicles

Several heavy duty bottom crawling tethered vehicles have been built to carry out trenching tasks on telephone cables and flowlines and lift heavy loads etc. These vehicles have had varying success and some are still engaged in oil-related work. Several new trenching vehicles are coming into service but are, as yet, unproven.

SEABUG I/II. A heavy duty four-wheeled seabed vehicle designed for trenching and pipeline surveys. Because of its stability Seabug can perform tasks outside the capabilities of ROVs or submersibles, such as operating in strong currents or lifting heavy loads. It is launched by winch and 'A' frame from its support vessel or platform. The system comprises an underwater vehicle and its handling equipment, a power generator, control cabin and gyrocompass. Though usually monitored and remotely directed from the support vessel, Seabug can also be controlled underwater by a manned submersible or a diver. Standard equipment includes three CCTV cameras, a video-tape system, still camera, lights, sonar, sub-bottom profiler (UDI), trench profiler (UDI) and a CD probe (UDI).

Specifications
Length: 3.9 m (13′)
Width: 2.2 m (7′ 3″)
Height: 1.4 m (4′ 10″)
Weight in air: 4082 kg (9000 lb)
Maximum operating depth: 305 m (1000′)+ (limited by umbilical length)
Maximum speed: 2½ kt submerged
Payload: 907 kg (2000 lb)
Operators: 2 (6 required for prolonged work)
Builders: UDI Group, Aberdeen UK

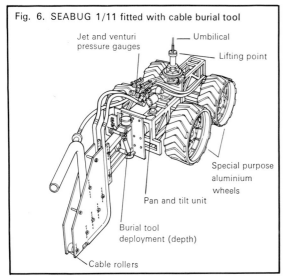

Fig. 6. SEABUG 1/11 fitted with cable burial tool

Jet and venturi pressure gauges
Umbilical
Lifting point
Special purpose aluminium wheels
Pan and tilt unit
Burial tool deployment (depth)
Cable rollers

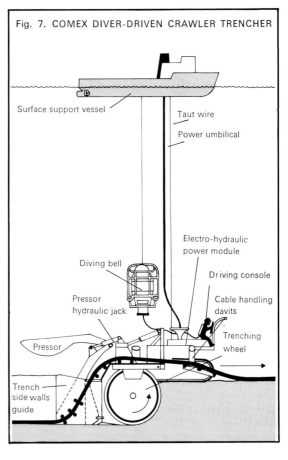

Fig. 7. COMEX DIVER-DRIVEN CRAWLER TRENCHER

Surface support vessel
Taut wire
Power umbilical
Electro-hydraulic power module
Diving bell
Driving console
Cable handling davits
Pressor hydraulic jack
Trenching wheel
Pressor
Trench side walls guide

COMEX DIVER DRIVEN CRAWLER TRENCHER. Designed to protect and stabilise any type of submarine pipeline or cable; consists of a crawler with interchangeable trenching tools. The trawler receives electrical power from the surface through an umbilical. Electro-hydraulic sources drive the tracked vehicle and power the trenching tools and ancillary systems. The crawler and the attached trenching tool are lowered to the seabed by a crane and then controlled by a diver. The line to be entrenched can be laid before or during the trench cutting operation. It is then guided through the machine, above the trenching tool. The performance of the machine and the diver are monitored from the surface by continuously recording data and TV video. The surface support can be anchored or dynamically positioned. Positioning of the support vessel in relation to the crawler is achieved using video (shallow water), acoustic beacons or a DP taut-wire connection (deep water). The two types of trenching tools are a plough with jetting nozzles and a trenching wheel. The plough is limited by the traction available from the crawler so a trenching depth of 0.8 m is the maximum obtainable in sand. The trenching wheel can perform over a large range of formations from medium consolidated sand to hard rock. Hard rock can be trenched 1 m deep at a mean speed of 0.6 m/min. The trenching wheel can be fitted with several types of cutting tools which are selected according to the soil to be trenched.

3. Towed vehicles

Towed vehicles are designed for specific tasks in deep-sea monitoring and seabed survey work, with particular emphasis on deep-sea mining. Towed vehicles are easier to operate for visual surveys than ROVs. Power is supplied from the support vessel via the tether to operate the instrumentation carried, such as low light level TV cameras and sonars.

DEEP-TOW. This vehicle is a powerful research tool for studying the geology of the seafloor. The precision of its complex instrumentation has produced data on the seabed unavailable before.

Specifications
Size: 3 m × 0.7 m × 1.3 m (10′ × 2′ 4″ × 4′ 3″)
Weight in air: 1000 kg (2450 lb)
Maximum tow speed: 2 kt
Operating depth: 6000 m (20 000′)
Builder: Scripps Institution of Oceanography, California, USA

There is another Deep-tow built in Germany by Dornier System GmbH, specially constructed for marine ore exploration. It is a high speed deep towing system in two stages, a passive controlled vehicle (Sep) and an active controlled vehicle (Gustav).

Specifications
Size: 3.3 m × 2.35 m × 0.7 m × 1.1 m (10′ 10″ × 7′ 10″ × 2′ 7″ × 3′ 6″)
Weight in air: 1361 kg (3969 lb)

Maximum tow speed: 8 kt
Maximum operating depth: 6000 m (20 000')
Builder: Dornier System GmbH, Germany

TELEPROBE. Operated by the US Naval Oceanographic
Office for survey and search work.

Specifications
Size: 3 m × 1.4 m × 2.1 m (10'× 4' 7" × 7')
Weight in air: 1588 kg (3600 lb)
Operating depth: 6000 m (20 000')
Maximum tow speed: 3 kt
Builder: US Naval Oceanographic Office, Washington DC, USA

4. Untethered self-propelled vehicles

Tether cables from ROVs to their support vessels
are restrictive and a potential hazard as they often
become twisted or fouled, sometimes even severed.
Although the technology for full control of untethered vehicles exists and several development
programmes are in progress, it is unlikely that their
use will become practical for commercial purposes
unless a major breakthrough in acoustic emission and
detection occurs.
However, there are several major programmes in
progress which have had some success. Two of these
are the University of Washington's Applied Physical
Laboratory's Spurv I and II, and the French
Epaulard vehicle developed by CNEXO.

SPURV I and II. There are three operational 'Spurvs'
(self propelled underwater research vehicle); the two
Mk Is are rated to 3000 m depths, and the one Mk II

rated to 1500 m. They are all acoustically tracked
and commanded from their support vessel which
carries a transducer array. Their 2 hp battery powered
motors drive a propeller which gives them a speed of
4–6 kt for 5–6 hr. The main pressure hull provides
buoyancy. Oceanographic data is multiplexed, digi-
tised and taped on a special recorder.
Builder: University of Washington, Applied Physics
         Laboratory, Seattle, USA

EPAULARD. The deepest operating untethered vehicle
at the present time with a depth capability of 6000 m
(20 000'). It has been designed for photographic and
bathymetric surveys of the seabeds. It navigates at a
constant altitude of 7 m above the seabottom. Epaulard is tear-drop shaped and is powered by its own
batteries driving one horizontal thruster. Standard
equipment includes a Benthos 377 still camera taking
up to 5000 pictures and a DC100 magnetic recorder.
Builder: Société ECA, Asnieres-sur-Seine, France

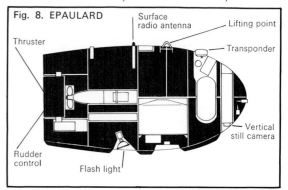

Fig. 8. EPAULARD
Surface radio antenna
Lifting point
Thruster
Transponder
Rudder control
Flash light
Vertical still camera

4.4 SUBMERSIBLE ELECTRONIC ANCILLARY EQUIPMENT

Except for the very specialised or lightweight submersibles, electronic and hydraulic instrumentation and equipment can be fitted to submersibles to suit any specific work to be done. Most will carry some form of lighting and CCTV, for monitoring, remote direction control and data collection. Many will be fitted with a mechanical arm (manipulator) and some with special hydraulic tools such as a cable-cutter or jetting gun. The electronic instrumentation might include underwater navigation systems, sonar and various NDT and surveying measuring instruments.

1. Navigation systems

Radio techniques used by surface vessels are inefficient underwater; instead, dead reckoning (calculating distances from a known position) or underwater sound (acoustic) systems are employed. The latter can be used by both surface and subsea craft. Acoustic techniques can be combined in various ways to form communication systems, telemetering systems, control and positioning systems.

If an array of transponders is placed in known positions on the seabed, submersibles can determine their position relative to them. Acoustic systems are classified by their baselines: Short (SBL) (5–20 m); Super Short (SSBL) (0.5 m); and Long (LBL) (20 m).

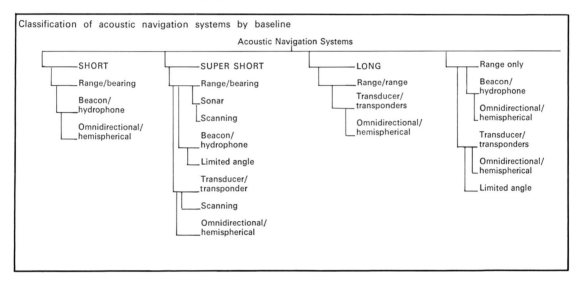

Classification of acoustic navigation systems by baseline

Acoustic Navigation Systems

- SHORT
  - Range/bearing
  - Beacon/hydrophone
  - Omnidirectional/hemispherical
- SUPER SHORT
  - Range/bearing
    - Sonar
    - Scanning
  - Beacon/hydrophone
    - Limited angle
  - Transducer/transponder
    - Scanning
  - Omnidirectional/hemispherical
- LONG
  - Range/range
  - Transducer/transponders
  - Omnidirectional/hemispherical
- Range only
  - Beacon/hydrophone
  - Omnidirectional/hemispherical
  - Transducer/transponders
  - Omnidirectional/hemispherical
  - Limited angle

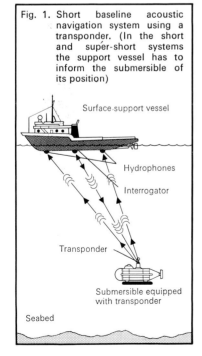

Fig. 1. Short baseline acoustic navigation system using a transponder. (In the short and super-short systems the support vessel has to inform the submersible of its position)

Surface support vessel
Hydrophones
Interrogator
Transponder
Submersible equipped with transponder
Seabed

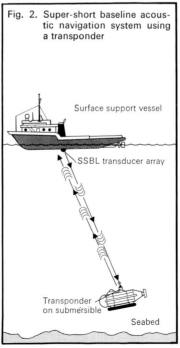

Fig. 2. Super-short baseline acoustic navigation system using a transponder

Surface support vessel
SSBL transducer array
Transponder on submersible
Seabed

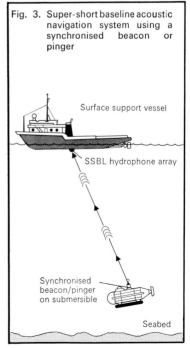

Fig. 3. Super-short baseline acoustic navigation system using a synchronised beacon or pinger

Surface support vessel
SSBL hydrophone array
Synchronised beacon/pinger on submersible
Seabed

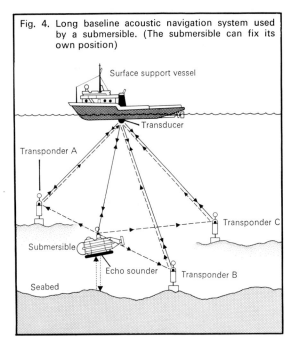

Fig. 4. Long baseline acoustic navigation system used by a submersible. (The submersible can fix its own position)

(vi) Scan trench profile sonar. Provides transversal profiles of a pipe trench by combining a high resolution scanning sonar with a very accurate echo-sounder.

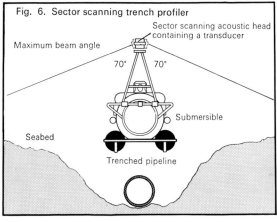

Fig. 6. Sector scanning trench profiler

2. Sonar systems

Sonar stands for 'sound and ranging' and is the detection of objects underwater by sound waves. There are many specialised applications, such as:

(i) Echo-sounder. Establishes the depth of water by measuring the time taken for a vertical sound pulse to reach the bottom and to the reflected back to the source.

(ii) Scan. (a) A continuous-sweep sonar to locate objects or for obstacle avoidance (OAS). (b) A continuous transmission frequency modulator (CTFM).

(iii) Side scan sonar. Fan-shaped sound beams provide a continuous shadow-graph of the surrounding ocean floor.

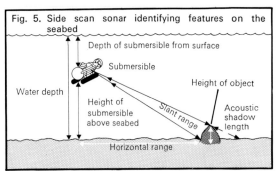

Fig. 5. Side scan sonar identifying features on the seabed

(iv) Sub-bottom profiler. Traces a reflection profile of the strata beneath the sea bottom, such as sedimentary rock layers forming the sub-bottom structure.

(v) Pinger/locater. Trainable receiver used to determine the direction of an underwater sound source, such as a submersible might use to locate a pinger on the seabed.

(vii) Through-water communications. Acoustic signals are modulated into speech in much the same way as in radio telephony.

Terms commonly used in acoustic systems

ACOUSTIC BEACONS

Transponder: A receiver/transmitter which will transmit a sound pulse through water on receipt of a suitably coded acoustic signal from another source. Most transponders on the seabed are positively buoyant and are fitted with a coded acoustic release for recovery. The source of the original signal can measure the range from the transponder by computing the time taken by the transmission.

Responder: Like a transponder, but with power and time trigger signal passed by umbilical—not acoustically transmitted or battery supplied.

Pinger: A battery-powered device which transmits continuous sound pulses through the water.

Transducer: A device for converting electrical signals into sound and vice versa.

Hydrophone: A device for converting underwater sounds into electrical signals. A fixed or directional receiver capable of detecting an underwater noise source.

Acoustic release: A method of releasing a positively buoyant package from its sinker on the seabed using sound pulses.

Velocimeter: An acoustic device for measuring the speed of sound in water.

Temperature and salinity meter: Gauge for measuring seawater temperature and salinity for use in calculating sound velocity.

4.5 DIVING SYSTEMS

Diving systems can be divided into two types: air or mixed gas. The mixed gas types can be further subdivided into bounce or saturation diving types.
As the depth of operation increases, first air diving is used, then mixed gas bounce diving followed by mixed gas saturation diving. There is, however, a considerable overlap with these techniques.
Figure 1 illustrates the major components of a saturation diving system.

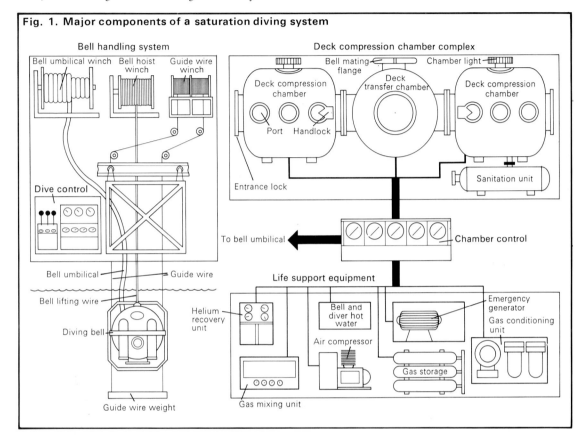

Fig. 1. Major components of a saturation diving system

The saturation diving system comprises five main parts:
Diving bell.
Bell handling and dive control.
Deck compression chamber complex.
Chamber control.
Life support equipment.

Diving bell

A variety of designs exists according to the individual requirements of the manufacturer, operator and the task. A bell may be a two or three man unit, the latter usually being used for construction tasks needing two divers out of the bell working together. It may be bottom-mating locking onto the top of a transfer chamber; it may have a rollover bottom-mating facility which connects with the side of a transfer chamber, or it may be side-mating using a second trunking and doors arrangement on the side of the bell. There are many variations of bell construction and the diver should familiarise himself thoroughly with the bell and its handling system before use.

BELL HANDLING AND DIVE CONTROL
The dive control station is the normal location of the diving supervisor during the dive. It is usually positioned alongside the launching point for the bell to allow easy control of the launch and recovery.
The diving bell may be launched over the side of a vessel or through a dedicated moonpool.
To launch over the side, an extendable A-frame, gantry or davit may be used to hoist the bell clear of the vessel.

In the moonpool arrangement, the bell usually has a specially built handling system for the particular vessel.

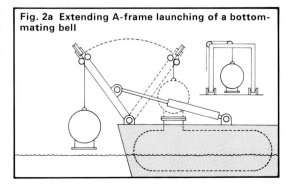

Fig. 2a Extending A-frame launching of a bottom-mating bell

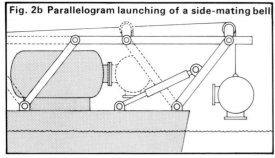

Fig. 2b Parallelogram launching of a side-mating bell

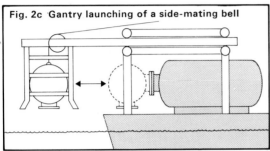

Fig. 2c Gantry launching of a side-mating bell

transfer chamber, receives the bell. It is used to store wet clothing, for kitting/de-kitting, showering and toilet.

Smaller 'hand' locks allow the transfer of food and small items in and out of the main chambers.

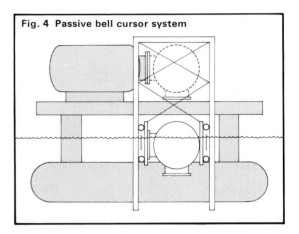

Fig. 4 Passive bell cursor system

A means of increasing the foul weather bell handling capability is provided by use of a bell cursor. The cursor may be 'active' or 'passive'. The passive cursor may be a heavy weight secured on vertical rails and can be attached to the bell. It is lowered by additional winches and allows the bell to sink steadily through the air/water interface. The bell is released from the weight near the bottom of the vessel where the water movement is not so great.

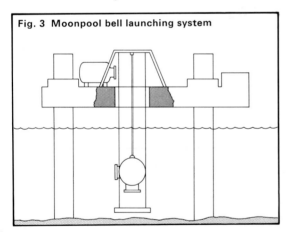

Fig. 3 Moonpool bell launching system

The 'active' cursor may have a similar means of restraining the bell against a vertical rail system. It would have, in addition, an active drive system to move the bell up and down the rails. Cursor systems are usually seen in dedicated DSVs with moonpools.

Deck compression chamber complex

The chamber complex may consist of up to five or more interconnecting chambers depending on the size of the task for which it is built. The chambers themselves may be subdivided internally by pressure bulkheads or simple partitions. The various locks provide sleeping, eating, showering, changing, toilet, storage facilities. One chamber, usually called the

CHAMBER CONTROL

This is the main base of the chamber operator/saturation technician and is the central point of life support control for all chambers and the bell.

Chamber control includes the following functions:

Regulation of all chamber compression and decompression procedures.

All routine gas analysis for the bell, chambers and gas banks.

All voice communications with chamber occupants.

Regulation of gas mix in chamber, its temperature and humidity control.

Control of handlocks including meals and materials transfers.

Control of all chamber electrics.

Control of any entertainment facilities such as radio, cassettetape, film etc.

Control of sanitation unit.

LIFE SUPPORT EQUIPMENT

The life support equipment tends to be grouped together for convenience. The exception is normally any oxygen handling equipment which should be located well away from areas of possible oil contamination, high temperatures, electrics and poor ventilation.

Bell diving operations

Bells may be used for routine diving in the following ways:

1 atmosphere observation dive.
Shallow air lock-out dive.
Shallow air (nitrox) saturation dive.
Deep mixed gas (heliox) bounce dive.
Deep mixed gas saturation dive.

The procedure for the main types of dive is summarised and illustrated in Figs 5a–d.

Some typical Diving Systems compared

Fig. 5a One atmosphere observation dive with diving bell

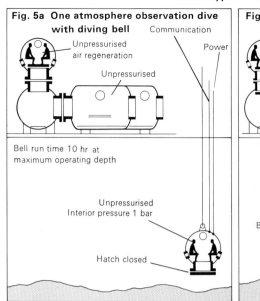

Unpressurised air regeneration

Communication

Power

Unpressurised

Bell run time 10 hr at maximum operating depth

Unpressurised Interior pressure 1 bar

Hatch closed

Fig. 5b Shallow, air lock-out dive

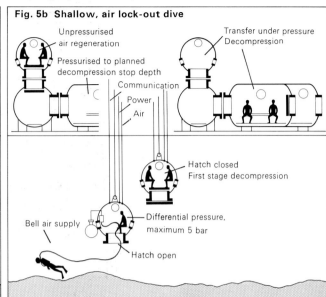

Unpressurised air regeneration

Transfer under pressure Decompression

Pressurised to planned decompression stop depth

Communication

Power

Air

Hatch closed First stage decompression

Bell air supply

Differential pressure, maximum 5 bar

Hatch open

Fig. 5c Mixed gas bounce dive

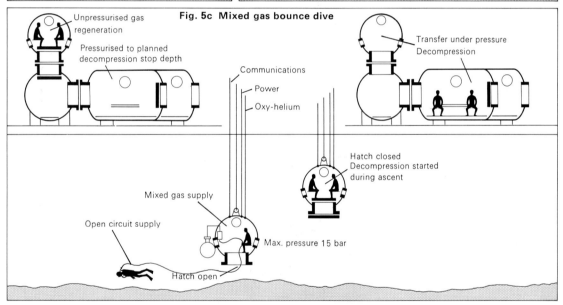

Unpressurised gas regeneration

Pressurised to planned decompression stop depth

Communications

Power

Oxy-helium

Transfer under pressure Decompression

Hatch closed Decompression started during ascent

Mixed gas supply

Open circuit supply

Max. pressure 15 bar

Hatch open

Fig. 5d Deep, mixed gas saturation dive

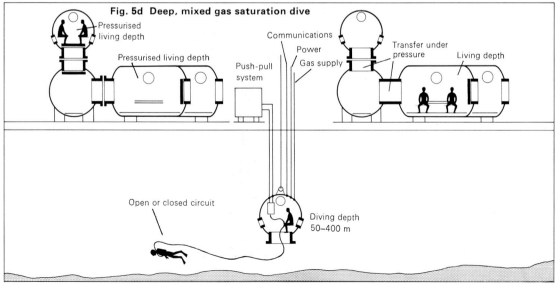

Pressurised living depth

Pressurised living depth

Communications

Power

Gas supply

Transfer under pressure

Living depth

Push-pull system

Open or closed circuit

Diving depth 50–400 m

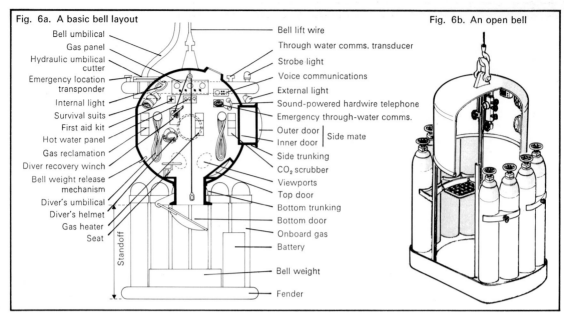

Fig. 6a. A basic bell layout

Bell umbilical
Gas panel
Hydraulic umbilical cutter
Emergency location transponder
Internal light
Survival suits
First aid kit
Hot water panel
Gas reclamation
Diver recovery winch
Bell weight release mechanism
Diver's umbilical
Diver's helmet
Gas heater
Seat
Standoff

Bell lift wire
Through water comms. transducer
Strobe light
Voice communications
External light
Sound-powered hardwire telephone
Emergency through-water comms.
Outer door ⎤ Side mate
Inner door ⎦
Side trunking
CO_2 scrubber
Viewports
Top door
Bottom trunking
Bottom door
Onboard gas
Battery
Bell weight
Fender

Fig. 6b. An open bell

Fig. 7a. IUC 310 m saturation diving system

Fig. 7b. Seaforth 206/290 m bounce diving system

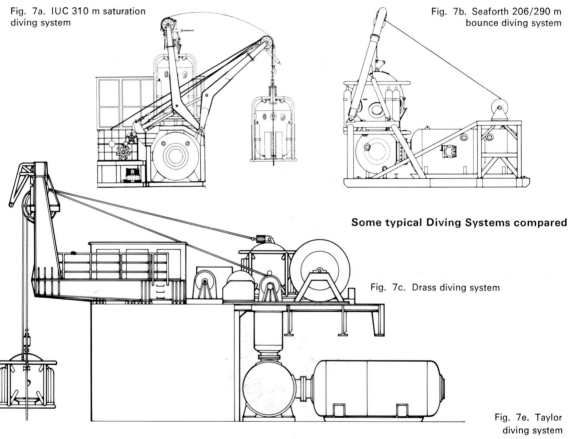

Some typical Diving Systems compared

Fig. 7c. Drass diving system

Fig. 7e. Taylor diving system

Fig. 7d. Comex 200 m diving system

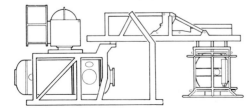

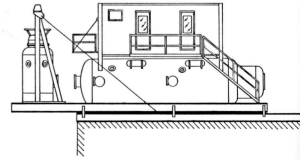

4.6 CHAMBER OPERATION AND LIFE SUPPORT

Chamber operators (life support technicians) are responsible for maintaining the internal environment of the compression chambers in a healthy condition. This involves constant maintenance of the correct oxygen level, keeping the carbon dioxide level to a minimum and controlling the temperature and humidity. It also includes management of the compression and decompression phases. This is a very technical and responsible position requiring a high professional standard essential for the maintenance of the health of the divers.

The following information provides general guidelines only and company procedures should always take precedence.

1. Time and Depth Control

a. Time

Accurate timing is always necessary and should be kept to the nearest second if possible, although the nearest minute is adequate. Control clocks, either digital or analogue, should be synchronised to local time by telephone or radio time checks. If a 'dive time' or running time is used, be sure to record time of day as well.

b. Pneumatic analogue or transducer digital depth gauges require frequent calibration checks. For diving beyond 250 msw, the relative density to which a gauge system is calibrated becomes increasingly important. In practice, many have adopted a standard for msw where 10 msw is exactly equivalent to 1 bar. Legislation in several countries lays down standards for the frequency and accuracy of gauge calibration.

2. Gas Composition

a. Air saturation

Chamber gas should be kept as close as possible to the normal composition of atmosphere air unless company procedure dictates a different arrangement.

	By volume	Suggested tolerance
Oxygen	20.946%	20–22%
Nitrogen	78.084%	78–80%
Carbon dioxide	0.033%	less than 0.005 bar
Relative humidity	50–60% preferred	50–80%

b. Oxy-helium saturation

Oxygen	0.2–0.6 bar; tolerance of ±0.01 bar
Nitrogen	Less than 0.10 bar; above 0.8 bar should be considered as Trimix
Carbon dioxide	Less than 0.005 bar
Helium	Remainder
Relative humidity	50–60% preferred; 50–80% tolerated (may be less for depths greater than 300 msw)

c. Oxy-helium-nitrogen saturation (Trimix)

As in b except that the nitrogen content will be specified either as a percentage of the volume or a constant partial pressure.

If percentage then ±0.5% should be achieved. If partial pressure than ±0.1 bar.

3. Oxygen Control

Very strict control of the oxygen levels must be maintained for several reasons.

—To provide for the diver's bodily requirements.
—To avoid hypoxia.
—To avoid oxygen toxicity.
—To maintain the effectiveness of the decompression schedule.
—To minimise fire hazard.

Company procedure will specify the required levels of oxygen to be maintained at the various stages of a dive. For any particular depth, different levels of oxygen may be specified for:

—The DCC when at living depth or during decompression.
—BIBS for therapeutic purposes.
—The diver's breathing supply during DLO.
—The bail-out gas supply.

Oxygen must be carefully added to the DCC to maintain the correct levels. Special care must be taken to ensure good mixing of the oxygen and that all fire hazard precautions are taken. The chamber oxygen should never exceed 25% by volume. The rate at which oxygen will be required will depend on the number of divers and their levels of physical activity, as shown in the following graph.

In general, raised partial pressures of oxygen can have advantages including:

—Faster decompression times.
—Reduced bend incidence.
—Greater tolerance to sudden loss of gas supply.
—Higher percentages for more accurate monitoring at depths greater than 300 m, when the percentage becomes very low.

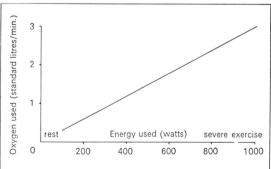

Graph 1. Amount of oxygen used up by a diver for various levels of work

But upper limits are imposed because:

—Oxygen poisoning can occur.
—An increased fire hazard may arise at depths shallower than 50 m.
—A reduced tolerance will occur to the higher

oxygen levels that may be required for therapeutic procedures.

The following graph shows how the time of exposure to high oxygen partial pressures must be reduced in the higher range to avoid oxygen poisoning.

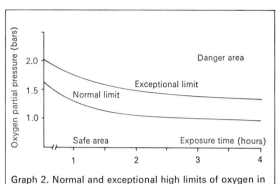

Graph 2. Normal and exceptional high limits of oxygen in in breathing gas

4. Carbon Dioxide Control

Carbon dioxide must be kept at very low levels for the comfort and safety of the divers.

The DCC CO_2 level should normally be kept below 5 mb, whilst a slightly higher level of 10 mb may be accepted for shorter periods spent, say, in the diving bell. If the level exceeds 50 mb then BIBS or ora-nasal CO_2 scrubbers should be used by the divers until the level returns to normal.

The following graph shows how a small increase in the CO_2 level can rapidly cause a dangerous situation.

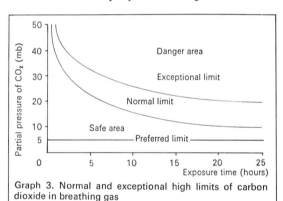

Graph 3. Normal and exceptional high limits of carbon dioxide in breathing gas

5. Gas Contaminants

Most life support gas analysis is concerned with monitoring only oxygen and carbon dioxide. However, other gases can sometimes appear. These can be highly toxic even at very low levels and therefore tests should be made to reduce the risk of such occurrences. These tests can be carried out using chemical colour-indicating tubes or electronic instrumentation.

As a rough guide, the following sources of contaminants and their relative degrees of toxicity should be appreciated.

SOURCES OF TOXIC GASES

a. Overheating or burning of electrical insulation and other materials.

Overheating can cause smoke without fire. The chemicals in the smoke and fumes can be highly poisonous. They affect the eyes, lungs and skin. When absorbed into the blood stream, they can attack the nervous system and quickly incapacitate the diver. Only very small quantities may be required to incapacitate. Slightly larger amounts can be fatal.

Just a few of the poisonous gases that can be formed are:

Ammonia	NH_3
Carbon dioxide	CO_2
Carbon monoxide	CO
Hydrogen chloride	HCl
Hydrogen cyanide	HCN
Hydrogen fluoride	HF
Nitrogen dioxide	NO_2
Sulphur dioxide	SO_2

Some of the materials in a diving system that can produce these gases include PVC, ABS, polystyrene, polyester, polyurethane, phenol-formaldehyde, wool, silk, acrylics, rubber, nylon, PTFE.

b. Gases produced from electrical arcing

Apart from ozone and oxides of nitrogen, most of these products are not a problem in the short term. But a long term exposure could be a problem.

c. Task-orientated contaminants

Contaminant gases can appear in a diving system via the diving bell. These can appear if divers return to the bell with contaminated equipment/suits, or if the bell is located over:

—An area of seabed which is degassing.

—A diver using oxy-arc equipment.

—A welding habitat.

—An open pipeline end.

All these sources can and should be avoided with proper diving practice.

Some additional gases which can appear are:

Acetone	CH_3COCH_3
Acetylene	C_2H_2
Benzene	C_6H_6
Ethylalcohol	C_2H_5OH
Hydrogen	H_2
Methane	CH_4
Oxygen	O_2
Other hydrocarbons	
Various halogens	

TOXIC LEVELS

The following table gives the relative toxicity of some example gas contaminants. Note the low concentrations.

Gas	SURFACE EQUIVALENT VALUES		
	Concentration to produce rapid death (ppm)	Concentration tolerable for a short time (ppm)	Threshold limit value (ppm)
NH_3	*	*	25
CO	4000–5000	400–500	50
HCl	1000–2000	50–100	5
HCN	100–300	*	10
HF	50–250	*	3
H_2S	800–1000	20	10
NO_2	200–700	*	5
SO_2	400–500	50	5

*No information available

6. Temperature Control

Chamber temperature levels are adjusted according to diver comfort requirements. As the depth increases, the comfortable temperature range narrows to plus or minus 1°C at around 300 m (1000').

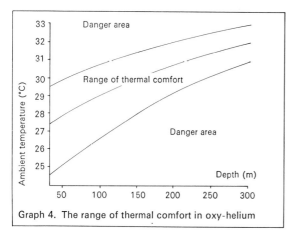

Graph 4. The range of thermal comfort in oxy-helium

Great care is required not only to maintain comfort, but also to avoid the danger of both overheating (hyperthermia) and cooling (hypothermia). Emergency procedures are required to cater for the accidental occurrence of both conditions.

The temperature of inspired breathing gas of a diver in the water also becomes increasingly important as depth increases. UK Regulations require special gas heating to be provided for the diver at 150 m (480') and deeper. The following data are based on US Navy information.

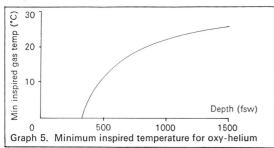

Graph 5. Minimum inspired temperature for oxy-helium

Diver suit heating is required by UK Regulations at 50 m and deeper.

7. Humidity Control

Chamber gas should be kept between about 50% and 60% relative humidity. Prolonged periods outside this range can cause respiratory problems. A high atmospheric humidity will reduce a diver's tolerance to ambient temperature changes and increase the risk of infections.

The main problem with controlling humidity is keeping it down. Apart from the use of dehumidifiers, care must be taken by the divers within the DCC to avoid unnecessary increases in humidity. This includes:
—Keeping wet equipment from the bell separate from the DCC.
—Prudent use of the shower.
—Regularly checking the DCC bilges for water and draining as necessary.

8. Use of Medical and Equipment Locks

Ideally the compression and decompression rates should be the same as for the divers. In practice however, if equipment is being locked in or out, the following rates may be used:

    Compression rate   20 m/min.
    Decompression rate   40 m/hr
    Medical samples such as blood should be decompressed at rates specified by a medical doctor.

The chamber operator must keep very strict control of every item that is locked into the chamber. He must examine every item and check:
—Is it a fire risk?
—Is there a toxicity risk?
—Is there a health risk?
—Is there a risk of explosion on decompression?
—Will it withstand the pressure (implosion)?
—Will it withstand the rate of compression (implosion)?

9. Emergency Procedures

LOSS OF PRESSURE
Causes:
1. Failure of O-rings or seals.
2. Failure of valve casings, fittings or pipe runs.
3. Cracked or damaged porthole.
4. Incorrect valve operation.

When pressure loss occurs the operator should endeavour to re-establish and maintain depth using the appropriate mix gas on-line because if helium were used in such a circumstance a risk of hypoxia may occur due to reduced PO_2 levels.

It is advisable that a treatment gas (10% or 20% O_2) should be on-line in saturation control ready for immediate use in the event of a sudden pressure loss. It also allows the controller to have the necessary gas on-line to deal with any case of decompression sickness which may occur.

Slow pressure loss:
Frequently caused through worn or damaged seals in handlock operating mechanisms or worn door or hatch seals. Where the cause of pressure loss is known and unlikely to require drastic action such as an evacuation of the chamber, then the leak should be rectified as soon as convenient.

Rapid pressure loss:
Whatever the cause, this must be considered as a serious problem as there is a decompression risk when the pressure cannot be maintained. If the fault cannot be rectified immediately, then the chamber must be evacuated and surfaced until the fault is repaired and further pressure tests have been carried out to the diving superintendent's satisfaction. BIBS gas must be on-line for immediate use in the event of the PO_2 dropping below the acceptable limits and if it cannot immediately be made up.

Avoidance of loss of pressure:
Regular maintenance and visual inspection of valves and door seals will minimise the risk of mechanical or seal failures. Before O-rings are fitted, it must be ascertained that they are of the correct size and type for the task they have to perform. When removing O-rings, care must be taken to avoid scratching the seating with the tool and causing a leak.
Particular attention must be paid to the operation

of handlocks, flush valves and drain valves. Before operation of the valves takes place, visual and, where possible, direct voice communication should be made between the tenders outside and the divers inside the chamber. None of these functions should be carried out without first checking with' the saturation controller. This is particularly critical when decompression is in progress.

FIRE IN CHAMBER

Causes:

1. Spontaneous ignition with high PO_2 content.
2. Spontaneous combustion of hydrocarbon-based materials under pressure.
3. Failure of electrical insulation.
4. Sparks from metal-to-metal impact.

Fires may be of the 'slow burn or smouldering' type or of the spontaneous 'flash fire or explosion' type. Whichever the type or cause, any fire is a very serious problem in a chamber.

The slow burn type of fire may occur without the divers being immediately aware of its presence and may produce toxic gases to which the divers may succumb before the danger is realised. If the oxygen content is high enough, a slow fire may develop into a sudden flash fire.

A sudden flash fire will usually result in severe burns to personnel, hypoxia and as already stated a danger from toxic gases produced from burning material.

If fire occurs, the chamber must be evacuated instantly. The divers may enter an adjacent lock or HRV and breathe on BIBS if necessary. Most complexes are now fitted with fire-drenching systems which operate automatically—and occasionally manually from the control area. All oxygen and electrical supplies to the affected chamber must be turned off.

If the fire is not of great intensity then it may be possible for the divers in the chamber to put on their BIBS masks and extinguish the fire themselves.

The chamber should be sealed off and brought to the surface to allow deck personnel to quench the fire. The manually operated fire extinguishers within the chamber may first be operated by one of the divers in the chamber—usually the last man out, and only if this does not expose him to additional risk.

FIRE IN SATURATION CONTROL ROOM OR OUTSIDE CHAMBER

In the event of this type of fire occurring, the following steps may be taken to regain control:

1. Saturation controller and other personnel to don breathing apparatus.
2. Isolate all oxygen and electrical supplies but maintain chamber communication.
3. Inform the diving superintendent and Dive Control of the situation.
4. Inform divers in chamber and, if necessary, put divers on the BIBS system.
5. Attempt to extinguish fire with locally sited appliances until help arrives.
6. Keep chambers cool by hosing down with cold water paying particular attention to O_2 lines and gas lines.
7. Prepare to transfer divers into the HRV or to another diving vessel with a compatible bell system.

CHAMBER HEATING FAILURE

When there is more than one chamber, the DCC heating supplies to each chamber are usually cross-connected in case one should fail.

If emergency heaters are fitted within the chamber they should be switched on.

Extra blankets and 'woolly bears' may also be provided.

4.7 OXYGEN BOOSTERS

Industrial gases are delivered under high pressure. When gas is decanted off the cylinders, the pressure progressively drops off as it is used up. If more high pressure gas is needed from the same bank, boosters will be required to recompress the gas. For example, low pressure gas cannot be transferred into a high pressure quad unless it is boosted higher than the pressure of the receiving gas supply.

In diving terms oxygen boosters are mainly used to mix gases and to transfer gas from a low pressure store to a high pressure store.

Since oxygen under pressure can be particularly dangerous, oxygen boosters are specially designed to avoid the risk of explosion. Stringent maintenance procedures must be carried out according to the manufacturer's instructions.

Other precautions include the use of special inert lubricants such as Voltalef, Fomblin and Brayco greases/fluids. They are not affected by the oxygen and also provide some corrosion protection. Utmost caution is recommended when handling these lubricants at high temperatures, since vapours may be given off which can irritate the skin and are toxic if inhaled. Smoking should be prohibited. Cigarettes should not be taken into an area where these lubricants are being handled because they can absorb the toxic vapours.

Oxygen boosters commonly used for handling diving gases include those made by Corblin, Maximator and Haskel Energy Systems Ltd.

Corblin electrically-driven, water-cooled boosters are of the diaphragm type. The flexing metal diaphragm separates the piston from the gas being handled and this sealed construction allows for higher pressures and eliminates contamination by lubricants.

Since most gas bottling applications involve pressures of 200 bars, the most commonly encountered unit is the A2 C250 package. It incorporates a single stage compressor capable of handling all diving gases including pure oxygen. The booster's capability of 250 bars allows slight overpressure filling, to compensate for the pressure drop when the gas cools down after transfer. The Corblin range includes single and two-stage boosters over a wide range of pressure and volume capacities, to suit the application.

The Haskell and Maximator type boosters are air-driven, air-cooled, and piston-operated.

Two stage boosters with a compression ratio of 15:1 are normally selected to achieve the pressures needed for diving gas handling, but the differential piston design can supply much higher pressures if required. These piston-type boosters consist of a large-area reciprocating air drive piston directly coupled by a connecting rod to a small-area gas piston.

The air drive section includes a cycling spool and pilot valves that provide continuous reciprocating action when compressed air is supplied to the air drive inlet. Conventional industrial, shipboard or contractor type compressed air sources are normally used for power. The gas piston operates in a high pressure gas barrel. The end cap of each gas barrel contains the high pressure gas inlet and outlet and their associated check valves. Three sets of seals isolate the compression chambers from the air drive section. The intervening two chambers are vented to atmosphere. This design prevents air-drive contamination from entering the gas stream.

Cooling is provided by directing the cold exhausted drive air through a jacket surrounding the gas barrel and also through an intercooler on the interstage line. All motive power and controls are pneumatic with no electrical connections. The inlet cylinder pressure and outlet receiver pressure are continually monitored by a pneumatic control package which stops the booster automatically when the desired outlet or minimum inlet pressure is reached—permitting unattended operation.

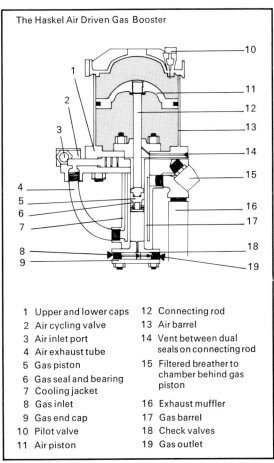

Corblin Diaphragm Compressor Head

1 Gas plate	9 Oil pressure limiter
2 Inlet valve	seat
3 Orifice plate	10 Oil pressure limiter
4 Outlet valve	11 Oil check valve
5 Diaphragm	12 Gudgeon pin
6 Plate gasket, oil side	13 Piston
7 Plate bolts	14 Luboil pump
8 Oil plate	15 Compensating pump

The Haskel Air Driven Gas Booster

1 Upper and lower caps	12 Connecting rod
2 Air cycling valve	13 Air barrel
3 Air inlet port	14 Vent between dual
4 Air exhaust tube	seals on connecting rod
5 Gas piston	15 Filtered breather to
6 Gas seal and bearing	chamber behind gas
7 Cooling jacket	piston
8 Gas inlet	16 Exhaust muffler
9 Gas end cap	17 Gas barrel
10 Pilot valve	18 Check valves
11 Air piston	19 Gas outlet

UK distributors: George Meller Ltd,
Orion Park, Northfield Avenue,
Ealing, London, W13 9SJ.
Tel: (01) 579 2111 Tlx: 27800

UK distributors: Haskel Energy Systems Ltd,
North Hylton Road, Sunderland,
SR5 3JD.
Tel: (0783) 491212 Tlx: 53624

Text continued on page 141.

Gas analysis

5.1 AIR AND MIXED GAS PURITY ANALYSIS

The development of subsea experience and technology has enabled a wider range of diving activities to take place at increasingly greater depths. In air diving, surface decompression procedures are widely used to maximise bottom time. Saturation diving is now the common commercial method of carrying out subsea operations at greater depth. The possible build up of gaseous impurities in the chambers, due to contamination or inadequate ventilation, becomes a major concern. Furthermore, at the deeper diving depths the required percentages of oxygen and the maximum allowable percentages of contaminants become very small (see Section 5.2, Air and mixed gas purity standards). Consequently the accuracy of breathing gas analysis takes on an increasingly important role. Nowadays oxygen and carbon dioxide are the main components measured in a diving system. With future diving methods, procedures and techniques, the need will arise to widen the range to encompass other possible toxic impurities. Hyperbaric welding is a special example.

Analytical instruments for hyperbaric monitoring cover a wide range. They depend on the type and concentration of components to be measured. The main factors to be considered when selecting such instruments should be:

—Compatibility with the environment where it will be used.
—Simplicity of operation.
—Accuracy of measurement.
—Repeatability of measurement accuracy.
—Response time to components being measured.
—Suitability for constant monitoring.
—Compatibility with electrical supply at the work place.
—Emergency power requirements.
—Robustness, reliability and maintenance requirements.

The offshore industry requires a rugged, fast, accurate and stable instrument. By meeting the criteria stated above, the instruments will provide the necessary safeguards to the diver.

The constituents of a gas mixture may be varied and therefore may be required to be analysed by different methods. The main commercial diving gas suppliers use a combination of mass spectrometry, infra-red spectrophotometry and gas chromatography to ensure that the gas purity meets the required standards.

A variety of instruments is available. Most of these maintain a constant visible read-out of the various gas concentrations in the chambers. Some systems are fitted with sophisticated electronic instruments which will illustrate the gas content either as a partial pressure equation or percentage at the flick of a switch. Many of these can leave the oxygen levels preset so that automatic O_2 injection is carried out by the instrument without manual assistance from the operator.

Most gas monitoring instruments are mounted on or adjacent to the control panel in the saturation system control room. The gas from the chamber is fed to the instruments using the same operating principle as depth gauges. Gas flow to the instruments is regulated according to the manufacturer's recommendations. All monitors should be calibrated daily against a known calibration gas usually stored or fed into the saturation control room. Methods of calibration are always contained in the instrument handbooks supplied by the makers.

The remainder of this section lists a selection of commercially available instruments for single component or multi-component analysis. Further details with regard to technical or operational matters should be discussed directly with the manufacturer.

ANALYSIS EQUIPMENT

Table 1. One-component analysers

Oxygen

Manufacturer	Type of detection	Ranges
Anacon	Electrochemical cells. Zirconia principle	Mainly ppm and low %. Multirange % and ppm
Analysis automation	Fuel cell	Multirange % and partial pressure
Beckmann	Paramagnetic and polarographic	Multirange % and partial pressure
Taylor instrument analytics	Paramagnetic	Multirange % Meter and digital readout

Carbon dioxide

Anatek	Infra-red	Varied ppm and %
Beckmann	Infra-red and electrochemical	Varied ppm and % also partial pressure
MSA	Infra-red	As above
Sabre	Infra-red	As above
Seiger	Infra-red	As above

Moisture

Anatek	Infra-red	O—ambient
Anacon	Electrochemical Infra-red	O—ambient **ppm and %**
Beckmann	Infra-red and electrochemical	O—ambient
Foxboro	Infra-red	O—ambient
Shaw	Sensor	Many ranges

Others, i.e. carbon monoxide, hydrocarbons, nitric and nitrous oxides, sulphur dioxide etc.
These can be done by the following:
Anacon, Anatek, Beckmann, Foxboro, Sabre and Seiger
Available in ppm or % ranges

Table 2. Multi-component analysers

These usually fall into two categories:

Manufacturer	Detector	Ranges
Ebra Science	Many	Many
Foxboro	Many	Many
Hewlett Packard	Many	Many
Pye Unicam	Many	Many
Perkin Elmer	Many	Many
Spectra Physics	Many	Many
Techmation	Many	Many
Varian	Many	Many

The reason for many different detectors is that, as application, components and concentrations vary, the instruments are modified to meet individual requirements.

Infra-red spectrophotometer

Beckmann	Infra-red	As required
Foxboro	Infra-red	As required
Pye Unicam	Infra-red	As required
Perkin Elmer	Infra-red	As required

These analysers can all be set up to give visual display and written printouts of component concentrations.

Name	Address	Tel. no.	Name	Address	Tel. no.
Anacon Instruments Ltd	*St Peters Road, Maidenhead, Berkshire, UK*	0628 39711	Perkin Elmer Ltd	*Post Office Lane, Beaconsfield, Buckinghamshire, UK*	049 46 6161
	FC Box 416, South Bedford Street, Burlington, Mass. 01803, USA	(617) 272 1313		*Main Avenue, Norwalk, Conn. 06856, USA*	(203) 762 1000
Anatek Ltd	*High Street, Mayfield, Sussex, UK*	04355 3477	Pye Unicam Ltd	*York Street, Cambridge, CB1 2PX, UK*	0223 58866
Analysis Automation Ltd	*Southfield House, Fynsham, Oxford, UK*	0865 881888	Sabre Safety Ltd	*225 Ash Road, Aldershot, UK*	0252 316611
Beckmann Ltd	*6 Stapledown Road, Orton, Southgate, Peterborough, UK*	0733 237055	Seiger	*31, Nuffield Estate, Poole, Dorset, UK*	0202 676161
	2500 Harbor Boulevard, Fullerton, Ca 92634, USA	(714) 871 4848	Shaw Moisture Meters Ltd	*Rawson Road, Westgate, Bradford, West Yorkshire, UK*	0274 33582
Erba Science (UK) Ltd	*Headlands Trading Estate, Swindon, Wiltshire, SN2 6JQ, UK*	0793 33551	Spectra Physics Ltd	*17 Brick Knoll Park, St Albans, Hertfordshire, UK*	0727 30131
				3333 North First Street, San Jose, Ca 95134, USA	946 6080
Foxboro (GB) Ltd	*Analytical Division, 28 Heathfield, Stacey Bushes, Milton Keynes, Buckinghamshire, UK*	0908 318222	Taylor Instruments Ltd	*Crowborough, Sussex, UK*	08926 2181
Hewlett Packard Ltd	*Nine Mile Ride, Easthampstead, Wokingham, Berkshire, UK*	03446 3100	Techmation Ltd	*58 Edgware Way, Edgware, Middlesex, UK*	01 958 3111
	Analytical Instruments Group, 1501 Page Mill Road, Palo Alto, Ca 94304, USA	(415) 857 1501	Varian Associates Ltd	*28 Manor Road, Walton on Thames, Surrey, UK*	093 22 43741
Mine Safety Appliances	*East Shawhead, Coatbridge, Scotland*	0236 24966		*611 Hansen Way, Palo Alto, Ca 94304, USA*	(415) 493 4000
	400 Penn Center Boulevard, Pittsburgh, Pa 15235, USA	(412) 273 5260			

5.2 AIR AND MIXED GAS PURITY STANDARDS

Every country has its own purity standards for air and some countries have standards for mixed gas. The following are the standards for UK and USA.

UNITED KINGDOM

Breathing gases should be blended from pure gases and the mixing process should not add any impurities at concentrations likely to cause toxic or other harmful effects when breathed continuously under pressure.

Air standards:

Purity—oxygen	$21\% \pm 0.5\%$
Maximum permissible contaminants:	
Carbon dioxide (CO_2)	500 ppm
Carbon monoxide (CO)	10 ppm
Nitrogen and inert gases	Balance
Odour	Nil
Moisture (measured in the cylinder filling line)	15 ppm

At present there are no mixed gas purity standards in the UK. The UK Department of Energy are establishing breathing gas purity standards for oxygen, nitrogen and helium. The following are the proposed standards.

It is important to note that these are not necessarily the final DEn specifications, only the proposed standards, and may be amended: they should only be used as a guide.

Mixed gas standards:

Oxygen	99.5%
Maximum permissible contaminants:	
Nitrogen	0.1%
Argon	0.4%
Hydrocarbons	3 ppm
Methane	25 ppm
Carbon dioxide (CO_2)	5 ppm
Carbon monoxide (CO)	1 ppm
Moisture (H_2O)	25 ppm
Nitrogen	99.5%
Maximum permissible contaminants:	
Oxygen (O_2)	50 ppm
Hydrocarbons	1 ppm
Carbon dioxide (CO_2)	1 ppm
Carbon monoxide (CO)	1 ppm
Moisture (H_2O)	25 ppm
Helium	99.97%
Maximum permissible contaminants:	
Oxygen (O_2)	50 ppm
Hydrocarbons	1 ppm
Carbon dioxide (CO_2)	1 ppm
Carbon monoxide (CO)	1 ppm
Moisture	25 ppm

Oil mist should not be present; however, if detected

after pumping, the level of contaminant should not exceed 1 mg/m³. The percentage of error in the mixture should be restricted to plus or minus 5% of the minor component.

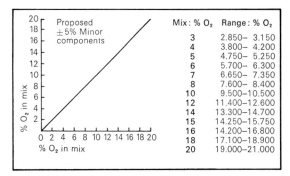

Mix: % O₂	Range: % O₂
3	2.850– 3.150
4	3.800– 4.200
5	4.750– 5.250
6	5.700– 6.300
7	6.650– 7.350
8	7.600– 8.400
10	9.500–10.500
12	11.400–12.600
14	13.300–14.700
15	14.250–15.750
16	14.200–16.800
18	17.100–18.900
20	19.000–21.000

UNITED STATES OF AMERICA
Respirable air standards:

Oxygen	20–22% by vol
Maximum permissible contaminants:	
Carbon monoxide (CO)	20 ppm
Carbon dioxide (CO₂)	1000 ppm
Oil	5 mg/m³
Noxious or pronounced odour	Nil

Air purity tests should be carried out every 6 months by means of samples taken at the connection to the distribution system. Non-oil lubricated compressors need not be tested for oil mist.
Breathing gases are classified as follows:

Type I—gaseous
Type II—liquid
Class 1—Oil-free
Class 2—Oil-tolerant
Grade A—99.95% pure
Grade B—99.5% pure
Grade C—99.5% pure (Type I only); moisture content not specified

Oxygen
Oxygen must meet the requirements of Federal Specification BB-0-925a, be Type I and grade A or B.

Nitrogen
Nitrogen must meet the requirements of Federal Specification BB-N-411c, be Type I, class 1 and Grade A, B or C.

Property	Requirement		
	Grade A	Grade B	Grade C
Purity minimum % by vol.	99.95	99.50	99.50
Oxygen maximum % by vol.	0.05	0.50	0.50
Moisture maximum mg H₂O/l of gas	0.02	0.02	*
Odour (see note 2)	none	none	none
*no limiting characteristics			

Notes:

1. Purity is the percentage of nitrogen and includes trace quantities of argon, neon and helium.

2. All types and grades of nitrogen shall be free of oil contamination and shall have a total hydrocarbon level less than 50 ppm as methane by volume, detectable by odour or by test when specified by the purchaser.

3. Type I nitrogen shall contain no solid particles larger than 50 microns. These particles are normally eliminated by using a filter at or close to the cylinder charging manifold.

Helium
Helium must be grades A, B or C and produced by the Federal Government or equivalent.

Diving equipment

6.1 HELMETS AND MASKS INTRODUCTION

Band masks differ from helmets in that the former make a water tight seal around the face only, whereas helmets keep the diver's head completely dry as the air seal is effected by a neck seal. In most band masks and helmets there are two alternative systems for breathing: a steady flow of gas, or by a demand regulator. Most divers breathe through the demand regulator and maintain a slight steady flow to keep the face plate clear.

The emergency supply is an independent system.

Helmets fitted with umbilicals which provide a continuous supply of air divide into two groups, heavyweight or lightweight. The distinction between the two is that the lightweight helmets are usually not integral with the diving dress. Examples of heavyweight helmets are the Siebe Gorman 12-bolt and the Divex M2000. The Superlite 17a is typical of a lightweight helmet.

The choice between wearing a helmet or mask usually depends upon which one the diver is most familiar with; as on most work sites both are available for use. Other factors should also be considered, such as the type of diving dress worn, the depth, how much swimming is involved, what type of work the diver is required to do, whether the water is polluted, and whether the head needs to be kept dry.

The depth of diving operations can influence the choice of equipment. Masks are worn commonly in shallow water diving because of the ease of putting them on, and their lightness. Should the diver become unconscious and fall in such a way as to dislodge his mask, the face seal might be broken, flooding the mask. This would not occur when wearing a helmet, which would retain an intact seal under any circumstances.

The nature of the dive task will also dictate which type of equipment to use. Should the job entail a lot of swimming, as in pipeline inspection, a mask is preferable and easier to swim in than a helmet.

Because it is difficult to look upwards when wearing a helmet, a diver working inside structures needs the protection a helmet affords. On the other hand, many masks may be fitted with a head protector.

Communications are considerably better in a helmet as opposed to a mask. A helmet is to be preferred in polluted water as the ears and skin are not exposed to the water.

A light smear of some liquid soap, such as Prell, on the inside of the faceplate makes an effective demisting agent.

Maintenance

The routine maintenance of both masks and helmets consists mostly of washing in clean fresh water after use, perhaps with a mild disinfectant. Always dilute the disinfectant with fresh water—never use neat disinfectant. Hygiene is important if the equipment is being used by different divers.

Avoid letting water enter orifices such as the emergency gas inlet.

When wearing a helmet, the neck dam should be inspected for tears or holes. The head cushion or lining should be secure and any chin strap adjusted to suit the individual diver.

When wearing a band mask, the hood should have some provision for venting any excess gas that might escape around the sides of the oral-nasal mask.

The diver should always be fastidious about checking the communication system and all moving parts such as the main gas supply handle, the nose clearing device and the regulator adjustment knob. Most important of all to check is the non-return valve on the air intake.

A monthly routine would include the detailed inspection of the regulator, lubrication of all 'O' rings and rubber components with silicon grease and a check of the one-way valve.

The following pages show the main components of, and describe the controls of, some of the more widely used helmets and masks. These are constantly being modified, and some parts are interchangeable.

Advantages of helmets over band masks

(1) Keeps the head dry and decreases risk of ear infections, especially in saturation diving.

(2) Some divers find helmets more comfortable to wear for long dives, especially saturations.

(3) Reduces infection risk in polluted waters.

(4) Provides integral physical protection to the head.

(5) Can provide better voice communications.

(6) Better suited to gas recovery systems.

(7) Can provide a stable platform for head-mounted TV camera/light.

Advantages of band-masks over helmets

(1) Lighter and smaller to wear.

(2) Allows for greater mobility of the head.

(3) Easier to swim in.

(4) Some types can be quicker to put on.

(5) Require less assistance to put on.

(6) Allows the use of the hot water hood to keep the head warm.

(7) Usually cheaper.

6.1a DIVING HELMETS   SUPERLITE 17A

Although the Superlite 17 is the seventeenth helmet designed by Kirby and Morgan, only a few of the previous designs have made it to full production. This positively buoyant helmet weighs 10.9 kg (24 lb) and weights of 1–3 lb can be added according to diver preference. It consists of two parts; the neck dam-yoke and the helmet. The diver slips on the neck dam with the attached yoke hinging into place. The neck clamp is then slipped up onto the helmet and locked. A special neck dam is available for cold water and hot water suits. Most of the breathing equipment parts on the front of the Superlite are interchangeable with the Heliox—18a/b masks. The only difference between the 17a and 17b is that in 17a the umbilical is worn in front of the diver, whereas in 17b it passes over the diver's shoulder.

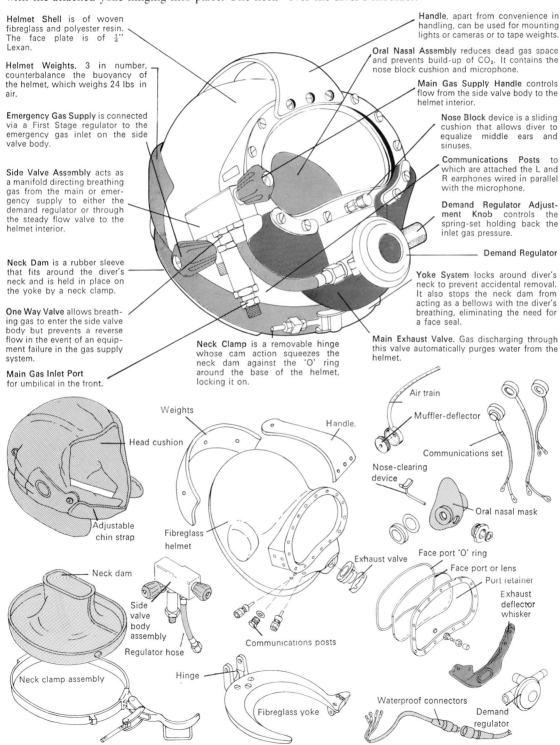

Helmet Shell is of woven fibreglass and polyester resin. The face plate is of $\frac{1}{4}''$ Lexan.

Helmet Weights, 3 in number, counterbalance the buoyancy of the helmet, which weighs 24 lbs in air.

Emergency Gas Supply is connected via a First Stage regulator to the emergency gas inlet on the side valve body.

Side Valve Assembly acts as a manifold directing breathing gas from the main or emergency supply to either the demand regulator or through the steady flow valve to the helmet interior.

Neck Dam is a rubber sleeve that fits around the diver's neck and is held in place on the yoke by a neck clamp.

One Way Valve allows breathing gas to enter the side valve body but prevents a reverse flow in the event of an equipment failure in the gas supply system.

Main Gas Inlet Port for umbilical in the front.

Neck Clamp is a removable hinge whose cam action squeezes the neck dam against the 'O' ring around the base of the helmet, locking it on.

Handle, apart from convenience in handling, can be used for mounting lights or cameras or to tape weights.

Oral Nasal Assembly reduces dead gas space and prevents build-up of CO_2. It contains the nose block cushion and microphone.

Main Gas Supply Handle controls flow from the side valve body to the helmet interior.

Nose Block device is a sliding cushion that allows diver to equalize middle ears and sinuses.

Communications Posts to which are attached the L and R earphones wired in parallel with the microphone.

Demand Regulator Adjustment Knob controls the spring-set holding back the inlet gas pressure.

Demand Regulator

Yoke System locks around diver's neck to prevent accidental removal. It also stops the neck dam from acting as a bellows with the diver's breathing, eliminating the need for a face seal.

Main Exhaust Valve. Gas discharging through this valve automatically purges water from the helmet.

Head cushion

Adjustable chin strap

Weights

Handle.

Neck dam

Side valve body assembly

Regulator hose

Neck clamp assembly

Hinge

Fibreglass helmet

Communications posts

Fibreglass yoke

Air train

Muffler-deflector

Communications set

Nose-clearing device

Oral nasal mask

Exhaust valve

Face port 'O' ring

Face port or lens

Port retainer

Exhaust deflector whisker

Waterproof connectors

Demand regulator

Illustration © Bob Kirby and Bev Morgan 1980. Patented USA 3, 958, 257: UK and other countries 1, 505, 803.

6.1b DIVING BAND MASKS HELIOX 18b COMMERCIAL DIVER'S MASK

This mask was evolved from the well-known Kirby Morgan series, and is manufactured by Diving Systems International of California. A similar mask, the KMB-10, is produced by US Divers Co. and most of the parts are interchangeable.

There are some innovations from models 9 and 10. The side valve assembly has been redesigned and the muffler deflector has been replaced with an 'air train' that smooths the steady gas flow across the diver's face. There is a new exhaust bubble deflector 'whisker' which keeps the gas bubbles away from the face port. An improved 'comfort insert' on the interior of the face seal/cushion makes the face seal more comfortable. The 18a differs from the 18b only in that in the former the umbilical passes across the diver's front, in the latter it passes over his shoulder.

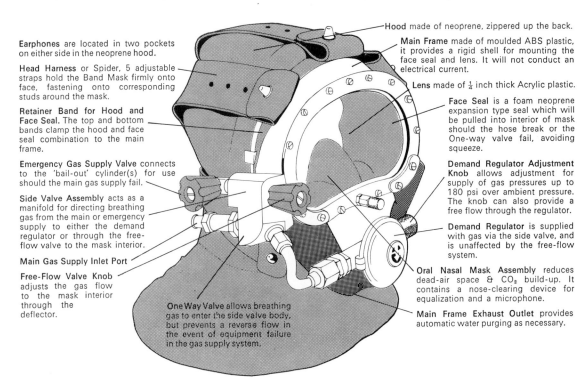

Earphones are located in two pockets on either side in the neoprene hood.

Head Harness or Spider, 5 adjustable straps hold the Band Mask firmly onto face, fastening onto corresponding studs around the mask.

Retainer Band for Hood and Face Seal. The top and bottom bands clamp the hood and face seal combination to the main frame.

Emergency Gas Supply Valve connects to the 'bail-out' cylinder(s) for use should the main gas supply fail.

Side Valve Assembly acts as a manifold for directing breathing gas from the main or emergency supply to either the demand regulator or through the free-flow valve to the mask interior.

Main Gas Supply Inlet Port

Free-Flow Valve Knob adjusts the gas flow to the mask interior through the deflector.

One Way Valve allows breathing gas to enter the side valve body, but prevents a reverse flow in the event of equipment failure in the gas supply system.

Hood made of neoprene, zippered up the back.

Main Frame made of moulded ABS plastic, it provides a rigid shell for mounting the face seal and lens. It will not conduct an electrical current.

Lens made of $\frac{1}{4}$ inch thick Acrylic plastic.

Face Seal is a foam neoprene expansion type seal which will be pulled into interior of mask should the hose break or the One-way valve fail, avoiding squeeze.

Demand Regulator Adjustment Knob allows adjustment for supply of gas pressures up to 180 psi over ambient pressure. The knob can also provide a free flow through the regulator.

Demand Regulator is supplied with gas via the side valve, and is unaffected by the free-flow system.

Oral Nasal Mask Assembly reduces dead-air space & CO_2 build-up. It contains a nose-clearing device for equalization and a microphone.

Main Frame Exhaust Outlet provides automatic water purging as necessary.

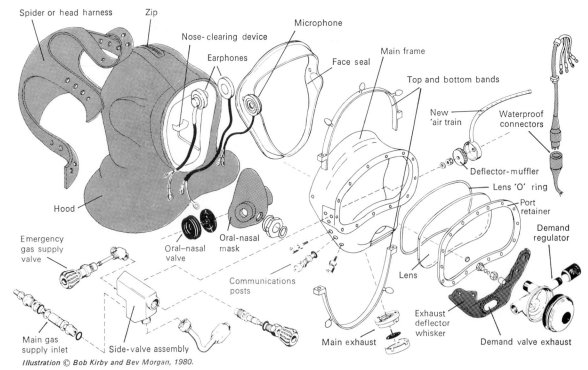

Spider or head harness · Zip · Nose-clearing device · Microphone · Earphones · Face seal · Main frame · Top and bottom bands · New 'air train' · Waterproof connectors · Deflector-muffler · Lens 'O' ring · Port retainer · Demand regulator · Hood · Emergency gas supply valve · Oral-nasal valve · Oral-nasal mask · Communications posts · Lens · Exhaust deflector whisker · Demand valve exhaust · Main exhaust · Main gas supply inlet · Side-valve assembly

Illustration © Bob Kirby and Bev Morgan, 1980.

6.1c DIVING MASKS COMEX PRO MASK

This neutrally buoyant band mask is available in two models, a European and a US standard.

The face plate is attached to the mask by two hinged screws. It is easily removable, so a protective visor can be substituted when welding or cutting, thus avoiding the necessity of a welding shield. The face plate is of Triplex which remains waterproof even when cracked.

The breathing gases, both emergency and normal, can be supplied to the interior of the mask via either the demand regulator or the free-flow valve. The demand regulator is the Comex Pro Super-Physalie which has been tested down to 610 m (61 bar). The Super-Physalie automatically regulates the gas flow to the mask at a pressure of 5–15 bars relative, flow rate 400 l/min under 5 mbars depression. On the US standard there is a manual control for switching to the emergency gas supply. There is an exhaust valve on the oral nasal mask as well as one on the demand valve, and another out of the side of the main frame.

The communications system consists of two waterproof earphones, a waterproof microphone and a four-pin moulded rubber watertight connector (two-pin on the European standard).

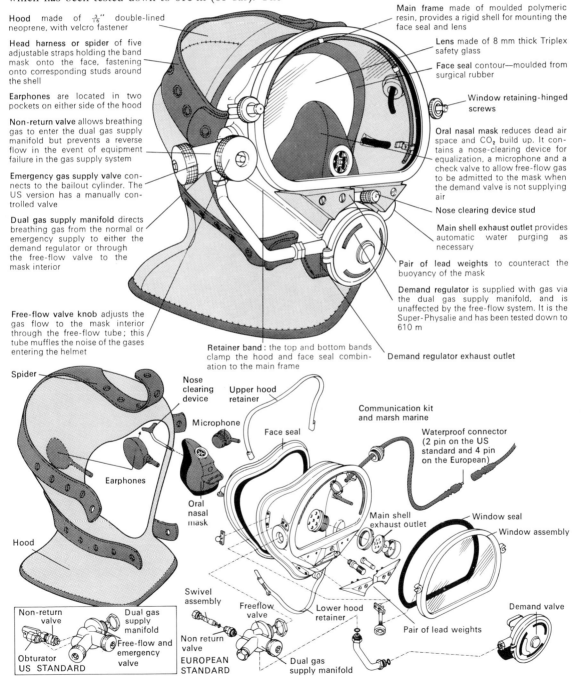

Hood made of $\frac{3}{16}''$ double-lined neoprene, with velcro fastener

Head harness or spider of five adjustable straps holding the band mask onto the face, fastening onto corresponding studs around the shell

Earphones are located in two pockets on either side of the hood

Non-return valve allows breathing gas to enter the dual gas supply manifold but prevents a reverse flow in the event of equipment failure in the gas supply system

Emergency gas supply valve connects to the bailout cylinder. The US version has a manually controlled valve

Dual gas supply manifold directs breathing gas from the normal or emergency supply to either the demand regulator or through the free-flow valve to the mask interior

Free-flow valve knob adjusts the gas flow to the mask interior through the free-flow tube; this tube muffles the noise of the gases entering the helmet

Main frame made of moulded polymeric resin, provides a rigid shell for mounting the face seal and lens

Lens made of 8 mm thick Triplex safety glass

Face seal contour—moulded from surgical rubber

Window retaining-hinged screws

Oral nasal mask reduces dead air space and CO_2 build up. It contains a nose-clearing device for equalization, a microphone and a check valve to allow free-flow gas to be admitted to the mask when the demand valve is not supplying air

Nose clearing device stud

Main shell exhaust outlet provides automatic water purging as necessary

Pair of lead weights to counteract the buoyancy of the mask

Demand regulator is supplied with gas via the dual gas supply manifold, and is unaffected by the free-flow system. It is the Super-Physalie and has been tested down to 610 m

Retainer band: the top and bottom bands clamp the hood and face seal combination to the main frame

Demand regulator exhaust outlet

Spider

Nose clearing device

Upper hood retainer

Microphone

Face seal

Communication kit and marsh marine

Waterproof connector (2 pin on the US standard and 4 pin on the European)

Earphones

Oral nasal mask

Main shell exhaust outlet

Window seal

Window assembly

Hood

Swivel assembly

Freeflow valve

Lower hood retainer

Pair of lead weights

Demand valve

Non-return valve

Dual gas supply manifold

Obturator

Free-flow and emergency valve

US STANDARD

Non return valve

EUROPEAN STANDARD

Dual gas supply manifold

Comex Pro, Avenue de la Soude, 13275 Marseille Cedex 2, France. Tel: (91) 410 107 Tlx: 410985

6.1d DIVING HELMETS COMEX PRO

This neutrally buoyant helmet was designed especially for construction diving and is available in two models, European and US standard.

The helmet divides into two halves; the upper half, made of brass, serves as ballast and protection, while the lightweight lower half houses the breathing and communication equipment.

The breathing gases (both normal and emergency) enter the helmet at the dual gas supply manifold. The gas is then supplied to the interior of the helmet through the free flow valve or the demand regulator. The regulator is the Comex 'Super-physalie', which has been tested at all depths down to 610 m. There are exhaust valves on the helmet and on the regulator. The diver's head is kept dry by the neck seal, so the helmet can be worn with any diving dress.

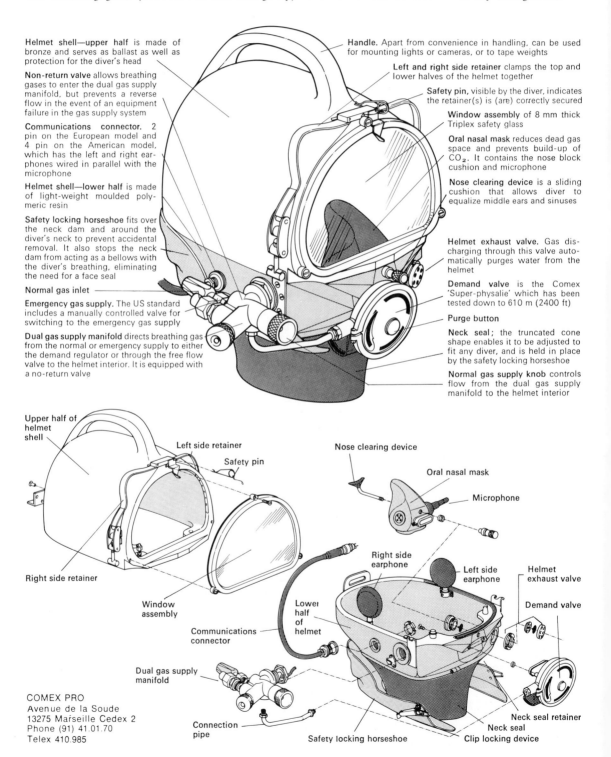

Helmet shell—upper half is made of bronze and serves as ballast as well as protection for the diver's head

Non-return valve allows breathing gases to enter the dual gas supply manifold, but prevents a reverse flow in the event of an equipment failure in the gas supply system

Communications connector. 2 pin on the European model and 4 pin on the American model, which has the left and right earphones wired in parallel with the microphone

Helmet shell—lower half is made of light-weight moulded polymeric resin

Safety locking horseshoe fits over the neck dam and around the diver's neck to prevent accidental removal. It also stops the neck dam from acting as a bellows with the diver's breathing, eliminating the need for a face seal

Normal gas inlet

Emergency gas supply. The US standard includes a manually controlled valve for switching to the emergency gas supply

Dual gas supply manifold directs breathing gas from the normal or emergency supply to either the demand regulator or through the free flow valve to the helmet interior. It is equipped with a no-return valve

Handle. Apart from convenience in handling, can be used for mounting lights or cameras, or to tape weights

Left and right side retainer clamps the top and lower halves of the helmet together

Safety pin, visible by the diver, indicates the retainer(s) is (are) correctly secured

Window assembly of 8 mm thick Triplex safety glass

Oral nasal mask reduces dead gas space and prevents build-up of CO_2. It contains the nose block cushion and microphone

Nose clearing device is a sliding cushion that allows diver to equalize middle ears and sinuses

Helmet exhaust valve. Gas discharging through this valve automatically purges water from the helmet

Demand valve is the Comex 'Super-physalie' which has been tested down to 610 m (2400 ft)

Purge button

Neck seal; the truncated cone shape enables it to be adjusted to fit any diver, and is held in place by the safety locking horseshoe

Normal gas supply knob controls flow from the dual gas supply manifold to the helmet interior

Upper half of helmet shell

Left side retainer

Safety pin

Right side retainer

Window assembly

Communications connector

Dual gas supply manifold

Connection pipe

Nose clearing device

Oral nasal mask

Microphone

Right side earphone

Left side earphone

Helmet exhaust valve

Demand valve

Lower half of helmet

Neck seal retainer

Neck seal

Safety locking horseshoe

Clip locking device

COMEX PRO
Avenue de la Soude
13275 Marseille Cedex 2
Phone (91) 41.01.70
Telex 410.985

6.1e DIVING HELMETS — DIVEX 2000 AIR HELMET (SWINDELL)

The Divex 2000 Air Helmet was developed originally by George Swindell and manufactured by Advanced Diving Equipment and Manufacturing Company. Beckman Instrument Company later joined Advanced, and Divex Ltd have now taken over so the helmet is known as a Swindell, Advanced, Beckman or Divex helmet. It is constructed from lightweight fibreglass which is electrically non-conductive so the helmet can be worn when cutting or welding underwater. Because the diver's head is kept dry by a neck seal it can be worn with any dry or wet suit. The helmet is positively buoyant and therefore is worn with a jock strap assembly. A special breast plate can be supplied for use with the standard dry suit and in this configuration the diver must be careful to avoid a blowup.

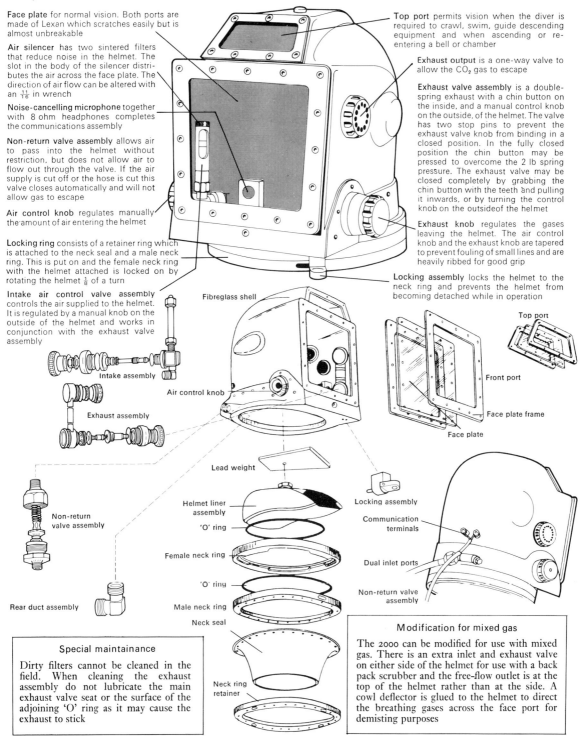

Face plate for normal vision. Both ports are made of Lexan which scratches easily but is almost unbreakable

Air silencer has two sintered filters that reduce noise in the helmet. The slot in the body of the silencer distributes the air across the face plate. The direction of air flow can be altered with an $\frac{11}{16}$ in wrench

Noise-cancelling microphone together with 8 ohm headphones completes the communications assembly

Non-return valve assembly allows air to pass into the helmet without restriction, but does not allow air to flow out through the valve. If the air supply is cut off or the hose is cut this valve closes automatically and will not allow gas to escape

Air control knob regulates manually the amount of air entering the helmet

Locking ring consists of a retainer ring which is attached to the neck seal and a male neck ring. This is put on and the female neck ring with the helmet attached is locked on by rotating the helmet $\frac{1}{8}$ of a turn

Intake air control valve assembly controls the air supplied to the helmet. It is regulated by a manual knob on the outside of the helmet and works in conjunction with the exhaust valve assembly

Top port permits vision when the diver is required to crawl, swim, guide descending equipment and when ascending or re-entering a bell or chamber

Exhaust output is a one-way valve to allow the CO_2 gas to escape

Exhaust valve assembly is a double-spring exhaust with a chin button on the inside, and a manual control knob on the outside, of the helmet. The valve has two stop pins to prevent the exhaust valve knob from binding in a closed position. In the fully closed position the chin button may be pressed to overcome the 2 lb spring pressure. The exhaust valve may be closed completely by grabbing the chin button with the teeth and pulling it inwards, or by turning the control knob on the outside of the helmet

Exhaust knob regulates the gases leaving the helmet. The air control knob and the exhaust knob are tapered to prevent fouling of small lines and are heavily ribbed for good grip

Locking assembly locks the helmet to the neck ring and prevents the helmet from becoming detached while in operation

Fibreglass shell

Intake assembly

Air control knob

Exhaust assembly

Non-return valve assembly

Rear duct assembly

Lead weight

Helmet liner assembly

'O' ring

Female neck ring

'O' ring

Male neck ring

Neck seal

Neck ring retainer

Top port

Front port

Face plate frame

Face plate

Locking assembly

Communication terminals

Dual inlet ports

Non-return valve assembly

Special maintainance

Dirty filters cannot be cleaned in the field. When cleaning the exhaust assembly do not lubricate the main exhaust valve seat or the surface of the adjoining 'O' ring as it may cause the exhaust to stick

Modification for mixed gas

The 2000 can be modified for use with mixed gas. There is an extra inlet and exhaust valve on either side of the helmet for use with a back pack scrubber and the free-flow outlet is at the top of the helmet rather than at the side. A cowl deflector is glued to the helmet to direct the breathing gases across the face port for demisting purposes

Divex (UK) Ltd, Unit 4, Brinell Way, Harfrey's Industrial Estate, Great Yarmouth, Norfolk, NR31 0LU, UK. Tel: (0493) 57927 Tlx: 975273
Divers Exchange Inc, 2245 Breaux Avenue, PO Box 504, Harvey, La. 70059, USA. Tel: (504) 368 2986 Tlx: 587 428

6.1f DIVING HELMETS AQUADYNE AIR-HELMET (AH–2)

A distinguishing feature of this lightweight, buoyant helmet is the two ports. The front port provides excellent vision for normal tasks while the top port permits vision when the diver is required to crawl, swim, guide descending equipment and when ascending or re-entering a bell or chamber. It can be fitted to a standard dry suit with a special breastplate or used with its own neoprene neck seal for diving with a dry suit, wet suit, hot water suit or boiler suit (jockey system available). The neck ring assembly has an external annular groove permitting attachment to certain dry suits. It has a free-flow system with an automatic exhaust and two-way communications, but no oral/nasal mask.

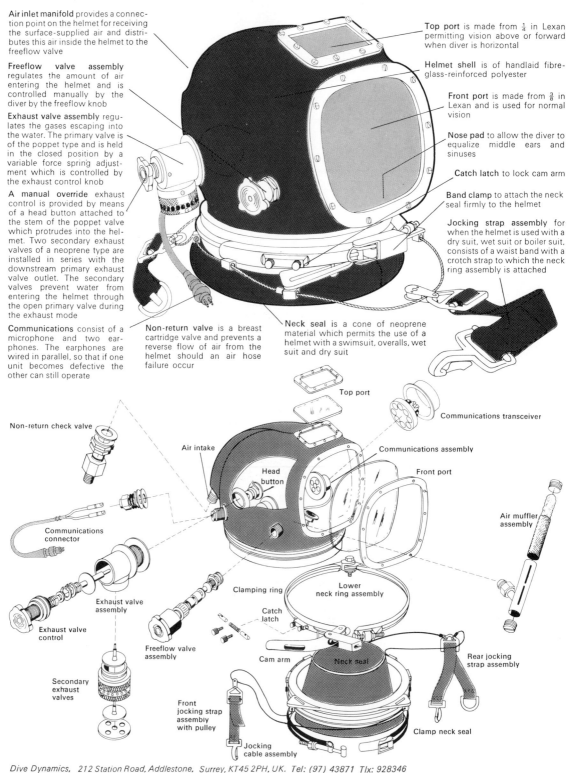

Air inlet manifold provides a connection point on the helmet for receiving the surface-supplied air and distributes this air inside the helmet to the freeflow valve

Freeflow valve assembly regulates the amount of air entering the helmet and is controlled manually by the diver by the freeflow knob

Exhaust valve assembly regulates the gases escaping into the water. The primary valve is of the poppet type and is held in the closed position by a variable force spring adjustment which is controlled by the exhaust control knob

A manual override exhaust control is provided by means of a head button attached to the stem of the poppet valve which protrudes into the helmet. Two secondary exhaust valves of a neoprene type are installed in series with the downstream primary exhaust valve outlet. The secondary valves prevent water from entering the helmet through the open primary valve during the exhaust mode

Communications consist of a microphone and two earphones. The earphones are wired in parallel, so that if one unit becomes defective the other can still operate

Non-return valve is a breast cartridge valve and prevents a reverse flow of air from the helmet should an air hose failure occur

Top port is made from $\frac{1}{4}$ in Lexan permitting vision above or forward when diver is horizontal

Helmet shell is of handlaid fibre-glass-reinforced polyester

Front port is made from $\frac{3}{8}$ in Lexan and is used for normal vision

Nose pad to allow the diver to equalize middle ears and sinuses

Catch latch to lock cam arm

Band clamp to attach the neck seal firmly to the helmet

Jocking strap assembly for when the helmet is used with a dry suit, wet suit or boiler suit, consists of a waist band with a crotch strap to which the neck ring assembly is attached

Neck seal is a cone of neoprene material which permits the use of a helmet with a swimsuit, overalls, wet suit and dry suit

Non-return check valve

Air intake

Head button

Communications transceiver

Communications assembly

Top port

Front port

Air muffler assembly

Communications connector

Exhaust valve assembly

Exhaust valve control

Freeflow valve assembly

Secondary exhaust valves

Clamping ring

Lower neck ring assembly

Catch latch

Cam arm

Neck seal

Rear jocking strap assembly

Front jocking strap assembly with pulley

Jocking cable assembly

Clamp neck seal

Dive Dynamics, 212 Station Road, Addlestone, Surrey, KT45 2PH, UK. Tel: (97) 43871 Tlx: 928346

6.1g DIVING HELMETS AQUADYNE DMC-7 HELMET

The distinctive feature of this neutrally buoyant helmet is its adjustable head pads. The pads are integral with the helmet and are adjusted by each diver to his own head and neck size without additional pads or parts. Adjustment can be made underwater for comfort during long dives.

Air or mixed gas is supplied through a demand regulator and/or flow valve. The regulator has an external adjustable orifice so does not require disassembly to keep in fine tune. The helmet exhausts through the tee on the demand regulator, and water escapes through the purge valve on the helmet.

Two alternative communication connections are provided, binding posts and Marsh-marine. The helmet has two earphones and a microphone wired in parallel.

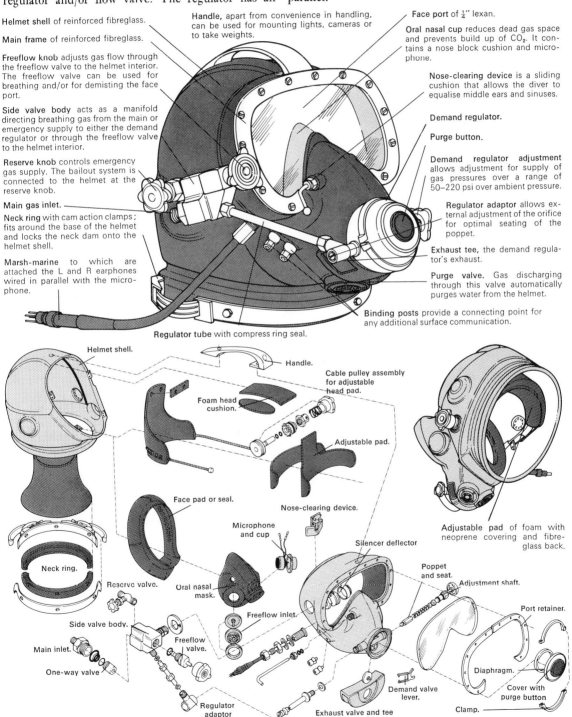

Helmet shell of reinforced fibreglass.

Main frame of reinforced fibreglass.

Freeflow knob adjusts gas flow through the freeflow valve to the helmet interior. The freeflow valve can be used for breathing and/or for demisting the face port.

Side valve body acts as a manifold directing breathing gas from the main or emergency supply to either the demand regulator or through the freeflow valve to the helmet interior.

Reserve knob controls emergency gas supply. The bailout system is connected to the helmet at the reserve knob.

Main gas inlet.

Neck ring with cam action clamps; fits around the base of the helmet and locks the neck dam onto the helmet shell.

Marsh-marine to which are attached the L and R earphones wired in parallel with the microphone.

Handle, apart from convenience in handling, can be used for mounting lights, cameras or to take weights.

Face port of ¼″ lexan.

Oral nasal cup reduces dead gas space and prevents build up of CO_2. It contains a nose block cushion and microphone.

Nose-clearing device is a sliding cushion that allows the diver to equalise middle ears and sinuses.

Demand regulator.

Purge button.

Demand regulator adjustment allows adjustment for supply of gas pressures over a range of 50–220 psi over ambient pressure.

Regulator adaptor allows external adjustment of the orifice for optimal seating of the poppet.

Exhaust tee, the demand regulator's exhaust.

Purge valve. Gas discharging through this valve automatically purges water from the helmet.

Binding posts provide a connecting point for any additional surface communication.

Regulator tube with compress ring seal.

Helmet shell.

Handle.

Cable pulley assembly for adjustable head pad.

Foam head cushion.

Adjustable pad.

Face pad or seal.

Nose-clearing device.

Microphone and cup.

Silencer deflector.

Neck ring.

Reserve valve.

Oral nasal mask.

Freeflow inlet.

Poppet and seat.

Adjustment shaft.

Port retainer.

Side valve body.

Freeflow valve.

Main inlet.

One-way valve.

Regulator adaptor

Exhaust valve and tee.

Demand valve lever.

Diaphragm.

Clamp.

Cover with purge button.

Adjustable pad of foam with neoprene covering and fibreglass back.

General Aquadyne Inc, 1009 Cindy Lane Carpinteria. Ca. 93013, USA. Tel: (805) 684 8339 Tlx: 658417
Underwater Instrumentation, 212 Station Road, Addlestone. Surrey, KT45 2PH, UK. Tel: (97) 43871 Tlx: 928346

6.1h DIVING MASKS AQUADYNE MASK—DM-5 AND DM-6

The Aquadyne Mask is a flexible system which can be surface-supplied with air or mixed gas. Both the DM–5 and DM–6 band masks can be converted easily to a DMC–7 helmet. Depending on the diver's needs and work load the mask's air intake can be free-flow or demand.

A contoured face seal bonded to the mask opening provides padding for the diver's face, forming the watertight seal. Comfort and sealing is achieved through proper adjustment of the rubber head harness which secures the mask to the diver's head. Excessive tension on the head harness adjustment straps only results in discomfort to the diver without improving the face seal.

Two-way communications consist of a microphone and an earphone, and are wired in parallel, preventing the failure of one unit from affecting the performance of the other. The DM-6 mask is exactly the same as the DM–5 but with two earphones instead of one, housed in pockets in the neoprene hood.

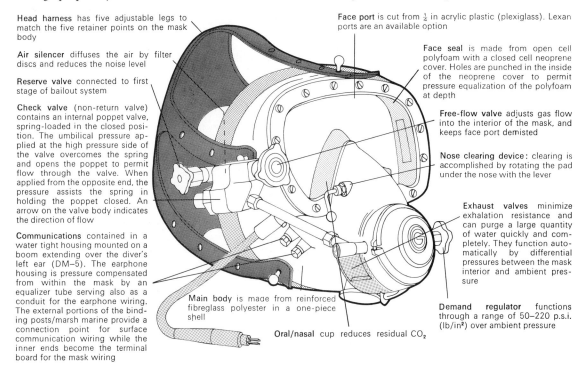

Head harness has five adjustable legs to match the five retainer points on the mask body

Air silencer diffuses the air by filter discs and reduces the noise level

Reserve valve connected to first stage of bailout system

Check valve (non-return valve) contains an internal poppet valve, spring-loaded in the closed position. The umbilical pressure applied at the high pressure side of the valve overcomes the spring and opens the poppet to permit flow through the valve. When applied from the opposite end, the pressure assists the spring in holding the poppet closed. An arrow on the valve body indicates the direction of flow

Communications contained in a water tight housing mounted on a boom extending over the diver's left ear (DM–5). The earphone housing is pressure compensated from within the mask by an equalizer tube serving also as a conduit for the earphone wiring. The external portions of the binding posts/marsh marine provide a connection point for surface communication wiring while the inner ends become the terminal board for the mask wiring

Face port is cut from $\frac{1}{4}$ in acrylic plastic (plexiglass). Lexan ports are an available option

Face seal is made from open cell polyfoam with a closed cell neoprene cover. Holes are punched in the inside of the neoprene cover to permit pressure equalization of the polyfoam at depth

Free-flow valve adjusts gas flow into the interior of the mask, and keeps face port demisted

Nose clearing device: clearing is accomplished by rotating the pad under the nose with the lever

Exhaust valves minimize exhalation resistance and can purge a large quantity of water quickly and completely. They function automatically by differential pressures between the mask interior and ambient pressure

Main body is made from reinforced fibreglass polyester in a one-piece shell

Oral/nasal cup reduces residual CO_2

Demand regulator functions through a range of 50–220 p.s.i. (lb/in²) over ambient pressure

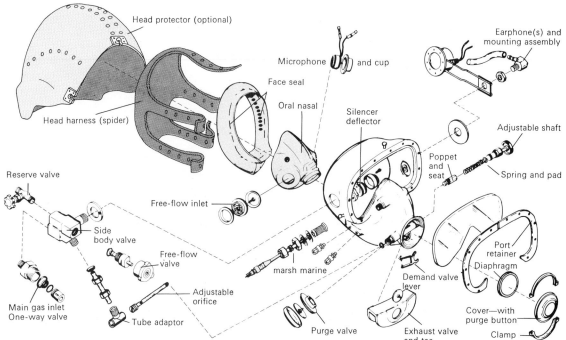

Head protector (optional)

Head harness (spider)

Microphone and cup

Earphone(s) and mounting assembly

Face seal

Oral nasal

Silencer deflector

Adjustable shaft

Spring and pad

Poppet and seat

Reserve valve

Free-flow inlet

Side body valve

Free-flow valve

Adjustable orifice

marsh marine

Main gas inlet One-way valve

Tube adaptor

Purge valve

Demand valve lever

Exhaust valve and tee

Port retainer

Diaphragm

Cover—with purge button

Clamp

General Aquadyne Inc, 1009 Cindy Lane, Carpinteria Ca. 93013, USA. Tel: (805) 684 8339 Tlx: 658417
Underwater Instrumentation, 212 Station Road, Addlestone, Surrey, KT45 2PH, UK. Tel: (97) 43871 Tlx: 928346

6.1i DIVING HELMETS MILLER 400 SERIES

This lightweight, neutrally-buoyant helmet is made entirely from metal; the helmet shell is bronze, while all the valves, hardware and fasteners are stainless steel or nickel-plated brass. The helmet moves with the diver's head because it is secured with an internal adjustable padded neck strap. The jam-proof, locking neck ring can be adjusted on all four external cams for an effective watertight seal, and can be matched to almost any type of diving suit. It has an optional bronze face guard and a flip-up welding shield.

There are two alternative breathing systems, one is free-flow, the other is by demand regulator. It is available with three different demand regulators: Miller, KMB-10 with Miller adaptor, and a Miller-10 (KMB 10 valve in a Miller regulator). It has 2 adjustable exhausts, one on the helmet and one on the regulator and has an optional bailout elbow.

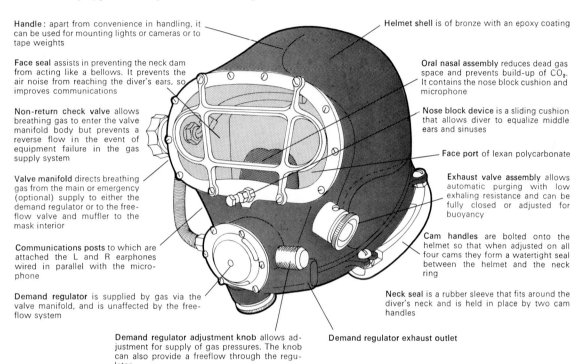

Handle: apart from convenience in handling, it can be used for mounting lights or cameras or to tape weights

Face seal assists in preventing the neck dam from acting like a bellows. It prevents the air noise from reaching the diver's ears, so improves communications

Non-return check valve allows breathing gas to enter the valve manifold body but prevents a reverse flow in the event of equipment failure in the gas supply system

Valve manifold directs breathing gas from the main or emergency (optional) supply to either the demand regulator or to the free-flow valve and muffler to the mask interior

Communications posts to which are attached the L and R earphones wired in parallel with the microphone

Demand regulator is supplied by gas via the valve manifold, and is unaffected by the free-flow system

Demand regulator adjustment knob allows adjustment for supply of gas pressures. The knob can also provide a freeflow through the regulator

Helmet shell is of bronze with an epoxy coating

Oral nasal assembly reduces dead gas space and prevents build-up of CO_2. It contains the nose block cushion and microphone

Nose block device is a sliding cushion that allows diver to equalize middle ears and sinuses

Face port of lexan polycarbonate

Exhaust valve assembly allows automatic purging with low exhaling resistance and can be fully closed or adjusted for buoyancy

Cam handles are bolted onto the helmet so that when adjusted on all four cams they form a watertight seal between the helmet and the neck ring

Neck seal is a rubber sleeve that fits around the diver's neck and is held in place by two cam handles

Demand regulator exhaust outlet

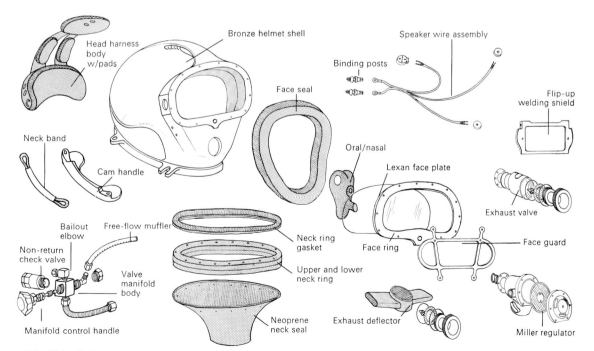

Head harness body w/pads

Bronze helmet shell

Speaker wire assembly

Binding posts

Face seal

Flip-up welding shield

Neck band

Cam handle

Oral/nasal

Lexan face plate

Exhaust valve

Bailout elbow

Free-flow muffler

Non-return check valve

Valve manifold body

Neck ring gasket

Upper and lower neck ring

Face ring

Face guard

Manifold control handle

Neoprene neck seal

Exhaust deflector

Exhaust valve

Miller regulator

Miller Diving Equipment Inc, London Route, Box 334, Harper, Tex. 78631, USA. Tel: (512) 864 4022

6.1j DIVING MASKS THE AGA DIVATOR

Aga developed a positive pressure mask for work in toxic atmospheres such as firefighting and rescue operations. There are two diving versions of the breathing valve, one colour-coded yellow and used by sports divers, and one which is an integral part of a professional face mask. The professional diving version is particularly suitable for cutting and welding in an underwater habitat as it eliminates the risk of inhaling toxic gases; and in an emergency the mask can be donned quickly by the bell diver.
The mask has a flat visor to prevent optical distortion.

To avoid disturbing reflections, but still let in light, the sides of the visor may be matted on the inside using a fine glass-paper. There is a nose-clearing device for equalising. The positive pressure should always be turned on underwater to automatically drain the mask should it become dislodged. It is easy to put on and can be worn with most types of diving dress. Communications are optional extras and are usually in the form of a microphone and a mastoid transmitter.

Dry air flushes over the visor clearing misting and enters into the inner mask through non-return valves.

Demist channels.

Speech diaphragm and space for connecting microphone.

Valve housing with two-position cover for turning on or off the positive pressure.

Quick release buckles.

Adjustable rubber head straps.

Inner oral–nasal mask reduces dead space and breathing resistance to a minimum.

Full face mask with large visor and wide sealing edge of soft rubber which makes a positive seal against the face by the positive pressure in the mask.

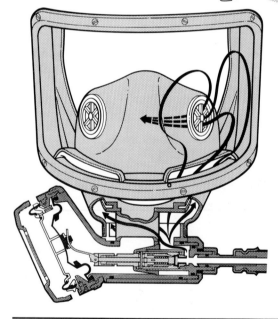
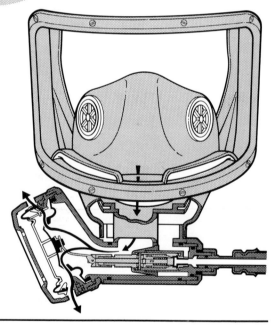

Inhalation
Switching on the positive pressure causes the diaphragm disc (1) to press on the lever (2) and open the air supply. On inhalation, air passes into the breathing valve and mask through channel A, flushing across the visor, and is drawn through the non-return valves of the inner mask, escaping through the exhalation valve (3) into the positive pressure chamber (7). The chamber is closed to any leakage of air, in or out, by the diaphragm disc (1) and the positive pressure diaphragm (5) tightened against the valve housing by the inner diaphragm ring (4). When the pressure in the chamber (7), mask and

breathing valve has risen to approximately 300 Pa (or 300 N/m², or 300×10^{-5} bar), the spring pressure on the diaphragm disc (1) is counteracted, pressing it outwards. The lever (2) then ceases to operate the inlet valve and the air supply is shut off.

Exhalation
During exhalation the pressure in the chamber (6) rises to above 300 Pa which causes the diaphragm disc (1) to be pressed further outwards, engaging the inner diaphragm ring (4) together with the positive pressure diaphragm (5) and the outlet is opened to allow exhaled air out.

When the exhalation cycle is over, the inner diaphragm ring (4) and diaphragm edge shut off the outlet and the whole procedure is repeated in the next breath.

Maintenance
The mask should only be cleaned with a detergent with a pH value of less than 10 and which does not contain Perborate. Liquid Fenom, Ajax and Extol are recommended by Aga.

Aga Spiro Ltd,
Halesfield 19, Telford, Shropshire, TF7 4QT, UK.
Tel: (0952) 582 822/847   Tlx: 35368

6.1k DIVING HELMETS THE RATCLIFFE HELMET (RAT HAT)

The 'Rat Hat' derives its name from its designer Bob Ratcliffe, and is now produced by Underwater Technology Services for the exclusive use of Oceaneering International.

It is positively buoyant by about 1 kg (2–3 lb). Different size head liners, a chin strap and jock strap keep the helmet in place on the diver's head.

Both the emergency and operational breathing gases are connected to a manifold on the back of the helmet. The manifold directs gas either to the freeflow valve or to the demand regulator system.

There are two different neck ring assemblies: one for dry suit diving (seldom used) and one for wet suit/hot water suit diving. The wet suit neck ring can also be used when wearing a Unisuit.

The microphone and earphone are connected by a Marsh-Marine connector to the diver's umbilical.

The helmet can be fitted with such options as a hot water breathing gas heater, a thermal regenerator breathing gas heater, a helium reclaim valve and a lamp mounted on the handle.

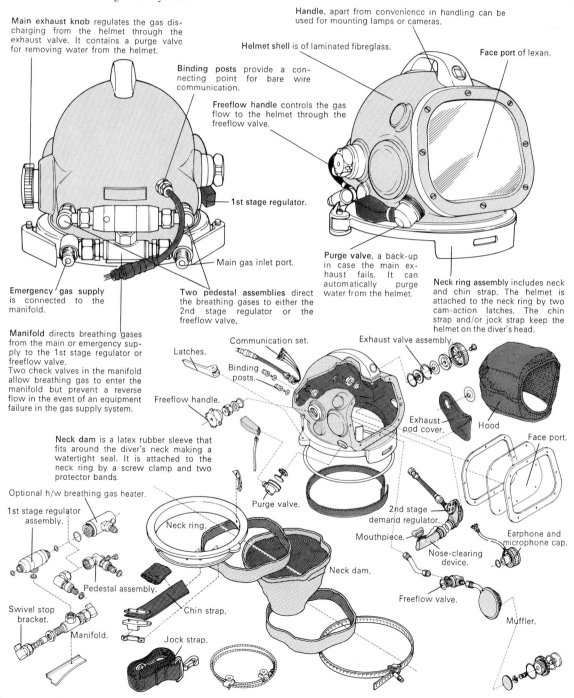

Main exhaust knob regulates the gas discharging from the helmet through the exhaust valve. It contains a purge valve for removing water from the helmet.

Handle, apart from convenience in handling can be used for mounting lamps or cameras.

Helmet shell is of laminated fibreglass.

Face port of lexan.

Binding posts provide a connecting point for bare wire communication.

Freeflow handle controls the gas flow to the helmet through the freeflow valve.

1st stage regulator.

Purge valve, a back-up in case the main exhaust fails. It can automatically purge water from the helmet.

Main gas inlet port.

Emergency gas supply is connected to the manifold.

Two pedestal assemblies direct the breathing gases to either the 2nd stage regulator or the freeflow valve.

Neck ring assembly includes neck and chin strap. The helmet is attached to the neck ring by two cam-action latches. The chin strap and/or jock strap keep the helmet on the diver's head.

Manifold directs breathing gases from the main or emergency supply to the 1st stage regulator or freeflow valve.
Two check valves in the manifold allow breathing gas to enter the manifold but prevent a reverse flow in the event of an equipment failure in the gas supply system.

Communication set.

Latches.

Binding posts.

Freeflow handle.

Exhaust valve assembly.

Exhaust pod cover.

Hood.

Face port.

Neck dam is a latex rubber sleeve that fits around the diver's neck making a watertight seal. It is attached to the neck ring by a screw clamp and two protector bands.

Purge valve.

Optional h/w breathing gas heater.

1st stage regulator assembly.

Neck ring.

2nd stage demand regulator.

Mouthpiece.

Nose-clearing device.

Earphone and microphone cap.

Pedestal assembly.

Neck dam.

Freeflow valve.

Swivel stop bracket.

Manifold.

Chin strap.

Jock strap.

Muffler.

Oceaneering International, PO Box 4488, Santa Barbara, Ca. 93103, USA. Tel: (805) 963 1414 Tlx: 658419

6.11 DIVING HELMETS SIEBE GORMAN 12 BOLT HELMET

The famous Siebe Gorman standard helmet has been developed directly from the original Siebe design patented in 1837. The original design was so sound and functional that it is the direct ancestor of today's deep-sea diving outfit.

The all metal, positively buoyant helmet can be used for diving to depths down to 61 m (200 ft). It is worn with a standard dry suit and attached to the dry suit by a 12 bolt corselet, so care should be taken to avoid a blow-up. The front window is removable so it can be interchanged with a protective faceplate when welding. The helmet is free-flow with two exhausts, a spitcock and a regulating exhaust valve.

The major advantages are the protection it gives to the diver in polluted waters, the large internal volume which is a built-in air reserve, and when well maintained it will last indefinitely. The major disadvantage is that it is heavy and bulky for the diver.

There are two alternative helmets, the 12 bolt with round corselet and the lightweight utility helmet with corselet.

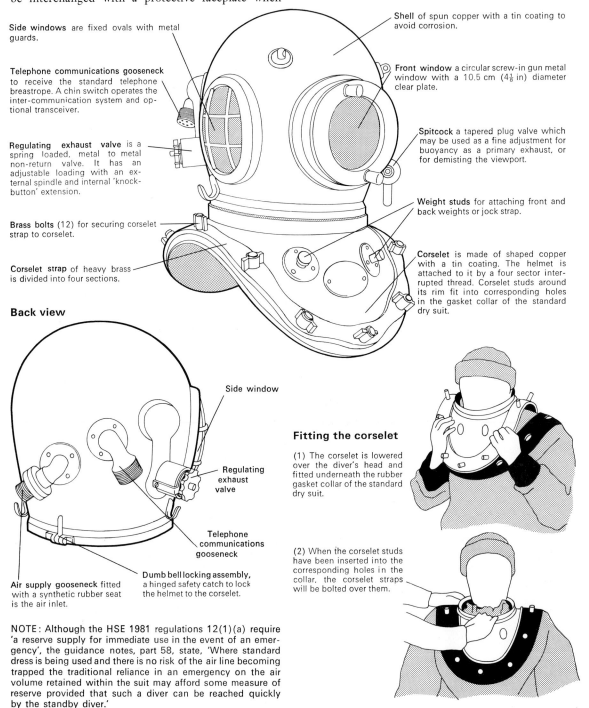

Side windows are fixed ovals with metal guards.

Telephone communications gooseneck to receive the standard telephone breastrope. A chin switch operates the inter-communication system and optional transceiver.

Regulating exhaust valve is a spring loaded, metal to metal non-return valve. It has an adjustable loading with an external spindle and internal 'knock-button' extension.

Brass bolts (12) for securing corselet strap to corselet.

Corselet strap of heavy brass is divided into four sections.

Shell of spun copper with a tin coating to avoid corrosion.

Front window a circular screw-in gun metal window with a 10.5 cm (4⅛ in) diameter clear plate.

Spitcock a tapered plug valve which may be used as a fine adjustment for buoyancy as a primary exhaust, or for demisting the viewport.

Weight studs for attaching front and back weights or jock strap.

Corselet is made of shaped copper with a tin coating. The helmet is attached to it by a four sector interrupted thread. Corselet studs around its rim fit into corresponding holes in the gasket collar of the standard dry suit.

Back view

Side window

Regulating exhaust valve

Telephone communications gooseneck

Air supply gooseneck fitted with a synthetic rubber seat is the air inlet.

Dumb bell locking assembly, a hinged safety catch to lock the helmet to the corselet.

Fitting the corselet

(1) The corselet is lowered over the diver's head and fitted underneath the rubber gasket collar of the standard dry suit.

(2) When the corselet studs have been inserted into the corresponding holes in the collar, the corselet straps will be bolted over them.

NOTE: Although the HSE 1981 regulations 12(1)(a) require 'a reserve supply for immediate use in the event of an emergency', the guidance notes, part 58, state, 'Where standard dress is being used and there is no risk of the air line becoming trapped the traditional reliance in an emergency on the air volume retained within the suit may afford some measure of reserve provided that such a diver can be reached quickly by the standby diver.'

6.2 DIVER GAS RECOVERY SYSTEMS

Saturation diving to depths in excess of 50 m requires a helium–oxygen breathing mixture. Helium, however, is very expensive and supply arrangements can occasionally cause problems, especially in remote areas or where bad weather conditions prevail.

In general, open circuit diving (where exhaled gas is released into the water) supplies gas from the surface to the diver at an average rate of 0.04 m³/min (1.5 ft³/min). Thus, a diver working at 200 m will require gas at the rate of 0.8 m³/min (30 ft³/min) (measured at atmospheric pressure). The gas alone could cost over £200 per hour; on top of this must be added the costs of transport and handling, bottle storage and interest etc.

A closed circuit gas recovery system can save about 80–85% of these costs by recovering the helium that would otherwise be vented into the water and by reconstituting it for reuse. It will also reduce the amount of helium required to be transported and stored, thus saving deck space and reducing deck weight.

Another advantage is that since the gas is recycled, a given amount of heliox will last longer than if used on open circuit supply. This means that where gas-carrying capacity is limited, such as in diver lock-out submersibles, the excursion times can be considerably extended before the supply has to be recharged.

Gas recovery systems fall into two general categories: those which require an umbilical gas supply, and self-contained backpack systems.

Umbilical-supplied systems

The umbilical-supplied systems recover the diver's exhaled gas via a special exhaust control valve, which regulates the flow of gas out of the helmet or mask such that the diver can exhale safely.

BELL-MOUNTED SYSTEM	TOPSIDE-MOUNTED SYSTEM
ADVANTAGES	ADVANTAGES
Generally less expensive Small, lightweight package Relatively simple to operate Minimal modification to bell umbilical (addition of power cable)	System not in hostile environment Can be serviced while dive is in progress Easily interfaced with bell Negligible weight and volume added to bell Allows greater excursions from the bell Generally provides demand system which allows open circuit operation
DISADVANTAGES.	
System in hostile environment If a problem arises bell must surface to await repair Difficult to mount on some bells All systems electrically operated, thus increasing the risk of electric shock Electrical operation may cause interference with communications or TV	DISADVANTAGES Slightly more expensive Generally requires more deck-space Bigger bell umbilical required

There are many different types of gas recovery systems available, of which nine umbilical-supplied and three backpack systems are discussed below, in alphabetical order.

COMEX INDUSTRIES
287 Chemin de la Madrague-ville,
13314 Marseille Cedex 3, Tel: (91) 69 90 03
France. Tlx: CX IND 401755

Specifications

Type of system	Surface-mounted
Name of system	Comex Gas Reclaim System
Dimensions	2.4 × 2.2 × 2.2 m (8 × 7 × 7′) and panel 60 × 40 × 25 cm (24 × 16 × 10″)
Operating range	50–over 300 m (165–1500′)
Gas recovery	80–95%

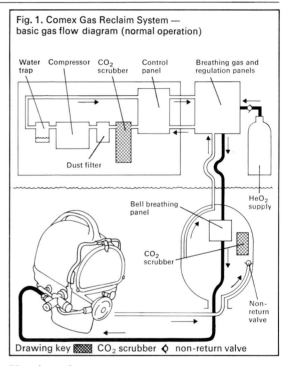

Fig. 1. Comex Gas Reclaim System — basic gas flow diagram (normal operation)

Water trap — Compressor — CO_2 scrubber — Control panel — Breathing gas and regulation panels

Dust filter

Bell breathing panel

CO_2 scrubber

HeO_2 supply

Non-return valve

Drawing key ▨ CO_2 scrubber ◇ non-return valve

How it works

The diver is supplied with breathing gas from the surface supply. Non-return valves on the inlet/outlet of the diver's helmet prevent any exhaled gas from returning to and contaminating his gas supply. His exhaled gas returns to the bell via the exhaust hose in the diver umbilical; a non-return valve on the end of the hose keeps the system water-tight and free from solid particles. The gas is released into the bell atmosphere where a scrubber removes CO_2, and where the consumed oxygen is replaced under the control of the bellman who also controls the emergency gas supply (from cylinders mounted on the outside of the bell). Gas from the bell atmosphere returns to the surface via the bell umbilical. At the surface it passes through a CO_2 scrubber which removes any remaining carbon dioxide, a filter to remove any solid particles and a water trap where condensation is removed. The reconstituted gas is then returned to the diver, thus completing the cycle. At every stage the gas in the system is carefully monitored by surface and bell control panels, with selected gas analysis.

Compressor
Corblin Suppressor AC 60.

Headgear
Comex Pro with inlet/outlet regulators.

Safety features
—A safety device on the diver exhaust hose to the bell automatically closes the exhaust line should the exhaust valve on the helmet remain open. The exhaust valve can also be manually closed and the exhaled gas released to the water.

—A non-return valve on the end of the return line to the bell prevents gas flowing back to the diver and inflating his mask when he is working above the bell.

COMEX INDUSTRIES
287 Chemin de la Madrague-Ville,
13314 Marseille Cedex 3,   Tel: (91) 69 90 03
France.   Tlx: CX IND 401755

Specifications
Type of system	Bell-mounted
Name of system	Closed Circuit Breathing System
Dimensions	$73 \times 57 \times 60$ cm ($29 \times 22 \times 24''$)
Weight	100 kg (220 lb) in air; 75 kg (165 lb) in water
Operating range	50–450 m (165–1500')
Gas recovery	80–90%

Fig. 2. Comex Closed Circuit Breathing System — basic gas flow diagram (normal operation)

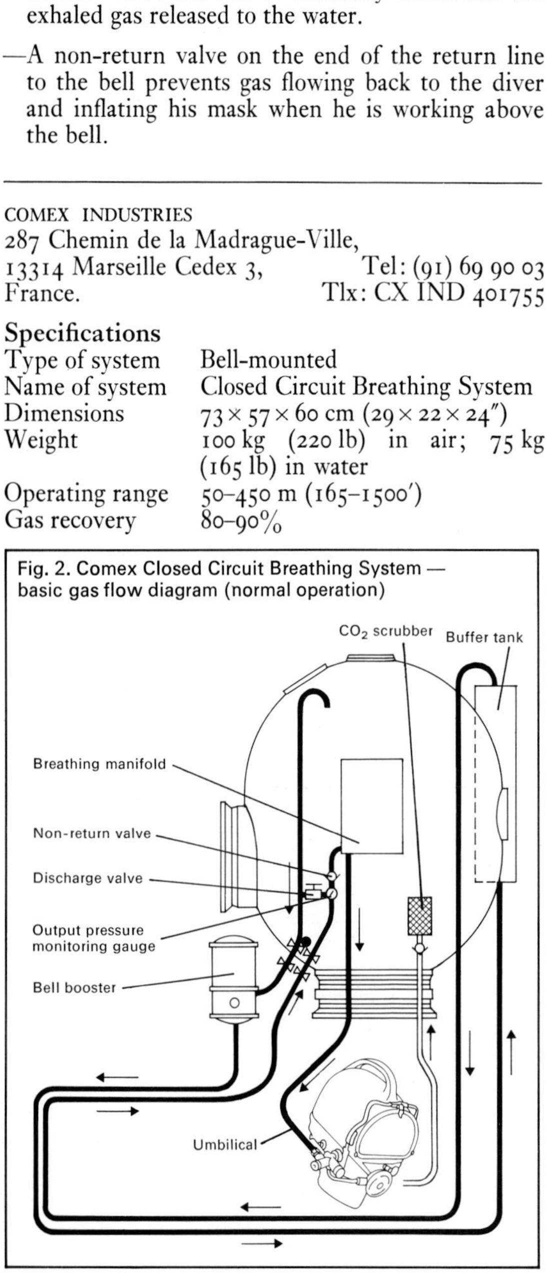

How it works
Gas from the bell atmosphere is compressed at the bell and pumped to the diver via a buffer tank which stabilises output pressure to the diver. An umbilical carries gas to the diver through a non-return valve which prevents exhaled gas from flowing back into the gas supply. Exhaled gas passes back to the bell via a return hose in the umbilical; it passes through a non-return valve into a CO_2 scrubber and is released to the bell atmosphere for rebreathing. Since this system depends on the hydrostatic head of pressure to return the exhaled gas upwards to the bell, the non-return valve on the return hose is important as it prevents exhaled gas from flowing back up to the diver when he is working above the bell. In this situation the diver adjusts the valve on his helmet and allows the exhaled gas to be vented to the water.

Compressor
Bell-mounted, 12 kW, electrically-driven, oil-free compressor. Pressure resistant internally and externally to 45 bars. Output pressure, 12 bars above pressure of the bell.

Headgear
Comex Pro helmet with inlet/outlet regulators.

Safety features
—Unit cooled by direct contact with seawater, so no pressure-resistant container required.

—If motor fails, the bellman switches to umbilical supply and diver adjusts his helmet valve to allow exhaled gas to be vented to the water.

—If the bellman opens umbilical supply without switching off closed circuit system, a non-return valve prevents exhaled gas returning to the diver.

—Noxious gas from compressor motor reaching the diver is minimised by double piston arrangement.

—Buffer tank provides gas reserve and stabilises output pressure.

—If closed circuit fails, manual or automatic switch over to umbilical supply available.

—If diver is working above the bell a non-return valve prevents his exhaled gas returning and inflating his mask.

Special features
Very low noise level.

DIVER'S EXCHANGE INC.   DIVEX (UK) LIMITED
2245 Breaux Avenue,   Unit 4, Brinell Way,
Harvey,   Harfrey's Industrial Estate,
Louisiana 70058,   Great Yarmouth,
USA.   Norfolk, NR3 0LU,
                            England.

Tel: (504) 368 2986   Tel: (0493) 57927
Tlx: 587428 DIVEX   Tlx: 975273 DIVEX

Specifications
Type of system	Bell-mounted
Name of system	Divex Push-Pull Breathing System Arawak V
Dimensions	pump unit: 1.6×0.4 m ($5 \times 1.25'$) backpack: approx. $61 \times 30 \times 15$ cm ($24 \times 11\frac{3}{4} \times 6''$) backpack
Weight	pump: 172 kg (380 lb) in air; neutral in water
	helmet: 9.3 kg (20.5 lb) in air; neutral in water

Operating range 60–457 m (200–1500′)
Gas recovery   85% approx.

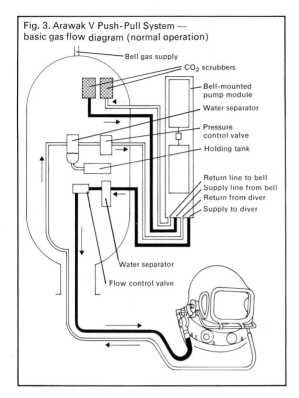

Fig. 3. Arawak V Push-Pull System —
basic gas flow diagram (normal operation)

- Bell gas supply
- CO₂ scrubbers
- Bell-mounted pump module
- Water separator
- Pressure control valve
- Holding tank
- Return line to bell
- Supply line from bell
- Return from diver
- Supply to diver
- Water separator
- Flow control valve

How it works
The Arawak V is a purpose-designed means of circulating bell gas to and from the diver.

The compressor module, located on the outside of the bell (or submersible), in a pressure-compensated capsule, draws the gas through a scrubber and passes it across a flow control valve to the diver's free flow helmet.

Exhaled and unused gas is returned via the back pressure regulator mounted on the diver's pack, through another control valve into the bell via the scrubber and water separater. The gas mixes with the existing bell gas and is ready for another cycle.

A gauge panel is provided for continuous system monitoring and all standard diving and electrical safety facilities are fitted.

The system is designed to enable the diver to work from 10 m (33′) above the bell to 30 m (100′) below the bell.

Compressor
A bell-mounted cylinder containing two electrically driven compressors and associated valving. Oil-free. One unit supplies one diver.

Headgear
Specially designed Arawak V helmet. One movement locks helmet on; five separate movements required to remove the helmet. A helmet liner (available in a selection of sizes) improves comfort and, together with cross-straps, helps the helmet move with the head. Free-flow supply means that there is no oral–nasal mask to encumber speaking into the microphone.

Safety features
—There are two independent emergency gas systems:
  from cylinders on the bell
  from cylinders in the backpack.

—An open circuit option is available in case the exhaust control system fails.

—Non-return valves on helmet prevent exhaled gas from returning to supply.

—Back pressure regulator in return line.

—Failsafe valve on helmet both automatic and manually operated.

Special features
—Specially designed helmet with high ventilation rate.

—System includes a backpack which contains two bail-out cylinders.

—Neck dam movement controls exhaust system on helmet.

GAS SERVICES OFFSHORE LIMITED
7 Westhill Industrial Estate, Westhill,
Aberdeen, AB3 6TQ,   Tel: (0224) 740145
Scotland.   Tlx: 73386 AIRCAL

Specifications
Type of system	Topside-mounted
Name of system	Gassaver and Gasmizer
Dimensions	1.22 × 0.61 × 1.68 m (4 × 2 × 5.5′)
Weight	850 kg (1870 lb)
Operating range	to 500 m (1650′)
Gas recovery	90% or more

How it works
Gassaver
Since this system depends on hydrostatic pressure to return diver-exhaled gas upwards to the bell, it cannot be used on closed circuits where excursions above the bell may occur.

The diver is supplied with breathing gas from surface control; his exhaled gas returns to the bell where the consumed oxygen is replaced. Bulk moisture and CO₂ are removed before it is released to the bell atmosphere. The exhaled gas flows back to the surface via an exhaust which is attached to the lower part of the bell; this ensures that the water level can never rise above the level of the exhaust penetration of the bell, even if the bellman is incapacitated. At the surface, remaining moisture and solid particles are removed before the gas is compressed and stored, ready for rebreathing.

Gasmizer
Breathing gas is supplied to the diver from topside control. The exhaled gas returns to the bell through a water trap which removes any bulk moisture; it then flows through a back pressure regulator which is set at a pressure lower than the ambient pressure within the bell so that, when the diver is working above the bell, his exhaled gas can still return to the bell under hydrostatic pressure. This enables gas recovery excursions to be made to 20 m (66′) above

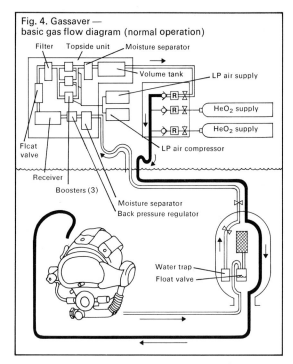

Fig. 4. Gassaver —
basic gas flow diagram (normal operation)

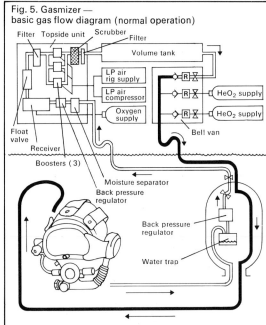

Fig. 5. Gasmizer —
basic gas flow diagram (normal operation)

Headgear

Most commonly, standard Kirby Morgan band mask or helmet fitted with Helinaut exhaust valve. Modification for other helmets is also possible. The valve operates by using two diaphragms to control the gas flow; it has no mechanical moving parts. Shifting from closed circuit to open circuit or vice versa requires a single action.

Safety features

—The Helinaut valve design makes leakage highly remote.

—Demand system provides back-up.

—A SAECO (supply actuated exhaust cut-off) valve on the return hose closes the exhaust circuit if the gas supply to the diver falls below a predetermined level.

—If all the above safety features fail, a flood valve deactivates the system.

—Standby gas can be automatically supplied if topside gas is interrupted for any reason.

—In the Gasmizer system the bell atmosphere can be scrubbed from topside.

Special features

—Det norske Veritas and Lloyd's approved.

—Simple operation and assembly.

—Takes less than one minute to check the system prior to use. Full manufacturer's repair kits supplied for gas boosters, valves, filters, regulators etc.

—Small size.

GENERAL DIVING SYSTEMS LIMITED
Deemouth Centre,
South Esplanade East,
Aberdeen,   Tel: (0224) 873150
Scotland.   Tlx: 739220 GDSABD

Specifications

Type of system	Topside-mounted
Name of system	Krasberg Return Line System
Dimensions	$3.1 \times 1.7 \times 2.8$ m ($10 \times 5 \times 9'$)
Weight	2730 kg (3 tons) in air
Operating range	30–230 m (100–800')
	Optional 460 m (1500')
Gas recovery	95–99%

Breathing gas is supplied to the diver from surface control, down the bell umbilical, through the bell supply regulator and diver's tether. The exhaled gas returns to the bell under hydrostatic pressure; it passes through water traps in the bell where bulk moisture is removed and flows back to the surface unit via a back pressure regulator. At the surface the gas is filtered to remove solids and any remaining water droplets before being dried in a twin tower drier. It is heated and scrubbed to remove CO_2 and oxygen is then added to the gas which is finally compressed and stored, ready for recycling.

the bell and 30 m (99') below the bell. From the bell the gas returns to the surface where a moisture separator removes any remaining moisture and metabolic oxygen is added. Before being filtered to remove solid particles and bacteria the gas passes through a float valve which prevents any water entering the system if, for instance, there were a loose hose fitting on the bell. The gas is compressed and scrubbed to remove CO_2 before being stored ready for reuse.

Gas boosters

Three topside-mounted, oil-free, air-driven boosters. Output pressure is up to 70 bars (1000 psi) maximum.

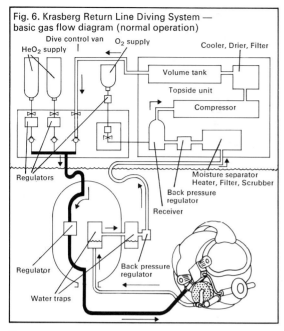

Fig. 6. Krasberg Return Line Diving System — basic gas flow diagram (normal operation)

Compressor
Topside-mounted. Oil-free. One or two 12 kW compressors. One compressor will handle two divers.

Headgear
Kirby Morgan Superlite 17B helmet fitted with Superflow valves.

Safety features
Unblemished safety record to date. Over 30 000 diver-hours. Fourteen systems worldwide.

—Two separate helmet back pressure regulators, one with a safety valve.

—Positive diver warning if any one regulator leaks.

—Demand system available if valves should ever leak.

—Topside unit has positive protection against toxic fumes from Teflon components and contains drier to prevent regulator icing up.

Special features
Mini surface unit available for bounce diving and short saturation dives.

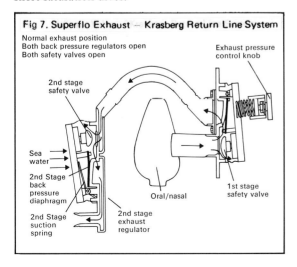

Fig 7. Superflo Exhaust — Krasberg Return Line System

Normal exhaust position
Both back pressure regulators open
Both safety valves open

NORMALAIR–GARRETT LIMITED
Yeovil,
Somerset, BA20 2YD,   Tel: (0935) 5181
England.   Tlx: 46132 NGLYEO

Specifications

Type of system	Topside or bell-mounted
Name of system	Push-pull Breathing Gas Re-circulation
Dimensions	90×40 cm ($36 \times 16''$)
Weight	182 kg (400 lb) in air, 28.6 kg (69.31 lb) in water
Operating range	55–457 m (180–1500')
Gas recovery	90% or more

How it works
Bell-mounted system
Breathing gas is circulated by a push-pull pump contained in a pressure vessel attached to the outside of the bell. Each unit contains one delivery (push) and one suction (pull) pump and can support one diver. Gas from the bell atmosphere enters an inlet strainer and is drawn through a penetration in the bell to the delivery pump in the external push-pull pump unit. This pump compresses the gas and returns it to the inside of the bell where it passes through a delivery filter (which removes solid particles) before flowing down the diver's umbilical to the diver. The diver's exhaled gas is pulled back to the bell by the suction pump. In the bell, it passes through a water trap where bulk moisture is removed before passing out through the bell penetration to the suction pump in the push-pull unit outside the bell. The suction pump delivers the gas back to the bell where it is scrubbed to remove CO_2. The gas is then released into the bell

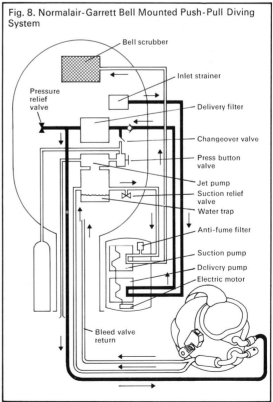

Fig. 8. Normalair-Garrett Bell Mounted Push-Pull Diving System

atmosphere and the cycle starts over again. The gas is monitored from inside the bell.

Topside-mounted system

The same push-pull pump units are used as for the bell-mounted system but the monitoring assembly is located on the deck of the support vessel. This means that the diving bell need contain only a water trap and umbilicals. Two pumps are used, one as an emergency reserve. The suction pump draws the gas to the push-pull pump unit. The delivery pump receives the gas and pumps it to a filter where solid matter is removed before the gass is passed on down the umbilical to the diver. The diver's exhaled gas is pulled up to the bell by the suction pump. Bulk moisture is removed when the gas passes through a water trap in the bell. The gas returns to the surface, where it is scrubbed to remove CO_2 before returning to the suction pump where the cycle repeats itself.

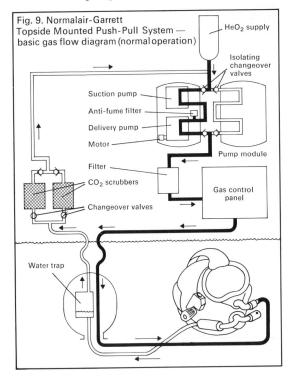

Fig. 9. Normalair-Garrett Topside Mounted Push-Pull System — basic gas flow diagram (normal operation)

HeO$_2$ supply

Isolating changeover valves

Suction pump
Anti-fume filter
Delivery pump
Motor

Pump module

Filter
CO_2 scrubbers
Changeover valves

Gas control panel

Water trap

Headgear
Various helmets can be modified, e.g. Kirby Morgan Superlite 17B.

Safety features
—Anti-fume filter prevents fumes from pump entering the breathing gas.

—When diver is working above the bell, surplus gas supply can be bled-off back to the bell.

—Non-return valves prevent unprocessed, exhaled gas returning to gas supply.

—If gas supply fails the gas is prevented from being drawn out of the helmet by a non-return valve on the gas inlet and an anti-suck valve on the helmet outlet.

—Self-adjusting pressure relief valve prevents excess internal helmet pressure.

—In an emergency, open circuit breathing option is available.

—Automatic oxygen top-up if oxygen content falls below set level.

—CO_2 units may be replaced without disrupting the dive.

—Pressure control valves automatically top-up gas if there is any leakage from the system.

—Pump can be repaired/replaced without interrupting the dive.

—Two pumps used, one for emergency/reserve.

—Automatic changeover to second pump if gas supply drops to a predetermined level.

Special features
—Gas in helmet is directed onto the visor to prevent misting and irritation of the diver's eyes.

SUBMARINE PRODUCTS LIMITED
Hexham,
Northumberland,   Tel: (0434) 604061
England.   Tlx: 537510 SUBPRO

Specifications
Type of system	Topside-mounted
Name of system	Push-Pull System
Dimensions	1.2×0.2 m $(44 \times 10\frac{1}{2}'')$
Weight	181 kg (400 lb)
Operating range	50–300 m (164–1000')
	to 30 m (100') below the bell
Gas recovery	80–90%

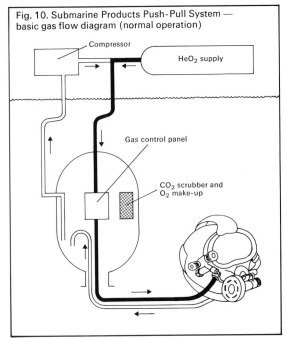

Fig. 10. Submarine Products Push-Pull System — basic gas flow diagram (normal operation)

Compressor

HeO$_2$ supply

Gas control panel

CO_2 scrubber and O_2 make-up

How it works
Topside-mounted system
Breathing gas from the surface is supplied to the bell where it is monitored before being pumped down

the diver's umbilical to the diver. The diver's exhaled gas returns via a dump valve on his helmet to the bell atmosphere where it is scrubbed to remove CO_2, and oxygen is added. The gas is drawn back to the surface where it is compressed and stored ready for recycling to the diver. Topside personnel control the gas flow.

Compressor
Electrically operated, oil-free and capable of withstanding an internal and external pressure of 40 bars. Air-cooled. Two or more compressors may be used. Provides sufficient gas flow for two divers on demand or one on free flow.

Headgear
Modified standard Kirby Morgan helmet or band mask. The inlet valve is the same (diver chooses demand or free-flow), but the outlet has a push-pull changeover valve. This valve is operated by a bar which, when pushed up, vents the exhaust gas to the water (open circuit) and, when pulled down, returns the exhaled gas to the bell. Hence the diver can operate on demand or on free-flow, open or closed circuit.

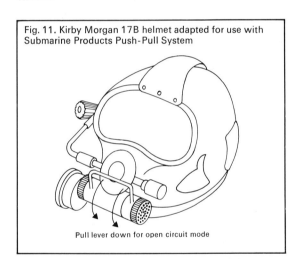

Fig. 11. Kirby Morgan 17B helmet adapted for use with Submarine Products Push-Pull System

Pull lever down for open circuit mode

Safety features
—If there is any malfunction, the dump (return) valve closes automatically and the exhaled gas is released into the water. Excess suction (over 30 mb) on the valve will cause it to flood and equalise pressure.

Special features
—The dump valve on the return line on the helmet is designed to operate over large pressure differentials, although exhalation may be difficult close under the bell when returning to it. In this case the diver changes to open circuit.

Self-contained backpack systems
Unlike systems which use an umbilical for primary life support and a diver-carried back-up system, self-contained backpack systems do not depend on the umbilical supply to operate, although, in fact they may use the umbilical supply option. They are compared with umbilical-supplied systems.
Self-contained backpack systems circulate the diver's

breathing gas within the equipment so that no gas is lost to the surrounding water. In deep diving the breathing gas is pure oxygen mixed with a diluent (helium or heliox), so called because it 'dilutes' the oxygen, making it safe to breathe.
At each breath the exhaled CO_2 and moisture is removed. Oxygen replacement is controlled by oxygen sensors which maintain the oxygen partial pressure at a safe preset level. Safety features include efficient oxygen sensors, a reliable battery and electronics system, diver and/or supervisor displays (with alarms) of oxygen partial pressure, battery voltage and gas cylinder pressures, and an emergency umbilical gas supply.

Advantages
(1) No gas reclamation system required.

(2) No duplication of controls necessary, though sometimes provided.

(3) Less costly than bell- or surface-mounted systems.

(4) Breathing gas is maintained at high purity level, hence no danger of contaminants building up.

(5) No maintenance of large equipment, compressors, safety valves or control panels. Only maintenance of the breathing sets themselves.

(6) Less deck space and logistic support required compared with surface-mounted system.

(7) Suitable for lock-out submersibles.

Disadvantages
(1) Extra weight for diver to carry. Size may also be an encumberance.

(2) No CO_2 sensor, therefore scrubber unit must be reliable and efficient.

(3) Careful servicing of breathing set, batteries, CO_2 scrubbers and recharging of bottles required.

(4) Breathing resistance increases with depth, since lungs have to power the gas circulation.

(5) No gas-heating system in backpack, although it may be provided via umbilical link.

(6) Good diver training essential.

(7) The larger backpack can be cumbersome when locking through narrow trunkings.

(8) The backpack may take up valuable space in a bell or DLO submersible.

COMEX INDUSTRIES
287 Chemin de la Madrague-Ville,
13314 Marseille Cedex 3,   Tel: (91) 69 90 03
France.   Tlx: 401755

Specifications
Name of system	Lock-out Breathing System (LBS)
Dimensions	35 × 25 × 12 cm (14 × 10 × 4″)
Weight	6 kg (13 lb) in air; neutral in water
Operating range	to 300 m (990′)
Duration	4 hr minimum
Gas recovery	85%–92%

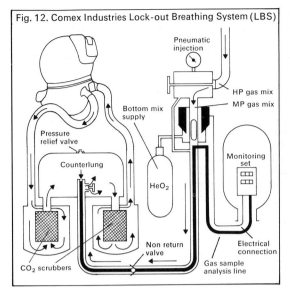

Fig. 12. Comex Industries Lock-out Breathing System (LBS)

The system is designed to relieve the diver of as many decisions as possible regarding the operation of his breathing system. Consequently, all diver monitoring and control is carried out by the supervisor in the bell/submersible. The diver wears a very lightweight backpack containing only a breathing bag, and CO_2 scrubbers and is connected to the bell by an umbilical. Breathing gas from the bell supply is delivered to the diver via the umbilical which also carries a communications link, hot water, an oxygen make-up hose and a gas-sampling hose. A non-return valve in the mouthpiece prevents exhaled gas from returning to and contaminating the gas supply.

The diver's exhaled gas passes into a flexible counterlung (breathing bag) in the backpack via a CO_2 scrubber. The counterlung contracts and expands as the diver breathes in and out and so maintains the gas circulation in the system. The consumed oxygen is replaced by the addition of an oxygen-rich breathing mix from the bell. Samples of the gas supply to the diver are continually returned to the bell for analysis. Whenever the partial pressure of oxygen falls below a predetermined minimum level an oxygen-rich breathing mix is injected into the counterlung; this raises the PO_2 by 150 mb. As the breathing circuit is closed between injections the PO_2 decreases until the minimum value is again reached and the cycle is repeated. When the diver is at rest, gas is added approximately every 2.5 min decreasing to every 1 min with heavy work.

A pressure relief valve on the counterlung prevents excess pressure building up should the admission valve remain open. The gas then returns to the diver via another CO_2 scrubber and the cycle is repeated. An oxygen bail-out bottle attached to the diver's harness provides a 5 min bail-out capability.

Headgear
Kirby Morgan band mask 10.

Safety features
—Visual and audible alarms indicate:
  no sample gas flow
  PO_2 less than 0.2 bar
  PO_2 more than 0.7 bar

more than 3 min between gas injections.
—A non-return valve in the umbilical prevents loss of gas and ensures that the backpack remains in closed-circuit in case the umbilical breaks.
—Emergency free-flow gas supply available via a back-up umbilical.

Pressure-relief valve on counterlung maintains system at ambient pressure.

Non-return valves on mouthpiece prevent exhaled gas from flowing back into the gas supply.

Special features
—All electronic monitoring carried out at atmospheric pressure in the bell. No electric/pneumatic mechanisms are immersed in water.
—Diving supervisor monitors/controls breathing system thus allowing the diver to concentrate on the job.
—Since all monitoring equipment is in the bell, the backpack is small and lightweight.

NORMALAIR–GARRETT LIMITED
Yeovil, Somerset, BA20 2YD,   Tel: (0935) 5181
England.   Tlx: 46132 NGLYEO

Specifications
Name of system	Deep Dive 500
Dimensions	$69 \times 41 \times 18$ cm ($27\frac{1}{4} \times 16 \times 7\frac{1}{4}''$)
Weight fully charged	39.5 kg (87 lb) in air; 11 kg (24 lb) in water
Operating range	to 250 m (810')
Duration	5 hr
Gas recovery	85% or more

How it works
An umbilical connects breathing gas (bottom mix) and communications to the helmet, the supervisor's display to the backpack and hot water to the diver or pack if required. The diver also wears a backpack which contains an emergency breathing gas supply, a CO_2 scrubber, oxygen and electronic package with built-in power source to drive the diver's and supervisor's monitor readout. The breathing gas, known as the diluent, is helium for deep diving and compressed air for shallow water diving.

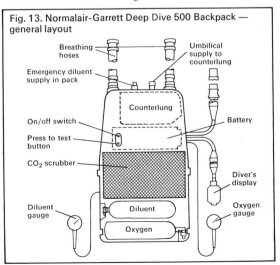

Fig. 13. Normalair-Garrett Deep Dive 500 Backpack — general layout

Before use, air is purged from the system by flushing it through with diluent from the umbilical supply. Because it is a closed circuit system (exhaled gas is not lost to the water), no further additions of diluent from the umbilical will be required except to make up the small amount of gas that may be absorbed by the diver's body and/or to prevent the counterlung from deflating. The diver then breathes in from the gas-filled counterlung (breathing bag) in the backpack; his exhaled gas is returned via an exhaust hose and passes through a CO_2 scrubber in the backpack. Excess moisture is removed when the gas flows over a water trap. It then passes over two PO_2 sensors which electronically monitor the oxygen content of the gas and maintain it within an acceptable preset limit by the controlled addition of oxygen. This oxygen replaces that consumed by the diver and is made up before the gas re-enters the counterlung. The reconstituted gas enters the counterlung and is then rebreathed by the diver, thus completing the closed circuit.

The counterlung is a flexible bag, surrounded by water, which contracts and expands as the diver breathes in and out. It is maintained at ambient water pressure by the addition or release of gas. For example, as the diver descends, gas from the umbilical supply is added to the system to balance the increase in pressure; as he ascends, ambient pressure decreases and gas is released to the water through a pressure relief valve in the counterlung. Should any of the valves fail, the first action should be to isolate the pack from the helmet by operating a shut-off lever on the left side of the helmet and then turn on the free flow to the helmet using the 'vent and blow' valve on the front of the helmet. If the umbilical supply fails, turning on the emergency supply valve on the right of the helmet will allow diluent gas to be taken from the emergency supply in the backpack (the closed circuit bail-out mode).

Manually operated bypass valves enable oxygen or diluent to be added directly to the system. However, these valves are not always fitted, since they are not recommended for deep saturation diving due to the risk of oxygen poisoning from incorrect use.

An expendable battery in the backpack powers the diver's display unit, but the supervisor's can be run from the battery or bell supply. The diver's display provides information on the partial pressure of oxygen, the battery voltage and the oxygen and diluent cylinder pressures (200 atm (3240 psi) when fully charged); the supervisor's display gives information on PO_2 only but can be modified to suit other requirements if required.

Headgear
Kirby Morgan Superlite 17B helmet, band mask or mouthpiece adapted for use with closed circuit equipment.

Safety features
—Non-return valves on the mouthpiece prevent exhaled gas from returning to the diver or gas supply.

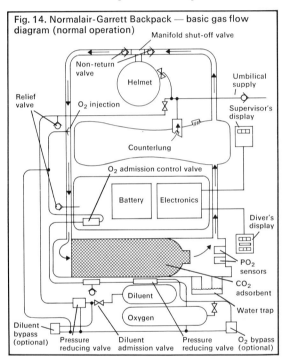

Fig. 14. Normalair-Garrett Backpack — basic gas flow diagram (normal operation)

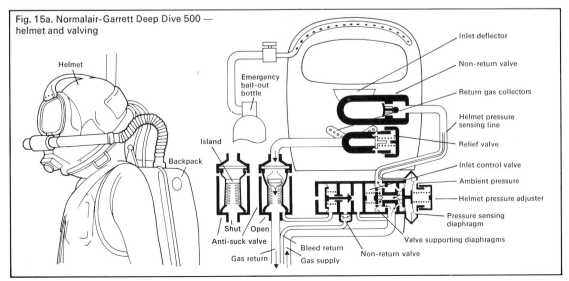

Fig. 15a. Normalair-Garrett Deep Dive 500 — helmet and valving

—Two bail-out modes are available:
a totally enclosed closed circuit rebreather option
in case the umbilical fails
a free-flow mode from umbilical supply should
anything in the backpack fail.

—Two manually operated bail-out modes are available—a self-contained closed circuit or a free-flow
through-helmet option.

—A relief valve prevents excess pressure build-up
in the counterlung.

—Manual bypass valves (optional fittings for shallow
water diving) enable the diver to add oxygen or
diluent to the system should the admission valves
fail.

—Oxygen input is limited to 3 litres/min in case the
admission valve remains open.

—Visual alarms on the diver's and supervisor's
display units indicate:

Diver's display
partial pressure of oxygen
sensor discrepancy
diluent cylinder pressure becoming low
oxygen cylinder pressure becoming low
battery voltage becoming low
secondary PO_2 showing high, normal and low.

Supervisor's display
partial pressure of oxygen
sensor discrepancy.
Audible alarms can be fitted if requested.

Special features
—Diver and/or supervisor display units available.
—Slim profile of unit is designed to allow re-entry
to bells/diver lock-out submersibles with 58 cm
(23″) diameter hatches.

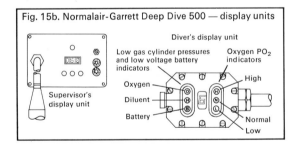

Fig. 15b. Normalair-Garrett Deep Dive 500 — display units

REXNORD SAFETY PRODUCTS
45 Great Valley Centre,
Malvern,
Pennsylvania 19355,   Tel: (215) 647 7200
USA.   Tlx: 902056 BIOMARINE MARN

Specifications

Name of system	CCR-1000 (Closed Cycle Rebreather—1000′)
Dimensions	$61 \times 38 \times 20$ cm $(24 \times 15 \times 8″)$
Weight fully charged	25 kg (55 lb) in air; neutrally buoyant in water
Operating range	to 300 m (1000′)
Duration	6 hr
Gas recovery	95%

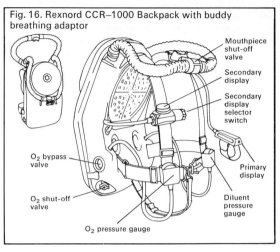

Fig. 16. Rexnord CCR-1000 Backpack with buddy breathing adaptor

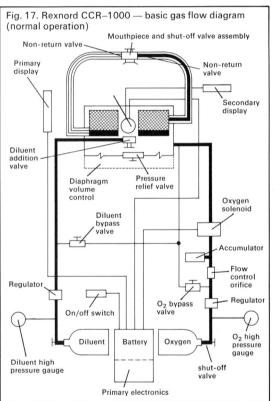

Fig. 17. Rexnord CCR-1000 — basic gas flow diagram (normal operation)

How it works

The diver wears a backpack which contains pure
oxygen plus a diluent mixture, a CO_2 scrubber, a
battery for the electronic controls and moisture
absorbent pads. The system does not require an
umbilical but takes advantage of one for communication, depth readings and decompression.

Before use, the system is flushed through with
breathing gas from the high-pressure cylinder in the
backpack. This removes air from the system and
ensures that it is full of breathing gas: heliox or
compressed air depending on the depth of the dive.
The breathing gas is known as the diluent, since its
primary function is to dilute the oxygen in the
system. Apart from the small amount that may be
absorbed by the body, helium is not consumed by the

diver. Therefore, after the initial filling of the system, more diluent will be required only to prevent the gas reservoir from becoming deflated or in the event of an emergency when it is used as the tertiary life support system.

The diver breathes from a flexible bag protected within the backpack. An exhaust hose carries his exhalation to the backpack where excess moisture is removed when it passes over water traps. A scrubber removes the CO_2, and three PO_2 sensors electronically monitor and add oxygen to make up for the oxygen consumed. The reconstituted gas is returned to the breathing bag and is then rebreathed by the diver, hence completing the closed circuit.

The diaphragm is exposed to water pressure, thus maintaining the complete system, including the diver's lungs, at ambient pressure. A pressure relief valve prevents build-up of excess pressure, whilst diluent is automatically added to the system to compensate for increase in pressure when, for example, the diver descends. Manual bypass valves enable the diver to add diluent and/or oxygen directly to the system should any of the valves fall: however, the oxygen bypass is restricted to prevent excessively high PO_2 developing.

The diver is also provided with two readouts. A helmet or wrist-mounted digital light display indicates the optimum level of oxygen in the breathing gas and has various alarms, while the secondary display indicates the battery voltage and output from each PO_2 sensor.

Headgear
The set can be fitted to the helmet or mask of the operator's choice.

Safety features
—Multiple redundancy system affords improved diver safety.

—Non-return valves on the mouthpiece prevent exhaled gas from returning to the diver or gas supply.

—Manual bypass valves enable the diver to admit diluent or oxygen directly to the system. Thus even in the event of total primary failure the diver can continue on secondary.

—A pressure relief valve prevents excess pressure building up in the counterlung.

—Oxygen input is automatically maintained even if a PO_2 sensor should fail.

—A cylinder of diluent in the backpack provides emergency bail-out facility.

—Alarm lights indicate high and low PO_2 and battery failure, sensor failure or flooding.

—A shut-off valve on the mouthpiece allows buddy breathing from one set.

Special features
—A buddy-breathing adaptor provides two mouthpieces, enabling two divers to breathe simultaneously from one set.

—The almost silent operation ensures enhanced diver communications.

—Considerable saving of diver heat loss in exhaled breath.

—Heating of the breathing gas is simply provided by extending the hot water supply to the backpack.

Conclusion
Gas economisation systems are certainly here to stay. The methods are available and proven in terms of cost effectiveness and operational safety. The future potential is very great. The choice of system and direction of development, however, depends on diver acceptability, the degree of safety, the client, the operator and any relevant legislation.

6.3 THERMAL PROTECTION

Proper thermal protection is imperative for divers working in cold water as it increases efficiency and prevents hypothermia. It is especially important on deep dives when breathing oxy-helium, since the danger of hypothermia is increased because of the pressure of the working depth and the breathing mix used. The pressure compresses the normal insulating material of the suit (e.g. foamed neoprene) rendering it ineffective, while oxy-helium rapidly conducts heat away from the diver's lungs and body, especially when it is under pressure. (Helium conducts heat at a rate of 6 times that of air.)

The main aim for any form of thermal protection is to maintain as normal the body's core and skin temperatures (see Section 12.3) so the diver can work at maximum efficiency. Thermal protection can be divided into 3 categories: (a) Operational, (b) Emergency and (c) Operational and emergency.

(a) OPERATIONAL

Operational thermal protection is used from day to day in any normal working situation. Apart from the main aim stated above, other considerations such as keeping the diver mobile, giving him free use of his hands and being as unencumbered as possible are major factors affecting the design of operational thermal protection equipment.

Types of operational thermal protection	
(1) Wet suit	
(2) Thermal underwear	
(3) Dry suit	Passive protection
(4) Hot water suit	Active protection
(5) Electrically heated undersuit	
(6) Diver gas heater	
(7) Surface heater unit and bell gas heater	

Passive thermal protection relies on the insulation, either of the air or water trapped inside the suit or of the suit itself, to protect the diver. Active protection means heat is supplied to the diver. In both cases the objective is to reduce the diver's normal heat loss to a rate the body can comfortably tolerate and control.

When active protection is used, especially in hot climates, care should be taken to avoid hyperthermia. The recommended maximum body temperatures to avoid hyperthermia are shown in Section 12.3.

(1) WET SUIT

How to use	A close-fitting garment worn next to the diver's skin. Water enters the suit at its edges, cuff and neck etc. and is retained against the wearer's skin by the close fit of the suit.	Other considerations	FIT: this is important as too loose a fit allows flushing, too tight restricts blood circulation, movement and breathing. BUOYANCY: because of the gas trapped in the wet suit it is very buoyant in water. To compensate for this a weight belt has to be worn. The pressure of water at depth compresses the gas-filled neoprene resulting in a loss of buoyancy. This poses a potential buoyancy problem as a diver who is weighted for neutral buoyancy on the surface will become negatively buoyant at depth and this may lead to problems during controlled ascent. Care should be taken to determine the optimum level at which a state of neutral buoyancy should be achieved. This can be overcome by using an adjustable buoyancy lifejacket (ABLJ).
Material	Closed-cell expanded foam neoprene, a synthetic rubber-like material full of minute 'closed cells' of nitrogen gas. These cells are not interconnected and the material does not soak up water.		
Design variations	One piece, trousers (with optional 'long john' extension to cover the chest), jacket, hood, bootees and gloves; neoprene thickness from 4 mm to 8 mm; nylon-lined or unlined.		
Thermal protection	The minute 'closed cells' of nitrogen gas within the neoprene form an insulating layer. The diver's body heats the film of water between the diver's skin and the wet suit and so assists in providing insulation.	Advantages	1. Relatively inexpensive. 2. Easy to repair. 3. If punctured the suit can still provide thermal protection and buoyancy. 4. Comfortable to wear. 5. Easy to swim in. 6. Little care and maintenance required. 7. Urination does not cause loss of efficiency.
Potential thermal protection problems	The pressure of water at depth compresses the gas-filled neoprene. At 20 m (65 ft) a diver's wet suit is about half its original thickness and its insulation quality is also approximately halved. Flushing (the action of pumping out of the layer of water between suit and skin) can occur if the suit is too loose or if there are too many tears. It is initiated by the frequent flexing of the body particularly at the waist and reduces thermal protection to almost zero. With age the neoprene cells develop interconnections, lose gas and soak up water, reducing their thermal protection capacity. Wet suits are not as effective in air. Divers can often get very cold on the way to and from a dive if the air temperature is low and especially if there is a wind chill factor.	Disadvantages	1. Flushing can occur if the suit is too loose or there are too many holes or zips. 2. Compresses with depth which reduces thermal protection. 3. Little thermal protection if there is a wind chill factor. 4. Loses buoyancy with depth.
		Companies producing wet suits	There are hundreds of manufacturers of wet suits throughout the world; consult distributors, dive shops and diving literature.

(2) THERMAL UNDERWEAR

How to use	Under a dry suit when conditions are cold.	Other considerations	Foamed neoprene underwear can be used when using hot water suits, both for added protection and for a back-up in case of malfunction.
Material	Flameproof wool, synthetic fibres, or foamed neoprene.		
Design variations	One piece; separate pants and jacket; some with feet enclosed; often with such extras as double zipper, boots and mittens.	Advantages	1. Protection can be varied to suit the conditions. 2. Rugged and easy to repair. 3. Inexpensive enough for every diver to own one, so fit and cleanliness is the individual diver's responsibility.
Thermal protection	The gas trapped in the material provides an insulating layer. The thickness of this insulating layer can be controlled by dry suit inflation and deflation facilities.	Disadvantages	1. When wet, loses most of its thermal protection. 2. Attention must be paid to maintenance to ensure personal hygiene.
Potential thermal protection problems	When heliox is used the gas trapped in the fibres does not provide a layer of insulation as helium rapidly conducts heat away from the diver, especially when it is under pressure.	Companies producing thermal underwear	DUI, Helly Hansen, Poseidon, Strentex Fabrics, Sub Sea Services, Windak.

(3) DRY SUIT

How to use	The diver is intended to remain dry in these suits, which have seals around the cuffs and the neck and/or face. Thermal underwear is usually worn underneath, either to provide insulation, as a protective layer, or to soak up sweat. In all cases gas must be able to flow into the suit, because under pressure the gas in the suit is compressed until the suit is squeezed against the body; this is painful, restrictive and causes loss of buoyancy.	Potential thermal protection problems	When used with heliox the dry suit's thermal protection is reduced as the heliox does not provide an insulating layer but rather conducts the diver's body heat away into the surrounding water. Consequently the dry suit is usually only used for diving in shallow cold waters, up to 50 m (165 ft).
Material	Rubberised canvas (for use with standard helmets), foamed neoprene, reinforced rubber or various synthetic materials.	Other considerations	BLOW UP. A most important aspect of the use of any dry suit is to learn to avoid a 'blow up'. This is when the suit inflates and forces the diver into an uncontrolled ascent. The suit pressure can, in some cases, completely immobilise the diver. Special care is therefore required to use the suits properly and to know the appropriate ways of dumping suit gas quickly. Any special dump valves must be carefully maintained and protected (from sand, for example) during a dive.
Design variations	There are four types of dry suits: standard, Unisuit, conventional dry and constant volume types. The standard suit, of canvas/rubber, is connected directly to the helmet by a breastplate so the air flows from the helmet into the suit; the Unisuit is a snug fitting foamed neoprene suit with inflation/deflation facilities on the suit; the conventional dry suit is a loose fitting, strong, thin skin with suit deflation/inflation facilities on the suit; the constant volume suit automatically maintains a constant volume within the suit regardless of the depth of the diver.	Advantages	1. Thermal protection can be varied to suit the conditions. 2. Can be very rugged. 3. Can protect the diver in polluted or infected water. 4. Fit is not so critical.
Thermal protection	The main thermal protection comes from the layer of gas trapped between the diver's skin, thermal underwear and the suit. This layer can be increased or decreased with suit inflation/deflation facilities, or in the case of the standard suit, with the helmet's intake/exhaust facilities. When the suit is made from foamed, neoprene the material also provides thermal protection from the layer of 'closed cells' of nitrogen.	Disadvantages	1. If punctured there is a loss of thermal protection, possibly some buoyancy and the dive may need to be aborted. 2. Blow up possible. 3. Urination leads to discomfort and loss of insulation. 4. Requires careful maintenance/repair.
		Companies producing dry suits	1. Siebe Gorman—standard suits. 2. Poseidon—Unisuit. 3. Avon, Comex, DUI, Dunlop, Poseidon —dry suits. 4. Spirotechnique—constant vol. suits. There are many other manufacturers of dry suits; consult distributors, dive shops and diving literature.

Andark Ltd,
Unit 1, Cabin Boatyard,
Bridge Road, Bursledon,
Southampton, UK.
Tel: (042121) 5558

Avon Industry Polymers,
Bumper Way,
Bristol Road,
Chippenham, Wiltshire,
UK.
Tel: (0249) 562 41
Tlx: 444 557

Comex Pro,
Avenue de la Soude,
13275 Marseille Cedex 2,
France.
Tel: (91) 41 01 70
Tlx: 410 985F

Divematics,
Nordstrom House,
North Broomhill,
Morpeth,
Northumberland,
NE65 9UJ, UK.
Tel: (0670) 760 365
Tlx: 537 859

Société ECA,
17 Avenue du Château,
92190 Meudon Bellevue,
France.
Tel: 626 71 11
Tlx: 200 336 F

The Unisuit

The Unisuit, a dry suit manufactured by Poseidon, is snug fitting and, as with all suits, care is required in dressing and undressing. Special attention must be paid to the maintenance of the waterproof zip fastener and relief valve.

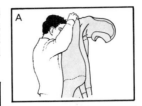

Prior to use

Apply a little grease along the metal part of the zip fastener and spray the rubber parts with silicone.

Putting on the Unisuit

1. Remove any neck chain, wrist watch or bracelet.
2. Spray the collar of the neck seal and all the inner side of all seals with silicone grease.
3. Open the zip fastener fully.
4. Fit the neck seal over the head (A).
5. With both hands take a firm grip of the top of the hood and around the collar of the neck seal. Stretch the hood (B) and slip it onto your head (C).
6. Straighten the hood after you have slipped it onto your head. Do not pull the face seal (D).
7. Fold the neck seal so that it lies evenly around your neck (E). Check that there is nothing between the seal and the neck. The neck seal should form a pocket which arrests the air and provides a uniform, comfortable seal (F).
8. Push your hands through the wrist seals (G). Avoid gripping the insides of the cuffs with your nails. Keep your fingers straight when you push your hand through the wrist seal.
9. Pull the sides of the suit forwards, over the shoulders, but make sure not to put too much strain on the zipper (H).
10. Put on the suit legs. The easiest way to do this is by sitting. Make sure that the suit legs are not twisted (I). Pull up the suit legs as far as possible (J).
11. Straighten out the shoulder.
12. Pull the zip fastener. You will need assistance to ensure that the zip is pulled up in the correct direction (K/L). Make sure that there is no undersuit material or any other debris trapped in the zipper which would cause a leak.
13. Move about inside the suit. Check that it fits correctly, that your freedom of movement is not restricted and that all seals are flat against your body.

Taking off the Unisuit

1. Open the zipper fully.
2. Grasp the zipper sides level with the hips and pull each side of the suit forwards to release from the rear (M).
3. Then pull one of the suit's shoulders over your shoulder so that your elbow is free (N).
4. Insert your fingers in under the sleeve cuff (O). Take a firm grip of the sleeve's nylon and pull the cuff off your hand.
5. Make sure that the hood is sitting properly on your head.
6. Remove the hood by twisting the suit over your head. Then insert both thumbs between the seal and the neck (P). Stretch out the neck seal and slide the hood off the head.
7. Sit down and pull off the legs.

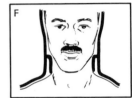

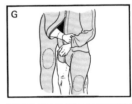

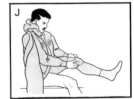

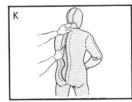

When heliox is used, active thermal protection is usually required as helium rapidly transfers body heat from the diver to the surrounding water. In the UK and Norway, the Department of Energy and the Norwegian Petroleum Directorate require all dives deeper than 50 m (165 ft) to use some means of suit heating and for dives deeper than 150 m (500 ft) the diver's gas should be heated. The USA have no thermal protection requirements regulations.

(4) HOT WATER SUIT

How to use

A loose-fitting suit with tubing to distribute the heated water around the inside of the suit. It has a control manifold so the diver can regulate the amount and distribution of hot water. It usually includes gloves and boots and should be worn with a protective undersuit to avoid scalding in case of malfunction.

Material

Foamed neoprene insulation material, with double-sided nylon lining.

Design variations

A one-piece suit which usually includes gloves and boots. The mixed-gas suit can include a heated hood. The hot water can either vent through the arm, leg and neck seal (open circuit and most common system) or recirculate (closed circuit) to the heater unit to be rewarmed; this is used in special applications such as DLO submersibles.

Andark Limited make a different sort of closed circuit hot water suit that is supplied with hot water from a unit carried on the diver's back; it is electrically powered from the surface, bell or submersible. It was originally designed for lock-out submersible operations, as the umbilical required is considerably smaller than those of other hot water suits; however, it can be used for all types of diving. It is recommended that the suit be worn underneath a dry suit to obtain greater efficiency of heat distribution and power economy.

Thermal protection

Hot water is produced at the surface and transferred, either directly or via the diving bell, through insulating tubing to the diver for use in his hot water suit. The circulation of the warm water around the diver's body creates an active insulation barrier which allows the diver to easily maintain a normal body temperature, and normal blood circulation. The hot water sacrifices its heat to the environment in place of the heat that would otherwise be drained from the diver's body. The diver himself is still losing metabolic heat from his body to the water in the suit. However he is losing heat slowly enough for his body to sustain the heat loss comfortably. The hot water around the diver should not fall below 32°C (90°F) or hypothermia can result nor should it rise above 45°C (113°F) or the diver can be burnt.

Potential thermal protection problems

FIT. This is important because if the suit is too tight the hot water in the suit will not circulate freely. The manufacturers usually recommend 1″ between the diver's body and the inside of the suit. A reduced circulation means the heat will not be distributed evenly throughout the suit and the diver will experience both hot and cold spots. SWIMMING. The average suit will hold 13–22 litres (3–5 gallons) of hot water. When a great deal of swimming is anticipated this 22 litres (5 gallons) of water becomes a hindrance. If for this reason the volume of water in the suit is reduced, the flow rate and the injection temperature must be carefully readjusted. INJECTION TEMPERATURE. The injection temperature of hot water into the suit should be carefully controlled as the diver is often not aware of a gradual increase/decrease in the water temperature and hyperthermia/hypothermia may result. In the initial stages of both hyperthermia and hypothermia the diver is often unaware of his deteriorating condition.

HEATER UNIT. Care should be taken to ensure that the heater unit is compatible with the hot water suits and the length and type of the umbilicals used.

Other considerations

The water temperature within the suit is affected by:
- (a) the injection temperature of the water entering the suit
- (b) the rate at which the flow of water enters the suit
- (c) the amount of water in the suit
- (d) the exchange rate within the suit which is obtained by dividing the number of litres/gallons of water in the suit (c) by the rate of flow of water entering the suit (b)
- (e) the insulation of the suit material
- (f) the depth and temperature of the water
- (g) the amount of surrounding water which gets into the suit, causing inefficiency.

Hot water suits are widely used within the diving industry, both offshore and in civil diving. As the diver requires an umbilical for communications, breathing gases and life line, the addition of a hot water hose is not in itself a major encumbrance.

Advantages

1. Safe, comfortable and effective.
2. Diver able to regulate the amount of thermal protection.

Disadvantages

1. Can be difficult to swim in.
2. In DLO submersible operations, special consideration should be given to efficiency of heat conservation.
3. In some open circuit suits constriction can cause burning.

Companies producing hot water suits

Andark, Comex, Divematics, DUI.

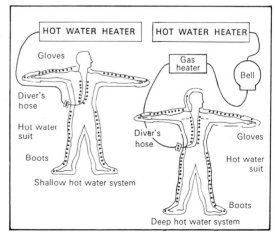

For hot water suits, specially insulated umbilicals are required to carry the hot water to the diver. Even so, heat loss from the umbilical can make controlling the temperature of the diver difficult, especially during deep dives.

(5) THE WINDAK ELECTRICALLY HEATED SUIT (EHS)

How to use	Light underwear (i.e. long johns, etc.) may be worn underneath the EHS, as it is more practical to wash than the suit, and a dry suit should be worn on top. Windak suggest that the diver wears thermal underwear between the EHS and the dry suit to increase efficiency of thermal protection.
Material	Electric heating wires on a wool material.
Design	A one-piece suit; the heating element extends over the whole body, including the feet, up as far as the base of the neck but not over the shoulders where the weight of the helmet corslet might compress it against the skin. Gloves are designed to function when wet. The suit is run from low DC voltage. Although normally dry, the heated suit is perfectly safe even when flooded and will still provide a good measure of thermal protection in this condition.
Thermal protection	The EHS uses an electrical heating element to actively heat the diver.
Potential thermal protection problems	Care must be taken to hang the suit up after use. Never turn it on unless the suit is being worn as this might short-circuit the heating element.

In the past misuse of the suit has led to some divers being burnt. One electrical element in the suit should never overlap with another element or the suit may short-circuit and burn the diver. Never turn the collar back upon the suit, or tuck the gloves up on the suit.

Other considerations	The EHS is mainly used by military divers. For offshore use its main advantages would be in manned submersibles where there is already an electric power source aboard the submersible and where the need to reduce the size of the umbilical is of paramount importance.
Advantages	1. Very efficient for heat produced. 2. Small heater unit required for maximum heat production. 3. Smaller umbilicals than hot water suits. 4. More effective at greater depths than open circuit suits. 5. More versatile for setting up at remote sites where hot water equipment is too cumbersome to install.
Disadvantages	1. Diver does not receive as much heat as with hot water suits. 2. As four layers are needed for thermal protection the diver's mobility can be reduced and care is needed in dressing.

(6) DIVER GAS HEATER

How to use	Diver gas heaters can be mounted on the diver or on the umbilical; they use hot water to heat the gas. This hot water usually comes from the hot water supply to the suits.
Material	Non-corrosive metals.
Design variations	There are designs for either free-flow or demand helmets/masks; and for different pressures of hot water from the suit. Windak produce a different gas heater using a sealed electric element which heats seawater surrounding a gas hose.
Thermal protection	Upon inhalation the body attempts to bring the vapour content of the inhaled gas up to 100% and bring the temperature up to that of the deep core temperature. If the gas is cold and dry it will take heat from the body to accomplish this. In air diving, because the diver is at a relatively shallow depth the gas is not very dense. As air is not a good conductor of heat, this is not a major problem. Helium, however, has six times the thermal conductivity of air and is only breathed at depths where it will be very dense. Consequently if the diver breathes cold, dry oxy-helium he loses an enormous amount of body heat whenever he exhales. This can cause inefficiency of operation and bring on hypothermia. For dives deeper than 150 m (500 ft) the diver's gas is usually heated to reduce this loss of body heat. This is a UK Department of Energy and Norwegian Petroleum Directorate requirement.
Potential thermal protection problems	As the heat usually comes from the diver's hot water supply, any malfunction in the supply can affect the gas heater.

Other considerations As the diver goes deeper the gas inhalation temperature needs to be increased to maintain a safe body temperature.

Minimum inspired gas temperatures			
Depth		Minimum temperature	
m	ft	°C	°F
150	490	6	42
200	655	16	60
250	820	22	71
300	985	26	78
350	1150	28	83

Advantages	1. Safe and effective. 2. Little care and maintenance required.
Disadvantages	1. No emergency back up if umbilical supply is lost.
Companies producing diver gas heaters	Comex, DUI, Kinergetics, Windak.

The design principle of a commonly used system (Kinergetics) is shown below.

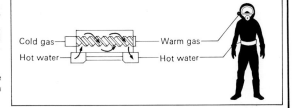

Cold gas — Warm gas
Hot water — Hot water

(7) SURFACE HOT WATER HEATER UNIT AND BELL

How to use	The surface heater unit (SHU) is placed in the ship or platform and should be near the diving spread. It is an important part of the diving system and its location on the ship/platform should be considered when the diving system is placed. The bell gas heater (BGH) is usually attached outside the bell.
Material	Non-corrosive metals.
Design variation	The surface heater units produce hot water which may be provided by steam from the ship's supply, propane, diesel or electrical immersion systems. Bell gas heaters use this hot water supplied from the insulated umbilical. Other variables such as fresh or salt water, depth of operation and number of divers using the heating, determine the selection of the heater. Some companies custom-build heaters to fit the power source and may provide a back-up heat supply as a safety feature. The most popular heating method is by electricity to heat hot water at the surface. Andark Ltd produce a slightly different electrically-powered heater unit which heats seawater and is carried on the diver's back. Bell gas heaters can also affect the choice of carbon dioxide adsorbent.
Thermal protection	In surface-supplied diving, the surface heater unit provides hot water directly to the diver for use in hot water suits and diver gas heaters. When a diving bell is used the surface heater unit sends the hot water to the bell. This hot water is used to heat the bell's breathing gases, the diver's hot water suit and his breathing gases.
Potential thermal protection problems	If the design of the heater is inadequate, fluctuations within the system can occur and the diver can be burnt. If the heater unit is unable to cope with the number of divers using the system, it may fail to heat the divers adequately, leading to hypothermia. Care should be taken to choose an adequate heater unit.
Advantages	1. Safe, simple and effective. 2. Rugged. 3. Good redundancy of heat/power supplies can be built in. 4. Excellent track record.
Disadvantages	1. If the heater failed, the dive would have to be terminated. 2. Adequate maintenance requires training. 3. Diver can be unaware of slow temperature changes.
Companies producing SHU and BGH	Andark, Comex, DUI, Kinergetics.

(b) EMERGENCY

A surface-supplied diver suffering from hypothermia would be brought to the surface and treated; however, when a bell is used it may not be possible to retrieve the diver to the surface since, in the worst possible case, the bell's umbilical would be severed. Consequently emergency equipment may be carried in the bell. The bell is already crowded with equipment so size is a major consideration for any emergency equipment.

Types of emergency thermal protection:

(1) Rebreather.
(2) Survival suit.
(3) Bell heater unit.

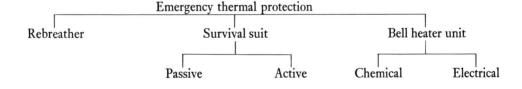

Emergency thermal protection — Rebreather — Survival suit (Passive, Active) — Bell heater unit (Chemical, Electrical)

DUI Inc,
1148 Delevan Drive,
San Diego,
Ca. 92102, USA.
Tel: (714) 236 1203
Tlx: 697 971

DUI Ltd,
Advance Unit 8, Farburn
Industrial Estate,
Dyce, Aberdeen, UK.
Tel: (0224) 724 093
Tlx: 739 130

General Diving Systems,
Deemouth Centre,
South Esplanade East,
Aberdeen, UK.
Tel: (0224) 873 150
Tlx: 739 220

Helly Hansen,
N—1501 Moss, Norway.
Tel: (032) 57 000
Tlx: 163 72

Helly Hansen (UK) Ltd,
College Street,
Kempson, Bedfordshire,
NK42 8NA, UK.
Tel: (0234) 41431
Tlx: 825537

Helly-Hansen Inc,
Box C-31,
Redmond, Washington,
98052, USA.
Tel: (206) 883 4313
Tlx: 152 555

Kinergetics Inc,
6029 Reseda Blvd.,
Tarzana,
Ca. 91356, USA.
Tel: (213) 345 2851
Tlx: 696 399

Kinergetics Ltd,
11 Greenfern Place,
Mastrick, Aberdeen, UK.
Tel: (0224) 681 020
Tlx: 739 675

Perry Oceanographics,
PO Box 10297,
Riviera Beach,
Fla. 33404, USA.
Tel: (305) 842 5261
Tlx: 513439

Perry Oceanographics,
Craigdarroch,
Kirkton of Raye,
Inverurie, Aberdeen,
AB5 9AH, UK.

Poseidon Industri AB,
Norra Gubberogatan 30,
Box 6095,
5400 60 Goteborg,
Sweden,
Tel: (031) 801 580
Tlx: 206 21 Posdive

Poseidon Systems USA,
241 Raritan Street,
South Amboy,
NJ 08879, USA.
Tel: (201) 721 5300
Tlx: 844 568

Siebe Gorman,
Avondale Way, Cwmbran,
Gwent, Wales, NP4 1YR,
UK.
Tel: (063 33) 612 11
Tlx: 498 108

Strentex Fabrics Ltd,
Huddlesdon Mills,
Darwen, DB3 3NW, UK.
Tel: (0254) 713 83
Tlx: 677 119

La Spirotechnique IC,
06510 Carros Ind. (T),
France.
Tel: 9308 1800
Tlx: 970 624

(1) REBREATHER

Why necessary

When a diver breathes cold oxy-helium, under pressure he loses body heat whenever he exhales. In an emergency where all heating to the bell is lost this can quickly incapacitate the diver, leading to hypothermia and eventually death. Under most bottom conditions divers without protection could be incapacitated in only a few hours.

Thermal protection

A rebreather acts as a 'heat exchanger'. The diver exhales into the rebreather which picks up the heat and moisture from the expired breath, this then warms and moistens the next inhalation. To avoid carbon dioxide (CO_2) build up, a passive scrubber is needed. Ordinary CO_2-adsorbing agents are inefficient at low temperatures so either Sodalime or Sodasorb must be used.

Other considerations

When wet: the CO_2 adsorbent can form a caustic solution if the rebreather gets wet. The rebreather can lose much of its effectiveness if it becomes wet although it will give some thermal protection. Oxygen deficiency can occur if the re-breather is deep inside a sleeping bag (part of the survival suit) with no ventilation.

A combination of CO_2 build up and oxygen deficiency can occur when the diver's breathing is shallow (due to hypothermia) and the rebreather's CO_2 adsorbent is almost used up. When the adsorbent is almost used up the amount of 'dead space' can increase by almost 50%. Dead space is the portion of an exhaled breath which is rebreathed in the next breath. If the diver is severely hypothermic or in a deep sleep he may become hypoxic.

CO_2 build up can occur when the CO_2 adsorbent is used up; however this alerts the diver by stimulating breathing, so is not a major problem.

Despite the potential problems it is much more dangerous to be without a re-breather than to risk the associated difficulties.

Companies producing rebreathers

Divematics, DUI, Kinergetics, Windak, Wharton Williams Taylor.

(2) SURVIVAL SUIT

Why necessary

At low temperatures the diver loses heat not only from exhaling but also from his body, unless he is wearing protective clothing. Pressure renders foamed neoprene suits ineffective as it compresses the material. In a helium environment the helium will diffuse into the gas spaces of the neoprene. Other protective materials such as goose down are inadequate when wet. When helium is used its heat-conducting properties make normal insulating materials ineffective. There are two types of survival suits: passive and active.

Thermal protection

PASSIVE. These suits have been designed to reduce body heat loss in a wet helium pressurised environment. Thermal protection is provided by the material the suit is made from. These suits vary in design. However, all cover the diver's entire body from the feet to the top of the head, except the nose and mouth so the diver can breathe.

ACTIVE. These suits use emergency heater units to heat the suit, with either hot water or an electrically heated undersuit. They can also be used as operational suits; however, unlike normal operational suits they are extremely efficient with low power consumption. The heater units required to heat these emergency suits are extremely small in comparison with surface heater units and are usually carried aboard the bell.

Other considerations

PASSIVE. Using either passive survival suits or a rebreather provides insufficient thermal protection to avoid hypothermia. DUI, Kinergetics and 2W-T produce emergency systems consisting of passive survival suits, a rebreather and, depending on the system: sanitary bags, rations, harness, stowage bag, mattress and towel.

ACTIVE. The same suit is used operationally and in an emergency. There are two power sources however, a surface power unit used operationally and an emergency power supply affixed to the bell or submersible. In an emergency active survival suits offer little or no protection if the emergency power supply is not fitted to the bell.

Companies producing survival suits

Passive: DUI, Kinergetics, Wharton Williams Taylor.
Active: Andark, Windak.

Comparison chart of the three major passive survival systems

	DUI-Polar Bear System	KI Survival System	2W-T Diver Survival Kit
(UK) DEn letter of 'non-objection'	Yes	Yes	
Passed NUI 300 m test	Yes		
Dimensions: main package	Pillow = 330 × 140 × 610 mm Mattress = 508 × 121 mm	Vest = 508 × 356 × 178 mm Bag = 914 × 152 dia mm	431 × 228 × 127 mm
Dimensions: scrubber	457 × 140 × 45 mm	203 × 152 × 76 mm	355 × 303 × 152
Urine collection system	Yes	No	Yes
Instructions for use	Included with each unit	No	Included with each unit
Head harness for mask	Yes	No	Yes
Ease of CO_2 adsorbent inspection	See-through design	Must open to inspect	See-through design
CO_2 adsorbent capacity	2.7 kg	2.3 kg	2.7 kg
Efficiency of regenerator	100%	95%	95%
Degree of water resistance	Waterproof	Water resistant	Waterproof

(3) BELL HEATER UNIT

Why necessary	In the worst possible case, power and hot water supply to the bell would be lost so normal bell heater units would not function. An emergency heater unit may be incorporated into the layout of the bell for use in such situations. Emergency heater units can be divided into two types, chemical and electrical.
Thermal protection	The chemical units produce an exothermic reaction (giving-off heat) when seawater is added. The seawater is then pumped through a heat exchanger equipped with blowers. The electrical units are battery cells which, with the addition of seawater, generate heat or power. When heat is generated, the seawater surrounding the

battery units is pumped through a heat exchanger equipped with blowers; when power is generated this can be used to heat the bell or submersible.

Other considerations	Some emergency gas heater units only operate if the heater is upright. If the umbilical breaks, the bell will not necessarily fall to the bottom in an upright position. Careful consideration should therefore be given to the placement of the heater unit.
Companies producing emergency heater units	General Diving Services, Kinergetics, Perry Oceanographics.

(c) OPERATIONAL AND EMERGENCY

Divematics and Société Eca produce active thermal protection systems that have both operational and emergency capabilities. Both companies manufacture systems for bells and submersibles.

How it works	DIVEMATICS. A pump especially designed to maximise heat output circulates and heats the seawater used in the system. The pump, which is affixed to the bell or submersible, is powered by electricity from the surface and circulates the water through the hot water suits and diver gas heaters. In an emergency when the supply is severed, an ethane gas heater unit, also affixed to the bell or submersible, provides an alternate power source. The emergency heater unit is activated from inside the bell or submersible. SOCIÉTÉ ECA. A molten salt storage unit, mounted on the bell or submersible powers the system. Molten salts were chosen for their high energy-storing capabilities. The storage unit is electrically charged on the surface and then disconnected from the onboard circuit. The storage unit is linked with a heat exchanger and the molten salts give up their heat to seawater which circulates through diver gas heaters and hot water suits.
Thermal protection	DIVEMATICS. A closed circuit hot water suit and a diver gas heater actively protect the diver. The hot water in the suit sacrifices its heat and reduces the diver heat loss so the diver can function safely and efficiently. As the suit is closed-circuit the diver remains dry, thus reducing the possibility of skin infection and irritation. The diver's breathing gases are actively heated by the hot water so that the heat loss from breathing is kept to a minimum. SOCIÉTÉ ECA. A specially designed low flow rate suit and diver gas heater actively protect the diver. The suit which

is open-circuit has a flow rate of 1–2 litre/min as compared with 5–8 litre/min with most other open-circuit hot water suits. The hot water sacrifices its heat so that the diver's body temperature remains stable. The two layers of 4 mm thick neoprene also provide some passive insulation. The diver's gas is actively heated by the hot water so that heat loss from breathing is kept to a minimum.

Other considerations	The system is designed to maximise space and equipment when providing operation and emergency thermal protection. Consequently it would be inadvisable to mix parts of the system with other equipment without checking with the manufacturers first. Because the systems are fitted to the bell or submersible, the equipment is in constant use and should be maintained in good working condition. The hot water umbilical is only from the bell/submersible to the diver so it is easier to control the diver's hot water temperature and heat loss from umbilical is reduced to a minimum. A lower injection temperature can be used which increases the efficiency of operation.
Advantages	1. Operational and emergency capabilities. 2. Reduces heat loss through umbilicals. 3. Independent of surface. 4. Very efficient for heat produced. 5. More efficient at greater depths than surface-supplied hot water suits.
Disadvantages	1. A limited storage capacity in submersibles. 2. Any serious malfunction can halt diving operations. 1. Operational and emergency.

Spirotechnique (UK),
Silverdale Road,
Hayes, Middlesex, UK,
Tel: (01) 573 7615
Tlx: 889 259

US Divers,
3323 West Warner
Avenue,
Santa Ana,
Ca. 92702, USA.
Tel: (714) 540 8010
Tlx: 067 8414

Underwater
Instrumentation,
212 Station Road,
Addlestone, Surrey,
KT45 2PH, UK.
Tel: (97) 438 71
Tlx: 928 346

Wharton Williams Taylor,
Farburn Ind. Estate,
Dyce, Aberdeen, UK.
Tel: (0224) 722 877
Tlx: 73368

Windak,
Woodside,
Poynton, Cheshire,
SK12 1AH, UK.
Tel: (0625) 872261

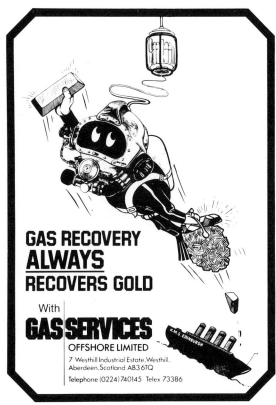

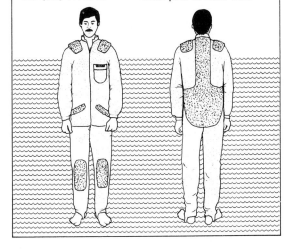

Communications

Divers will often find themselves in situations where they need to communicate over long distances with ships, the shore or with aircraft. The basis for most forms of communication is the International Code of Signals (published by HMSO) which provides for nine languages and is understood all over the world. Unfortunately, some signal systems vary from country to country or company to company. It is important to establish which code is being used. The main methods are listed below.

7.1 RADIO TELEPHONY (RT)

Radio telephony is the method of communication used between vessels and the shore. A vessel or platform can be connected to the worldwide telecommunication network via the Coast Station Radio Telephony Service. RT is used widely by offshore installations to nearby ships or aircraft, or to the nearest shore radio station for onward relay, as the range is short.
RT is transmitted by voice over radio circuits, usually in plain language, but can be by ICS where language difficulties are encountered. A 'simplex' arrangement is where one party only can transmit at any one time. A 'duplex' type of communication is like an ordinary telephone arrangement when both parties can talk at the same time and can, therefore, interrupt each other.

There are three ranges of frequency.

(1) Long range high frequency (HF) world wide service. (In UK—through Portishead Radio.)

(2) Medium frequency (MF) which has a range of about 200 miles.

(3) Very high frequency (VHF) has a range limited to little more than line of sight between aerials and 35–40 miles between coastal shipping and coastal radio stations. It is the system most used by offshore installations. UHF is occasionally used in place of VHF to avoid interference in busy areas. UHF is suitable for walkie-talkies.

VHF CALL PROCEDURE
Make sure that you know:
- how to operate the radio/telephone
- to whom you are speaking
- on what frequency to transmit
- and be prepared for any possible questions.

(1) Turn on your receiver to Channel 16 and listen before calling. If the channel is engaged wait until it is free.

(2) Transmit the name or Call Sign of the station that you are calling (up to three times only).

(3) Transmit the words, 'This is', and then:

(4) Transmit the name or Call Sign of your own station (up to three times only).

(5) When contact is established:
- transmit your own name or Call Sign once
- nominate your working channel/frequency and ensure that the other station has that particular channel facility
- transfer to your chosen working frequency. Many offshore companies use their own channels. NOTE: Do not use channel 16 for working dialogue
- transmit, 'How do you hear me? Over'
- wait for response, 'I hear you loud and clear/weak but clear/loud but distorted', etc.
- deliver message.

(6) If you require an answer or continuation with the conversation, end your transmission with, 'Over'. If you do not require an answer or continuation of the conversation use, 'Out'.

(7) Use the **phonetic alphabet** for spelling difficult or unusual words.

(8) Use **prowords** (procedure words) wherever possible.

(9) On completion of transmission return the radio channel selector to '16'.

VHF OPERATING TECHNIQUE
Always give precedence to distress or urgent calls.

Do not jam channels with unnecessary conversation.

Avoid interrupting.

Avoid swearing.

Try not to say 'er' or 'um' between phrases.

Speak steadily and at a medium speed.

Speak only slightly louder than normal conversation.

Always keep your mouth close to the microphone.

Pitch your voice slightly higher than usual.

There are a variety of short phrases or words that make conversation easier. These are called PROCEDURE WORDS or PROWORDS.

PHONETIC ALPHABET
Syllables to be emphasized are emboldened

A Alfa	**ALF**AH	N November	NO**VEM**BER
B Bravo	**BRAH**VOH	O Oscar	**OSS**CAR
C Charlie	**CHAR**LEE	P Papa	PAH**PAH**
D Delta	**DELL**TAH	Q Quebec	KEH**BEK**
E Echo	**ECK**OH	R Romeo	**ROW**MEOH
F Foxtrot	**FOKS**TROT	S Sierra	SEE**AIR**RAH
G Golf	**GOLF**	T Tango	**TANG**O
H Hotel	HOH**TELL**	U Uniform	**YOU**NEEFORM
I India	**IN**DEEAH	V Victor	**VIK**TAH
J Juliet	**JEW**LEEETT	W Whiskey	**WISS**KEY
K Kilo	**KEY**LOH	X X-ray	**ECKS**RAY
L Lima	**LEE**MAH	Y Yankee	**YANG**KEY
M Mike	**MIKE**	Z Zulu	**ZOO**LOO

NUMERALS
Apart from Call Signs and Grid References all figures should be preceded by the word, 'Figures'.

0	**ZEERO**	5	**FIVER**
1	**WUN**	6	**SICKS**ER
2	**TOO**	7	**SEH**VEN
3	THUH-**REE**	8	**ATE**
4	**FOW**-ER	9	**NINER**

PROWORDS (Procedure Words)

PROWORD	USE OR MEANING	PROWORD	USE OR MEANING
MAYDAY (3 times)	The distress signal; used when threatened by grave or imminent danger; a request for immediate assistance. (Remember, your call sign and position are of vital importance and should follow the proword 'Mayday').	How do you read?	Can you understand what I am saying?
		I read back	In response to 'Read back'; the message already sent then follows.
		I say again	When conditions are bad it is used by the sender to emphasize the important areas, or when a repetition is requested.
PANPAN (3 times)	The urgency signal; used for a message concerning the safety of a ship or of a person. If you require medical assistance ask your coast radio station for Medico Service and you will be connected to the casualty department of a local hospital (no charge).	I spell	Used when spelling out a word or abbreviation.
		Negative	'No' or 'Permission not granted'.
		Net message	Message for all stations.
		*Out	Transmission over and no reply expected.
SÉCURITÉ (SAY CURE EETAY) (3 times)	The safety signal; mostly important navigational or metereological warnings. (Usually originate ashore).	*Over	Transmission over but a reply is expected.
		Read back	Please repeat back the whole message.
Acknowledge	Have you received and understood this message?	Roger	Message received and understood.
Affirmative	'Yes' or 'Permission granted'.	Say again	Used by receiver when requiring the whole message to be repeated.
All after....	To identify part of a message.		
All before...	Used in conjunction with other words.	Seelonce	All stations maintain a radio silence and await direction.
Break	Separation between address/text/signature of a spoken telegram.	Seelonce fini	Silence is lifted.
		Wait	The station requires to consider the reply to a transmission. 'Wait' followed by a number indicates the time (in minutes) required to consider.
Confirm	My version is .... is that correct?		
Correct	You are correct.		
Correction	Cancels the word or phrase just sent or indicated.	* NOTE: The combination 'Over and out' is contradictory and should **never** be used.	
Go ahead	Proceed with your message.		

7.2 RADIO TELEGRAPHY (WT)

WT is employed mostly ship-to-ship or ship-to-shore. It is very fast, precise and capable of being transmitted over long distances. WT is sent in morse code and thus requires a skilled operator.

There is a range of services, which includes:

(1) Long range WT; for onward transmission to any ship or station; via Portishead Radio in the UK.
(2) Medium range WT; in the UK there are 11 coast stations on the 405–525 kHz bands, and 3 stations on the 1605–3800 kHz band.
(3) Medium Range Radio Telegram Service.
(4) Weather and navigational broadcasts.

When making Morse it is most important to get the right rhythm and spacing. If a dot is taken as the unit of time, the correct spacing is as follows:

Dot 1 unit	Dash 3 units
Space between each dot or dash in a letter	1 unit
Space between each letter or symbol	3 units
Space between each word or group	7 units

By whatever method Morse is being sent, it must be remembered that a dash is three times the length of a dot, and that there must be a slight pause between each letter—otherwise, for example, EE would be read as I, or AE as R. The pause between each word must be even more pronounced.

ALPHABET

A ·—	J ·———	T —	3 ···——
B —···	K —·—	U ··—	4 ····—
C —·—·	L ·—··	V ···—	5 ·····
D —··	M ——	W ·——	6 —····
E ·	N —·	X —··—	7 ——···
F ··—·	O ———	Y —·——	8 ———··
G ——·	P ·——·	Z ——··	9 ————·
H ····	Q ——·—	**NUMERALS** 0 —————	
I ··	R ·—·	1 ·————	
	S ···	2 ··———	

North European coastal radio stations

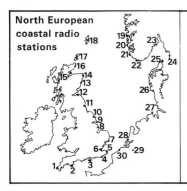

	Station	Telephone number
1.	Land's End	Sennen (0736) 87363
2.	Start Point	Sennen (0736) 87363
3.	Niton	Niton (0983) 730495
4.	Hastings	Thanet (0843) 20592
5.	North Foreland	Thanet (0843) 20592
6.	Thames	Thanet (0843) 20592
7.	Orfordness	Thanet (0843) 20592
8.	Bacton	Mablethorpe (05213) 3447
9.	Humber	Mablethorpe (05213) 3447
10.	Whitby	Whitley Bay (0632) 531318
11.	Cullercoats	Whitley Bay (0632) 531318
12.	Forth	Stonehaven (0569) 62917
13.	Stonehaven	Stonehaven (0569) 62917
14.	Buchan	Stonehaven (0569) 62917
15.	Cromarty	Wick (0955) 2271
16.	Wick	Wick (0955) 2271
17.	Orkney	Wick (0955) 2271
18.	Shetlands	Wick (0955) 2271
19.	Floro	(45) 41500
20.	Bergen	(5) 218080
21.	Rogaland	(45) 73297
22.	Farsund	(43) 49100
23.	Tjome	(33) 90588
24.	Goteborg	(0300) 62000
25.	Skagen	(458) 443727
26.	Blavand	(455) 279004
27.	Nordfriesland	(494721) 22066
	Eiderstedt	(494721) 22066
	Hamburg	(494721) 22066
	Elbe-Weser	(494721) 22066
	Helgoland	(494721) 22066
	Bremen	(494721) 22066
	Norddeich	(494721) 22066
28.	Scheveningen	(312550) 19104
29.	Antwerp	(31) 193820
30.	Ostend	(59) 702438

Gulf of Mexico coastal radio stations

	Station	State	Telephone number
1.	Key West	Florida	(305) 294 6655
2.	Marathon	Florida	(305) 743 9081
3.	Naples	Florida	(813) 649 8311
4.	Fort Myers	Florida	(813) 542 6001
5.	Venice	Florida	(813) 959 7702
6.	Palmetto	Florida	(813) 247 3669
7.	St Petersburg	Florida	(813) 895 5583
8.	Tampa	Florida	(813) 877 6752
9.	Clearwater	Florida	(813) 229 9111
10.	Crystal River	Florida	(904) 795 4811
11.	Cedar Key	Florida	(813) 247 3669
12.	Apalachicola	Florida	(904) 229 5000
13.	Panama City	Florida	(904) 769 1611
14.	Fort Walton Beach	Florida	(904) 243 4713
15.	Pensacola	Florida	(904) 432 9034
16.	Coden	Alabama	(205) 666 5110
17.	Mobile	Alabama	(205) 666 5110
18.	Pascagoula	Mississippi	(601) 762 9525
19.	Gulfport	Mississippi	(601) 388 9924
20.	Slidell	Louisiana	(504) 362 2967
21.	Hopedale	Louisiana	(504) 362 2967
22.	Venice	Louisiana	(504) 362 2967
23.	Leeville	Louisiana	(504) 693 3111
24.	Cocodrie	Louisiana	(504) 837 8330
25.	Morgan City	Louisiana	(504) 872 9001
26.	Delcambre	Louisiana	(318) 685 2344
27.	Erath	Louisiana	(318) 232 1622
28.	Cameron	Louisiana	(318) 583 2111
29.	Port Arthur	Texas	(713) 521 8123
30.	La Porte	Texas	(713) 521 8123
31.	La Marque	Texas	(713) 521 8123
32.	Freeport/Bay City	Texas	(713) 245 9151
33.	Port Lavaca	Texas	(512) 552 5751
34.	Corpus Christi	Texas	(512) 884 1915
35.	Brownsville	Texas	(512) 682 3171
36.	Tampico	Tamaulipas, Mexico	(XFS) 25582/25583
37.	Veracruz	Veracruz, Mexico	(XFU) 73809/73821
			(XFU) 73843/73865
38.	Coatzacoalcos	Veracruz, Mexico	(XFF) 23037/23141
39.	Cuidad del Carmen	Campeche, Mexico	(XFB) 21428/20007
40.	Progreso	Yucatan, Mexico	(XFN) 73200/73488
41.	Cozumel	Qunitana Roo, Mexico	(XFC) 20094/20183

Gulf of Guinea coastal radio stations

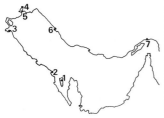

	Station	Telephone number
1.	Abidjan Ivory Coast	352219
2.	Takoradi/Sekondi Ghana Takoradi	3322, 3297, 3107
3.	Cotonou Benin	312051, 312531, 313099
4.	Lagos Nigeria	59666 Ext 254
5.	Douala Cameroon	425055

Gulf, Middle East coastal radio stations

	Station	Telephone number
1.	Bahrain	681259/252047
2.	Ra's Tannurah Saudi Arabia	Dhahran 65295*
		*for use by authorised Aramco personnel only
3.	Kuwait	814959/814079/439091
4.	Port Khomeini Iran (previously Shapoor)	Telex contact only: Tehran 21 2271
5.	Kormussa Iran	Telex contact only: Tehran 21 2271
6.	Bushir Iran	(03721) 2576
7.	Abbas Iran	(0361) 4045/4046

7.3 DIVER VOICE COMMUNICATIONS

Voice communication by underwater telephone is the primary source of diver/surface communication. Line pull signals serve as a back-up. Direct diver-to-diver conversations are possible without apparatus where both divers are wearing helmets; by touching the helmets together an acoustic connection is made and the divers are able to talk to each other. Standard visual hand signals also supplement diver-to-diver communications.

Basically there are four types of diver voice communications.

(1) **Through-water acoustic system**: consists of a microphone, amplifier, power supply and transducer. It transduces speech into the water through the underwater loudspeaker. This signal is picked up by a hydrophone or by nearby divers.

(2) **Through-water amplitude modulated (AM) system**: consists of a microphone, amplifier, power supply modulator and underwater transducer. In this system a carrier wave is modulated by the speech signal and can be understood only by a diver or tender with a receiver and modulator.

(3) **Hardwire system**: similar to a telephone; a microphone, a cable through which the signal is transmitted and a receiver. This system requires an umbilical and is the most used for surface-supplied and lock-out diver communications. Hardwire systems are of three kinds. The original intercommunication system, consisting of an amplifier, a diver's reproducer and a combination lifeline/amplifier cable, operated by a surface tender controlling tender-to-diver or diver-to-diver communication by switching. Another DIS (diver inter-communication system; sometimes called DUCS—diver underwater communication system) is similar to the above except that it is a party line system in which any diver may speak to another without switching. DIS I and II are used mostly with hard-hat equipment. The third DIS set is a surface/underwater system between the tender and up to three divers in surface-supplied helmets or masks and includes voice correction circuitry to compensate for speaking in an oxy-helium atmosphere.

(4) **Non-acoustic wireless system**: an electric field, a voice-actuated microphone and carried on the back. It is designed for diver-to-diver communications with a range of only 30–60 m (100–200 ft), also for diver-surface or surface-surface communication.

Procedure

(1) Speak clearly, at a steady pace and normal volume.

(2) Topside should pay attention to the diver's breathing rhythm. Try not to talk over loud diver inhalation noises.

(3) Break long messages into short sections, the length of one breath or shorter. This is because the diver may have to shut off his air to hear you. Gas recovery systems, which have no exhaust noises, are much quieter.

(4) Keep each message as simple as you can, es-

FACTORS WHICH CAN IMPROVE DIVER VOICE COMMUNICATIONS INTELLIGIBILITY

1. **System design.**
   - Use of high quality components
   - Use of compatible components
   - Use of robust components
   Acoustics of mask/helmet
   Elimination of electrical interference

2. **Reduction of ambient noises.**
   - diver exhaust gas noises
   - diver free-flow noises
   - task noises such as:
     air-driven tools
     hydraulic tools
     gas escape
     water escape
     surface machinery
     vibrations
     explosives
   - marine animal noises
   - pingers and transponders
   - surface vessel noises, especially DP vessels

3. **Use of divers and tenders.**
   - of the same nationality
   - with similar regional accents
   - no speech impediments.

4. **Training and familiarity with the use of standard vocabulary, prowords and procedures.**

---

pecially on the diver-to-surface links which are particularly difficult.

(5) If you want a message repeated to you say, 'Say again'.

(6) When there has been a pause in communications, identify yourself and the person to whom you are talking at the start of the next message.

(7) Never **assume** that a message has been received; repeat it until you get a response.

(8) A message which needs to be repeated should be repeated in the same words. When it is obvious that the repeats are not being understood you should say 'Rephrasing message', and say the message in a different way.

(9) If a message is failing to get through and you suddenly need to say something different, indicate the change of subject by saying 'Cancel that last' before giving the new, different message.

(10) When acknowledging a message it is better to repeat back the message, or a summary of it, rather than just saying 'Roger'. 'Roger' on its own does not indicate that the message has been received correctly.

(11) In general, the worse the communications link and the more important the message that you are trying to get through, the more essential it is that you check that your message has been correctly understood.

(12) Diving tasks should be arranged so as to avoid long periods of continuous talking by the diver, as talking reduces breathing efficiency.

(13) The telephone operator should not speak to the diver whenever power is applied, or when cables are moving, as it prevents the diver from warning the surface of any problems.

(14) Complete recordings should be made of all dives, including pre-dive checks and blow-down, and the recordings retained until it is clear that no problems were met during or after the dive.

(15) Tapes of incidents or accidents should be carefully removed and stored in a secure place pending investigation.

Language

(1) Agreed names should be developed and used for tools, components, positioning and other aspects of the diver's work.

(2) If possible these names and words should be three syllables long as they are easier to understand.

(3) Mark and label tools and equipment with sizes and/or reference numbers before use so as to avoid making mistakes and wasting time.

(4) Use the phonetic alphabet wherever needed.

(5) Use metric measurements whenever possible; always say what units you are using (e.g. 'six metres').

(6) Avoid using fractions where possible. If you have to use a fraction, repeat it in a different way (e.g. 'one sixth, that is, one over six').

(7) For all 'teens' repeat in a different way (e.g. 'thirteen, that is, one three').

(8) For all 'tens' repeat in a different way (e.g. 'thirty, that is, three zero').

(9) Be specific. Don't add endings such as '. . . ish'; say 'red' not 'reddish'.

(10) Always use the word 'zero'. Do not use 'nought', 'oh', or 'nothing'.

7.4 LIGHT SIGNALS

These can have the same meanings as flags in the ICS but are transmitted by lamp light using Morse Code. Messages can be sent in plain language, but there are a variety of procedure signals which can save time. The ICS can be understood in nine languages.
- Single letter signals are urgent, important or frequently used.
- Two letter signals are general signals.

Light signals are particularly effective for attracting the attention of a specific recipient, and can be seen by day as well as by night.

Procedure
A signal by flashing light comprises the following.

(1) THE CALL
This may be either the general call ($\overline{AA}$ $\overline{AA}$ $\overline{AA}$, etc.) if it is required to attract the attention of all stations within sight or of a station whose identity is not known. The call is repeated until response is made in the form of the answering signal ($\overline{TTT}$, etc.).

(2) THE IDENTITY
The transmitting station then makes 'DE' followed by its identity signal or name. This is repeated back by the receiving station, which then signals its own identity signal.

(3) THE TEXT
This may consist of plain language or code groups, the latter being preceded by the signal 'YU'. The receiving station acknowledges the receipt of each word or code group by the letter 'T'.

(4) THE ENDING
The transmitting station indicates the end of the signal with letters 'AR', which are acknowledged by the receiving station with 'R' meaning 'received'.

PROCEDURE SIGNALS					
Sign	Morse symbol	Meaning	Sign	Morse symbol	Meaning
$\overline{AA}$ $\overline{AA}$ $\overline{AA}$ etc. (until answered)	· — · — · — · — · — etc.	Call up	WA	· — — ·	Word or group after
$\overline{TTTTTT}$ etc. (until call up stops)	— — — — — — etc.	Answering signal	WB	· — — — · · ·	Word or group before
T	—	Word received	BN	— · · · — ·	Word or group between
AAA	· — · — · —	Full stop or decimal point	$\overline{AR}$	· — · — ·	Message ends
EEEEEE etc.	· · · · · · · etc.	Erase	$\overline{AS}$	· — · · ·	Waiting signal or period signal
(Note: the five signals above are used only when sending Morse by light. The remaining procedure signals below can be used with other methods, as well as when using light.)			C	— · — ·	Affirmative—YES
			R	· — ·	Received
DE	— · · ·	From	YT4	— · — — — · · · · —	I cannot read your morse signalling lamp
RPT	· — · · — — · —	Repeat signal			
AA	· — · —	All after	YU	— · — — · · —	Am going to communicate by International Code
AB	· — — · · ·	All before			

7.5 DIVER HAND SIGNALS DIVER TO DIVER AND DIVER TO SURFACE

These signals are used widely throughout the diving industry, with some variations between different countries. Check first that you are both using the same code. Signals should be given slowly and consciously exaggerated and acknowledged if understood. At night the diver should illuminate his hand, making the signals with a torch held in his other hand.

Stop
Stay where you are

OK?
Is all well?

Go up

Go down

You OR me

Something wrong

Distress

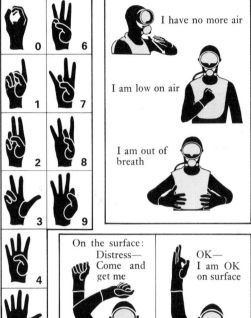

0
6
1
7
2
8
3
9
4

On the surface:
Distress—
Come and get me

OK—
I am OK on surface

I have no more air

I am low on air

I am out of breath

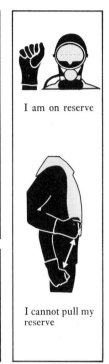

I am on reserve

I cannot pull my reserve

7.6 DIVER ROPE SIGNALS EXTRACTS FROM THE RN STANDARD CODE

There are a number of situations where a diver should be in physical contact with his partner or his tender by means of a rope. Such a situation might be a low visibility search or a failure of the telephone link. All signals are to be preceded by one pull to attract attention and the signal itself is made when the diver has replied with one pull. Roped signals are either pulls or bells given by (a) long, steady pulls (b) short, sharp tugs as striking a ship's bell.

If a lifeline gets fouled, or has turns around the shot rope, it may be impossible to get signals through.

DIRECTION & WORKING SIGNALS

Signal	Tender	Diver
ONE PULL	Search where you are.	
TWO BELLS	Go to end of distance line.	
THREE BELLS	Face shot, then go right.	
FOUR BELLS	Face shot, then go left.	
FIVE BELLS	Come into your shot.	
ONE PULL		Hold on/stop.
TWO BELLS		Pull up.
THREE BELLS		Lower.
FOUR BELLS		Take up slack/ You are holding me too tightly.
FIVE BELLS		Have found/ started/ completed work.

GENERAL SIGNALS

Signal	Tender	Diver
ONE PULL	To call attention Are you OK?	To call attention I am OK. Arrived or left bottom.
TWO PULLS	Am sending down a rope.	Send down a rope.
THREE PULLS	You have come up too far, Go down slowly until I stop you.	I am going down.
FOUR PULLS SUCCESSION OF PULLS (More than four)	Come up. Emergency signal. Come up immediately.	May I come up? Emergency signal. Pull me up immediately.
FOUR PULLS+ TWO BELLS	Come up, hurry up. Come up— surface D/C.	I want to come up. Assist me up.
FOUR PULLS+ FIVE BELLS	Come up on your SMB?	May I come up on my SMB?
SUCCESSION OF TWO BELLS		Am foul and need assistance.
SUCCESSION OF THREE BELLS		Am foul but can clear myself.

(US Navy signals differ from those above.)

7.7 CRANE OPERATOR SIGNALS STANDARD HAND SIGNALS UK AND USA

UK

Hoist — Clench and unclench fingers to signal take the strain

Lower

Slew left

Slew right

Derricking jib — Jib up — Jib down

Travel to me — Travel from me — Signal with both hands

Telescoping jib — Extend jib — Retract jib
Horizontal jib — Trolley in — Trolley out
Signal with one hand other on head

Stop — Clench and unclench fingers to signal inch the load

Emergency stop

USA

Hoist — Move hand in horizontal circle

Lower

Bridge travel — Make pushing motion in direction of travel

Trolley travel — Thumb pointing in direction of motion, jerk hand horizontally

Stop — Hold position rigidly

Emergency stop — Move hand rapidly right and left

Multiple trolleys — One finger for block '1' two fingers for block '2'

Move slowly — Use one hand to give any motion signal other hand motionless over it

Magnet is disconnected

Crane signals recommended by the National Federation of Building Trades Employers and Federation of Civil Engineering Contractors.

Crane signals recommended by the US Department of Health, Education and Welfare.

7.8 DISTRESS AT SEA

There are a number of emergencies that the diver may be faced with and which will demand immediate action on his part. Diving Superintendents will have worked out procedures for dealing with diving emergencies before they happen, and many operating companies have their own instructions. Every diver ought to be familiar with these and be ready to apply them the moment things start to go wrong. Chaos often attends disaster and at such times it is easy to make the wrong decisions.

Distress is critical, life-threatening circumstances from which the victims are unable to extricate themselves and therefore need immediate assistance.

Some examples of distress at sea might be the collapse of a structure; a collision of two ships; an uncontrollable blow-out followed by a fire; the ditching of a helicopter. In all such events, the first call for help would probably be by radiotelephone (R/T). The signal also might be given by radiotelegraphy (W/T) by the transmission of an alarm signal followed by SOS in morse code. A third method might be by visual signal, see page 187

Search and rescue (SAR) organization

Coastal radio stations in the UK keep watch on the International distress frequency which is 2182 kHz MF on the radio telephone and 500 kHz by radiotelegraphy. Most ships and coastguard radio stations keep watch on Channel 16, 156.8 MHz.

Most maritime countries maintain a life-saving service for anyone in distress. Around the UK coast and between latitudes 45° to 61°N and as far west as longitude 30°W, HM Coastguard will normally co-ordinate and initiate search and rescue measures.

To be effective, a MAYDAY call must be accompanied by the victim's position, and if possible, the nature of the distress and the aid required. Failure to furnish these details may greatly reduce the chances of being found.

Good communications are essential and of great importance in order to keep the rescue under control.

There are some fundamental rules for surviving distress.
1. Try to stay with the boat or wreckage so that you can be spotted more easily. Keep together.
2. If obliged to swim, reduce the amount of activity to a minimum to conserve heat and energy.
3. If being rescued by a helicopter, abandon any support or craft that could endanger the helicopter. Allow the winch wire to dip (earth) in the sea. Never secure the winch wire to a boat or structure.
4. Use flares sparingly and only when they are likely to be seen.
5. Never give up hope. Many a rescue has been successful after all chances apparently had faded.

7.9 VISUAL DISTRESS SIGNALS

A rocket parachute red light flare | A hand-held red light flare | Rockets/shells firing red stars | Orange coloured smoke

Flames on the vessel | Square flag above/below ball | Some article of clothing | Raising and lowering arms

Ensign hoisted upside down | ICS flags N C

ASSISTANCE SIGNALS

I require assistance — V · · · —

I require medical assistance — W · — —

7.10 NAVIGATION LIGHTS AND DAYMARKS DISPLAYED AT SEA

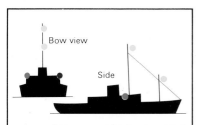

Power-driven vessel over 50 m under way

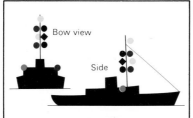

Vessel restricted in ability to manoeuvre

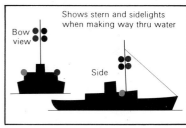

Vessel under way but not under command

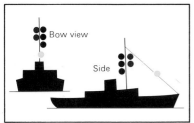

Vessel aground over 7 m in length

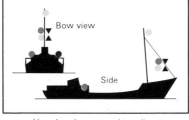

Vessel under way and trawling

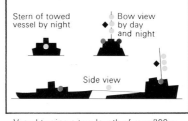

Vessel towing a tow length of over 200 m

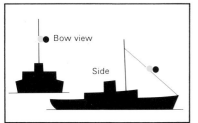

Vessel at anchor

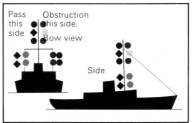

Vessel at anchor engaged in u/w operations.

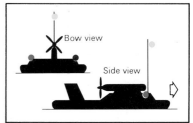

Hovercraft under way

7.11 FLAG SIGNALS FROM THE INTERNATIONAL CODE OF SIGNALS, VOL. I

Method used by ship or shore authorities where a continuous message is displayed for general information, in daylight only. Flags are divided into classes, either alphabetical or numerical. Substitutes allow for the repetition of up to three more letters or numerals. The first Sub repeats the first flag of the group in the class immediately superior to it. The second Sub repeats the second flag of that class, and the third Sub, the third flag.

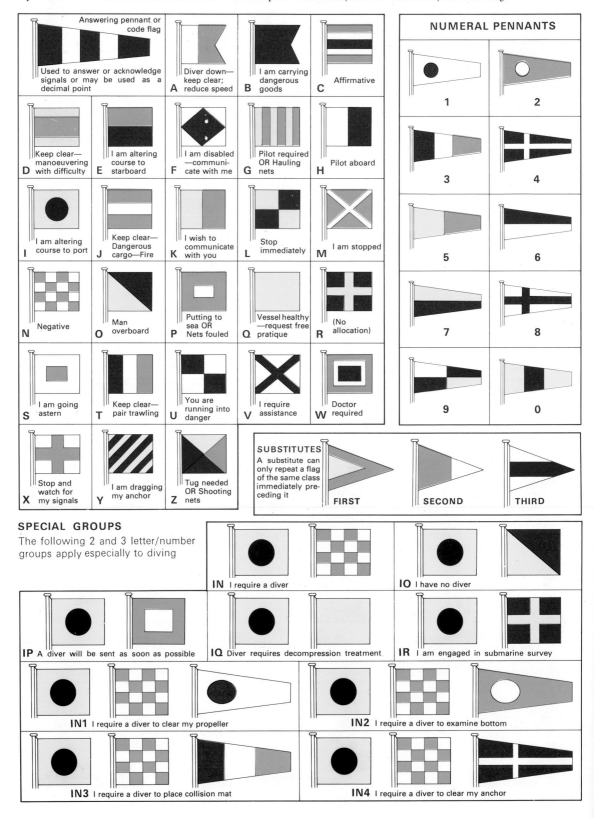

SPECIAL GROUPS

The following 2 and 3 letter/number groups apply especially to diving

8.1 CYLINDER IDENTIFICATION

Extreme care must be taken when identifying gas cylinders by colour coding only. This is because there is not yet an International Colour Code Standard for diving gases.

The Norwegians have developed a colour coding especially for diving. It is based on the International Standard for cylinders for medical use (ISO 32) and stipulates that the important area for colour coding is the valve end. The name and chemical formula of the gas is required to be printed on each cylinder and each quad or rack should have a sign with the name of the gas.

The UK have standards for various categories such as industrial, medical and research grade gases. However, there is no stipulation as to which grade of gas should be used for diving. The name and chemical formula of the gas should be clearly labelled on the shoulder of the cylinder. These standards were set out some years ago and are outdated with regard to diving as often the storage system may obscure the information on the cylinder. For example, only the neck of the cylinder at the valve end may be visible. Since British coding relies on being able to see the sides and shoulder of cylinders in order to differentiate between their contents, this new system of storage can lead to confusion where British Standards are used. Consequently, many of the North Sea suppliers prefer to use the Norwegian coding.

In the USA there is no colour coding for diving gases, and the DoT requires a stencil or label for identification. As there is no stipulation regarding where this stencil or label should appear, most companies follow the Norwegian coding.

Cylinder colours for Norway and UK are shown below.

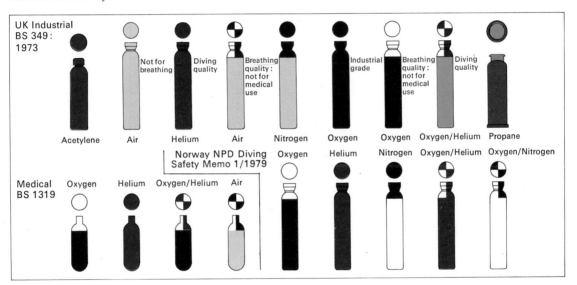

HANDLING AND STORING

1. Never drop cylinders or permit them to strike each other violently. Avoid dragging, rolling, or sliding cylinders even for a short distance. They should be moved by a suitable hand truck.

2. Cylinders may be stored in the open but, in such cases, should be protected against extremes of weather and, to prevent rusting, from the dampness of the ground. In areas where extreme temperatures are prevalent, cylinders should be stored in the shade. Store filled cylinders vertically with the valve upwards, or horizontally. Never store a cylinder in an inverted position. For long-term storage, leave slight positive pressure in the cylinder.

3. Do not store full and empty cylinders together. Serious suckback can occur when an empty cylinder is attached to a pressurized system.

4. The valve protection cap should be left on each cylinder until it has been secured against a wall or bench, or placed in a cylinder stand and is ready to be used.

5. Remove valve and inspect internally at regular intervals and test hydraulically at specified times. Never tamper with safety devices in valves or cylinders. When refitting valve, coat the thread lightly with silicone grease or PTFE paste but no other.

6. No part of a cylinder should be subjected to a temperature higher than 52°C (125°F). A flame should never come in contact with a compressed gas cylinder.

7. Do not place cylinders where they may become part of an electric circuit. When electric arc welding, precautions must be taken to prevent striking an arc against a cylinder.

8. Keep paintwork in good condition. Touch up damaged areas with suitable primers and paints, preferably air-drying. When removing old paintwork do not use heat or chemical strippers on any type of cylinder. When repainting do not use paints that require stoving for longer than $\frac{1}{2}$ hr at temperatures greater than 150°C.

9. Never fill to a pressure greater than the working pressure stamped on the cylinder.

10. Ensure that the inside of the cylinder is dry after testing.

11. Do not modify the cylinder in any way.

12. After diving, rinse the outside of cylinders in clean fresh water and let them dry thoroughly.

13. Where possible, use a self-draining boot on a scuba cylinder. It should be removed regularly for cleaning and to check for rust or damage.

An underwater structure unfortunately provides an ideal site for marine growth colonisation. This increases the size and weight of the structure, causing it to suffer greater waveloading and current forces. To maintain its safety, it is necessary to assess the extent and nature of the marine growth. Local variations in the type and density will occur according to environmental conditions; for example, the warmth derived from the hot products in the risers can encourage local growth

Fig. 1 Seaweeds: *Ulva lactuca* (green); *Polysiphonia* (dull red)

Fig. 2. Kelp: *Laminaria hyperborea*

Seaweeds are present on most structures on sunlit surfaces less than 15 m deep. Annual species such as the green ribbon-like and dull red feathery seaweeds in Fig. 1, may grow to 15 cm long in summer. Perennial kelps (roots living for more than 2 years) as in Figs. 2 and 3, are slower to colonise but may grow to 50–150 cm.

Fig. 3. Mussels: *Mytilus edulis.* Kelp: *Laminaria digitata*

Fig. 4. Mussels: *Mytilus edulis.* Seaweeds: *Polysiphonia; Ectocarpus*

Fig. 5. Mussels: *Mytilus edulis*

Mussels are characteristic fouling organisms which grow most densely on the upper surfaces of horizontal members in the 0–20 m depth range. Fig. 3 shows a typical mussel bed about 4 cm thick composed of animals up to 5 cm long. In sunlit areas, mussels themselves bear an overgrowth of filamentous red and green seaweeds up to 15 cm long, like those in Fig. 4. Mussel shells on offshore structures are smooth, glossy brown or black in contrast to the abraided blue-black shells of inshore mussels.

Fig. 6. Tubeworm: *Pomatoceros triqueter*

Fig. 7. Hydroids: *Bougainvillia ramosa*

Fig. 8. Hydroids: *Tubularia larynx*

A dense cover of solitary tubeworms, so crowded that their hard calcareous ('chalk') tubes are growing away from the steel surface, forming a brittle layer 0.5 to 1.5 cm thick.

Plant-like colonial animals called hydroids are the principal members of the layer of soft growth found on most structures offshore. Many, like those in Fig. 7 (4–6 cm long), may be confused with seaweeds, but individuals of up to 6 cm long (Fig. 8) are easily recognised by their large pink 'heads'.

arine growth can be described as either hard or soft. Hard owths include mussels, barnacles, hard corals and calcareous be worms etc. Soft growths include anemones, sponges, soft rals, kelps, sea squirts etc. It is important to be able to fferentiate between these two groups since they will affect e engineering stress calculations and also the choice of

cleaning method used to remove them.

Marine fouling makes it difficult for divers to apply NDT and inspection techniques. Divers often spend far longer removing the marine growth than doing the actual inspection.

Here are some common varieties likely to be encountered in the North Sea for example.

Fig. 9. Dead men's fingers: *Alcyonium digitatum*

This colonial soft coral is one of the soft organisms that usually overgrows the initial hard fouling layer of tubeworms or barnacles. Individuals here are 3 to 12 cm high and range from white or pale yellow to deep orange.

Fig. 10. Plumose anemones: *Medridium senile*

Present on most structures, particularly those deeper than 30 m. Fig. 10 shows a typical dense cluster of individuals 8 to 15 cm long. Colour ranges from palest yellow through orange to reddy-brown.

 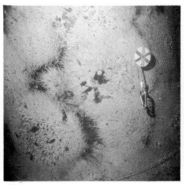 

Fig. 11. Colonial tubeworm: *Filograna implexa*   Fig. 12. *Filograna implexa*

Fig. 13. Deep water barnacle: *Balanus hameri*

This colonial tubeworm is often present at depths greater than 50 m. Individual tubes of the worm are only 0.5 mm wide and 4 to 7 mm long, but may form large dome-shaped growths up to 50 cm in dia. and 20 cm high (Fig. 11). Another form is a thin, spreading, disc-shaped area of tubes. In Fig. 12 discs 10 to 40 cm in dia. have almost run together forming a layer 1 cm thick.

Various species of barnacles are found at varying depths. Individuals in Fig. 13 are 2 to 3 cm in dia. and 3 to 4 cm high and this photograph illustrates a characteristic cluster of these barnacles in a silt-free area.

Fig. 14. Breadcrumb sponge: *Halichondria panices*

Encrusting sponges may be recognised on some structures. Size and shape are very variable but the surface pattern and holes of the breadcrumb sponge may be noted by the diver.

Fig. 15. Sea squirts: *Ciona intestinalis*

Sea squirts, such as those in Fig. 15, may be abundant in regions free from silt. The individuals in this photograph are 4 to 6 cm long growing over a background cover of solitary tubeworms.

Because of the moisture content and temperature variations of our atmosphere, clouds are formed with almost any and every movement of air masses. As a result, clouds provide a useful indication of these movements. The six pictures on this page are a sequence showing the typical approach pattern of clouds in the development of a warm front.

1.1 CIRRUS. Cirrus clouds are composed of ice crystals. A criss-crossed effect is clouds on more than one level being influenced by winds from different directions. Upper clouds moving rapidly are often a sign of unsettled weather. When thickening, with a falling barometer, it is the first sign of an approaching warm front. Wind tends to increase and back.* Temperature falls. Barometer: ↘

1.2 CIRRUS–CIRROSTRATUS. Largely as a result of variations in their altitude, cirrus may thicken into cirrostatus, and subsequently thin out again. However, should the sun become veiled by cirrostratus clouds it is a sure sign of approaching bad weather. The wind still tends to increase and the temperature to fall. Barometer: ↘

1.3 CIRROSTRATUS. Closer to the warm front the stratified cloud covers the sky completely, paling though not obscuring the sun. A halo may be noticeable. Visibility at this point is still quite good, but will almost certainly deteriorate into rain within the next 12 hours. The wind will rise and back* more rapidly. Barometer: ↓

1.4 ALTOCUMULUS–ALTOSTRATUS. As the height of the cloud base drops, the clouds thicken more rapidly. Here altocumulus is present on several levels. The denser, lower cloud in the distance is approaching altostratus. But note that in summer, ragged altocumulus may indicate thunderstorms. Barometer: ↓

1.5 ALTOSTRATUS. By this time, the thickening altostratus has reached the observer, and so probably have the first spots of rain. The sun looks watery. The wind is consistent in direction, and freshening. The temperature may start to increase from this point. Barometer: ↓

*In S. Hemisphere, for 'backing' read 'veering' and vice versa.

1.6 NIMBOSTRATUS. A uniformly grey sky, with the sun totally obscured and continuous rain, announce the impending arrival of the warm front. Visibility is seriously impaired, as the cloud base is unlikely to be higher than 2000 m. In summertime the passage of the front will often lead to an improvement in the weather with nimbostratus lightening into stratus, or thinning into stratocumulus. Barometer: ↔

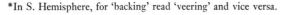

The first two pictures (2.1, 2.2) show warm sector weather. 3.1 shows the approach of a cold front and the last three (4.1–4.3) show the growth of cumulus cloud.

The symbols aim to show the tendency of the barometer.

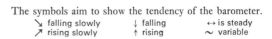

| ↘ falling slowly | ↓ falling | ↔ is steady |
| ↗ rising slowly | ↑ rising | ∼ variable |

2.1 STRATUS. The area immediately behind the warm front is known as the warm sector and can be an area of relative improvement. Because the air is relatively warm and moist, sea fog can occur when the air temperature is higher than that of the sea. Barometer: ↔

2.2 STRATOCUMULUS. In areas well away from frontal activity, small scale convection and turbulence in the lower layers will often give rise to sheets of stratocumulus. Cloud cover may be complete or the sun may break through from time to time. Barometer: ↔

3.1 CUMULUS–CUMULONIMBUS. Unlike a warm front, which gives plenty of warning of its approach, the first that is learnt of a cold front is the appearance of a towering mass of cumulus cloud. Visual indications are important here, for the impending weather conditions are similar to the behaviour of the cloud mass. Barometer: ↑ ↓

4.1 CUMULUS HUMILIS (fair weather cumulus). Not all cloud patterns are rapidly changing. These small cumulus show little sign of growth as the day goes on. This type of cloud is seen mostly over land—less often at sea. If accompanied by a constant barometer, they indicate a spell of fine weather. Barometer: ↔

4.2 CUMULUS CONGESTUS. Cumulus cloud does not always tower high into the air. Where there is a temperature inversion in the middle layer of the atmosphere the cloud is likely to spread horizontally, but it may still produce squalls and variable winds. Barometer: ∼

4.3 CUMULONIMBUS. Low lying cumulonimbus can sometimes resemble nimbostratus, but generally produces heavy showers rather than continuous rain. An approaching bank of cumulonimbus may well bring with it a line squall with a definite veer in wind direction. Barometer: ∼

10.1 BUOYAGE — IALA SYSTEM COMBINED LATERAL AND CARDINAL SYSTEMS

Buoys mark the approximate position of underwater features, such as an obstruction, or they are moorings for vessels. The International Hydrographic Organisation (IHO) has been endeavouring to standardize world-wide buoyage by introducing the IALA System, Region A and B.

Region A differs from B only in the colour of the lateral marks; for example, the US(B) starboard marks are red, in Europe(A) they are green. As a very general guide, the Old World is region A, the New World is region B. It may take ten years before all maritime systems are the same.

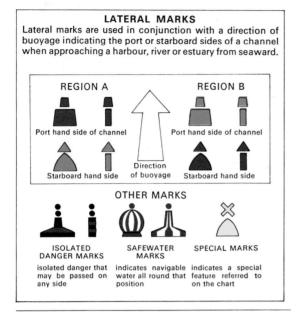

LATERAL MARKS
Lateral marks are used in conjunction with a direction of buoyage indicating the port or starboard sides of a channel when approaching a harbour, river or estuary from seaward.

REGION A — Port hand side of channel — REGION B — Port hand side of channel — Direction of buoyage — Starboard hand side — Starboard hand side

OTHER MARKS
ISOLATED DANGER MARKS — isolated danger that may be passed on any side
SAFEWATER MARKS — indicates navigable water all round that position
SPECIAL MARKS — indicates a special feature referred to on the chart

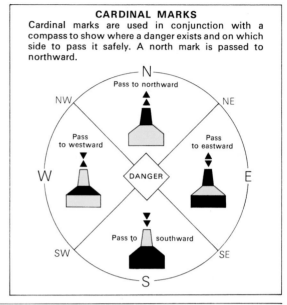

CARDINAL MARKS
Cardinal marks are used in conjunction with a compass to show where a danger exists and on which side to pass it safely. A north mark is passed to northward.

N — Pass to northward
NW — NE
Pass to westward — Pass to eastward
W — DANGER — E
SW — SE
Pass to southward
S

10.2 ADMIRALTY CHARTS — A SELECTION OF SYMBOLS ON METRIC CHARTS

Admiralty Chart 5011 is a booklet which gives the meaning of every symbol used on both fathom and metric charts. The Admiralty follows the International Hydrographic Organisation conventions, as do most of the maritime nations. Soundings of less than 21 m are in metres and decimetres. Drying heights on rocks and banks which uncover are shown underlined, and are in metres and decimetres above chart datum.

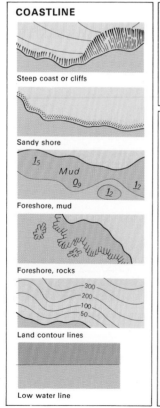

COASTLINE
Steep coast or cliffs
Sandy shore
Foreshore, mud
Foreshore, rocks
Land contour lines
Low water line

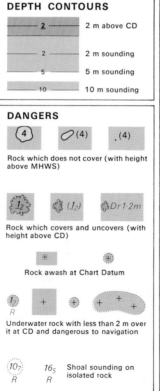

DEPTH CONTOURS
2 — 2 m above CD
2 — 2 m sounding
5 — 5 m sounding
10 — 10 m sounding

DANGERS
Rock which does not cover (with height above MHWS)
Rock which covers and uncovers (with height above CD)
Rock awash at Chart Datum
Underwater rock with less than 2 m over it at CD and dangerous to navigation
Shoal sounding on isolated rock

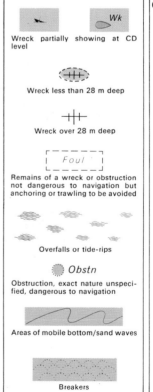

Wreck partially showing at CD level — Wk
Wreck less than 28 m deep
Wreck over 28 m deep
Foul — Remains of a wreck or obstruction not dangerous to navigation but anchoring or trawling to be avoided
Overfalls or tide-rips
Obstn — Obstruction, exact nature unspecified, dangerous to navigation
Areas of mobile bottom/sand waves
Breakers

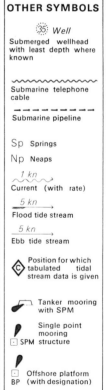

OTHER SYMBOLS
35 Well — Submerged wellhead with least depth where known
Submarine telephone cable
Submarine pipeline
Sp Springs
Np Neaps
1 kn — Current (with rate)
5 kn — Flood tide stream
5 kn — Ebb tide stream
C — Position for which tabulated tidal stream data is given
Tanker mooring with SPM
Single point mooring
SPM structure
Offshore platform BP (with designation)

Weather and sea

The diver needs to understand something about the weather since it limits many of his activities. The area covered by an individual forecast may include a large area as big as 50 000 square miles, but the weather conditions within that area may vary considerably in different parts of it. The offshore diver is in a unique position to observe the weather regularly and to be able to make quite accurate forecasts based on what he can see, his built-up experience and the available information.

Weather is wind and wind is sea state. The more the diver knows about these three, the safer and more effective will be his diving.

11.2 WEATHER

Weather is the result of the interaction of many phenomena, including solar energy input, temperature, wind and humidity. The key factor, however, is that hot air rises.

The sun heats the Earth's surface which in turn warms the air immediately above it causing it to rise. However, not all parts of the Earth's surface receive the same amount of heat from the sun. As the Earth moves around the sun areas of the Earth's surface receive differing amounts of heat (Fig. 1(a)). Areas nearer the equator usually receive the most direct sunlight and therefore tend to be hotter than areas nearer the poles where the sun's rays have to travel further and through a thicker section of the atmosphere (Fig. 1(b)).

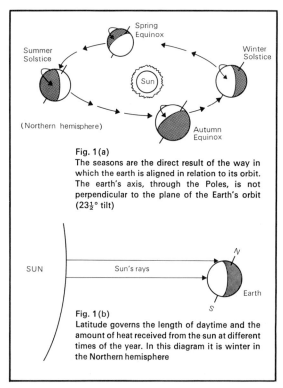

Fig. 1(a)
The seasons are the direct result of the way in which the earth is aligned in relation to its orbit. The earth's axis, through the Poles, is not perpendicular to the plane of the Earth's orbit ($23\frac{1}{2}°$ tilt)

Fig. 1(b)
Latitude governs the length of daytime and the amount of heat received from the sun at different times of the year. In this diagram it is winter in the Northern hemisphere

General circulation of the atmosphere

The amount of heat received by the atmosphere varies with latitude, resulting in the coolness in the polar regions and warmth at the equator. The resultant temperature differentials cause related variations in the atmospheric pressure. Like all natural forces that seek to establish an equilibrium, air tends to move from areas of high pressure to areas of low pressure. This movement is called wind. Considered on a global scale, low pressure areas occur where warm air rises; high pressure areas occur where cooler air descends to replace the warm air.

These differing pressures are shown on 'weather maps' by concentric ring patterns called isobars, formed by joining points of equal pressure. There are broad 'bands' of high and low pressure areas over the Earth's surface and the circulation between them forms the prevailing winds. If the Earth were not rotating, air would move directly towards low pressure from high pressure.

Figure 2(a) shows how the general circulation of cold air would flow from the poles towards the equator. There is a great variation in winds in the upper and lower atmosphere. Lower layers up to 600 m (2000 ft) decrease in speed as they go downwards because the air flow is slowed by friction. In general, winds will be stronger at platform level than at sea level. In the upper atmosphere, between 9000 m and 12 000 m, there are narrow bands of intense winds (100–200 knots). These jet streams transport heat from the equator to the poles on a wavy course in a west–east direction, thus contributing to the easterly deflexion of other winds, and they also steer and develop depressions.

Because the Earth rotates it imparts a rotational motion to any moving object on its surface. In the Northern hemisphere moving objects, such as winds or oceans, deviate to the right (eastwards), whereas in the Southern hemisphere they deviate to the left. For example, a northward flowing upper wind from the tropics would swing to become a westerly (Fig. 2(b)). This is known as the Coriolis Effect and causes any movement of the airstream to be progressively deflected into a curved path or a circle. This swing is also affected by the speed of the Earth's eastward movement, which varies with the latitude (Fig. 2(c)). The heat differential of the air and the rotation of the earth lead to semi-permanent high pressure areas over the poles and in a belt around the earth in subtropical latitudes (30°N and 30°S) (Fig. 2(b)). These are high pressure areas containing circulating weather

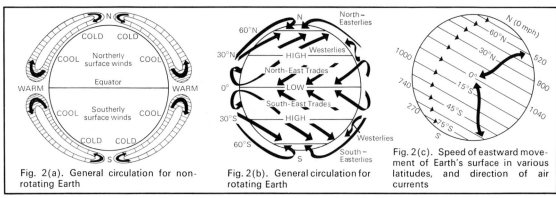

Fig. 2(a). General circulation for non-rotating Earth

Fig. 2(b). General circulation for rotating Earth

Fig. 2(c). Speed of eastward movement of Earth's surface in various latitudes, and direction of air currents

patterns called anticyclones which are areas where air descending to the earth's surface spreads away from the centres of high pressure. Air from the polar 'high' meets air from the subtropical 'high' in mid-latitudes (60° N and S) and where they meet is an area which often develops into clearly defined areas of low pressure or depression. In the Northern hemisphere these 'lows' travel in an eastward direction, separated by local areas of descending air or high pressure. In the Northern hemisphere winds blow around 'lows' in an anti-clockwise direction and around 'highs' in a clockwise direction. These directions are reversed in the Southern hemisphere.

Figure 2(b) shows that in temperate regions (30°–60°N & S) the weather systems move in a west to east direction, and the cloud types indicate weather activities. However, in tropical and subtropical regions (0°–30°N & S) most systems move in an east to west direction and are generally shallow and indeterminate: they do not carry frontal systems like the temperate weather systems, but usually have an 'easterly wave' area of less fine weather, sometimes with heavy thundery conditions. The exceptions to this are the hurricanes, cyclones and tropical storms. These are slow-moving, usually no more than 5–12 knots, but have intense cyclonic circulations of winds of 100 knots or more, heavy thundery rain and very rough seas. The swell will often advance rapidly well to the west of such a system so that divers should keep in touch with their nearest meteorological service for adequate warning of its approach.

Air masses: north-western Europe

Air reaching the North Sea originates either from the polar or subtropical 'high', but will be affected by its passage over land or sea. Fig. 3 shows the air masses which influence North Sea weather, with the characteristics due to their origins.

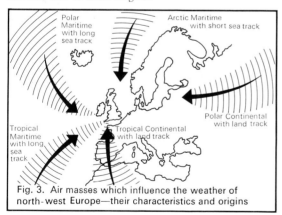

Fig. 3. Air masses which influence the weather of north-west Europe—their characteristics and origins

Air masses may be composed of warm or cool air, in which case there will often be a marked boundary (front) between the two. Air from the pole, initially cold, may become warmed as it travels south; air from across the Atlantic also may be warmed; air from the Continent may have some warming in the summer, but probably none in winter. Air from the subtropics (30°N & S), such as the Azores High, is cooled as it moves northward over progressively colder seas.

Depressions and fronts

Because warm air rises, it will climb over (or be pushed up by) an adjacent mass of colder air depending on whether it is overtaking or being overtaken. The first condition is called a warm front, the latter a cold front. When these two become combined, usually at altitude, the fronts are said to be occluded. An occlusion may be of either type, warm occluded or cold occluded. Both are represented in the same way on the weather map.

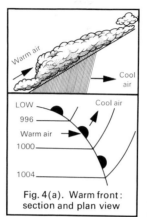

Fig. 4(a). Warm front: section and plan view

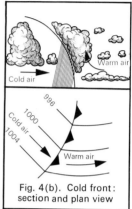

Fig. 4(b). Cold front: section and plan view

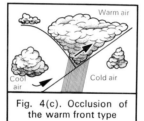

Fig. 4(c). Occlusion of the warm front type

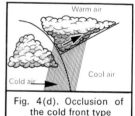

Fig. 4(d). Occlusion of the cold front type

Clouds

The North Sea lies between latitude 50° and 65°N, close to an interface between low and high pressure air masses. Cool air from higher latitudes and warm air from lower latitudes are brought together in a broad band which stretches across the Atlantic Ocean from the eastern United States to north-west Europe. Along this band warm air pushes into the cold, setting up a pattern of large depressions moving eastward. Such depressions bring a variety of weather, mostly unsettled. Whether they arrive in the North Sea depends on whether they are deflected by the positions of the Azores or polar Highs. The Azores High pushes them north towards Iceland, and the polar High steers them south towards the Bay of Biscay. Highs such as these are slow moving and usually cause settled weather for several days.

As warm air rises it cools and its water vapour condenses to form clouds. The moisture content of air varies according to its temperature and the surface over which it travels before it is forced to rise. The higher the temperature of the air, the more moisture it can contain. However, a warm air mass over land will not pick up as much moisture as a similar air mass over the sea. Thus a warm wind blowing onshore generally carries more moisture than a wind blowing off the land onto the sea.

Because of the moisture content and temperature variations of our atmosphere, clouds follow the movement of air masses and thus clouds provide a useful indication of these movements. The many varieties of cloud make it possible to extract much more information than just the direction (and perhaps speed) of the air mass (see Section 11.1, Cloud types as weather indicators).

Clouds can be divided into three major groups:
(1) low cloud—with bases from sea level up to 2 km (7000 ft); stratus, nimbostratus, cumulus, cumulonimbus
(2) medium cloud—with bases from 2 km up to 8 km (25 000 ft); altostratus, altocumulus
(3) high cloud—with bases from 5 km up to 13 km (16 000 ft–45 000 ft); cirrus, cirrostratus, cirrocumulus.

The base levels tend to sink below their lower limits in winter, and in higher latitudes.

Cloud types can also be divided into three classifications:
(1) layer clouds (stratiform)
(2) heaped clouds (cumuliform)
(3) feathery clouds (cirroform).
'Alto' used with a cloud name means medium level and 'nimbus' means rain-bearing. Cloud sub-types can be more precisely specified by combinations of these names, i.e. altostratus, cumulonimbus.

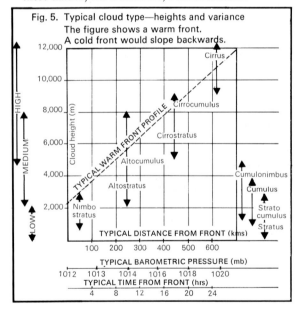

Fig. 5. Typical cloud type—heights and variance
The figure shows a warm front.
A cold front would slope backwards.

Winds

As has been described, wind is caused by temperature differences between one area and another, which in turn give rise to pressure differences. The pressure difference over a unit distance is known as the pressure gradient—the steeper, the stronger the wind.

There are three main types of wind
• Trade winds—permanent oceanic winds which blow in the same direction most of the year.

• Seasonal winds—regular winds, such as the monsoons of the Indian Ocean, which depend on the declination of the sun, the season and the pressure distribution.

• Winds associated with individual weather systems.
The direction of the wind is the point from which it blows. Thus a wind blowing in a north eastwards direction is called a sou'westerly wind. Because of its position (lat. 50°–60°N) the North Sea lies well within the temperate low pressure region, so that the prevailing winds are therefore westerly. Wind speed is measured in knots by an anemometer, and its force is classified in the Beaufort Scale (Section 11.4). When estimating wind force and speed from a structure it should be remembered that at platform height, which could be 50 m above sea level, the wind will probably be stronger than at the surface.

As a general rule, in the Northern hemisphere, if the observer stands with his back to wind, the area of lowest barometric pressure will lie to his left, the highest to his right.

Wind is said to 'back' or 'veer' when it changes direction. In the northern hemisphere a backing wind would blow anti-clockwise, i.e. north through east, south through west; a veering wind is the opposite, and in the northern hemisphere is often a sign of approaching bad weather.

Offshore and onshore breezes

Land heats up and cools down faster than the sea. In summer the sun warms the land faster than it does the sea. The warm air rises off the land and is replaced by cooler air off the sea, causing an onshore breeze. At night, as the land cools to below sea temperature, the effect is reversed, producing an offshore breeze.

A coastline may form a zone of change.
(a) Coastline clouds over the sea indicate that the air is unstable over the sea but stable inland. This happens when the sea is warmer than the land, occurring most often in autumn and winter. Should the wind change direction towards the shore, or should the warming up of the land bring an onshore sea breeze, showers might be expected to migrate inland.
(b) Coastline clouds over the land only indicate that the air is stable over the sea and unstable over the land. If the wind should blow offshore, cloud may migrate over the coast.

Fog

Fog results from the condensation of water vapour due to the high humidity of the air; it is usually caused by the cooling of the air. Sea fog is sometimes formed by warm air moving over a cold sea surface (advection fog), and may be due to a change of wind or a cold sea current. If the air mass above the sea is warmer than the land it is approaching, the increased moisture that it is carrying will form fog when it cools on reaching land. This is known as 'Haar' on North Sea coasts. In the same way, warm moist air crossing a warm land mass will form fog when it reaches the cold sea water.

11.3 WEATHER FORECASTS

When trying to forecast the approaching weather by watching the changing cloud formations it is important to note the sequence of the changes. A pattern of weather watching should be established. Temperature and humidity; windspeed and direction (especially high-altitude estimates), and barometric pressure are all valuable considerations likely to increase the accuracy of any forecast.

The pattern of differing barometric pressures is the most important factor in producing a 'weather map'. Differing pressures are shown on these maps, properly known as synoptic charts, by the familiar pattern of contours. These are called 'isobars' and are defined as lines joining points of equal barometric pressure.

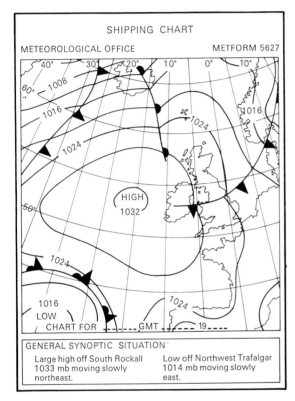

SHIPPING CHART
METEOROLOGICAL OFFICE   METFORM 5627

HIGH 1032
LOW 1016
CHART FOR ____ GMT ____ 19 ____

GENERAL SYNOPTIC SITUATION
Large high off South Rockall 1033 mb moving slowly northeast.   Low off Northwest Trafalgar 1014 mb moving slowly east.

In general, the higher the latitude the more unsettled and unpredictable will be the weather. Diving operations in the Persian Gulf, the Gulf of Guinea, the Gulf of Mexico and around the coasts of Indonesia are each subject to quite different constraints. Close to the equator weather conditions tend to remain stable for much longer periods.

Forecasts from the Radio

Most national radio systems broadcast regular weather forecasts and most nations supplement these with forecasts for shipping. To take the British Broadcasting Corporation as an example, forecasts are given for home waters in the following form:

O Gale warnings.
O General synopsis.
O Forecasts for home water forecast areas or coastal/inshore areas.
O Reports from selected coastal stations.

Refer to a nautical almanac or to the relevant Broadcasting Authority for comprehensive details of all bulletins, but BBC announcements covering UK Home waters are broadcast daily on Radio 4 – 200kHz (1500m) at 0015, 0625, 1355 and 1750 hours. Local Radio 4 stations also broadcast the same bulletins on local frequencies and they are also available on Radio 4 VHF. Coastal water forecasts are given on BBC Radio 3 or 4 at 0020, 0655 and 0755 hours.

Gale warnings are broadcast on BBC Radio at the first opportunity after receipt. 'Gale imminent' means that it can be expected within 6 hours; 'Gale soon' – between 6 and 12 hours; 'Gale later' – after 12 hours.

Weather Maps

In order to study how a weather pattern is developing and how the local situation relates to what is being forecast over a much wider area, it is a good idea to record a forecast bulletin. These are best written down in a standard form and may be tape-recorded if necessary. It is useful to have to hand a reference map of the area of interest, with prominent features marked.

There are many forms of weather maps available, such as the METFORM 5627 (Shipping Chart) from HMSO or the METMAP published by the Royal Meteorological Society and the RYA.

Reports from coastal stations can be transferred to these forms to produce a weather map, useful in forming a sequential record and to reinforce cloud and barometer observations. The information given in these sections of the weather forecast is rarely more than two hours old and thus is of immediate use in identifying current tendencies. Pay particular attention to those areas from which the weather is coming. Coastguard Stations will report on the present weather situation in their particular area.

Since the introduction of Facsimile Transmission (FAX) hardware during the past ten years high quality weather information has become available at even the remotest of sites. However, it uses professionally-evolved symbols which may be difficult to understand to those without specialist training.

Specialised Forecasting Service

In addition to the free and publicly available information it is possible to obtain tailored weather reports on a commercial basis. Special local weather reports for the North Sea are issued by the Meteorological Office. They are delivered either by telex or by facsimile transmission. Subscribers to the UK Meteorological Office's services receive information covering a specified location, and contain details of expected winds, weather, visibility, sea and swell for the next 24 hours. Ten metres altitude above sea level is a standard reporting and forecasting height. Forecasts are issued at 0800 and 2000 hours and cover two further periods of 24 hours, extending predictions to three days ahead.

A specimen bulletin form and weather map is shown on the following page.

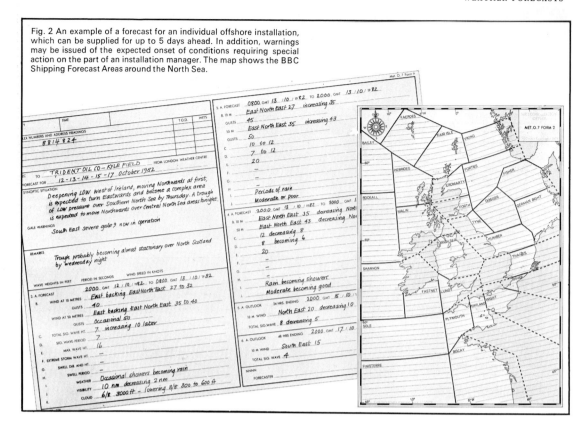

Fig. 2 An example of a forecast for an individual offshore installation, which can be supplied for up to 5 days ahead. In addition, warnings may be issued of the expected onset of conditions requiring special action on the part of an installation manager. The map shows the BBC Shipping Forecast Areas around the North Sea.

11.4 SEA STATE

Waves

Sea state is the result of weather conditions. The surface friction between the wind and the sea surface slows the wind and the energy produced becomes a wave.

Waves at sea travel in the same general direction as the wind which causes them, although the water itself makes little progress. Waves can be compared to a stretched out rope which is given an upward flick—a wave travels along the rope which itself does not move forward.

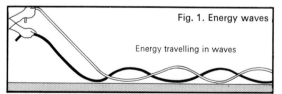

Fig. 1. Energy waves

Energy travelling in waves

As a wave undulates past, each particle of water describes a circular path, the circles diminishing as they descend from the surface. In deep water its effect is felt to a depth equal to about half the wave length, so that a wavelength of 20m may cause turbulence down to 10m.

In shallow water the surface wave energy cannot be absorbed in this way, and breakers result.

Much of the measurable properties of a wave, such as its length, height, shape and speed may be changed by the nature and situation of a wave. The only

WAVE DEFINITIONS

1. **THE WAVE FORM** is the curve of the surface of the sea seen in elevation. Any one wave form extends from a point on a wave surface (for example a crest) to the equivalent point on the next wave.

2. **THE WAVE LENGTH** is the horizontal distance between one crest to a preceding or a succeeding one, along the line of advance.

3. **THE WAVE HEIGHT** is the vertical distance from trough to crest on one wave form.

4. **THE WAVE SPEED** is that with which the wave form is moving relative to the undisturbed body of water, measured horizontally in the direction of the advance of the wave form.

5. **THE STILL WATER LEVEL** is that which a body of water will assume when unaffected by wave forms.

6. **THE WAVE TRAIN** is a succession of waves proceeding as a group in a given direction.

7. **THE PERIOD OF A WAVE** is the time interval between the passing of two successive crests or troughs.

relationship that does not change is that wave speed is equal to the wave length divided by the period.

There is a common belief that every seventh wave is larger than the rest. There is no 'law' about this, but it can sometimes happen when two nearly similar wave trains coincide. The pattern arising from several wave trains becomes complex because of the

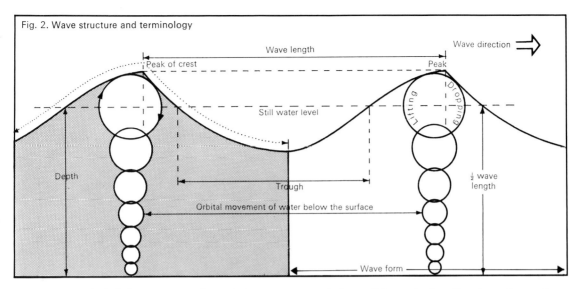

Fig. 2. Wave structure and terminology

many and varied influences on them. However, considered very generally, some useful predictions may be made.

When a wind of constant velocity blows for a long time across an ocean unaffected by other wave trains, the waves will reach their maximum size. In such conditions, the average wave height (in metres) will be equal to half the wind speed (in knots). The largest waves will attain a height of 2.5m for every 10kt of wind. A strong wind of 50kt (Beaufort Scale Force 9) has been known to produce a largest storm wave of some 12m high.

Sea and swell

For those working on or below the surface of the sea, the most important aspect of the weather is likely to be its effect on the sea surface. Apart from tides and currents, all the sea's activities are the results of wind which affects the sea in three distinct ways: by the speed of the wind, by the length of time that the wind has been blowing and by the distance that the wind has blown over the water (the fetch). Locally-produced disturbances are called seas and are different from remotely-produced ones called swells. Swells may even be the product of a weather system from across the ocean.

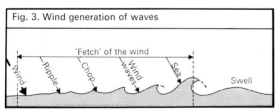

Fig. 3. Wind generation of waves

A cross swell is caused by a fresh swell being formed from a different direction from the residual swell. The result can produce a most uncomfortable motion which may complicate shallow water operations.

Maximum wave height

This is the maximum height of crest to trough over a 10 minute period. This includes swell.

In addition to the freely available shipping fore-

casts, it is possible to obtain tailored weather and sea state reports on a commercial basis. These bulletins are sent by telex or facsimile transmission. Subscribers to the UK Meteorological Office's service receive information pertinent to a specified installation. Other services tend to be by field, or a portion of a standard forecasting area.

Significant wave height

Most of the terms in the UK Meteorological Office's subscribers' reports are self-explanatory, but one deserves further explanation. 'Significant wave height' is defined as the average height of the largest one third of all waves recorded over a period of 10 minutes. A close approximation of significant wave height may be obtained by observing the height of the largest wave in any 2 minute period. Observers should note that the foreshortening effect of looking down from the deck of an installation is considerable. Eye-ball estimates can be very inaccurate. A convenient scale should be marked on one or more of the installation's legs to aid more accurate assessment.

Ten metres above sea level is a standard reporting and forecasting height. The units used throughout are the knot (kt), the second (sec), the foot (ft) and the nautical mile (nm). WMO reports are coded in half metres of wave height. (See Fig. 4 overleaf.)

Specialist information

The Institute of Oceanographic Sciences at Wormley (042 679 4141) will provide on request what is called wave climate. This is an average of the wave conditions for any locality for any time of the year. Such information would be essential when any large scale operation is being planned.

The Marine Forecasting Division of the Meteorological Office will supply Real Time Climate data, which are the weather conditions at any locality for any given time, today, tomorrow or next week.

Wind-driven currents

The wind also causes the sea surface to move as a current. The direction of this wind-driven surface current is not the same as that of the wind but at an angle of 45° to it. In the northern hemisphere it is 45°

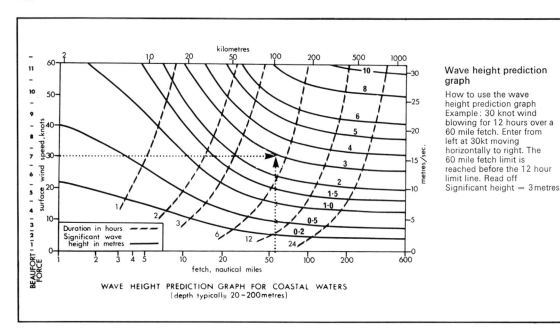

WAVE HEIGHT PREDICTION GRAPH FOR COASTAL WATERS
(depth typically 20–200 metres)

Wave height prediction graph

How to use the wave height prediction graph
Example: 30 knot wind blowing for 12 hours over a 60 mile fetch. Enter from left at 30kt moving horizontally to right. The 60 mile fetch limit is reached before the 12 hour limit line. Read off Significant height = 3 metres

to the right of the wind direction, while in the southern hemisphere it is 45° to the left. This effect is due to the earth's rotation and is called the Coriolis effect.

The strength of the wind-driven current lessens with increasing depth. Also the direction of travel turns progressively away from the direction of the wind. For example, at 11m, the current direction is 90° to the wind direction. This spiralling change of direction is known as the Ekman spiral. Its effect increases with its distance from the equator.

Except in very shallow water, the surface current speed is equivalent to approximately 3% of wind speed. It decreases, however, at a rate which depends on the stability of the entire water column, the length of time the wind has been blowing, the uninterrupted distance over which it has blown (the 'fetch'), and the size of the waves present.

Sea state tables
Sea states are normally expressed in tabular form. This usually corresponds quite closely to the Beaufort Scale which attempts to relate wind speed to the behaviour of the environment. The difference between the 'sea states' and the Beaufort Scale is that sea state has the advantage of referring to the actual sea condition at the time of the observation. The Beaufort Scale refers to the sea condition in a fully arisen sea; this can take hours to achieve in any wind condition.

As an example, in open reaches of the North Sea, a wind speed of 30 knots from one direction for an hour results in a sea state of 5/6.

There are several scales of sea states in use today. It is therefore important to be sure of the scale being used when quoting any particular sea state value.

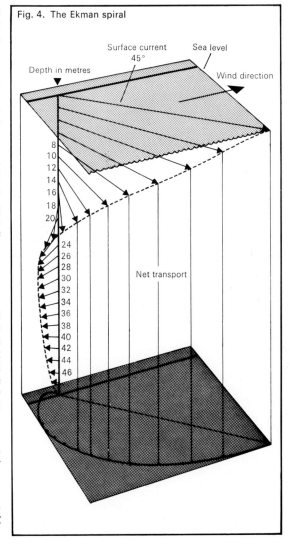

Fig. 4. The Ekman spiral

A Comparison of Sea State Scales

Sea State (US Navy)		Douglas	SeaTech magazine	Reed's Nautical Almanac	Shell oil contracts	Beaufort Wind Scale		Wind speed (knots)
0	Sea like a mirror	1	1	0	1	0	Calm	0–1
	Ripples without crests		2		2	1	Light air	1–3
1	Small wavelets					2	Light breeze	4–6
2	Large wavelets	2	3	1	3	3	Gentle breeze	7–10
	Small waves	3		2		4	Moderate breeze	11–16
3				3				
4	Moderate waves			4	4	5	Fresh breeze	17–21
5	Large waves form	4	4	5	5	6	Strong breeze	22–27
6	Heaped-up sea			6				
		5	5	7	6	7	Near gale	28–33
7	Moderately high waves	6	6		7	8	Gale	34–40
8	High waves		7			9	Severe gale	41–47
				8	8	10	Storm	48–55
9	Very high waves							
	Exceptionally high waves	7				11	Violent storm	56–63
			8		9	12	Hurricane	64 and over

11.5 TIDES AND TIDAL STREAMS

Tides

Tides are the periodic vertical movements of the sea, and tidal streams are its horizontal movements resulting from the tides. Both are caused by the attraction of the moon and sun.

Tides are of little concern to the offshore deep water diver as the rise and fall is insignificant to diving operations. To the inshore or shallow water offshore diver, however, determining the height and duration of the tide at a given time and place may be of great importance, for example, when repairing the piles of a pier or salvaging a sunken object. For this information it is necessary to find the time of the next high or low water at the nearest standard or secondary port and to extrapolate the exact details by a simple calculation. High water times and heights may be obtained from the Admiralty Tide Tables or most nautical almanacs.

Tidal streams

Tidal streams are a horizontal oscillation of particles of water which usually flow in one direction for a known period of time and then return along much the same path for another period. The two periods may not be the same.

Tidal streams concern all divers in the sea because they can affect working capacity and safety. Any stream in excess of 1 kt will make underwater swimming difficult, especially when hauling an umbilical. In streams above 1 kt, the diver may have to wear additional weights or find some shelter from the main force of the stream.

There are two ways of determining the rate and direction of the tidal stream at the surface in any area. In each case the time of local high water must be known.

(1) Refer to an appropriate tidal atlas.
(2) Using a local chart, find the tidal stream diamond nearest to the dive site. Note the letter initial in the diamond and find the information that relates to it by referring to the tidal stream table positioned near the edge of the chart.

The velocity or rate of the stream is influenced by the shape of the adjoining land and the configuration of the bottom. This rate is often miscalculated by divers; usually it is exaggerated.

Tidal stream direction depends on the direction of the flood tide, and usually it flows the opposite way on the ebb. Slack water is the time of change of flow from one direction to its opposite, and although this is often coincidental with high or low water, it need not necessarily be so. Along open coasts the turn of the tide most often occurs at half-tide. Tidal streams are strongest during spring tides and weakest during neaps, and are usually strongest in inshore areas. Tidal streams on the bottom in deep water often differ in strength and direction from those on the surface. Information on bottom tidal streams and current can often be obtained from the client's records. However, in some areas information may only be built up from practical experience.

In the southern North Sea, strong streams are caused by the funnel effect of the English Channel. As a result of these strong streams, dive times are considerably restricted ($\frac{3}{4}$–1 hr).

In the northern North Sea, north of latitude 56°N, tidal streams are not so affected and dive times are only limited by diver endurance levels, typically 4 hr.

THE TIDAL STREAMS IN THE NORTH SEA

→ indicate weak streams. → indicate strong streams. ⟨s⟩ indicate slack

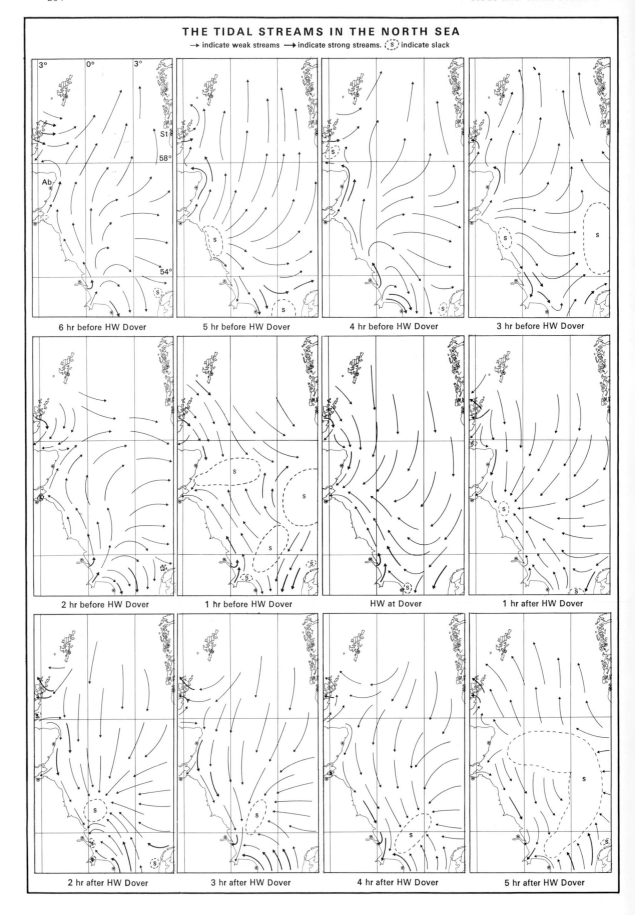

6 hr before HW Dover   5 hr before HW Dover   4 hr before HW Dover   3 hr before HW Dover

2 hr before HW Dover   1 hr before HW Dover   HW at Dover   1 hr after HW Dover

2 hr after HW Dover   3 hr after HW Dover   4 hr after HW Dover   5 hr after HW Dover

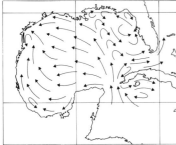

PREVAILING SURFACE CURRENTS
in the Gulf of Mexico

General surface current
circulation throughout
the year

Branch 1.
Mean rate: $\frac{1}{2}$–$1\frac{1}{2}$ kt,
increasing with
southerly winds in
summer.

Branch 2.
Mean rate: 1 kt,
increasing with easterly
winds, decreasing with
westerlies.

Branch 3.
Mean rate: 1–$1\frac{1}{2}$ kt;
there is a westerly set off
the delta.

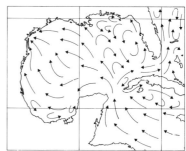

Winter (January, February, March)

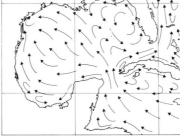

Spring (April, May, June)

Summer (July, August, September)

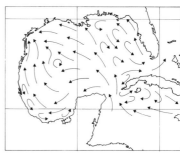

Autumn (October, November, December)

EFFECT OF WIND ON TIDES

The sea level tends to be raised in the direction towards which the wind is blowing and lowered in the direction from which it is blowing. A strong southerly wind blowing in the North Sea for example may cause lower low waters in the Thames Estuary. Strong winds may also have the effect of advancing or retarding the time of high water by as much as 1 hr.

Gulf of Mexico

The range of tides in this area is small (av. 0.6 m) and the tides have a marked diurnal inequality, i.e. one high water of the day is much higher than the other. Tidal streams in general are weak and in many places there is only one stream a day, running for about 12 hr continuously in one direction. As a general rule, the streams offshore set to the northward and westward on the rising tide and vice versa on the falling tide.

Comparatively strong currents tend to predominate in the Gulf. The main current is the Equatorial, which circuits the Gulf in three main branches before flowing out to become the Gulf Stream. The map shows the general current circulation throughout the year. To a very large extent the flow of water within this area is very variable and dependent on prevailing winds.

Currents

Currents are not the same as tidal streams. Currents are different in that they are an onward flow of water, not an oscillating one. They are of two types. Ocean currents include regular horizontal movements of water in one direction, such as the Gulf Stream. The second type is usually the result of meteorological conditions such as wind, or the geographical nature of the adjacent land and the sea bottom.

Specialist information

The Marine Information and Advisory Service of the IOS at Wormley (Tel: Wormley (042-879) 4141) will supply specialist advice and any published oceanographic information or numerical data relating to the marine environment. The MIAS will, for example, be able to produce details of bottom-currents for pipeline inspection over the period involved. Inshore, for port operations, tidal data may be processed to provide local tidal stream atlases. The nature of the seabed, its structure and strong bottom currents are of vital importance to the installation of sub-sea structures and for submersibles.

The MIAS Enquiry Office is set up to provide a fast efficient service, and where appropriate will put an enquirer into direct contact with a member of the IOS research staff. The MIAS will advise on locations all over the world.

11.6 TEMPERATURE AND THERMOCLINES

Water temperature is a significant factor in diving as it may influence the type of equipment used, and possibly the duration and safety of the dive.

The sea temperature at the surface can range from sub-zero temperatures up to 27°C (80°F), because it is affected by the air temperature directly above it. The deeper one goes, the less the temperature varies, until eventually a depth is reached where it can be constant all the year round.

There is a sandwich-like layering of cold and warm water masses. The warmer, more saline layers lie on top of colder layers, which get colder and less saline as the depth increases. As the lowering temperatures make each layer denser than the one above it, each layer rests stably upon the one below. There is little mixing because the process of layering is one of constant renewal.

The boundaries between the layers of different water temperatures are called thermoclines. These may occur at any level, close to the surface or in deep water, and the temperature may vary from layer to layer by as much as 7°C (20°F).

The most important effect on divers is that of currents. The layers of water between the thermo-

clines can be moving independently of each other, so a freely descending diver may drift in several different directions on his way down. Also, the current on the surface is not necessarily going in the same direction as the current on the sea bed. Consequently, if the direction of the current is to be used for navigation purposes, the orientation of its movement must be determined on the bottom, not on the surface.

The other effect on the diver is, of course, the temperature drop suffered while descending through the thermocline. Thus even if the surface conditions indicated a warm dive, the bottom conditions could lead to a much shorter and colder dive.

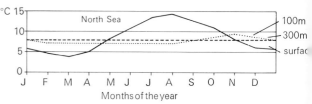

This graph shows temperature variation at the surface with steady levels at 100m & 300m.

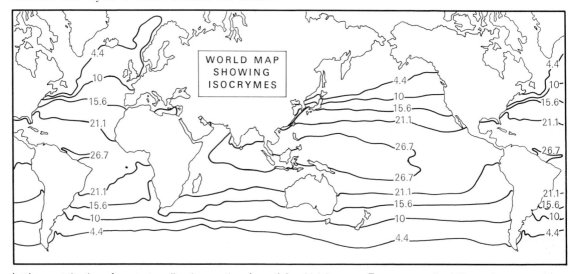

Isotherms at the time of greatest cooling, irrespective of month in which it occurs. Temperatures should be read equatorwards.

Isotherms at the time of greatest warming, irrespective of month in which it occurs. Temperatures should be read polewards.

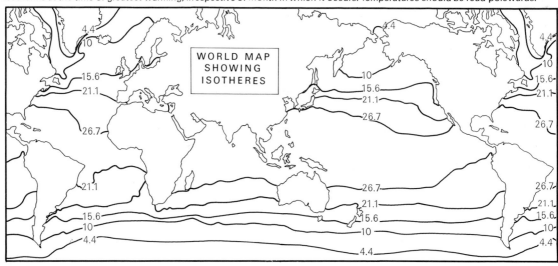

SECTION TWELVE

Health and safety

12.1 FIRST AID.

The first aid described in this Handbook is limited to the treatment of diving accidents, including the treatment of injuries while under pressure. It is assumed that little or no first aid equipment is to hand. Remember that near drowning may complicate or mask other injuries.

The basic guidelines are

1. Remove victim from danger.
2. Check breathing using 'Feel and listen' method.
3. If breathing absent, check pulse.
4. Stop major bleeding.
5. Treat for shock.
6. Treat any other conditions.
7. Summon expert medical advice.

(1) REMOVE VICTIM FROM DANGER
This will usually mean remove victim from the water.

(2) CHECK BREATHING USING THE 'FEEL AND LISTEN' METHOD
First extend the victim's airway. In a bell it may be dark and there may be excessive noise and vibration, so use the 'Feel and listen' method by placing your cheek over the victim's open mouth to check if he is breathing.

(3) IF BREATHING ABSENT CHECK THE PULSE
A victim's pulse may be weak, erratic or very slow, and so may be difficult to feel. When searching for a victim's pulse, allow at least 10 seconds to find it. The wearing of a neck-dam may make it difficult to feel the diver's carotid pulse. Alternatives would be the wrist pulse or the auricular pulse (the small flap at the front entrance to the ear).

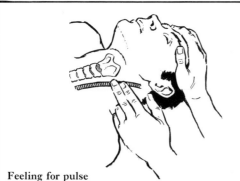

Feeling for pulse
Maintain backward tilt of the head with one hand, while feeling for the victim's carotid pulse with the other. Feel for the pulse by placing your index and middle fingers (not the thumb) gently on the victim's larynx (Adam's apple); then slide the fingers off to the side. Palpate with the flat part of your fingers, rather than with the tips. Palpate long enough (at least 10 seconds) to ensure that you do not miss a slow heart rate.

(4) STOP MAJOR BLEEDING
Apply direct pressure to the bleeding point. In most cases the best treatment for staunching an external wound is to apply a pressure pad on the wound itself. The origin of the bleeding should be exposed, but unless the bleeding is very severe or inaccessible leave the victim's suit on.

Control of external bleeding

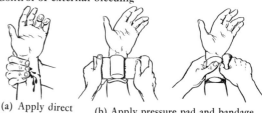

(a) Apply direct manual pressure   (b) Apply pressure pad and bandage

How to apply a pressure pad:
(i) Elevate the bleeding site above the level of the heart, if practical.
(ii) Apply pressure over the wound with the hands until a pad is available.
(iii) Replace hands with a pressure pad. It doesn't matter what the pad is made of, but ideally an effective pad should consist of a sterile dressing, a self-adhesive elastic bandage strip and a semi-rigid styrene block over the pad. An elastic bandage wrapped over the block applies pressure against the wound and stops bleeding.

How to apply a tourniquet:
Only use a tourniquet if bleeding cannot be stopped by applying a pressure pad.
(i) Place the tourniquet between the heart and the wound.
(ii) Make sure that the time is recorded.
(iii) Loosen for 10 seconds every 20 minutes.

(5) TREAT FOR SHOCK
Any serious injury causes shock. It is the result of a loss of blood or a drop in blood pressure causing decreased circulation. Shock and fright are not the same thing.

(a) Symptoms (not all may be present)
(i) Weak rapid pulse.　(iv) Low blood pressure.
(ii) Cold, clammy skin.　(v) Thirst.
(iii) Pale ashen skin.　(vi) Sometimes cyanosis.

(b) Treatment
(i) Victim should be reassured, made to lie down. Keep him warm and quiet, but do not overheat.
(ii) If conscious, he may be given a warm drink, but not alcohol. Do not massage his limbs.
(iii) Except in the case of chest and head injuries, it may help to elevate the lower extremities.
(iv) Administer oxygen if needed.

(6) TREAT SPECIAL CONDITIONS
Divers are constantly injuring their hands because of the nature of the work and the tools they use. Low temperatures will have a numbing effect which will cause less efficient handling of tools. It is even possible to be unaware of an injury. Many of these will be burns from cutting and welding. Treatment is to seek medical aid promptly.

One particular type of injury that deserves special attention is that caused by high pressure water jets, used primarily for cleaning surfaces in non-destructive testing (NDT) work. Superficial damage to the skin may appear trivial and give little indication of the extent of the injury and the damage to deeper tissue beneath. On site, first aid is confined to dressing the wound. The victim should be observed for the next few hours for developing symptoms. In the event of fever, pain or a rising pulse rate occurring before medical advice is available, give a course of antibiotics.

CHECK-LIST OF POSSIBLE CAUSES OF UNCONSCIOUSNESS IN DIVER

Remember that unconsciousness could be due to more than one of these causes. Some important examples include:

(1) Hypoxia/anoxia (insufficient O_2 in breathing gas)
(2) Asphyxia/drowning
(3) Arterial gas embolism
(4) Carbon dioxide poisoning
(5) Serious decompression sickness (type II), severe central nervous system (CNS) or cardio-respiratory involvement
(6) Hyperoxia (acute oxygen poisoning; too much oxygen in breathing gas)
(7) Inert gas narcosis (only significant on air at depths greater than 80 m)
(8) Hypothermia (body cooling)
(9) Hyperthermia (body overheating)
(10) Toxic gas contamination of breathing gas,' e.g.
    — carbon monoxide
    — consequences of u/w processes such as:
        — gases associated with welding/cutting
        — epoxy-resin gases
        — decomposing organic matter gases
(11) HPNS (high pressure nervous syndrome, 'microsleep', but only at depths over 400 m)
(12) Head injury
(13) Psychological factors such as fainting
(14) Electrocution
(15) Unassociated medical problems such as brain haemorrhage or heart attack.

Drowning

Drowning is basically asphyxia due to immersion in a liquid and is the fatal termination of a sequence of preventable events. Among the many causes of drowning, the most common is hypothermia.
The victim of immersion both inhales and swallows water, however in the majority of cases comparatively little water enters the lungs. Whether it does or not the result is the same: breathing stops. It is unimportant whether immersion occurs in fresh or salt water, drowning is lung damage and failure of oxygen transfer. Death usually occurs within about 8 minutes. Occasionally survival may be prolonged by profound hypothermia. People have recovered after being totally immersed and without breathing for 40 minutes. In all cases of drowning, attempts to restore respiration must be commenced without delay. Even though the survivor of near drowning may appear to have recovered, he should not be allowed home, as possible complications may develop rapidly during the next day or so.

Resuscitation

The basic technique of rescue from drowning is called cardiopulmonary resuscitation (CPR). The treatment is always the same although the technique may vary with the expertise of the rescuer and the equipment available.

CPR can be a lengthy treatment. For convenience it can be divided into 3 phases.

Phase 1: BASIC LIFE SUPPORT (BLS), known as the ABC of lifesaving.

Phase 2: ADVANCED LIFE SUPPORT (ALS) which is the restoration of spontaneous breathing and circulation by trained personnel only. This involves the insertion of a tube into the throat to control the airway, the administration of drugs and the use of de-fibrillation equipment.

Phase 3: PROLONGED LIFE SUPPORT (PLS) which is long-term resuscitation, involving intensive care in a hospital. Phases 2 and 3 are beyond the scope of this book.

COMMON PITFALLS IN RESUSCITATION TECHNIQUES

Pitfall No. 1 The airway is not properly extended so that the air passes into the victim's stomach instead of into his lungs. The rescuer will know this if the victim's stomach bulges. This may cause vomiting, so be prepared to tilt the victim's head down and onto the side.

Pitfall No. 2. The rescuer makes himself dizzy if he ventilates too fast. EAR should not exceed 20 breaths a minute.

Pitfall No. 3. Rescuer giving ECC must maintain an uninterrupted steady rhythm with the other rescuer giving EAR. One ventilation should be given with every 5 ECCs (at a rate of 60 per minute) without interrupting the rhythm of the compressions.

Some points in rescuing

(1) Speed in commencing EAR is essential. Unconsciousness will result from depriving the brain of oxygen for more than 30 seconds. An absolute deprivation of oxygen (anoxia) for more than 3 minutes may result in brain damage followed by death, though survival up to 40 minutes has been recorded.
(2) Immersion victims usually suffer from respiratory arrest before cardiac arrest, which is the opposite to what happens in most other modes of death. In many immersion victims the heart continues to beat although breathing has stopped, so that ECC is unnecessary; concentrate on ventilation.
(3) Be prepared to have to force open the victim's mouth, as drowning victims often clench their teeth. Use the 'crossed-finger' manoeuvre for a moderately relaxed jaw; the 'finger-behind-the-teeth' for a tightly clenched jaw. A solid object placed between the teeth to one side of his mouth will keep it open.
(4) 50% of victims will vomit during resuscitation. Check constantly that the airways remain clear.
(5) Victims of near-drowning may or may not have water in their lungs. You can check this by putting your ear on the back of the victim's chest at the bottom part of the lung wall, and listen.
(6) The treatment of wounds takes second place to resuscitation except in the case of a severe haemorrhage.
(7) A drowning victim's pulse may be weak, erratic or very slow. When searching for a victim's pulse, allow at least 10 seconds to find it.
(8) When performing ECC, a square wave sequence should be adopted, i.e. depress sternum 4–5 cm (1½–2 in.) for ½ second (50% of cycle), then release rapidly and wait for another ½ second (the other 50% of the cycle) to let the heart fill with blood.
(9) The use of artificial airways is only effective if the

Basic life support (BLS)

(1) Airway—tilt back head

(a) With head forward the tongue obstructs the airway
(b) Tilting back head clears the airway of the obstruction
(c) Lifting the neck and supporting the jaw gives better control of opening the mouth

(2) Breathing—expired air resuscitation (EAR)

Give breaths 12 times per minute

Inflation   Exhalation

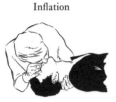

(a) Mouth-to-mouth (with head tilt by neck support)

Inhalation   Exhalation

(b) Mouth-to-nose (with head tilt by chin support)

(3) Circulation—external cardiac compression (ECC)

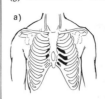

(a) **Identifying the pressure point**
Feel for lower end of breastbone and apply pressure about 4 cm above it, using heels of both hands

ECC given by 1 operator

(b) **Technique of** ECC
Body and hand position for ECCs. Press straight downwards 4 to 5 cm using part of your body weight. Keep arms straight and hands off ribs

(c) Release of pressure to let heart fill

(d) Compress and release for 50% of each cycle

External CPR with 2 operators; EAR and ECC simultaneously

rescuer is trained to use them. There are many to choose from, starting with a simple 'S'-shaped plastic airway tube, up to an oesophageal obturator airway.
(10) Cardiopulmonary resuscitation, if done effectively, is a most exhausting procedure. It is recommended that the rescuers set themselves a half-hour target to re-establish breathing, otherwise there may be more than one victim. The decision to stop resuscitation should be left to a qualified person. Efforts may reasonably be discontinued, however, after a minimum of half an hour if the victim remains pulseless. An exception might be made for a victim who has been immersed in very cold water, so that in this kind of situation CPR should be continued for at least up to one hour.
(11) If CPR is successful, arrange victim into recovery position.
(12) Following recovery, **never** relax your vigilance. Stay with the victim, observe him closely and be ready to furnish medical staff with details of the accident. Admission to hospital is mandatory for all drowning victims. If water has entered the lungs the victim may drown after a successful rescue, or his lungs may suddenly react and fill up with his own body fluids. Many victims have died days after an apparently successful recovery.

Note:
(1) ECC is not recommended in the diving bell because of the practical limitations with space and the positioning of the victim. Simply concentrate on EAR.
(2) The rescuer should be alert for symptoms of hypothermia: shallow, slow breathing, mental confusion, heart rate decrease, unconsciousness.

(3) If the victim is shivering, EAR will not be necessary as he has a pulse and is breathing.

Recovery position

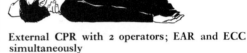

(a) Flex leg closest to you
(b) Put hand closest to you under his buttocks

(c) Gently roll him onto his side

(d) Tilt his head backward keeping his face low
Put his upper hand under his lower cheek to maintain head-tilt and to prevent him from rolling onto his face
The lower arm behind his back prevents him from rolling backward

RESCUE OF AN UNCONSCIOUS SURFACE-SUPPLIED DIVER
Practical intervention by a standby diver from the surface can take place only down to a limit of 75 m.

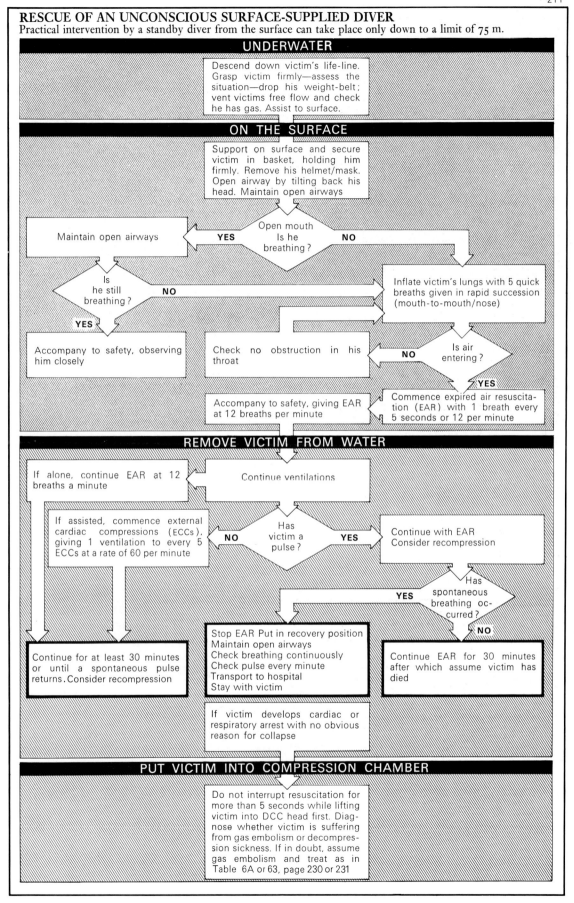

UNDERWATER

Descend down victim's life-line. Grasp victim firmly—assess the situation—drop his weight-belt; vent victims free flow and check he has gas. Assist to surface.

ON THE SURFACE

Support on surface and secure victim in basket, holding him firmly. Remove his helmet/mask. Open airway by tilting back his head. Maintain open airways

Open mouth Is he breathing?

YES → Maintain open airways

NO → Inflate victim's lungs with 5 quick breaths given in rapid succession (mouth-to-mouth/nose)

Is he still breathing?

NO →

YES → Accompany to safety, observing him closely

Check no obstruction in his throat

Is air entering?

NO →

YES → Commence expired air resuscitation (EAR) with 1 breath every 5 seconds or 12 per minute

Accompany to safety, giving EAR at 12 breaths per minute

REMOVE VICTIM FROM WATER

If alone, continue EAR at 12 breaths a minute

Continue ventilations

If assisted, commence external cardiac compressions (ECCs), giving 1 ventilation to every 5 ECCs at a rate of 60 per minute

Has victim a pulse?

NO →

YES → Continue with EAR Consider recompression

Has spontaneous breathing occurred?

YES →

NO →

Continue for at least 30 minutes or until a spontaneous pulse returns. Consider recompression

Stop EAR Put in recovery position
Maintain open airways
Check breathing continuously
Check pulse every minute
Transport to hospital
Stay with victim

Continue EAR for 30 minutes after which assume victim has died

If victim develops cardiac or respiratory arrest with no obvious reason for collapse

PUT VICTIM INTO COMPRESSION CHAMBER

Do not interrupt resuscitation for more than 5 seconds while lifting victim into DCC head first. Diagnose whether victim is suffering from gas embolism or decompression sickness. If in doubt, assume gas embolism and treat as in Table 6A or 63, page 230 or 231

RESCUE OF AN UNCONSCIOUS BELL DIVER

When a diver becomes unconscious out of a bell, or does not respond for whatever reason, it must be assumed that he is not breathing or not breathing sufficiently.

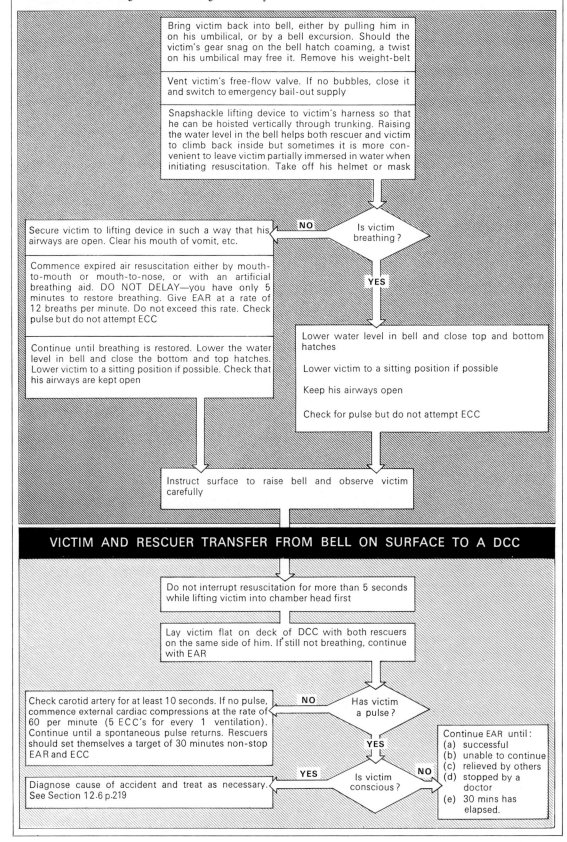

Bring victim back into bell, either by pulling him in on his umbilical, or by a bell excursion. Should the victim's gear snag on the bell hatch coaming, a twist on his umbilical may free it. Remove his weight-belt

Vent victim's free-flow valve. If no bubbles, close it and switch to emergency bail-out supply

Snapshackle lifting device to victim's harness so that he can be hoisted vertically through trunking. Raising the water level in the bell helps both rescuer and victim to climb back inside but sometimes it is more convenient to leave victim partially immersed in water when initiating resuscitation. Take off his helmet or mask

Is victim breathing?

NO

Secure victim to lifting device in such a way that his airways are open. Clear his mouth of vomit, etc.

Commence expired air resuscitation either by mouth-to-mouth or mouth-to-nose, or with an artificial breathing aid. DO NOT DELAY—you have only 5 minutes to restore breathing. Give EAR at a rate of 12 breaths per minute. Do not exceed this rate. Check pulse but do not attempt ECC

Continue until breathing is restored. Lower the water level in bell and close the bottom and top hatches. Lower victim to a sitting position if possible. Check that his airways are kept open

YES

Lower water level in bell and close top and bottom hatches

Lower victim to a sitting position if possible

Keep his airways open

Check for pulse but do not attempt ECC

Instruct surface to raise bell and observe victim carefully

VICTIM AND RESCUER TRANSFER FROM BELL ON SURFACE TO A DCC

Do not interrupt resuscitation for more than 5 seconds while lifting victim into chamber head first

Lay victim flat on deck of DCC with both rescuers on the same side of him. If still not breathing, continue with EAR

Check carotid artery for at least 10 seconds. If no pulse, commence external cardiac compressions at the rate of 60 per minute (5 ECC's for every 1 ventilation). Continue until a spontaneous pulse returns. Rescuers should set themselves a target of 30 minutes non-stop EAR and ECC

NO

Has victim a pulse?

YES

Continue EAR until:
(a) successful
(b) unable to continue
(c) relieved by others
(d) stopped by a doctor
(e) 30 mins has elapsed.

Diagnose cause of accident and treat as necessary. See Section 12.6 p.219

YES

Is victim conscious?

NO

12.2 EAR INFECTIONS PREVENTION AND TREATMENT

Ear infections are a continual problem for divers, especially for those involved in saturation diving. No preventative (prophylactic) treatment of the ears can be guaranteed to be 100% effective because of the enclosed atmosphere of the compression chambers in which divers spend so much time. A real physical effort is required to maintain a high standard of personal hygiene. No one should enter a chamber with any kind of ear or skin infection, however slight.

(1) Prevention of infections

The following must comprise a regular routine for every day of a saturation dive; these preventative measures have no chance of success otherwise.

1. Ensure that the ears are clean and dry.
2. Apply ear drops; either aluminium acetate in a 2% acetic acid solution, or Otic Domeboro solution ear drops. Avoid drops containing steroids or antibiotics.
3. Label the bottles, one for each ear, with your name to prevent cross-infection.
4. Put 3 to 4 drops in one ear, tilting the head on one side for 5 minutes. Repeat for the other ear.
5. Start 24 hours before each dive and then use each morning and evening of the saturation as well as after each immersion or shower.
6. Dry the outside of the ears with a towel—do not push anything into the ears. Avoid the use of ear buds.

NOTE: Treatment drops should **not** be used as a preventative measure.

(2) Ear infections

There are two types of infection and they can be identified only in a laboratory. One type is due to *Pseudomonas aeruginosa* and known as 'Pyo'; the other is due to other gram negative bacilli, and known as 'gram negative not Pyo'.
Divers suffering from Pyo must be removed from saturation as soon as possible. Divers with other ear infections may continue in saturation under treatment, although this is undesirable.

(3) Treatment of infections

Irritation or pain in the ears are the symptoms of an infection.
Have swabs of both ears, and of the ears of all others in the chamber, sent to a laboratory for analysis.
Inform a doctor of the situation.

Label all ear-drop bottles (two for each person) with the name of the diver and whether right or left ear. One bottle should be used for each ear and this rule must be rigorously observed.
Begin treatment only when there is a positive indication—significant ear pain and/or the results of the laboratory bacteriological studies.
Preventative treatment drops must **stop** before any curative treatment drops are used.
Use curative treatment as recommended by medical advice. If this is not available use polymixin/gentimicin ear drops. Use Otosporin only if pain is very severe.
The head should be tilted to one side and three drops allowed to fall into the ear canal. The dropper must not touch the ear or anything else. It would be easier if one diver applied the drops to another's ears. Do not exceed the dose, as toxic side effects may occur.
The head should be kept tilted to one side for at least 30 seconds while the tragus (the cartilaginous lump in front of the external ear orifice) is gently massaged with a circular motion. Repeat for the other ear.
Repeat this procedure four times daily (every 6 hours) for seven full days—even if the symptoms disappear. Discard any remaining drops after this time.
Do not keep drops for more than 3 weeks at +30°C (saturation environment), or more than 5 months at +4°C (fridge). Do not put in a freezer.
Panadol (Paracetamol) may be taken as a painkiller (2 tablets every 6 hours—do not exceed this dose). Beware of hiding pains due to decompression sickness.
If divers develop any other symptoms other than ear pain while under treatment, ask for medical advice.
Ear swabs must **not** be taken during treatment—results during this time are misleading. At the end of a course of treatment, drops should not be used for a further 2 days, then ear swabs taken on the third day. If these swabs are clear a cure can be assumed. If the infection persists seek medical advice.
Repeated infections in a DCC require investigation—check that the DCC is not contaminated.
Oral nasal masks and the linings of helmets should be sterilized from time to time in a solution of Hycalin or similar development.

NOTE: The proper use of treatment drops, while simple, is not a trivial matter. Treatment must be supervised and carried out with close attention to detail.

MEDICAL TERMS

Eustachian tube The canal, partly bony and partly cartilaginous, connecting the throat (pharynx) with the middle ear (tympanic cavity), serving as an air channel by which air pressure within the middle ear is equalized with that outside.

External ear That portion of the ear from the outermost portion to the tympanic membrane encompassing the external canal.

Inner ear That portion of the ear located within the bony confines of the temporal bone of the skull, and containing the organs of equilibrium and hearing.

Middle ear That portion of the ear between the tympanic membrane and the bony enclosure of the inner ear.

Sinuses Cavities within the bones of the skull lined by epithelium and connected by small openings to the nasal passageways.

Tympanic membrane A thin membranous partition (eardrum) separating the external ear from the middle ear.

12.3 HYPOTHERMIA

Definition

Hypothermia is the condition of a person when the deep body temperature is abnormally low.

Description

When body temperature first falls below the normal level (37°C, 98.4°F) the body will try to prevent a further fall and try to return to normal by

—increasing heat production by shivering
—reducing heat loss by restricting blood flow to the skin and limbs.

If the skin temperature falls below 10°C (due to, say, immersion in cold water) the blood vessels lose the ability to restrict the blood flow; they relax and the skin becomes red. At this time the body loses control of heat retention by the skin.

Only when these preventive measures fail does the body progress from merely 'being cold' towards true 'hypothermia'.

Heliox gas is a good conductor of heat. The thermal conductivity of helium is six times that of air, and at pressure it is also quite dense. Deep divers therefore can lose body heat via their breathing gas as well as from the body surface. This can be minimized while in the water by heating the respiratory gas to a suitable temperature. The chamber gas will also require to be maintained at elevated temperatures (see section 4.6 Chamber Operation).

> A deep diver can become hypothermic when breathing cold heliox even though his skin temperature is kept high.

Signs and symptoms

SHIVERING. The degree of shivering increases as the body temperature falls to about 35°C. If the body temperature continues to fall, the shivering decreases and disappears and the muscles become stiff.

CONFUSION AND DISORIENTATION. The victim becomes irrational and confused. Logical thinking and the ability to take corrective action are lost.

SWITCH-OFF PHENOMENON. It is impossible to communicate with the victim and he is unable to listen to or pay attention to even the simplest instructions.

AMNESIA. The victim will have no recollection of events while his body is at or below this temperature.

CARDIAC ARRHYTHMIAS. The heart beat becomes irregular and inefficient and the danger of heart failure is considerably increased.

SEMI-CONSCIOUSNESS. The victim is unable to perform any useful action.

UNCONSCIOUSNESS. The victim is rigid and unconscious.

VENTRICULAR FIBRILLATION. Heart failure. Recovery from this stage is unlikely and would require specialist medical equipment and supervision.

DEATH. A serious hypothermic victim may have no detectable signs of life. The only way to discover if the victim has died is to observe for signs of life (pulse, breathing) during rewarming.

Survival times

The thermal insulation provided by diving suits offers a major advantage where accidents result in divers drifting on the surface for long periods. This has a most important effect on the requirement for subsequent search and rescue operations, which would need to be maintained much longer than in conventional 'man overboard' situations. This length of time should be a minimum of 48 hours.

When drifting for long periods in the sea it is most important to retain the mask if possible, in order to keep the water from entering the eyes.

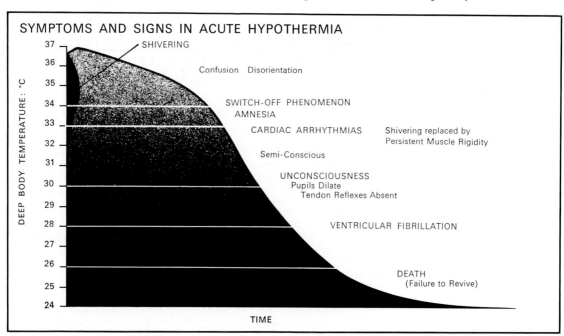

SYMPTOMS AND SIGNS IN ACUTE HYPOTHERMIA

DEEP BODY TEMPERATURE: °C

SHIVERING

Confusion   Disorientation

SWITCH-OFF PHENOMENON
AMNESIA

CARDIAC ARRHYTHMIAS   Shivering replaced by
                             Persistent Muscle Rigidity

Semi-Conscious

UNCONSCIOUSNESS
Pupils Dilate
Tendon Reflexes Absent

VENTRICULAR FIBRILLATION

DEATH
(Failure to Revive)

TIME

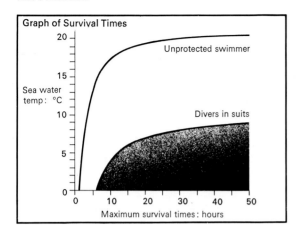

Graph of Survival Times

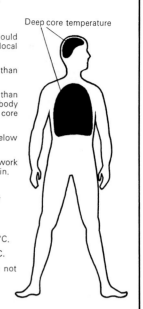

Deep core temperature

Recommended criteria for protecting divers against hypothermia:

Skin/head temperatures should not fall below 25°C, nor local temp. below 20°C.

Net respiratory loss no more than 175 W.

Net body heat loss no more than 12 kJ/kg (3.3 Wh/kg) of body weight (assuming a starting core temperature of 37°C).

Deep core temp. not to fall below 35.5°C.

Limbs above 15°C for useful work and above 10°C to prevent pain.

Recommended criteria for protecting divers against hyperthermia:

Deep core temp. not above 39°C.

Max skin temp. not above 42°C.

Inspiration temp. of dry gas not exceeding 35°C.

Methods of revival

DEEP BODY TEMPERATURE 34°C—37°C
Hot bath at 40°C if fully conscious.
DEEP BODY TEMPERATURE BELOW 33°C
If unconscious to semi-conscious, isolate from cold, prevent further heat loss. Maintain victim in a horizontal position. Maintain ventilation and assist circulation where necessary and gradually rewarm. Summon medical assistance.

Notes
1. It is normal for the deep body temperature to continue to fall, perhaps several degrees further (the afterdrop), during the initial phase of re-warming. Special care must be taken of the patient during this time because the ensuing rapid circulatory changes can jeopardise the victim.
2. If the body temperature falls below 35°C, the body will lose progressively the ability to shiver. At this stage the body's active protective mechanisms are beginning to fail. Remember therefore that a cold person who is not shivering could actually be seriously hypothermic.

Surface oriented, wet suit diving

It should be remembered that the chilling effect on the wet-suited diver in an open boat in a cold wind can be considerably greater than while he was in the water. Special precautions should be taken to provide protection against a long exposure to cold wind, especially following a dive.

Department of Energy (UK) requirements

The UK Regulations require that divers deeper than 50 m (mixed gas) will have suit heating and those deeper than 150 m will have gas heating.

Lost diving bell

Provision for a minimum life support endurance of 24 hours, including protection from hypothermia, should be made in the equipping of diving bells, to cater for the accidental disconnection of the bell from the surface support.

Protective devices/equipment

Dealt with in (6.3) Thermal protection.

EQUIVALENT WIND CHILL TEMPERATURE CHART

In cold, windy weather, divers on the surface may become very chilled by the movement of cold air over exposed skin. The chart on the left shows the decrease in air temperature caused by the increase in wind velocity. Winds above 40 mph have little additional effect.

Boldest type indicates greatest danger (flesh may freeze within 1 minute).

	Wind MPH															
		5		10		15		20		25		30		35		40	
°F	°C	°F	°C	°F	°C	°F	°C	°F	°C	°F	°C	°F	°C	°F	°C	°F	°C
40	4	35	2	30	−1	25	−4	20	−7	15	−9	10	−12	10	−12	10	−12
35	2	30	−1	20	−7	15	−9	10	−12	10	−12	5	−15	−5	−15	0	−17
30	−1	25	−4	15	−9	10	−12	5	−15	0	−17	0	−17	−5	−21	−5	−21
25	−4	20	−7	10	−12	0	−17	0	−17	−5	−21	−10	−23	−10	−23	−15	−26
20	−7	15	−9	5	−15	−5	−21	−10	−23	−15	−26	−20	−29	−20	−29	−20	−29
15	−9	10	−12	0	−17	−10	−23	−15	−26	−20	−29	**−25**	**−32**	**−30**	**−34**	−30	−34
10	−12	5	−15	−10	−23	−20	−29	**−25**	**−32**	−30	−34	−30	−34	−35	−37	−35	−37
5	−15	0	−17	−15	−26	**−25**	**−32**	−30	−34	−35	−37	−40	−40	−40	−40	−45	−43
0	−17	−5	−15	−20	−24	**−30**	**−34**	−35	−37	−45	−43	−50	−46	−50	−46	−55	−48
−5	−21	−10	−23	**−25**	**−32**	−40	−40	−45	−43	−50	−46	−55	−48	−60	−51	−60	−51
−10	−23	−15	−26	**−35**	**−37**	−45	−43	−50	−46	−60	−51	−65	−54	−65	−54	−70	−57
−15	−26	−20	−29	**−40**	**−40**	−50	−46	−60	−51	−65	−54	−70	−57	−75	−60	−75	−60
−20	−29	**−25**	**−32**	**−45**	**−43**	−60	−51	−65	−54	−75	−60	−80	−62	−80	−62	−85	−65
−25	−32	**−30**	**−34**	**−50**	**−46**	−65	−54	−75	−60	−70	−62	−85	−65	−90	−68	−95	−71

Equivalent chill temperature °F °C

12.4 HYPERTHERMIA

Hyperthermia (heat stroke) occurs when the body is unable to lose the heat which it produces and/or when it is forced to absorb heat from its surroundings. The raising of the body temperature more than 2°C above normal (from 37 to 39°C) produces a serious condition. A further increase as far as 41°C results in an emergency condition, and the temperature must be lowered quickly to prevent permanent brain damage or death.

The body is less capable of surviving an increase in temperature than a reduction of the same order. Damage to the body caused by hyperthermia can be irreversible and is therefore more serious than the more recoverable effects of hypothermia.

In hot, humid climates, and especially when the compression chamber is on deck, the heat from the sun combined with the heat produced during pressurization can lead to extremely high temperatures within the chamber. The conductivity of oxy-helium is six times that of air and if the humidity in the chamber is high (more than 85%) the diver will not lose heat by sweating. The victim will then be absorbing heat without losing any and hyperthermia will result. The danger is greater for fat people.

Treatment

Lower the chamber temperature—see check list. Lower the body temperature as quickly as possible by bathing the victim in cold water, or if possible by completely immersing the body. Sponge the head and neck with the same cool water. The victim must drink copious fluids. A weak solution of salt water (1 teaspoon salt to 1 quart (2 pints) water) is beneficial. The victim should be examined by a physician.

Check list of ways of reducing the temperature of a chamber either routinely or in an emergency

1. In hot climates any compression chamber on deck should be protected from the sun by an awning.

2. The deck compression chamber (DCC) can be kept cool by covering it with a blanket or sacking and dowsing it with cold water, as water evaporating has a great cooling effect. If necessary, and possible, the outside of the chamber may be packed with ice, particularly on top.

3. Ice may be passed through the medical lock.

4. Anyone inside the chamber should drink plenty of cool fluids.

5. Clothing reduces the cooling effect of sweating; so remove all clothing.

6. Sponge the body with cool water.

7. Flush the chamber with the appropriate gas mix. Gas from a high pressure source is cooled as its pressure reduces on entering the chamber.

8. In an emergency, stop compression immediately and decompress as soon and as fast as safety allows.

A lack of understanding of these points has in the past led to fatalities caused by hyperthermia.

Signs and symptoms

Rise in body temperature	Convulsions	Extremely rapid and feeble pulse
Sudden collapse	Dilated pupils	Breathing deep at first, then
Skin extremely dry and hot	Weakness	very shallow and rapid

12.5 HIGH PRESSURE NERVOUS SYNDROME (HPNS)

High pressure nervous (or neurological) syndrome can occur at depths over 200 m (660 ft) when breathing helium/oxygen mixtures. It is probably caused by the pressure itself and not by the gas. HPNS is the major limiting factor in very deep diving, at present around 670 m (2200 ft) (1976).

Symptoms

Tremors of the hands; jerky movements of the limbs; dizziness; nausea; decreased alertness; a tendency to sleep if the diver does not stay active. Also there are changes in the electrical activity of the brain.

From studies on animals it has been shown that tremors are followed by convulsions, coma and death. If the convulsion stage is reached, even with immediate decompression, death may result.

Ways of avoiding or reducing the effects of HPNS

(1) For dives of about one hour duration at depths of less than 200 m (660 ft) use a compression rate of 30 m/min. (100 ft/min.).

(2) For dives over 200 m (660 ft) use a compression rate of less than 3 m/min. (10 ft/min.), ideally 1 m/min. (3 ft/min.).

(3) Compression stops at various levels reduce the severity of the HPNS symptoms and allow deeper dives.

(4) Symptoms may be reduced, allowing deeper dives and more rapid compressions by adding small quantities of nitrogen to the breathing mixture.

12.6 DECOMPRESSION

Decompression is a drop in pressure which may occur
(a) when climbing to altitude in an aircraft (atmospheric to sub-atmospheric pressure), or
(b) when ascending to the surface after a dive (raised pressure back to sea level or atmospheric pressure).

The importance of decompression lies in the effect that it has on the dissolved inert gas in the body.

Decompression sickness (DCS) occurs when a diver is subjected to reduced environmental pressure sufficient to cause the formation of bubbles from the inert gases dissolved in his tissues. If the elimination of gas by the blood flowing through the lungs is inadequate to parallel the rate of reduction of the ambient pressure, the super-saturation of gas in the tissues will cause the gas to come out of solution in the form of bubbles. Bubbles collecting in the bloodstream may block circulation, while those in the tissues will distort the tissues as the bubbles expand. Visible symptoms will depend on where the bubbles arise, whether in the joints, muscles, bones, nerves, and so on.

Recognition of the symptoms of DCS, which may occur up to 36 hours after the dive has ended, is very important. Omitted decompression is when a diver has neglected to carry out the required decompression procedure, either by ascending too rapidly or by missing decompression stops due to an emergency such as an exhausted air supply or bodily injury. The diver should be recompressed to depth, as appropriate, using USN Table 5, or Table 1A if no oxygen is available. Consider any illness during or after this procedure as a recurrence.

In-water decompression is to be avoided except in the most favourable circumstances.

Stage decompression is a technique, used mostly in air diving, of bringing the diver safely back to the surface without suffering DCS by ascending in a series of programmed stages. It is safer and more comfortable to decompress in a surface chamber, but this can be carried out only when there is a deck compression chamber (DCC) ready to repressurize the diver to beyond the depth of his last stop within five minutes of leaving that stop.

A bounce dive, either on air or mixed gas, is where the bottom time is limited to no more than about one hour to avoid the diver's tissues becoming saturated. A saturation dive is a deep dive of unlimited bottom time made possible by the diver's tissues becoming completely saturated with inert gas in a submersible compression chamber (SCC) or DCC before and during the dive.

Decompression procedures

The diving company which employs the diver is responsible for determining the decompression procedures, which may be derived from several sources
1. US Navy   4. Diving company in house
2. Royal Navy (UK) 5. Diving consultant
3. Other navies
(In UK waters schedules have to be approved by DEn)
These procedures will cover both air and mixed-gas diving and therapeutic recompression requirements.

The US Navy and Royal Navy tables are freely available while those of proprietary sources, such as the diving companies, specialist consultants or other navies, tend to be confidential, though not necessarily any better. The most widely used procedures in the professional diving field worldwide are provided by the US Navy. It is a safe principle to avoid mixing compression/decompression/therapeutic recompression procedures.

It is important to use also the corresponding advice on repetitive diving, diving at altitude and flying after diving. If changing from one procedure to another, perhaps due to a change of diving company, it is extremely important to learn the new procedure in full detail. This is because there can be basic differences between the procedures. Notable examples include whether the excursion time between two stops is taken out of the stop being left, or the stop being approached, and what gas mixes/partial pressures are used routinely for operational and therapeutic purposes.

If there is a choice of whose tables to use, bear in mind the following:
- What gases are available?
- What DCCs are available?
- How available are the DCCs?
- What diving medical support is available?
- Which procedure is the most conservative?
- Is a conservative table needed, say due to very cold conditions, hard work, lack of medical and therapeutic support?
- Are tables metricated to match charts?

Symptoms appear usually within six hours after surfacing but can be delayed up to 36 hours afterwards. There are two types of symptoms of decompression sickness. For all practical purposes all or any of them should be regarded as an emergency.

TYPE I (Mild)

These are often described as mild, which is not always necessarily true. Symptoms include pain and itching and occasionally the skin may show a blotchy mottled rash or red spots of varying size. Sometimes the skin looks like marble. Usually fatigue is an important symptom of mild decompression sickness and may precede serious problems.

A typical example of decompression sickness might begin with itching or burning of a particular area of the body, which may spread and later reduce. There is also a tingling of the skin. Pain, which is the most frequent symptom, is deep and usually felt in or near a joint, and can become progressively worse until it is unbearable. Distinguish between this and a muscle or joint sprain, which is usually painful to the touch, and swollen and discoloured.

TYPE II (Serious)

These are often called the serious symptoms, but all decompression symptoms are to be managed as serious. Type II, however, are extremely urgent and dangerous. Symptoms are much more random than for Type I and are easy to confuse with those of gas embolism. In either case, immediate treatment by recompression is indicated. Shock, nausea, and hearing difficulties are common signs. Abdominal pain is frequently followed by a weakness, paralysis or numbness of the limbs. There is often dizziness. Pain in the chest, shortness of breath, extreme fatigue, collapse and unconsciousness, are other symptoms of serious decompression sickness. The most common signs are sensory and muscular changes of a scattered nature affecting one or more limbs.

It is quite easy to be misled when an obvious and painful symptom masks another which may develop into a more serious symptom later on, e.g. the presentation of a joint pain may seem dominant, diverting attention from some patch of numbness that demands a more vigorous approach.

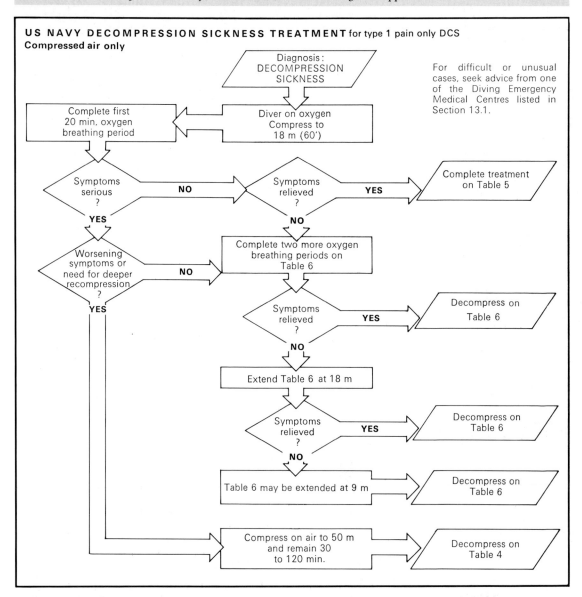

US NAVY DECOMPRESSION SICKNESS TREATMENT for type 1 pain only DCS
Compressed air only

Diagnosis:
DECOMPRESSION
SICKNESS

For difficult or unusual cases, seek advice from one of the Diving Emergency Medical Centres listed in Section 13.1.

Diver on oxygen
Compress to
18 m (60')

Complete first
20 min. oxygen
breathing period

Symptoms serious ? — NO → Symptoms relieved ? — YES → Complete treatment on Table 5

YES ↓ / NO ↓

Worsening symptoms or need for deeper recompression ? — NO → Complete two more oxygen breathing periods on Table 6

YES ↓

Symptoms relieved ? — YES → Decompress on Table 6

NO ↓

Extend Table 6 at 18 m

Symptoms relieved ? — YES → Decompress on Table 6

NO ↓

Table 6 may be extended at 9 m → Decompress on Table 6

Compress on air to 50 m
and remain 30
to 120 min. → Decompress on Table 4

Diagnosing Decompression Sickness

A major problem with divers is that they tend to ignore mild symptoms of decompression sickness that may develop into a more serious problem later on. If there is no hyperbaric chamber on site, divers suspected of having serious DCS should be administered oxygen immediately and placed in the Trendelenberg Position. The victim should then be transferred immediately to the nearest hyperbaric chamber and compressed to 18 m on O_2. If the symptoms are relieved or improving within 10 min the victim should be kept on oxygen for 30 min. If the symptoms get worse, follow the recommendations of the flowchart shown above. If, however, arterial gas embolism is suspected, the victim should be compressed to 50 m without delay

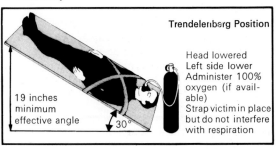

Trendelenberg Position

Head lowered
Left side lower
Administer 100% oxygen (if available)
Strap victim in place but do not interfere with respiration

19 inches
minimum
effective angle

30°

SYMPTOMS OF DECOMPRESSION ILLNESS

This table is a guide to recognising the many forms that decompression illness may take. D/C sickness is graded into two types, Type I and Type II. Type I is represented by joint pains and rashes which are defined as 'mild'. Type II is serious and dangerous, usually involving either the central nervous system or pulmonary effects, such as air embolism. Symptoms such as those due to the failure of a middle-ear or sinus to clear, or an escape of air from a tear in the lungs (Pneumothorax) can occur during or immediately after an ascent.

Symptoms due to bubbles of gas in the bloodstream or tissues (the bends), may occur during or up to 36 hr after ascent, though most occur within 1 hr.

Symptom	Type	Common and/or Technical Name	Urgency	Action
Discomfort, or slight pain in a limb	I	Niggle	Vigilance	Observe. Possibly recompress
Rash; Itching	I	Skin Bend; Pruritis; Mild Decompression Sickness	Vigilance	Observe. Possibly recompress
Deep pain in joint	I	Bend; Hit; Decompression Sickness	Urgent	Recompress
Localised soft swelling	I	Oedema; Lymphatic Bend; Lymphatic Decompression Sickness	Vigilance	May need recompression
Swelling in neck with crackling under skin	I	Interstitial Emphysema; Surgical Emphysema	Non Urgent	Observe. Do *not* recompress
Pins & needles; "Wooliness" of feet	II	Bend; Spinal Bend; Serious Decompression Sickness	Very Urgent	Recompress. Consult nearest diving doctor
Excessive tiredness; General "unwellness"	II	Bend; Decompression Sickness	Very Urgent	Probably recompress. Consult nearest diving doctor
Unconsciousness; Headache; Difficulty with vision or speech	II	Bend; Cerebral Bend; Serious Decompression Sickness; Air Embolism	Extremely Urgent	Recompress. Send for nearest diving doctor
Unsteadiness; Dizziness; Nausea; Vomiting	II	Staggers; Cerebral Bend; Vestibular Bend; Vestibular Hit; Vertigo; Serious Decompression Sickness	Extremely Urgent	Recompress. Send for nearest diving doctor
Pain in chest; Breathing difficulty; Shortness of breath; Coughing; Blue colour	II	Pneumothorax; Chokes	Extremely Urgent	Give O₂. Recompress for chokes only. Send for nearest diving doctor

If there is no recompression chamber on site, it is essential that another diver accompanies the affected diver, preferably his companion or the Supervisor, in the ambulance and during treatment. A careful note should be made of the deepest depth and the duration of the dive: entonox, a nitrous oxide analgesic should not be administered by the ambulance crew, as it makes the bends worse.

Where no special recompression facilities exist locally, a telephone call should be made to the Superintendent of Diving, HMS Vernon (Portsmouth (0705) 822351 ext. 872375 during the day; or 0705 822351 ext. 872413/4/5 at other times).

In the USA, anyone needing emergency help may call 919 684-8111 [call collect if required] and ask for the Diving Accident Network (DAN).

A common problem in the management of diving accidents is an initial misdiagnosis. To minimize the likelihood of overlooking serious symptoms of decompression sickness or gas embolism, an attending diving doctor should give a neurological examination which usually takes about 30 minutes and requires certain diagnostic equipment and training to interpret the results. As a diving doctor is rarely at the scene of a diving accident, however, a preliminary four minute neurological evaluation has been developed which requires no equipment and can be carried out by non-medical persons. The results can then be communicated to a diving doctor by telephone or other system. The information from this check list will assist the doctor to make a fast and accurate decision without actually examining the diver himself.

INITIAL NEUROLOGICAL EXAMINATION BY NON-MEDICAL PERSONNEL

NOTE
When interpreting the results of this examination, try to ascertain whether the abnormalities are a result of the diving disorder and not the result of a previous disorder, i.e. some divers may have a hearing impairment caused by working near noisy equipment. If in doubt, assume it is DCS.

Mental condition or status

As very little interference is required to impair functioning of the higher mental faculties, test for subtle signs of serious decompression sickness by observing:
(1) ORIENTATION
Time (the first function to go). E.g. 'What day is this?'
Place (the next to go). E.g. 'Where are you?'
Person (severe impairment). E.g. 'What is your name?'
(2) MEMORY
Immediate (test with a series of numbers).
Recent (happenings within last 24 hours).
Remote (background).
(3) MENTAL FUNCTION
Test by using serial 7's. Subtract 7 from 100, then 7 from the answer, and so on. If an error is repeated, like '93, 90, 83, 80, 73, 70', there is a condition called perseveration that usually indicates impairment.
(4) LEVEL OF CONSCIOUSNESS
Watch for any fluctuation.
(5) SEIZURES
These are obvious.

Cranial nerves (nerves that come directly from the brain)

What to check and how to test the twelve cranial nerves. Test one side versus the other side.
(1) SENSE OF SMELL (Olfactory nerves)
Test with coffee, for example, one nostril at a time. Do not delay if appropriate material for this test is not available.
(2) SIGHT (Optic nerve)
Hold up fingers for the diver to count; test one eye at a time.
(3) EYE MOVEMENT (Oculomotor, Trochlear, and Abducens nerves)
Have the diver's eyes follow your finger as you move it up and down, left and right.
(4) CHEWING (Trigeminal nerves)
Can the teeth be clenched? Feel the jaw muscles on both sides simultaneously.
(5) MOUTH (Facial nerves)
Can the diver smile?
Can both corners of the mouth be lifted simultaneously?
(6) HEARING (Auditory nerves)
Test one ear at a time by whispering or rubbing your fingers together approximately 2 cm away from the ear.
(7) TALKING (Glossopharyngeal, Vagus nerves)
Check for gagging and proper pronunciation of words.
(8) SHOULDER MUSCLES (Spinal Accessory nerves)
Have diver shrug his shoulders while you press down on them. Note any weakness on one side.
(9) TONGUE (Hypoglossal nerves)
Can the diver stick his tongue out straight? Does it move to one side?

Sensory nerves

(1) SHARP VERSUS DULL (check one hand versus other)
Using sharp and dull objects, see if the diver can distinguish between them by testing
  (i) back of hand
  (ii) base of thumb
  (iii) base of little finger.

Motor nerves (nerves that operate muscles)

(1) MUSCLE STRENGTH
Have the diver grip two of your fingers with each hand. Is the strength the same in each hand?
With the diver sitting or lying down, place your hands on the legs just above the ankle and press down lightly; have the diver try to lift his legs. Is the strength equal in both?
(2) RANGE OF MOTION
Check normal movement of both arms and legs.
(3) MUSCLE TONE
Check if the muscles are spastic (in a state of contraction) or flaccid (totally relaxed).

Muscle co-ordination (cerebellar function)

(1) POINT IN SPACE
Can the diver touch your finger held in front of his nose?
(2) FINGER TO NOSE
Can the diver move a finger from touching your finger to the tip of his nose, and repeat the motion?
(3) GAIT
Walking gait—check for rubber legs, staggering and unsteadiness.
Tandem gait—walking heel to toe.
(4) BALANCE (sharpened Romberg)
Have a diver stand straight, feet together, arms folded in front and eyes closed.

Reflexes

(1) BASIC REFLEXES (check both sides with a blunt instrument)
  biceps   knee   forearm
  triceps   ankle.
(2) BABINSKI REFLEX
Run a blunt object up the sole of the foot. If the toes curl down towards the sole of the foot, a normal Babinski is present. If nothing happens, no conclusion can be drawn, but if the toes flex backwards, upwards, and spread, this is a reliable sign of probable spinal involvement.

Language problem

(1) APHASIA (speech impairment)
Check for misplaced words and incorrect word order.

Although there is usually little time in which to examine the diver, especially under pressure in a DCC, do not skimp the examination. In all cases of doubt treat the diver by recompression. If you are not sure that he is completely free from serious symptoms, use the longer table. Time and air are cheaper than joints and brain tissue.
For a comparative summary of the symptoms of both DCS and gas embolism, see previous page.

Youngblood and Clarke, 1978

Diving casualty examination checklist

(for recording results)

Patient
Date

Life-threatening conditions
1. Airway
2. Breathing
3. Circulation
4. Hemorrhage
5. Shock

Mental condition or status

1. Orientation — Time
   Place
   Person
2. Memory — Immediate
   Recent
   Remote
3. Mental function
4. Level of consciousness
5. Seizures

Cranial nerves

1. Sense of smell (Olfactory)	R	L
2. Sight (Optic)	R	L
3. Eye movement (Oculomotor, Trochlear, Abducens)	R	L
4. Chewing (Trigeminal)	R	L
5. Mouth, smile (Facial)	R	L
6. Hearing (Acoustic)	R	L
7. Talking (Glossopharyngeal, Vagus)	R	L
8. Shoulders (Spinal Accessory)	R	L
9. Tongue (Hypoglossal)	R	L

Sensory nerves

1. Sharp vs. Dull	R	L

Motor nerves

1. Muscle strength	R	L
2. Range of motion	R	L
3. Muscle tone	R	L

Co-ordination

1. Point in space	R	L
2. Finger to nose	R	L

3. Gait: Walking
   Tandem
4. Balance

Reflexes

1. Basic:	Biceps	R	L
	Triceps	R	L
	Forearm	R	L
	Knee	R	L
	Ankle	R	L
2. Babinski reflex		R	L

Language
1. Aphasia
Comments or conclusions
Examiner

Diving at altitude

When air diving at altitudes of less than 100 m, no adjustments to the decompression tables will be necessary. Higher than 100 m, where surface pressure is less than 1 bar absolute, adjust as shown in the table below. Decompression stops should always be calculated for sea water as a safety precaution.

Depth corrections for diving at altitude

Altitude	Correction
under 100 m	no adjustment
100–300 m	add $\frac{1}{4}$ of actual depth to give effective depth
300–2000 m	add $\frac{1}{3}$ of actual depth to give effective depth
2000–3000 m	add $\frac{1}{2}$ of actual depth to give effective depth

For oxy-helium diving at altitude, consult special tables compiled by Professor Buhlmann, Zurich University.

Flying after diving

To avoid the risk of decompression sickness by flying after having dived, it is best to wait for 24 hours. However, the following rules apply:

Altitude restrictions—flying after diving

AIR DIVING	Time before flying at cabin altitude	
	610 m (2000')	2438 m (8000')
No-stop dives. Total time under pressure less than 60 minutes within previous 12 hours	2 hours	4 hours
All other air diving (Less than 4 hours under pressure)	12 hours	12 hours
Air or Nitrox saturation (More than 4 hours under pressure). Caution. Experience in this range extremely limited.	24 hours	48 hours

MIXED GAS DIVING (Diver on air at sea level)
No flying at all for AT LEAST 12 hours following return to atmospheric pressure following heliox and trimix bounce and saturation diving.

*Commercial aircraft normally fly at an effective cabin altitude of 1500–3000 m.

These rules would not apply to a very low flying aircraft (less than 300m/1000 ft) such as a helicopter transporting a decompression victim to a DCC.

Post-treatment restrictions

Divers who have been carrying out a decompression involving stops should remain in the vicinity of a DCC
(1) for 8 hr following an air dive
(2) for 5 hr following a heliox dive, including saturation.
Divers surfacing after therapeutic treatment are to be kept close to a DCC for 6 hours and within 1 hour's travelling time for the next 18 hours. Mild cases, with successful treatment, are not to be allowed to dive for 24 hours, and no deeper than 10 m for an additional 2 days. In serious cases the examining doctor would normally consider a lay-off of 7 days after a complete recovery. If any signs of DCS persist, the diver is to be re-examined before diving. After all the above intervals, a diver may travel by boat without further restriction or fly by helicopter not higher than 300 m. It is advisable to wait for 12 hours after an air or heliox dive, prior to flying.

Action in the absence of a compression chamber

If no DCC is immediately available on site
(1) Contact by telephone the nearest authority controlling a chamber and request it be made available. If no DCC is available locally, telephone HMS Vernon, as detailed in Section 13.1.
(2) Dispatch patient by quickest available means; if by air, at a pressure equivalent to less than 300 m (1000 ft).
(3) If available, victim to breathe O_2 during transfer.
(4) The victim should be accompanied by the diving supervisor and, if possible, a diving doctor. If none of these are available, another diver fully conversant with details of the accident should be sent.

Mixed gas decompression

The term 'mixed gas' refers to any breathing medium other than air. Mixed gas might consist of an oxygen/nitrogen mixture in different proportions to atmospheric air, or oxygen alone, or of a mixture of oxygen with inert gases. Helium is usually the inert gas used because of its low density; it is non-inflammable and non-toxic. The other inert gas that is sometimes used is nitrogen. Air is sometimes used in phases of a mixed gas dive.

There are two main reasons for breathing mixed gas instead of air on dives deeper than 50 m (165 ft). One is that the partial pressure of oxygen becomes toxic at such depths; the other is that nitrogen narcosis impairs diver performance severely. The main difference between surface-supplied air and helium/oxygen decompression methods is that in the former the depth of the dive is the controlling factor whereas in helium/oxygen diving it is the pressure of the inert gas.

Mixed gas diving is a complex operation requiring detailed planning, specialized equipment and extensive surface support. Mixed gas operations require their own decompression tables, according to whether they are Scuba or surface-supplied and whether helium/oxygen or nitrogen/oxygen is used.

Decompression sickness occurring in non-saturation mixed gas diving is treated in the same manner as decompression sickness in air diving. The preferred method is the oxygen treatment tables.

Decompression sickness as a result of a saturation exposure has its established treatment procedures.

Having diagnosed decompression sickness, Type I or Type II, or gas embolism, a suitable therapeutic recompression table must be selected. Summaries of the US Navy and the Royal Navy tables are listed below.

RULES FOR RECOMPRESSION TREATMENT
Always
1. Follow the Treatment Tables accurately.
2. Have qualified tender in chamber at all times during recompression.
3. Maintain the normal descent and ascent rates.
4. Examine patient thoroughly at depth of relief or treatment depth.
5. Treat an unconscious patient for gas embolism or serious decompression sickness unless the possibility of such a condition can be ruled out without question.
6. Use air tables only if oxygen is unavailable.
7. Be alert for oxygen poisoning if oxygen is used.
8. In the event of oxygen convulsion, remove the oxygen mask and keep the patient from harming himself.
9. Maintain oxygen usage within the time and depth limitations.
10. Check patient's condition before and after coming to each stop and during long stops.
11. Observe patient for at least 6 hours after treatment for recurrence of symptoms.
12. Maintain accurate timekeeping and recording.
13. Maintain a well stocked medical kit at hand.

Never
— Permit any shortening or other alteration to the tables except under the direction of a trained Diving Medical Officer.
— Let patient sleep between depth changes or for more than one hour at any one stop.
— Wait for a bag resuscitator. Use mouth-to-mouth immediately if breathing ceases.
— Break rhythm during resuscitation.
— Permit the use of oxygen below 60 feet.
— Fail to report symptoms early (diver).
— Fail to treat doubtful cases.
— Allow personnel in the chamber to assume any cramped position which may interfere with complete blood circulation.

NOTE: The utilization of a He/O₂ breathing medium is an option to be considered at the discretion of the cognizant medical officer as determined by the circumstances of the individual case.

SUMMARY OF U.S. NAVY RECOMPRESSION TREATMENT TABLES*

5	Oxygen Treatment of Pain-only D/C Sickness	Treatment of pain-only decompression sickness when symptoms are relieved within 10 minutes at 60'.
6	Oxygen treatment of Serious D/C Sickness	Treatment of serious decompression sickness or pain-only decompression sickness when symptoms are not relieved within 10 minutes at 60'.
6A	Air and Oxygen Treatment of Gas Embolism	Treatment of gas embolism. Use also when unable to determine whether symptoms are caused by gas embolism or severe decompression sickness.
1A	Air Treatment of Pain-only D/C Sickness— 100' treatment	Treatment of pain-only decompression sickness when oxygen unavailable and pain is relieved at depth less than 60'.
2A	Air Treatment of Pain-only D/C Sickness— 165' treatment	Treatment of pain-only decompression sickness when oxygen unavailable and pain is relieved at a depth greater than 60'.
3	Air Treatment of Serious D/C Decompression Sickness or Gas Embolism	Treatment of serious symptoms or gas embolism when oxygen unavailable and symptoms are relieved within 30 minutes at 165'.
4	Air Treatment of Serious D/C Sickness or Gas Embolism	Treatment of worsening symptoms during the first 20-minute oxygen breathing period at 60' on Table 6, or when symptoms are not relieved within 30 min. at 165' using air treatment Table 3.

*This summary presents oxygen treatment tables before air treatment tables because the oxygen breathing method is preferred. Use of Table 5A has been discontinued.

SUMMARY OF ROYAL NAVY RECOMPRESSION TREATMENT TABLES

52	Air recompression therapy	Tables 52, 53, 54 and 55 are the air tables normally employed for therapeutic decompression and used at the following rates of descent:
53	Air recompression therapy	—10 m/min for mild DCS symptoms —30 m/min for serious DCS symptoms.
54	Air recompression therapy	Table 55 is to be used instead of 54 when O₂ is not available. Both diver and attendant are to breathe O₂ during the later stages of decompression.
55	Air recompression therapy	
61	Oxygen recompression therapy	Tables 61 and 62 are used when O₂ is available and required for the greater part of the therapy. They form the therapeutic approach for the majority of cases of DCS. Only life-threatening DCS or cases of arterial gas embolism would normally be compressed to 50 m on air as the initial treatment.
62	Oxygen recompression therapy	
63	Air/oxygen recompression therapy	For arterial gas embolism therapy. See section 12.7, p 231.
71	Modified air recompression therapy	Tables 71 and 72 may be used instead of the air tables 52–55 on the advice of a diving doctor.
72	Modified air recompression therapy	
73	Modified air recompression therapy	For arterial gas embolism therapy. Table 73 may be used in place of Tables 54 and 55, and is preferred in cases of gas embolism or incomplete relief of DCS. See section 12.7, p 231.

TABLE 5 OXYGEN TREATMENT OF PAIN-ONLY DECOMPRESSION SICKNESS

1. Treatment of pain-only decompression sickness when symptoms are relieved within 10 minutes at 60 feet.
2. Descent rate—25 ft/min.
3. Ascent rate—1 ft/min. Do not compensate for slower ascent rates. Compensate for faster rates by halting the ascent.
4. Time at 60 feet begins on arrival at 60 feet.
5. If oxygen breathing must be interrupted, allow 15 minutes after the reaction has entirely subsided and resume schedule at point of interruption.
6. If oxygen breathing must be interrupted at 60 feet, switch to TABLE 6 upon arrival at the 30 foot stop.
7. Tender breathes air throughout. If treatment is a repetitive dive for the tender or tables are lengthened, tender should breathe oxygen during the last 30 minutes of ascent to the surface.

KEY TO BREATHING GASES

 Oxygen

 Air

 Air decompression

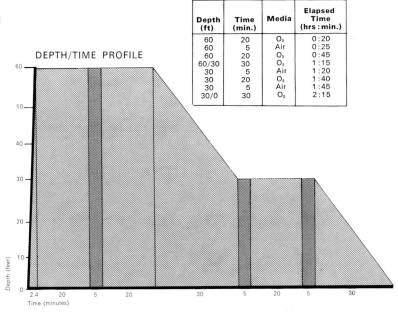

DEPTH/TIME PROFILE

Depth (ft)	Time (min.)	Media	Elapsed Time (hrs : min.)
60	20	O₂	0:20
60	5	Air	0:25
60	20	O₂	0:45
60/30	30	O₂	1:15
30	5	Air	1:20
30	20	O₂	1:40
30	5	Air	1:45
30/0	30	O₂	2:15

TABLE 6 OXYGEN TREATMENT OF SERIOUS DECOMPRESSION SICKNESS

1. Treatment of serious or pain-only decompression sickness when symptoms are not relieved within 10 minutes at 60 feet.
2. Descent rate—25 ft/min.
3. Ascent rate—1 ft/min. Do not compensate for slower ascent rates. Compensate for faster rates by halting the ascent.
4. Time at 60 feet—begins on arrival at 60 feet.
5. If oxygen breathing must be interrupted, allow 15 minutes after the reaction has entirely subsided and resume schedule at point of interruption.
6. Tender breathes air throughout. If treatment is a repetitive dive for the tender or tables are lengthened, tender should breathe oxygen during the last 30 minutes of ascent to the surface.
7. Table 6 can be lengthened by an additional 25 minutes at 60 feet (20 minutes on oxygen and 5 minutes on air) or an additional 75 minutes at 30 feet (15 minutes on air and 60 minutes on oxygen), or both.

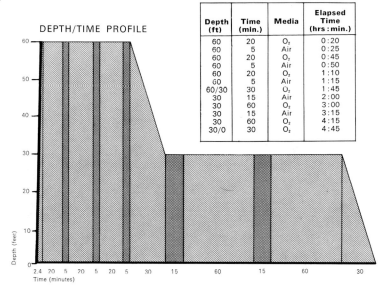

DEPTH/TIME PROFILE

Depth (ft)	Time (min.)	Media	Elapsed Time (hrs : min.)
60	20	O₂	0:20
60	5	Air	0:25
60	20	O₂	0:45
60	5	Air	0:50
60	20	O₂	1:10
60	5	Air	1:15
60/30	30	O₂	1:45
30	15	Air	2:00
30	60	O₂	3:00
30	15	Air	3:15
30	60	O₂	4:15
30/0	30	O₂	4:45

TABLE 1A AIR TREATMENT OF PAIN-ONLY DECOMPRESSION SICKNESS—100-FOOT TREATMENT

1. Treatment of pain-only decompression sickness when oxygen unavailable and pain is relieved at a depth less than 66 feet.
2. Descent rate—25 ft/min.
3. Ascent rate—1 minute between stops.
4. Time at 100 feet—includes time from the surface.
5. If the piping configuration of the chamber does not allow it to return to atmospheric pressure from the 10 foot stop in the one minute specified, disregard the additional time required.

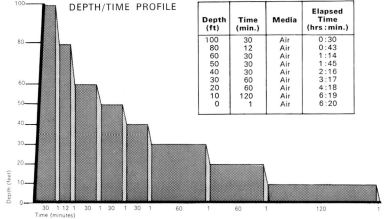

DEPTH/TIME PROFILE

Depth (ft)	Time (min.)	Media	Elapsed Time (hrs : min.)
100	30	Air	0:30
80	12	Air	0:43
60	30	Air	1:14
50	30	Air	1:45
40	30	Air	2:16
30	60	Air	3:17
20	60	Air	4:18
10	120	Air	6:19
0	1	Air	6:20

TABLE 2A AIR TREATMENT OF PAIN-ONLY DECOMPRESSION SICKNESS—165-FOOT TREATMENT

1. Treatment of pain-only decompression sickness when oxygen unavailable and pain is relieved at a depth greater than 66 feet.
2. Descent rate—25 ft/min.
3. Ascent rate—1 minute between stops.
4. Time at 165 feet—includes time from the surface.

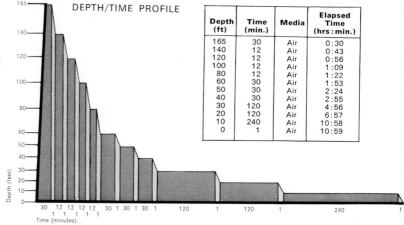

DEPTH/TIME PROFILE

Depth (ft)	Time (min.)	Media	Elapsed Time (hrs : min.)
165	30	Air	0:30
140	12	Air	0:43
120	12	Air	0:56
100	12	Air	1:09
80	12	Air	1:22
60	30	Air	1:53
50	30	Air	2:24
40	30	Air	2:55
30	120	Air	4:56
20	120	Air	6:57
10	240	Air	10:58
0	1	Air	10:59

TABLE 3 AIR TREATMENT OF SERIOUS DECOMPRESSION SICKNESS OR GAS EMBOLISM

1. Treatment of serious symptoms or gas embolism when oxygen unavailable and symptoms are relieved within 30 minutes at 165 feet.
2. Descent rate—as rapidly as possible.
3. Ascent rate—1 minute between stops.
4. Time at 165 feet—includes time from the surface.

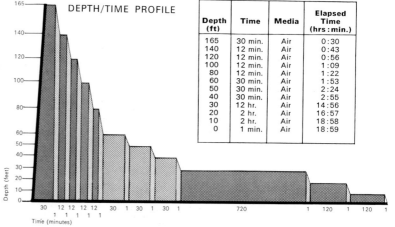

DEPTH/TIME PROFILE

Depth (ft)	Time	Media	Elapsed Time (hrs : min.)
165	30 min.	Air	0:30
140	12 min.	Air	0:43
120	12 min.	Air	0:56
100	12 min.	Air	1:09
80	12 min.	Air	1:22
60	30 min.	Air	1:53
50	30 min.	Air	2:24
40	30 min.	Air	2:55
30	12 hr.	Air	14:56
20	2 hr.	Air	16:57
10	2 hr.	Air	18:58
0	1 min.	Air	18:59

TABLE 4 AIR TREATMENT OF SERIOUS DECOMPRESSION SICKNESS OR GAS EMBOLISM

1. Treatment of worsening symptoms during the first 20-minute oxygen breathing period at 60 feet on Table 6, or when symptoms are not relieved within 30 minutes at 165 feet using air treatment Table 3.
2. Descent rate—as rapidly as possible.
3. Ascent rate—1 minute between stops.
4. Time at 165 feet—includes time from the surface.

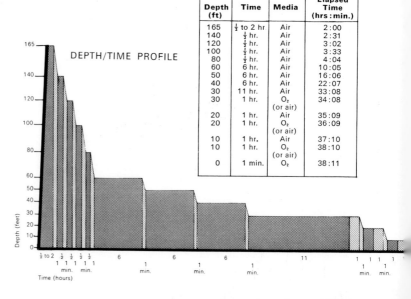

DEPTH/TIME PROFILE

Depth (ft)	Time	Media	Elapsed Time (hrs : min.)
165	½ to 2 hr	Air	2:00
140	½ hr.	Air	2:31
120	½ hr.	Air	3:02
100	½ hr.	Air	3:33
80	½ hr.	Air	4:04
60	6 hr.	Air	10:05
50	6 hr.	Air	16:06
40	6 hr.	Air	22:07
30	11 hr.	Air	33:08
30	1 hr.	O₂ (or air)	34:08
20	1 hr.	Air	35:09
20	1 hr.	O₂ (or air)	36:09
10	1 hr.	Air	37:10
10	1 hr.	O₂ (or air)	38:10
0	1 min.	O₂	38:11

ROYAL NAVY TABLES FOR TREATMENT OF DECOMPRESSION SICKNESS FOLLOWING AIR OR N₂O₂ MIXTURE DIVING

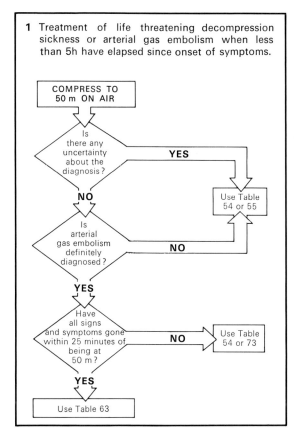

1 Treatment of life threatening decompression sickness or arterial gas embolism when less than 5h have elapsed since onset of symptoms.

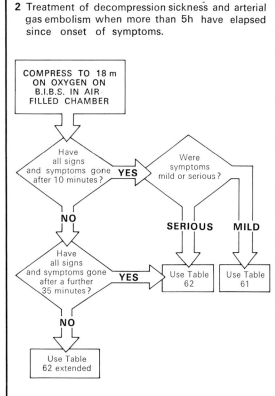

2 Treatment of decompression sickness and arterial gas embolism when more than 5h have elapsed since onset of symptoms.

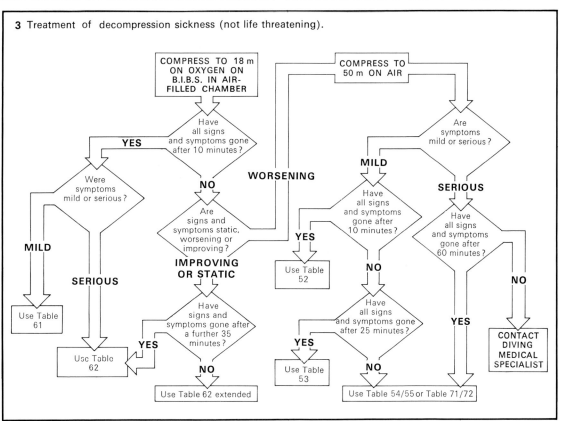

3 Treatment of decompression sickness (not life threatening).

ROYAL NAVY THERAPEUTIC TABLES

Different therapeutic tables are provided for different sets of circumstances and may be selected by reference to the flow diagram on page 225. There are some common factors, which are outlined below.

(a) *Descent time.* Descent time, which varies between tables, is not included in the elapsed time.

(b) *Elapsed time.* The timing of each table starts when maximum pressure is reached, and is given in hours and minutes opposite each step of the table.

(c) *Stoppages.* The duration of stoppages is given, oxygen being breathed as indicated.

(d) *Ascent.* The rate of ascent varies between tables,

but with all tables the ascent becomes critical near the surface, where the rate of change of pressure is greatest. If, as the compression chamber nears the surface, air begins to escape round the door seal, compensation by admitting more compressed air may be needed. In addition, the gauges may indicate that the surface has been reached when there is still some pressure in the chamber. If this occurs the chamber must continue to be vented at the established rate until pressure is equalized.

(e) *Surfacing.* On arrival at the surface both patient and attendant must remain in the chamber for one minute in case of return of symptoms.

Tables 52 to 55 : air-recompression therapy

These tables are applied as described above and are those normally employed for therapeutic recompression, but with the following modifications:

(a) RATE OF DESCENT
(1) In mild cases—at a rate of 10 m/min.
(2) In serious cases—as fast as can be tolerated.

This is normally of the order of 30 m/min.

(b) ASCENT. Ascent between stoppages is to take five minutes. This is not included in the stoppage times, but allowed for in the elapsed times.

(c) OXYGEN. Both patient and attendants are to breathe oxygen as indicated in Table 54.

TABLE 52. AIR RECOMPRESSION THERAPY

GAUGE DEPTH: m	STOPPAGES: h and min.	ELAPSED TIME: h and min.	RATE OF ASCENT
50	30 min.	0000—0030	5 minutes be-
42	12 min.	0035—0047	tween stoppages
36	12 min.	0052—0104	throughout
30	12 min.	0109—0121	
24	12 min.	0126—0138	
18	30 min.	0143—0213	
15	30 min.	0218—0248	
12	30 min.	0253—0323	
9	2 h	0328—0528	
6	2 h	0533—0733	
3	2 h	0738—0938	
Surface		0943	

TABLE 53. AIR RECOMPRESSION THERAPY

GAUGE DEPTH: m	STOPPAGES: h and min.	ELAPSED TIME: h and min.	RATE OF ASCENT
50	30 min.	0000—0030	5 minutes be-
42	12 min.	0035—0047	tween stoppages
36	12 min.	0052—0104	throughout
30	12 min.	0109—0121	
24	12 min.	0126—0138	
18	30 min.	0143—0213	
15	30 min.	0218—0248	
12	30 min.	0253—0323	
9	12 h	0328—1528	
6	2 h	1533—1733	
3	2 h	1738—1938	
Surface		1943	

TABLE 54. AIR RECOMPRESSION THERAPY

GAUGE DEPTH: m	STOPPAGES: h and min.	ELAPSED TIME: h and min.	RATE OF ASCENT
50	2 h	0000—0200	5 minutes be-
42	30 min.	0205—0235	tween stoppages
36	30 min.	0240—0310	throughout
30	30 min.	0315—0345	
24	30 min.	0350—0420	
18	6 h	0425—1025	
15	6 h	1030—1630	
12	6 h	1635—2235	
9	11 h	2240—3340	
	1 h (O₂)	3340—3440	
6	1 h	3445—3545	
	1 h (O₂)	3545—3645	
3	1 h	3650—3750	
	1 h (O₂)	3750—3850	
Surface		3855	

TABLE 55. AIR RECOMPRESSION THERAPY

GAUGE DEPTH: m	STOPPAGES: h and min.	ELAPSED TIME: h and min.	RATE OF ASCENT
50	2 h	0000—0200	5 minutes be-
42	30 min.	0205—0235	tween stoppages
36	30 min.	0240—0310	throughout
30	30 min.	0315—0345	
24	30 min.	0350—0420	
18	6 h	0425—1025	
15	6 h	1030—1630	
12	6 h	1635—2235	
9	12 h	2240—3440	
6	4 h	3445—3845	
3	4 h	3850—4250	
Surface		4255	

This table is to be used instead of Table 54 when Oxygen is not available.

Tables 61, 62: oxygen-recompression therapy

Tables 61 and 62 are employed when oxygen is available and is required for the greater part of the therapy.

Tables 61 and 62 are applied as described on a previous page but with the following modifications

(a) DESCENT. The descent is to take 1 to 2 min.

(b) ASCENT. Conduct as follows:

  (1) It is to be at a continuous bleed rate of 3 m in 10 minutes.

  (2) If the rate is slowed it is not to be compensated for by subsequent acceleration.

  (3) The ascent should be halted if the rate is exceeded, or if the ascent cannot be controlled during flushing of the chamber.

(c) OXYGEN. Oxygen is to be breathed before descent. The attendant may remain on air unless it is a repetitive dive, when he must breathe oxygen for the final 9 m ascent. To help prevent oxygen poisoning, the patient is to be kept at rest, lying down, during all oxygen breathing periods at 9 m or deeper.

Oxygen poisoning is not likely to occur with these Tables, but the supervisor must be prepared and take the following action:

(a) If ascending, halt the ascent and maintain depth.

(b) Instruct the attendant to remove the oxygen mask and protect the tongue of the convulsing patient, and prevent him from injuring himself.

(c) Wait until 15 minutes after all symptoms of oxygen poisoning have subsided, then resume the oxygen treatment table at the point of interruption. In the unlikely event of a second episode of oxygen poisoning, act as in (b), then change to decompression on Table 55 or 73 from the same depth. However, if the patient is free of decompression sickness symptoms, and the depth is less than 9 m, continue the bleed to the surface on air.

If relief from signs and symptoms is incomplete after 75 minutes on Table 62, a further one or two periods of oxygen breathing may be introduced at 18 m. These periods would be of 20 minutes duration interspersed with 5 minutes air breathing. Decompression from 18 m to 9 m should be preceded by 5 minutes' air breathing. Similarly, one further 60 minutes' oxygen breathing period may be introduced at 9 m following an intervening period of 15 minutes air breathing. Final decompression to the surface will still be on oxygen. Should any of these extra oxygen breathing periods be employed, the attendant will breathe oxygen during the final 60 minutes at 9 m and during the final decompression to the surface.

TABLE 61.
OXYGEN RECOMPRESSION THERAPY
If symptoms relieved in 10 mins at 18 m

GAUGE DEPTH: m	STOPPAGES/ ASCENT: min.	ELAPSED TIME: h and min.	RATE OF ASCENT m/min.
18	20 (O$_2$)	0000—0020	—
18	5	0020—0025	—
18	20 (O$_2$)	0025—0045	—
18–9	30 (O$_2$)	0045—0115	3 m in 10 mins
9	5	0115—0120	—
9	20 (O$_2$)	0120—0140	—
9	5	0140—0145	—
9–0	30 (O$_2$)	0145—0215	3 m in 10 mins
Surface		0215	

TABLE 62.
OXYGEN RECOMPRESSION THERAPY
If symptoms not relieved after 10 mins at 18 m

GAUGE DEPTH: m	STOPPAGES/ ASCENT: min.	ELAPSED TIME: h and min.	RATE OF ASCENT m/min.
18	20 (O$_2$)	0000—0020	—
18	5	0020—0025	—
18	20 (O$_2$)	0025—0045	—
18	5	0045—0050	—
18	20 (O$_2$)	0050—0110	—
18	5	0110—0115	—
18–9	30 (O$_2$)	0115—0145	3 m in 10 mins
9	15	0145—0200	—
9	60 (O$_2$)	0200—0300	—
9	15	0300—0315	—
9	60 (O$_2$)	0315—0415	—
9–0	30 (O$_2$)	0415—0445	3 m in 10 mins
Surface		0445	

TABLE 71.
MODIFIED AIR RECOMPRESSION THERAPY
Alternative tables, used only on specialist advice

GAUGE DEPTH: m	STOPPAGES/ ASCENT: min.	ELAPSED TIME: h and min.	RATE OF ASCENT m/min.
70	30 min.	0000—0030	—
70–63	7 min.	0030—0037	60 m/h
63–51	2 h	0037—0237	6 m/h
51–39	4 h	0237—0637	3 m/h
39–29	5 h	0637—1137	2 m/h
29–20	6 h	1137—1737	1.5 m/h
20–10	10 h	1737—2737	1 m/h
10–0	20 h	2737—4737	0.5 m/h
Surface		4737	

TABLE 72.
MODIFIED AIR RECOMPRESSION THERAPY
Alternative tables, used only on specialist advice

GAUGE DEPTH: m	STOPPAGES/ ASCENT: min.	ELAPSED TIME: h and min.	RATE OF ASCENT m/min.
50	2 h (see Note)	0000—0200	—
50–39	3 h 40 min.	0200—0540	3 m/h
39–29	5 h	0540—1040	2 m/h
29–20	6 h	1040—1640	1.5 m/h
20–10	10 h	1640—2640	1 m/h
10–0	20 h	2640—4640	0.5 m/h
Surface		4640	

NOTE: The period of two hours can be reduced and decompression started earlier if the patient's symptoms have cleared.

12.7 BURST LUNG (PULMONARY BAROTRAUMA)

Definition

Pressure damage to the lungs, brought about by excess differential pressures causing tearing of the lung tissue. It may occur from compression but it is usually a decompression injury.

Description

This is the cause of unconsciousness immediately following, or within 10 minutes of, an important decompression. Burst lung is usually caused when a diver ascends through the water holding his breath. It is a very real risk if the diver abandons his breathing set and returns to the surface by a free ascent. It can also be caused by local retention of gas in a diver who is exhaling correctly during ascent. This may be due to a chronic or a recent chest illness. If, for any reason, the expanding air in the chest cannot escape it will rupture the lung membranes and can pass into the blood circulation and/or into the tissue between the lungs, heart and rib-cage.

There are three presentations of Pulmonary Barotrauma:

(1) INTERSTITIAL EMPHYSEMA, SOMETIMES CALLED MEDIASTINAL EA. The gas may escape inwards into the central tissues within the chest cavity and appear under the skin in the neck and/or around the heart. A voice change is quite common if the gas extends into the neck (tinny quality). It is from this site that the gas may cause pneumothorax and respiratory distress.

(2) PNEUMOTHORAX. The gas can escape through the alveolar walls, track back to the root of the lungs and end up between the lung sac and the chest wall. This causes the lung to collapse and can lead to respiratory distress and hypoxia.

(3) ARTERIAL GAS EMBOLISM. Where expanding gas in the lungs enters the blood stream (pulmonary veins) via the damaged tissue. If these bubbles in the bloodstream find their way into the brain circulation arteries they may block the oxygen supply and cause brain damage. More rarely, the bubbles may cause the sudden cessation of heartbeat and breathing by direct blockage of the coronary arteries or by a reflex effect from the brain. Gas embolism is a major cause of death in diving. It can be complicated

DIAGNOSIS OF DECOMPRESSION SICKNESS AND GAS EMBOLISM

■ Probable □ Possible

Summary chart of what various presentations could mean, but remember that any abnormality after a dive should be treated as Decompression Illness unless proved otherwise.

SYMPTOMS AND SIGNS	DECOMPRESSION SICKNESS				GAS EMBOLISM		
			SERIOUS		SERIOUS		
	Skin	Pain-only	CNS	Chokes	CNS symptoms	Pneumo-thorax	Mediastinal emphysema
Pain–back			□				■
Pain–neck						□	□
Pain–chest			□	■			
Pain–stomach			■				
Pain–arms/legs		■					
Pain–shoulders		■					
Pain–hips		■					
Unconsciousness			■	□	■	□	
Shock			□	□	□		
Vertigo			■		■		
Visual difficulty			■		■		
Nausea/vomiting			■		□		
Hearing difficulty			■		□		
Speech difficulty			□		□		
Lack of balance			■		■		
Numbness	□		■		■		□
Weakness		□	■		■		
Swollen neck			■		■		
Short of breath							
Cyanosis			□	■	□	■	□
Skin changes	■			□	□	□	□
'Cellophane' crackling							
Bloody frothy sputum							■
Paralysis						□	□
Irregular pulse						□	
Coughing/pain on breathing				■			

by DCS if the tissues are pre-loaded with dissolved gas. There may be more than one of the above conditions present at the same time. Any diver who has obtained a breath from any source at depth, and who becomes unconscious at the surface, should be assumed to be suffering from a gas embolism.

Signs and symptoms

It is easy to confuse the symptoms of gas embolism with those of serious decompression sickness. Both are caused by gas bubbles. If no differentiation can be made between the diagnosis of decompression sickness and gas embolism, give the treatment for gas embolism. The commonest symptom by far is chest pain.

Note: Any abnormal situation that starts within 10 minutes of the accident should be treated as a gas embolism, no matter how shallow the depth. Any doubt about the correct diagnosis must be resolved in favour of the victim—treat for gas embolism.

(1) SYMPTOMS OF INTERSTITIAL EMPHYSEMA
Pain under the breastbone, or elsewhere in the chest
Shortness of breath and difficulty in breathing
Feeling of fullness in neck area
Crushing sensation on skin, like crumpled cellophane, particularly near the front of the neck just above the collarbone
Change in sound of voice (tinny)

(2) SYMPTOMS OF PNEUMOTHORAX
Bloody, frothy sputum
Shortness of breath—rapid shallow breathing
Pain anywhere in the chest, especially when breathing in, and made worse by deep breathing
Coughing
Swelling of neck veins

Cyanosis (blueness of fingertips, lips and earlobes)
Irregular pulse
The pneumothorax that accompanies pul. barotrauma is usually found by X-ray and is seldom troublesome.

(3) SYMPTOMS OF ARTERIAL GAS EMBOLISM
Chest pain
Visual disturbances, sometimes even blindness
Dizziness
Weakness or paralysis, usually one-sided
Numbness and tingling, usually one-sided
Headache
Sudden unconsciousness, often on surfacing
Confusion, stupor
Cessation of breathing
Bloody frothy sputum (quite rare)
Respiratory distress (rare)

Pulmonary barotrauma without arterial gas embolism is quite rare and accounts for only 10% of pulmonary overinflation. However, careful examination and observation are vital.

Treatment

(1) INTERSTITIAL EMPHYSEMA (IE)
If diagnosis is uncertain, recompress as for gas embolism. Treatment as for pneumothorax, but in IE the needle is less likely to be ineffective. The therapeutic decompression will be a slow procedure requiring very close medical supervision.

(2) PNEUMOTHORAX
If diagnosis is uncertain, recompress as for gas embolism. Pneumothorax does not usually require recompression for itself. However, if recompression is needed for concurrent embolism, manifestations of pneumothorax will be improved. Recompression is useful if symptoms are serious (e.g. pneumothorax of both sides) and if no hollow

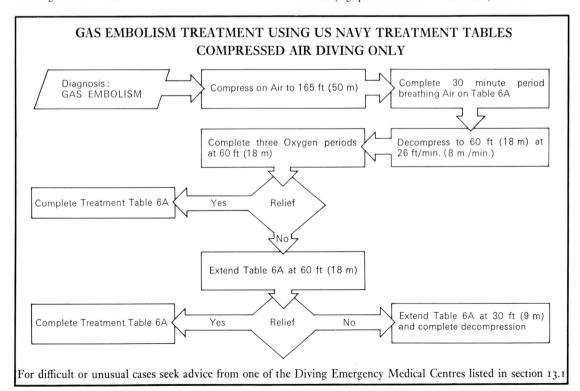

GAS EMBOLISM TREATMENT USING US NAVY TREATMENT TABLES COMPRESSED AIR DIVING ONLY

Diagnosis: GAS EMBOLISM → Compress on Air to 165 ft (50 m) → Complete 30 minute period breathing Air on Table 6A

Complete three Oxygen periods at 60 ft (18 m) ← Decompress to 60 ft (18 m) at 26 ft/min. (8 m /min.)

Complete Treatment Table 6A ← Yes — Relief — No → Extend Table 6A at 60 ft (18 m)

Complete Treatment Table 6A ← Yes — Relief — No → Extend Table 6A at 30 ft (9 m) and complete decompression

For difficult or unusual cases seek advice from one of the Diving Emergency Medical Centres listed in section 13.1

needle is available to remove trapped air. If the victim is under pressure, stop any further decompression. Treatment can include administering oxygen-rich mixtures at appropriate depths. If breathing is very impaired, or in order to continue a decompression, a suitably skilled person can withdraw most of the entrapped gas by inserting a hollow needle into the affected part.

(3) ARTERIAL GAS EMBOLISM

This is extremely urgent and very serious. Immediate recompression in a DCC is required, as detailed in Tables 6A and 63. As victims are often also near-drowning victims, CPR may have to be initiated. The chances of recovery decreases rapidly with each minute lost in getting the victim under pressure.

US NAVY TABLE 6A. AIR AND OXYGEN TREATMENT OF GAS EMBOLISM

1. Treatment of gas embolism. Use also when unable to determine whether symptoms are caused by gas embolism or severe decompression sickness.

2. Descent rate—as fast as possible.

3. Ascent rate—1 ft/min. Do not compensate for slower ascent rates. Compensate for faster ascent rates by halting the ascent.

4. Time at 165 feet—includes time from the surface.

5. If oxygen breathing must be interrupted, allow 15 minutes after the reaction has entirely subsided and resume schedule at point of interruption.

6. Tender breathes air throughout. If treatment is a repetitive dive for the tender or tables are lengthened, tender should breathe oxygen during the last 30 minutes of ascent to the surface.

7. Table 6A can be lengthened by an additional 25 minutes at 60 feet (20 minutes on oxygen and 5 minutes on air) or an additional 75 minutes at 30 feet (15 minutes on air and 60 minutes on oxygen), or both.

DEPTH: (ft)	TIME: (min.)	BREATHING MEDIA	TOTAL ELAPSED TIME: hr:min.
165	30	Air	0:30
165 to 60	4	Air	0:34
60	20	Oxygen	0:54
60	5	Air	0:59
60	20	Oxygen	1:19
60	5	Air	1:29
60	20	Oxygen	1:44
60	5	Air	1:49
60 to 30	30	Oxygen	2:19
30	15	Air	2:34
30	60	Oxygen	3:34
30	15	Air	3:49
30	60	Oxygen	4:49
30 to 0	30	Oxygen	5:19

TABLE 6A DEPTH/TIME PROFILE

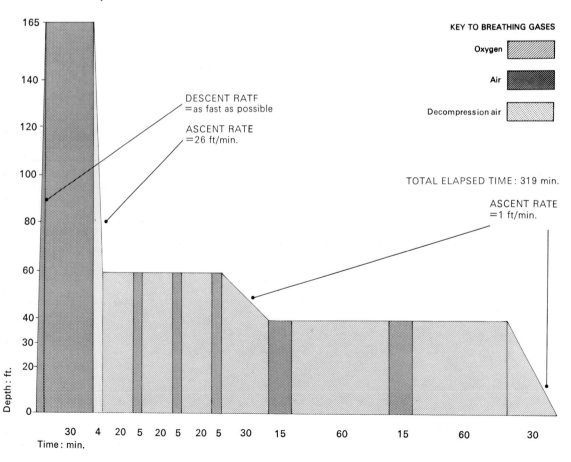

ROYAL NAVY TABLE 63. DEEP AIR-OXYGEN RECOMPRESSION THERAPY

(1) In cases of definite arterial gas embolism, when the patient is completely relieved of symptoms within 25 minutes at 50 m, Table 63 may be used.

(2) Table 63
a. *Rate of descent*—as fast as tolerable.

b. *Rate of ascent*
(1) From 50 m to 18 m in 4 minutes.
(2) From 18 m to 9 m and 9 m to the surface—at 3 m in 10 minutes.

c. The attendant must always breathe oxygen during the final 60 minutes at 9 m and the subsequent ascent.

GAUGE DEPTH: m	STOPPAGES: min.	ELAPSED TIME: h and min.	RATE OF ASCENT: m/min.
50	30	0000–0030	—
50–18	4	0030–0034	8
18	20 (O₂)	0034–0054	—
18	5	0054–0059	—
18	20 (O₂)	0059–0119	—
18	5	0119–0124	—
18	20 (O₂)	0124–0144	—
18	5	0144–0149	—
18–9	30 (O₂)	0149–0219	0.3
9	15	0219–0234	—
9	60 (O₂)	0234–0334	—
9	15	0334–0349	—
9	60 (O₂)	0349–0449	—
9–0	30 (O₂)	0449–0519	0.3
Surface		0519	

ROYAL NAVY TABLE — MODIFIED AIR RECOMPRESSION THERAPY

Descent time—is not included in the elapsed time.

Elapsed time—the timing of each table starts when max. pressure is reached, given in hours and min. opposite each step of the table.

Stoppages—the duration of stoppages is given, oxygen being breathed as indicated.

Ascent—becomes critical near the surface where the rate of change is greatest.

This table approximates the bleed rate of the final 18 m of Decompression Tables 71 and 72. Medical advice may recommend a period of oxygen breathing during the shallower depths.

Surfacing—on surfacing both victim and attendant must remain in the chamber for 1 min. in case of return of symptoms.

GAUGE DEPTH: m	STOPPAGES: h and min.	ELAPSED TIME: h and min.	RATE OF ASCENT m/h	GAUGE DEPTH: m	STOPPAGES: h and min.	ELAPSED TIME: h and min.	RATE OF ASCENT m/h
50	2 h	0000—0200	5 minutes between stoppages throughout	11	55 min.	1630—1725	5 minutes between stoppages throughout
42	30 min.	0205—0235		10	1 h 55 min.	1730—1925	
36	30 min.	0240—0310		9	1 h 55 min.	1930—2125	
30	30 min.	0315—0345		8	1 h 55 min.	2130—2325	
24	30 min.	0350—0420		7	1 h 55 min.	2330—2525	
18	6 h	0425—1025		6	1 h 55 min.	2530—2725	
17	55 min.	1030—1125		5	1 h 55 min.	2730—2925	
16	55 min.	1130—1225		4	1 h 55 min.	2930—3125	
15	55 min.	1230—1325		3	1 h 55 min.	3130—3325	
14	55 min.	1330—1425		2	1 h 55 min.	3330—3525	
13	55 min.	1430—1525		1	1 h 55 min.	3530—3725	
12	55 min.	1530—1625		Surface		3730	

MEDICAL TERMS

Alveolus A small sac, which is the end portion of the respiratory system in the lung, where the gaseous exchange takes place.

Apnea The stopping of breathing for short intervals of time.

Dysbarism A general term applied to any clinical condition caused by a difference between the surrounding atmospheric pressure and the total gas pressure in the various tissues, fluids and body cavities.

Embolus A plug brought by the blood from another vessel and forced into a smaller one so as to obstruct the circulation.

Emphysema A swelling or inflation caused by the presence of air or other gas in body tissue.

Hyperventilation Excessively deep breathing.

Mediastinum That portion of the chest cavity located between the right and left lungs, containing the heart, the major vessels and some of the major nerves traversing from the neck to the abdomen.

Pneumothorax The presence of air or gas in the pleural cavity resulting from a rupture of an alveolus, which allows the pleural space to come into equilibrium with the external pressure.

Thrombus A plug or clot in the blood vessel or in one of the cavities of the heart.

Trachea That portion of the breathing system that extends from the posterior portion of the mouth to the chest cavity.

12.8 HYPOXIA AND ANOXIA

Hypoxia means a reduced amount of oxygen, while anoxia means total lack of oxygen. Both conditions could result in death or decreased efficiency of the body.

Causes of hypoxia

Continuing life depends on the combined reactions of the heart, blood and lungs. If the heart stops, the body will use up all the oxygen left in the tissues and then die of anoxia. If the heart is not strong enough to pump sufficient blood around the body various parts will suffer from hypoxia. If the blood volume is decreased because of bleeding, the amount of oxygen that can be carried around the body will be reduced and, again, the body will suffer. Some substances, such as carbon monoxide, can poison the blood and prevent the carriage of oxygen.

If the interchange of gases in the lungs is interfered with, either because breathing has stopped or because the breathing gas cannot reach the lungs, the body will continue to use the oxygen which remains in the bloodstream, reducing the blood's oxygen further. The skin will take on a blue-grey tinge particularly noticeable at the lips, earlobes and finger nail beds—characteristic of cases of hypoxia. If normal breathing is not restored, or resuscitation not applied, the body will suffer from a lack of oxygen and die.

Hypoxia will also occur if the breathing gas in the lungs does not contain sufficient oxygen for the body's needs. Different parts of the body vary in their sensitivity to hypoxia and, therefore, the time it takes to cause damage from which they cannot recover. The cells of the brain are most sensitive and if the heart stops, the brain is likely to be irrevocably damaged within 4 min. Other tissues are much more resistant and can tolerate an oxygen debt: a muscle, for example, will eventually recover its full strength and function, even if its blood supply has been stopped for as much as 30 min.

Signs and symptoms of hypoxia

It is almost impossible to detect the onset of these in oneself, especially during a dive. It is more likely that they would cause a change in behaviour in the diver that would be noticed by the buddy diver, supervisor or tender.

They include:
—Tiredness.

—Headache.

—'Drunkenness', over-confidence.

—Unconsciousness in or under the water.

—Unconsciousness after surfacing, possibly from a free ascent.

—Strong breathing efforts.

—Blueness of lips, ear-lobes and finger nail beds.

Treatment of hypoxia

If normal breathing is not present, restore normal breathing applying EAR. Apply pure oxygen or a high oxygen mix as appropriate. Treat for shock and get medical help; keep the victim under observation.

Avoidance of hypoxia

—Use the correct gas mixture for each particular range of depths.

—Check and double check, by analysis, oxygen levels in gas banks before use.

—Avoid the use of pure helium for mixing on dive sites as far as possible; try to use heliox mixtures for mixing. This reduces the risk of accidental use of pure helium in breathing circuits.

—Ensure efficient mixing of gases during oxygen make-up in life-support systems.

—Carefully monitor the bell oxygen level during long lock-outs.

—Consciously control efficient breathing whilst diving.

—Keep talking to a minimum whilst wearing a mask or helmet.

—When using closed circuit or semi-closed circuit breathing equipment, avoid rapid ascents, especially near the surface, and comply strictly with manufacturer's operating rules.

MEDICAL TERMS

Bradycardia Slowness of the heart beat.

Cyanosis A bluish discoloration of the skin from insufficient oxygenation of the blood.

Dyspnea Difficulty in breathing.

Expiratory reserve The amount of air that can be exhaled out of the lungs after normal expiration.

Hypercapnia Undue amount of carbon dioxide in the blood, causing overactivity in the respiratory centre.

Normoxic A breathing gas mixture that supplies the diver with a 'normal' partial pressure of oxygen, about 0.21 ata, at any specific depth.

Residual nitrogen A theoretical concept that describes the amount of nitrogen remaining in a diver's tissue after a hyperbaric exposure.

Residual nitrogen time Time (in minutes) added to actual bottom time for calculating the decompression schedule for a repetitive dive, based on the concept of residual nitrogen.

Residual volume The amount of air left in the lungs after a maximal expiratory effort.

Tachycardia Excessive rapidity of heart beat.

Tidal volume The amount of air breathed in and out of the lungs during normal respiration.

Vital capacity Maximal volume of air which can be expired after maximal inhalation.

12.9 GAS HAZARDS   a. OXYGEN POISONING

Types of oxygen poisoning

There are two basic types: acute and chronic.
Acute means a short term effect while chronic means a long term effect.

The following is a list of possible symptoms of acute oxygen poisoning which may be experienced by a diver.

(*a*) Lip-twitching and twitching of other facial muscles.

(*b*) Dizziness (vertigo).

(*c*) Feeling sick (nausea).

(*d*) Unusual tiredness.

(*e*) Disturbances of breathing, e.g. overbreathing (hyperpnoea), temporary stoppage (apnoea) or difficulty in breathing (dyspnoea).

(*f*) Unusual mental states, e.g. euphoria.

(*g*) Disturbances of sight, e.g. tunnel vision.

(*h*) Unconsciousness and general convulsions similar to a major (grand mal) epileptic fit.

By far the most dangerous symptoms to the diver are the unconsciousness and convulsions, since each condition could easily lead to his losing the mouthpiece or mask and drowning. The other symptoms may or may not occur prior to the convulsions, and experience shows that in the case of divers there is most often no warning whatever before convulsive seizure and unconsciousness interrupts their dive.

Oxygen convulsions

There are three distinct phases experienced by the unsuspecting diver. A diver succumbing to oxygen convulsions would first become unconscious and enter the 'tonic phase', which lasts about half a minute to 2 minutes; during this phase the diver arches backwards as all his voluntary muscles contract simultaneously and completely, his body becoming quite rigid. Following immediately after the tonic phase would come the 'clonic phase', which is the familiar convulsive stage. In this phase the diver would jerk violently and spasmodically perhaps for 2 or 3 minutes. As the clonic phase subsided the diver would pass into a relaxed, though exhausted and unconscious, stage called the 'post-convulsive depression'. Once this series is begun there is no means of stopping the natural progression to the post-convulsive stage.

The rescuer should return the stricken diver to air-breathing or back into the bell as soon as possible and then support him until he can be laid in a comatose position and allowed to sleep it off and recover. Once he is returned to air-breathing he may or may not have another convulsion. The diver should slowly recover consciousness over 5 to 30 minutes after returning to air-breathing, but he should not be regarded as having revived since he will be in an exhausted state, mentally confused and likely to become unconscious or fall asleep without warning.

No permanent neurological injury would be expected to have occurred as a direct cause of one or two convulsions. However, the violent muscular contractions which occur during the tonic and clonic phases are so complete (a condition which would never occur in normal life) that the forces exerted occasionally tear the muscle tissue itself, tear its tendons from their bone insertions or even break the bones to which the tendons are attached.

There is often a strong desire to fall asleep if the diver regained consciousness shortly after returning to air-breathing. This is even beneficial so long as he can be kept warm and safe from further accidents. When he regains consciousness he should be talked to calmly, reassuringly and in simple terms; warm clothing should be provided as soon as possible. He will not have any recollection of his previous experience (amnesia) from the time when he became unconscious, or perhaps a little while before that.

One important item remains to be noted: the diver would automatically be holding his breath (apnoeic) during the tonic phase and consequently it would be hazardous to try to bring him to the surface during this brief period due to the danger of burst lung (pulmonary barotrauma). Even though it would be more difficult to surface a convulsive body rather than a rigid one, it would be safer to await the onset of the clonic or convulsive phase before ascending. However, the tonic phase is rarely noticed underwater and the rescuing diver's attention will probably be first drawn by the convulsions, so it is unlikely that the necessity of waiting before surfacing will arise.

When a diver might suffer acute oxygen poisoning

Acute oxygen poisoning occurs when a particularly high concentration of oxygen appears in the blood and the brain. This is brought about by breathing a gas mixture with a particularly high partial pressure of oxygen. The danger arises whenever the partial pressure of oxygen exceeds 1.6 bars. Under ideal conditions such as in the comfort of a chamber, 2.0 bars can be tolerated for many hours. This figure reduces towards 1.6 bars whenever additional stresses are incurred such as:

physical exercise, cold (hypothermia) and carbon dioxide.

Certain types of closed circuit breathing equipment automatically change the oxygen concentration in the

Oxygen partial pressure limits table											
	Exposure time (minutes)	30	40	50	60	80	100	120	180	240
Maximum oxygen partial pressure 6 bars	Normal exposure	1.6	1.5	1.4	1.3	1.2	—	1.1	—	1.0
	Exceptional exposure	2.0	1.9	—	1.8	1.7	1.6	1.5	1.4	1.3
Oxygen partial pressure limits for nitrogen–oxygen SCUBA and surface-supplied helium–oxygen mixed-gas diving.											

breathing gas mixture as the diver varies his depth, thus maintaining a constant and safe partial pressure of oxygen.

Oxygen poisoning does not occur immediately the diver is exposed to a high partial pressure; there is a delay or 'latent period' while the oxygen reaching the brain gradually builds up. Logically, the higher the partial pressure of oxygen (due to a greater depth or a richer gas mixture), the shorter the latent period. It is unfortunate, however, that it is impossible to predict the latent period or even an individual diver's susceptibility to acute oxygen poisoning. Both susceptibility and latency vary widely from individual to individual and from day to day. Certain broad generalizations can be made in some cases. For example, it is known that fatigue, stress, hard work, high carbon dioxide concentration, cold water, 'hang-over' and poor physical condition increase susceptibility and reduce the latency to acute oxygen poisoning.

Chronic oxygen poisoning

This form of poisoning can be suffered at a lower partial pressure of oxygen than that which produces 'acute' oxygen poisoning, and the time taken to the onset of symptoms is much longer. This particular type shows itself initially as soreness of the chest. As the lungs themselves become further irritated by the high level of oxygen, there develops a condition similar to pneumonia, with congestion, coughing and considerable discomfort.

More pertinent to the diver would be the case of mixed gas and saturation dives, in which case the diver is exposed to a high-pressure gas environment for days or even weeks. Thus, if the oxygen partial pressure of the gas were too high, he would be a likely candidate for chronic oxygen poisoning. The condition is even more likely during therapeutic schedules.

If 100% oxygen is breathed at atmospheric pressure (that is, at a partial pressure of 1 bar) the irritation would probably be experienced within 24 hours. However, breathing 60% oxygen at atmospheric pressure (partial pressure of 0.6 bars) for an indefinite period appears to result in no ill effects to most people.

When increased pressures of oxygen are used in the treatment of more serious diseases such as severe decompression sickness or gas gangrene, it may be reasonable to accept a greater degree of pulmonary toxicity in order to treat the illness. The primary requirement of any therapy is that the treatment is not worse than the disease. The degree of pulmonary oxygen toxicity which produces a 10% decrease in lung vital capacity is associated with coughing and pain in the chest on deep inspiration. This degree of impairment of the lungs has been shown to be reversible within a few days. However, symptoms and signs of toxicity can increase for a few hours following the ending of the high oxygen exposure. Greater oxygen exposure may not be reversible.

A system of assessing and predicting the possible complications of chronic oxygen poisoning has been devised which uses values of 'unit pulmonary toxic dose' or UPTD. This system can be a useful and worthwhile guide but it should not be regarded as infallible.

$$UPTD = t \times KP$$

Where t = time of exposure in minutes
KP is a constant to each PPO_2 6 bars

See the table of KP numbers for each PPO_2 to work out the UPTD.

A UPTD of 615 produces no symptoms at all.

A UPTD of 1425 can produce symptoms of congestion and a 10% reduction in lung vital capacity. This is regarded as the upper safe limit.

\ PPO₂ represented below																	

KP value table

PPO₂	KP	PPO₂	KP	PPO₂	KP	PPO₂	KP	PPO₂	KP	PPO₂	KP	PPO₂	KP	PPO₂	KP	PPO₂	KP
0.50	0.00	0.78	0.61	1.06	1.10	1.34	1.54	1.62	1.96	1.90	2.36	2.18	2.74	2.46	3.12	2.74	3.49
0.51	0.03	0.79	0.63	1.07	1.11	1.35	1.56	1.63	1.97	1.91	2.37	2.19	2.76	2.47	3.13	2.75	3.51
0.52	0.05	0.80	0.65	1.08	1.13	1.36	1.57	1.64	1.99	1.92	2.39	2.20	2.77	2.48	3.14	2.76	3.52
0.53	0.08	0.81	0.67	1.09	1.14	1.37	1.59	1.65	2.00	1.93	2.40	2.21	2.78	2.49	3.16	2.77	3.53
0.54	0.10	0.82	0.69	1.10	1.16	1.38	1.60	1.66	2.01	1.94	2.42	2.22	2.80	2.50	3.17	2.78	3.54
0.55	0.13	0.83	0.70	1.11	1.18	1.39	1.62	1.67	2.03	1.95	2.43	2.23	2.81	2.51	3.18	2.79	3.56
0.56	0.16	0.84	0.72	1.12	1.19	1.40	1.63	1.68	2.04	1.96	2.44	2.24	2.83	2.52	3.20	2.80	3.57
0.57	0.18	0.85	0.74	1.13	1.21	1.41	1.65	1.69	2.06	1.97	2.46	2.25	2.84	2.53	3.21	2.81	3.58
0.58	0.21	0.86	0.76	1.14	1.22	1.42	1.66	1.70	2.07	1.98	2.47	2.26	2.85	2.54	3.23	2.82	3.60
0.59	0.23	0.87	0.78	1.15	1.24	1.43	1.68	1.71	2.08	1.99	2.49	2.27	2.87	2.55	3.24	2.83	3.61
0.60	0.26	0.88	0.79	1.16	1.26	1.44	1.69	1.72	2.10	2.00	2.50	2.28	2.88	2.56	3.25	2.84	3.62
0.61	0.28	0.89	0.81	1.17	1.27	1.45	1.71	1.73	2.12	2.01	2.51	2.29	2.90	2.57	3.27	2.85	3.64
0.62	0.30	0.90	0.83	1.18	1.29	1.46	1.72	1.74	2.13	2.02	2.53	2.30	2.91	2.58	3.28	2.86	3.65
0.63	0.32	0.91	0.85	1.19	1.30	1.47	1.74	1.75	2.15	2.03	2.54	2.31	2.92	2.59	3.30	2.87	3.66
0.64	0.34	0.92	0.86	1.20	1.32	1.48	1.75	1.76	2.16	2.04	2.56	2.32	2.94	2.60	3.31	2.88	3.67
0.65	0.37	0.93	0.88	1.21	1.34	1.49	1.77	1.77	2.18	2.05	2.57	2.33	2.95	2.61	3.32	2.89	3.68
0.66	0.39	0.94	0.90	1.22	1.35	1.50	1.78	1.78	2.19	2.06	2.58	2.34	2.96	2.62	3.34	2.90	3.70
0.67	0.41	0.95	0.92	1.23	1.37	1.51	1.80	1.79	2.21	2.07	2.60	2.35	2.98	2.63	3.35	2.91	3.71
0.68	0.43	0.96	0.93	1.24	1.38	1.52	1.81	1.80	2.22	2.08	2.61	2.36	2.99	2.64	3.36	2.92	3.72
0.69	0.45	0.97	0.95	1.25	1.40	1.53	1.83	1.81	2.23	2.09	2.63	2.37	3.00	2.65	3.38	2.93	3.74
0.70	0.47	0.98	0.97	1.26	1.42	1.54	1.84	1.82	2.25	2.10	2.64	2.38	3.01	2.66	3.39	2.94	3.75
0.71	0.49	0.99	0.98	1.27	1.43	1.55	1.86	1.83	2.26	2.11	2.65	2.39	3.03	2.67	3.40	2.95	3.76
0.72	0.51	1.00	1.00	1.28	1.45	1.56	1.87	1.84	2.28	2.12	2.67	2.40	3.04	2.68	3.41	2.96	3.77
0.73	0.52	1.01	1.02	1.29	1.46	1.57	1.89	1.85	2.29	2.13	2.68	2.41	3.05	2.69	3.43	2.97	3.78
0.74	0.54	1.02	1.03	1.30	1.48	1.58	1.90	1.86	2.30	2.14	2.69	2.42	3.07	2.70	3.44	2.98	3.80
0.75	0.56	1.03	1.05	1.31	1.50	1.59	1.92	1.87	2.32	2.15	2.70	2.43	3.08	2.71	3.45	2.99	3.81
0.76	0.59	1.04	1.06	1.32	1.51	1.60	1.93	1.88	2.33	2.16	2.72	2.44	3.09	2.72	3.47	3.00	3.82
0.77	0.60	1.05	1.08	1.33	1.53	1.61	1.94	1.89	2.35	2.17	2.73	2.45	3.11	2.73	3.48		

12.9b OXYGEN HANDLING

Oxygen, especially at pressure, vigorously supports burning and explosion. Metal, clothing and flesh can burn like paper, and oils and grease will ignite spontaneously in the presence of HP oxygen.

For these reasons, the properties of oxygen should be understood and the greatest care must be taken when handling it. The following guidelines are aimed at ensuring safe operations.

1. All materials that come into contact with HP O_2 must be carefully selected.

2. Stainless steel fittings should be avoided. Brass, copper and tungum should be used wherever possible.

3. Rigid piping should be used in preference to flexible whips wherever possible. If flexible whips are used, keep them as short as possible, use minimum number of inter-connectors and protect them from damage.

4. Pipework should be protected from any form of damage, especially from objects being dropped on it.

5. Oxygen and mixes in excess of 30% should be in pipework separate from other pipework.

6. Any gas containing 30% or more oxygen should be treated as if it was pure oxygen.

7. Oxygen should be piped at low to medium pressure rather than high pressure.

8. The pressure should be reduced immediately at the oxygen bank to 50 bar or less before being transferred.

9. Decanting should be the main system of transferring oxygen. Pumping should be used as little as possible.

10. A buffer, medium pressure, oxygen bank near the DC chambers can be helpful if there is a long pipe run from the HP bank. It provides a continuity of supply whilst changing over HP banks, or if there is a failure somewhere along the pipe run. Check valves and isolation valves would be needed upstream of the medium pressure bank.

11. Never use quarter turn ball valves in HP oxygen lines because quarter turn valves can cause too rapid a pressure-up with consequent heating effect and fire risk. Quarter turn valves may be used as emergency isolation valves in low to medium pressure oxygen lines.

12. Slow pressure-up, HP oxygen compatible valves only should be used.

13. When opening an oxygen valve, always do it slowly.

14. HP oxygen banks should be stored in open air safe areas. They should be well secured against movement during poor weather conditions offshore.

15. HP oxygen banks should be separate from other HP gas banks and any high fire risk materials.

16. HP oxygen banks should be well protected from any form of damage.

17. The area around the HP oxygen banks, pipework, and fittings should be clean and free of oil and grease.

18. All pipework or end fittings should be sealed carefully to avoid contamination when not connected up.

19. Any pipework or related fittings which have been or are suspected to be contaminated and are likely to carry oxygen should be very carefully cleaned.

20. If compressed air has been allowed into piping or fittings which are likely to carry oxygen, assume they are oil-contaminated and clean as necessary.

21. The cleaning of oxygen pipework and fittings can be done using special solvents. If possible, avoid using toxic solvents such as trichlorethylene, a typical toxic degreasant, and always ensure complete drying after cleaning.

22. Keep rigorously to gas colour codes.

23. In fighting an oxygen fire, give priority to sealing off the source of the oxygen.

24. Assume everything will burn in HP oxygen.

25. Develop a healthy respect for oxygen and keep an acute awareness of the danger of fire and explosion.

Note: See Section 12.11, Chamber hygiene, for a list of substances that must never be brought in contact with HP O_2.

12.9c NITROGEN NARCOSIS

This is a state of stupor experienced by a diver due to the introduction of nitrogen under pressure into his body tissue at too high a rate. Narcosis dulls the senses and is most likely to occur when compressed air is used as a breathing gas. This is one of the factors limiting the use of compressed air to shallow dives. It is occasionally met by divers involved in nitrox (oxygen and nitrogen mixtures) or in trimix (oxygen, helium and nitrogen diving). The effect is very similar to that of drinking alcoholic drinks. Symptoms may manifest themselves at depths of 28 m or deeper.

It is important to realise that there are two different effects of narcosis on the mental activities of the diver.

FIRST, a change can occur in the personality of the diver. This is potentially the most serious effect, but only affects some divers. A normally careful and disciplined diver may suddenly become totally carefree and undisciplined with disastrous results. This is important to watch for, especially in inexperienced divers. Generally speaking, such individuals should not be allowed to dive deep on air.

SECOND, there is a progressive reduction in thinking ability as divers go deeper on air. This affects every diver without exception. It is usually not noticeable until it is necessary to work out a task such as setting up a camera. Only then is the difficulty apparent.

As the depth increases, it can become impossible to work out even simple tasks. For this reason, the supervision of deep air divers must be very tight. The diver must be carefully briefed and if necessary, his job rehearsed. The amount of thinking and decision-making required of the diver must be kept to a minimum.

If any important diver observations need to be recorded, they should be done during rather than after the dive. This is because the memory also is reduced in capability by nitrogen narcosis.

Whilst experience will help overcome both these effects of nitrogen narcosis, it will never eliminate them. So the problem must always be treated with the greatest respect. Regular diving tends to reduce the likelihood of nitrogen narcosis.

Certain other aspects of diving can greatly increase the effects of nitrogen narcosis and should be avoided wherever possible. These will include:

—Heavy exercise and high CO_2 levels.

—Inefficient breathing equipment.

—Cold.

—Bad visibility.

—Fear.

—Hangover.

—Poor physical condition.

Signs and symptoms

—Personality changes.

—Dizziness.

—Apparent drunkenness or general euphoria.

—Loss of co-ordination.

—Numbness of the lips.

—Tunnel vision.

The only way to avoid nitrogen narcosis is to return to shallower water and lower pressure. Nitrogen narcosis disappears immediately on such action and leaves no after-effects.

12.9d CARBON MONOXIDE POISONING

Carbon monoxide (CO) can very occasionally contaminate a diver's air supply, usually because of the exhaust fumes from a petrol/diesel engine being drawn into the compressor intake.

Carbon monoxide is particularly dangerous because it is virtually undetectable in very small concentrations and as little as 0.00001 bar abs can kill a diver. One of the dangers of breathing contaminated air is that on the surface it can easily be undetected. As the diver's water depth increases the partial pressure of the CO can rise to lethal levels. Divers who smoke will already have a relatively high concentration of CO in their blood, making them more sensitive to the contaminated air.

The effect on the body is to cause hypoxia, except that in CO poisoning the blood does not turn blue in colour. The skin remains an apparently healthy colour whilst the body is being robbed of its oxygen. This is because the CO is taken up by the red blood cells in preference to the oxygen, but the result is to make the blood cells bright red.

Symptoms of CO poisoning

The most likely effect of CO poisoning in a diving situation would be diver unconsciousness before any of the less serious symptoms are noticed.

—Dizziness, headache and tiredness.

—Staggering, mental confusion and slurred speech.

—Flushed lips and cheeks.

—Nausea and vomiting.

—Unconsciousness.

—Coma and death.

Treatment of CO poisoning

The victim should breathe pure oxygen or a high percentage of oxygen, preferably under pressure. The high PO_2 speeds up the elimination of CO from the blood and pushes extra O_2 into simple solution in the blood.

The following schedule provides a possible treatment for a severe case of CO poisoning and should be administered with the greatest possible urgency.

CARBON MONOXIDE TREATMENT

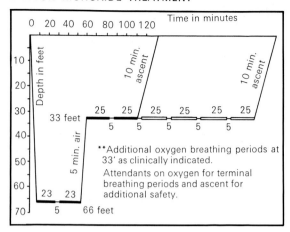

Prevention of CO poisoning

CO poisoning is easily preventable and should never happen. The entry of CO with the air supply is the result of negligence on the part of the compressor operator which can be avoided by good maintenance and sound operational practice of the compressors.

12.9e CARBON DIOXIDE POISONING

Carbon dioxide (CO_2) is a waste product of the body that is eliminated through the lungs. The body monitors the CO_2 level in the blood and regulates the breathing rate based on this information. A rise in the CO_2 level will cause an increase in the depth and rate of breathing (hypercapnoea). If it continues to rise, this may cause a headache and breathlessness increases until confusion occurs. In extreme cases, consciousness is lost.

Anything that prevents normal breathing efficiency can cause CO_2 poisoning. Examples of these are:

—Overexertion.

—An inefficient demand valve.

—A large dead space in the breathing circuit.

—Restricting clothing or harness.

—Inefficient or exhausted CO_2 scrubber in a breathing set or life-support unit.

—Inadequate or badly-sited CO_2 scrubber in a bell or chamber.

—Improper use of a free-flow helmet, such as too low a setting for the free-flow rate, or too much shutting off the free-flow for better voice communication.

Symptoms

A level of 0.02 bar of CO_2 in the lungs causes little disturbance to the diver. Levels of 0.05 bar will cause breathlessness and a feeling of discomfort. An increase of up to 0.1 bar will cause a marked increase in breathing effort with mental confusion and headaches. Levels in excess of 0.1 bar will be accompanied by marked mental effects leading to unconsciousness. Higher quantities will cause convulsions, unconsciousness and eventually death.

Avoidance of CO₂ poisoning

It is not as easy as it may seem to notice the problem in oneself. If however, it is recognised, the following action should be taken.

—Stop any physical exertion immediately.

—Ensure a stable position and relax the body as much as possible. Try to remain calm.

—Concentrate on regaining a controlled breathing rate.

—Flush the mask or helmet with air.

—Do not attempt talking until a stable breathing rate has been established.

—Breathe deeply rather than in rapid shallow breaths.

—If breathing on an inefficient demand valve, take long, slow, deep breaths. Sucking hard is to be avoided.

—If on a closed or semi-closed breathing set, change to an open circuit as soon as possible.

12.9f HYDROGEN SULPHIDE POISONING

Hydrogen sulphide (H_2S) is a dangerous gas that can be released from the crude oil or the gas produced by drilling operations. It smells strongly of rotten eggs so it can be easy to detect in small concentrations. But the sense of smell adapts quickly and after a short while the smell may seem to have gone; however, the H_2S may not have gone.

H_2S is very poisonous, even in small quantities, and great care should be taken to avoid exposure to it. Over 1000 ppm at atmospheric pressure can kill instantaneously.

Signs and symptoms

—Strong smell of rotten eggs that 'disappears' quickly.

—Irritation of the eyes and lungs.

—Dizziness, headache, nausea, vomiting.

—Loss of consciousness.

—Death.

Avoidance of H_2S poisoning

Wherever there are hydrocarbons, there is a potential risk from H_2S poisoning. The risk is greatest in confined spaces.

—Avoid contaminating diving equipment with crude oil.

—Avoid bringing equipment and materials contaminated with crude oil into a diving bell.

—Avoid locating a diving bell over an area of gassing.

—If in doubt, go onto BIBS or breathing mask/helmet immediately.

—Be particularly careful when first entering a confined space such as an SPM compartment. In such cases, never work alone.

—If a contaminated atmosphere is suspected, carry out gas tests such as the use of chemical indicator tubes (Draeger, MSA for example) before attempting to breathe the atmosphere.

12.9g EPOXY RESIN DEGASSING

Epoxy resins are being increasingly used underwater to provide protective coatings and for making various types of repairs such as on concrete.

During the curing phase of some resins, gases can be given off which are potentially very harmful. The risk concerns the possibility of causing cancer and increases if the exposure to the contamination is over a long period. This may occur if the gases appear in a compression chamber with its closed circuit life-support system, because these harmful gases are not removed by ordinary scrubbing systems.

Avoidance of resin degassing risks

—Avoid contaminating diving equipment and clothing with the resin.

—Avoid bringing equipment and materials contaminated with the resin into a bell or chamber.

—Carefully follow the manufacturer's operating instructions.

12.10 CHAMBER HYGIENE

Chamber hygiene is of paramount importance to the health and safety of divers undergoing pressurization, particularly in saturation. Divers should be aware of the potential hazards to their health that simple exposure to pressure may present. To maintain a habitable environment within a chamber, oxygen and carbon dioxide concentrations, temperature and humidity must be kept within the following limits.

1 Oxygen content	The pp O_2 must lie between 0.25 and 0.5 ata (250 and 500 millibar). The percent by volume should never exceed 25%.
2 Carbon dioxide content	The pp CO_2 should not exceed 0.005 ata (5 millibar).
3 Temperature	Temperature must be between 75°F and 85°F (24°C and 30°C) and/or as directed by the chamber occupants.
4 Humidity	Between 60% and 75% relative humidity.

Infection

Viruses, bacteria and fungi are microscopic organisms of which there are many types. Many are capable of causing infections in humans; they can destroy tissues and produce poisonous products within the body. Some bacteria, for instance, are actually necessary for the body functions and occur normally within and on the human body. Others are controlled by the body's protective mechanisms.

Three common ways of contracting an infection are
(1) Direct physical contact with a person
(2) Inhaling infective organisms from a person
(3) Eating contaminated food

There are four common categories of disease that particularly concern divers in chambers.

(1) Internal disorders such as gastro-enteritis
(2) Fungal infections such as athlete's foot
(3) Outer ear infections such as otitis externa
(4) Respiratory infections such as colds

Because of the confined nature of the chamber environment, great attention must be given to a preventative (prophylactic) hygiene regime. Such a regime could be considered in two parts.
(a) Personal hygiene
(b) Chamber hygiene

(a) Personal hygiene

BEFORE ENTERING A CHAMBER

(1) You should not be suffering from any kinds of infection whatsoever. Any disorder, or even a suspected oncoming disorder, must be reported to the diving supervisor and, if necessary, be given clearance by a diving doctor before recommencing diving.
(2) You should shower immediately before entering a chamber and don clean clothes.

INSIDE A CHAMBER

(3) You should apply prophylactic (preventative) eardrops and maintain a meticulous regime.

(4) You should use only soap in the shower once in every 24 hours so as not to remove the skin's natural oils and defences.
(5) Use only your own personally marked towels and bed linen.
(6) Change your clothing every day after showering.

(b) Chamber hygiene

The only practical method of disinfecting a chamber is by chemical means. A suitable disinfectant must be
(a) Unaffected by pressure
(b) Non-toxic
(c) Non-allergic
(d) Non-volatile
(e) Non-inflammable
(f) Non-corrosive
(g) Odourless, if possible

Dichlorophen is such a chemical, trade named 'Panacide'. When diluted by a factor of 1 : 2000 by volume, it is used to scrub the whole chamber complex and as it dries it deposits a film which inhibits bacterial growth. 'Panaclean' is 'Panacide' mixed with a detergent, which when diluted 1 : 100 by volume in water is used for the physical cleaning of the inside of the chamber before disinfection with 'Panacide'.

Disinfection routine

BEFORE PRESSURIZATION

(1) Scrub the chamber with 'Panaclean' (1 : 100).
(2) Disinfect the chamber with 'Panacide' (1 : 2000).
(3) Mattresses and bedding which have been washed should have had a final rinse in 'Panacide' (1 : 1000).
(4) A container of 'Panacide' solution (1 : 2000) may be placed in the transfer trunking prior to locking on the bell or, alternatively, a 10 l container of neat 'Panacide' together with a 10 ml syringe could be passed through the medical lock for use during saturation.
(5) Urine spilt outside the pan or on the toilet seat must be wiped up immediately.

DURING PRESSURIZATION

(6) Washbasins and toilets should be washed with 'Panacide' (1 : 2000) every 24 hours.
(7) Pour a small amount of the 'Panacide' solution into the toilet bowl each time it is used and just prior to flushing.
(8) Wipe over the medical lock door, tables, seats and deck plates daily.
(9) Wipe down the chamber bulkheads every 3–4 days.
(10) Be meticulous in cleaning up spilt food.
(11) It is recommended that bedding is changed every 48 hours, unless it has been rinsed in 'Panacide' when it can be extended to 72 hours.
(12) Used clothing and towels must be placed in a plastic bag and passed out through the lock.

AFTER DECOMPRESSION

(13) When the chamber is unpressurized, 'Panacide' (1 : 2000) should be left on all surfaces, with the door closed, for at least 12 hours.
(14) Diving suits and hoods should be soaked in 'Panacide' (1 : 2000) for at least 12 hours.

DILUTION
Examples of how to achieve the required dilutions.

PANACIDE		PANACLEAN
1 : 1000 in clean fresh water	1 : 2000 in clean fresh water	1 : 100 in clean fresh water
Panacide + water	Panacide + water	Panaclean + water
1 ml + 1 l	1 ml + 2 l	1 ml + 0.1 l
0.3 ml + 0.3 l	0.3 ml + 0.6 l	0.3 ml + 0.03 l
2.4 ml + 2.4 l	2.4 ml + 4.8 l	2.4 ml + 0.24 l
12 ml + 12 l	12 ml + 24 l	12 ml + 1.2 l

COMPARATIVE MEASURES		
LITRES	US GALLONS	IMPERIAL GALLONS
PANACIDE/WATER		
1 ml × 1.0	1 cm³ × 0.26	1 cm³ × 0.22
0.3 ml × 0.3	0.3 cm³ × 0.08	0.3 cm³ × 0.07
2.4 ml × 2.4	2.4 cm³ × 0.63	2.4 cm³ × 0.53
12 ml × 12	12 cm³ × 3.17	12 cm³ × 2.64
1 ml × 2	1 cm³ × 0.53	1 cm³ × 0.44
0.3 ml × 0.6	0.3 cm³ × 0.16	0.3 cm³ × 0.13
2.4 ml × 4.8	2.4 cm³ × 1.27	2.4 cm³ × 1.06
12 ml × 24	12 cm³ × 6.34	12 cm³ × 5.28
1 ml × 0.1	1 cm³ × 0.026	1 cm³ × 0.022
0.3 ml × 0.03	0.3 cm³ × 0.008	0.3 cm³ × 0.007
2.4 ml × 0.24	2.4 cm³ × 0.063	2.4 cm³ × 0.053
12 ml × 1.2	12 cm³ × 0.317	12 cm³ × 0.264

BIBS equipment

Visually check the BIBS masks, hoses and their fittings that are to be installed in the chamber. The masks and lines should be oxygen cleaned, then tested and disinfected with Panacide 1:2000 before fitting. Enclosing the equipment in a plastic bag ensures that it stays free of dust.

Oral nasal masks and the linings of helmets should be sterilised from time to time in a solution of Hycalin or similar disinfectant.

Remember that the saturation diving environment is ideal for the growth of bacteria because of the high temperatures and humidities. The atmosphere is totally enclosed and constantly recirculated by the life support system. All this means that each man is exposed to any infection that may be present. Any diver who contracts an infection in a chamber should report it immediately. One man's ill-considered action could mean that the entire team in the chamber stands to lose good health and money, and even, perhaps, job prospects.

DIET IN CHAMBER

There are two basic considerations affecting the choice of foodstuff entering the chamber:

(i) to maintain a healthy diet (see Section 12.9, Keeping Fit)

(ii) to avoid introducing a fire risk (see 4.5 DCC Operation). Certain substances, for example sugar (especially if finely ground), butter, oils, etc., can introduce a major fire hazard and should therefore not be locked into a chamber. This also applies to certain powder-based medications and alcoholic solutions.

LIST OF ITEMS THAT SHOULD NEVER BE LOCKED INTO A DCC UNDER PRESSURE

Butter

Oil (such as salad dressings)

Sugar in fine powders

Alcohol

Drugs, other than those provided

Thermos flasks

If you require sugar in drinks, dissolve it before transfer into the chamber. When passing in medication, loosen the tops of bottles first.

12.11 KEEPING FIT

Physical fitness is necessary to maintain a state of good health for efficient operation and to help avoid and overcome dangers. A physically fit diver is able to withstand fatigue for longer periods, is better equipped to tolerate physical stress, is less likely to suffer from decompression sickness, is more resistant to hypoxia, and has a stronger heart than the unfit.

How to estimate personal fitness

A simple way of estimating fitness is to step up and down onto a 50 cm (20″) chair for 5 minutes at a rate of 30 times a minute. Lie down immediately afterwards. Take and note the pulse (for 30 sec.) after 30 seconds, 2 minutes and 4 minutes of rest.

Physical fitness is calculated from: $\dfrac{t \times 100}{p \times 2}$

where t = time taken in seconds to complete the exercise

p = the sum of the three pulse counts (for those who complete the entire exercise, t = 300 seconds or 5 minutes)

HOW TO SCORE

Below 41 = Unfit	75 to 90 = Good
41 to 74 = Average	Over 90 = Excellent

Recent research into fitness training has revealed that a certain level, the threshold level, of heart beats per minute has to be reached and maintained for a minimum of 15 minutes to achieve a training effect on the cardio-respiratory system. This training effect must be achieved at least three times per week in order to improve fitness.

The following is a guide to calculating the threshold level:

Formula:

$$60\% \times (220 - \text{age} - \text{resting pulse (RP)}) + \text{RP} = \text{threshold level}$$

Example for a person aged 30, with a resting pulse of 70:

$$220 - 30 - 70 = 120 \times 60/100\%$$
$$= 72 + 70\,(\text{RP}) = 142$$

Threshold level = 142 beats per minute (bpm)

Any type of exercise routine involving total muscular activity which invokes the threshold level principle is acceptable.

Running, swimming, and circuit training are some ways. The exercise outlined below shows a series of general body exercises which can be used in confined quarters to help you maintain your personal fitness. The importance of warming up before exercise cannot be overstressed and a simple warm-up routine is shown on Chart A.

Make a record card laid out as shown in this diagram.

Exercise Record		Date	Initial exercise circuit time		Target time
Exercise no.	Max. no. of repeats of each exercise in 30 seconds	No. of exercises for the circuit	Exercise no	Max. no. of repeats of each exercise in 30 seconds	No. of exercises for the circuit
1 2 3 4 5 6			7 8 9 10 11 12		
Progress					
Date					
Time					

EXERCISE ROUTINE

1. Warm up using suggested routine on Chart A.
2. Using Chart B, carry out, in order, as many repetitions as you can in 30 seconds, of each exercise. Record the number on your Exercise Record Sheet.
3. Take a 1 minute rest between each exercise.
4. Warm down using initial warm up routine × 10 repetitions of each exercise.

The next training session

5. Halve your recorded maximum for each exercise and note this on your Exercise Record Sheet.
6. Carry out three continuous circuits of the exercises using your new ½ maximum repetition.
7. Write down the time this takes in the space at the top of the Exercise Record Sheet under 'Initial exercise circuit time' and insert the date.
8. Calculate 2/3 of that time. This is now your new target time in which you must aim to complete the continuous three circuits. Fill in this new time on the top right corner of the Exercise Record Sheet.
   For example:
   Max. repeats in 30 sec.   20
   ½ max. for circuit repetitions   10
   Time of × 3 circuits   12 min.
   Target time   12 × 2/3 = 8 min.
9. Once you reach your target time, retest your 30 sec. maximum repetitions. It should have increased. Reset your new target time.
10. The boxes at the base of the card allow you to record your progress. During the early stages of the training check your pulse after each circuit. Are you reaching your threshold level? If not,

you are *not* working hard enough. Conversely, if your pulse is over your allowed maximum (i.e. 220 − age), you are pushing yourself too hard.

Progression is by gradually reaching your target time and resetting it once you reach it. However, once a good level of fitness is achieved you may find that you are unable to improve your 30 sec. maximum repetitions. Once this occurs, you may want to increase your maximum repetition time by 10 seconds so that the maximum repetitions are recorded over 30 seconds, 40 seconds, 50 seconds and so on. This will further increase your work time over 3 exercise circuits and in so doing, increase the time that you are working above your threshold level.

DOs and DON'Ts

DO   Train regularly.
DO   Warm up before exercise.
DO   Wear suitable clothing (working up a sweat by wearing a tracksuit does not increase fitness).
DO   Give up smoking immediately.
DO   Diet if you are overweight, but only under medical supervision whilst undergoing this training schedule.
DO   Limit excessive alcohol intake.

DON'T Train until at least 1 hour after a meal, longer if the meal has been large.
DON'T Train if you have a heavy cold or if you are feeling particularly off colour.

CHART A. Warm up routine

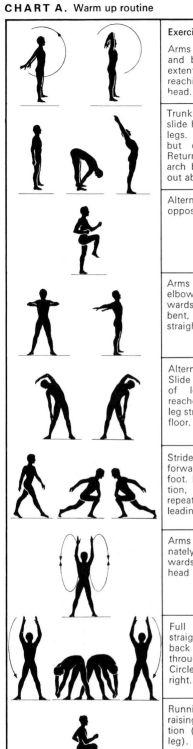

	Exercise Description
	Arms swinging forward and bend elbows at full extent of swing, hands reaching down behind head.
	Trunk bending forwards, slide hands down front of legs. Keep legs straight, but do not overstrain. Return to standing and arch back, arms reaching out above head.
	Alternate high knee raising, opposite arm forward.
	Arms horizontal bend at elbow, arm pressing backwards. One press arms bent, one press arms straight.
	Alternate side bending: Slide hand down outside of leg, opposite arm reaches over head. Keep leg straight, feet flat on the floor.
	Stride standing, lower forward until knee over foot. Return to start position, pivot round and repeat with opposite leg leading.
	Arms full circling alternately forward and backwards. Keep arms close to head during inward circle.
	Full trunk circling, legs straight throughout. Arch back whilst passing through upright position. Circle alternately left and right.
	Running on the spot, thigh raising to horizontal position (10 repetitions each leg).

The need for warming up before exercise cannot be over-stressed. Main muscle groups and joints should be taken through a full range of movement. All movements should be carried out ten times, slowly and smoothly at first so that the muscles and joints have time to adapt to the new tensions placed on them. Finally repeat the exercises again ten times with more vigour, but with the movements remaining smooth and comfortable.
Your body is now ready to take the extra stresses of an exercise routine.

CHART B. Exercises

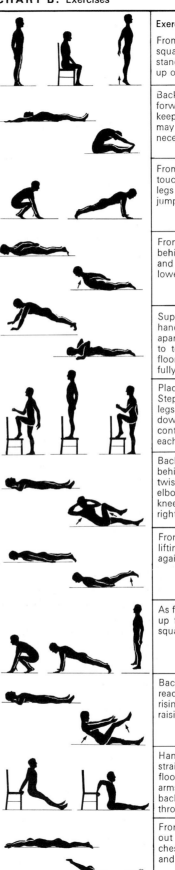

	Exercise Description
	From standing position, squat to chair. Return to standing position and rise up onto toes.
	Back lying: Sit up, reach forward towards toes keeping legs straight. Feet may be fixed/held if necessary.
	From squat position, knees touching elbows, thrust legs back straight and jump back to start position.
	Front lying: Hands clasped behind back, raise head and chest from floor and lower.
	Support position with hands shoulder width apart, body straight. Lower to touch chest lightly on floor, push back up to arms fully extended.
	Place one foot on chair. Step up onto chair with legs fully extended; step down leaving same foot in contact with chair (30 sec. each leg).
	Back lying: Hands clasped behind head, sit up and twist upper body to touch elbow on opposite rising knee. Alternate left and right.
	Front lying: Double leg-lifting from floor and lower again to floor.
	As for exercise 3 but stand up fully in between each squat thrust.
	Back lying: Sit up and reach towards ankle of rising leg. Alternate leg raising.
	Hands on chair, legs straight, lower towards floor and push back until arms fully extended. Keep back close to chair throughout.
	Front lying: Arms straight out by head, raise arms, chest and legs off the floor and lower.

Exercise charts prepared by the Staff of the Army Physical Training Corps at RMA Sandhurst.

SMOKING

Cigarette smoking reduces fitness. It also has the following effects:

○ It reduces breath-holding endurance.

○ It increases risk of burst lung.

○ It reduces heart efficiency.

○ It reduces breathing efficiency.

○ It causes lung disease.

○ It causes heart disease.

○ It causes cancer.

Think about it.

Diet

Diet plays an important role in keeping fit because if more food is eaten than the body can consume it is stored as fat. Obesity should be avoided. Overweight people are a liability in an emergency because they move more slowly than if they were their correct weight. Offshore they are often an added handicap as they are unable to move swiftly in small places and if they suffer an accident, they are difficult to lift and manoeuvre. Divers should be particularly weight conscious as fat people are more prone to decompression sickness. Note the following table and ensure that the recommended weights for height and build are exceeded by no more than 20%.

Height without shoes		Correct weight unclothed		20% over correct weight	
m	ft	kg	lb	kg	lb
1.55	5′ 1″	50.8	112	61.0	134
1.60	5′ 3″	54.4	120	65.3	144
1.65	5′ 5″	57.6	126	69.0	152
1.70	5′ 7″	60.6	133	72.7	160
1.75	5′ 9″	63.9	140	76.7	169
1.80	5′ 11″	67.1	148	80.5	177
1.85	6′ 1″	70.5	155	84.6	186

Age Allowances
18—29 years as above
30—39 years, add 2.3 kg (5 lb)
40—44 years, add 4.5 kg (10 lb)
(Adapted from Kemsley W. F. F. *et al.*, *Brit. J. prev. soc. Med.* **16**, 189, 1962)

To maintain a healthy diet avoid fried foods and limit sugar and fat intake. Don't overeat to the point of feeling bloated. Alcohol is very fattening and can increase blood pressure. Eat fruits, salads, fresh vegetables, bran cereals, wholemeal bread, lean meat and polyunsaturated fats in preference to fried, fatty and sweetened foods. During decompression in chambers, avoid dehydration; drink plenty of liquid to increase resistance to decompression sickness.

12.12 THE DIVING MEDICAL EXAMINATION

A diving medical is required so the diver can safely and competently carry out his profession.

In the UK and Norway only certain approved doctors can examine divers (see Section 12.13, Diving medical examiners). The UK examination is recorded on special forms and one copy sent to the National Centre at the Decompression Central Registry at Newcastle upon Tyne. Consequently a long-term evaluation of the individual diver's health is possible as well as an evaluation of any adverse effects of diving on health. In Norway an examination similar to the UK examination is required. In the USA the medical examination can be carried out by any qualified doctor.

The following information is intended as a guide to what a diving medical involves and what may disqualify a person from taking up or continuing a diving career.

United Kingdom

The medical examination forms (Diver's Questionnaire and Doctor's Records) and guidelines to be used with them are available on open sale from UEG, 6 Storey's Gate, London, SW1 3AU, UK. Doctors approved to examine divers under the Diving Operations at Work Regulations (1981) receive the forms direct from the central registry.

GENERAL

Any disease or condition which may require urgent treatment will disqualify a diver. Serious disturbances of the endocrine system, such as diabetes or other hormonal disturbances, will exclude him, as will a history of a serious allergic disease. Any minor chronic, recurring or temporary mental or physical illness which may distract the diver and cause him to ignore factors concerned with his own or others' safety must be given careful consideration.

AGE

Minimum age should be at least 18 years because of the need for physical and psychological maturity. There is no upper limit providing all the medical standards can be met. A man older than 25 years should not normally start diving if he wishes to become a mixed gas saturation diver. For air diving, he would not normally be accepted for training after the age of 35 years. Divers over the age of 40 may not have adequate reserves of pulmonary and cardiovascular fitness for use in an emergency so their professional diving career may have to be terminated on these grounds.

HEIGHT

There is no set limit, but the man must be judged to have sufficient strength to work as a diver.

WEIGHT

Obesity may increase the chances of decompression sickness and implies a general lack of fitness. The diver should not exceed by more than 20% the standard weight for his height and age (see Section 12.10, Physical fitness). This table does not allow for variations in body type so this may have to be taken into account.

SKIN

Some skin disorders will be aggravated by diving. Friction from dry diving suits, prolonged immersion, prolonged exposure to high humidity, and elevated temperature environments encountered by saturation divers can all adversely affect skin conditions. They can give rise to social problems when sharing suits and lead to psychological problems due to embarrassment.

Contagious (catching) skin diseases, such as scabies, warts on the feet and impetigo must be cured before diving is allowed. Other skin diseases of a more chronic nature must be assessed on their seriousness.

EARS, NOSE AND THROAT

The ear drums and sinuses are directly exposed to changes of pressure associated with diving. The ear drums should be healthy and the eustachian tubes functioning normally. A diver must be able to 'clear his ears' to be able to dive. Any infection of the middle or outer ear will disqualify until it is cleared up. Chronic outer ear disease, perforations and scarring of the eardrum, history of chronic or repeated acute ear infection, deafness sufficient to affect hearing normal speech, recurrent nose bleeds, chronic or recurrent sinusitis will all disqualify, until resolved.

RESPIRATORY SYSTEM

It is essential that the respiratory system should be normal as, like the ears, nose and throat, it is directly exposed to changes in pressure associated with diving. Any condition that might cause retention and trapping of expanding gas in any part of the lungs during decompression must disqualify. In particular asthma (except childhood asthma of which there has been no recent evidence), chronic or recurrent bronchitis, bronchiectasis, pneumothorax, or tuberculosis, cysts, emphysema and bullae (blister) will disqualify. The diver's pulmonary function test must be normal.

TEETH

Teeth in an unsatisfactory state of conservation or unhealthy gums will disqualify. Inability to retain an unmodified diving equipment mouthpiece after removal of dentures because of malformation of the gums will disqualify.

CARDIOVASCULAR SYSTEM

There must be no evidence of heart disease. Heart sounds should be normal. Any abnormality should be referred to a cardiological expert. Diseases of the blood or blood-forming organs will disqualify. Performance of an exercise tolerance test should be satisfactory. An ECG (sometimes called EKG) is often given after the exercise tolerance test as exercise may reveal malfunctions of the heart. A haemoglobin or haematocrit estimation should be normal. The resting blood pressure should be 140/90. Severe varicose veins may disqualify until they are treated.

ABDOMEN

Peptic ulceration will disqualify unless there is evidence of healing and the candidate has been untroubled for 1 year; herniation (when because of weakness of the abdominal muscles an abnormal bulge occurs in which gut may be caught) should be cause for rejection until satisfactory treatment has taken place; impaired kidney function, gall stones and kidney stones will disqualify as an attack underwater could be fatal.

Venereal disease will disqualify until adequately treated. Varicocele (varicose veins of the testicles) or hydrocele (cysts of the testicles) will disqualify until treated.

BONES AND JOINTS

A diver has to undertake a good deal of heavy work both in and out of the water as part of his job. Although the physical strain can be less when working under the water than doing the same job on land, there should be no gross limitation in functions of any major joints. The potential diver with 'recurrent back trouble' will need to be carefully assessed. Bone necrosis is an occupational hazard of diving

so all joints and long bones should be X-rayed periodically. Every case should be decided on its own merit, taking into account the nature and location of the lesion, the diver's past history, age, general fitness and his future diving intentions. Any disease or injury that could be potentially disabling will disqualify.

CENTRAL NERVOUS SYSTEM

A full and careful examination is essential at the initial medical examination and any abnormalities should be documented.. Fits, blackouts, epilepsy or recurrent headaches will disqualify as underwater these could prove fatal. Severe or repeated head injury resulting in prolonged unconsciousness or requiring surgery will disqualify. Diseases or damage to the nervous system with abnormal function and disturbances of the blood supply to the brain will disqualify.

PSYCHOLOGICAL FITNESS

Owing to the nature of the work it is unlikely that many psychologically unsuitable people will wish to become divers, but it is essential for a diver to have a stable personality, an equable temperament and no history of mental illness. Any person taking psychotherapeutic drugs is unsuitable. Alcoholics and drug addicts must be excluded.

EYES

Minor defects are not a bar to diving. Colour vision will be tested at the initial examination and any abnormality detailed in the diver's log book and certificate of fitness. Any reduction in the field of vision or uncorrected vision 15% worse than average may disqualify.

All divers must be examined annually. If an injury or illness prevents a diver from diving for 7 days or more his certificate of fitness must be renewed. The occurrence of Type II decompression sickness requires a renewal of the diver's certificate of fitness.

United States of America

The following table shows the tests for the diving medical examination required by the Occupational Safety and Health Administration.

Test	Initial examination	Annual re-examination
Chest X-ray	×	
Visual acuity	×	×
Colour blindness	×	
EKG: Standard 12L*		
Hearing test	×	×
Hematocrit or hemoglobin	×	×
Sickle cell index	×	
White blood count	×	×
Urinalysis	×	×
* To be given to the employee once, at age 35 or over.		

The decision on the employee's fitness to be exposed to hyperbaric conditions, including any recommended restrictions or limitations, is the examining physician's; however a second and third opinion can be sought. Unlike the UK, there is no available list of diseases or illnesses that may disqualify a person from diving.

12.13 DIVING MEDICAL EXAMINERS

UNITED KINGDOM

Doctors approved by the Health and Safety Executive and the Secretary of State for Trade to issue certificates of medical fitness in connection with the diving operations regulations. This list is continually updated and information can be obtained from Employment Medical Advisory Services (EMAS), Tel: (01) 262 3277.

NORTHERN REGION

Dr W. Howe,*
EMAS,
Vincent House,
2 Woodland Road,
Darlington, DL3 7PJ.
0325 56148

Dr R. I. McCallum,
21 Claremont Place,
Newcastle-upon-Tyne,
NE2 4AA.
0632 28511 Ext 3254

Dr J. N. O'Neill,
The Health Centre,
PO Box 101 (B),
20 Cleveland Square,
Middlesbrough, Cleveland.
0642 247257

Mr J. Pooley,
Sunderland District Hospital,
Kayll Road, Sunderland,
Tyne and Wear.
0783 56256

Dr S. G. Shaw,
Ashleigh House,
Seaburn Court, Sunderland,
Tyne and Wear, SR6 8EF.
0783 76691 or 74293

Dr I. H. Thomas,
Department of Surgery,
University of Newcastle,
Royal Victoria Infirmary,
Newcastle-upon-Tyne,
NE1 4LP.
0632 28511 Ext 3159

Prof. D. N. Walder,
Department of Surgery,
Royal Victoria Infirmary,
Newcastle-upon-Tyne,
NE1 4LP.
0632 25131 Ext 365

Dr J. F. Wollaston,
British Shipbuilders
(North East) Training and
Safety Co. Ltd,
Ellison Street,
Hebburn, Tyne and Wear.
0632 832231

NORTH EAST REGION

Dr J. D. Brackenridge,
75 High Street,
Boston, Lincs.
0205 65881

Dr J. E. H. Ellis,
West Yorkshire Metropolitan
Police,
Western Area Headquarters,
The Tyrls,
Bradford, BD1 1TR.
0274 23422

Dr H. M. Kidd,
15 Hartington Road,
Buxton,

Derbyshire, SK17 6JP.
0298 2338

Dr R. Rogerson,
3–5 Mizzen Road,
Beverley High Road,
Hull, HU6 7AG.
0482 854574

EASTERN AND SOUTH EAST MIDLANDS REGIONS

Dr I. K. Anderson,
North Sea Medical Centre,
Central Surgery,
Sussex Road,
Gorleston-on-Sea,
Gt Yarmouth,
Norfolk, NR31 6QB.
0493 600011

Dr C. H. Brookings,
North Sea Medical Centre,
Central Surgery,
Sussex Road,
Gorleston-on-Sea,
Gt Yarmouth,
Norfolk, NR31 6QB.
0493 600011

Dr R. A. Davenport,
201 Hamilton Road,
Felixstowe, Suffolk.
03942 3197

Dr N. V. Edwards,
Alderford Grange,
Sible Hedingham,
Halstead,
Essex, CO9 3RD.
0787 60260

Dr H. A. Evans,
North Sea Medical Centre,
3 Lowestoft Road
Gorleston-on-Sea,
Gt Yarmouth,
Norfolk, NR31 6QB.
0493 600011

Dr G. C. Liddle,
North Sea Medical Centre,
Central Surgery,
Sussex Road
Gorleston-on-Sea,
Gt Yarmouth,
Norfolk, NR31 6QB.
0493 600011

Dr N. M. Livingstone,
North Sea Medical Centre,
Sussex Road,
Gorleston-on-Sea,
Gt Yarmouth,
Norfolk, NR31 6QB.
0493 600011

Dr N. K. I. McIver,
North Sea Medical Centre,
Central Surgery,
Sussex Road,
Gorleston-on-Sea,
Gt Yarmouth,
Norfolk, NR31 6QB.
0493 600011

Dr D. G. Watson,
North Sea Medical Centre,
Central Surgery,
Sussex Road,
Gorleston-on-Sea,
Gt Yarmouth,
Norfolk, NR31 6QB.
0493 600011

LONDON NORTH REGION

Dr J. C. Betts,
82A Roman Road,
London, E2.
01 980 3023

Dr E. S. Blackadder,
British Broadcasting
Corporation,
Broadcasting House,
Portland Place,
London, W1A 1AA.
01 580 4468

Dr R. A. F. Cox,
Phillips Petroleum,
Portland House,
Stag Place, London, SW1.
01 828 9766

Dr K. P. Duncan,*
Health and Safety Executive,
25 Chapel Street,
London, NW1 5DT.
01 262 3277

Surg. Cdr D. H. Elliot,
Consultant Undersea
Activities,
Shell UK Ltd,
Shell Mex House,
Strand,
London, WC2R 0DY.
01 438 3000

Dr W. L. B. Leese,
Mobil Producing,
North West-Europe Inc,
Medical Department,
54–60 Victoria Street,
London, SW1E 6QB.
01 828 9777

Dr G. W. Mears,
Senior Flight Medical Officer,
Y.142 Speedbird House,
London (Heathrow) Airport,
Hounslow, Middx. TW6 2JA.
01 759 5511 x 3063

Dr A. H. Pickering,
Gulf Oil Company,
Eastern Hemisphere,
2 Portman Street,
London, W1H 0AN.
01 493 8040

Dr F. S. Preston,
British Airways Medical
Service,
Heathrow Airport,
Hounslow,
Middlesex, TW6 2JA.
01 897 5372

Dr D. Rossdale,
Esso Petroleum Co. Ltd,
Esso House,
Victoria Street, London, SW1
01 834 6677

Dr G. S. Sorrie,*
EMAS,
25 Chapel Street,
London, NW1 5DT.
01 262 3277

Dr R. Stubbings,
Medical Department,
The British Petroleum Co. Ltd,
Britannic House,
Moor Lane,
London, EC2Y 9BU.
01 920 7799

LONDON SOUTH AND SOUTH EAST REGION

Dr W. Crosbie,
13 Eastlands Crescent,
Dulwich,
London, SE21 7LG.
01 693 4894

Surg. Lt T. J. R. Francis,
Medical Centre,
HM Dockyard,
Chatham, Kent.
0634 44422 Ext 2972

Dr C. Harris,
Sutton Place,
Sutton Road,
Maidstone, ME15 9DU.
0622 53040

Dr J. D. King,
126 Ferndene Road,
London, SE24.
01 274 3171
(Appointments)
or
144 Harley Street,
London, W1.
01 935 0023

Dr J. H. Lewis,
Lancing Health Centre,
Penstone Park, Lancing,
Sussex, BN15 9AG.
09063 63144

Dr W. F. Parrott,*
EMAS,
1 Long Lane, Borough,
London, SE1 4PG.
01 407 8911

Dr A. J. Raw,
Farnham Health Centre,
Brightwells, East Street,
Farnham, Surrey, GU9 7SA.
0252 723122

Dr K. P. Walker,
Canterbury House,
Sydenham Road,
Croydon, Surrey.
01 688 3430

Dr J. T. Weir,
Surrey County Council,
County Hall,
Kingston Upon Thames,
KT1 2DN.
01 546 1050 X 3560

SOUTH WESTERN REGION

Dr M. W. Calder,
23 Beaumont Road,
Plymouth, Devon.
0752 63776

*Employment Medical Adviser

Dr M. Cross,
Fort Bovisand Underwater
Centre,
Plymouth, Devon.
0752 42570

Dr A. J. G. Davis,
Health Centre,
St Marys, Isles of Scilly.
0720 22628

Dr G. F. Devey,
HMS Osprey,
Portland, Dorset.
0305 820311 Ext 2432

Surg. Cdr C. W. Evans,
Dockyard Medical Centre,
HM Dockyard,
Devonport, Plymouth.
0752 553740

Dr J. B. Evans,
Powderham,
Lanlivery,
Cornwall, PL30 5BH.
020 887 272

Dr J. J. S. Fisher,
The Health Centre,
Osborn Road,
Fareham, Hants.
0329 282911

Dr J. M. Fisher,
2 Hanway Road,
Portsmouth,
Hants, PO1 4ND.
0705 815317

Dr M. E. Glanvill,
Jocelyn House,
Chard, Somerset, TA20 1QL.
046 06 3380

Surg. Lt Cdr R. F. Goad,
Institute of Naval Medicine,
Alverstoke,
Gosport, Hants, PO12 2DL.
0705 22351 Ext 41509

Dr E. P. Hamblett,
Avon County Council,
Central Health Clinic,
Tower Hill,
Bristol, BS2 0JD.
0272 291010

Surg. Cdr R. de G. Hanson,
Admiralty Marine,
AMTE Physiological
Laboratory,
Fort Road, Alverstoke,
Gosport, Hants, PO12 2DU.
0705 22351

Surg. Lt Cdr J. Haydon,
Institute of Naval Medicine,
Alverstoke, Gosport,
Hants, PO12 2DL.
0705 22351 Ext 41120

Dr I. D. Hewett,
The Health Centre,
Trevaylor Road,
Falmouth, Cornwall.
0326 312143
0326 312596

Dr G. W. Hickish,
Medical Centre,
Bransgore,

Hants, BH23 8AD.
0425 73484

Dr W. L. J. Houston,
23 Beaumont Road,
Plymouth, PL4 9BL.
0752 63776

Dr A. P. Lees,
'Brooklands',
Warfield Street,
Bracknell,
Berkshire, RG12 6GB.
0344 21774

Surg. Capt. D. E. Mackay,
Director of Medical Staff
Training,
Training Division,
RN Hospital,
Haslar, Gosport,
Hants, PO12 2AA.
0705 22351 Ext 41590

Dr D. P. Markby,
The Medical Centre,
Hythe,
Southampton, SO4 52B.
0590 612451

Dr G. C. Mathers,
99 London Road,
Gloucester.
0452 23126

Surg. Capt. T. P. Oliver,
Principal Medical Officer,
HM Naval Base,
Portsmouth, PO1 3ND.
0705 822351 Ext 22955

Surg. Cdr R. R. Pearson,
Institute of Naval Medicine,
Alverstoke, Gosport,
Hants, PO12 2DL.
0705 22351 Ext 41769

Dr J. F. Preece,
378 Pinhoe Road,
Exeter, Devon, EX4 8EG.
0392 67700

Surg. Cdr G. N. Shell,
Occupational Health Centre,
HM Naval Base,
Devonport, Plymouth.
0752 552335

Dr T. G. Shields,
Institute of Naval Medicine,
Alverstoke, Gosport.
Hants, PO12 2DL.
0705 22351

Dr A. K. Smeeton,
46 Northumberland Road,
Redland,
Bristol, BS6 7BD.
0272 44714

Dr J. J. W. Sykes,
Admiralty Marine Technology
Establishment,
Physiology Laboratory,
Fort Road,
Alverstoke,
Hants, PO12 2DU.
0705 22351
Ext 41842 or 41569

Dr M. S. Taylor,
18 Kirkway,

Broadstone,
Dorset, BH18 8EE.
0202 697307

Dr I. R. Thomas,
8 Kings Avenue,
St Austell, Cornwall.
0726 5555

Dr J. D. Thomas,*
EMAS,
Intercity House,
Mitchell Lane,
Victoria Street,
Bristol, BS1 6AN.
0272 290681

Dr C. B. Thomson,*
2nd Floor,
Intercity House,
Mitchell Lane,
Victoria Street,
Bristol, BS1 6AN.
0272 290681

Surg. Cdr M. G. Williams,
HMS Osprey,
Portland, Dorset.
0305 820311

Surg. Capt. J. M. Young,
Institute of Naval Medicine,
Alverstoke, Gosport.
Hants, PO12 2DU.
0705 22351

Dr Z. Torok,
AMTE Physiological
Laboratory,
Fort Road, Alverstoke,
Gosport, PO12 2DU.
0705 22351

WALES

Dr D. C. Beckingham,
Royal Gwent Hospital,
Newport, NPT 2UB.
0633 52244 Ext 607

Dr J. C. Bignall,
The Surgery,
Newport, Pembroke,
Dyfed, SA42 0TS.
023 976 397

Dr W. T. George,
22 Hamilton Terrace,
Milford Haven,
Dyfed, SA73 3JA.
064262 2674

Dr D. H. Lloyd,
Craig Hyfrid,
Cambria Street, Holyhead,
Anglesey, Gwynedd.
0407 2735

Dr R. H. G. Lloyd,
Roath House,
100 Penylan Road,
Roath Park, Cardiff, CF2 5HY.
0222 498482

Dr G. S. Lodwig,
25 Neath Road,
Maesteg,
Mid-Glamorgan, CF34 9PG.
0656 733200

Dr J. B. Williamson,*

EMAS,
Brunel House,
2 Fitzalan Road,
Cardiff, CF2 1SH.
0222 497777

WEST MIDLANDS REGION

Dr P. M. Brown,*
EMAS,
McLaren Building,
2 Mass House Circus,
Queensway,
Birmingham, B4 7NP.
021 236 5080

Dr P. P. Keith,*
EMAS,
McLaren Building,
2 Mass House Circus,
Queensway,
Birmingham, B4 7NP.
021 236 5080

Dr G. Krishnan,*
EMAS,
McLaren Building,
2 Mass House Circus,
Queensway,
Birmingham, B4 7NP.
021 236 5080 Ext 362

Dr C. R. Weatherley,
The Robert Jones & Agnes
Hunt Orthopaedic Hospital,
Oswestry, Salop.
0691 5311

NORTH WESTERN REGION

Dr M. J. Blyth,
72 Harrowside,
Blackpool, Lancs, FY4 1LR.
0253 41793

Dr B. J. Charlick,*
EMAS,
The Triad, N/E Wing,
19th Floor,
Stanley Road, Bootle,
Merseyside, L20 3PG.
051 922 7211

Dr W. Kerns,
42 Woodstock Drive,
Worsley, Manchester.
061 794 3488
061 245 7251
061 245 7239

Dr A. Y. Jones,
Shell UK Oil Ltd,
PO Box 3,
Stanlow Refinery,
Ellesmere Port,
South Wirral, L65 4HB.
051 355 3600

Dr A. D. Lawson,
Medical Department,
British Nuclear Fuels Ltd,
Sellafield,
Cumbria, CA20 1PG.
0940 28000

Dr A. C. Maclean,
PO Box No 3,
Stanlow, Ellesmere Port,
Cheshire, L65 4HB.
051 355 3600 Ext 4195

Dr P. L. Zacharias,
54 Rodney Street,
Liverpool, L1 9AB.
                    051 709 6979

SCOTLAND

Dr T. A. Anderson,
Offshore Medical Support,
Ashgrove Road West,
Aberdeen, AB2 5EF.
                    0224 683111

Dr A. W. Baird,*
Health and Safety Executive,
314 Vincent Street,
Glasgow, GS 8XG.
                    041 638 6366

Dr A. G. Beattie,
Shieldaig,
296 Queens Road,
Aberdeen, AB1 8DT.
                    0224 36280

Dr E. M. Botheroyd,
EMAS,
21 Albyn Place,
Aberdeen, AB1 1YN.
                    0224 56363

Dr B. Brown,
Offshore Medical Support,
Ashgrove Road West,
Aberdeen, AB2 5ES.
                    0224 683111

Dr R. McN. Cadenhead,
6 Burgh Road,
Lerwick,
Shetland Isles, ZE1 0LB.
                    0595 2535

Dr C. W. Childs,
Institute of Environmental and
Offshore Medicine,
9 Rubislaw Terrace,
Aberdeen, AB1 1XE.
                    0224 55595

Dr J. D. M. Douglas,
Tweedale Surgery,
Fort William, Inverness.
                    0397 3136/7

Surg. Cdr T. L. Fallowfield,
Comex Diving Ltd,
Bucksburn House,
Howes Road, Bucksburn,
Aberdeen, AB2 9RQ.
                    0336 714101

Dr D. E. Fraser,
11 Glen Road,
Dyce, Aberdeen, AB2 0FB.
                    0224 722594

Dr W. A. Freeland,
Institute of Environmental and
Offshore Medicine,
9 Rubislaw Terrace,
Aberdeen.
                    0224 55595

Dr P. B. James,
University Department of
Community and Occupational
Medicine,
Medical School,
Nine Wells,
Dundee, DD1 9SY.
                    0382 60111 Ext 2417

Dr D. D. Johnstone,
Ness House,
Stromness, Orkney.
                    085685 205

Dr I. McA. Ledingham,
University Department of
Surgery,
Western Infirmary,
Glasgow, G11 6NT.
                    041 339 8822 Ext 626

Dr I. D. Levack,
41 Queens Road,
Aberdeen.
                    0224 30860

Dr V. R. F. de Lima,
Medical Centre,
Heriot-Watt University,
Riccarton,
Currie,
Midlothian, EH14 4AS.
                    031 449 5111 Ext 2234

Dr J. N. MacAskill,
Tweedale Surgery,
High Street,
Fort William, PH33 6EU.
                    0397 3136/7

Dr T. W. Manson,
5 Hermitage Terrace,
Edinburgh, EN10 4RP.
                    031 447 6277

Dr J. H. Mawdsley,
Foresterhill Health Centre,
Westburn Road,
Aberdeen, AB9 2AY.
                    0224 695949

Dr I. M. McEwan,
Medical Centre,
HM Naval Base,
Rosyth, Fife.
                    0436 5878

Dr N. I. P. McKie,
Headlands of Findon,
Old Inn Road, Findon,
Aberdeen, AB1 4RN.
                    0224 780362

Dr W. D. S. McLay,
Police Headquarters,
173 Pitt Street,
Glasgow, G2 4JS.
                    041 204 2626

Dr A. H. Milne,
Offshore Medical Support,
Ashgrove Road West,
Aberdeen, AB2 5ES.
                    0224 683111

Dr J. Morrison,
Health and Safety Executive,
Meadow Bank House,
153 London Road,
Edinburgh, EH8 7AU.
                    031 661 6171

Dr E. A. Muir,
Boswell House,
Argyll Square, Oban.
                    0631 3522

Dr D. S. Munro,
Ashfield House,
Milngavie, Glasgow, G62.
                    041 956 1339

Dr J. N. Norman,
Department of Surgery,
University Medical Buildings,
Foresterhill,
Aberdeen, AB9 2ZD.
                    0224 55595

Dr J. G. Page,
16 Stronsay Drive,
Aberdeen, AB2 6EA.
                    0224 31640

Surg. Lt R. Payne,
HM Dockyard,
Rosyth, KY11 2BG.
                    0383 412121

Dr N. M. Piercy,
Castlegate,
25 Bridge Street, Montrose,
Angus, DD10 8AH.
                    0674 2554

Dr P. V. Powell,
Tweedale Surgery,
Fort William,
Inverness-shire, PH33 6EU.
                    0397 3136/7

Dr C. Robinson,
Tweedale Surgery,
Fort William,
Inverness-shire, PH33 6EU.
                    0397 3136/7

Dr I. Ross,
The Foresterhill Health Centre,
Westburn Road,
Aberdeen, AB9 2AY.
                    0224 695949

Dr H. D. Rycroft,
51 Hillhouse Road,
Edinburgh, EH4 3TH.
                    031 332 7696

Dr W. J. C. Scott,*
The Surgery,
75 Bank Street, Alexandria,
Dumbartonshire, G83 0NB.
                    0389 52626

Dr G. G. Shirriffs,
7 Rubislaw Place,
Aberdeen.
                    0224 28968

Dr R. Strachan,
The Foresterhill Health Centre,
Westburn Road,
Aberdeen, AB9 2AY.
                    0224 695949/867516

Dr W. S. Wallace,
The Surgery,
16 Glasgow Street, Millport,
Isle of Cumbrae.
                    047553 338

Dr M. A. White,
The House of Corse,
Lumphanan, Aberdeen.
                    033 983662

Dr I. C. F. Wisley,
Dyce Health Centre,
23A Altronrea Gardens,
Dyce, Aberdeen.
                    0224 722345

NORTHERN IRELAND

Dr J. E. Galway,

Tara,
Brompton Park.
Derryhale, Portadown,
N. Ireland, BT62 3SP.
                    0762 871757

Dr J. T. Sweetnam,
EMAS,
Department of Manpower
Services,
Netherleigh, Massey Avenue,
Belfast, BT4 2JP.
                    0232 63244 Ext 227

CHANNEL ISLANDS

Dr P. D. M. Costen,
Grange End Group Practice,
St Peter Port, Guernsey.
                    0481 24184

ISLE OF MAN

Dr R. Hamm,
46 Lock Promenade,
Douglas, Isle of Man.
                    0624 5490

OTHER COUNTRIES

AUSTRALIA

Dr I. P. Unsworth,
The Southside Diving Clinic,
40 Borrodale Road,
Kingsford, Sydney NSW, 2032.
                    02 663 5108

Dr P. Laverick,
Bass Strait Medical Services,
281 Main Street,
Bairnsdale, Victoria, 3875.
                    051 52 3055

BRUNEI, BORNEO

Dr J. M. Davidson,
Panaga Hospital,
Brunei Shell Petroleum
Co. Ltd, Seria.
                    Panaga 2200

Dr W. G. Bridgwood,
Panaga Hospital,
Brunei Shell Petroleum
Co. Ltd, Seria.
                    Panaga 2200

Dr G. M. Duff,
PML,
Brunei Shell Petroleum
Co. Ltd, Seria.
                    Not known

FRANCE

Dr M. B. Comet,
Comex,
Avenue de la Soude,
13009 Marseille.
                    091 410170

Dr X. Fructus,
Comex,
Traverse de la Jarre,
13275 Marseille Cedex 2.
                    091 410170

IRISH REPUBLIC

Dr D. Donovan,
Cork Offshore Medical Centre,

Silverdale,
Ballinlough, Cork.
    Cork 33863/33438/33624

Prof. J. D. Kennedy,
University Department of
Pathology,
Regional Hospital,
Galway.
    Galway 4141 Ext 417

Dr B. F. M. Powell,
12 Cullenswood Park,
Ranelagh,
Dublin 6.
        974588

ITALY

Dr C. Barnini,
Corso Plebisciti 15,
20123 Milan.
    02 4983141

Dr A. Marroni,
PO Box 876,
Milan.
    02 4045210

Dr G. Oriani,
Via Bergognone Da Fossano
31, Milan.
    02 8326426

Dr Zannini,
Instituto di Medicina Del
Lavoro,
Universita Di Genova,
Ospedali Civili—16132,
Genova.
    0 10 509093

THE NETHERLANDS

Dr P. D. Boomsma,
Medical Adviser,
Duik-Berginsbedrijf,
'Energie' BV,
PO Box 27, Dracten.
    0 5120 12852

Dr A. A. Schouten,
Moerbeiboom 37,
4104 WC Culemborg.
    Not known

Dr L. M. Schrier,
Royal Netherlands Navy,
Mijnendienst,
Bassingracht 106,
1781 Den Helder.
    0 2230 11234

Dr W. Sterk,
Liniewegs 5,
7921 VK Zuidwolde.
    0 5287 1834

NEW ZEALAND

Dr A. G. Slark,
6 Victoria Road,
Devon Port, Auckland 9.
    09 543 483

Dr P. D. Veitch,
Shell BP+Todd Oil Services
Ltd,
167 Devon Street West,
New Plymouth.
    0 67 87609

NIGERIA

Dr R. J. Hamshere,
MEDW,
Shell Development Co.
of Nigeria Ltd,
Private Mail Bag 2418,
21/22 Marina, Lagos.
    Not known

NORWAY

Surg. Lt Cdr S. Eidsvik SJ,
Sj Forsvarets UVB—
Dykkerlege,
Postboks 26,
5078 Haakonsvern.
    05 212000 Ext 699

Dr J. J. Jorgensen,
Mobile Exploration Norway
Inc,
Borehaugen 1,
PO Box 510,
4001 Stavanger.
    045 33500

Dr B. Minsaas,
Oljedirektoratet,
Postboks 600,
4001 Stavanger.
    045 32100

Dr T. Nome,
Ovre Holmegt 15,
400 Stavanger.
    045 21520

Dr J. Smith-Sversten,
PO Box 73,
N 5078 Haakonsvern.
    05 212000 Ext 700

SAUDI ARABIA

Dr A. Downie,
Arabian American Oil Co.,
Occupational Medicine
Division,
Rm K-108 Clinic C,
PO Box 76, Dhahran.
    Not known

SINGAPORE

Dr G. Chan,
Chan Clinic,
Blk. 452 1773 Avenue 10,
Ang Mo K10,
Singapore 2056.
    4531007

TRINIDAD

Dr H. J. M. Spicer,
9A Stanmore Avenue,
Port of Spain,
Trinidad.
    809 62 53959

USA

Dr C. G. Daugherty,
Medical Arts Clinic,
1120 Avenue G,
Bay City, Tex. 7714.
    713 245 5721

Dr A. Dick,
Duke University Medical
Centre,
Box 3823,
Durham, NC 27710.
    919 684 3305

Dr T. S. Dunn,
914 Union Street,
New Orleans, La.
    504 561 1051

Dr H. D. Greer,
Santa Barbara Medical
Foundation Clinic,
PO Box 1200,
Santa Barbara, Ca. 93102.
    805 964 6211

Dr W. Kime,
Dive-Med International,
The Gruehn Building,
3001 South Hanover Street,
Baltimore, Md 21225.
    301 539 2787

Dr E. P. Kindwall,

Department of Hyperbaric
Medicine,
St Lukes Hospital,
2900 West Oklahoma Avenue,
Milwaukee, Wis. 53215.
    414 647 6423

Dr P. G. Linaweaver,
Santa Barbara Medical
Foundation Clinic,
PO Box 1200, Ca. 93102.
    805 964 6211

Dr J. R. Serio,
Belle Chasse Medical
Services,
1301 Belle Chasse Highway
North,
Belle Chasse, La 70037.
    504 394 3880

Dr E. L. Sherrer,
Dive-Med International,
The Gruehn Building,
3001 South Hanover Street,
Baltimore, Md 21225.
    301 539 2787

Capt. J. Vorosmarti Jr, USN,
Naval Medical Research Inst.,
National Naval Medical
Centre,
Bethesda, Md 20014.
    Not known

Dr D. A. Youngblood,
Belle Chasse Medical
Services,
1301 Belle Chasse Highway
Belle Chasse, La 70037.
    504 394 3880

UNITED ARAB EMIRATES

Dr I. S. Ayoub,
c/o McDermott Dubai,
PO Box 3098,
Dubai.
    25360

Dr I. Masarik,
Dubai Polytechnic,
PO Box 557,
Dubai.
    Not known

WEST GERMANY

Dr J. Holtaus,
GKSS,
Institut fur Anglagentechnik,
Reaktorstrasse 1,
Postfach 1160,
2054 Geesthact-Tesperhude.
    Not known

NORWAY

All doctors approved by the Secretary of State for Energy and the Secretary of State for Trade in the United Kingdom are also approved by the Norwegian Directorate of Health to perform medical examination of commercial divers and to issue certificates of fitness.
In addition the Norwegian Directorate of Health has approved the following Norwegian doctors to perform medical examination of commercial divers and to issue certificates of fitness. This list is continuously updated and information can be obtained from the Norwegian Petroleum Directorate or The Directorate of Health.

Aasgaard, H. U.,
Sørlandet sjøforsvarsdistrikt,
4600 Kristiansand S.

Andersen, Harald T.,
Flymedisinsk institutt,
Box 281,
Blindern, Oslo 3.

Bang, Arve,
Storhamar legesenter,
2300 Hamar.

Benestad, Hans,
Tynset sykehus,
2500 Tynset.

Bertelsen, Sevald,
Box 274,
9401 Harstad.

Alnæs, Egil,
Flymedisinsk institutt,
Box 281,
Blindern, Oslo 3.

Brekke, Dag,
Fannebakken 21,
6400 Molde.

Brubakk, Alf,
Regionsykehuset i Trondheim,
7000 Trondheim.

Bryne, Tormod,
Elf Aquitaine Norge A/S,
Box 168,
4001 Stavanger.

Christensen, Jan Krogh,
Olavsvern,
9000 Tromsø.

248

Eidsvik, Svein,
5078 Håkonsvern.

Gauperaa, Tore,
Ortopedisk avd,
Regionsykehuset,
9012 Tromsø.

Gjellestad, Axel,
9600 Hammerfest.

Grindheim, Martha,
Oslo brannvesen,
Arne Garborgspl 1,
Oslo 1.

Hansen, Klaus,
Ørland flystasjon,
7130 Brækstad.

Hasselgård, Terje,
6460 Eidsvåg i Romsdal.

Helle, Arthur Odd,
Breivika,
6017 Åsestranda.

Hoddevik, Gunnar Martin,
Bjerkelundsvn 36,
1342 Jar.

Holder, Arild,
Mølnåsen,
9440 Evenskjær.

Høie, Erik,
Langvn 52,
6500 Kristiansand N.

Høstmark, F. O.,
Teglverksvn 2,
3100 Tønsberg.

Ingebrigtsen, Helge,
Andreas Markussonsvei 28,
8015 Hunstad.

Johnsen, Knut Kristian
Strømdalåsen 42,
3700 Skien.

Jørgensen, Knut Jørgen,
Mobil Exploration Norway Inc
Postboks 510,
4001 Stavanger.

Karlsen, Kåre,
Mobil Exploration Norway Inc
Postboks 510,
4001 Stavanger.

Kvamme, Odd,
5454 Sæbøvik.

Lehmann, Egil H.,
Institutt for samfunnsmedisin

9010 Åsgård sykehus.

Lindholm, Lars Tvete,
1620 Gressvik.

Loven, Jens-Øyvind,
Mellomveien 92,
9000 Tromsø.

Malde, Kjeld,
Bioddgt 20,
4890 Grimstad.

Midgard, Rune,
Box 26,
5078 Håkonsvern.

Minsaas, Børge,
Oljedirektoratet,
Box 600,
4001 Stavanger.

Moe, Jens,
Elleveien 4,
1440 Drøbak.

Molvær, Otto Inge,
Gravdalsveien 255,
5034 Ytre Laksevåg.

Mortensen, Vidar,
9440 Evenskjær.

Nome, Tor,
Phillips Petroleum Company
Norway,
Box 69,
4001 Stavanger.

Offer-Ohlsen, Dag,
Legekontoret for sjømenn i
Oslo,
Grev Wedelspl 7,
Oslo 1.

Olafsrud, Arve,
Sentrum Felles
Bedriftslegekontor,
Kirkegt 14-16-18^v,
Oslo 1.

Olaussen, Jørg Petter,
Box 10,
6420 Aukra.

Olsen, Pål,
9442 Ramsund.

Owe, Jan Ove,
Flymedisinsk Institutt,
Box 281,
Blindern,
Oslo 3.

Pettersen, Jon Elling,

Vindalsringen 25,
3700 Skien.

Ragnum, Tor William,
Marinebasen,
3190 Horten.

Schaaning, Jan,
Havstenlia 1,
7000 Trondheim.

Schumann-Andersen, Jon,
Helneveien 51,
1600 Fredrikstad.

Sivertsen, Olav M.,
Anestesiavd,
Regionsykehuset i Tromsø,
9012 Tromsø.

Sleire, Laura,
Markeveien 8-10,
5000 Bergen.

Smith-Sivertsen, Jens,
5078 Håkonsvern.

Sollie, Per,
Ullevålsveien 58,
Oslo 4.

Stordahl, Arvid,
Sentralsykehuset i
Kristiansand,
4600 Kristiansand S.

Stray, Per Andreas,
Haukelandsbakken 18A,
5000 Bergen.

Sugar, Endre,
Åsveien 23,
1320 Stabekk.

Syverstad, Odd T.,
Smidsrødveien 7,
3130 Teie.

Tamber, Einar Rolf,
Box 40,
7733 Namdalseid.

Thorsvik, Dagfinn,
7650 Verdal.

Tyssebotn, Ingvald Mikal,
Fysiologisk Institutt,
Årstadveien 19,
5000 Bergen.

Tønjum, Stein,
5016 Haukeland sjukehus.

Vea, Gunnar,
5078 Håkonsvern.

Wolff, Stein Sydengen,
1674 Vesterøy.

The Norwegian Directorate of
Health has also approved the
following foreign doctors.

Charlick, B. J.,
Merseyside,
England.

Childs, C. M.,
Aberdeen,
Scotland.

Conrad, G. W.,
New York,
USA.

Fallowfield, T. L.,
Aberdeen,
Scotland.

Greer, H. G. III,
California,
USA.

Jacquin, M.,
Marseille,
France.

Norman, J. N.,
Aberdeen,
Scotland.

Serio, J. R.,
California,
USA.

Sterk, W.,
Zuidwolde,
The Netherlands.

Garfield, J. W.,
Mobil Oil Corporation,
New York.

Meredith, J. R.,
Mobil Oil Corporation,
Princeton,
New Jersey.

Grisdale, W. R.,
Mobil Oil Canada Ltd,
Calgary,
Alberta.

UNITED STATES OF AMERICA

The patient has the right to
consult the doctor of his
choice.

12.14 PROCEDURES FOLLOWING A FATAL ACCIDENT

It is the responsibility of a medical practitioner to certify the fact of death. This should be done as soon as possible. In the UK, the body is the legal property of the Coroner from the time of death.

What to do with the body

DECOMPRESSION
Standard decompression schedules are not applicable to a dead body. After death has been confirmed, the body should first be left at pressure for about one hour. Decompression at about 2 m/min. can then be carried out. This should allow the release of free gas without causing excessive tissue damage. Too slow a decompression will cause greater tissue damage due to decomposition.

STORAGE
The optimum temperature conditions for the preservation of a body are between 0°C and 4°C, and on no account should it be frozen before an autopsy has been performed. When no refrigeration is available, enclosing the body in a polythene bag and surrounding it with ice is sufficient. Minimal interference should be maintained and the diving suit left intact. The body should remain in the diving suit until the time of autopsy.

TRANSPORTATION
The body should be transported ashore as soon as possible.
In the UK, arrangements should be made with the local Coroner's Officer to transport the body to a mortuary.
Outside the UK, the services of an undertaker with experience in this field should be sought. In the absence of such help, the following outline of procedures to be adopted may be helpful.

RETURN OF A BODY TO THE UNITED KINGDOM
A medical certificate, giving the cause or circumstances of death, must be obtained from the appropriate authorities who will also give written authorisation for export of the body. Several copies of such documents should be made immediately. For air transportation, the body has to be embalmed before being sealed in a zinc-lined box. Embalming may have to be performed by a medical officer where local custom dictates. On arrival in the UK the body passes into the custody of the Coroner into whose area it is imported. The Coroner will decide whether to order an autopsy. The foreign certificate is usually acceptable to the Registrar of Births, Marriages and Deaths of the district in which burial is to take place. A Certificate of No Liability to Register is issued giving authorisation for burial. When cremation is required the procedure can become more complicated. The foreign certificate may not be acceptable to the medical referee of the crematorium who may then require an autopsy or have the case reported to the Coroner for autopsy.

EXPORT OF A BODY FROM THE UNITED KINGDOM
Embalming and sealing in a zinc-lined coffin is necessary. An Out of England Certificate from the Coroner is required before authorisation can be obtained from the Home Office to allow the body to leave the country. A similar procedure holds in Scotland involving the Procurator Fiscal and the Scottish Home and Health Department. In addition, some countries require a certificate stating that no infectious or communicable disease was present at the time of death.

LEGAL CONSIDERATIONS AFFECTING THE BODY
Once the fact of death is established, there is usually a process of law to be followed. Around the world, systems of investigation of sudden, violent or unexplained death fall into three main groups.

1. CORONER SYSTEM
   Countries with a common law background which include England and many of its colonies, ex-colonies and dominions.
   In Scotland a similar system is operated through the Procurator Fiscal.
   In Britain, when the order for the autopsy is given by the Coroner or Procurator Fiscal, the body passes into his custody. Only following the conclusion of the investigation is it released to the next of kin.

2. MEDICAL EXAMINER SYSTEM
   In the United States a medically qualified executive officer is appointed.

3. CONTINENTAL SYSTEM
   In this system, those deaths which have aroused the suspicions of the police are investigated. In the Netherlands, for example, the public prosecutor appoints the Lijkschouwer to investigate unexplained deaths or cases for cremation; in Denmark there is the Ligsynsmand, who has a similar duty which is, however, very rarely performed.

Autopsies are not allowed in Muslim countries as a general principle.

What to do with the diver's personal equipment

After the recovery of the body there must be minimal interference with its associated equipment. Open valves should be turned off. A safe record must be made of any turns of valves, if necessary marking their position with paint before sealing to await expert technical examination. Closed valves should be left closed. Everything must be sealed off and the equipment placed in a polythene bag for later examination by the authorities.
When gas cylinders are to be sent for laboratory analysis, it should be noted that, under current air transport freight regulations, they cannot be transported by air whilst containing pressurised gas. It will probably be necessary to have the gas tested on-site before transporting the equipment.
The equipment remains the property of the diving company but it will have to be presented to the local police, Coroner, or equivalent local legal authority.

Organisation of accident investigation

Following a fatal accident an investigation is essential for three reasons.

1. To establish the facts of the case.
2. To establish the cause of the accident.
3. To enable changes in procedure and equipment to be made to prevent a future recurrence.

It is usually mandatory that at some time the local legal authorities are involved, and this may also be so where injuries are non-fatal.

In the offshore situation most accidents require the expertise of medical, engineering and technical personnel to arrive at a satisfactory explanation. Team work with a central co-ordinator such as the Coroner or Procurator Fiscal is therefore very important. In the UK, the Department of Energy Diving Inspector takes charge of the investigation.

Even where there is no authority such as a Coroner, such a team, investigating on behalf of the employer or operator, will be most likely to arrive at factual, objective conclusions. Such a team may also be welcomed by local authorities who lack the technical expertise to conduct their own investigations in this specialised field.

ACCIDENT HISTORY

It is imperative that a proper and detailed history of the events leading up to the accident is obtained. This may be a difficult and tedious procedure, but if it is not properly performed it can prejudice the whole investigation. In any accident situation, witnesses' accounts are often confused. They can be simplified by establishing a strict chronological plan. All witnesses should be interviewed alone at the earliest possible time after the accident. More accurate descriptions are obtained if witnesses are questioned directly than if they are just asked to submit statements. If possible, the interviews should be tape-recorded and the recordings written out.

At every stage, photography must be used to record the scene and equipment. Ideally, shots should be taken from each quarter with a measurement scale appearing in each picture.

When a detailed report is being compiled, all original notes must be kept for future reference in court.

Log books and tapes should be examined before commencing any interviews. No details should be omitted and facts such as subjective indications of trivial illness and the time of the last meal should be recorded. A check list can be used so that all aspects are covered. It is to be remembered that accidents are more usually caused by passive negligence rather than active negligence.

Accident check list

1. MEDICAL HISTORY OF VICTIM
   Pre-existing disease.
   Recent illness.
   Last physical examination.

2. PERSONAL HISTORY OF VICTIM
   Diving experience and training.
   Previous diving accidents/near-accidents.

3. ENVIRONMENT
   Location.
   Weather.
   Sea state.
   Visibibility.
   Wind.
   Temperature: at surface, at working depth.
   Hazards: cables, rig legs, underwater obstructions, valves, pipes, propellers, tides, currents, visibility, water jets, any explosive demolition in the vicinity, any other.

4. DIVE PROFILE
   History of recent dives.
   Depth and duration.
   Current dive profile.
   Dive of tender or buddy.
   Ascent speed.
   Stops and untoward incidents.
   Pre-dive events.
   Food.
   Alcohol.
   Drugs.
   Pre-dive behaviour.
   Events in recovery, resuscitation, therapy, recompression.

5. DIVING EQUIPMENT
   Suit and gloves.
   Helmet/mask.
   Valves.
   Weight belt.
   Gas bottles.
   Gas mixture and flow rates.
   Purity of gas.
   Buoyancy vest.
   Depth gauge.
   Cylinder contents.
   Safety line/umbilical.
   Knife.

6. TIMING
   Establish precise chronological order of events.

7. DIVING TASK DETAILS

8. PERSONNEL
   Names, with respective duties, of all involved.

13.1 EMERGENCY MEDICAL CENTRES

Australia

Diving Medical Centre,
2B Hale Road, Mosman,
New South Wales 2088.
Tel: (02) 905 422
(02) 771 3333

Dr Carl Edmonds,
25 Battle Boulevarde,
Seaforth,
New South Wales 2092.
After hrs Tel: (02) 949 5547

The Prince Henry Hospital,
Casualty Department,
Little Bay, Sydney.
Tel: (02) 661 0111
Request diver aid

HMAS Penguin,
Balmoral, Sydney.
Tel: (02) 960 0444
Request medical officer on duty

Diving Medical Centre,
132 Yallambee Road,
Jindalee, Brisbane,
Queensland 4074.
Tel: (07) 376 1414

Diving Medical Clinic, Perth,
135 Dunedin Street,
Mt Hawthorn,
Western Australia 6016.
Tel: (09) 444 8296
(09) 383 1636

Dr George Clegg,
2 Aristride Avenue,
Kallaroo,
Western Australia 6025.
Tel: (09) 401 2167
(09) 451 3667

Dr Greg Deleuil,
135 Dunedin Street,
Mt Hawthorn,
Western Australia 6016.
Tel: (09) 444 8296

Bass Strait Medical Services,
Main Street Medical Centre,
281 Main Street,
Bairnsdale, Victoria 3875.
Tel: (051) 52 3055

Brunei

Hospital Panaga,
Brunei Shell Petroleum Co. Ltd,
Seria.
Tel: (Panaga) 2200

Denmark

Denmark has no 24-hour emergency facility; however, the Naval Rescue Centre have helicopters available for emergency transportation and, as they work in conjunction with other Naval facilities, would be able to advise on available chamber facilities.

Sovaernets Opperative Komando,
(Naval Rescue Centre),
PO Box 483,
DK 8100 Aarhus C.
Tel: (06 123 099)

Greece

No official diving centre exists, but the three hyperbaric facilities can be consulted. Telephone confirmation of availability is indispensible.

Naval Hospital of Piraeus,
65 Akti Mutsopulu,
Piraeus.
Tel: 451 2466

Naval Hospital of Crete,
Arsenal of Crete,
Soudha/Chania.
Tel: (0821) 89306
(0821) 89309

General Hospital of Kalymnos
(Vouvalion).
Tel: (0243) 28851

Italy

Hyperbaric Medical Centre CMI,
Zigonia Bergamo,
Corso Venezia, 5.
Tel: (035) 884 406

Ospedale S. Martini Istituto
Medicina del Lavoro
Genova, Via S. Benedetto XV, 10.
Tel: (010) 504158

Japan

Japan has no 24-hour facility

Kyushu Rosai Hospital,
1-3-1- Takamatsu Kuzuhara,
Kokura Minami-ku,
Kitakyushu-shi, 800-02.
Tel: (093) 471 1121

Department of Public Health,
School of Medicine,
Tokyo Medical and Dental University,
1-5-45 Yushima,
Bunkyo-ku, Tokyo, 113.
Tel: (03) 813 6111

Department of Hygiene,
Saitama Medical School,
38 Morohongo,
Moroyama, Iruma-gun,
Saitama, 350-04.
Tel: (04929) 4 1212

JMSDF
2-7-1 Nagase,
Yokosuka-shi, 239.
Tel: (0468) 41 7650

Department of Anaesthetics,
585 Yogi,
Naha-shi, 902.
Tel: (0988) 87 0101

Netherlands

Diving Medical Centre,
Royal Netherlands Navy,
MCM Barracks,
Bassingracht 106,
1781 CJ Den Helder.
Tel: (02230) 11234 ext 3306
or 3273. After hrs and
weekends: (02230) 11234 and
ask for the duty officer MCM
Barracks or the duty officer
of the Commander in Chief.

New Zealand

Royal New Zealand Naval Hospital,
6 Victoria Street,
Devonport,
Auckland.
Tel: 454 000
Ask for the duty staff officer
of the naval base.
Recompression chamber
O_2 and air only.

Princess Margaret Hospital,
Christchurch.
Tel: 792 900 or 799 160
Contact Dr H. Guy.
Air recompression chamber only.

Shell BP Todd Oil Services,
New Plymouth.
Tel: 87609
or New Plymouth Police.

The MV Stena Constructor, 22 miles offshore, has a 12 man saturation diving and air diving system where casualties can be treated. It operates all year.

Nigeria

No formal arrangements exist.   Telephone home base.

Norway

Diving Medical Centre,
Stavanger.
Tel: (010) 47045
(010) 50119
(010) 51190

Rogaland Hospital,
Stavanger.
Tel: (4) 53 10 00
Ask for the oil duty doctor
(will inform about
diving doctor on call).

The Provisional Regulations for diving on the Norwegian continental shelf (issued by the Norwegian Petroleum Directorate 1980) state that:

'The diving contractor shall have a liaison agreement with a medical doctor experienced in hyperbaric medicine and approved by the Directorate of Health. Name and address of the doctor shall be submitted to the Norwegian Petroleum Directorate.'

List of doctors approved by the Norwegian Ministry of Health

Professor C. J. Lambertsen, MD,
217 Glenn Road, Ardmore,
Pa. 19003, USA.
Tel: (010 39)
2 498 3141

Mr Cesare Barnini, MD,
Corso Pleibisciti 15,
20123 Milano, Italy.

Dr P. B. James,   Tel: (0382) 60111
University Department of   ext 2417
Community & Occupational Medicine,
Medical School,
Ninewell, Dundee,
DD1 9SY, Scotland, UK.

Dr C. Childs,   Tel: (0224) 555 95
Institute of Environmental
and Offshore Medicine,
9 Rubislaw Terrace,
Aberdeen, AB1 1XE, UK.

Dr J. N. Norman,   Tel: (0224) 555 95
Department of Surgery,
University Medical Buildings,
Foresterhill,
Aberdeen, AB9 2ZD, UK.

Dr W. Sterk,   Tel: (010 31) 5287 1834
Liniewegs 5,
7921 UK Zuidwolde,
The Netherlands.

Dr N. I. P. MacKie,   Tel: (09) 425 1211
Medical Adviser,
Woodside Petroleum Ltd,
77 St George's Terrace,
Perth,
Western Australia, 6000.

Stein Tønjum,
Norsk Undervannsinstitutt,
Gravdalsveien 255,
5035 Ytre Laksevag,
Norway.

Dr X. Fructus,   Tel: (010 3391) 410170
Comex,
Traverse de la Jarre,
Marseille, France.

Saudi Arabia

Arabian American Oil Company,   Tel: (Ras Tanura)
West pier, Ras Tanura,   81248
Dhahran.

Dr A. Downie,   Tel: (Dhahran) 48790
Arabian American Oil Company, After hrs: (Dhahran) 62959
Medical Services Organisation,
Dhahran.

Singapore

Naval Diving Unit Medical Centre,   Tel: (01065) 456 2244
Terror Camp, Sembawang,   ext 51140
Singapore, 27.

If the diving company provides chamber facilities:

Dr Gene Chan,   Tel: (01065) 453 1007
Chan Clinic,
1773, Blk 452, Avenue 10,
Ang Mo Kio,
Singapore, 20.

Spain

Cencro de Recuperacion e   Tel: (343) 318 7749
Investigaciones Submarinas
Pelayo 32,
Barcelona 1.

Sweden

Diving Medical Centre,   Tel: (0750) 63000
Marinens Dykericentrum,   Office hours only.
S-130 61 Horsfjarden.

Switzerland

Diving Medical Centre,   Tel: (01) 255 1111
Universitatsspital Zurich,   (01) 255 2036
Druckkammerlabor,   (01) 252 6454
Ramistrasse 100,
CH-8091 Zurich.

Hospital Cantonal,   Tel: (021) 411 111
CH-1000 Lausanne.

United Arab Emirates

Dubai Polyclinic,   Tel: 422 225 or 422 215
PO Box 557, Dubai.   After hrs: 443 519

In conjunction with
Hydrospace International   Tel: 470 605
Division of Oceaneering.   After hrs: 440 243

United States of America

The National Diving   Tel: (919) 684 8111
Accident Network,
F. G. Hall Laboratory,
Duke University Medical Center,
Box 3823, Durham,
NC 27710.

Telephone collect if necessary and ask for **Diving Accident
Network or DAN.** The Network serves seven regions: South-
east, North-east, Mid West, Gulf, North-west, South-west
and the Pacific.

United Kingdom

Offshore Medical Support,   Tel: (0224) 871848
12 Sunnybank Road,   Aircall.
Aberdeen, AB2 5EF.   Tlx: 73677 CASVAC G

North Sea Medical Centre,   Tel: (0493) 61617
3 Lowestoft Road,   After hrs: (0493) 63264
Gorleston-on-Sea,   Tlx: 975118 NORMED G
Great Yarmouth,
Norfolk, NR31 6QB.

HMS Vernon   Tel: (0705) 22351 ext 2375/7
Portsmouth,   Superintendent of Diving.
Hampshire.   After hrs: (0705) 22351 ext 2413/4/5
                                     Duty Lieutenant Commander.

London Hyperbaric   Tel: 935 0023 or 274 3171
(Medical Services)   or Securicor radio network
126 Ferndale Road,   (01) 233 1901 call to be
London, SE24 0AA.   relayed to 'Ray Hazel One.'

Diving Medical Service, Plymouth,   Tel: (0752) 261 910
This is a private line   Ask for the duty diving doctor.
'Aircall' and the duty
doctor is equipped with a pager.

West Germany

Naval Medical Institute,   Tel: (0431) 54391
Schiffahrtsmedizinisches,
Institut der Bundesmarine.
2300 Kiel-Kronshagen.

13.2 OFFSHORE DIVING EMERGENCY PROCEDURES

The management and co-ordination requirements of a major offshore diving accident will involve a heavy commitment by both the diving company and the client oil company.

The level of capability of this effort will vary greatly in different parts of the world. The following example illustrates the arrangements that apply to the UK sector of the North Sea.

Sector clubs

The North Sea has been divided into sectors, each of which can be conveniently co-ordinated by one of the principal oil operators. The major accidents which can be effectively handled include rig abandonment or lost bell situations where assistance from other diving support vessels might be needed.

The system provides a weekly status of vessels in any sector with emergency support capability, including diving and submersible support vessels. The same information is available from other sectors through the sector club co-ordinators. This helps in the selection of the best available vessel to help in a diving emergency from the point of view of distance, state of readiness, capability, etc.

The ultimate responsibility for any emergency lies with the oil operator, but primary safety responsibility for the divers remains with the diving contractor. The choice of the centralised co-ordination facilities site is extremely important and depending on circumstances could be set up either at the oil operator's or the diving contractor's offices.

The actual arrangements are made as a part of the contract negotiations and take into consideration the local capabilities.

The onshore plan will ensure good communications arrangements, the recall of key personnel, and establishment of the centre for operations. Liaison would be set up with the sector club co-ordinators, other vessels, diving contractors, coastguard, police, helicopter services, Department of Energy, press, etc. Offshore, an onboard procedure would include the general organisation, individual responsibilities and communications. In particular, a very clear line of communication would be established between the vessel (Master and diving supervisor), installation/platform and shore.

A TYPICAL EXAMPLE OF PROCEDURES
An example of the organisation needed to deal with a diving emergency might be as follows.

1. Offshore field personnel
(a) Diving supervisor handles emergency action as necessary, calling his duty personnel and informing vessel's master, oil operator's representative and his own head office.

(b) Oil operator's representative calls his duty engineer/operations personnel onshore as required, and alerts OIM of nearest platform if appropriate. He sets up a communication link and undertakes liaison responsibility between the diving supervisor, vessel, platform and shore as required.

(c) The responsibility for diving action must remain with the diving contractor's offshore diving supervisor, with advice from their own management as necessary, and back-up from the oil operator if required.

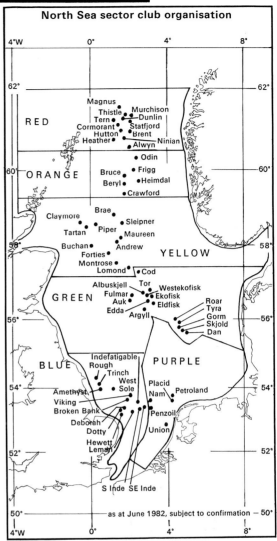

North Sea sector club organisation

as at June 1982, subject to confirmation

Consultation should take place as soon as possible between the two supervisors, but it is likely that the supervisor of the rescue vessel (who has responsibility for his own divers and diving equipment) will take charge of the rescue operation. If, due to poor or nonexistent communications, it is not possible to obtain this endorsement, then the diving supervisor of the rescue vessel should assume responsibility for the rescue if his own divers and equipment are going to be used.

2. Oil company shore representative

(a) Immediately calls diving contractor's contact staff and other emergency personnel as required. He clears the lines of communication from offshore, and sets up an emergency room. He contacts sector club co-ordinator.

(b) This should be all in accordance with an established procedure previously agreed with all departments and the contractor. Subsequent actions would be in accordance with developing requirements.

It must be emphasised that a co-ordinated effort with good communications and a clear channel of command is the key to success.

HYPERBARIC RESCUE

Hyperbaric rescue is the means by which a diver or divers may be taken from within their normal diving system location to another system without any change in pressure, for medical or safety reasons.

Hyperbaric evacuation must be regarded as the very last resort in an emergency. This is because premature evacuation, or the evacuation itself, may introduce a greater risk to the divers than the initial emergency. This will depend greatly on the circumstances at the time.

A special procedure is produced for each evacuation system and this should take into account the possibility of the vessel listing, the loss of mains electrical power and the possible loss of the use of a crane.

At present Norway is the only country that requires the full hyperbaric evacuation capability by law. The UK requires only the capability to use the transfer under pressure diver rescue system.

The rescue of divers under pressure may arise from any of the following situations:

—Their support vessel being in danger of capsizing or sinking.

—The presence of an unacceptable fire or explosion risk or an occurrence such as a blow-out.

—A fire or other disaster within the diving system.

—A medical problem with one or more of the divers that can be more safely treated elsewhere and does not incur unreasonable risk during transfer.

—A lost bell.

There are several options which can be used, depending on the circumstances and location. These include:

1. The TUP diver rescue system.

2. A hyperbaric lifeboat.

3. A hyperbaric rescue chamber.

4. A bell-to-bell transfer.

5. A bell used as a rescue chamber.

1. The TUP (transfer under pressure diver rescue system).

For a medical evacuation, the medical team managing the case needs to satisfy itself that the patient's condition is stable enough to cope with hyperbaric evacuation. In such a case, it is anticipated that there would be adequate time to organise the hyperbaric transfer.

If the need arises for the evacuation of a whole diving crew from a pressurised system offshore under emergency conditions, the use of these flying hyperbaric rescue chambers may be considered among the possible alternatives.

The system, which currently operates for the North Sea, comprises:

—One single man transfer chamber made of titanium 2.34×0.81 m (7′ 8″×2′ 8″), weighing 277 kg (610 lb) and having a maximum working pressure of 23 bar (335 psi).

The transfer chamber is meant to allow the transfer of a patient from a diving complex to the bigger helicopter chamber. Although it is designed as a one-man chamber, two men could be crammed into it for a short time. It requires six men to carry it.

—One helicopter chamber made of titanium, 2.6× 1.14 m (8′ 6″×4′), weighing 794 kg (1750 lb) and having a maximum working pressure of 23 bar (335 psi).

This chamber is light enough to be transported by a Sikorski S-61 helicopter along with the transfer chamber and the life support equipment.

Although it is designed primarily to allow a doctor to administer care to a patient during transport, up to 8 men could be fitted into it if necessary.

—All this equipment is compatible with the hospital hyperbaric therapeutic chamber set up in Dyce at the premises of IUC (International Underwater Contractors) in the ownership of the Grampian Health Board Hyperbaric Centre (GHB).

MOBILISATION

The need to transfer a sick diver from an offshore installation to shore would normally be identified by the doctor retained by the diving contractor. He would advise the supervisor who would then liaise through his head office with the client oil company requesting the use of transfer chambers from Offshore Medical Support (OMS).

Grampian Health Board's agreement is required before a final decision is made to transfer the diver into the GHB hospital chambers in Dyce. This agreement is sought by OMS. If it is impossible (GHB chambers technically unavailable or already in use, etc.), the use of alternative chambers may be contemplated.

Compatibility of these rescue chambers with all the UK offshore worksites is a UK Department of Energy requirement. Adaptor/spool pieces are normally stored offshore with the diving spread.

OPERATION OF THE TRANSFER CHAMBERS

—They belong to a group of oil companies.

—They are administered by OMS.

—They are managed technically by IUC.

—Compatibility and smooth transfer from the offshore installation to the rescue chambers is the responsibility of the diving contractor involved.

—The medical management of the patient being transferred by the rescue chamber remains with the doctor contracted to the diving company. When the diver has been locked into the hospital chamber at Dyce the effective transfer is complete. The GHB assume responsibility thereafter.

OPERATION OF THE SHORE-BASED HOSPITAL CHAMBERS

—They belong to the GHB.

—They are managed technically by IUC.

—They are located at the premises of IUC.

—The medical management is the responsibility of the GHB.

—They are maintained in a state of readiness for major surgery.

There can be many variations depending on circumstances, such as the use of a boat instead of a helicopter and variations in the gas handling.

TYPICAL TUP DIVER RESCUE OPERATION

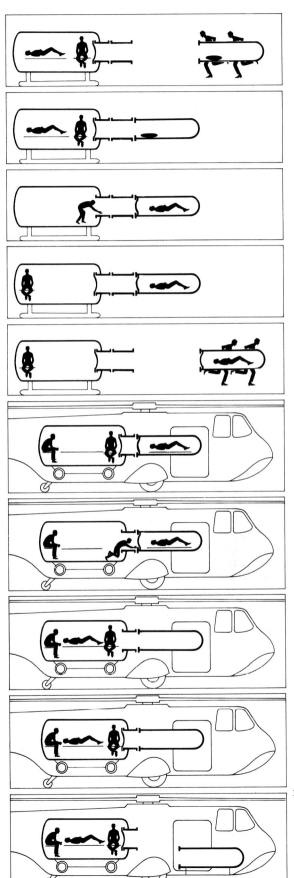

1.—The adaptor spool is connected to the DCC.
  —The helicopter carrying the system arrives.
  —An electrical lead with special plug is led to the helicopter to provide a 24V supply to conserve its batteries for running the chamber's life-support system on the way inshore.
  —An HP gas hose with a special quick connector is passed to the helicopter to pressure-up the helicopter chamber.
  —The transfer chamber is manhandled from the helicopter to the DCC.

2.—The transfer chamber is connected to the adaptor spool and its door is left open. The transfer chamber and trunking can be equalised with the DCC. The equalisation can be by direct piping to the DCC (in which case the DCC chamber pressure will require to be maintained) or by a separate whip connection to the trunking or transfer chamber from a suitable gas supply.

3.—The attendant opens the door of the DCC.
  —The attendant transfers the diver into the transfer chamber.

4.—When everything is ready for a quick transfer, the attendant fits and shuts the door of the transfer chamber. It is held shut until a seal is obtained. At this point, the helicopter chamber with medic(s) is pressured up.
  —The attendant shuts the door of the DCC and holds until a seal is obtained by venting the trunking.
  —The trunking is then fully depressurised and the DCC pressure adjusted if necessary.

5.—The crew disconnect the transfer chamber and manhandle it (using a crane if necessary) to the helicopter.
  The period whilst the diver is alone and inaccessible in the transfer chamber should be as short as possible and the chamber should be handled gently.

6.—The transfer chamber is connected to the helicopter chamber.
  —The medical attendants in the helicopter equalise the trunking with the helicopter and transfer chamber.

7.—The helicopter chamber attendant opens the doors to allow the diver through.

8.—The diver is brought through into the helicopter chamber and attended by the doctor and attendant.

9.—The attendant shuts the helicopter chamber door and holds until a seal is obtained by venting the transfer chamber and trunking.

10.—The transfer chamber is disconnected when completely depressurised.

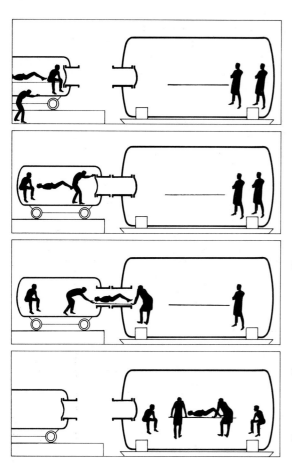

11.—The helicopter delivers the system to the nearest heliport or helipad. From there it is conveyed by the diver system hydraulic trolley to the GHB facility at Dyce.
  —The helicopter chamber is transported to the hospital chamber which has been prepared with the correct pressure, gas mix and medical equipment, materials and personnel.

12.—The helicopter chamber is connected to the hospital chamber.
  —The trunking is equalised with the two chambers.

13.—The chamber doors are opened and the diver transferred into the hospital chamber.

14.—All personnel under pressure locate in the hospital chamber.
  —The door is closed.
  —The trunking is vented to obtain a seal.

15.—The patient can then receive a very high standard of medical attention.

2. Hyperbaric lifeboat

The hyperbaric lifeboat consists of a compression chamber housed inside a lifeboat. It provides a means of evacuating an entire team of divers whilst under pressure from a vessel.

To be able to carry this out, the hyperbaric lifeboat's compression chamber is kept pressured up and mated with the deck chamber system via a trunking arrangement. If used, the divers transfer under pressure into the lifeboat and the trunking clamp is released. The boat, with its crew and divers under pressure, is then launched into the sea. The lifeboat can head away under its own power. It is then intended to be lifted out of the water and mated with another system to undertake the decompression.

3. Hyperbaric rescue chamber

Hyperbaric rescue chambers are compression chambers provided with ballast and buoyancy to ensure a stable floating configuration when launched into the sea. They will also have fenders and a basic life-support package.

They differ from hyperbaric lifeboats in not having an outside crew or any motive power. The self-help capability is therefore minimal and the system requires greater assistance from topside personnel than a hyperbaric lifeboat.

Like the hyperbaric lifeboat, the rescue chambers are normally kept mated with the DCC system. They may be ready pressured up and available for immediate use. A deck crane or dedicated launching

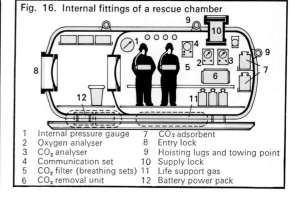

Fig. 15. Hyperbaric lifeboat

1	Hyperbaric chamber	6	Control panel
2	Entry pressure door	7	Mixed gas
3	Exit pressure door	8	Lifeboat cockpit
4	Supply lock	9	Propulsion unit (engine)
5	Oxygen		

Fig. 16. Internal fittings of a rescue chamber

1	Internal pressure gauge	7	CO_2 adsorbent
2	Oxygen analyser	8	Entry lock
3	CO_2 analyser	9	Hoisting lugs and towing point
4	Communication set	10	Supply lock
5	CO_2 filter (breathing sets)	11	Life support gas
6	CO_2 removal unit	12	Battery power pack

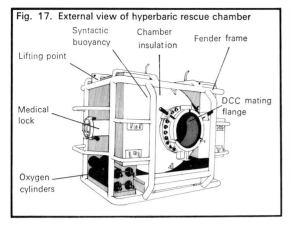

Fig. 17. External view of hyperbaric rescue chamber

Lifting point
Syntactic buoyancy
Chamber insulation
Fender frame
Medical lock
DCC mating flange
Oxygen cylinders

Bell Emergency Communication

For use between the crew of a lost craft and rescue divers

Code	Situation
3.3.3	Communication opening procedure (inside & outside)
1	Yes or affirmative or agreed
3	No or negative or disagreed
2.2	Repeat please
2	Stop
5	Have you got a seal?
6	Stand by to be pulled up
1.2.1.2	Get ready for through water transfer (open your hatch)
2.3.2.3	You will NOT release your ballasts
4.4	Do release your ballast in 30 minutes from now
1.2.3	DO increase your pressure
3.3.3	Communication closing procedure (inside & outside)

system may be used for the launching and assistance is required from the surface diving crew. In practice, the chamber is either dropped onto another vessel alongside or into the water and towed away for later retrieval. The decompression would normally be carried out after the divers have been transferred under pressure to another DCC system.

There is considerable variation in the design of these systems but a common feature of all is the general capability to evacuate an entire team of divers under pressure.

4. Bell-to-bell transfer

Bell-to-bell transfer may be carried out to rescue divers from a lost or entrapped bell, or to evacuate a diving spread. The following illustration shows how a bell-to-bell transfer may be carried out from a trapped bell.

In this procedure, one or more divers swim from the bell of their own diving spread to the bell of a second spread at the same depth. The two diving spreads may be on the same vessel or on separate vessels.

In the case of a lost or entrapped bell, the UK AODC has produced a tapping code to assist with communicating with the divers inside the stricken bell. This is reproduced above and is normally written on

a plastic card kept within the bell.

Emergency bell location arrangements are required by law by the UK and Norwegian Governments. These include the use of a 37.5 kHz acoustic transponder on the bell and a diver-held transponder which provides range and bearing data. Full details are given in the AODC publication, *Emergency diving bell recovery: Location of a diving bell.*

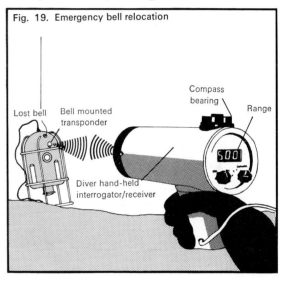

Fig. 19. Emergency bell relocation

Lost bell
Bell mounted transponder
Compass bearing
Range
Diver hand-held interrogator/receiver

5. Bell used as a rescue chamber

In this case, a diving bell is used as a rescue chamber. The divers would prepare the bell as well as possible for the transfer. Umbilicals, helmets, etc., can be removed and additional life-support materials, provisions and equipment could be taken in.

Special provision can be made in the bell to make this possible. This can include additional life-support capability, special ballast/buoyancy arrangements, restraining harnesses on seats and special launch and recovery facilities.

The number of divers that can be rescued using this method is limited. Ideally it should only be considered as viable when there is a second diving system within easy reach which has a compatible flange mating facility.

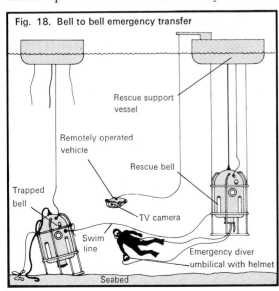

Fig. 18. Bell to bell emergency transfer

Rescue support vessel
Remotely operated vehicle
Rescue bell
Trapped bell
TV camera
Swim line
Emergency diver umbilical with helmet
Seabed

13.3 COASTGUARD

The United Kingdom and United States Coastguard are responsible for co-ordinating search and rescue (SAR) operations in the waters under their jurisdiction. In this capacity, both Coastguards maintain and operate public rescue facilities co-ordinating the services of appropriate authorities such as the Navy, Air Force, Lifeboats, Police and a network of coastal radio stations.

United Kingdom

HM Coastguard (HMCG) is divided into six regions, each under a Regional Controller based at a regional Maritime Rescue Co-ordinating Centre (MRCC). Each region is further divided into districts known as Maritime Rescue Sub-Centre (MRSCs). All these centres, MRCCs and MRSCs, are equipped to enable the Coastguard to make and maintain contact with any maritime distress call and to despatch appropriate rescue units. Each centre is manned and on watch for 24 hours each day throughout the year, and it is from them, should a distress call be received, that the necessary rescue services will be mobilised.

As a general rule, because they are equipped for the task, offshore operators will manage and co-ordinate their own rescue services for their rigs and platforms. They will however, always keep the Coastguard informed of what rescue operations they are conducting and will call upon the Coastguard to supplement their requirements if necessary.

To avoid gas flares being mistaken for fires at sea all operating companies are requested to notify the MRCC or MRSC of any proposed well testing operations involving the flaring of gas. Similarly any proposed detonation of explosives should be reported to the Coastguard.

When civil engineering divers are working from boats they should keep the Coastguard informed of their plans and movements.

In an emergency, the UK Coastguard can be contacted immediately by telephone by dialling 999 and asking for the Coastguard.

Check list of the information needed by the Coastguard in case of an emergency:

Type of vessel or installation.
Name of vessel or installation, how and where displayed.
Number of persons on board.
Colours of hull and topside.
Speed and endurance.
Special identification features.
Life-raft and serial number.
Life boat type and colour.
Life jackets carried.
Radio—HF/MF/trans./rec., VHF channels and call sign.
Type of distress signal carried.
Usual base, mooring, activity and sea areas.
Shore contact's name, address, telephone number.
Owner's name, address, telephone number.
Date.

HM COASTGUARD, MARITIME RESCUE CO-ORDINATION CENTRES (MRCCS)

A. ABERDEEN	Blaikies Quay, Aberdeen	Aberdeen	(0224) 873347
B. YARMOUTH	Great Yarmouth, Norfolk.	Great Yarmouth	(0493) 63444
C. DOVER	Langdon Battery, Swingate, Dover, Kent.	Dover	(0304) 210008
D. BRIXHAM	Brixham, Devon.	Brixham	(08045) 2156
E. SWANSEA	Mumbles, Swansea, West Glamorgan.	Swansea	(0792) 66534
F. CLYDE	Navy Buildings, Eldon Street, Greenock, Renfrewshire.	Greenock	(0475)29988

HM COASTGUARD, MARITIME RESCUE SUB-CENTRES (MRSCS)

1. SHETLAND	Lerwick, Shetland.	Lerwick	(0595) 2976
2. ORKNEY	Kirkwall, Orkney.	Kirkwall	(0856) 3268
3. WICK	Wick, Caithness.	Wick	(0955) 2332
4. MORAY	Peterhead, Aberdeenshire.	Peterhead	(0779) 4278
5. FORTH	Fife Ness, Crail, Fife.	Crail	(03335) 666
6. TYNE	Tynemouth, North Shields, Tyne and Wear.	North Shields	(0632) 572691
7. TEES	Teesmouth, Southgare, Redcar, Cleveland.	Redcar	(0642) 474639
8. HUMBER	Spurn Point, Nr Hull, North Humberside.	Spurn Point	(09646) 351
9. THAMES	Hall Lane, Walton-on-the-Naze, Essex.	Frinton-on-Sea	(02556) 5518
10. SHOREHAM	Shoreham-by-Sea, West Sussex.	Shoreham	(07917) 2226
11. SOLENT	Totland Bay, Freshwater, Isle of Wight.	Freshwater	(0983) 832265
12. PORTLAND	Grove Point, Portland, Dorset.	Portland	(0305) 820441
13. FALMOUTH	Castle Drive, Falmouth, Cornwall.	Falmouth	(0326) 314481
14. LANDS END	Gwennap Head, Cornwall.	Sennen	(073687) 351

15. HARTLAND	Hartland, Bideford, Devon.	Hartland (02374) 235
16. MILFORD HAVEN	Castle Way, Dale, Haverfordwest, Dyfed.	Dale (06465) 218
17. HOLYHEAD	Holyhead, Anglesey.	Holyhead (0407) 2051
18. LIVERPOOL	Formby, Liverpool.	Formby (07048) 72903
19. RAMSEY	Ramsey, Isle of Man.	Ramsey (0624) 813255
20. BELFAST	Bangor, Co. Down.	Groomsport (024784) 284
21. OBAN	Boswell House, Argyll Square, Oban, Argyll.	Oban (0631) 3720
22. STORNO-WAY	Stornoway, Isle of Lewis.	Stornoway (0851) 2013

United States

The Coast Guard in the USA (USCG) divides its maritime SAR region into subregions under the guidance of 14 Rescue Co-ordination Centres (RCCs). USCG resources include their own fleet of cutters, aircraft and numerous radio and communication stations. The USCG also administer commercial diving operations regulations offshore and is involved in most spheres of diving activities, such as operations/equipment requirements and standards for construction and maintenance. They are also the investigating authority in the case of fatal or serious accidents.

UNITED STATES COAST GUARD, GULF OF MEXICO

AIR STATIONS
A. **NEW ORLEANS**   (504) 589 2153
B. **HOUSTON**   (713) 481 1400 (ext. 2316)
C. **CORPUS CHRISTI**   (512) 939 2251

BASES
1. **MOBILE**   (205) 690 2231
2. **NEW ORLEANS**   (504) 589 7145 & 6856
3. **GALVESTON**   (713) 763 1635

UK Rescue Centres

USA Rescue Centres in the Gulf of Mexico

14.1 REGULATIONS UK HSE DEPARTMENT OF ENERGY

Arrangement of Regulations

1. Citation and commencement

These Regulations may be cited as the Diving Operations at Work Regulations 1981 and will come into operation on 1st July 1981.

2. Interpretation

(1) In these Regulations, unless the context otherwise requires—

breathing mixture means air or any other mixture of gases which is fit for breathing;

concession owner means a person who has been granted a licence pursuant to the Petroleum (Production) Regulations 1976;

diver shall be construed in accordance with paragraph (2)(*b*);

diving bell means any compression chamber which is capable of being manned and is used or designed for use under the surface of water in supporting human life being a chamber in which any occupant is or may be subjected to a pressure of more than 300 millibars above atmospheric pressure during normal operation; and *bell diving* shall be construed accordingly;

diving contractor has the meaning assigned by Regulation 5(4);

diving operation shall be construed in accordance with paragraph (2)(*a*) & (*c*);

diving rules means the rules required by Regulation 5(1) (*b*);

diving supervisor means, in relation to any diving operation, the competent person referred to in Regulation 6 who has been appointed in relation to that operation by the diving contractor;

emergency means an emergency affecting or likely to affect the health or safety of a diver engaged in a diving operation;

offshore installation has the meaning assigned by the Health and Safety at Work etc. Act 1974 (Application outside Great Britain) Order 1977;

pipe-line and *pipe-line works* have the meanings assigned respectively by section 26(2) of the Petroleum and Submarine Pipe-lines Act 1975 with the addition of the provision of internal or external protection for a pipe-line;

self-contained in relation to any diving plant and equipment, means diving plant and equipment in which the supply of breathing mixture is carried by the diver independently of any other source.

(2) For the purposes of these Regulations—

(*a*) a diver shall be deemed to be engaged in a diving operation from the time when he commences to prepare to dive until—
 (i) if he entered the water he has left it and returned to a place from which the diving operations are being carried on, and
 (ii) he is no longer subject to raised pressure, and
 (iii) it may reasonably be anticipated that he will not need therapeutic recompression,
except that heads (ii) and (iii) shall not apply when for the purposes of receiving medical treatment he has been transferred to a hospital or other place which is not under the control of the diving contractor or the diving supervisor;

(*b*) a person shall be deemed not to be a diver if he—
 (i) is in a submersible chamber or craft or in a pressure-resistant diving suit, and is not exposed to a pressure exceeding 300 millibars above atmospheric pressure during normal operation, or
 (ii) uses no underwater breathing apparatus or uses only snorkel type apparatus, or
 (iii) is taking part in the diving operation in a capacity other than as an employee or self-employed person, or
 (iv) is on duty as a member of the armed forces of the Crown or visiting forces and is engaged in operations or operational training;

(*c*) a person who is engaged in any activity as a diving supervisor, or as a member of a diving team or in connection with the recompression or decompression of a diver engaged in a diving operation shall be deemed to be engaged in a diving operation.

(3) In these Regulations, unless the context otherwise requires, a reference to—

(*a*) a numbered Regulation or Schedule is a reference to the Regulation of, or Schedule to, these Regulations bearing that number;

(*b*) a numbered paragraph is a reference to the paragraph bearing that number in the Regulation in which the reference appears.

3. Application of these Regulations

(1) Subject to paragraph (2), these Regulations shall apply to and in relation to all diving operations in which any diver taking part is at work as an employee or a self-employed person within the meaning of section 53 of the Health and Safety at Work etc. Act 1974, being diving operations either—
(*a*) in Great Britain, or
(*b*) outside Great Britain in circumstances in which sections 1 to 59 of that Act apply by virtue of the Health and Safety at Work etc. Act 1974 (Application outside Great Britain) Order 1977.

(2) These Regulations shall apply to a diving operation only if at least one of the persons going under water is a diver for the purposes of the Regulations.

(3) Where a person is exposed to a pressure greater than 300 millibars above atmospheric pressure in a surface compression chamber in connection with—
(*a*) any diving operation, or
(*b*) the testing or evaluation of any plant or equipment designed for use in diving operations,
then these Regulations shall apply to, and in relation to, him as if he were a diver engaged in a diving operation except Regulations 5(3)(*b*)(ii), 7(1)(*a*), 8(2), (3) and (4), 10, and 12(1)(*b*), (*f*), (*g*), (*i*) and (*j*); but this paragraph shall not apply to a diver engaged in a diving operation or to a person to whom Regulation 2(2)(*b*)(iv) applies.

4. Duty to ensure compliance with these Regulations

(1) In addition to any specific duty placed on him by these Regulations—
(*a*) every diving contractor and every other person who to any extent is responsible for, has control over or is engaged in a diving operation, and
(*b*) in the case of—
 (i) an offshore installation, the owner,
 (ii) a proposed offshore installation, the concession owner,
 (iii) a pipe-line, the owner,
 (iv) a proposed pipe-line, the person who will be the owner when it is laid,
shall ensure so far as is reasonably practicable—
(*c*) that these Regulations are complied with, and
(*d*) that they are complied with in such a way that persons involved are not exposed to risks to their health or safety.

(2)
(*a*) An employer shall not permit any employee of his to take part in a diving operation as a diver unless there is a diving contractor for that operation.
(*b*) A person employed under a contract for services or who would be diving on his own account shall not take part in a diving operation as a diver unless there is a diving contractor for that operation.

5. Diving contractors

(1) Every diving contractor shall in respect of each diving operation—

(a) appoint one or more diving supervisors in accordance with paragraph (3) to be in immediate control of the operation;

(b) issue diving rules in accordance with Regulation 9 and Schedule 1 for regulating the conduct of all persons engaged in the diving operation;

(c) provide a diving operations log book, which is to be maintained in accordance with Regulation 6, and shall keep it for at least two years after the date of the last entry in it;

(d) ensure that all plant and equipment, including any plant and equipment required by Regulation 12, which is necessary for the safe conduct of the diving operation is available for immediate use;

(e) not permit the use of compressed natural air as the breathing mixture in any diving operation at a depth exceeding 50 metres except where the use is for therapeutic purposes.

(2) Every diving contractor shall so far as is reasonably practicable ensure that—

(a) each diving operation is carried out from a suitable and safe place with the consent of any person having control of that place;

(b) emergency services are available including in particular in the cases of diving—
   (i) using saturation techniques, or
   (ii) at a depth exceeding 50 metres, facilities for transferring the divers safely under a suitable pressure to a place where treatment can be given safely under pressure;

(c) there are effective means of communication between the place at which operations are being or are to be carried out and—
   (i) persons having control of that place, and
   (ii) the emergency services.

In this paragraph, *saturation techniques* means procedures by means of which a diver avoids repeated decompressions to atmospheric pressure by being continuously subjected to an ambient pressure greater than atmospheric pressure so that his body tissues and blood become saturated with the inert element of the breathing mixture.

(3)(a) Each diving supervisor shall be appointed in writing and where two or more diving supervisors are appointed in respect of any diving operation, the diving contractor shall specify which part or parts of the diving operation each is to supervise at any one time; except that the diving contractor may permit two duly appointed supervisors to arrange between themselves the time at which one is to take over from the other.

(b) A person shall not be appointed to be a diving supervisor unless—
   (i) he is a competent person with adequate knowledge and experience of the diving techniques to be used in the diving operation for which he is appointed, and either—

(ii) he has qualified as a diver, in respect of the diving techniques to be used, under these Regulations or under any of the Regulations revoked or modified by Regulation 16 of these Regulations or under the Submarine Pipe-lines (Diving Operations) Regulations 1976, or

(iii) during the period of two years immediately preceding the coming into operation of these Regulations he acted as a diving supervisor of a diving operation in which the same diving techniques were used,

except that heads (ii) and (iii) shall not apply where the diving operation is to be carried on in water which is not more than 1.5 metres deep.

(4) For the purposes of these Regulations, *diving contractor* in relation to any diving operation, means—

(a) in any case where any of the divers taking part are employees—
   (i) their employer, or
   (ii) if there is more than one employer, such one of them as those employers may appoint in writing;

(b) if there is no diving contractor by virtue of the preceding sub-paragraph and the operation is carried on—
   (i) from or in connection with an offshore installation, the manager of the installation appointed pursuant to section 4 of the Mineral Workings (Offshore Installations) Act 1971 or where no such manager has been appointed, the person made responsible by the owner for health and safety on the installation,
   (ii) in connection with a proposed offshore installation, the concession owner,
   (iii) in connection with a pipe-line, the owner of the pipe-line,
   (iv) in connection with a proposed pipe-line, the person who will be the owner of the pipe-line when it is laid;

(c) if there is no diving contractor by virtue of either of the preceding sub-paragraphs, any diver employed under a contract for services or diving on his own account and if there is more than one such person, such one of them as they may appoint in writing.

In this paragraph—

'in connection with an offshore installation' and 'in connection with a proposed offshore installation' does not include any pipe-line works;

'in connection with a pipe-line' and 'in connection with a proposed pipe-line' means in connection with that part of it with which the diving operation is concerned and includes pipe-line works; and 'the owner' means the owner of that part.

6. The diving supervisor

(1) Every diving supervisor shall, so far as is reasonably practicable, ensure that each diving operation for which he is appointed is carried out in accordance with the diving rules and under his

immediate control.

(2) In relation to each diving operation the diving supervisor shall—

(a) ensure that plant and equipment is not used unless Regulation 13(1)(c) and (d) have been complied with;

(b) comply with Regulation 9(4);

(c) enter in the diving operations log book provided under Regulation 5(1)(c) an accurate record of the matters specified in Schedule 2 and shall sign the entries daily during the course of the diving operation;

(d) countersign the entries relating to the diving operation in the diver's log book of each diver who took part in that operation.

(3) A person shall not dive while he is the diving supervisor for the time being in charge of a diving operation or any part of it.

7. Divers

(1) A person shall not take part in any diving operation as a diver unless he—

(a) has a valid certificate of training issued under Regulation 10, and

(b) has a valid certificate of medical fitness to dive issued under Regulation 11, and

(c) is competent to carry out safely the work which he is called upon to perform in that operation;

but sub-paragraph (b) shall not apply to a person who enters a compression chamber in order to provide treatment in an emergency.

(2) Every diver engaged in a diving operation shall inform the diving supervisor appointed in respect of that operation if he is unfit or if there is any other reason why he should not go or remain under water or in a compression chamber as the case may be.

(3)(a) Every diver engaged in a diving operation shall maintain a personal log book ('diver's log book') in which he shall enter his name and which shall contain his signature and a photograph which is a reasonable likeness of him.

(b) On every day on which he takes part in a diving operation a diver shall record in his log book the matters set out in Schedule 3, and he shall sign each entry and it shall be countersigned by the diving supervisor.

(4) Every diver shall present his diver's log book to the doctor examining him for the purposes of Regulation 11.

(5) Every diver shall retain his diver's log book for at least two years from the date of the last entry in it.

8. Diving team

(1) At all times when any diving operation is, or is about to be, carried out there shall be present a sufficient number of divers and other competent persons (*the diving team*) necessary to—

(a) ensure that so far as is reasonably practicable the operation can be undertaken safely;

(b) operate plant, equipment or other facilities necessary for the safe conduct of the operation.

(2) Subject to paragraphs (4) and (5), in addition to the diver or divers who will be diving in a diving operation—

(a) there shall be another diver (*the standby diver*) who shall—

   (i) where a diving bell is being used, descend in the bell to the depth from which work is to be carried out and shall remain in the bell to monitor the diver or divers who leave it and be in immediate readiness to render assistance to them,

   (ii) in all other cases, be in immediate readiness to dive except that two divers in the water at the same time who are near enough to be able to communicate with and to render assistance to each other in an emergency may each be regarded as the standby diver for the other;

(b) in the following cases there shall be an extra diver on the surface in addition to the standby diver—:

   (i) where diving stops are required for the purposes of routine decompression,

   (ii) where the diving will be at a depth of 30 metres or more,

   (iii) where there is a special hazard and in particular where a diver will be endangered in a current or where there is a risk of a diver being trapped or his equipment entangled.

(3) The standby diver and any diver required by paragraph (2)(b) shall be in addition to—

(a) any members of the team required to attend or work any plant, equipment or other facilities;

(b) the diving supervisor;

except that the standby diver and the extra diver required by paragraph (2)(b) may perform other duties in the diving team where to do so would not prejudice the safety of any person in the water if he is called upon to dive.

(4) Paragraph (2) shall not prevent the standby diver or any diver required by paragraph (2)(b) from going to the assistance of any other diver in an emergency.

(5) Paragraph (2) shall not apply where the diving operation is to be carried on in water which is not more than 1.5 metres deep.

9. Diving rules

(1) The diving rules required by Regulation 5(1)(b) shall include provisions for securing the health and safety of persons engaged in the diving operation and in particular shall—

(a) make provision relating to such of the matters specified in Schedule 1 as are relevant to the diving operation to be undertaken;

(b) require the use of such of the plant and equipment specified in Regulation 12 as is relevant to the diving operation to be undertaken.

(2) The diving contractor shall, if an inspector appointed pursuant to section 19 of the Health and Safety at Work etc. Act 1974 so requires, supply the inspector with a copy of the diving rules issued by him for any diving operation or intended operation or such part of those rules as the inspector may require.

(3) The diving contractor shall supply the diving supervisor with a copy of the diving rules.

(4) The diving supervisor shall make available to each member of the diving team a copy of the part or parts of the diving rules relevant to that member.

10. Qualification of divers

(1) The certificate of training required by Regulation 7(1)(a) shall be valid only if—

(a) it has been issued by the Health and Safety Executive or by a person or body of persons approved by the Executive for the purposes of this subparagraph, and

(b) it states—

   (i) the name of the individual to whom it relates (*the diver*),

   (ii) the category or categories of diving to which it relates,

   (iii) that the person or body issuing the certificate is satisfied that the diver has attained a satisfactory standard of competence (whether by training, experience or a combination of both) in the matters specified in Schedule 4 which are relevant to the category or categories of diving to which the certificate relates, except that where the person or body is not satisfied on all such matters, but nevertheless considers it appropriate to issue a certificate subject to restrictions within a category of diving, those restrictions shall be stated in the certificate;

(c) it has not ceased, in accordance with paragraph (2), to be valid.

(2) If—

(a) the person or body which issued a certificate declares it to be no longer valid, or

(b) the Executive declares a certificate to be no longer valid, whether or not the certificate was issued by the Executive,

then that certificate shall cease to be a valid certificate for the purposes of paragraph (1).

(3) The certificate of training shall be kept in the diver's log book.

(4) The preceding provisions of this Regulation shall not apply to a person taking part in a diving operation as part of training approved for the time being by the Executive or by a person or body of persons approved by the Executive for the purposes of this paragraph.

(5) Without prejudice to the generality of paragraph (1)(a), where a person or body approved for the purposes of this Regulation or the Executive

(a) refuses to issue a certificate of training, or

(b) declares a certificate of training it has issued to be no longer valid,

the Executive, upon application being made to it by the person aggrieved, within 28 days of his being notified of the refusal or declaration as the case may be, shall review that decision and if it is satisfied that it should be reversed or altered shall in either case issue a certificate of training.

11. Certificate of medical fitness to dive

(1) The certificate of medical fitness to dive required by Regulation 7(1)(b)

shall be valid in respect of a particular diving operation only if—

(a) it has been issued by an approved doctor or by the Health and Safety Executive in accordance with the following provisions of this Regulation,

(b) the diving undertaken does not contravene any limitation contained in the certificate pursuant to paragraph (3)(a)(v),

(c) the period mentioned in paragraph (3)(a)(vi) has not expired.

(2) A certificate of medical fitness shall only be issued for the purposes of paragraph (1) after the person concerned has undergone an examination carried out by an approved doctor in such manner and including such tests as the Executive may require either generally or for that case or class of case.

(3) The certificate of medical fitness to dive shall—

(a) state—

   (i) the name of the person to whom it relates,

   (ii) the date of the medical examination,

   (iii) the date of any X-ray taken for the purposes of that examination,

   (iv) that the person is considered fit to dive,

   (v) any limitation on the diving or compression for which the person is considered fit,

   (vi) the period not exceeding 12 months for which the person is considered fit,

   (vii) the name, address and telephone number of the approved doctor issuing the certificate;

(b) be signed by the doctor issuing it, or on behalf of the Executive as the case may be.

(4) The certificate of medical fitness shall be entered in the diver's log book; and the entry shall be in such form as the Executive may approve.

(5) If an approved doctor decides, after examination, that a person is unfit to dive, he shall enter this fact in the diver's log book together with the information required by paragraph (3)(a)(i)-(iii) and (vii) and shall sign the entry.

(6) An employment medical adviser may on medical grounds revoke a certificate of medical fitness after, where reasonably practicable, consulting the doctor who issued that certificate.

(7) Without prejudice to the generality of paragraph (1)(a), where an approved doctor decides—

(a) that a person is unfit to dive, or

(b) that a person is fit to dive subject to limitations,

the Executive, upon application being made to it by that person within 28 days of the decision, shall review the decision and if it is satisfied that it should be reversed or altered shall issue a certificate of fitness to dive subject to such limitations, if any, as it considers appropriate.

(8) In this Regulation, *an approved doctor* means a medical practitioner

approved for the time being by an employment medical adviser for such purposes of these Regulations as he may specify in the instrument of approval; and *employment medical adviser* means a person appointed under Part II of the Health and Safety at Work etc. Act 1974 to be such an adviser and who is authorized by the Executive to give approvals under this paragraph or to make revocations under paragraph (6) as the case may be.

12. Plant and equipment

(1) The plant and equipment mentioned in Regulation 5(1)(*d*) shall—

(*a*) include a means of supplying a breathing mixture (including a reserve supply for immediate use in the event of an emergency or for therapeutic recompression or decompression)—
   (i) suitable in content and temperature and of adequate pressure, and
   (ii) at an adequate rate,
to sustain prolonged vigorous physical exertion at the ambient pressure for the duration of the diving operations;

(*b*) include a lifeline for each diver except—
   (i) where the nature of the diving operations renders a lifeline unsuitable and an alternative system for ensuring the diver's safety is used, or
   (ii) in a case where two divers are at a depth not exceeding 30 metres and each is acting as standby diver for the other and one of them is connected to the surface by a lifeline;
and in this sub-paragraph *lifeline* means a rope, gas hose, communication cable or any combination thereof which is adequate in strength and suitable for recovering and lifting the diver and his equipment from the water;

(*c*) enable each diver to communicate with the diving supervisor except—
   (i) where paragraph (1)(*b*)(i) applies,
   (ii) where paragraph (1)(*b*)(ii) applies in which case one of the divers shall be able to communicate with the supervisor,
and in a case where a diving bell is being used enable the diver who leaves the bell to communicate with the diver remaining in it;

(*d*) in addition to the means of communication required by sub-paragraph (*c*) above, include where reasonably practicable a system enabling oral communication to be made between each diver and the diving supervisor;

(*e*) include such plant and equipment as may be necessary to ensure that divers may safely enter and leave the water;

(*f*) in the case of any of the following diving operations, include a surface compression chamber with all necessary ancillary equipment; and the chamber and equipment shall comply with Schedule 5—
   (i) at a depth in excess of 50 metres,
   (ii) at a depth exceeding 10 but not

exceeding 50 metres where the routine decompression time exceeds 20 minutes,
   (iii) at a depth exceeding 10 but not exceeding 50 metres where the routine decompression time is 20 minutes or less and effective arrangements have not been made for the rapid conveyance of any diver requiring therapeutic recompression from the location of the diving operations to a suitable two-compartment chamber,
   (iv) from or in connection with an offshore installation, a proposed offshore installation or pipe-line works;

(*g*) for a diving operation at a depth exceeding 50 metres include a diving bell which shall have all necessary ancillary equipment and shall comply with the requirements of Schedule 6;

(*h*) include such plant and equipment, if any, as may be necessary to ensure that each diver's body temperature is kept within safe limits and in all cases where the diving operation is—
   (i) at a depth exceeding 50 metres there shall be a means of heating the diver, and
   (ii) at a depth exceeding 150 metres there shall also be a means of heating the diver's breathing mixture;

(*i*) where a diving operation is to be carried on during the hours of darkness include—
   (i) a lamp or other device attached to the diver to indicate his position when he is on the surface, and
   (ii) such plant and equipment as may be necessary to illuminate adequately the place on the surface from which the diving is being carried on, except where the nature of the diving operations render such illumination undesirable;

(*j*) include depth measuring devices which where reasonably practicable shall be suitable for surface monitoring.

(2) Where a person is deemed to be engaged in a diving operation by virtue of Regulation 3(3), the surface compression chamber and its ancillary equipment shall comply with Schedule 5.

(3) Where any vessel, hovercraft, floating structure or offshore installation is used in a diving operation there shall be means of securing that it is—

(*a*) at anchor or aground, or

(*b*) made fast to the shore, to a fixed structure or to an offshore installation which is in a fixed position, or

(*c*) maintained in position using its propulsion system or a dynamic positioning system with adequate precautions to secure the safety of the diver from these systems and the flow of water created.

(4) All plant and equipment used in a diving operation shall—

(*a*) be properly designed, of adequate strength and of good construction from sound and suitable material;

(*b*) be suitable for the conditions in which it is intended to be used;

(*c*) where its safe use depends on the depth or pressure at which it is used, be marked with its safe working pressure or the maximum depth at which it may be used;

(*d*) at whatever temperature it is to be used, be adequately protected against malfunctioning at that temperature.

(5) Each gas cylinder used in a diving operation shall be legibly marked with the name and the chemical formula of its contents.

13. Maintenance, examination and testing of plant and equipment

(1) The plant and equipment specified in Regulation 12(1), (2) and (5) shall not be used in any diving operation unless—

(*a*) it is maintained in a condition which will ensure so far as is reasonably practicable that it is safe while it is being used;

(*b*) the register maintained under paragraph (4) contains—
   (i) a certificate by a competent person that it complies with Regulation 12(4), and
   (ii) in the case of a surface compression chamber or a diving bell, sufficient information, including information relating to the materials used in its construction, to enable it to be safely used, repaired or altered;

(*c*) there is in force a certificate issued under paragraph (2) by a competent person that it has been examined and tested and that it may be safely used;

(*d*) it has been examined by a competent person within the six hours immediately before the diving operation commenced.

(2) The certificate referred to in paragraph (1)(*c*) shall—

(*a*) state—
   (i) the plant and equipment to which it relates,
   (ii) that the competent person has examined it,
   (iii) that it has been tested by him or under his close supervision,
   (iv) the pressure, depth or other conditions under which it can be safely used, and
   (v) the period during which it can be safely used which shall not exceed six months;

(*b*) cease to be valid—
   (i) when any repair or alteration has to be made to the plant or equipment which affects its safe working,
   (ii) on the expiration of six months or such shorter period as may be certified under sub-paragraph (*a*)(v) above.

(3) For the purposes of paragraph (2)(*a*)(iii) the competent person need not cause a pressure leak test or an internal pressure test to be repeated—

(*a*) in the case of a surface compression chamber or a diving bell—
   (i) if a pressure leak test to a safe working pressure has been carried out and certified within the previous two years, or as the case may be,
   (ii) if an internal pressure test has been carried out and certified

within the previous five years;

(b) in the case of a seamless gas cylinder not taken under water if either a pressure leak test to a safe working pressure or an internal pressure test has been carried out and certified within the previous five years;

(c) in the case of any other item of plant or equipment which will be subjected to an internal pressure in excess of 500 millibars above external pressure, if either a pressure leak test to a safe working pressure or, an internal pressure test has been carried out and certified within the previous two years.

(4) The diving contractor shall—

(a) enter in, attach to or insert into a register kept for the purpose, the certificates and information required by paragraph (1)(b) and (c);

(b) retain each such register—

(i) in the case of a register containing certificates relating to any surface compression chamber or diving bell or seamless gas cylinder not taken under water, for at least five years from the date of the last such certificate,

(ii) in any other case, for at least two years from the date of the last certificate it contains.

14. Exemption certificates

(1) Subject to paragraph (2), the Health and Safety Executive may, by a certificate in writing, exempt any person or class of persons, any diving operation or class of diving operations and any plant and equipment or class of plant and equipment from any requirement or prohibition imposed by any provision of these Regulations, and any such exemption may be granted subject to conditions and to a limit of time and may be revoked at any time.

(2) The Executive shall not grant any such exemption unless, having regard to the circumstances of the case, and in particular to—

(a) the conditions, if any, which it proposes to attach to the exemption, and

(b) any other requirements imposed by or under any enactment which apply to the case,

it is satisfied that the health and safety of persons who are likely to be affected by the exemption will not be prejudiced in consequence of it.

15. Transitional provisions

(1) It shall be a sufficient compliance with Regulation 10 if instead of the certificate of training the diver's log book includes a certificate issued by the diving contractor during the first six months immediately after the coming into operation of these Regulations that he is satisfied that the diver's experience during the two years immediately preceding the issue of the certificate is such that he is competent to take part in diving operations of the category stated in the certificate; in this paragraph *the diving contractor* means the first relevant diving contractor after these Regulations come into operation.

(2) The Health and Safety Executive may revoke a certificate issued under paragraph (1) at any time if, after making such enquiries as it considers necessary, it considers that in all the circumstances of the case it is appropriate to do so.

(3) A certificate of medical fitness issued under any of the Regulations revoked or modified by Regulation 16 of these Regulations or under the Submarine Pipe-lines (Diving Operations) Regulations 1976 shall have effect for the purposes of these Regulations as if it had been issued under Regulation 11(1) of these Regulations as the case may be.

16. Revocations and modification

(1) The Diving Operations Special Regulations 1960 and the Offshore Installations (Diving Operations) Regulations 1974 are hereby revoked.

(2) For Regulation 2(1) of the Merchant Shipping (Diving Operations) Regulations 1975 there shall be substituted the following paragraph—

'(1) These Regulations shall apply to all diving operations (other than diving operations to which the Diving Operations at Work Regulations 1981 apply) carried on from, on, in or near any submersible or supporting apparatus to which Part IV of the Act applies, being diving operations carried on in the course of or in connection with any trade or business (not including archaeology or non-commercial research) other than a school for the training of divers'.

SCHEDULE 1
Regulations 5(1)(b) and 9
Matters in respect of which provision is to be made in Diving Rules

1. PLANNING
Consideration of—

(a) metereological conditions, including forecasted conditions;

(b) tidal information including local tide tables and indications of speed of current to be expected;

(c) proposed shipping movements;

(d) air and water temperatures;

(e) underwater hazards of the diving site, including any culverts, penstocks, sluice valves or areas where differences in hydrostatic pressure may endanger the diver;

(f) depth and type of operation;

(g) suitability of plant and equipment;

(h) availability and qualifications of personnel;

(i) the effect on a diver of changes of air pressure if he flies after diving;

(j) the activities of any person who will be diving in connection with the diving operation whether or not he is a diver for the purposes of these regulations.

2. PREPARATIONS

(a) Consultation with persons having any control over or information related to the safety of any diving operations; and in particular persons having control of lifting appliances or having control of or information about shipping movements;

(b) selection of the breathing apparatus and mixtures;

(c) check of plant and equipment;

(d) allocation of personnel;

(e) personal fitness of divers for underwater operations;

(f) precautions against cold in and out of the water;

(g) signalling procedures;

(h) precautions against underwater hazards of the diving site.

3. PROCEDURES DURING DIVING

(a) Responsibilities of diving supervisor, divers and surface support;

(b) use of all types of personal diving equipment;

(c) supply of gas and gas mixture, including maximum and minimum partial pressure of gases;

(d) operations direct from an installation, work site or craft;

(e) operations in relation to diving bell;

(f) working in different locations;

(g) operations and use of equipment under water;

(h) limits on depth and time under water;

(i) descent, ascent and recovery of divers;

(j) descent, ascent and recovery of diving bell;

(k) diving tables for use in decompression procedures for both single and repetitive diving and in therapeutic decompression procedures; and for inland waters the need to take account of the effect on pressure of the altitudes at which the diving takes place;

(l) control in changing conditions;

(m) time for which divers are to remain in vicinity of the surface compression chamber;

(n) maintenance of log books.

4. EMERGENCY PROCEDURE

(a) Emergency signalling;

(b) emergency assistance under water and on the surface;

(c) therapeutic recompression and decompression and the availability of chambers for that purpose;

(d) first aid;

(e) medical assistance;

(f) calling assistance from emergency services including advance liaison with those services where appropriate;

(g) precautions in the event of evacuation of the installation, work site, vessel, hovercraft or floating structure;

(h) provision of emergency electrical supplies.

SCHEDULE 2
Regulation 6
Matters to be entered in the Diving Operations Log Book

The following matters shall be entered in the diving operations log book in respect of each diving operation:

(a) the name of the diving contractor;

(b) the dates on which and the period during which the diving operation was carried on;

(c) the name or other designation of the craft or offshore installation or work site in connection with which the diving operation was carried on and the location of that craft or offshore installation or work site;

(d) the name of the diving supervisor and the period for which he is acting in that capacity in respect of that diving operation;

(e) the names of the other persons engaged in the diving operation including those operating any diving plant or equipment and their respective duties;

(f) the arrangements for emergency support;

(g) the procedures followed in the course of the diving operation including details of the decompression schedule used;

(h) the maximum depth reached in the course of the operation for each diver;

(i) for each diver, in respect of each dive he makes, the time he leaves the surface, his bottom time (that is the period from the time he leaves the surface until he starts to ascend) and the time he reaches the surface;

(j) the type of breathing apparatus and mixture used;

(k) the nature of the diving operation;

(l) any decompression sickness, other illness, discomfort or injury suffered by any of the divers;

(m) particulars of any emergency which occurred during the diving operation and any action taken;

(n) any defects that are discovered in any plant or equipment used in the diving operations;

(o) particulars of any environmental factors affecting the diving operation;

(p) any other factors relevant to the safety or health of the persons engaged in the operation.

SCHEDULE 3
Regulation 7
Matters to be entered in the Diver's Log Book

The following matters shall be entered in the diver's log book in respect of each diving operation in which he takes part:

(a) the name and address of the diving contractor;

(b) the date;

(c) the name or other designation and the location of the offshore installation, work site, craft or harbour from which the diving operation was carried on;

(d) the name of the diving supervisor;

(e) the maximum depth reached on each occasion;

(f) the time he left the surface, his bottom time and the time he reached the surface on each occasion;

(g) where the dive includes time spent in a compression chamber, details of any time spent outside the chamber at a different pressure;

(h) the type of breathing apparatus and mixture used by him;

(i) any work done by him on each occasion and the equipment (including tools) used by him in that work;

(j) any decompression schedules followed by him on each occasion;

(k) any decompression sickness or other illness, discomfort or injury suffered by him;

(l) any other factor relevant to his safety or health.

SCHEDULE 4
Regulation 10(1)(b)(iii)
Matters in respect of which a diver has to attain a satisfactory standard of competence

Part I BASIC AIR DIVING

1. The theory of air diving.
2. Use of self-contained and surface supplied diving equipment.
3. Diving safely and competently in various conditions not exceeding 50 metres in depth, including the safe use of hand tools and hand held power tools and equipment.
4. Use of diver communication systems appropriate to air diving.
5. Emergency procedures for air diving.
6. Surface compression chamber operation, therapeutic recompression, decompression and the decompression tables appropriate to air diving.
7. First aid appropriate to emergencies arising in air diving.
8. Relevant legislation and guidance.

Part II MIXED GAS OR BELL DIVING

1. All the matters specified in Part I of this Schedule.
2. The theory of mixed gas and bell diving.
3. Gases and gas systems.
4. Diving safely and competently to representative depths exceeding 50 metres from a diving bell.
5. Use of diver communication systems appropriate to mixed gas and bell diving.
6. Diving bell operation, transferring to surface compression chamber, recompression on mixed gas and decompression and decompression tables appropriate to mixed gas diving.
7. Emergency procedure for mixed gas and bell diving.
8. First aid appropriate to emergencies arising in mixed gas and bell diving.
9. Legislation and guidance relevant to mixed gas diving not covered under paragraph 8 of Part I of this Schedule.

Part III AIR DIVING WHERE NO SURFACE COMPRESSION CHAMBER IS REQUIRED ON SITE

1. The theory of air diving.
2. Use of surface-supplied diving equipment.
3. Use of self-contained diving equipment.
4. Diving safely and competently in various conditions.
5. Use of diver communication systems appropriate to air diving.
6. Emergency procedures for air diving.
7. Therapeutic recompression, decompression and the decompression tables appropriate to air diving.
8. First aid appropriate to emergencies arising in air diving.
9. Relevant legislation and guidance.

Part IV AIR DIVING WITH SELF-CONTAINED EQUIPMENT WHERE NO SURFACE COMPRESSION CHAMBER IS REQUIRED ON SITE

All matters specified in Part III except the use of surface-supplied diving equipment.

SCHEDULE 5
Regulation 12(1) (f)
Surface Compression Chambers

A surface compression chamber shall:

(a) have at least two compartments with doors each of which acts as a pressure seal and can be opened from either side (a *two-compartment chamber*); or alternatively a single compartment chamber may be used where—

  (i) the divers do not go to a depth exceeding 50 metres, and

  (ii) the diving operations are not carried on from or in connection with an offshore installation or pipe-line works, and

  (iii) facilities are provided for transferring persons under pressure from that chamber to a two-compartment chamber within four hours;

(b) in the case of a two-compartment chamber, have sufficient space in at least one of its compartments to enable two adults to lie down inside the chamber without difficulty and if the chamber is to be used in circumstances in which a person is intended to remain inside under pressure for a continuous period of 12 hours or more, excluding any therapeutic decompression, it shall have a minimum internal diameter of two metres, except that in the case of equipment taken into use for the first time before 1st July 1982 the minimum internal diameter shall be 1.75 metres;

(c) where a diving bell is used, be capable of allowing a person to transfer under pressure from the bell to the surface compression chamber and vice versa;

(d) provide a suitable environment and suitable facilities for the persons who are to use it, having regard to the kind of operation in connection with which it is used and the period during which the pressure is raised;

(e) be so designed as to mimimize the risk of fire;

(f) have a lock through which food and medical supplies may be passed into the chamber while its occupants remain under pressure;

(g) be equipped with such valves, gauges and other fittings (which are to be made of suitable materials and so designed as to minimize the noise inside the chamber during rapid pressurization) as are necessary to control and indicate the internal pressures of each compartment from outside the chamber;

(h) be fitted with adequate equipment, including reserve facilities, for supplying and maintaining the appropriate breathing mixture to persons inside it;

(i) be equipped with a two-way oral communication system;

(j) be fitted with equipment for heating and lighting the chamber and adequate first aid and sanitary facilities.

SCHEDULE 6
Regulation 12(1)(g)
Diving Bells

A diving bell shall:

(*a*) be equipped with means by which each diver using the bell is able to enter and leave it without difficulty;

(*b*) be capable of allowing a person to transfer under pressure from it to a surface compression chamber and vice versa;

(*c*) be equipped with doors which act as pressure seals and which may be opened from either side;

(*d*) be equipped with such valves, gauges and other fittings (which are to be made of suitable materials) as are necessary to control and indicate the pressure within the bell and to indicate to those inside the bell and to the diving supervisor the external pressure on the bell;

(*e*) be fitted with adequate equipment including reserve facilities for supplying the appropriate breathing mixture to persons occupying or working from the bell;

(*f*) be equipped with a two-way oral communication system which enables contact to be maintained both with persons at the place from which the diving operation is carried on and with divers while they are outside the bell;

(*g*) be fitted with equipment for lighting and heating the bell;

(*h*) contain adequate first aid facilities and be fitted with lifting equipment sufficient to enable an unconscious or injured diver to be hoisted into the bell by a person inside it;

(*i*) be provided with means by which, in the event of any energency, it can be rapidly located by through water signals from the stricken bell and the lives of trapped persons can be sustained for at least 24 hours or, where that is not practicable, sustained for as long as is practicable;

(*j*) be used in association with lifting gear which enables the chamber to be lowered to the depth from which the diving operations are to be carried on, maintained in its position and raised, in each case without excessive lateral, vertical or rotational movement taking place; and

(*k*) be provided with a means by which, in the event of failure of the main lifting gear, the chamber can be returned to the surface; if those means involve the shedding of weights, they shall be capable of being shed from the bell by a person inside it and a means shall be incorporated to prevent their accidental shedding.

EXPLANATORY NOTE
(*This Note is not part of the Regulations*)

These Regulations apply to diving operations in which the divers are at work either in Great Britain or outside Great Britain in circumstances covered by the Health and Safety at Work etc. Act 1974 (Application outside Great Britain) Order 1977. They also apply when a surface compression chamber is being used in connection with a diving operation or the testing of equipment for use in a diving operation.

The principal provisions of the Regulations are that for each diving operation there must be a diving contractor whose main duties are to provide safe and suitable plant and equipment, to make diving rules laying down the procedures to be followed in the operation and to appoint a diving supervisor to have immediate control of it. Duties are placed on the diving supervisor, who must have certain qualifications or experience, on the divers themselves and on all persons having any control over the diving operation. Divers are required to have certificates of training in the type of diving to be undertaken and of medical fitness to dive.

Certain divers are excluded from the Regulations (Regulation 2(2)(*b*)), principally those using snorkel type apparatus or no underwater breathing apparatus at all and those in submersible craft or pressure-resistant suits at less than 300 millibars above atmospheric pressure.

Existing Regulations relating to diving at work are revoked or modified by Regulation 16 or will be revoked separately.

The Regulations also contain transitional and incidental provisions including requirements for the keeping of records.

█ REGULATIONS █ US COAST GUARD

SUBCHAPTER V—
MARINE OCCUPATIONAL
SAFETY AND HEALTH
STANDARDS

Part 197—
General Provisions

SUBPART B—COMMERCIAL DIVING OPERATIONS

AUTHORITY: (46 U.S.C. 239; 46 U.S.C. 390b; 46 U.S.C. 391a; 33 U.S.C. 1509(b); 43 U.S.C. 1333(d)(1); 43 U.S.C. 1331 et seq., as amended by Sec. 203 and 208 of Pub. L. 95-372; 46 U.S.C. 395; 46 U.S.C. 375; 46 U.S.C. 391; 46 U.S.C. 392; 46 U.S.C. 416; 49 U.S.C. 1655(b); 49 CFR 1.46 (b) and (s).)

Subpart B—Commercial Diving Operations

General

197.200 PURPOSE OF SUBPART.
This subpart prescribes rules for the design, construction, and use of equipment, and inspection, operation, and safety and health standards for commercial diving operations taking place from vessels and facilities under Coast Guard jurisdiction.

197.202 APPLICABILITY.
(a) This subpart applies to commercial diving operations taking place at any deepwater port or the safety zone thereof as defined in 33 CFR 150; from any artificial island, installation, or other device on the Outer Continental Shelf and the waters adjacent thereto as defined in 33 CFR 147 or otherwise related to activities on the Outer Continental Shelf; and from all vessels required to have a certificate of inspection issued by the Coast Guard including mobile offshore drilling units regardless of their geographic location, or from any vessel connected with a deepwater port or within the deepwater port safety zone, or from any vessel engaged in activities related to the Outer Continental Shelf; except that this subpart does not apply to any diving operation—

(1) Performed solely for marine scientific research and development purposes by educational institutions;

(2) Performed solely for research and development for the advancement of diving equipment and technology; or

(3) Performed solely for search and rescue or related public safety purposes by or under the control of a governmental agency.

(b) Diving operations may deviate from the requirements of this subpart to the extent necessary to prevent or minimize a situation which is likely to cause death, injury, or major environmental damage. The circumstances leading to the situation, the deviations made, and the corrective action taken, if appropriate, to reduce the possibility of recurrence shall be recorded by the diving supervisor in the logbook as required by § 197.482(c).

197.204 DEFINITIONS.
As used in this subpart:
ACFM means actual cubic feet per minute.
ANSI Code means the B31.1 American National Standards Institute 'Code for Pressure Piping, Power Piping'.
ASME Code means the American Society of Mechanical Engineers 'Boiler and Pressure Vessel Code'.
ASME PVHO-1 means the ANSI/ASME standard 'Safety Standard for Pressure Vessels for Human Occupancy'.
ATA means a measure of pressure expressed in terms of atmosphere absolute (includes barometric pressure).
Bell means a compartment either at ambient pressure (open bell) or pressurized (closed bell) that allows the diver to be transported to and from the underwater work site, allows the diver access to the surrounding environ-

ment, and is capable of being used as a refuge during diving operations.
Bottom time means the total elapsed time measured in minutes from the time the diver leaves the surface in descent to the time to the next whole minute that the diver begins ascent.
Breathing gas/breathing mixture means the mixed-gas, oxygen, or air as appropriate supplied to the diver for breathing.
Bursting pressure means the pressure at which a pressure containment device would fail structurally.
Commercial diver means a diver engaged in underwater work for hire excluding sport and recreational diving and the instruction thereof.
Commercial diving operation means all activities in support of a commercial diver.
Cylinder means a pressure vessel for the storage of gases under pressure.
Decompression chamber means a pressure vessel for human occupancy such as a surface decompression chamber, closed bell, or deep diving system especially equipped to recompress, decompress, and treat divers.
Decompression sickness means a condition caused by the formation of gas or gas bubbles in the blood or body tissue as a result of pressure reduction.
Decompression table means a profile or set of profiles of ascent rates and breathing mixtures designed to reduce the pressure on a diver safely to atmospheric pressure after the diver has been exposed to a specific depth and bottom time.
Depth means the maximum pressure expressed in feet of seawater attained by a diver and is used to express the depth of a dive.
Dive location means that portion of a vessel or facility from which a diving operation is conducted.
Dive team means the divers and diver support personnel involved in a diving operation, including the diving supervisor.
Diver means a person working beneath the surface, exposed to hyperbaric conditions, and using underwater breathing apparatus.
Diver-carried reserve breathing gas means a supply of air or mixed-gas, as appropriate, carried by the diver in addition to the primary or secondary breathing gas supplied to the diver.
Diving installation means all of the equipment used in support of a commercial diving operation.
Diving mode means a type of diving requiring SCUBA, surface-supplied air, or surface-supplied mixed-gas equipment, with related procedures and techniques.
Diving stage means a suspended platform constructed to carry one or more divers and used for putting divers into the water and bringing them to the surface when in-water decompression or a heavy-weight diving outfit is used.
Diving supervisor means the person having complete responsibility for the safety of a commercial diving operation including the responsibility for the safety and health of all diving personnel in accordance with this subpart.
Facility means a deepwater port, or an artificial island, installation, or other

device on the Outer Continental Shelf subject to Coast Guard jurisdiction.
Fsw means feet of seawater (or equivalent static pressure head).
Gas embolism means a condition caused by expanding gases, which have been taken into and retained in the lungs while breathing under pressure, being forced into the bloodstream or other tissues during ascent or decompression.
Heavy-weight diving outfit means diver-worn surface-supplied deep-sea dress.
Hyperbaric conditions means pressure conditions in excess of surface atmospheric pressure.
Injurious corrosion means an advanced state of corrosion which may impair the structural integrity or safe operation of the equipment.
Liveboating means the support of a surfaced-supplied diver from a vessel underway.
Maximum working pressure means the maximum pressure to which a pressure containment device can be exposed under operating conditions (usually the pressure setting of the pressure relief device).
No-decompression limits means the air depth and bottom time limits of appendix A.
Pressure vessel means a container capable of withstanding an internal maximum working pressure over 15 psig.
Psi(g) means pounds per square inch (gage).
PVHO means pressure vessel for human occupancy but does not include pressure vessels for human occupancy that may be subjected to external pressures in excess of 15 psig but can only be subjected to maximum internal pressures of 15 psig or less (i.e., submersibles, or one atmosphere observation bells).
Saturation diving means saturating a diver's tissues with the inert gas in the breathing mixture to allow an extension of bottom time without additional decompression.
SCUBA diving means a diving mode in which the diver is supplied with a compressed breathing mixture from diver carried equipment.
Standby diver means a diver at the dive location available to assist a diver in the water.
Surface-supplied air diving means a diving mode in which the diver is supplied from the dive location or bell with compressed breathing air including oxygen or oxygen enriched air if supplied for treatment.
Surface-supplied mixed-gas diving means a diving mode in which the diver is supplied from the dive location or bell with a compressed breathing mixture other than air.
Timekeeping device means a device for measuring the time of a dive in minutes.
Treatment table means a depth, time, and breathing gas profile designed to treat a diver for decompression sickness.
Umbilical means the hose bundle between a dive location and a diver or bell, or between a diver and a bell, that supplies the diver or bell with a life-line, breathing gas, communications, power,

and heat as appropriate to the diving mode or conditions.

Vessel means any waterborne craft including mobile offshore drilling units required to have a Certificate of Inspection issued by the Coast Guard or any waterborne craft connected with a deepwater port or within the deepwater port safety zone, or any waterborne craft engaged in activities related to the Outer Continental Shelf.

Volume tank means a pressure vessel connected to the outlet of a compressor and used as an air reservoir.

Working pressure means the pressure to which a pressure containment device is exposed at any particular instant during normal operating conditions.

197.205 AVAILABILITY OF STANDARDS

(a) Several standards have been incorporated by reference in this subchapter. The incorporation by reference has been approved by the Director of the FEDERAL REGISTER under the provisions of 1 CFR Part 51.

(b) The standards are available from the appropriate organizations whose addresses are listed below:

(1) American National Standards Institute, 1430 Broadway, New York, N.Y. 10018.

(2) American Society of Mechanical Engineers, United Engineering Center, 345 East 47th Street, New York, N.Y. 10017.

197.206. SUBSTITUTES FOR REQUIRED EQUIPMENT, MATERIALS, APPARATUS, ARRANGEMENTS, PROCEDURES, OR TESTS.

(a) The Coast Guard may accept substitutes for equipment, materials, apparatus, arrangements, procedures, or tests required in this subpart if the substitute provides an equivalent level of safety.

(b) In any case where it is shown to the satisfaction of the Commandant that the use of any particular equipment, material, apparatus, arrangement, procedure, or test is unreasonable or impracticable, the Commandant may permit the use of alternate equipment, material, apparatus, arrangement, procedure, or test to such an extent and upon such condition as will insure, to his satisfaction, a degree of safety consistent with the minimum standards set forth in this Subpart.

197.208 DESIGNATION OF PERSON-IN-CHARGE.

(a) The owner or agent of a vessel or facility without a designated master shall designate, in writing, an individual to be the person-in-charge of the vessel or facility.

(b) Where a master is designated, the master is the person-in-charge.

197.210 DESIGNATION OF DIVING SUPERVISOR.

The name of the supervisor for each commercial diving operation shall be—

(a) Designated in writing; and

(b) Given to the person-in-charge prior to the commencement of any commercial diving operation.

Equipment

197.300 APPLICABILITY.

(a) Each diving installation used on each vessel or facility subject to this subpart must meet the requirements of this subpart.

(b) In addition to the requirements of this subpart, equipment which is permanently installed on vessels and is part of the diving installation must meet subchapters F and J of this chapter.

(c) All repairs and modifications to pressure vessels used for commercial diving operations must be made in accordance with the requirements of section VIII, division 1 or division 2 of the ASME Code, ASME PVIIO-1, part 54 of this chapter, or 49 CFR 173.34, as applicable.

(d) All repairs and modifications to pressure piping used for commercial diving operations must be made in accordance with the requirements of the ANSI Code or part 56 of this chapter, as applicable.

197.310 AIR COMPRESSOR SYSTEM.

A compressor used to supply breathing air to a diver must have—

(a) A volume tank that is—

(1) Built and stamped in accordance with section VIII, division 1 of the ASME Code with—
(i) A check valve on the inlet side;
(ii) A pressure gage;
(iii) A relief valve; and
(iv) A drain valve; and

(2) Tested after every repair, modification, or alteration to the pressure boundaries as required by § 197.462;

(b) Intakes that are located away from areas containing exhaust fumes of internal combustion engines or other hazardous contaminants;

(c) An efficient filtration system; and

(d) Slow-opening shut-off valves when the maximum allowable working pressure of the system exceeds 500 psig.

197.312 BREATHING SUPPLY HOSES.

(a) Each breathing supply hose must—

(1) Have a maximum working pressure that is equal to or exceeds—
(i) The maximum working pressure of the section of the breathing supply system in which used; and
(ii) The pressure equivalent of the maximum depth of the dive relative to the supply source plus 100 psig;

(2) Have a bursting pressure of four times its maximum working pressure;

(3) Have connectors that—
(i) Are made of corrosion-resistant material;
(ii) Are resistant to accidental disengagement; and
(iii) Have a maximum working pressure that is at least equal to the maximum working pressure of the hose to which they are attached; and

(4) Resist kinking by—
(i) Being made of kink-resistant materials; or
(ii) Having exterior support.

(b) Each umbilical must—

(1) Meet the requirements of paragraph (a) of this section; and

(2) Be marked from the diver or open bell end in 10-foot intervals to 100 feet and in 50-foot intervals thereafter.

197.314 FIRST AID AND TREATMENT EQUIPMENT.

(a) Each dive location must have—

(1) A medical kit approved by a physician that consists of—
(i) Basic first aid supplies; and
(ii) Any additional supplies necessary to treat minor trauma and illnesses resulting from hyperbaric exposure;

(2) A copy of an American Red Cross Standard First Aid handbook;

(3) A bag-type manual resuscitator with transparent mask and tubing; and

(4) A capability to remove an injured diver from the water.

(b) Each diving installation must have a two-way communications system to obtain emergency assistance except when the vessel or facility ship-to-shore, two-way communications system is readily available.

(c) Each dive location supporting mixed-gas dives, dives deeper than 130 fsw, or dives outside the no-decompression limits must meet the requirements of paragraph (a) of this section and have—

(1) A decompression chamber;

(2) Decompression and treatment tables;

(3) A supply of breathing gases sufficient to treat for decompression sickness;

(4) The medical kit required by paragraph (a)(1) of this section that is—
(i) Capable of being carried into the decompression chamber; and
(ii) Suitable for use under hyperbaric conditions; and

(5) A capability to assist an injured diver into the decompression chamber.

197.318 GAGES AND TIMEKEEPING DEVICES.

(a) A gage indicating diver depth must be at each dive location for surface-supplied dives.

(b) A timekeeping device must be at each dive location.

197.320 DIVING LADDER AND STAGE.

(a) Each diving ladder must—

(1) Be capable of supporting the weight of at least two divers;

(2) Extend 3 feet below the water surface;

(3) Be firmly in place;

(4) Be available at the dive location for a diver to enter or exit the water unless a diving stage or bell is provided; and

(5) Be—(i) Made of corrosion-resistant material; or
(ii) Protected against and maintained free from injurious corrosion.

(b) Each diving stage must—

(1) Be capable of supporting the weight of at least two divers;

(2) Have an open-grating platform;

(3) Be available for a diver to enter or exit the water from the dive location and for in-water decompression if the diver is—
(i) Wearing a heavy-weight diving outfit; or
(ii) Diving outside the no-decompression limits, except when

a bell is provided; and

(4) Be—(i) Made of corrosion-resistant material; or
(ii) Protected against and maintained free from injurious corrosion.

197.322 SURFACE-SUPPLIED HELMETS AND MASKS.

(a) Each surface-supplied helmet or mask must have—
(1) A nonreturn valve at the attachment point between helmet or mask and umbilical that closes readily and positively;
(2) An exhaust valve; and
(3) A two-way voice communication system between the diver and the dive location or bell.

(b) Each surface-supplied air helmet or mask must—
(1) Ventilate at least 4.5 ACFM at any depth at which it is operated; or
(2) Be able to maintain the diver's inspired carbon dioxide partial pressure below 0.02 ATA when the diver is producing carbon dioxide at the rate of 1.6 standard liters per minute.

197.324 DIVER'S SAFETY HARNESS.

Each safety harness used in surface-supplied diving must have—
(a) A positive buckling device; and
(b) An attachment point for the umbilical life line that—
(1) Distributes the pulling force of the umbilical over the diver's body; and
(2) Prevents strain on the mask or helmet.

197.326 OXYGEN SAFETY.

(a) Equipment used with oxygen or oxygen mixtures greater than 40 per cent by volume must be designed for such use.

(b) Oxygen systems with pressures greater than 125 psig must have slow-opening shut-off valves except pressure boundary shut-off valves may be ball valves.

197.328 PVHO—GENERAL.

(a) Each PVHO, contracted for or purchased after February 1, 1979, must be built and stamped in accordance with ASME PVHO-1.

(b) Each PVHO, contracted for or constructed before February 1, 1979, and not Coast Guard approved, must be submitted to the Coast Guard for approval prior to February 1, 1984.

(c) To be approved under paragraph (b), a PVHO must be—
(1) Constructed in accordance with Part 54 of this Chapter; or—
(2) Be built in accordance with section VIII, division 1 or division 2 of the ASME Code; and
(i) Have the plans approved in accordance with § 54.01-18 of this chapter;
(ii) Pass the radiographic and other V welded joints required by section VIII, division 1 or division 2, as appropriate, of the ASME Code; and
(iii) Pass—(A) The hydrostatic test described in § 54.10-10 of this chapter; or
(B) The pneumatic test described in § 54.10-15 of this

chapter and such additional tests as the Officer-in-Charge, Marine Inspection (OCMI) may require.

(d) Each PVHO must—
(1) Have a shut-off valve located within 1 foot of the pressure boundary on all piping penetrating the pressure boundary;
(2) Have a check valve located within 1 foot of the pressure boundary on all piping exclusively carrying fluids into the PVHO;
(3) Have the pressure relief device required by ASME PVHO-1;
(4) Have a built-in breathing system with at least one mask per occupant stored inside each separately pressurized compartment;
(5) Have a two-way voice communications system allowing communications between an occupant in one pressurized compartment of the PVHO and—
(i) The diving supervisor at the dive location;
(ii) Any divers being supported from the same PVHO; and
(iii) Occupants of other separately pressurized compartments of the same PVHO;
(6) If designed to mechanically couple to another PVHO, have a two-way communications system allowing communications between occupants of each PVHO when mechanically coupled;
(7) Have a pressure gage in the interior of each compartment that is—
(i) Designed for human occupancy; and
(ii) Capable of having the compartment pressure controlled from inside the PVHO;
(8) Have viewports that allow observation of occupants from the outside;
(9) Have viewports that meet the requirements of ASME PVHO-1 except those PVHO's approved under paragraph (b) of this section which have nonacrylic viewports;
(10) Have means of illumination sufficient to allow an occupant to—
(i) Read gages; and
(ii) Operate the installed systems within each compartment;
(11) Be designed and equipped to minimize sources of combustible materials and ignition;
(12) Have a protective device on the inlet side of PVHO exhaust lines;
(13) Have a means of extinguishing a fire in the interior;
(14) Have a means of maintaining the oxygen content of the interior atmosphere below 25 per cent surface equivalent by volume when pressurized with air as the breathing mixture;
(15) Have a means of maintaining the interior atmosphere below 2 per cent surface equivalent carbon dioxide by volume;
(16) Have a means of overriding and controlling from the exterior all interior breathing and pressure supply controls;

(17) Have a speech unscrambler when used with mixed-gas;
(18) Have interior electrical systems that are designed for the environment in which they will operate to minimize the risk of fire, electrical shock to personnel, and galvanic action of the PVHO; and
(19) Be tested after every repair, modification, or alteration to the pressure boundaries as required by § 197.462.

197.330 PVHO—CLOSED BELLS.

(a) Except as provided in paragraph (b) of this section, each closed bell must meet the requirements of § 197.328 and—
(1) Have underwater breathing apparatus for each occupant stored inside each separately pressurized compartment;
(2) Have an umbilical;
(3) Have lifting equipment attached to the closed bell capable of returning the occupied closed bell when fully flooded to the dive location;
(4) Be capable of recompressing on the surface to the maximum design diving depth;
(5) Be constructed and equipped as required by § 197.332;
(6) Have an emergency locating device designed to assist personnel on the surface in acquiring and maintaining contact with the submerged PVHO if the umbilical to the surface is severed;
(7) Have a capability to remove an injured diver from the water; and
(8) Have a life support capability for the intact closed bell and its occupants for—
(i) Twelve hours after an accident severing the umbilical to the surface when the umbilical to the surface is the only installed means of retrieving the closed bell; or
(ii) A period of time, at least equal to 1 hour plus twice the time required to retrieve the bell from its designed operating depth and attach an auxiliary lifesupport system, after an accident severing the umbilical to the surface when the umbilical is one of the two independent installed means of retrieving the closed bell, each meeting the requirements of paragraph (a)(3) of this section.

(b) A closed bell that does not meet the requirements of paragraphs (a)(3), (a)(4), and (a)(5) of this section, must be capable of attachment to another PVHO that—
(1) Allows the transfer of personnel and diver's equipment under pressure from the closed bell to the PVHO;
(2) Meets the requirements of paragraph (a)(3) of this section;
(3) Is capable of attachment to a decompression chamber meeting the requirements of paragraphs (a)(4) and (a)(5) of this section; and
(4) Allows the transfer of personnel

and diver's equipment under pressure from the PVHO to the decompression chamber.

197.332 PVHO—
DECOMPRESSION CHAMBERS.
Each decompression chamber must—
(a) Meet the requirements of § 197.328;
(b) Have internal dimensions sufficient to accomodate a diver lying in a horizontal position and another person tending the diver;
(c) Have a capability for ingress and egress of personnel and equipment while the occupants are under pressure;
(d) Have a means of operating all installed man-way locking devices, except disabled shipping dogs, from both sides of a closed hatch;
(e) Have interior illumination sufficient to allow visual observation, diagnosis, and medical treatment of an occupant.
(f) Have one bunk for each two occupants;
(g) Have a capability that allows bunks to be seen over their entire lengths from the exterior;
(h) Have a minimum pressure capability of—
  (1) 6 ATA, when used for diving to 300 fsw; or
  (2) The maximum depth of the dive, when used for diving operations deeper than 300 fsw, unless a closed bell meeting the requirements of § 197.330(a) (3), (4), and (5) is used;
(i) Have a minimum pressurization rate of 2 ATA per minute to 60 fsw and at least 1 ATA per minute thereafter;
(j) Have a decompression rate of 1 ATA per minute to 30 fsw;
(k) Have an external pressure gage for each pressurized compartment;
(l) Have a capability to supply breathing mixtures at the maximum rate required by each occupant doing heavy work; and
(m) Have a sound-powered headset or telephone as a backup to the communications system required by § 197.328(c) (5) and (6), except when that communications system is a sound-powered system.

197.334 OPEN DIVING BELLS.
Each open diving bell must—
(a) Have an upper section that provides an envelope capable of maintaining a bubble of breathing mixture available to a diver standing on the lower section of the platform with his body through the open bottom and his head in the bubble;
(b) Have lifting equipment capable of returning the occupied open bell to the dive location;
(c) Have an umbilical; and
(d) Be—
  (1) Made of corrosion-resisting material; or
  (2) Protected against and maintained free from injurious corrosion.

197.336 PRESSURE PIPING.
Piping systems that are not an integral part of the vessel or facility, carrying fluids under pressures exceeding 15 psig must—
(a) Meet the ANSI Code;
(b) Have the point of connection to the integral piping system of the vessel or facility clearly marked; and

(c) Be tested after every repair, modification, or alteration to the pressure boundaries as set forth in § 197.462.

197.338 COMPRESSED GAS CYLINDERS.
Each compressed gas cylinder must—
(a) Be stored in a ventilated area;
(b) Be protected from excessive heat;
(c) Be prevented from falling;
(d) Be tested after any repair, modification, or alteration to the pressure boundaries as set forth in § 197.462; and
(e) Meet the requirements of—
  (1) Part 54 of this Chapter; or
  (2) 49 CFR 173.34 and 49 CFR 178 Subpart C.

197.340 BREATHING GAS SUPPLY.
(a) A primary breathing gas supply for surface-supplied diving must be sufficient to support the following for the duration of the planned dive:
  (1) The diver.
  (2) The standby diver.
  (3) The decompression chamber, when required by § 197.432 (e)(2) or by § 197.434(a) for the duration of the dive and for one hour after completion of the planned dive.
  (4) A decompression chamber when provided but not required by this subpart.
  (5) A closed bell when provided or required by § 197.434(d).
  (6) An open bell when provided or required by § 197.432(e)(4) or by § 197.434(c).
(b) A secondary breathing gas supply for surface-supplied diving must be sufficient to support the following:
  (1) The diver while returning to the surface.
  (2) The diver during decompression.
  (3) The standby diver.
  (4) The decompression chamber when required by § 197.432(e)(2) or by § 197.434(a) for the duration of the dive and one hour after the completion of the planned dive.
  (5) The closed bell while returning the diver to the surface.
  (6) The open bell while returning the diver to the surface.
(c) A diver-carried reserve breathing gas supply for surface-supplied diving must be sufficient to allow the diver to—
  (1) Reach the surface.
  (2) Reach another source of breathing gas; or
  (3) Be reached by a standby diver equipped with another source of breathing gas for the diver.
(d) A primary breathing gas supply for SCUBA diving must be sufficient to support the diver for the duration of the planned dive through his return to the dive location or planned pick-up point.
(e) A diver-carried reserve breathing gas supply for SCUBA diving must be sufficient to allow the diver to return to the dive location or planned pick-up point from the greatest depth of the planned dive.
(f) Oxygen used for breathing mixtures must—
  (1) Meet the requirements of Federal Specification BB-0-925a; and
  (2) Be type 1 (gaseous) grade A or B.

(g) Nitrogen used for breathing mixtures must—
  (1) Meet the requirements of Federal Specification BB-N-411c;
  (2) Be type 1 (gaseous);
  (3) Be class 1 (oil free); and
  (4) Be grade A, B, or C.
(h) Helium used for breathing mixtures must be grades A, B, or C produced by the Federal Government, or equivalent.
(i) Compressed air used for breathing mixtures must—
  (1) Be 20 or 22 per cent oxygen by volume;
  (2) Have no objectionable odour; and
  (3) Have no more than—
    (i) 1000 parts per million of carbon dioxide;
    (ii) 20 parts per million carbon monoxide;
    (iii) 5 milligrams per cubic meter of solid and liquid particulates including oil; and
    (iv) 25 parts per million of hydrocarbons (includes methane and all other hydrocarbons expressed as methane).

197.342 BUOYANCY-CHANGING DEVICES.
(a) A dry suit or other buoyancy-changing device not directly connected to the exhaust valve of the helmet or mask must have an independent exhaust valve.
(b) When used for SCUBA diving, a buoyancy-changing device must have an inflation source separate from the breathing gas supply.

197.344 INFLATABLE FLOATATION DEVICES.
An inflatable floatation device for SCUBA diving must—
(a) Be capable of maintaining the diver at the surface in a faceup position;
(b) Have a manually activated inflation device;
(c) Have an oral inflation device;
(d) Have an over-pressure relief device; and
(e) Have a manually operated exhaust valve.

197.346 DIVER'S EQUIPMENT.
(a) Each diver using SCUBA must have—
  (1) Self-contained underwater breathing equipment including—
    (i) A primary breathing gas supply with a cylinder pressure gage readable by the diver during the dive; and
    (ii) A diver-carried reserve breathing gas supply provided by
      (A) A manual reserve (J valve); or
      (B) An independent reserve cylinder connected and ready for use;
  (2) A face mask;
  (3) An inflatable floatation device;
  (4) A weight belt capable of quick release;
  (5) A knife;
  (6) Swim fins or shoes;
  (7) A diving wristwatch; and
  (8) A depth gage.
(b) Each diver using a heavyweight diving outfit must—
  (1) Have a helmet group consisting of helmet, breastplate, and as-

sociated valves and connections;
(2) Have a diving dress group consisting of a basic dress that encloses the body (except for head and hands) in a tough, waterproof cover, gloves, shoes, weight assembly, and knife;
(3) Have a hose group consisting of the breathing gas hose and fittings, the control valve, the lifeline, communications cable, and a pneumofathometer; and
(4) Be provided with a helmet cushion and weighted shoes.
(c) Each surface-supplied dive operation using a heavyweight diving outfit must have an extra breathing gas hose with attaching tools available to the standby diver.
(d) Each diver using a lightweight diving outfit must have—
(1) A safety harness.
(2) A weight assembly capable of quick release.
(3) A mask group consisting of a lightweight mask and associated valves and connections;
(4) A diving dress group consisting of wet or dry diving dress, gloves, shoes or fins, and knife; and
(5) A hose group consisting of the breathing gas hose and fittings, the control valve, the lifeline, communications cable, and a pneumofathometer (if the breaking strength of the communications cable is at least equal to that required for the lifeline, the communications cable can serve as the lifeline).
(e) Each surface-supplied air dive operation within the no-decompression limits and to depths of 130 fsw or less must have a primary breathing gas supply at the dive location.
(f) Each surface-supplied dive operation outside the no-compression limits, deeper than 130 fsw, or using mixed-gas as a breathing mixture must have at the dive location—
(1) A primary breathing gas supply; and
(2) A secondary breathing gas supply.
(g) Each diver diving outside the no-decompression limits, deeper than 130 fsw, or using mixed-gas must have a diver-carried reserve breathing gas supply except when using a heavyweight diving outfit or when diving in a physically confining area.

Operations

197.400 APPLICABILITY.
Diving operations may only be conducted from a vessel or facility subject to the subpart if the regulations in this subpart are met.

197.402 RESPONSIBILITIES OF THE PERSON-IN-CHARGE
(a) The person-in-charge shall—
(1) Be fully cognizant of the provisions of this subpart;
(2) Prior to permitting any commercial diving operation to commence, have—
(i) The designation of the diving supervisor for each diving operation as required by § 197.210;
(ii) A report on—

(A) The nature and planned times of the planned diving operation; and
(B) The planned involvement of the vessel or facility, its equipment, and its personnel in the diving operation.
(b) Prior to permitting any commercial diving operation involving liveboating to commence, the person-in-charge shall insure that—
(1) A means of rapid communications with the diving supervisor while the diver is entering, in, or leaving the water is established; and
(2) A boat and crew for diver pick-up in the event of an emergency is provided.
(c) The person-in-charge shall insure that a boat and crew for SCUBA diver pickup is provided when SCUBA divers are not line-tended from the dive location.
(d) The person-in-charge shall co-ordinate the activities on and off the vessel or facility with the diving supervisor.
(e) The person-in-charge shall insure that the vessel or facility equipment and personnel are kept clear of the dive location except after co-ordinating with the diving supervisor.

197.404 RESPONSIBILITIES OF THE DIVING SUPERVISOR.
(a) The diving supervisor shall—
(1) Be fully cognizant of the provisions of this subpart;
(2) Be fully cognizant of the provisions of the operations manual required by § 197.420;
(3) Insure that diving operations conducted from a vessel or facility subject to this subpart meet the regulations in this subpart;
(4) Prior to the commencement of any commercial diving operation, provide the report required by § 197.402 to the person-in-charge;
(5) Co-ordinate with the person-in-charge any changes that are made to the report required by § 197.402; and
(6) Promptly notify the person-in-charge of any diving related casualty, accident, or injury.
(b) The diving supervisor is in charge of the planning and execution of the diving operation including the responsibility for the safety and health of the dive team.

197.410 DIVE PROCEDURES.
(a) The diving supervisor shall insure that—
(1) Before commencing diving operations, dive team members are briefed on—
(i) The tasks to be undertaken;
(ii) Any unusual hazards or environmental conditions likely to affect the safety of the diving operation; and
(iii) Any modifications to the operations manual or procedures including safety procedures necessitated by the specific diving operation;
(2) The breathing gas supply systems, masks, helmets, thermal

protection, when provided, and bell lifting equipment, when a bell is provided or required, are inspected prior to each diving operation;
(3) Each diver is instructed to report any physical problems or physiological effects including aches, pains, current illnesses, or symptoms of decompression sickness prior to each dive;
(4) A depth, bottom time profile, including any breathing mixture changes, is maintained at the dive location for each diver during the dive, except that SCUBA divers shall maintain their own profiles;
(5) A two-way voice communication system is used between—
(i) Each surface-supplied diver and a dive team member at the dive location or bell (when provided); and
(ii) The bell (when provided) and the dive location;
(6) A two-way communication system is available at the dive location to obtain emergency assistance;
(7) After the completion of each dive—
(i) The physical condition of the diver is checked by—
(A) Visual observation; and
(B) Questioning the diver about his physical well-being;
(ii) The diver is instructed to report any physical problems or adverse physiological effects including aches, pains, current illnesses, or symptoms of decompression sickness or gas embolism;
(iii) The diver is advised of the location of an operational decompression chamber; and
(iv) The diver is alerted to the potential hazards of flying after diving;
(8) For any dive outside the no-decompression limits, deeper than 130 fsw, or using mixed-gas as a breathing mixture—
(i) A depth, time, decompression profile including breathing mixture changes is maintained for each diver at the dive location;
(ii) The diver is instructed to remain awake and in the vicinity of the dive location decompression chamber for at least one hour after the completion of a dive, decompression, or treatment; and
(iii) A dive team member, other than the diver, is trained and available to operate the decompression chamber; and
(9) When decompression sickness or gas embolism is suspected or symptoms are evident, a report is completed containing—
(i) The investigation for each incident including—
(A) The dive and decompression profiles;
(B) The composition, depth, and time of breathing mixture changes;
(C) A description of the symptoms including depth and time

of onset; and

(D) A description and results of the treatment;

(ii) The evaluation for each incident based on—

(A) The investigation;

(B) Consideration of the past performance of the decompression table used; and

(C) Individual susceptibility; and

(iii) The corrective action taken, if necessary, to reduce the probability of recurrence.

(b) The diving supervisor shall ensure that the working interval of a dive is terminated when he so directs or when—

(1) A diver requests termination;

(2) A diver fails to respond correctly to communications or signals from a dive team member;

(3) Communications are lost and cannot be quickly re-established between—

(i) The diver and a dive team member at the dive location; or

(ii) The person-in-charge and the diving supervisor during liveboating operations; or

(4) A diver begins to use his diver-carried reserve breathing gas supply.

197.420 OPERATIONS MANUAL.

(a) The diving supervisor shall—

(1) Provide an operations manual to the person-in-charge prior to commencement of any diving operation; and

(2) Make an operations manual available at the dive location to all members of the dive team.

(b) The operations manual must be modified in writing when adaptation is required because of—

(1) The configuration or operation of the vessel or facility; or

(2) The specific diving operation as planned.

(c) The operations manual must provide for the safety and health of the divers.

(d) The operations manual must contain the following:

(1) Safety procedures and checklists for each diving mode used.

(2) Assignments and responsibilities of each dive team member for each diving mode used.

(3) Equipment procedures and checklists for each diving mode used.

(4) Emergency procedures for—

(i) Fire;

(ii) Equipment failure;

(iii) Adverse environmental conditions including, but not limited to, weather and sea state;

(iv) Medical illness; and

(v) Treatment of injury.

(5) Procedures dealing with the use of—

(i) Hand-held power tools;

(ii) Welding and burning equipment; and

(iii) Explosives.

Specific Diving Mode Procedures

197.430 SCUBA DIVING.

The diving supervisor shall insure that—

(a) SCUBA diving is not conducted—

(1) Outside the no-decompression limits;

(2) At depths greater than 130 fsw;

(3) Against currents greater than one (1) knot unless line-tended; and

(4) If a diver cannot directly ascend to the surface unless line-tended;

(b) The SCUBA diver has the equipment required by § 197.346(a);

(c) A standby diver is available while a diver is in the water;

(d) A diver is line-tended from the surface or accompanied by another diver in the water in continuous visual contact during the diving operation;

(e) When a diver is in a physically confining space, another diver is stationed at the underwater point of entry and is line-tending the diver; and

(f) A boat is available for diver pickup when the divers are not line-tended from the dive location.

197.432 SURFACE-SUPPLIED AIR DIVING.

The diving supervisor shall insure that—

(a) Surface-supplied air diving is conducted at depths less than 190 fsw, except that dives with bottom times of 30 minutes or less may be conducted to depths of 220 fsw;

(b) Each diving operation has a primary breathing gas supply;

(c) Each diver is continuously tended while in the water;

(d) When a diver is in a physically confining space, another diver is stationed at the underwater point of entry and is line-tending the diver;

(e) For dives deeper than 130 fsw or outside the no-decompression limits—

(1) Each diving operation has a secondary breathing gas supply;

(2) A decompression chamber is ready for use at the dive location;

(3) A diving stage is used except when a bell is provided;

(4) A bell is used for dives with an in-water decompression time greater than 120 minutes, except when the diver is using a heavy-weight diving outfit or is diving in a physically confining space;

(5) A separate dive team member tends each diver in the water;

(6) A standby diver is available while a diver is in the water; and

(7) Each diver has a diver-carried reserve breathing gas supply except when using a heavy-weight diving outfit or when diving in a physically confining space;

(f) The surface-supplied air diver has the equipment required by § 197.346 (b) or (d).

197.434 SURFACE-SUPPLIED MIXED-GAS DIVING.

The diving supervisor shall insure that—

(a) When mixed-gas diving is conducted, a decompression chamber or a closed bell meeting the requirements of § 197.332 is ready for use at the dive location;

(b) A diving stage is used except when a bell is provided;

(c) A bell is used for dives deeper than 220 fsw or when the dive involves in-water decompression times greater than 120 minutes, except when the diver is using a heavy-weight diving outfit or is diving in a physically confining space;

(d) A closed bell is used for dives at depths greater than 300 fsw, except when diving is conducted in a physically confining space;

(e) A separate dive team member tends each diver in the water;

(f) A standby diver is available during all nonsaturation dives;

(g) When saturation diving is conducted—

(1) A standby diver is available when the closed bell leaves the dive location until the divers are in saturation; and

(2) A member of the dive team at the dive location is a diver able to assist in the recovery of the closed bell or its occupants, if required;

(h) When closed bell operations are conducted, a diver is available in the closed bell to assist a diver in the water;

(i) When a diver is in a physically confining space, another diver is stationed at the underwater point of entry and is line-tending the diver;

(j) Each diving operation has a primary and secondary breathing gas supply meeting the requirements of § 197.340; and

(k) The surface-supplied mixed-gas diver has the equipment required by § 197.346 (b) or (d).

197.436 LIVEBOATING.

(a) During liveboating operations, the person-in-charge shall insure that—

(1) Diving is not conducted in seas that impede station-keeping ability of the vessel;

(2) Liveboating operations are not conducted—

(i) From 1 hour after sunset to 1 hour before sunrise; or

(ii) During periods of restricted visibility;

(3) The propellers of the vessel are stopped before the diver enters or exits the water; and

(4) A boat is ready to be launched with crew in the event of an emergency.

(b) As used in paragraph (a)(2)(ii) of this section, 'restricted visibility' means any condition in which vessel navigational visibility is restricted by fog, mist, falling snow, heavy rainstorms, sandstorms or any other similar causes.

(c) During liveboating operations, the diving supervisor shall insure that—

(1) Diving is not conducted at depths greater than 220 fsw;

(2) Diving is not conducted in seas that impede diver mobility or work function;

(3) A means is used to prevent the diver's hose from entangling in the propellers of the vessel;

(4) Each diver carries a reserve breathing gas supply;

(5) A standby diver is available while a diver is in the water;

(6) Diving is not conducted with in-water decompression times greater than 120 minutes; and

(7) The person-in-charge is notified before a diver enters or exits the water.

Periodic Tests and Inspections of Diving Equipment

197.450 BREATHING GAS TESTS.
The diving supervisor shall insure that—
(a) The output of each air compressor is tested and meets the requirements of § 197.340 for quality and quantity by means of samples taken at the connection point to the distribution system—
   (1) Every 6 months; and
   (2) After every repair or modification.
(b) Purchased supplies of breathing mixtures supplied to a diver are checked before being placed on line for—
   (1) Certification that the supply meets the requirements of § 197.340; and
   (2) Noxious or offensive odor and oxygen percentage;
(c) Each breathing supply system is checked, prior to commencement of diving operations, at the umbilical or underwater breathing apparatus connection point for the diver, for noxious or offensive odor and presence of oil mist; and
(d) Each breathing supply system supplying mixed-gas to a diver, is checked, prior to commencement of diving operations, at the umbilical or underwater breathing apparatus connection point for the diver, for percentage of oxygen.

197.452 OXYGEN CLEANING.
The diving supervisor shall ensure that equipment used with oxygen or oxygen mixtures greater than 40 per cent by volume is cleaned of flammable materials—
(a) Before being placed into service; and
(b) After any repair, alteration, modification, or suspected contamination.

197.454 FIRST AID AND TREATMENT EQUIPMENT.
The diving supervisor shall ensure that medical kits are checked monthly to insure that all required supplies are present.

197.456 BREATHING SUPPLY HOSES.
(a) The diving supervisor shall insure that—
   (1) Each breathing supply hose is pressure tested prior to being placed into initial service and every 24 months thereafter to 1.5 times its maximum working pressure;
   (2) Each breathing supply hose assembly, prior to being placed into initial service and after any repair, modification, or alteration, is tensile tested by—
      (i) Subjecting each hose-to-fitting connection to a 200 pound axial load; and
      (ii) Passing a visual examination for evidence of separation, slippage, or other damage to the assembly;
   (3) Each breathing supply hose is periodically checked for—
      (i) Damage which is likely to affect pressure integrity; and
      (ii) Contamination which is likely to affect the purity of the breathing mixture delivered to the diver; and
   (4) The open ends of each breathing supply hose are taped, capped, or plugged when not in use.
(b) To meet the requirements of paragraph (a)(3) of this section, each breathing supply hose must be—
   (1) Carefully inspected before being shipped to the dive location;
   (2) Visually checked during daily operation; and
   (3) Checked for noxious or offensive odor before each diving operation.

197.458 GAGES AND TIMEKEEPING DEVICES.
The diving supervisor shall insure that—
(a) Each depth gage and timekeeping device is tested or calibrated against a master reference gage or timekeeping device every 6 months;
(b) A depth gage is tested when a discrepancy exists in a depth gage reading greater than 2 per cent of full scale between any two gages of similar range and calibration;
(c) A timekeeping device is tested when a discrepancy exists in a timekeeping device reading greater than one-quarter of a minute in a 4-hour period between any two timekeeping devices; and
(d) Each depth gage and timekeeping device is inspected before diving operations are begun.

197.460 DIVING EQUIPMENT.
The diving supervisor shall insure that the diving equipment designated for use in a dive under § 197.346 is inspected before each dive.

197.462 PRESSURE VESSELS AND PRESSURE PIPING.
(a) The diving supervisor shall insure that each volume tank, cylinder, PVHO, and pressure piping system has been examined and tested every 12 months and after any repair, modification, or alteration to the extent necessary to determine that they are in condition and fit for the service intended.
(b) The following tests must be made to meet the annual requirements of paragraph (a) of this section:
   (1) An internal and external visual examination for mechanical damage or deterioration. If a defect is found that may impair the safety of the pressure vessel, a hydrostatic test must be performed.
   (2) A leak test.
   (3) A pneumatic test.
   (4) A hydrostatic test every fifth year instead of the pneumatic test.
(c) The following tests must be made after any repair, modification, or alteration to meet the requirements of paragraph (a) of this section:
   (1) An internal and external visual examination for correctness and adequacy of repair, modification, or alteration.
   (2) A leak test.
   (3) A hydrostatic test when the repair, modification, or alteration affects the pressure boundary.
(d) When the pneumatic test on pressure vessels is conducted—
   (1) The test pressure must be the maximum allowable working pressure stamped on the pressure vessel; and
   (2) The test may be conducted only after suitable precautions are taken to protect personnel and equipment.
(e) When the pneumatic test on pressure piping is conducted
   (1) The test pressure must be no less than 90 per cent of the setting of the relief device; and
   (2) The test may be conducted only after suitable precautions are taken to protect personnel and equipment.
(f) When a hydrostatic test on a pressure vessel is made, the test pressure must be—
   (1) $1\frac{1}{4}$ times the pressure stamped on the pressure vessel built to division 2 of the ASME Code; and
   (2) $1\frac{1}{2}$ times the pressure stamped on the pressure vessel built to division 1 of the ASME Code.
(g) When a hydrostatic test on pressure piping is conducted, the test must be conducted in accordance with the ANSI Code.
(h) When the leak test on pressure vessels or pressure piping is conducted—
   (1) The test must be conducted with the breathing mixture normally used in service;
   (2) The test must be conducted at the maximum allowable working pressure; and
   (3) The test pressure must be maintained for a minimum of 10 minutes to allow checking all joints, connections, and regions of high stress for leakage.

Records

197.480 LOGBOOKS.
(a) The person-in-charge of a vessel or facility required by 46 U.S.C. 201 to have an official logbook shall maintain the logbook on form CG-706.
(b) The person-in-charge of a vessel or facility not required by 46 U.S.C. 201 to have an official logbook, shall maintain, on board, a logbook for making the entries required by this subpart.
(c) The diving supervisor conducting commercial diving operations from a vessel or facility subject to this subpart shall maintain a logbook for making the entries required by this subpart.

197.482 LOGBOOK ENTRIES.
(a) The person-in-charge shall insure that the following information is recorded in the logbook for each commercial diving operation:
   (1) Date, time and location at the start and completion of dive operations.
   (2) Approximate underwater and surface conditions (weather, visibility, temperatures, and currents).
   (3) Name of the diving supervisor.
   (4) General nature of work performed.
(b) The diving supervisor shall insure that the following information is recorded in the logbook for each commercial diving operation:

(1) Date, time, and location at the start and completion of each dive operation.

(2) Approximate underwater and surface conditions (weather, visibility, temperatures, and currents).

(3) Names of dive team members including diving supervisor.

(4) General nature of work performed.

(5) Repetitive dive designation or elapsed time since last hyperbaric exposure if less than 24 hours for each diver.

(6) Diving modes used.

(7) Maximum depth and bottom time for each diver.

(8) Name of person-in-charge.

(9) For each dive outside the no-decompression limits, deeper than 130 fsw, or using mixed-gas, the breathing gases and decompression table designations used.

(10) When decompression sickness or gas embolism is suspected or symptoms are evident—
(i) The name of the diver; and
(ii) A description and results of treatment.

(11) For each fatality or any diving related injury or illness that results in incapacitation of more than 72 hours or requires any dive team member to be hospitalized for more than 24 hours—
(i) The date;
(ii) Time;
(iii) Circumstances; and
(iv) Extent of any injury or illness.

(c) The diving supervisor shall insure that the following is recorded in the logbook for each diving operation deviating from the requirements of this subpart:
(1) A description of the circumstances leading to the situation.
(2) The deviations made.
(3) The corrective action taken, if appropriate, to reduce the possibility of recurrence.

(d) The diving supervisor shall insure that a record of the following is maintained:
(1) The date and results of each check of the medical kits.
(2) The date and results of each test of the air compressor.
(3) The date and results of each check of breathing mixtures.
(4) The date and results of each check of each breathing supply system.
(5) The date, equipment cleaned, general cleaning procedure, and names of persons cleaning the diving equipment for oxygen service.
(6) The date and results of each test of the breathing supply hoses and system.
(7) The date and results of each inspection of the breathing gas supply system.
(8) The date and results of each test of depth gages and timekeeping devices.
(9) The date and results of each test and inspection of each PVHO.
(10) The date and results of each inspection of the diving equipment.
(11) The date and results of each test and inspection of pressure piping.
(12) The date and results of each test and inspection of volume tanks and cylinders.

(e) The diving supervisor shall insure that a notation concerning the location of the information required under paragraph (d) is made in the logbook.
NOTE.—R.S. 4290 (46 U.S.C. 201) requires that certain entries be made in an official logbook in addition to the entries required by this section; and R.S. 4291 (46 U.S.C. 202) prescribes the manner of making those entries.

197.484 NOTICE OF CASUALTY.
(a) In addition to the requirements of subpart 4.05 of this chapter and 33 CFR 146.01-20, the person-in-charge shall notify the Officer-in-Charge, Marine Inspection, as soon as possible after a diving casualty occurs, if the casualty involves any of the following:
(1) Loss of life.
(2) Diving-related injury to any person causing incapacitation for more than 72 hours.
(3) Diving-related injury to any person requiring hospitalization for more than 24 hours.

(b) The notice required by this section must contain the following:
(1) Name and official number (if applicable) of the vessel or facility.
(2) Name of the owner or agent of the vessel or facility.
(3) Name of the person-in-charge.
(4) Name of the diving supervisor.
(5) Description of the casualty including presumed cause.
(6) Nature and extent of the injury to persons.

(c) The notice required by this section is not required if the written report required by § 197.486 is submitted within 5 days of the casualty.

197.486 WRITTEN REPORT OF CASUALTY.
The person-in-charge of a vessel or facility for which a notice of casualty was made under § 197.484 shall submit a report to the Officer-in-Charge, Marine Inspection, as soon as possible after the casualty occurs, as follows:
(a) On form CG-924E, when the diving installation is on a vessel.
(b) Using a written report, in narrative form, when the diving installation is on a facility. The written report must contain the information required by § 197.484.
(c) The report required by this section must be accompanied by a copy of the report required by § 197.410(a)(9)

when decomp / sickness is involved.

197.488 RETENTION OF RECORDS AFTER CASUALTY.
(a) The owner, agent, or person-in-charge of a vessel or facility for which a report of casualty is made under § 197.484 shall retain all records on-board that are maintained on the vessel or facility and those records required by this subpart for 6 months after the report of a casualty is made or until advised by the Officer-in-Charge, Marine Inspection, that records need not be retained onboard.
(b) The records required by paragraph (a) of this section to be retained on board include, but are not limited to, the following:
(1) All logbooks required by § 197.480.
(2) All reports required by § 197.402 (a)(2)(ii), §197.404(a)(4), § 197.410(a)(9).
(c) The owner, agent, person-in-charge, or diving supervisor shall, upon request, make the records described in this section available for examination by any Coast Guard official authorized to investigate the casualty.

APPENDIX A

The Table gives the depth versus bottom time limits for single, no-decompression, air dives made within any 12-hour period. The limit is the maximum bottom time in minutes that a diver can spend at that depth without requiring decompression beyond that provided by a normal ascent rate of 60 fsw per minute. (Although bottom time is concluded when ascent begins, a slower ascent rate would increase the bottom time thereby requiring decompression.) An amount of nitrogen remains in the tissues of a diver after any air dive, regardless of whether the dive was a decompression or no-decompression dive. Whenever another dive is made within a 12-hour period, the nitrogen remaining in the blood and body tissues of the diver must be considered when calculating his decompression.

Air No-Decompression Limits

Depth	No decompression limits
35 (feet)	310 (minutes)
40	200
50	100
60	60
70	50
80	40
90	30
100	25
110	20
120	15
130	10

These Regulations apply to offshore diving only. OSHA Safety and Health Standards cover inland diving.

14.2 DEPARTMENT OF ENERGY SAFETY MEMOS

These memoranda can be obtained from: The Diving Inspectorate, Petroleum Engineering Directorate, Department of Energy, Thames House South, Millbank, London SW1P 4QJ, England.

Memo Number	Date	Title
15/81	Dec 1981	Fatal Accident Inquiry—Recommendations
14/81	23 Oct 1981	Offshore Installations/Unmanned Diving Systems
13/81	20 Oct 1981	Diver's Certificate of Competence
12/81	12 Oct 1981	Hydraulic Handling System
11/81	18 Aug 1981	Diving Breathing Gases
10/81	17 Aug 1981	Diving Certificate of Training and Certificate of Medical Fitness to Dive
9/81	18 Aug 1981	Lost Bell Relocation
8/81	Jun 1981	British Standards 5045 (Cylinder Standards)
7/81	6 Jul 1981	Silicon Fluid Filled Diving Chamber Lighting
6/81	8 Jun 1981	Diver Training Standards—revised 6 Jul 1981
5/81	24 Apr 1981	Diving Operations at Work Regulations, 1981
4/81	26 Jan 1981	KMB Mark 10 Non-return Valves
3/81	2 Jan 1981	The Offshore Diving Industry/Government Responsibilities
2/81	1 Jan 1981	Decompression Sickness—Reporting Status
1/81	1 Jan 1981	Diving Medical Emergencies
13/80	31 Oct 1980	Emergency Diving Medical Service—superseded by 1/81
12/80	10 Oct 1980	Underwater Welding/Cutting and Burning Explosives Hazards
11/80	22 Aug 1980	Diver Training Requirements/Standards for Air and Mixed Gas/Bell Diving
10/80	8 Aug 1980	Norwegian Petroleum Directorate Bell Diving Certification
9/80	7 Aug 1980	Tunnelling—The Use of Jetting Equipment
8/80	3 Jul 1980	Oxy-Helium Diving Tables 1970
7/80	10 Apr 1980	Diving Bell Buoyancy
6/80	9 Apr 1980	KMB–10 Mushroom Valves
5/80	8 Apr 1980	Diver/Bell Umbilicals (amended 30 Jun 1981)
4/80	7 Apr 1980	Lost Diving Bell Emergency
3/80	7 Apr 1980	Underwater Electrical Safety
2/80	Jan 1980	Welding Equipment—Unsafe Knife Switches
1/80	Jan 1980	Diving Medical Emergencies (amended)—superseded 1/81
13/79	30 Oct 1979	Potential Danger to Divers
12/79	30 Oct 1979	Diving Emergencies

Memo Number	Date	Title
11/79	30 Oct 1979	Corrosion in Diving Life Support System
10/79	13 Sep 1979	Through-Water Communications
9/79	Jun 1979	Underwater Jetting Practice
8/79	May 1979	Diver Heating
7/79	22 May 1979	Ship Dynamic Positioning System
6/79	22 May 1979	Dysbaric Osteonecrosis
5/79	28 Mar 1979	Dynamically Positioned Vessels
4/79	Jan 1979	Sea Bottom Debris—Danger to Divers
3/79	16 Jan 1979	Diving Bell Sealing Doors
2/79	16 Jan 1979	Diver Operating from a Dynamically Positioned Vessel
1/79	6 Jan 1979	Diving Medical Emergencies (amended 6 Mar 1979)—superseded by 1/81
25/78	Dec 1978	Multigas Detection Tubes
24/78	Dec 1978	Craftsweld UA–10 Underwater Cutting Torch
23/78	22 Dec 1978	Diving Near Culverts, other Inlets and Pipelines
22/78	24 Oct 1978	Accident Investigation System
21/78	24 Oct 1978	Security of Diving Plant and Equipment
20/78	24 Oct 1978	Medical Certificates for Diving Supervisors
19/78	4 Aug 1978	Ship Dynamic Positioning System
18/78	27 Jul 1978	The Offshore Installations (Inspectors and Casualties) Regulations 1973
17/78	25 Jul 1978	Responsibilities of a Diving Supervisor
16/78	21 Jul 1978	High Pressure Half-inch Re-usable Brass Hose End Fittings
15/78	21 Jul 1978	Corrosion in Steel High Pressure Air Cylinders
14/78	17 Jul 1978	Underwater Welding
13/78	30 Mar 1978	Use of French Chalk (talcum) for the Storage and Use of Rubber Items of Operational Equipment
12/78	22 Mar 1978	Transfer Under Pressure System/Medical Casualties
11/78	28 Mar 1978	Charges in the Inspectorate
10/78	7 Apr 1978	Qualification of Divers
9/78	3 Mar 1978	Snark 11 Silver Demand Valve
8/78	2 Mar 1978	Diagnosis of Decompression Sickness
7/78	2 Mar 1978	Amendment to Diving Safety Memorandum 1/78
6/78	2 Mar 1978	Independent Examination of Lifting Appliances and Gear
5/78	23 Feb 1978	Electrically-heated Under-suits
4/78	24 Feb 1978	Diving Medical Emergencies—superseded by 1/81

Memo Number	Date	Title
3/78	6 Jan 1978	Decompression Meters
2/78	6 Jan 1978	Snark 11 Silver Demand Valve
1/78	6 Jan 1978	Diving Medical Emergencies—superseded by 1/81
15/77	7 Dec 1977	Accident Reporting (amended 13 Jan 1978)
14/77	1 Dec 1977	US Divers Regulators
13/77	11 Nov 1977	Kirby Morgan 16 Neck Clamp
12/77	18 Aug 1977	Hoses for Diving
11/77	18 Aug 1977	Transfer of Diver Under Pressure by Helicopter
10/77	Jun 1977	Protective Headgear
9/77	Jun 1977	Cathodic Protection on Offshore Installations
—	17 Jun 1977	Safe Evacuation of Divers Under Pressure
8/77	9 May 1977	Lifting Appliances
7/77	17 Mar 1977	Manning Levels and Frequency of Diver Practice
6/77	17 Mar 1977	Warning: High Oxygen Partial Pressure in NOAA Saturation Excursion Tables
5/77	17 Mar 1977	Surface-Orientated Diving
4/77	24 Feb 1977	Diver Heating
3/77	2 Mar 1977	Diesel Fired Heating Systems; Defective Synflex Fittings
2/77	4 Jan 1977	Qualifications of Divers (amended 2 Mar 1977)
1/77	1 Jan 1977	Diving Medical emergencies—superseded by 1/81
18/76	4 Nov 1976	Bulk Stowage of High Pressure Oxygen; Diver Hot Water Heating Systems
17/76	15 Oct 1976	Checking Contents of Breathing Mixtures
16/76	15 Oct 1976	Oxygen Safety in Diving Systems
15/76	1 Oct 1976	The Merchant Shipping (Registration of Submersible Craft) Regulations 1976. No 940
14/76	30 Jul 1976	Equipment Design; Offshore Installations, Merchant Shipping, Submarine Pipelines (Diving Operations) Regs
13/76	1 Jul 1976	The Submarine Pipelines (Diving Operations) Regulations 1976

Memo Number	Date	Title
12/76	22 Jun 1976	Cathodic Protection on Offshore Installations
11/76	22 Jun 1976	Self-contained Underwater Breathing Apparatus (Air Diving)
10/76	22 Jun 1976	Fatal Accident Report
9/76	29 Apr 1976	Self-contained Underwater Breathing Apparatus (Air Diving)
8/76	29 Apr 1976	Danger from suction on Ballast Weights for Diving Bells
7/76	8 Apr 1976	First Aid Emergency Medical Equipment; Equipment to be held within a Diving Bell
6/76	19 Mar 1976	KMB–9 Band Mask
5/76	17 Feb 1976	Diving Medical Emergencies—superseded by 1/81
4/76	5 Feb 1976	High Pressure Oxygen in Diving Breathing Systems
3/76	5 Feb 1976	Diving Bell Weight Systems
2/76	3 Feb 1976	Diving from Craft and Vessels
1/76	15 Jan 1976	Diving Information Bulletin
—	Dec 1975	Amendment to Royal Navy Diving Manual; Evacuation of Offshore Installation
—	Nov 1975	Diver's Medical Examination
—	Sept 1975	Hyperthermia
—	6 Aug 1975	Diving near Culverts, other Inlets and Pipelines
—	6 Aug 1975	The Effects of Cold on the Diver
—	16 Jul 1975	Diving Panel
—	Jun 1975	Diver Training
—	Jun 1975	Oxygen Safety in Diving Systems
—	6 May 1975	The Offshore Installations (Diving Operations Regulations, 1974: Gas Storage Cylinders)
—	14 Apr 1975	Diving Accidents/General Information
—	20 Mar 1975	The Offshore Installations (Diving Operations) Regulations, 1974
—	6 Dec 1974	Report of Diving Accidents and 'Near Misses'
—	Jan 1974	Diving Supervision

Cross-referenced index of Department of Energy Diving Safety Memoranda

14.3 UK EQUIPMENT TEST REQUIREMENTS

The testing of equipment is an important aspect of care and maintenance. Each country has its own requirements regarding type and frequency of testing. The information below is based on a table compiled by UEG for the revision of 'The Principles of Safe Diving Practice' which was available in draft in July 1982. The revised 'Principles' are to be published by UEG in association with the Department of Energy and the Association of Offshore Diving Contractors in late 1982/early 1983.

Diving bells and surface compression chambers

Person competent to carry out or supervise the test: Engineer specialising in such work.*

Type of test (I): Pressure leak test at maximum rated working pressure, using typical gas or gas mixture. The object of this test is to ensure that the system as a whole does not leak beyond acceptable limits and, therefore, neither the system nor any of its constituent parts can be stripped for examination after the test. Any subsequent repairs, modifications or replacements would require that the whole system be retested to this standard.

Periodicity: 2 years.

Test standard: To a recognised international or national standard. Typically a leakage rate of up to 1% pressure drop in 24 hours is acceptable. Acceptable standards will include those published by Classification Societies and other bodies having experience in this type of work, e.g. Lloyd's and DnV.

Type of test (II): Type of test is to be determined by the competent person, depending on the specific circumstances of the equipment. This will include either:
(a) internal hydraulic pressure test at 1.5 times the maximum rated working pressure, or
(b) internal air pressure test at 1.1 times the maximum rated working pressure. (The object of this test is to check the integrity of the pressure vessel and its constituent parts, including windows, door seals, penetrations etc).

Periodicity: 5 years.

Test standard: To a recognised international or national standard.

Other hydraulic pressure vessels and associated pipework and fittings of the hydraulic type including hot and cold water tanks, sewage tanks etc. It does not include any type of gas storage vessel.

Person competent to carry out or supervise test: Engineer specialising in such work.*

Type of test: Internal hydraulic pressure test at 1.5 times maximum rated working pressure.

Periodicity: 2 years.

Test standard: To a recognised international or national standard.

Umbilicals:
—Surface demand hoses.
—Diver's umbilicals.
—Other hoses (pressure containing parts only).

Person competent to carry out or supervise the test: Engineer specialising in such work.*

Type of test: Either:
(a) a pressure leak test, or
(b) an internal hydraulic pressure test. A pressure leak test should be carried out if the item normally carries a gas and the test pressure should be at the maximum rated working pressure of the item using typical gas or gas mixture.

An internal hydraulic pressure test should be carried out if the item normally carries a liquid and the test pressure should be at 1.5 times the maximum rated working pressure.
In addition, for hoses designed to carry hot water, additional tests should be carried out entailing circulating hot water at design pressure.

Periodicity: 2 years (UK guidance note 86 states that in the case of items carrying gases, a hydraulic internal pressure test is not required after initial commissioning, but may be used thereafter in the place of the leakage test proposed at the discretion of the competent person).

Test standard: To a recognised international or national standard.

Gauges

Person competent to carry out or supervise the test: Engineer specialising in such work.*

Type of test: Calibration test and necessary adjustments, including the production of a calibration chart if appropriate. Tests to be carried out over the full range of the gauge using the typical gas, gas mixture or fluid medium which would be used in practice.

Periodicity: 6 months.

Test standard: In accordance with equipment suppliers' standard procedures.

Heating systems:
—Chambers, bells, and divers.
(Heat generating devices and their

associated control equipment, as well as all pipework, heat exchangers and fittings.)

Person competent to carry out or supervise the test: Engineer specialising in such work.*

Type of test: (a) An internal hydraulic pressure test at 1.5 times the maximum rated working pressure, and
(b) function test at the maximum rated working pressure and flow rate.
(The objects of these two tests are to ensure the pressure integrity of the whole system and that all constituent parts, including the various controls, are functioning correctly.)

Periodicity: 2 years.

Test standard: In accordance with equipment suppliers' standard procedures.

Breathing systems

(The whole system from, but not including, the gas cylinders to the diver's personal diving equipment, but excluding any umbilicals. It does however include the BIBS system and all on/off valves, reducing valves, check valves, pipe runs and flexible hoses, pipe fittings, gauges and control panels.)

Person competent to carry out test: Engineer specialising in such work.*

Type of test: These types of test are to be carried out as follows:

(a) An internal pressure test at 1.5 times the maximum rated working pressure using any gas stipulated by the competent person with a view to ensuring the integrity of the system.
(b) An internal pressure leak test at maximum rated working pressure using a gas or gas mixture stipulated by the competent person. (The object of this test is to ensure that the system as a whole does not leak beyond the acceptable limits and, therefore, neither the system nor any of its constituent parts can be stripped for examination after the test. Any subsequent repairs, modifications, or replacements, would require that the whole system be retested to this standard.)
(c) A test to determine purity of gases or gas mixture being supplied to the diver(s).

Periodicity: 2 years (UK Official Guidance Note 86 states that in the case of items carrying gases, a hydraulic internal pressure test is not required after initial commissioning, but may be used thereafter in the place of the leakage test proposed at the discretion of the competent person.)

Test standard: To a recognised international or national standard. For the pressure leak test, various maximum leakage rates may apply, e.g. 1% pressure drop in 24 hours for the whole system; 0.3% per hour for BIBS system. (Acceptable standards will include those published by Classification Societies and other bodies having experience in this type of work, e.g. Lloyd's and DnV.)

Compressors

Person competent to carry out or supervise test: Engineer specialising in such work.*

Type of test: Compressors are to be tested for the pressure and delivery rates intended, and for the purity of the pressurised gas.

Periodicity: 2 years.

Test standard: To a recognised international or national standard with particular emphasis on the purity of pressurised gas produced.

Electrical systems

Person competent to carry out test: Engineer specialising in such work.*

Type of test: All electrical circuits and equipment must be tested for insulation using suitable instrumentation as appropriate.

Periodicity: 6 months.

Test standard: To a recognised international standard, but also taking into account specific recommendations in the DEn Guidance Notes for the safe use of electrical equipment underwater.

Fire extinction equipment

Person competent to carry out or supervise test: Engineer specialising in such work. Proprietary fire extinguishing equipment should be examined and functionally checked, if appropriate, by an authorised representative of the supplier. Other systems, including sprays and drenches, should be examined and tested by an employee of the owner of the equipment if his duties include this type of work on a regular basis and his responsibilities are such that he is able to act independently and in a professional manner.

Type of test: For fixed and mobile sprinkler or drenched systems, a functional test and examination as required. For proprietary fire extinguishing equipment, the test and examination should be stipulated and carried out by the independent examiner.

Periodicity: At intervals not exceeding 6 months or such shorter periods as may be required for proprietary items.

Test standard: To a recognised international or national standard.

Portable gas detection equipment

Person competent to carry out or supervise test: Engineer specialising in such work.*

Type of test: The equipment should be tested using standard test kits compatible with the equipment and the possible environmental hazards.

Periodicity: 28 days.

Test standard: In accordance with equipment suppliers' standard procedures.

Gas cylinders: All cylinders, bailout bottles, SCUBA cylinders, gas cylinders mounted on a diving bell or habitat which are taken underwater.

Person competent to carry out or supervise test: Suitably qualified engineer employed by the original manufacturer or other firm specialising in this type of work.

Type of test: Internal hydraulic pressure test, together with detailed examinations of the cylinder and all associated and constituent parts.

Periodicity: 2 years.

Test standard: To a recognised international or national standard as determined by the competent person. Typically BS 5430-1977, Part 1.

Gas cylinders: All single cylinders, cylinders in quads, portable tubes, built-in tubes and air reservoirs which are not taken underwater.

Person competent to carry out test: Suitably qualified engineer employed by the original manufacturer or other firm specialising in this type of work.

Type of test: Internal hydraulic pressure test, together with detailed examinations of the cylinder and all associated and constituent parts.

Periodicity: 5 years which may be extended to 10 years if it can be shown to the satisfaction of the HSE that the dryness of the gas charged into the cylinders is always controlled to a predetermined standard. 10 years' approvals have to be given in writing by the HSE.

Test standard: To a recognised international or national standard as determined by the competent person. Typically BS 5430-1977 Parts 1 and 2 and BS 5500-1976.

Lifting gear forming part of diving plant and equipment: All items of lifting gear which are part of the plant and equipment necessary to operate a diving system.

Person competent to carry out or supervise test: Engineer specialising in such work.* SI 1019-1976 Clause 2 specifically states that the competent person should be 'neither the owner of the installation nor his employee'. Installation is defined in Section 2 of the Principles and clearly does not cover the diving contractor who operates the plant and equipment.

Type of test: Functional test at maximum normal working load to ensure that all items are operating correctly. This test to be carried out through the full working range of the equipment, including the operation of brakes. All equipment to be examined after test for possible defects. HSE regulations, Clause 13(2)(a)(v) specifically requires all plant and equipment to be tested and examined at 6 monthly intervals, with certain exceptions. However, to apply proof loads at 6 monthly intervals could overstress the gear and would not be in line with requirements under Clause 6 and Part III of Schedule 1 of SI 1019-1976, or of the requirements for periodic examination of other items of lifting gear.

Periodicity: 6 months.

Test standard: To a recognised international or national standard. (Acceptable standards will include those published by Classification Societies and other relevant bodies having experience in this type of work, subject to qualifications noted above.)

All lifting gear not forming part of the diving plant and equipment
Person competent to carry out or supervise test: Engineer specialising in such work.* SI 1019-1976 Clause 2 specifically states that the competent person should be 'neither the owner of the installation nor his employee'. Installation is defined in Section 2 of the Principles and clearly does not cover the diving contractor who operates the diving plant and equipment.

Type of test: A thorough examination of all items to ensure that they are in good condition and working order. The 'competent person' may require that particular items be tested prior to a thorough examination if, in his considered judgement, it is necessary.

Periodicity: 6 months.

Test standard: To a recognised international or national standard. (Acceptable standards will include those published by Classification Societies and other relevant bodies having experience in this type of work, subject to qualifications noted above.)

---

* The engineer specialising in such work may be an employee of an independent company or an employee of the owner of the equipment. In the latter case, however, his duties should include this type of work on a regular basis, and his responsibilities be such that he is able to act independently and in a professional manner.

14.4 CLASSIFICATION AND CERTIFICATION

It is the job of the Classification Societies and Certification Authorities to set standards of design, construction and maintenance of ships and structures and to carry out periodic checks to ensure that they are fit and safe for their intended service. The classification of vessels is long established and many countries have their own Classification Societies. Certification, however, is a more recent development that applies largely to the offshore industry. Most countries with offshore installations have appointed organizations such as Classification Societies to act as Certification Authorities for offshore structures.

The fundamental difference between classification and certification is that, in the case of classed equipment and systems, plan approval, surveys during construction and subsequent periodical surveys are carried out in accordance with the classification society's own rules. Certification, however, is carried out in accordance with the statutory requirements issued by the relevant government departments. In most cases, certification of equipment is compulsory, but it is up to the owner to decide whether or not he wishes his equipment to be classed.

In either case the procedures followed during construction are the same. The owner submits to the Classification Society or Certification Authority plans, data, design calculations etc. which are vetted and, if satisfactory, approved. The apparatus is then constructed under the supervision of the societies' surveyors to ensure that the approved standards are complied with. On completion the apparatus will be given a final test and survey and, if up to standard, will be classed or certified.

In the UK, the Government requires that all offshore installations must have an in-date Certificate of Fitness, issued by an approved Certification Authority, before they are able to operate. Such a certificate assures that an installation is safe, in every respect, for its designed purpose and that the regulations are observed. Periodic checks must also be carried out during the time that the certificate is still valid.

Certification of an offshore structure usually requires special underwater inspection procedures using divers and ROVs to investigate wear and corrosion using photography, TV and various NDT techniques. However, in the case of diving systems, the certification procedure does not require diver involvement, as inspection and pressure testing of equipment is carried out on shore or aboard a ship or platform. Divers may be involved in the following aspects of the periodical survey programme for offshore structures.

—A complete general visual survey of structures and risers.

—A close visual survey of about 10% of nodes annually, including critical nodes. Certification requirements may dictate that non-destructive testing be carried out, depending on the structure. On older platforms, non-destructive testing of selected critical node welds is specified.

—Where a cathodic protection system is installed, a pattern of cathodic potential readings covering 10–20% sacrificial anodes.

—Preparation of a scour map (topographical survey of the seabed immediately surrounding the structure).

—A visual survey of riser connections to jackets.

The following is a list of the main Classification/Certification Authorities in the world.

*American Bureau of Shipping,
65 Broadway,
New York, NY 10006.
Tel: (212) 440 0300
Tlx: ITT 421966

*Bureau Veritas,
31 rue Henri-Rochfort,
Paris 17E, France.
Tel: 766 5105
Tlx: 290226

*Germanischer Lloyd,
PO Box 111606,
D-2000 Hamburg 11,
Germany.
Tel: (040) 361 491
Tlx: 21-2828

*Lloyd's Register of Shipping,
71 Fenchurch Street,
London, EC3M 4BS, UK.
Tel: (01) 709 9166
Tlx: 888379

Nippon Kaiji Kyokai,
4–7 Kioi-Cho, Chiyoda-Ku,
Tokyo 102, Japan.
Tel: (03) 230 1201
Tlx: J22975, 2324280

*Det Norske Veritas,
PO Box 300,
N-1322 Hoevik, Norway.
Tel: (02) 129 955
Tlx: 16192

*The Offshore Certification Bureau,
3 Shortlands, Hammersmith
London, W6 8BT, UK.
Tel: (01) 741 8788
Tlx: 916148

Polski Rejestr,
Waly Tiastowskie 24,
80-855 Gdansk, Poland.
Tel: 317223
Tlx: 0512373

Registro Italiano Navale,
Casella Postale N1195,
Via Corsica 12,
16100 Genoa, Italy.
Tel: (10) 53851
Tlx: 270022

Register of Shipping of the USSR,
8 Dvortsovaya Naberezhnaya,
Leningrad 192041, USSR.
Tel: 2157802, 2116327
Tlx: 121525

---

* Approved by UK Department of Energy for UK concessionary waters.

14.5 DIVING LOGBOOKS AND DIVING QUALIFICATIONS

The diving operation logbook

In Norway and the UK the diving contractor must supply a diving operation logbook which the diving supervisor maintains. The logbook must be retained by the diving contractor for 2 years after the date of last entry. The Norwegian Petroleum Directorate are issuing new diving regulations which will come into force in January 1983. These are intended to harmonise as far as possible with the UK Regulations. The US Regulations also require the diving supervisor to maintain a logbook. This should be kept by the employer for 1 year from the date of last entry, or 5 years if there has been an incident of decompression sickness.

Table 1 shows the items required to be entered into the diving operation logbook in Norway, UK and USA.

Items to be entered into the diving operation logbook	Norway (7.1)	UK (Schedule 2)	USA (197.182)
Name of the diving contractor	×	×	—
Date of diving operation	×	×	×
Period during which the diving operation was carried out	×	×	—
Name/designation and location of craft/installation/worksite on which the diving operations were carried out	×	×	×
Name of the diving supervisor	×	×	×
Name of person in charge	—	—	×
Period diving supervisor acting in that diving operation	—	×	—
Name of other persons engaged in diving operations including those operating any diving plant/equipment and their respective duties	×	×	×
Procedures followed including decompression schedules	×	×	×
Maximum depth reached by each diver	×	×	×
For each diver: Time leaving surface Bottom time Time reached surface	— × —	× × ×	× × ×
Type of equipment used	×	×	—
Breathing mixture used	×	×	(only outside no-decompression limits, deeper than 130 fsw or using mixed gas)
Nature of diving operation	×	×	×
Diving modes used	—	—	×
Repetitive dive designation or elapsed time since last hyperbaric exposure if less than 24 hr for each diver	—	—	×
Any decompression sickness/illness/discomfort or injury suffered by any diver	×	×	×
Particulars of any emergency and action taken	×	×	×
Any defects discovered in plant/equipment used in diving operations	—	×	—
Particulars of any environmental factors affecting diving operations	×	×	×
Other factors relevant to the safety/health of the persons engaged in the operation	×	×	—

The diver's logbook

The Norwegian and UK regulations require every diver to keep a personal logbook. The logbook must contain the diver's name, signature, photograph, certificate of medical fitness and training certificate. Every dive must be recorded and the diver should sign each entry and have it countersigned by the diving supervisor. The logbook must be retained for 2 years from the date of last entry. There are no US regulations regarding diver's logbooks.

Table 2 shows the items the Norwegian and UK regulations require to be entered into the logbook.

Table 2. Item to be entered into logbook after each dive	UK (Schedule 3)	Norway (8.1)
Name of diving contractor	×	×
Address of diving contractor	×	×
Date	×	×
Name and location of installation/worksite/craft/harbour from which the diving operation was carried on	×	×
Name of diving supervisor	×	×
Time left surface	×	—
Bottom time	×	×
Time reached surface	×	—
Maximum depth reached	×	×
Type of equipment used	×	×
Breathing mixture used	×	×
Work done	×	×
Decompression procedures followed	×	×
Any decompression sickness or other illness, discomfort or injury	×	×
Any other factor relevant to diver's safety or health	×	×

Qualifications

Training requirements for divers vary from country to country. The training requirements for Norway, the UK and the USA are tabulated below.

	Norway		UK		USA	
	Surface orientated < 50 m	Bell diving > 50 m	Surface orientated < 50 m	Bell diving > 50 m	Surface orientated	Bell diving
General requirements	a certificate issued by an institution approved by the Norwegian Petroleum Directorate	the diver(s) and standby diver(s) shall have a Bell Diver Certificate issued by the Norwegian Petroleum Directorate or an institution approved by the Directorate	a certificate issued by the Health and Safety Executive or by a person or body approved by the Executive		experience or training in: (i) tools equipment and systems; (ii) techniques of diving modes; (iii) diving operations and emergency procedures	training in diving-related physics and physiology
Approved schools	the Norwegian State Diving School does not issue certificates for surface orientated diving; the certificate/diploma from the UK MSC-recognised schools is acceptable for surface diving in Norwegian waters	Statens Dykkerskole (Norwegian State Diving School); Centravim	Plymouth Ocean Projects; Prodive; (MSC-approved schools)	(since UTC's closure, none)	the employer determines the training and experience necessary; a first aid qualification (American Red Cross standards course or equivalent) is mandatory for every diver	

15.1 DIVING COMPANIES ADDRESSES AND TELEPHONE NUMBERS

Company name	Head Office Address	Estimated number of divers	Specialisation	Other Address
Abu Dhabi Petroleum Ports Operating Company	PO Box 61, Abu Dhabi, UAE. Tel: 336 700 Tlx: 22209	12 on station.	Oil export terminal maintenance.	Ports of Jebel Dhanna and Ruwais Zirqu Island Terminal.
Atlantic Marine and Diving Co.	500 Beaverbrook Court, Fredricton, New Brunswick, Canada, E3B 5X4. Tel: (506) 455 3720 Tlx: 014 46208	High season—20 Low season—5	Submarine pipeline and cable installation and repair; inspection; general pipeline construction.	
B.I.X. Offshore Limited	Unit No. 1, Suffolk Road, Great Yarmouth, NR31 OLN, UK. Tel: (0493) 57329 Tlx: 975 116	High season—40 Low season—10	Non-destructive testing (NDT).	B.I.X. Offshore Limited, Greenbank Road, East Tullos Industrial Estate, Aberdeen, UK. Tel: (0224) 879 189 Tlx: 739 344
Binali Diving Services	PO Box 3687, Doha, State of Qatar, Arabian Gulf. Tel: Doha 416 180 Tlx: 4234 DH	High season—60 Low season—30	Diving services for oil industry and underwater civil engineering projects; repair, projects; maintenance and NDT contracts.	Binali Diving Services, PO Box 6985, Abu Dhabi, UAE. Tel: 32474 Tlx: 231719 Binali Diving Services, PO Box 2876, Dubai, UAE. Tel: 480 832 Tlx: 45922
Bource—ETRS Pty Ltd	Ashley Street, West Footscray, Victoria 3012, Australia. Tel: (03) 68 0551 Tlx: AA 31130	High season—20 Low season—6	Underwater non-destructive testing, inspection and photography.	
CCC (Underwater Engineering) Ltd	PO Box 11, Sharjah, UAE. Tel: 22555 & 354616 Tlx: 68032		Diving and underwater services; engineering support; project management; method and operational planning; marine facilities. Jeddah Office. Tel: 6824632 & 6827283 Tlx: 401284	PO Box 224, Abu Dhabi, UAE. Tel: 324015 & 324019 Tlx: 23084 PO Box 34, Dhahran Airport, Dhahran, Saudi Arabia. Tel: 8948487 & 8948903 Tlx: 671461 113/115 Queens Road, Reading, Berkshire, RG1 4DA, UK. Tel: (0734) 586601 Tlx: 848471
Celtic Sea Divers Ltd	Crosses Green, Frenches Quay, Cork, Ireland. Tel: (021) 963 450 & 963 069 After hours: (021) 811 286 Tlx: 4912		Deep sea; oilfield; civil engineering.	
Comex Houlder Diving Ltd	Bucksburn House, Howes Road, Bucksburn, Aberdeen, AB2 9RQ, UK. Tel: (0224) 714 101 Tlx: 73394	High season—365 Low season—145		
Comex Services SA	Avenue de la Soude, 13275 Marseille Cedex 2, France. Tel: (91) 41 01 70 Tlx: 410 985 F	About 450	Comex Marine Services Inc. USA, 15535 West Hardy, Suite 100, Houston, Tex. 77060, USA. Tel: (713) 820 52 50 Tlx: 0775701 Comex Middle East, PO Box 6273, SYD Ahmed BS Sullyyem Bldg, Sheikh Khalifa St, Abu Dhabi, UAE. Tel: (2) 33 95 51 Tlx: 22210 Comex Services Morocco, C/- Hamid Hasnaoui, PO Box 705, Rabat-Aguedal, Morocco. Tel: (7) 504 05 Comex Norge AS, Dusevik Base, PO Box 549, Stavanger 4001, Norway. Tel: (45) 41 955 & 41 998 Tlx: 33265 Comex Far East Pte Ltd, Thong Teck Building, 15 Scotts Road, Singapore 0922. Tel: 737 50 98 & 737 58 33 Tlx: 21 856 Comex Services India, C/- Lt. Colonel Kl. Suri, Resident Representative Officer, C. 484 Defence Colony, New Delhi, 110024, India. Tel: 621 954 Tlx: 312 347 P.T. Komaritim Indonesia, Five Pillars Office Park, Jl. Letjen M.T. Haryono 58, PO Box 379 KBY Jakarta, Indonesia. Tel: 793 808 Tlx: 47285 P.T. Komaritim Indonesia, Operations Base, Jln. K.S. Tubun, PO Box 108, Kampung Damai, Sepinggan, Balikpapan (East Kalimantan), Indonesia. Tel: 2316 Comex Services, C/- Condux SA DE CV, Mariano Escobedo 375, Piso 16, Mexico, 5-DF. Tel: (2) 545 6881 & 250 7801 Tlx: 22210	Comex Services Argentina, Viamonte 877, Piso 4to-Dept.16, CP Nr.1053, Buenos Aires, Argentina. Tel: 392 33 65 & 392 76 29 Tlx: 17898 & 17459 Comex Offshore Australia Pty Ltd, C/- Alan Healy, 18 Orchard Way, Doncaster, Victoria, 3108, Australia. Tel: (3) 848 49 73 Tlx: 30333 Comex Do Brazil, Rua Sendor Dantas 71, Salle 1402, Rio de Janeiro, Brazil. Tel: (21) 220 6060 Tlx: 2122 104 Comex Congo, PO Box 850, Pointe Noire, Congo. Tel: 94 21 36 & 94 11 54 Tlx: 8211 Comex España, Calle Cid N° 4, Madrid 1, Spain. Tel: (1) 276 88 39 Tlx: 43931 Comex Gabon, PO Box 621, Port Gentil, Gabon. Tel: 75 21 28 & 75 27 13 Tlx: 8239

Company name	Head Office Address	Estimated number of divers	Specialisation	Other Address
	Geomex Surveys (S) Pte Ltd, Block 1 Units 701–706, 7th Floor, PSA Multi Storey Complex, Pasir Panjang Road, Singapore 0511. Tel: 272 93 11 Tlx: 23 777 & 34 921		Comex Services Philippines, Xavier et Marianne Remaux, C/- Panda Services, Universaire Buildings, 106 Paseo de Roxas, Le Gaspi Village, Makati-Metro Manila, Philippines. Tel: 87 41 62 Tlx: 455 33 & 452 11	Comex Services Canada, C/- Underwater Specialists Ltd, 3601-19 Street NE, Calgary, Alberta, Canada, T2E 6SE. Tel: (403) 230 22 96 Tlx: 038228-16 Comex Malaysia SDN BHD, Lot A-B 10th Floor, Abgkasa Raya Bld, Jalan Ampang, Kuala Lumpur, Malaysia. Tel: 488 292 & 487 827
Commercial & Industrial Diving Co.	2714 Sharon Street, PO Box 2114, Kenner, La. 70063, USA. Tel: (504) 469 4711		Black water work; in-plant services; inland waterways; offshore construction and inspection.	
C.U.E. (Diving) Ltd	Unit 1, Bessemer Way, Harfrey Industrial Estate, Great Yarmouth, Norfolk, UK. Tel: (0493) 2752 Tlx: 97360	High season—45 Low season—30	NDT Works (to Lloyds Certifying Standard); scour control; consultancy and inspection services.	
Danish Diving Services	Islandsgade 54, 6700 Esbjerg, Denmark. Tel: (05) 136 868 & 116 961 Tlx: 54271	High season—7–10 Low season—3–4	Inspection.	
Divemex Ltd	Unit 38, Vastre, Newtown, Wales, UK. Tel: (0686) 25167	High season—20 Low season—8	Fire underwater; underwater welding, burning and explosives.	
Divemasters (Far East) Pte Ltd	27 Lorong Tukang Satu, Jurong Town, Singapore, 2261. Tel: 265 0658 & 265 1264 Tlx: RS 35095	High season—12 Low season—6		
Dive Task Limited	150 Haydn Road, Sherwood, Nottingham, NG5 2LB, UK. Tel: (0602) 621 738 After hrs: (0602) 264 901	High season—20 Low season—10	Civil engineering diving.	
Dockland Diving Engineers Ltd	44/52 River Road, Barking, Essex. Tel: (01) 594 4998 & 594 4999 & 594 4646 & 594 4647	High season— 10–15 Low season— 10–15	Civil engineering diving.	
Dockyard Diving Services	59 Whinfield Lane, Ashton, Preston, Lancs, UK. Tel: (0772) 727 026	High season—4 Low season—4	Harbour installations.	Glenoe, St Nicholas Road, Blackpool, Lancs, UK. Tel: (0253) 691 753
C. G. Doris Services UK Ltd	Unit 4E, Dyce Industrial Park, Dyce, Aberdeen, UK. Tel: (0224) 724 624 Tlx: 73771	High season—80 Low season—20		
Duikbedrijf Vriens BV	Van Konijnenburgweg 151–153, 4612 PL Bergen op Zoom, Holland. Tel: (01640) 40552 Tlx: 78199	High season—55 Low season—55	Marine construction, repair and maintenance; underwater concrete constructions.	
Dulam International Ltd	PO Box 3334, Dubai, UAE. Tel: 222 578 & 222 814 Tlx: 46154	High season—60 Low season—30		PO Box 6771, Abu Dhabi, UAE.
East Coast Divers	West Pitkierie, Near Anstruther, Fife, UK. Tel: (0333) 310 768	High season— 12–20 Low season—6–8	Underwater cutting.	
Felixarc Marine Ltd	The Docks, Felixstowe, Suffolk, IP11 8SY, UK. Tel: (039 42) 2497 Tlx: (504) 987129	High season—6 Low season—6	Harbour and general ship maintenance.	
Fraser Diving International Ltd	Rimaco Building, 146 Gul Circle, Jurong 2262, Singapore. Tel: 268 5466 Tlx: RS 22010	High season—60 Low season—30	Underwater construction.	Bermuda House, St Julian's Avenue, St Peter Port, Guernsey, Channel Islands, UK
Global Divers & Contractors Inc	PO Box 68, Maurice, La. 70555, USA. Tel: (318) 984 7600 Tlx: 784801	High season—50 Low season—40	Construction, saturation and RCV.	PO Box 491, Harvey, La. 70059, USA. 1770 St James Place, Suite 515, Houston, Tex. 77056, USA.

Company name	Head Office Address	Estimated number of divers	Specialisation	Other Address
Holland Diving International BV	Kon. Wilhelminahaven ZZ 13a, PO Box 276, 3130 AG Vlaardingen, The Netherlands. Tel: (010) 35 72 31 (24 hours) Tlx: 27399	High season—25 Low season—10	All offshore diving services; underwater cleaning.	
Humber Divers Ltd	1A Corby Park, North Ferry, Hull, UK. Tel: (0482) 796 203 & 561 634	High season—10 Low season—3		17 Woodlands End, Anlaby Park, Hull, UK.
Hydrospace International (a branch of Oceaneering)	PO Box 346, Dubai, UAE. Tel: 470605 Tlx: 47455		Complete diving services; NDT inspection; hull cleaning; classification surveys; oceanographic surveys; welding services; vessel supply; diving support vessels.	
Independent Divers Inc	PO Box 23123, New Orleans, La. 70183, USA. Tel: (504) 466 2800 Tlx: IWU Address 'Endive'	High season—16 Low season—16	Submarine cable; outfall pipeline; general underwater work.	
Indive	27 Beldoir Street, Rochdale, Lancs, UK. Tel: (0706) 44234	High season—12 Low season—6	Inland diving work; high altitude diving; inshore diving.	
International Underwater Contractors Inc	222 Fordham Street, City Island, NY 10464, USA. Tel: (212) 885 0600 Tlx: 147242		Bounce and saturation diving; diver lockout submersibles; deep diving submersibles 8300 feet; diver submersible support boat; mantis 1 atmosphere tethered vehicles; remotely operated vehicles; exploration and production support, salvage, construction and repair.	Deepsea International, 1 Allen Center, Suite 500, Houston, Tex. 77002, USA. Tel: (713) 759 9637 Tlx: 775002 404 Glenmeade, Gretna, New Orleans, La. 70053, USA. Tel: (504) 392 1472 35 Tozer Road, Beverly, Boston, Mass. 01915, USA. Tel: (617) 927 3422
I.U.C. International Inc	Unit 16 Woodlands Drive, Kirkhill Industrial Estate, Dyce, Aberdeen, AB2 0EF, UK. Tel: (0224) 724 915 & 724 838 Tlx: 739 272	High season—136 Low season—136	Diving support on exploratory drillrigs; operation of deep submersibles and atmospheric diving systems; salvage and marine construction.	PO Box 1661, Hamilton 5, Bermuda. Tel: (809) 295 0384 Tlx: 3433 Deepsea International, 1 Allen Center, Suite 500, Houston, Tex. 77002, USA. Tel: (713) 759 9637 Tlx: 775002
Jydsk Dykker & Entreprenørselskab Aps.	Broagervej 5, 7500 Holstebro, Denmark. Tel: (07) 426351	High season—6 Low season—6		
K. D. Marine (UK) Limited	Pitmedden Road Industrial Estate, Dyce, Aberdeen, UK. Tel: (0224) 723 415 Tlx: 73375 Celtic Sea Divers Ltd, Crosses Green, Frenches Quay, Cork, Ireland. WW Marine Inc, 292 Mecca Drive, Lafayette, La, USA. Tel: (318) 264 1310 Tlx: 586 608	High season— 200+ Low season—90+	All sub-sea engineering and inspection. KD Marine Australasia Pty Ltd, BMA Tower, Chatswood, NSW, Australia. Tel: (2) 411 4955 Tlx: 27882 KD Marine NV, 16-A Piefermaai, Curacao, Netherland Antilles. Tel: 613 502 Tlx: 390 1120	K.D. Marine (Atlantic) Ltd, Suite 303, 1 Canal Street, Dartmouth, Nova Scotia, Canada. Tel: (902) 463 8527 Tlx: 019 21707 K.D. Marine (Atlantic) Ltd, Topsail Road, PO Box 1447, St John's, Newfoundland, Canada. Tel: (709) 368 6266 Tlx: 016 4925
Keliston Marine Limited	Liverpool House, 15/17 Eldon Street, London EC2, UK. Tel: Ipswich 217 658 Tlx: 98 7874	High season—25 Low season—25	Civil engineering diving and slope protection.	Orwell Quay, Duke Street, Ipswich, Suffolk, IP3 0AQ, UK.
L'Orsa Diving, Arnulf L'Orsa A/S	Oscarsgt 34, Oslo 2, Norway. Tel: (02) 56 69 75 Tlx: 71187	High season—20 Low season—5	Underwater dry welding of anodes; brush-kart hull cleaning in Scandinavia.	
Maritime Diving	50-52 Beaumont Road, Middlesborough, Cleveland, UK. Tel: (0642) 211 756 Tlx: 587533	High season—12 Low season—6	Burning; welding; explosives; video.	
Maritime Offshore Projects Ltd	Marine Base, Southtown Road, Great Yarmouth, Norfolk, UK. Tel: (0493) 57101 & 50551 Tlx: 975345		High pressure cleaning and steam cleaning.	

Company name	Head Office Address	Estimated number of divers	Specialisation	Other Address
Mersey Docks and Harbour Company	Pierhead, Liverpool, L3 1BZ, UK. Tel: (051) 200 2020 After hrs: (051) 200 4124 Tlx: 627 013 After hrs: 627 458	High season— 2 + Supervisor Low season— 3 + Supervisor In both cases only one diving team is available at any one time.		
Midland Diving Services	59 Weeland Road, Knottingley, West Yorkshire, WF11 8BE, UK. Tel: (0977) 82921	High season—20 Low season—8	Inshore underwater civil engineering and hydrojetting.	
Mobell (Marine) Limited	23 North Street, Havant, Hampshire, PO9 1PW, UK. Tel: (0705) 472 092/471 300 Tlx: 86774	High season—30 Low season—12	Air diving operations for pipeline inspection and sub-sea surveys including NDT; submarine pipeline and cable bury tools operations; underwater explosive expertise; general diving operations.	
Multi Scan Dykker Service	Fr. Nansensvej 32, DK 8200 Aarhus N, Denmark. Tel: Denmark 6-168 297 Tlx: 64103		Harbour construction; discharging pipes at sea; salvage operations; all types of diving work.	
Al Musharekh Marine Equipment and Services	PO Box 2249, Abu Dhabi, UAE. Tel: 825412 Tlx: 22786	High season—15 Low season—10		
McDermott International Inc	Avenue Henri Matisse 16, 1140 Brussels, Belgium. Tel: (02) 242 1000 Tlx: 62831	High season—100 Low season—20	Diving Superintendents; diving supervisors; rack operators; saturation divers with NPD and DOE Bell Diving Certificates; welder divers; NDT qualified saturation divers; experienced construction divers; diving technicians (mechanical and electrical); diving tenders.	
McGregor Marine Services	Blackness Pier, Scalloway, Shetland, UK. Tel: (059-588) 637 226 Tlx: 75262	High season—20 Low season—6	Underwater blasting, obstructions, trenching etc.; underwater wet welding; underwater cutting; civil engineering; harbour maintenance and repairs; ship repairs; survey work; seabed clearance.	
Nautilus Sermares Ltda	Edifico Roca, Oficina 303, Punta Arenas, Chile. Tel: 23538 & 25874 Tlx: 80137 & 40158	High season—25 Low season—12	Estrecho de Magallanes diving.	Nautilus Sermares Ltda, Merced 116-B, Santiago, Chile.
Nordex Willco A/S	Tanager Marina, PO Box 75, N- 4056 Tanager, Norway. Tel: (04) 69 69 00 Tlx: 40119	High season—55 Low season—15	Operate manned and unmanned submersibles.	
Nordive A/S, see SSOS				
Northern Diving Engineering Limited	Tower Street, Hull, North Humberside, HU9 1TU, UK. Tel: (0482) 227 276 Tlx: 527064	High season—30–40 Low season—10–20	Civil engineering diving to 50 m.	The Quay, Newburgh, Aberdeenshire, Scotland. Tel: (03586) 538/9
North Western Marine Salvage	1 South Avenue, Chorley, Lancs, UK. Tel: (02572) 74610 & 76185	High and low season—4 permanent divers, but always 15–20 subcontracted divers on 24 hour call	Oxy-arc cutting and blasting.	24 Duke Street, Chorley, Lancs, UK.
Oceaneering International Services Ltd (Western Hemisphere Head Office)	10575 Katy Freeway, Suite 400, PO Box 19464, Houston, Tex. 77024, USA. Tel: (713) 461 4477 Tlx: 775 181	Western Hemisphere: High season—800 Low season—600 Eastern Hemisphere: High season—700 Low season—425	Diving contractor.	Commercial Diving Centre (Oceaneering Diver Training School), 272 South Fries Avenue, Wilmington, Ca. 90744, USA. Tel: (213) 834 2501 Underwater Technology Services Inc (West Coast Division), PO Box 4488, Santa Barbara, Ca. 93103, USA. Tel: (805) 963 1414 Tlx: 658 419

Company name	Head Office Address	Estimated number of divers	Specialisation	Other Address
	Oceaneering International, PO Box 889, Kuala Belait, State of Brunei. Tel : SKB 223 Tlx : 786 21012		Trinidad Marine Services, PO Box 765, 59 Sackville Street, Port of Spain, Trinidad, West Indies, 20,000. Tel : 625 1691 Tlx : 387 3446	Can-Dive Services Ltd, 250 East Esplanade Avenue No. 3, North Vancouver, British Columbia, Canada, V7L 1A3. Tel : (604) 984 9131 Tlx : 043 52566
	DHB Construction Ltd, Alton, England, UK. Tel : (420) 82554 Tlx : 851 858 179		P.T. Calmarine, JLN Dr. Saharjo 141, Tebet, Jakarta Selatan, Indonesia. Tel : 827 858 Tlx : 796 46351	Can Dive Services Ltd (Great Lakes Division), 22-7171 Torbram Road, Mississauga, Ontario, Canada, L4T 3W4. Tel : (416) 671 1883
	Oceaneering Ireland, Elm House, Clanwilliam Court, Lower Mount Street, Dublin, Ireland. Tel : 685222 Tlx : 30488		Oceaneering Australia Pty Ltd, PO Box 509, 308 Raglan Street, Sale, Victoria 3850, Australia. Tel : (51) 442 587 Tlx : 790 55233	Oceaneering International Inc (Gulf Coast Division), Highway West 90, Bayou Vista, Morgan City, La. 70380, USA. Tel : (504) 395 5247 Tlx : 586 445
	Oceaneering International-Egypt. Cairo, Egypt. Tel : 804 057 Tlx : 927 93660		Oceaneering International Services Ltd (Eastern Hemisphere Head Office)	Oceaneering International Inc (Texas Operation Division), 448 Commerce Avenue, Clute, Tex. 77531, USA. Tel : (718) 265 3336
	Oceaneering-Hydrospace International, Dubai, UAE. Tel : 470 605 Tlx : 958 47455		Pitmedden Road, Dyce, Aberdeen, Aberdeenshire, Scotland. Tel : (0224) 770444 Tlx : 73459	Oceaneering do Brasil Ltda, Rua Cendor Dantas 75, Grupo 1901, Rio de Janerio, RJ Brazil. Tel : (21) 220 5571 Tlx : 391 2133202
	Diving Services Khalifa A. Algosaibi, Dhahran, Saudi Arabia. Tel : 86 41643 Tlx : 928 670 137		Oceaneering Norway A/S, Verksgaten 41-43, 4001 Stavanger, Norway. Tel : 29101/32660 Tlx : 40115	Oceaneering Australia Pty Ltd, 5 Yampi Way, Willetton, Western Australia 6155. Tel : (9) 457 1211 Tlx : 790 93 416
	Oceaneering International Services Ltd, Riverside Road, Gorsleston, Great Yarmouth, Norfolk, NE31 6QP, UK. Tel : (0493) 64161 & 600914 & 600915 & 601029 Tlx : 97241		Oceaneering International AG, Zug, Switzerland. Tlx : 845 78797	
Oceanic Underwater Services (Ptd) Ltd	67 Bright Centre, Lorong L, Telok Kurau Road, Singapore, 1542. Tel : 345 5043 & 344 1274 & 440 8504 Tlx : RS 35404	High season—12 Low season—6	All types of underwater services to the shipping and engineering companies.	
Ocean Technical Services Ltd	43-44 Albermarle Street, London, W1X 3FE, UK. Tel : (01) 493 9577 Tlx : 264 066	High season—130 Low season—60	SBM maintenance ; platform inspection ; air and saturation diving.	Ocean Technical Services Ltd, Hudson Eurocentre, North River Road, Great Yarmouth, Norfolk, UK. Tel : (0493) 59455 Tlx : 975 424
Odd Berg (UK) Ltd	35 Albert Street, Aberdeen, AB1 1XU, UK. Tel : (0224) 22307/8 Tlx : 739 481	High season—120 Low season—120	Hyperbaric welding, RCV operator.	Odd Berg-Bergship A/S, Postboks 233, 9001 Tromso, Norway. Tel : (83) 850 40 Tlx : 64133
Offshore Diving and Salvaging Inc	PO Box 2236, Port Arthur, Tex. 77640, USA. Tel : (713) 985 5507	High season—25 Low season—15		
Oilfield Inspection Services	14 Brinell Way, Harfrey Industrial Estate, Great Yarmouth, UK. Tel : (0493) 58646 Tlx : 975 161	High season—6 Low season—6	NDT Testing Personnel and Equipment. PO Box 4074, Abu Dhabi, UAE. PO Box 100, South Freemantle, Western Australia 6162.	Silverburn Place, Bridge of Don, Aberdeen. 2nd Floor, Administration Bld., Jurong Marine Base, 45 Shipyard Road, Singapore, 2262.
Peter Madsen Rederi A/S	Industrievej 6, DK-8680 Ry, Denmark. Tel : (06) 89 19 11	High season—11 Low season—11	Laying pipelines ; levelling of stone beds ; drilling and blasting.	
P.M.D. Subsea Inspection Limited	14 Brinell Way, Harfrey Industrial Estate, Great Yarmouth, Norfolk, NR31 0LU, UK. Tel : (90493) 59229 & 55666 Tlx : 97170	High season—10 Low season—4	Consultancy and underwater inspection equipment hire.	
Rock Bottom Divers Inc	1702 West Church Street, Hammond, La. 70401, USA. Tel : (504) 542 0000	High season—12 Low season—5		
Saipem SpA	PO Box 12072, 20097 San Donato Milanese, Milan, Italy. Tel : (02) 5201 Tlx : 310246	High season—47 Low season—47	Deep water diving.	Saudi Arabian Saipem Ltd, PO Box 248, Dhahran Airport, Alkhobar, Saudi Arabia. Tel : 864 4148 Tlx : 670160

Company name	Head Office Address	Estimated number of divers	Specialisation	Other Address
	Saipem SpA, Stanhope House, 47 Park Lane, London, W1Y 4BP, UK. Tel: 493 7917 Tlx: 21959		Saipem Australia Pty Ltd, Associated National House, 8-12 Bridges Street, Sydney, NSW 2000, Australia. Tel: 277 031 Tlx: AA 21176 attn: Saipem.	Iran Saipem, Persian Marine, North Mirzaye Shirazi Av. 15, PO Box 13/1157, Tehran, Iran. Tel: 624 372 Tlx: 212 310
	Saipem SpA, 1 El Sadd El Aaly Str., El Mohandissin, Dokky, Cairo, Egypt. Tel: 817106 & 811217 Tlx: 94010		Intermare Sarda SpA, 21 Via Rugabella, 20122, Milano, Italy. Tel: 805 2291 Tlx: 310246	Rio Colorado SA, Sarmiento 663, Buenos Aires, Argentina. Tel: (46) 3211 & 3221 & 3231 Tlx: 18930 attn: Rio Colorado
	Saipem SpA, PO Box 2294, Sciara Bagdad, Tripoli, Libya. Tel: 43363 Tlx: 20491		Saipem SpA, 16 Lotissement Guellati, Algeria. Tel: 810713 Tlx: 53067	Rio Colorado, 330 North Belt E., Suite 100, Houston, Tex. 77060, USA. Tel: (713) 445 2231 Tlx: 790 007
	Saipem SpA, PO Box 1802, Sharjah, UAE. Tel: 354140 & 354414 Tlx: 68093		Saipem SpA, PO Box 7117, Abu Dhabi. Tel: 333 800 Tlx: 23827	Saipem AG, Schutzengasse 4, 8001 Zurich, Switzerland. Tel: 211 3290-91-92 Tlx: 812 221
	Saipem SpA, Lot no. 6, Rue Khereddine Pacha, Prolongee, BP 1087, El Menzah VI, Tunis, Tunisia. Tel: 238 414 & 238 634 & 238 844 Tlx: 13637		Saipem SpA, BP 774, Pointe Noire, Congo. Tel: 940542 Tlx: AGIPRECH 8213 K.G.	Saipem Argentina, Avenida Hipolito Yrigoyen 1628, Buenos Aires, Argentina. Tel: (46) 3695 & 7900 Tlx: 9223
	Saipem SpA, University Road, Jadryah House 2/2/14, PO Box 2298, Alwiya, Baghdad, Iraq. Tel: 776 3076/7/8 Tlx: 2251		Saipem SpA, Schwanthalerstrasse 2-6 D-8000 Munchen 15, Germany. Tel: 591261 & 529748 Tlx: AGIP M D 529 748	Saipem Nigeria Ltd, PO Box 1909, Plot 1028 Ologun Agbaje, Street Victoria, Nigeria. Tel: 618 258 Tlx: 22541
Salvage and Transport Co. Van den Akker	Piet Heinkade 59, 4381NG Vlissingen, Holland. Tel: (1184) 15120 (24 hrs) Tlx: 37808	High season—6 Low season—6	Salvage, inspection and clearance divers.	
Santa Fe International Corporation	PO Box 4000, Alhambra, Ca. 91802, USA. Tel: (213) 570 4470	High season—175 Low season—150	Diving services on Santa Fe vessels for the construction industry; the company owns Cachalot saturation diving systems and remotely controlled underwater video scanners: RCV-225 and RCV-150.	Santa Fe Diving Services Inc, Bayou DuLarge Route, Crozier Road, Houma, La. 70360, USA. Tel: (504) 876 7592 Tlx: 584 332 Santa Fe (UK) Ltd, Shed 4, Victoria Dock, Leith, Edinburgh, EH6 7DZ, UK. Tel: (31) 554 9311 Tlx: 727173 Santa Fe Diving Services Inc, 216A La Rue France, Lafayette, La. 70508, USA. Tel: (318) 232 6305
Scan Dive (UK) Ltd	Howe Moss Place, Kirkhill Industrial Estate, Dyce, Aberdeen, AB2 0ES, UK. Tel: (0224) 724466 Tlx: 73716		Operators of DSV 'Witch Queen'.	Lervigsveien 22, N-4000 Stavanger, Norway.
Scandyk A/S	Refshalevej 340, 1433 København K, Denmark. Tel: (01) 572 476 & 576 121 Tlx: 16600 attn: Scandykas	High season—8-10 Low season—4	Diving boats; TV—video; cathodic protection; underwater welding; repair of pipelines.	Manager Jørgen Krumbaek Hansen, Natskyggevej 20, 4600 Køge, Denmark. Tel: (03) 650 963
Schaefer Diving Company Inc	10707 Corporate Drive, Suite 106, Stafford, Tex. 77477, USA. Tel: (713) 494 1143	High season—50 Low season—25	Deep air, surface gas and saturation.	225 W. Broad, PO Box 1096, Freeport, Tex. 77541, USA. 1996 Pelican Island Blvd, PO Box 2458, Galveston, Tex. 77550, USA.
Scillonian Diving Services Ltd	'Warleggan', St Marys, Isles of Scilly, UK. Tel: (0720) 22563 & 22595	High season—6 Low season—4	Location of survey work; underwater blasting.	
Sequest Diving Services, also Douglas Seaquest Diving Services Co. Ltd	8 Kirkton Road, Dumbarton, UK. Tel: 933 1941	High season—14 Low season—8	Explosives, welding, cutting, civil engineering.	C/o R. A. Clement, 62 Sinclair Street, Helensburgh, Dumbartonshire, G84 7TF, UK.
Seaway Diving, see Stolt-Nielsen Seaway				
Seaweld Divers Limited	The Limes, The Street, Acle, Norfolk, NR13 3QJ, UK. Tel: (0493) 751 421 Tlx: 975101	20		

Company name	Head Office Address	Estimated number of divers	Specialisation	Other Address
Shiers Diving	21 Miller Lane, Stanstead Abbotts, Ware, Hertfordshire, SG12 8AF, UK. Tel: (0920) 871 151 Tlx: 817765	High season—150 Low season—40–50	Civil engineering diving.	
Smit Tak Internationaal Bergingsbedrijf BV	PO Box 1042, 3000 BA Rotterdam, Netherlands. Tel: (010) 54 99 11	40	Salvage and wreck-removal; underwater demolition (surveys, cutting and welding work); work with air tools (hydraulic driven tools, cox-guns, explosives, hot-tap installation); removal of bunkers and oil-cargo from sunken ships.	
Smit Vriens Offshore Diving BV	Van Konijnenburgweg 151-153, 4612 PL Bergen op Zoom, Netherlands. Tel: (01640) 43553 Tlx: 78199	High season—70 Low season—50	Underwater repair and maintenance; underwater coating (Blastcoat/Wetcoat); offshore soil investigation; NDT techniques and saturation diving techniques.	
Solus Ocean Systems (Americas Regional Base)	1441 Park 10 Boulevard, Houston, Tex. 77084 USA. Tel: (713) 492 2800 Tlx: 762214	High season—400 Low season—200	Hyperbaric welding; deep and shallow diving; inspection; construction; maintenance; ROV operators. Solus Ocean Systems (Pacific Regional Base), 1 Kwong Min Road, PO Box 204, Jurong, Singapore, 22. Tel: 261 3211 Tlx: 24760	Solus Ocean Systems (Europe and West Africa Regional Base), West Tullos Industrial Estate, Abbottswell Road, Aberdeen, AB1 4AD, UK. Tel: (0224) 876060 Tlx: 73264 Solus Shall (Nigeria) Ltd, Oluka Compound, PO Box 230, Warri/Sapele Road Warri, Nigeria. Tlx: 43295.
SSOS Sub Sea Oil Services SpA	Via San Vittore 45, 20123 Milan, Italy. Tel: 498 3141 Tlx: 332204 R & D, Via Berlino 5, Zingonia (Bg), Italy. Tel: (035) 882 252 Tlx: 301129 Operations Base, Via della Scafa 19, 00054 Fiumicino, Rome, Italy. Tel: (06) 644 1762 Tlx: 611156 Nordive A/S, Posboks 470, Tromsoe, Norway. Tel: 838 4480 Tlx: 64336		Undersea engineering and diving contractors; submarine pipeline surveys; design and construction of submersibles; pipeline trenching; hyperbaric welding. Sub Sea Española SA, Calle Segre 29, Madrid, Spain. Tel: 457 7937 Tlx: 42124	Thalassa Offshore (Scotland) Ltd Mains of Kirkhill, Kirkhill Industrial Estate, Dyce, Aberdeen, Scotland, UK. Tel: (0224) 724 666 Tlx: 73728 Technosub Engenharia e Servious Submarinos, Rua Bonfin 309, Rio de Janeiro, Brazil. Tel: 264 9047 Tlx: 213136
Star Offshore Services Ltd	Nordive House, Main Cross Road, Great Yarmouth, Norfolk, NR30 3NX, UK. Tel: (0493) 555 72 Tlx: 97116	High season—60 Low season—25–30	NDT ultrasonic inspection; salvage; SBM work; underwater photography.	
Stolt-Nielsen Seaway	Nedre Slottsgt. 15, PO Box 9570, Egertorget, Oslo 1, Norway. Tel: (02) 33 15 72 Tlx: 16600	High season—250 Low season—150	Sub-sea engineering; construction; diving; unmanned ROV operation; sub-sea inspection/ maintenance; hyperbaric welding; stand-by/fire-fighting; rescue and salvage operations; project management; vessel management.	Stolt-Nielsen Seaway, Haraldsgt. 125, PO Box 373, 5501 Haugesund, Norway. Tel: (047) 288824. Tlx: 42483 Stolt-Nielsen Seaway, Ovre Stokkavei 42, PO Box 740, 4001 Stavanger, Norway. Tel: (04) 53 5550 Tlx: 33 146
	Stolt-Nielsen Seaway, 11 Cambridge Square, PO Box 64, London, W2 2XJ, UK. Tel: (01) 402 1258 Tlx: 22294		Stolt-Nielsen Seaway, Cerrada de Vertientes 39, Apartado Postal 41-604, Mexico 10 DF. Tel: 596 0425 Tlx: 0177 3270	Stolt-Nielsen Seaway, Unit 2, Deemouth Centre, South Esplanade East, Aberdeen, AB1 3PB, UK. Tel: (0224) 879 797 Tlx: 73 270
SubSea Dolphin A/S	PO Box 63, N-4056 Tananger, Norway. Tel: (04) 69 67 22 & 69 61 82 Tlx: 33235	High season—45 Low season—10	All aspects of oilfield diving; remote and manned vehicle operations; hyperbaric welding.	Sub-Sea Offshore Ltd, Tyseal Base, Craigshaw Craigshaw Crescent, Aberdeen, AB1 4AW, UK.
SubSea International Inc	1440 Canal Street, New Orleans, La, USA. Tel: (504) 523 3617 Tlx: 230 584213	High season—100 Low season—60		SubSea International, 8748 Clay Road—Suite 320, Houston, Tex. 77080, USA. SubSea International, 1507 Centre Street, New Iberia, La. 70560, USA.
SubSea Offshore Ltd	Tyseal Base, Craigshaw Crescent Aberdeen, AB1 4AW, UK. Tel: (0224) 896 505 Tlx: 73494	High season—250–300 Low season—50–90	All forms of underwater NDT photography and welding.	SubSea International Inc, PO Box 61780, New Orleans, La, 70161, USA. Tel: (504) 523 3617 Tlx: 230 584213

Company name	Address of Head Office	Estimated number of divers	Specialisation	Other Address
Taylor Diving and Salvage Company Incorporated	701 Engineers Road, Belle Chasse, La. 70037, USA. Tel: (504) 394 6000 Tlx: 0584152	High season—175 Low season—25	Heavy undersea construction; pipeline repair by hyperbaric welding.	Taylor Diving (S.E.A.) Pte Ltd, No. 30 Joo Koon Circle, Locked Bag Service No. 11, Jurong Town Post Office, Singapore 2262. Tel: (65) 261 3311 Tlx: (786) RS 25381 Taylor Diving Services, A division of Brown and Root, SA, PO Box 807, Manama, Bahrain, Arabian Gulf. Tel: (973) 243455 Tlx: (955) 8279
Thalassa Offshore (Scotland) Ltd	Mains of Kirkhill, Kirkhill Industrial Estate, Dyce, Aberdeen, UK. Tel: (0224) 724 666 Tlx: 73728	High season—75 Low season—30	Underwater engineering; DP diving vessels; manned and unmanned submersibles; hyperbaric welding.	
T.I. Diving Services International Ltd	Unit 31, Wellheads Crescent, Wellhead Industrial Estate, Dyce, Aberdeen, UK. Tel: (0224) 770613 Tlx: 739522		Diving and diving training consultancy; saturation diving operations; deep salvage operations; RCV operation.	
Tracor Marine Inc	PO Box 13107, Port Everglades Station, Fort Lauderdale, Fla. 33316, USA. Tel: (305) 463 1211 Tlx: TWX 510 955 9864	High season—25 Low season—10	Underwater inspection; cable laying; ship repair. Tracor Marine Inc, PO Box 6865, San Diego, Ca. 92106, USA.	Tracor Marine Inc, Norfolk Operations, 1409 Air Rail Avenue, Virginia Beach, Va. 23455, USA. Tracor Marine Inc, Gallows Bay, Christiansted, St. Croix, US Virgin Islands 00820
Undersea Systems Inc	108 West Main Street, Bay Shore, NY 11706, USA. Tel: (516) 666 3127 & 665 2526 Tlx: 144599	High season—45 Low season—12	Diving services, including nuclear reactor diving services.	
Underwater Completion Team Inc	PO Box 383, New Iberia, La. 70560, USA. Tel: (318) 364 0413	High season—60 Low season—25	Sub-sea completions.	Highway 90 East, Highway 182 East, Port of Iberia, La., USA.
Underwater Construction Corporation	PO Box 698, Plains Road, Essex, Ct. 06426, USA. Tel: (203) 767 8256	High season—30 Low season—24	Marine construction and maintenance and repair for public utilities, refineries, telephone companies, etc.; travelling water screen, preventive maintenance programme, etc.	
Underwater Maintenance Company Ltd	Mayflower Close, Chandlers Ford Industrial Estate, Eastleigh, Hants, UK. Tel: (04215) 69866 Tlx: 477750	4	Underwater maintenance of commercial shipping; underwater hull cleaning; underwater hull inspectors; underwater scan surveys (to classification requirements); underwater colour TV/video; ultrasonic hull thickness measuring.	
Universal Diving Developments	Anchor House, 225 Station Road, Nether Whitacre, Coleshill, Birmingham, B46 2JG, UK. Tel: (0675) 63637	High season—4 Low season—2	Swimming pool repairs; water authority work; power station C/W work; explosives.	
U.W.R. Diving Services	Bridge Service Station, Appleton Roebuck, York, YO5 7DP, UK. Tel: (0904) 84 301	High season—20 Low season—8	Underwater burning and salvage.	
Wharton Williams Taylor	Farburn Industrial Estate, Wellheads Road, Dyce, Aberdeen, UK. Tel: (0224) 722 877 Tlx: 73368	High season—500 Low season—200	Underwater construction, repair and maintenance; underwater welding including the use of hyperbaric techniques; NDT, inspection and monitoring; underwater video and photographic inspection and monitoring; atmospheric diving systems and unmanned submersibles; project engineering and general diving services.	Wharton Williams Taylor, Dusavikn 17, N-4000 Stavanger, Norway.
Wijsmuller	Sluisplein 34, PO Box 510, 1970 AM Ijmuiden, Holland. Tel: (02550) 19010 Tlx: 41110	High season—25 Low season—25	Salvage and offshore diving.	

15.2 ADDRESSES OF TRAINING CENTRES

All the addresses of the European training centres were obtained from Volume II of the Guidance Notes for Safe Diving, compiled by the European Diving Technology Committee, and reproduced by the Commission of the European Communities, Directorate General for Employ- ment, Social Affairs and Education (July 1981 edition). Neither the Commission of the European Community, nor the European Diving Technology Committee nor any person acting on their behalf is responsible in any way for any use which might be made of this information.

Country: **Australia**
Training centre: **Underwater Training Centre**
Address: 40 Kingsway,
Cronulla, 2230, NSW.
Tel: 527 1744
Tlx: AA 23976
Courses: Air and mixed-gas diver training
Recognised by: The Professional Diver's Association of Australia

Country: **Belgium**
Training centre: **Mine clearance divers group Navclearmin**
Address: Naval Base,
Slijkenssteenweg 1,
8400 Oostende.
Tel: (059) 801402 Ext 345

Country: **Denmark**
Training centre: **The Royal Danish Navy School (Dykkerkursus Nyholm)**
Address: Holmen,
1433 Copenhagen K.

Country: **France**
Training centre: **Centravim**
Address: Port de la Pointe Rouge,
13008 Marseille.
Tel: (91) 733 462
Tlx: 410091

Country: **Germany (West)**
A German professional diver has to work for 2 years in an approved diver company, where there is at least one Master Diver and two professional divers. He must have more than 200 hours in the water before he can qualify to take the papers for the examination. There are two examination boards. These boards are constituted on governmental basis. If the diver passes the examination, he has to work for at least 5 years as a professional diver before it is possible for him to enter the master-course. If he is able to pass this course, then he is rated as a professional Master Diver and he is allowed to give instruction to trainee divers.

Examining board: Straatliche Prufungskommission fur das Tauchergewerbe in Schleswig-Holstein,
Spohienblatt 50,
2300 Kiel.
Tel: (0431) 61014

Chairman: Dipl.-Phys. Borisch (Regierungsgewerbedirektor) Prufungsausschuss fur Taucher und Tauchermeister der Industrie und Handelskammer Rhein-Neckar

Chairman: Dipl.-Ing. Breitel,
Dostowjewskistrasse 4
Postfach 3140,
6200 Wiesbaden 1.
Tel: (06121) 817-3361

There is only one company which prepares professional divers for the Master Diver examination.
Rhein-Main-Donau AG,
Postfach 40 15 69,
8000 Munchen 40.
Tel: (089) 38071

In addition to this commercial diving school for Master Divers there will be about 15 working divers groups with a Master Diver. These groups can train and prepare men for the examination.
Gesellschaft fur Kernenergiever- wertung in Schiffbau und Schiffahrt mbH,
Postfach 160,
2054 Geesthacht.
Tel: 04152/121
The GKSS has the capacity and the capability to train professional divers in mixed gas diving. The GKSS is funded by public authorities, mainly by the Ministry for Science and Technology.

Training centre: Bugsier, Reederei und Bergungs Ag
Address: Johannisbollweg 10,
2000 Hamburg 11.
Tel: 040/311 281

Training centre: Eisen und Metall AG
Address: Am Sandauhafen 31
2000 Hamburg 95.
Tel: 040/740 1041

Training centre: M. A. Flint
Address: Elleerholzdamm 17-19,
2000 Hamburg-Steinwerder.
Tel: 040/311 515-18

Training centre: Ottar Harmstorf & Sohne
Address: Falkensteiner Ufer 8,
2000 Hamburg-Blankensee.
Tel: 040/865 656

Training centre: Jade-Dienst GmbH
Address: Schleuseninsel 4,
2940 Wilhelmshaven.
Tel: 04421/42061

Training centre: Taucher Krause
Address: Rethbrook,
2300 Kiel.
Tel: 0431/34803

Training centre: August Runge
Address: Kieler Strasse 63,
2300 Kronshagen uber Kiel.
Tel: 0431/589 528

Training centre: Bundesgrenzschutz, Schule fur den technischen Dienst und ABC-Schutz
Address: Ratzeburger Landstrasse 4,
2400 Lubeck.
Tel: 0451/500 4561

Training centre: Taucherlehrbetrieb der Bundes marine
Address: 2430 Neustadt in Holstein.
Tel: 04561/6023

Training centre: Taucherlehrbetrieb Pionierschule
Address: 8136 Percha/Starnberger See.
Tel: 08151/3491-315

Training centre: Taucherlehrbetrieb Rhein-Main-Donau AG
Address: Leopoldstrasse 28,
8000 Munchen 40.
Tel: 089/3807-1

Training centre: Taucherlehrbetrieb der Wasser und Schiffahrtsverwaltung per Adresse
Address: Wasser und Schiffahrtsamt Rheine,
Bauhof Bergeshovede,
4440 Rheine/Westfalen.

Training centre: Ulrich Harms
Address: Vorsetzen 54,
2000 Hamburg 11.
Tel: 040/311316

Training centre: Taucher Heros GmbH & Co KG
Address: Larchenweg 1,
2114 Eversenheide.
Tel: 04165/6266

Training groups for scientific divers

Training centre: Biologische Anstalt Helgoland
Address: Meersstation,
2192 Helgoland.
Tel: 04723/577

Training centre: Tauchergruppe det Universitat beim Geologisch Palaontologischem Institut und Museum det Universitat Kiel
Address: Olshausenstrasse 40/60,
2300 Kiel.
Tel: 0431/880 2850

Training centre: Tauchergruppe bei dem Forschungszentrum Geesthacht GmbH
Address: Reaktorstrasse 7-9,
2054 Geesthacht.
Tel: 04152/121

Country: **Greece**
Training centre: Kartelias School of Diving
Address: 3 Karageorgi Servias Kastella,
Piraeus.
Tel: 412 2047

Training centre: Liamis School of Diving
Address: 54 Akti Mutsopulu,
Piraeus.
Tel: 451 0477 & 413 8026

Training centre: Milioglu School of Diving
Address: 62 T Oikonomidi Str,
Karaburnaki,
Thessaloniki.
Tel: 031/412 878

Training centre: Ciussi School of Diving
Address: 91 Chaina Str,
Chalkis.
Tel: 0221/21435

Training centre: Club Baracuda
Address: Paleokastritsa/Corfu.
Tel: 0663/41211

Training centre: International Centre of Diving Education
Address: 74 Dinostratou Street,
Neoskosmos, Athens.
Tel: 901 7470 & 922 9685

There are also the schools of Navy divers,

as well as the Public School of Divers of Kalymnos (running courses according to the needs of sponge-diving).

Country: **Italy**

The Italian Navy Diving School does not train commercial divers on a routine basis, but is sometimes involved in commercial diving training programmes. Two official schools are now training commercial divers for the air range only. However, the school operated by Subsea Oil Services (diving school) is training personnel for the air range, mixed-gas diving and saturation diving to professional standards.

Training centre: Istituto Technico Industriale Statale 'Alessandro Rossi'
Address: 52 Via Legione Gallieno, 36100 Vicenzia.
Tel: 044/506040 & 506101
Courses: Perito meccanico per lavori subacquei ed iperbarici (General Certificate of Education 'Industrial Expert Diver and Hyperbaric')
Recognised by: Ministero della Pubblica Istruzione

Training centre: Scuola professionale subacquea e iperbarica 'Marco Polo'
Address: Via Salaria n° 1075, Roma-00138.
Tel: 06/840 1650
Courses offered: Corsi per OTS (Operator Technici Subacquei) e OTI (Operatori Technici Iperbarici) svolti ai sensi delle Peggi Nazionali e Regionali in materia di Formazione e Qualificazione Professionale.

Training centre: Centro Professionale Di Immersione (Professional Diving Centre) Subsea Oil Services
Address: Via Venezia 3, Zingonia (BG).
Tel: 35 882077
Tlx: 301129
Courses offered: Basic air diving; bell diving; saturation diving; hyperbaric welding; NDT; hyperbaric first aid; underwater photography and video; diving supervision; life support technician; atmospheric bell pilot; submersible pilot; ROV operator; atmospheric suit operator; specific task training courses
Certification: Regione Lombardia (Regional Authority)

Country: **New Zealand**
Training centre: Underwater Training Centre
Address: 46 Karaka Park Place, St Heliers, Auckland, 5.
Tel: 542 460

Country: **Norway**
Training centre: Statens Dykkerskole (SDS) (Norwegian State Diving School)
Address: PO Box 6, 5034 Ytre Lakesevag.

Offshore divers in Norway must have a Bell Diver's Certificate when using a bell for diving. From 1 September 1980 the Bell Diver's Certificate is issued only to divers having attended an approved diving school. The above-mentioned school and the two following schools are approved in Norway.

Country: **Sweden**
Training centre: Royal Swedish Navy Diving Schools
Address: Marinens Dykericentrum, S130 61 Horsfjarden.
Tel: 0750/63000

Country: **Switzerland**
Training centre: Ausbildungszentrum fur Polozei-Taucher, Oberrieden
Tel: 01/720 7021

Training centre: Ausbildungszentrum fur Armeetaucher Brugg
Tel: 056/410311

Country: **United Kingdom**
Training centre: Fort Bovisand Underwater Centre
Address: Plymouth, Devon, PL9 0AB.
Tel: (0752) 42570 & 45641
Tlx: 45639
Courses offered: Commercial air diving up to and including HSE Part 1 Certification; NDT, explosives, first aid, chamber operating, and cleaning
Recognised by: Health and Safety Executive, CSWIP.

Training centre: Institute of Environmental and Offshore Medicine
Address: 9 Rubislaw Terrace, Aberdeen.
Tel: (0224) 55595
Courses offered: Life support; first aid; paramedic courses; food hygiene; rig medic course; occupational health nursing course; diving medicine for nurses and doctors

Training centre: Institute of Naval Medicine
Address: Alverstoke, Gosport, Portsmouth, Hants, PO12 2DL.
Tel: (0705) 822 351 Ext 41769
Courses offered: Underwater medicine for doctors

Training centre: Medicor
Address: 51 Murrayfield Gardens, Edinburgh, EH12 6DH.
Tel: (031) 337 4581
Tlx: 739446
Courses offered: Paramedic courses

Training centre: North Sea Medical Centre
Address: 3 Lowestoft Road, Gorleston-on-Sea, Great Yarmouth, Norfolk, NR31 6QB.
Tel: (0493) 600 011
Tlx: 975118
Courses offered: Diving medicine for divers and rig medics

Training centre: Northumbria Police National Diving School
Address: Marine Police Office, Pipewellgate, Gateshead, Tyne and Wear, NE8 2BJ.
Tel: (0632) 323 451 Ext 2691 or 2697
Courses offered: Three types of course are organised, all of which are specifically designed for the training of Police Officers in underwater search and recovery techniques, in addition to the preservation of evidence
(a) Basic air diving course—8 weeks
(b) Diving supervisor/leader course—3 weeks
(c) Diver refresher course—2 weeks
The school and courses are approved by the Health and Safety Executive

Training centre: Prodive Limited
Address: Commercial Diving Centre Services Area, Falmouth Oil Exploration Base, Falmouth Docks, Cornwall, TR11 4NR.
Tel: (0326) 315691
Tlx: 45362
Courses offered: Commercial air diving up to and including HSE Part 1 Certification; NDT, diver inspector full certification preparatory course; Lloyd's in-water assessment examination; professional underwater offshore photographic technician courses
Recognised by: Prodive is an 'Approved Training Centre'; this approval is given by the Health and Safety Executive

Training centre: Robert Gordon Institute of Technology
Address: 352 King Street, Aberdeen, AB9 2TQ.
Tel: (0224) 633 611 Ext 608
Courses offered: Offshore survival; firefighting; first aid; helicopter underwater escape
Recognised by: DOT (certain courses only)

Training centre: Royal Engineers Diving Establishment
Address: Marchwood Military Port, Near Southampton, SO4 4ZG.
Tel: 0703 4821 Ext 330
Courses offered: Courses offered only to Ministry of Defence (Army) military and civilian staff and foreign servicemen sponsored by Ministry of Defence (Army).
1. Army compressed air diving course—4–5 weeks—to H & S Diving Operations at Work Categories 4 and 3.
2. Army advanced diving course —7 weeks—to H & S Diving Operations at Work Category 1.
3. Army and unit diving supervisors course—3 and 2 weeks respectively.

Training centre: SANDT (School of Applied NDT)
Address: Abington Hall, Abington, Cambridge, CB1 6AL.
Tel: (0223) 891162
Tlx: 81183
Courses offered: NDT courses including CSWIP
Approved by: The Welding Institute

Training centre: SCOTA Ltd
Address: The Training Centre, Blackness Road, Altens, Aberdeen.
Tel: (0224) 873983
Courses offered: Offshore installation manager training courses

Training centre: Scottish School of NDT, Paisley College of Technology
Address: High Street, Paisley, Renfrewshire, TA1 2BE.
Tel: (041) 887 1241
Courses offered: NDT courses including CSWIP

Training centre: School of Welding Technology
Address: Abington Hall, Abington, Cambridge, CB1 6AL.
Tel: (0223) 891162
Tlx: 81183
Courses offered: Welding technology; design for welding; quality control and inspection
Approved by: Welding Institute

Training centre: Wells-Krautkramer

Address: Blackhorse Road,
            Letchworth, Herts, SG6 1HF.
            Tel: (04626) 78151 Tlx: 82329
Courses   NDT
offered:

Country: **United States of America**
Training   **Coastal Diving Academy**
centre:
Address: 108, West Main Street,
            Bay Shore, NY 11706.
            Tel: (516) 666-3127
            Tlx: 144599
Courses   Underwater photography; diver
offered: technician-tender; commercial
            scuba; scuba instructor; deep
            sea commercial diver
Recognised Member of the Association of
by: Commercial Diving Educators,
            New York State Education
            Department, Veteran's
            Administration

Training   **Divers Training Academy, Inc.**
centre:
Address: RFD 1 Box 193-C,
            Link Port, Fort Pierce,
            Fla 33450.
            Tel: (305) 465-1994
Courses   Commercial deep sea-air/mixed
offered: gas divers course
Recognised State Board of Independent Post
by: Secondary, Vocational, Technical,
            Trade and Business Schools of
            Florida, Accredited by National
            Association of Trade and
            Technical Schools

Training   **Commercial Diving Center**
centre:
Address: 272 S. Fries Avenue,
            Wilmington, Ca 90744.
            Tel: (213) 834 2501
            Dom. Tlx: 664839
            Int. Tlx: 188235
Courses   Commercial diver training in air/
offered: mixed gas; bell saturation;
            diver medical technician;
            underwater inspection/NDT
Recognised State and Federal Government
by:

Training   **Divers Institute of Technology**
centre: **Inc.**
Address: 4601 Shilshole Avenue NW,
            PO Box 70312,
            Seattle, Wa. 98107.
            Tel: (206) 783 5542
Courses   6 month professional deep sea
offered: diving course
Approved   US Coast Guard, Occupational
by: Safety and Health Administration,
            Department of Labor

Training   **Florida Institute of Technology**
centre:
Address: Underwater Technology
            Department,
            1707 NE Indian River Drive,
            Jensen Beach, Fla 33457.
            Tel: 305 334 4200
Courses   1. Underwater technology
offered: programme Associate of Science
            degree—gives 2 year degree and
            commercial diver certificate

            sanctioned by the Association of
            Commercial Diving Educators.
            2. Commercial Diver Certificate
            programme—22 week programme
            offering commercial diver
            certificate.

Training   **Highline Community College**
centre:
Address: Diving Technician,
            S 240th and Pacific Hwy S,
            Midway,
            Wa. 98031.
            Tel: (206) 878-3710
            Ext 512 or 391
Courses   2 year Associate in Applied
offered: Science degree; Life Saving and
            Industrial First Aid Certificate

Training   **Santa Barbara City College**
centre:
Address: Marine Diving Technical
            Programme,
            721, Cliff Drive,
            Santa Barbara,
            Ca. 93105.
Courses   2 year degree programme in
offered: marine diving technology;
            includes diving training through
            bell/saturation and a number of
            support courses

15.3 UNDERWATER ASSOCIATIONS AND PUBLICATIONS

Admiralty Marine Technology
Establishment,
(Experimental Diving Unit),
HMS Vernon,
Portsmouth,
Hampshire PO1 3ER, UK.
    Tel: (0705) 22351 ext 872376

Admiralty Marine Technology
Establishment
(Physiological Laboratory),
Fort Road,
Alverstoke,
Gosport,
Hampshire PO1 3ER, UK.
    Tel: (0705) 22351 ext 41381

Association of British
Offshore Industries,
11 Dartmouth Street,
London SW1, UK..

Association of Offshore
Diving Contractors,
28/30 Little Russell Street,
London, WC1A 2HN, UK.
    Tel: (01) 405 7045
            Tlx: 267568

British Society of Underwater
Photographers (BSoUP),
c/o Mr Jan Lenart,
122 Rannoch Road,
London W6, UK.
    Tel: (01) 748 6813

The British Sub-Aqua Club,
16 Upper Woburn Place,
London WC1, UK.
    Tel: (01) 387 9302

C-Core News,
Memorial University of
Newfoundland,
St John's, Newfoundland,
Canada, A1B 3X5.
    Tel: (709) 737 8354
            Tlx: 016 4794

Commercial Diving Journal,
1799 Stumpf Blvd,
Gretna, La, 70053, USA.

Committee for Nautical
Archaeology,
Mrs Margaret Rule FSA,
The Roman Palace,
Fishbourne,
Chichester, Sussex, UK.

Department of Agriculture
and Fisheries for Scotland,
PO Box 101, Victoria Road,
Aberdeen, AB9 8DB, UK.

Department of Energy,
Petroleum Production Division,
Thames House South,
Millbank,
London, SW1P 4QJ, UK.
    Tel: (01) 211 3000

Offshore Supplies Office,
Alhambra House,
45 Waterloo Street,
Glasgow, G2 6AS, UK.

Department of Environment,
2 Marsham Street,
London SW1, UK.
    Tel: (01) 212 3434

Department of Industry,
1 Victoria Street,
London SW1, UK.
    Tel: (01) 212 3395

Department of the Navy,
Naval Sea Systems Command,
Washington, DC 20362, USA

Det Norske Veritas,
PO Box 300,
N-1322 Hovik, Oslo,
Norway.
    Tel: (02) 129 900 & 129 955

Diver,
Magazine of the British
Sub-Aqua Club,
40 Grays Inn Road,
London WC1, UK.
    Tel: (01) 405 0224

European Diving Technology
Committee,
Commission of the European
Communities,
Directorate-General
Employment and Social
Affairs, Floor A2,
Jean Monet Building,
The Kirchberg,
Luxembourg.

The Health and Safety
Executive,
25 Chapel Street,
London, NW1 5DT, UK.
    Tel: (01) 262 3277

The Hydrographic Journal,
c/o Alan Rackley,
67 Kingtree Avenue,
Cottingham,
North Humberside,
HU16 4DR, UK.
    Tel: (0482) 846 2000

The Hydrographic Society,
North East London Polytechnic,
Forest Road,
London E17 4JB, UK.
    Tel: (01) 508 9908

Institution of Civil Engineers,
26–34 Old Street,
London EC1, UK.
    Tel: (01) 253 9999

Institute of Diving,
PO Box 876,
Panama City,
Fla 32401, USA.
    Tel: (904) 769 7544

The Institute of Environmental
and Offshore Medicine,
9 Rubislaw Terrace,
Aberdeen, Scotland.
    Tel: (0224) 55595

The International Journal of
Nautical Archaeology,
Academic Press,
24–28 Oval Road,
London NW1, UK.
    Tel: (01) 267 4466

The Institute of Marine Engineers,
c/o Marine Management
(Holdings) Ltd,
76 Mark Lane,
London EC3R 7JN, UK.
    Tel: (01) 481 8493

Institute of Oceanographic
Sciences,
Brook Road,
Wormley,
Godalming,
Surrey GU8 5UB, UK.
    Tel: (042 879) 4141

International Underwater
Systems Design,
USD Publications,
322 St John Street,
London, EC1V 4QH, UK.
    Tel: (01) 278 1102

Journal of the Society for
Underwater Technology (SUT),
1 Birdcage Walk,
London SW1, UK.
    Tel: (01) 222 8658

Journal of Undersea
Biomedical Research,
Undersea Medical Society,
9650 Rockville Pike,
Bethesda, Md 20014, USA.

Institute of Petroleum,
6 New Cavendish Street,
London W1M 8AR, UK.
Tel: (01) 636 1004

Manpower Training Centre,
162–168 Regent Street,
London, W1R 6DE, UK.
Tel: (01) 214 8006

Marine Information and
Advisory Service,
Institute of Oceanographic
Sciences,
Brook Road,
Wormley,
Godalming,
Surrey GU8 5UB, UK.
Tel: (042879) 4141

Marine Technology Society,
1730 M Street N W,
Washington,
DC 20036, USA.
Tel: (202) 659 3251

The Mary Rose Trust,
Old Bond Store,
48 Warblington Street,
Portsmouth, Hants, UK.

Medical Research Council,
Decompression Sickness
Central Registry,
University of
Newcastle upon Tyne,
21 Claremont Place,
Newcastle upon Tyne
NE2 4AA, UK.
Tel: (0632) 24987

Ministry of Defence,
Navy Department Bank Block,
Old Admiralty Buildings,
Whitehall, London SW1, UK.
Tel: (01) 218 9000

Ministry of Agriculture
Fisheries and Food,
Gt Westminster House,
Horseferry Road,
London SW1, UK.
Tel: (01) 217 3000

National Association of
Underwater Instructors (NAUI),
PO Box 630, Colton,
Ca. 92324, USA.

National Institute for
Occupational Safety
and Health,
5600 Fishes Lane,
Rockville, Md, 20852, USA.

National Oceanic and
Atmospheric Administration
(NOAA),
US Department of Commerce,
11400 Rockville Pike,
Room 429, Rockville,
Md 20852, USA.

National YMCA Scuba
Headquarters,
1611 Candler Building,
Atlanta, Ga 30303, USA.

Natural Environment Research
Council,
27–33 Charing Cross Road,
London WC2, UK.
Tel: (01) 930 9162

Noroil,
50 Gresham Street,
London, EC2V 7AY, UK.
Tel: (01) 606 3266

North Sea Letter,
Bracken House,
10 Cannon Street,
London, EC4P 4BY, UK.
Tel: (01) 248 8000

Norwegian Petroleum Directorate,
Lagardsveien 80,
PO Box 600,
N-4001 Stavanger,
Norway.
Tel: (045) 33160
Tlx: 33100

Ocean Industry,
PO Box 2608,
Houston, Tex. 77001, USA.
Tel: (713) 529 4301
Tlx: 762 908

The Oceanic Society,
Executive Offices,
Magee Avenue,
Stamford,
Conn. 06902, USA.
Tel: (203) 327 9786

Offshore,
PennWell Publishing Company,
1421 S. Sheridan Road,
Tulsa, Okla. 74101, USA.

Offshore Engineer,
26–34 Old Street,
London EC1, UK.
Tel: (01) 253 9999

Offshore Oil International,
Morton Offshore Ltd,
Suite D,
Silkhouse Court,
Tithebarn Street,
Liverpool, Merseyside,
L2 2LZ, UK.
Tel: (051) 227 4832

Offshore Services and
Technology,
Kingston Publication,
54 Eden Street,
Kingston-upon-Thames,
Surrey, KT1 1EE, UK.
Tel: (01) 549 9482

Petroleum Industry Training
Board,
York House,
Empire Way, Wembley,
Middlesex, UK.

Petroleum Review,
Institute of Petroleum,
61 New Cavendish Street,
London W1, UK.
Tel: (01) 636 1004
Tlx: 264380

Petroleum Times,
IPC Press,
Quadrant House,
The Quadrant,
Sutton, Surrey, UK.
Tel: (01) 661 3500

Pipeline Industry,
Gulf Publishing Co.,
PO Box 2608,
Houston, Tex. 77001, USA.
Tel: (713) 529 4301
Tlx: 762 908

Professional Association of
Diving Instructors (PADI),
2064 North Bush Street,
Santa Ana, Ca. 92706, USA.

Professional Divers' Association
of Australasia,
90 Queen Street,
Melbourne,
Victoria, Australia.
Tel: (03) 67 4636

Roustabout,
64 Great Northern Road,
Aberdeen, UK.
Tel: (0224) 46267

Royal Institute of Naval
Architects,
10 Upper Belgrave Street,
London SW1X 8BG, UK.
Tel: (01) 930 9162

The Salvage Association,
Bankside House,
107–112 Leadenhall Street,
London EC3A 4AP, UK.
Tel: (01) 623 1299

Science Research Council,
State House, High Holborn,
London, WC1R 4IA, UK.
Tel: (01) 930 9162

Scientific Civil Service,
Alencon Link,
Basingstoke,
Hants, UK.

SCOTA Ltd,
The Training Centre,
Blackness Road,
Altens, Aberdeen, UK.
Tel: (0224) 873 983

Sea Technology,
Suite 1000,
1117 North 19th Street,
Arlington, Va. 22209, USA.
Tel: (703) 524 3136

Skin Diver,
Petersen Publishing Co.,
8490 Sunset Blvd,
Los Angeles,
Ca. 90069, USA.

Society of Petroleum Engineers,
6200 North Central Expressway,
Dallas,
Tx. 75206, USA.
Tel: (214) 361 6601

The Society for Underwater
Technology (SUT),
1 Birdcage Walk,
London, SW1 9JJ, UK.
Tel: (01) 222 8658

South Pacific Underwater
Medicine Society,
c/o C. Louwrey,
43 Canadian Bay Road,
Mount Eliza,
Victoria 3930, Australia.

Sports Diver,
Ziff-Davis Publishing Company,
1 Park Avenue,
New York, NY 10016, USA.

The Undersea Medical Society,
9650 Rockville Pike,
Bethesda, Md 20014, USA.

The Underwater Association
for Scientific Research Ltd,
c/o Napier Lodge,
46 Monkton Road,
Minster-in-Thanet,
Kent, CT12 4EB, UK.

Underwater Conservation
Society (UCS),
Dr R. Earll,
Zoology Department,
University of Manchester,
Oxford Road,
Manchester, M13 9PL, UK.

Underwater Engineering Group
(UEG),
6 Storey's Gate,
Westminster,
London, SW1P 3AU, UK.
Tel: (01) 222 8891

Underwater Equipment and
Apparel Manufacturers
Association,
7 Swallow Street,
London W1R 7HD, UK.
Tel: (01) 437 7281

The World Underwater
Federation (CMAS),
34 Rue du Colisee,
75008 Paris, France.

US Coast Guard,
Department of Transportation,
Washington, DC 20590, USA.

US Navy Experimental Diving
Unit,
Panama City,
Fla 32407, USA.

16.1 METRICATION

The oil industry had developed in the United States long before the metric system was established in Europe and some other countries. Consequently, many units of measurement are unique to that industry, and some were even invented specially for it. Two of the measurements which are peculiar to the oil industry are the unit of force, the Kip, which equals 1000 lb force, and the unit of liquid volume, the barrel, which is a multiple of the US gallon. The American Petroleum Institute eventually rationalised standards for the measurement of length, mass, time and temperature.

In 1948 the International Committee of Weights and Measures began to study the establishment of a worldwide practical system of units of measurement. However, because the API still has not agreed to the adoption of the metric system, the subsea industry has to work in many incomparable units, such as SI (International System of Units), metric units, imperial units and API units. Conversion tables covering some of these systems will be found on pages 297-298.

The metric system

The International System of Units (SI) is a modern version of the metric system in use throughout the scientific and industrial world. Its universal use avoids confusion in international trade and scientific work.

The SI is based on seven units:

1. The metre (m) is the unit of length.

2. The kilogram (kg) is the unit of mass.

3. The second (s) is the unit of time.

4. The ampere (A) is the unit of electric current.

5. The kelvin (K) is the unit of thermodynamic temperature.

6. The mole (mol) is the unit of the amount of substance.

7. The candela (cd) is the unit of luminous intensity.

Other SI units are called derived units, formed by combining base units according to their corresponding physical properties. Some of these are described below:

Note: all symbols are written in lower case roman type, without full points and without any plural form (never hs for hours). The exception to this rule is when the symbol is taken from a proper name, i.e. W for Watt. Symbols written in italics are physical quantities, i.e. g = gravitational acceleration.

When a unit for a physical quantity is divided by a unit for another physical quantity, an oblique line (solidus) may be used, or the denominator may be expressed to the appropriate negative power, for example, m/s or ms^{-1}.

Quantity	SI unit	Symbol
Area	square metre	m^2
Volume	cubic metre	m^3
Velocity, speed	metre per second	m/s or ms^{-1}
Acceleration	metre per second squared	m/s^2 or ms^{-2}
Moment of force	newton metre	Nm
Mass per unit length	kilogram per metre	kg/m
Density	kilogram per cubic metre	kg/m^3

The following derived units have special names and symbols:

Quantity	Name	Symbol	Expressed in terms of Other SI units	Expressed in terms of SI base units
Activity (of a radio-active source)	bequerel	Bq		s^{-1}
Quantity of electricity (electric charge)	coulomb	C		As
Electrical capacitance	farad	F	C/V	s^{4}A^2(m^{2}kg)
Inductance	henry	H	Wb/A	m^{2}kg/(s^{2}A^2)
Frequency	hertz	Hz		s^{-1}
Energy, work, quantity of heat	joule	J	Nm	m^{2}kg/s^2
Luminous flux	lumen	lm		cd sr
Illuminance	lux	lx	lm/m^2	cd sr/m^2
Force	newton	N		m kg/s^2
Electrical resistance	ohm	Ω	V/A	m^{2}kg/(s^{3}A^2)
Pressure	pascal	Pa	N/m^2	kg/(ms^2)
Electrical conductance	siemens	S	A/V	s^{3}A^2/(m^{2}kg)
Magnetic flux density	tesla	T	Wb/m^2	kg/(s^{2}A)
Electrical potential difference	volt	V	W/A	m^{2}kg/(s^{3}A)
Power	watt	W	J/s	m^{2}kg/s^3
Magnetic flux	weber	Wb	Vs	m^{2}kg/(S^{2}A)

There are other units, not themselves SI units, which are often used in conjunction with them.

minute (min) (of time)	degree (°) (of angle or temp.)
hour (h)	minute (′) (of angle)
day (d)	second (″) (of angle)
litre (l)	tonne (t)
bar (b)	nautical mile (nm)
atmosphere absolute (ata)	knot (k)

Prefixes

In SI there is only one unit for each physical quantity, e.g. the metre for length. If a unit seems too large or small, a multiple should be used, called a prefix.

Prefix	Symbol	Factor by which unit is multiplied	
mega	M	1 000 000	= 10^6
kilo	k	1 000	= 10^3
hecto	h	100	= 10^2
deca	da	10	= 10^1
deci	d	0.1	= 10^{-1}
centi	c	0.01	= 10^{-2}
milli	m	0.001	= 10^{-3}
micro	μ	0.000 001	= 10^{-6}

There are some symbols which might be ambiguous. The symbol for litre is l. This is often confused with the numeral 1. The symbol for the metric tonne is t, which is often used for imperial tons. In such cases confusion can be avoided by spelling out the whole word, litre or tonne.

Decimal markers

The decimal point may be either a full point or a comma, written on the line. To avoid confusion, the comma should never be used as a thousands marker (as in 3,500). For the same reason, the use of a hyphen is recommended when writing sums of money on cheques.

16.2 CONVERSION TABLES

To convert	Into	Multiply by	To convert	Into	Multiply by
atmospheres	cm of mercury	76.0	gallons (US)	gallons (Br. Imp.)	0.83267
	ft of water (4°C)	33.9	inches	millimetres	25.4
	fsw	33.072		centimetres	2.54
	in of mercury (0°C)	29.92		feet	0.08333
	kg/cm²	1.0333		metres	0.0254
	kg/m²	10332		yards	0.02778
	pounds/in² (psi)	14.7	kilograms	grams	1000
	tons/ft²	1.058		pounds	2.205
bars	atmospheres	0.9869		tons (long)	0.0009842
	kg/m²	10200		tons (short)	0.001102
	kg/cm²	1.02	kilometres	feet	3281
	pounds/ft² (psi)	2089		miles	0.6214
centigrade	Fahrenheit	(°C × 9/5) + 32		yards	1094
centimetres	inches	0.3937	kilometres/hr	cm/sec	27.78
	feet	0.0328		feet/min	54.68
	yards	0.01094		feet/sec	0.9113
centimetres	atmospheres	0.01316		knots	0.5396
of mercury	ft of water (4°C)	0.4461		metres/min	16.67
	kg/m²	136		miles/hr	0.6214
	pounds/ft²	27.85	knots	feet/hr	6080.2
	pounds/in² (psi)	0.1934		kilometres/hr	1.8532
centimetres/sec	feet/min	1.9685		metres/sec	0.5144
	feet/sec	0.03281		statute miles/hr	1.1516
	km/hr	0.036		yards/hr	2,027
	knots	0.01943		feet/sec	1.689
	metres/min	0.6	litres	cu. cm (cc)	1000
	miles/hr	0.02237		cu. metres (m³)	0.001
	miles/min	0.0003728		cu. inches (in³)	61.02
cubic centimetres	cu. inches (in³)	0.06102		cu. ft (ft³)	0.03531
	cu. feet (ft³)	0.00003531		cu. yards (yd³)	0.001308
	cu. yards (yd³)	0.000001308		gallons (US liquid)	0.2642
	gallons (US liquid)	0.0002642	metres	inches	39.37
	litres	0.01		feet	3.281
	ounces	0.03381		miles (naut.)	0.0005396
cubic feet	cu. cm (cc)	28320		miles (stat.)	0.0006214
	cu. inches (in³)	1728		yards	1.094
	cu. metres (m³)	0.02832	metres/min	cm/sec	1.667
	cu. yards (yd³)	0.03704		feet/min	3.281
	gallons (US liquid)	7.48052		feet/sec	0.05468
	litres	28.32		km/hr	0.06
cubic feet/min	cu. cm/sec (cc/sec)	472		knots	0.03238
	gallons/sec	0.472		mile/hr	0.03728
cubic feet/sec	gallons/min	448.831	metres/sec	feet/min	196.8
cubic inches	cu. cm (cc)	16.39		feet/sec	3.281
	cu. feet (ft³)	0.0005787		km/hr	3.6
	cu. metres (m³)	0.00001639		km/min	0.06
	cu. yards (yd³)	0.00002143		miles/hr	2.237
	gallons (US liquid)	0.004329		miles/min	0.03728
	litres	0.01639	miles (nautical)	metres	1853.248
cubic metres	cu. inches (in³)	61023		kilometres	1.853248
	cu. feet (ft³)	35.31		feet	6080
	cu. yards (yd³)	1.308		yards	2025.4
	gallons (US liquid)	264.2		miles (stat.)	1.1516
	litres	1000	miles (statute)	centimetres	160900
feet	millimetres	304.8		metres	1609
	centimetres	30.48		kilometres	1.609
	metres	0.3048		feet	5280
	miles (naut.)	0.0001645		yards	1,760
	miles (stat.)	0.0001894		miles (naut.)	0.8684
feet of water (fsw)	atmospheres	0.0295	miles/hr	cm/sec	44.7
	in of mercury	0.8826		feet/min	88
	kg/cm²	0.03048		feet/sec	1.467
	kg/m²	304.8		miles/min	0.1667
	pounds/ft²	62.43		km/hr	1.609
	pounds/in² (psi)	0.4335		km/min	0.02682
feet/min	cm/sec	0.5080		knots	0.8684
	feet/sec	0.01667		metres/min	26.82
	km/hr	0.01829		metres/sec	0.447
	metres/min	0.3048	millimetres	inches	0.3937
	miles/hr	0.01136		feet	0.003281
feet/sec	cm/sec	30.48		yards	0.001094
	km/hr	1.097	ounces	pounds	0.0625
	knots	0.5921		cu. inches (in³)	1.805
	metres/min	18.29		litres	0.02957
	miles/hr	0.6818	ounces/in²	pounds/in²	0.0625
	miles/min	0.01136	pounds	kilograms	0.4536
gallons (Br. Imperial)	cu. cm (cc)	3785		ounces	16
	cu. feet (ft³)	0.1337	pounds/ft³	kg/m³	16.02
	cu. inches (in³)	231	pounds/in³	pounds/ft³	1728
	cu. metres (m³)	0.003785	pounds/ft	kg/m	1.488
	cu. yards (yd³)	0.004951	pounds/in	gm/cm	178.6
	litres	3.785	pounds/ft²	atmospheres	0.0004725
	pounds of water	8.33		kg/m²	4.882
	gallons (US)	1.20095			

To convert	Into	Multiply by
	pounds/in² (psi)	0.006944
pounds/in² (psi)	atmospheres	0.06804
	feet seawater	2.250482
	kg/m²	703.1
	pounds/ft²	144
pounds of water	gallons	0.12004
square feet	sq. mm (mm²)	92900
	sq. cm (cm²)	929
	sq. metres (m²)	0.929
	sq. inches (in²)	144
	sq. yards (yd²)	0.111
square inches	sq. mm (mm²)	645.2
	sq. cm (cm²)	6.452
	sq. feet (ft²)	0.006944
square kilometres	sq. miles	0.3861
square metres	sq. feet (ft²)	10.76
	sq. inches (in²)	1550
	sq. yards (yd²)	1.196
square miles	sq. kilometres	2.590
square millimetres (mm²)	sq. inches	0.00155
square yards	sq. metres (m²)	0.8361
temperature (°C) + 273	absolute temperature (°K)	1
temperature (°C) + 17.78	temperature (°F)	1.8
temperature (°F) + 460	absolute temperature	1
temperature (°F) — 32	temperature (°C)	5/9
tons (long)	kilograms	1016
	pounds	2240
	tons (short)	1.12
tons (short)	kilograms	907.1848
	ounces	32000
	pounds	2000
	tons (long)	0.89287
yards	centimetres	91.44
	metres	0.9144

Specific Gravity of Gases
(At 60°F and 29.92″ Hg)

Dry air (1 cu. ft at 60°F and 29.92″ Hg weighs .07638 pound)		1.000
Acetylene	C_2H_2	0.91
Ethane	C_2H_4	1.05
Methane	Ch_4	0.554
Ammonia	NH_3	0.596
Carbon dioxide	CO_2	1.53
Carbon monoxide	CO	0.967
Butane	C_4H_{10}	2.067
Butene	C_4H_8	1.93
Chlorine	Cl_2	2.486
Helium	He	0.138
Hydrogen	H_2	0.0696
Nitrogen	N_2	0.9718
Oxygen	O_2	1.1053

Water Pressure to Feet Head / Feet Head of Water to PSI

Pounds per square inch	Feet head	Pounds per square inch	Feet head	Feet head	Pounds per square inch	Feet head	Pounds per square inch
1	2.31	100	230.90	1	0.43	100	43.31
2	4.62	110	253.98	2	0.87	110	47.64
3	6.93	120	277.07	3	1.30	120	51.97
4	9.24	130	300.16	4	1.73	130	56.30
5	11.54	140	323 25	5	2.17	140	60.63
6	13.85	150	346.34	6	2.60	150	64.96
7	16.16	160	369.43	7	3.03	160	69 29
8	18.47	170	392.52	8	3.46	170	73.63
9	20.78	180	415.61	9	3.90	180	77.96
10	23.09	200	461.78	10	4.33	200	86.62
15	34.63	250	577.24	15	6.50	250	108.27
20	46.18	300	692.69	20	8.66	300	129 93
25	57.72	350	808.13	25	10.83	350	151.58
30	69.27	400	922.58	30	12.99	400	173.24
40	92.36	500	1154.48	40	17.32	500	216.55
50	115.45	600	1385.39	50	21.65	600	259.85
60	138.54	700	1616.30	60	25.99	700	303.16
70	161.63	800	1847.20	70	30.32	800	346.47
80	184.72	900	2078.10	80	34.65	900	389.78
90	207.81	1000	2309.00	90	38.98	1000	433.00

NOTE: One pound of pressure per square inch of water equals 2.309 feet of water at 62° Fahrenheit. To find the feet head of water for any pressure not given in the table above, multiply the pressure pounds per square inch by 2.309.

NOTE: One foot of water at 62° Fahrenheit equals 0.433 pounds pressure per square inch. To find the pressure per square inch for any feet head not given in the table above, multiply the feet head by 0.433.

Fraction–Decimal–Metric Conversion

Fraction	Decimal	MM	Fraction	Decimal	MM
1/64	.015625	0.3969	33/64	.515625	13.0969
1/32	.03125	0.7938	17/32	.53125	13.4938
3/64	.046875	1.1906	35/64	.546875	13.8906
1/16	.0625	1.5875	9/16	.5625	14.2875
5/64	.078125	1.9844	37/64	.578125	14.6844
3/32	.09375	2.3812	19/32	.59375	15.0812
7/64	.109375	2.7781	39/64	.609375	15.4781
1/8	.125	3.1750	5/8	.625	15.8750
9/64	.140625	3.5719	41/64	.640625	16.2719
5/32	.15625	3.9688	21/32	.65625	16.6688
11/64	.171875	4.3656	43/64	.671875	17.0656
3/16	.1875	4.7625	11/16	.6875	17.4625
13/64	.203125	5.1594	45/64	.703125	17.8594
7/32	.21875	5.5562	23/32	.71875	18.2562
15/64	.234375	5.9531	47/64	.734375	18.6531
1/4	.25	6.3500	3/4	.75	19.0500
17/64	.265625	6.7469	49/64	.765625	19.4469
9/32	.28125	7.1438	25/32	.78125	19.8438
19/64	.296875	7.5406	51/64	.796875	20.2406
5/16	.3125	7.9375	13/16	.8125	20.6375
21/64	.328125	8.3344	53/64	.828125	21.0344
11/32	.34375	8.7312	27/32	.84375	21.4312
23/64	.359375	9.1281	55/64	.859375	21.8281
3/8	.375	9.5250	7/8	.875	22.2250
25/64	.390625	9.9219	57/64	.890625	22.6219
13/32	.40625	10.3188	29/32	.90625	23.0188
27/64	.421875	10.7156	59/64	.921875	23.4156
7/16	.4375	11.1125	15/16	.9375	23.8125
29/64	.453125	11.5094	61/64	.953125	24.2094
15/32	.46875	11.9062	31/32	.96875	24.6062
31/64	.484375	12.3031	63/64	.984375	25.0031
1/2	.5	12.700	1	1	25.400

Feet to metres, metres to feet

Explanation: The central columns of figures in bold type can be referred in either direction. To the left to convert metres into feet, or to the right to convert feet into metres. For example, five lines down: 5 feet=1.52 metres, and 5 metres=16.40 feet.

Feet		Metres	Feet		Metres
3.28	1	0.30	88.58	27	8.23
6.56	2	0.61	91.86	28	8.53
9.84	3	0.91	95.14	29	8.84
13.12	4	1.22	98.43	30	9.14
16.40	5	1.52	101.71	31	9.45
19.69	6	1.83	104.99	32	9.75
22.97	7	2.13	108.27	33	10.06
26.25	8	2.44	111.55	34	10.36
29.53	9	2.74	114.83	35	10.67
32.81	10	3.05	118.11	36	10.97
36.09	11	3.55	121.39	37	11.28
39.37	12	3.66	124.67	38	11.58
42.65	13	3.96	127.95	39	11.89
45.93	14	4.27	131.23	40	12.19
49.21	15	4.57	134.51	41	12.50
52.49	16	4.88	137.80	42	12.80
55.77	17	5.18	141.08	43	13.11
59.06	18	5.49	144.36	44	13.41
62.34	19	5.79	147.64	45	13.72
65.62	20	6.10	150.92	46	14.02
68.90	21	6.40	154.20	47	14.33
72.18	22	6.71	157.48	48	14.63
75.46	23	7.01	160.76	49	14.94
78.74	24	7.32	164.04	50	15.24
82.02	25	7.62	328.08	100	30.48
85.30	26	7.92	3280.80	1000	304.8

1 nautical mile=approx. 1.853 km (6080 ft).
1 statute mile=1.609 km (5280 ft).

Tonnage

DISPLACEMENT TONNAGE is the weight of water displaced by a ship and is equal to the weight of the ship and its contents. It therefore varies with the ship's draft.

DEADWEIGHT TONNAGE is the weight, in tons (2240 lb) or tonnes (2204.62 lb), of the total contents of a fully laden ship. It is the difference in displacement of a ship light or fully laden.

GROSS TONNAGE is the official registered tonnage, usually calculated from all the spaces within the ship (1 gross ton = 100 cu ft). Net tonnage is similar with certain deductions, leaving only the cargo space.

Tonnage conversion table—long tons, short tons and metric tons

Long	Short	Metric	Short	Metric	Long	Metric	Long	Short
1	1.1	1.02	1	0.91	0.9	1	0.98	1.1
2	2.2	2.03	2	1.81	1.8	2	1.97	2.2
3	3.7	3.05	3	2.72	2.7	3	2.95	3.3
4	4.5	4.06	4	3.63	3.6	4	3.94	4.4
5	5.6	5.08	5	4.54	4.5	5	4.92	5.5
6	6.7	6.10	6	5.44	5.4	6	5.91	6.6
7	7.8	7.11	7	6.35	6.3	7	6.89	7.7
8	9.0	8.13	8	7.26	7.1	8	7.87	8.8
9	10.1	9.14	9	8.16	8.0	9	8.86	9.9
10	11.2	10.16	10	9.1	8.9	10	9.84	11.0
20	22.4	20.3	20	18.1	17.9	20	19.7	22.0
30	33.6	30.5	30	27.2	26.8	30	29.5	33.1
40	44.8	40.6	40	36.3	35.7	40	39.4	44.1
50	56.0	50.8	50	45.4	44.7	50	49.2	55.1
60	67.2	61.0	60	54.4	53.6	60	59.1	66.1
70	78.4	71.1	70	63.5	62.5	70	68.9	77.2
80	89.6	81.3	80	72.6	71.5	80	78.7	88.2
90	100.8	91.4	90	81.7	80.4	90	88.6	99.2
100	112.0	101.6	100	90.7	89.3	100	98.4	110.2
200	224.0	203.2	200	181.4	178.6	200	196.8	220.5
300	336.0	304.8	300	272.2	267.9	300	295.3	330.7
400	448.0	406.4	400	362.9	357.2	400	393.7	441.0
500	560.0	508.0	500	453.6	446.6	500	492.1	551.2
600	672.0	609.6	600	544.3	535.9	600	590.5	661.4
700	784.0	711.2	700	635.0	625.2	700	688.9	771.6
800	896.0	812.8	800	725.8	714.5	800	787.4	881.8
900	1008.0	914.4	900	816.5	803.8	900	885.8	992.1
1000	1120.0	1016.1	1000	907.2	893.1	1000	984.2	1102.3
2000	2240.0	2032.1	2000	1814.4	1786.2	2000	1968.4	2204.6
3000	3360.0	3048.1	3000	2721.6	2679.3	3000	2952.6	3306.9
4000	4480.0	4065.2	4000	3628.8	3572.4	4000	3936.8	4409.2
5000	5600.0	5080.2	5000	4536.0	4465.5	5000	4921.0	5511.5
6000	6720.0	6096.3	6000	5443.2	5358.6	6000	5905.2	6613.8
7000	7840.0	7112.3	7000	6350.4	6251.7	7000	6889.4	7716.1
8000	8960.0	8128.4	8000	7257.6	7144.8	8000	7873.6	8818.4
9000	10 080.0	9144.4	9000	8164.8	8037.9	9000	8857.8	9920.7
10 000	11 200.0	10 160.5	10 000	9071.9	8931.0	10 000	9842.0	11 023.0

Factors: 1 long ton: 2240 lb. 1 short ton: 2000 lb. 1 metric tonne: 2204.6 lb. or 1000 kg.

Comparison of cylinder pressures

lbf/sq. in	MN/sq. m	ats	bar
1800	12.4	122	124
2000	13.8	136	138
2250	15.5	153	155
2500	17.2	170	172
2650	18.2	180	183
3000	20.7	204	207

From	To	Multiply by
fsw	msw	0.3048
psi	fsw	2.250482
bar	psi	14.503774
psi	pascals	6894.757
bar	pascals	100 000
atmospheres	pascals	1 013 250
sq. km	pascals	9.806650
dyne/sq. cm	pascals	0.1
atmospheres	psi	14.696
atmospheres	fsw	33.072

1 bar = 100 kN/sq. m = 100 kPa

Comparison of cylinder capacities and mass of air contained

Capacity of cylinder			Mass of air	
cu. feet	litres	cu. metres	lb	kg
40	1133	1.133	3.1	1.39
45	1274	1.274	3.4	1.56
50	1416	1.416	3.8	1.74
55	1557	1.557	4.2	1.91
60	1699	1.699	4.6	2.08
65	1841	1.841	5.0	2.26
70	1982	1.982	5.4	2.43
75	2124	2.124	5.7	2.60
80	2265	2.265	6.1	2.78

16.3 ABBREVIATIONS

Which may be used in this Handbook or which may be found in diving-related literature.

A	International code 'Divers down'
ABDS	Association of British Diving Schools
ABLJ	Adjustable buoyancy life jacket
ABS	American Bureau of Shipping
a.c.	Alternating current
a.c.-d	Alternating current drop (NDT)
acfm	Absolute cubic feet per minute
ACU	Atmospheric conditioning unit
ACUC	Association of Canadian Underwater Councils
ADC	Association of Diving Contractors
ADS	Atmospheric diving suit
AF	Audio frequency
AFC	Automatic frequency control
AgCl	Silver chloride (chemical symbol)
AISI	American Iron and Steel Institute
ALP	Articulated loading platform
AM	Amplitude modulation
AMTE (EDU)	Admiralty Marine Technology Establishment (Experimental Diving Unit)
AMTE (PL)	Admiralty Marine Technology Establishment (Physiological Laboratory)
ANSI	American National Standards Institute
AODC	Association of Offshore Diving Contractors (UK)
API	American Petroleum Institute
ARLEMS	Articulated leg mooring system
ASA	American Standards Association
ASME	American Society of Mechanical Engineers
ASSY	Assembly
ASTM	American Society for Testing Materials
ata	Atmospheres (absolute)
atm	Atmosphere(s)
AUF	Australian Underwater Federation
AWG	American wire gauge
b	Bar (unit of pressure, 1 ata)
BA	British Association (screw thread)
BAD	Basic Air Diving (UK)
bbls	Barrels
BDV	Breakdown voltage
bhp	Brake horse power
BIBS	Built-in breathing system
BM	Bench mark (UK)
BOP	Blow out preventer
BOT	Board of Trade (UK)
BOTM	Buoyant off-bottom tow method
BP	Blood pressure
BSC	British Standard Cycle
BSF	British Standard Fine
BSG	British Standard Gauge
BSI	British Standards Institution
BSP	British Standard Pipe
BSPF	British Standard Pipe fastening
BSPT	British Standard Pipe taper
BST	British Summer Time
BSUP	British Society of Underwater Photographers
BSW	British Standard Whitworth
Btu	British thermal unit(s)
BV	Bureau Veritas
BWRA	British Welding Research Association
°C	Degrees Celsius/centigrade
CA	Certification authority
CAF	Compressed asbestos fibre gasket

cal	Calorie (unit of heat)
CALM	Catenary anchor leg mooring
cath	Cathode
CB	Centre of buoyancy
CBM	Conventional berthing mooring
C-Core	Centre for Cold Ocean Research
CCTV	Closed circuit television
CD	Chart datum
CD	Clearance diver (RN)
CDBA	Clearance diver's breathing apparatus (RN)
CDC	Commercial Diving Centre (USA)
CDJ	Commercial Diving Journal (USA)
cfm	Cubic feet per minute
cg	Centre of gravity
CG	Coastguard
CIRIA	Construction Industries Research and Information Association (UK)
clo	Unit of clothing insulation
cm	Centimetre
CMAS	World underwater federation
cm Hg	Centimetres of mercury (pressure)
cm H$_2$O	Centimetres of water (pressure)
CNS	Central nervous system
CO	Carbon monoxide (chemical symbol)
CO$_2$	Carbon dioxide (chemical symbol)
COP	Composite offshore platform
C/P	Charter Party
CP	Cathodic protection
CP	Corrosion potential
CPA	Critical path analysis
CPR	Cardio-pulmonary resuscitation
cps	Cycles per second
CRT	Cathode ray tube
CSWIP	Certification Scheme for Welding Inspection Personnel (UK)
CTW	Constant tension winch
CV	Curriculum vitae
cwt	Hundredweight
CWU	Compression wave ultrasonics
cyl	Cylinder
d	Draught
DAN	National Diving Accident Network
DAWS	Diver alternative work system
dB	Decibel(s)
DB	Derrick barge
d.c.	Direct current
DCC	Deck compression chamber (also DDC)
DCS	Decompression sickness
DDU	Deep diving unit
DEn	Department of Energy (UK)
D/F	Direction finding
DHSV	Down hole safety valve
dia.	Diameter
DIN	Deutsche Industrie Norman
DLO	Diver lock-out
DLT	Dead load testing
DMAC	Diving Medical Advisory Committee (UK)
DnV	Det norske Veritas (Norway)
DoT	Department of Trade (UK)
DoT	Department of Transportation (USA)
DP	Dynamic positioning
DPV	Diver propulsion vehicle (USA)
DRG	Drawing
DSL	Deep scattering layer
DSRV	Deep submergence rescue vehicle
DSV	Diving support vessel
DUC	Down hole utility capsule
DUCS	Diver underwater communication system (UK)
dwt	Deadweight tonnage
EAD	Equivalent air depth (nitrox diving)

EAR	Expired air resuscitation
EBHU	Emergency bell heating unit
ECC	External cardiac compression
ECG	Electrocardiograph (heart activity)
ECS	Environmental control system
ECU	Environmental control unit
EDTC	European Diving Technology Committee
EDTS	Emergency diver transfer system
EDU	Experimental Diving Unit
EEG	Electroencephalograph (brain)
EHP	Effective horse power
EL	Entrance lock
ELCB	Earth leakage circuit breaker
ELSBM	Exposed location single buoy mooring
EMI	Electromagnetic interrogation
EMT/D	Emergency medical technician/diver
EOR	Enhanced oil recovery
EP	Estimated position
EPS	Early production system
ERA	Electrical Research Association
ESD	Emergency shutdown
ESV	Emergency service vessel
ETA	Estimated time of arrival
ETD	Estimated time of departure
EUBS	European Undersea Biomedical Society
Ex	Exhaust
f	Frequency
°F	Degrees Fahrenheit
fa	Free alongside
FAO	For the attention of
FAUI	Federation of Australian Underwater Instructors
FAX	Facsimile
FCAW	Flux core arc welding
FCV	Flow control valve
FEV	Forced expiratory volume (lungs)
ffa	Free from alongside
fm	Fathoms
FM	Frequency modulation
fob	Free on board
foq	Free on quay
for	Free on rail
fot	Free on truck
fp	Freezing point
FPF	Floating production facility
fpm	Feet per minute
FSU	Floating storage unit
fsw	Feet of seawater
FVC	Forced vital capacity (lungs)
FW	Flash-butt welding
fwd	Forward
FX	Forecastle
g	Gram (also **gm**)
gal	Gallon
GDS	Guidelineless drilling system
GFD	Ground fault detection (USA)
GL	Germanischer Lloyd (CA)
GMAW	Gas metal arc welding
GMT	Greenwich mean time
GOR	Gas-oil ratio
GP	General practitioner (doctor)
gpm	Gallons per minute
GRP	Glass reinforced plastic
GRT	Gross registered tonnage
gr wt	Gross weight
GTAW	Gas tungsten arc welding
h	Hour(s) (time taken)
H$_2$	Hydrogen
HAT	Highest astronomical tide
HAZ	Heat affected zone
He	Helium (chemical symbol)
HE	High explosive
Heliox	Helium-oxygen mixture
He/O$_2$	Heliox (gas mixture)
HF	High frequency
Hg	Mercury (chemical symbol)
hi/lo	Butt edge misalignment (welding)

HME	Helicopter Medical Evacuation Inc.
HMPC	Hyperbaric Medicine Program Center (USN)
HOAL	Home Office specification for aluminium cylinders (UK)
hp	Horsepower
HP	High pressure
HPNS	High pressure nervous syndrome
hrs	Hours (24 hour clock)
HSE	Health and Safety Executive (UK)
HSW	Health and Safety at Work (UK)
HT	High tension (electrical)
HW	High water (tides)
HYD	Hydraulic
Hydrox	Hydrogen-oxygen mixture
Hz	Hertz (cycles per second)
IB	In bond
IC	Inspiratory capacity (lungs)
IC	Integrated circuit
ICAD	Integrated control and display
ICUE	International Conference of Underwater Education
id	Inside (internal) diameter
IDS	International diver's symposium (USA)
IGPM	Imperial gallons per minute
ihp	Indicated horse power
IMEP	Indicated mean effective pressure
in Hg	Inches of mercury (pressure)
IOD	Institute of Diving (USA)
IOE	Institute of Offshore Engineering
IOS	Institute of Oceanographic Sciences
IP	Indicated power
IP	Institute of Petroleum (UK)
IR	Infra-red
IR	Insulation resistance
ISIT	Intensified silicon intensified target
ISO	International Standards Organisation
JU	Jack-up (drilling rig)
k	Kilo (one thousand)
°K	Degrees Kelvin (absolute)
kg	Kilogram (one thousand grams)
kg/cm²	Kilograms per square centimetre
kgf/cm²	Kilograms force per square centimetre
kHz	Kilohertz (one thousand hertz)
km	Kilometres (one thousand metres)
kn	Knot (also Kt)
kN/m²	Kilonewtons per square metre
kVA	Kilovolt amps (thousand volt amps)
kW	Kilowatt (one thousand watts)
l	Litre
L/A	Lloyd's agent
Lat	Latitude
LAT	Lowest astronomical tide
lb	Pound(s) (weight)
LB	Lay barge
lbf/in²	Pounds force per square inch
L/C	Letter of credit
LBL	Long baseline (navigation)
LED	Light emitting diode
LF	Low frequency
LICB	Low induction circuit breaker
LIM	Line insulation monitor (welding)
LL	Lloyd's List
LMR	Lower marine riser
LNG	Liquid natural gas
loa	Length overall
Lo/Hy	Low hydrogen electrodes (welding)
Long	Longitude
LOP	Lack of penetration (welding)
LR	Lloyd's Register (CA)
LRA	Lower riser assembly
LRP	Lower riser package
LS	*Locus sigilii* (place of the seal)
LS	Lump sum
LSF	Lack of side wall fusion (welding)
LSS	Life support system (USN)
LT	Low tension (electricity)
LW	Low water (tides)
m	Metre
MA	Mechanical advantage Material
MaTSU	Marine Technology Support Unit
mb	Millibar(s)
MB	Motor boat
mbar	Millibar(s)
MBC	Maximum breathing capacity
MC	Manifold centre
MCC	Main control console (USN)
MDU	Mobile diving unit
MF	Medium frequency
mg	Milligram(s)
MHW	Mean high water (tides)
MHWN	Mean high water neaps (tides)
MHWS	Mean high water springs (tides)
MIG	Machine inert gas (welding)
min	Minimum (also minute(s))
ml	Millilitre(s) (same as cc)
ML	Motor launch
MLW	Mean low water
MLWN	Mean low water neaps (tides)
MLWS	Mean low water springs (tides)
mm	Millimetre(s)
MMA	Manual metal arc welding
mm Hg	Millimetres of mercury (pressure)
MOB	Mobile observation bell (also OMB)
MPCD	Magnetic particle crack detection
MPI	Magnetic particle inspection (NDT)
MRCC	Man-rated chamber complex (USA)
MRS-C	Maritime Rescue Sub-Centre (UK)
ms	Milliseconds
MSA	Merchant Shipping Act (UK)
MSC	Manpower Services Commission
MSL	Mean sea level
MSV	Multi-function service vessel
MSW	Metres of sea water
mt	Tonne (metric ton)
M/T	'Empty'
MTBF	Mean time between failures
MTL	Mean tide level
mV	Millivolt
MV	Motor vessel
MWL	Mean water level
MWMPS	Multiple well manifold production station
N₂	Nitrogen gas (chemical symbol)
N/A	Not applicable
NASDS	National Association of Skin Diving Schools (USA)
NAUI	National Association of Underwater Instructors (USA)
NBS	National Bureau of Standards (USA)
NDAC	National Diving Advisory Council
NDL	No decompression limit
NDT	Non-destructive testing
Ne	Neon (gas, chemical symbol)
NELP	North East London Polytechnic (UK)
NGL	Natural gas liquid(s)
NHP	Nominal horse power
Nitrox	Nitrogen-oxygen mixture
njj	'No-joint-juice'
nm	Nautical mile (also n mile)
N/m²	Newton(s) per square metre
NMRI	Naval Medical Research Institute
NOAA	National Oceanographic and Atmospheric Agency (USA)
NOHD	Nominal ocular hazard distance (lasers)
NPD	Norwegian Petroleum Directorate
NPS	American straight pipe
NPSH	Net positive suction head
NPT	American Taper Pipe
NPT	National pipe thread
NPTF	National pipe thread fine (USA)
NRT	Net registered tonnage
nt	Net tonnage
NUI	Norwegian Underwater Institute
NUTEC	Norwegian Underwater Technology Centre
O₂	Oxygen (gas, chemical symbol)
OBA	Oxygen breathing apparatus
Oce	Circumference
OCVR	Open circuit voltage reducer
od	Outside diameter
OIM	Offshore installation manager
OMB	Mobile observation bell
OMS	Offshore medical support (UK)
OSHA	Occupational Safety and Health Administration (USA)
OTC	Offshore Technology Conference
OVB	Over bottom pressure
p	Partial pressure (e.g. pO₂) (also pp)
P	Pressure (also PRESS)
Pa	Pascal(s) (unit of pressure)
PA	Public address system
PADI	Professional Association of Diving Instructors (USA)
Pb	Lead (chemical symbol)
PBM	Pipe burying machine
PCV	Packed cell volume (blood)
PCV	Pressure control valve
PDAA	Professional Divers Association of Australasia
PDTP	Passive diver thermal protection
PED	Petroleum Engineering Directorate (DEn, UK)
PERT	Programme evaluation and review technique (management)
PFD	Personal flotation device (USA)
pH	Acidity/alkalinity, measure of
PLEM	Pipeline end manifold
PLS	Prolonged life support
PNEU	Pneumatic
pp	Partial pressure (e.g. ppO₂)
PPB	Positive pressure breathing
PPI	Plan position indicator
ppm	Parts per million
ppu	Pipeline protection unit
psi(a)	Pounds per square inch (absolute)
psi(g)	Pounds per square inch (gauge)
PTC	Personnel transfer capsule (USA)
PTFE	Polytetrafluoroethylene
PVHO	Pressure vessels for human occupancy
PVC	Polyvinylchloride
Q	Volume flow rate
QED	Which had to be proved (from Latin)
r	Radius
RBI	Rigid bottom inflatable
RDX	Research and development 'X' (UK, type of explosive)
RE	Resident engineer (UK)
RF	Radio frequency
rh	Relative humidity
Rh	Rhesus factor (blood)
RIV	Rapid intervention vessel
RNLI	Royal National Lifeboat Institution
rob	Remaining on board
ROV	Remotely operated vehicle

rpm	Revolution per minute	**SPU**	Swimmer propulsion unit (USA)	**UA**	Underwater Association (UK)
RRPS	Riser recoil prevention system	**SRC**	Submarine rescue chamber	**UD**	Upper deck
RSJ	Rolled steel joist	**SRTJ**	Swivel ring type joint (flange)	**UDTC**	Underwater dry transfer chamber
RT	Radio telephone	**SS**	Semi-submersible	**UEG**	Underwater Engineering Group (UK)
RTJ	Ring type joint (flangeing)	**SS**	Steam ship	**UFN**	Until further notice
RV	Residual volume (lungs)	**SSALM**	Submerged single anchor leg mooring	**UHF**	Ultra high frequency (radio)
SABA	Swimmer's air breathing apparatus	**SSB**	Single side band (radio)	**UKOOA**	United Kingdom Offshore Operator's Association
SAE	Society of Automotive Engineers	**SSBA**	Surface supplied breathing apparatus	**ULCC**	Ultra large crude carrier
SAE	Standard Average European	**SSBL**	Super short baseline (navigation)	**UNC**	Unified coarse series
SALM	Single anchor leg mooring	**SSDV**	Side stone dumping vessel	**UNEF**	Unified extra fine series
SALS	Single anchor leg storage	**SSS**	Side scan sonar	**UNF**	Unified fine (screw thread)
SAR	Search and rescue	**SSTT**	Subsea test tree	**UNS**	Unified selective series
Sat	Saturation	**SSV**	Surface safety valve	**UPTD**	Unit pulmonary toxic dose
SAWS	Single atmosphere welding system	**SSV**	Surface support vessel	**U/S**	Out of service
SBL	Short baseline (navigation)	**SSW**	Stainless steel spiral wound gasket	**USCG**	United States Coast Guard
SBS	Single buoy storage	**STD**	Standard	**USGPM**	United States gallons per minute
SC	Salvaged charges	**STP**	Standard temperature and pressure	**UT**	Ultrasonic test (NDT)
SCC	Stress corrosion cracking	**SUBMISS**	Submarine missing (RN and USN)	**UT**	Universal time
SCC	Submersible compression chamber	**SUB-SMASH**	Submarine accident (RN and USN)	**UTC**	Underwater Training Centre (UK)
scfm	Standard cubic feet per minute	**SUT**	Society for Underwater Technology	**UTM**	Universal transverse meridian
scfm	Surface cubic feet per minute	**SWC**	Single wellhead completion	**UTV**	Underwater tethered vehicle
Scuba	Self contained underwater breathing apparatus	**SWC**	Submersible work chamber	**UUV**	Unmanned underwater vehicle
SD	Ship's diver (RN)	**SWG**	Imperial (standard) wire gauge	**UV**	Ultraviolet
SD	Stop depth	**SWL**	Safe working load	**UVS**	Underwater vehicle system
SDBA	Surface demand breathing apparatus			**UWC**	Underwater completion
SDC	Submersible decompression chamber	**T**	Absolute temperature	**UWH**	Underwater welding habitat
SDDE	Surface demand diver's equipment	**TBP**	Tethered buoy platform	**UWT**	Underwater telephone (also UQC)
SDHU	Submersible diver's heating unit	**TCV**	Temperature control valve		
SDS	Salvage diving system	**TDC**	Top dead centre	**V**	Voltage, volts
SDV	Silicon diode vidicon	**TDCS**	Total diver communication system	**VA**	Volt ampere
SEIS	Submarine emergency identification signal	**TDP**	Touch down point	**VAC**	Vacuum
sg	Specific gravity (also Sp Gr)	**TFL**	Transfer flow line (production well)	**VC**	Vital capacity (lungs)
shp	Shaft horsepower	**TIG**	Tungsten inert gas (welding)	**VDU**	Visual display unit
SI	International system of units	**TL**	Transfer lock	**VHF**	Very high frequency
SI	Statutory Instrument (UK)	**T/L**	Total loss	**VLCC**	Very large crude carrier
SIT	Silicone intensified target (TV)	**TLP**	Tension leg platform	**VLF**	Very low frequency (radio)
SIT	Spontaneous ignition temperature	**TLV**	Threshold limit value	**VMP**	Vertically moored platform
Sitrep	Situation report	**TLV**	Tolerance limit value	**Vol**	Volume
SLJ	Surface life jacket	**TNT**	Trinitrotoluene	**VRU**	Vertical reference unit
SLR	Single lens reflex	**TOPS**	Training Opportunities Scheme (UK)	**VVDS**	Variable volume dry suit
SMA	Shielded metal arc welding	**TP**	Test pressure		
S/N	Shipping note	**TPI**	Threads per inch	**W**	Watt
SOP	Standard operating procedure	**TPI**	Tons per inch (immersion)	**wbs**	Without benefit of salvage
SPEC	Specification(s)	**TPP**	Tethered production platform	**wef**	With effect from
SPM	Single point mooring	**TSS**	Total saturation system	**WOW**	Waiting on weather
SPS	Subsea production system	**TUP**	Transfer under pressure	**WP**	Weather permitting
SPT	Storage production terminal	**TV**	Tidal volume (lungs)	**WP**	Working pressure
		TVD	True vertical depth	**WSP**	Work system package
				Wt	Weight
				WT	Wireless telegraphy
				XIP or XIPS	Extra improved
				yd	Yard (measurement)
				Zn	Zinc (chemical symbol)

16.4 USEFUL INFORMATION APPLYING FOR A DIVING JOB

There is often a great deal of competition for any one diving job. In order to secure the best chances of landing the job, it is as important to present your case properly as it is to have the necessary experience.

The following points should be regarded as essential to presenting yourself properly to a diving company.

Interview: Press for an interview with the Operations Manager rather than simply sending details in the post.

Visits: This means physically visiting the diving companies at their operational bases. But make an appointment first rather than walking in on spec.

Personal Résumé (also referred to as Curriculum Vitae or CV): You will need to leave one at every diving company visited.

The contents and presentation are very important. As an example the following should be included:

—Full name.
—Nationality.
—Date of birth.
—Passport number, date of issue, place of issue, details of any visas held.
—Marriage status.
—Home address and telephone number.
—Next of kin: name, address and telephone number.
—Details of any professional and/or academic qualifications held.
—Details of any additional, useful skills.
—Membership to any relevant Associations or Institutes.
—Details of any sports, hobbies or special interests.
—Summary of career to date. Use half a page only.

Visas and Vaccinations

A visa is a stamp of approval placed on the page of a passport by an official of the country to be visited. It does not guarantee entry to the country and is usually valid for one entry/transit only. Multiple entry visas are obtainable at extra cost. When

—List of previous jobs held. Start with the most recent and work backwards.

Give full company names. State position held. Give details of any responsibilities held. Give details of types of tasks performed and any special experience gained. Give details of any experience with ADSs or ROVs. Give geographical locations.

—Give list of individual references. Include details of person to contact and job title. Attach copies of written references to the résumé.

It should be typed neatly and clearly.

Keep a plentiful supply of copies of the résumé at hand and keep them up-dated as necessary. If you find it difficult to produce, get someone to help you. This is a very important document.

Take with you: When attending an interview with a diving company it is very important to have with you the following documents:

—Personal résumé.
—Passport.
—Details of any jobs.
—Diving log book(s).
—Diving Medical Certificate (in date).
—Any trade certificates e.g.:
Welding/burning, Inspection and testing (NDT), Explosives.
Any EMT/first aid certificates.
Any photocopies of these documents that can be left with the company for their files will help.

—10 spare photographs. Some of these may be required for urgent visa applications if you are accepted.

applying for a business visa, a letter from the company sponsoring the visit is usually required. Evidence of financial standing may also be necessary.

A visa and work permit are not the same thing. Many countries

The table below shows the vaccination requirements for selected countries where offshore diving occurs.

Country visited	Vaccinations		Comments	Country visited	Vaccinations		Comments
	Required	Advised	* Required if travelling through an infected area		Required	Advised	* Required if travelling through an infected area
Angola	Cholera	Y. Fever Malaria		Ivory Coast	Y. Fever	Malaria	
Australia	* Cholera * Y. Fever			Malaysia	* Y. Fever	Malaria	
Brazil	* Y. Fever	Malaria	Only if visiting Belem area.	Mexico	* Y. Fever	Malaria	Malaria risk greater during Jun–Nov.
Brunei	* Cholera * Y. Fever			Nigeria	Y. Fever	Malaria	
Cameroon United Republic	Y. Fever	Cholera Malaria	Y. Fever not necessary if staying less than 15 days.	Oman	Cholera * Y. Fever	Malaria	
Ecuador	* Y. Fever	Malaria	Y. Fever	Saudi Arabia	* Y. Fever	Malaria	
				Singapore	* Y. Fever		
Egypt Arab Republic	* Cholera * Y. Fever	Malaria	Malaria risk Jun–Oct. in Nile delta, El Faiyum, parts Upper Egypt, Oases.	South Africa Republic	* Cholera * Y. Fever	Malaria	Malaria risk in north, east and western Transvaal and Natal coast.
Gabon	* Y. Fever * Y. Fever	Malaria	Y. Fever required if staying longer than 2 weeks.	Trinidad and Tobago	* Y. Fever		
India	* Y. Fever	Cholera Malaria	Malaria risk March–Oct.	United Arab Emirates	* Cholera		
Indonesia	* Y. Fever	Cholera Malaria		Venezuela		Y. Fever Malaria	Y. Fever for Amazon area.
Iran Islamic Republic	* Y. Fever * Cholera	Malaria	Malaria risk July–Nov.				
Iraq	* Y. Fever	Malaria	Malaria risk northern region May–Nov.	The following countries have no vaccination requirements: Canada, Denmark, France, Israel, Italy, Republic of Ireland, Japan, Jordan, Kuwait, Netherlands, New Zealand, Norway, Spain, Sweden, United Kingdom and United States of America.			

do not require a visa but require a work permit. Work permits are usually obtained outside the country to be visited. Each country has its own restrictions, so the Consulate or Embassy of the country to be visited should be consulted.

Local health authorities may require proof of vaccination against smallpox, cholera and/or yellow fever. The period of immunity varies for each. For cholera it becomes effective on the 6th day and is valid for 6 months thereafter; for smallpox, it is valid from the 8th day for the following 3 years; and for yellow fever, from the 10th day to 10 years thereafter. Where a risk of malaria exists, anti-malaria drugs should be taken starting 10 days before departure until one month after leaving the country. Tablets can be obtained from chemists.

16.4b WORLD TIME ZONES

When travelling or making overseas telephone calls it is useful to know the time differences between countries.

The world is divided into 24 time zones. Each zone generally represents 15° of longitude or 1 hour of time. The countries east of the Greenwich Meridian are ahead of Greenwich Mean Time (GMT) and the countries to the west are behind.

The times shown in the map below are based on noon in Greenwich, London, although there may be inconsistencies of 1 or 2 hours in some cities caused by the seasonal use of daylight saving.

British Summer Time (GMT + 1 hour) is generally observed in the UK from the last Sunday in March until the end of October. Other countries which also observe BST are Belgium, France, Greece, Hong Kong, Ireland, Israel, Italy, New Zealand, Spain, and Yugoslavia.

In the USA, Daylight Saving Time (1 hour ahead of local standard time) is used in all states except Arizona and Hawaii from 2 am on the last Sunday in April to 2 am of the last Sunday in October.

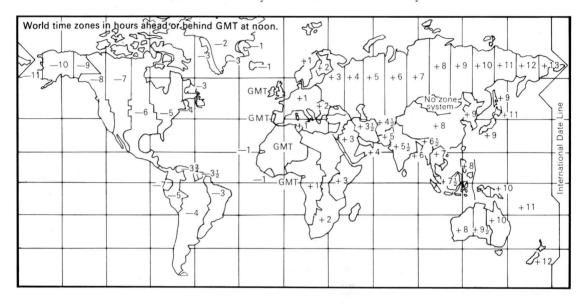

INDEX